Observations on the Language of Chaucer's Troilus

STUDIES AND NOTES

IN

PHILOLOGY AND LITERATURE

VOL. III.

PUBLISHED UNDER THE DIRECTION OF THE
MODERN LANGUAGE DEPARTMENTS OF HARVARD UNIVERSITY
BY GINN & COMPANY, TREMONT PLACE, BOSTON
1894

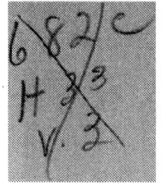

THE present volume, issued in 1894 as one of the Publications of the Chaucer Society for 1891 (Second Series, No. 28), is, by an arrangement with the Society, republished as Volume III. of Studies and Notes in Philology and Literature.

Observations on the Language of Chaucer's Troilus.

BY

GEORGE LYMAN KITTREDGE,

ASSISTANT PROFESSOR OF ENGLISH IN HARVARD UNIVERSITY.

PUBLISHT FOR THE CHAUCER SOCIETY
By KEGAN PAUL, TRENCH, TRÜBNER & CO.,
PATERNOSTER HOUSE, CHARING-CROSS ROAD
1891.

Moffitt fund

Second Series, 28.

R. CLAY & SONS, LIMITED, LONDON & BUNGAY.

TO

Professor Francis James Child

IN

GRATITUDE AND AFFECTION

PREFACE.

THE following Observations are intended to furnish some materials for the large induction necessary to reasonable certainty in the matter of Chaucer's language, particularly his use of final -*e*. Other matters than final -*e* are of course dealt with from time to time; but to this in particular the Observations are directed. In other words, the study here presented to members of the Chaucer Society is a study in forms, not in phonology. This study was begun in August 1887, and has been frequently interrupted. The printing has of necessity extended over an unconscionable length of time. It is hoped that these facts may serve as the excuse for some trifling inconsistencies of typography, and perhaps even for some slight vacillations in plan and method. For actual blunders no excuse is offered; but it is hoped that the work may contain enough that is useful to make scholars indulgent for such errors as they may observe. Corrections will be gratefully received.

A paper by Professor John M. Manly, of Brown University, extending the method of inquiry here followed to *The Legend of Good Women*, will be found in vol. ii. of the Harvard *Studies and Notes in Philology and Literature* (Boston, 1893), pp. 1 ff. The relations of Professor Manly's paper to the present study are explained in his Introductory Note. Both papers, it will be observed, are under special obligations to Professor Child's *Observations on the Language of Chaucer*.

My acknowledgments are due to Professor E. S. Sheldon and Professor J. M. Manly for a number of valuable suggestions. Dr. Furnivall, with his usual kindness, has furnished me with indispensable copies and collations. To Professor Child, who suggested the investigation, and has furthered it by his counsel and encouragement throughout, my obligations of every kind are innumerable.

G. L. K.

Cambridge, March 17th, 1894.

TABLE OF CONTENTS.

	PAGE
INTRODUCTORY NOTE	XV
COMPARATIVE TABLES OF LINE-NUMBERS	xix
ABBREVIATIONS AND SIGNS	xxiv

I. GRAMMATICAL CHAPTER.

NOUNS.

§§ 1—5. Nouns of the *n*- declension	1—9
§ 2. Masculines	1—5
§ 3. Feminines	5—8
§ 4. Neuters	8
§ 5 *Lady, play, fo, feldefare*	9
§§ 6, 7. Masculine and neuter nouns with A.S. nominative in *-e* or *-u*	9—12
§ 6. Ending in *-e* in the *Troilus*	9—11
§ 7. Exceptions to § 6	11—12
§ 8. Feminine nouns with A.S. nominative in *-u*	12—15
§§ 9—11. Monosyllabic feminine nouns with long stem-syllable in A.S.	15—34
§ 9. Ending in *-e* in the *Troilus*	15—27
§ 10. Nouns in *-yng, -ynge*	27—31
§ 11. Ending in a consonant in the *Troilus*	31—34
§ 12. Apocope of A.S. *-n* in nouns	34—35
§ 13. *Hond, honde*	35—36
§ 14. Masculine and neuter nouns ending in a consonant in A.S. but in *-e* in the *Troilus* (including so-called dative *-e's*)	36—47
§ 15. Germanic nouns, not A.S., ending in *-e* in the *Troilus*	47—51
§ 16. *Gle, se, stre, tre*	51
§ 17. *Body, day, iuy, uery*	51—52
§ 18. Masculine and neuter A.S. nouns ending in a consonant in the *Troilus*	52—63
§ 19. Other Germanic nouns ending in a consonant	63—64

viii *Table of Contents.*

	PAGE
§§ 20—31. Romance nouns in -*e* mute	64—87
§ 21. Miscellaneous nouns : -*e* retained	64—74
§ 22. Exceptions to § 21	74—75
§ 23. Nouns in -*aunce*	75—77
§ 24. Nouns in -*ence*	77—78
§ 25. I. Abstract nouns in -*esse*	78—79
II. Feminine *nomina agentis* in -*esse*	79
§ 26. Nouns in -*yce*, -*yse*	79—80
§ 27. Nouns in -*ure*	80—81
§ 28. Nouns in -*ère*	81—83
§ 29. Nouns in consonant + *re*	83—84
§ 30. Nouns in -*ye*, -*ie*	84—86
§ 31. Nouns in -*ye* (unaccented)	86—87
§ 32. Romance nouns that end in a consonant in French but take -*e* in the *Troilus*	87—88
§ 33. Nouns ending in Old French in -*é*, -*ée*	88—89
§ 34. Romance (and Latin) nouns without final -*e*	89—97
I. Nouns in -*er*	90
II. Nouns in -*our*	90—91
III. Nouns in -*ent*, -*ment*	91—92
IV. Nouns in -*aunt*	92
V. Nouns in -*s*	92—93
VI. Nouns ending in a vowel (not -*e*)	93—94
VII. Miscellaneous	94—97
§§ 35—37. Genitive singular of nouns	97—100
§ 35. Genitive singular in -*es*	97—98
§ 36. Genitive identical in form with nominative (*lady*, *brother*, etc.)	98—99
§ 37. Proper names in -*s*	99—100
§§ 38—45. Plural of nouns	100—110
§ 38. Plurals in -*es*, -*is*, -*ys* (after consonants), -*s* (after -*e*)	100—103
§ 39. Exceptions to § 38 : words in -*aunt*, -*ent*, -*ioun*, -*en*, -*on*, -*an*, -*r*; monosyllables in -*e*	104—106
§ 40. Plurals in -*en*	106—107
§ 41. Plurals in -*en* by imitation	107
§ 42. Plurals with umlaut	107
§ 43. Plural identical with singular	108—109
§ 44. Genitive plural	109—110
§ 45. Dative plural	110

ADJECTIVES.

§§ 46—52. Singular adjectives in the indefinite use	110—122
§ 46. A.S. adjectives in -*e*, -*a*	110—113
§ 47. *Allone, lame*	113—114
§ 48. *Lyté, muche*	114—115

Table of Contents.

ix

	PAGE
§ 49. A.S. adjectives ending in a consonant that take -e in the *Troilus*	115—118
§ 50. Germanic (not A.S.) adjectives that show -e in the *Troilus*	119—120
§ 51. Romance adjectives in -e	120—121
§ 52. Romance adjectives with -e in the *Troilus* but none in French	121—122
§§ 53—54. Monosyllabic singular adjectives in the definite use	122—127
§ 53. Taking -e	122—126
I. Ordinals	123
II. Superlatives	123—124
III. Miscellaneous	124—125
IV. Words sometimes showing -e in the indefinite use (cf. § 49)	125—126
V. *owene, owen, owne*	126
§ 54. -e dropped	126—127
§ 55. Vocative singular of monosyllabic adjectives	127—128
§§ 56—62. Adjectives singular of more than one syllable in definite and vocative constructions	128—134
§ 56. Rules	128—129
§ 57. I. Dissyllabic paroxytones (following word accented on first syllable)	129—132
§ 58. II. Dissyllabic oxytones (following word accented on second syllable)	132
§ 59. III. Trisyllabic proparoxytones (following word not accented on second syllable)	132—133
§ 60. IV. Trisyllabic proparoxytones (following word accented on second syllable)	133
§ 61. V. Trisyllabic paroxytones (following word accented on first syllable)	133
§ 62. Vocative of adjectives of more than one syllable	133—134
§ 63. French inflection of adjectives	134—135
§ 64. Comparative degree	135—137
(a) -er (-ere)	135
(b) *lenger*	135
(c) *bettre, bet; lasse, lesse; more, mo, moo; worse, wers*	135—137
§ 65. Comparative and superlative with *more* and *most*	137—138
§ 66. Superlative (-est)	138
§§ 67—71. Plural of adjectives	138—149
§ 67. Monosyllabic adjectives: plural in -e	138—149
(a) Miscellaneous	138—142
(b) *fele, fewe*	142
(c) Monosyllabic superlatives	142
(d) Cardinal numerals	142—144
§ 68. Monosyllabic perfect participles standing in the predicate	144—145

x *Table of Contents.*

PAGE

§ 69. Monosyllabic adjectives standing in the predicate: *e* sometimes omitted .. - .. 145—146
Other exceptions to § 67 146
§ 70. Adjectives of more than one syllable (in the interior of the verse) .. ... 146—148
§ 71. Adjectives of more than one syllable at the end of the verse ... . 148—149
§ 72. Adjectives in A.S. *-lìc (-lic)*, O.N. *-ligr* . . 149—150

PRONOUNS.

§ 73. Personal pronouns ... ... 150—154
§ 74. Possessive pronouns ... ... 154—157
§ 75. Reflexive and intensive pronouns ... ... 157—160
§ 76. Demonstrative pronouns ... ... 160—161
§ 77. Interrogative pronouns 161
§ 78. Relative pronouns (and pronominal adjectives), and the interrogative (etc.) *which* .. . . 161—164
§ 79. Other pronominal words (*same, som, somwhat, other, ech, euery, euerychon, any, eyther, bothe, men, oon (o), noon (no), ought, nought* .. . 164—169
§§ 80, 81. The adjective *al* . .. . 169—175
§ 80. I. Adjective use, singular; *al* .. . 169
II. Substantive uses, singular; *al* . . , 169—170
III. Singular *alle* ... . .. 170—171
IV. Plural of *al* .. .. . 171—175
§ 81. The genitive plural of *al* 175

ADVERBS AND OTHER PARTICLES.

§ 82. Adverbs in A.S. *-e* which preserve their termination .. .. 175—180
§ 83. Exceptions to § 82 180
§ 84. Adverbs in *-liche, -lich, -ly* _ ... . 180—187
§ 85. Adverbs without vowel-ending . .. 187—190
§§ 86, 87. Comparison of adverbs .. . 190—193
§ 86. Comparative degree . .. ., 190—192
§ 87. Superlative degree 193
§ 88. Miscellaneous particles which sometimes or always have *-e* in the *Troilus* .. ... . 193—201
§ 89. *Atwixen, -e, bytwyxen, -e, aweye, ehe, often, -e, saue; here, there, where* ... ... 201—206
§ 90. *Ever* and *never* .. ' .. .. ., 206—208
§ 91. Particles in *-es* ... ... 208—211

Table of Contents. xi

VERBS.

	PAGE
§§ 92—98. Present indicative	212—231
§ 92. First person singular	212—215
§ 93. Second person singular	216
§ 94. Third person singular in *-eth, -eth, -th*	217—220
§ 95. Third person singular in *-t (abit, halt, stant,* etc.)	220—222
§ 96. Plural in *-en, -e*	222—229
§ 97. Plural in *-eth, -th*	229—230
§ 98. Plural in *-es*	230—231
§§ 99—105. Preterite indicative (first and third persons) of weak verbs	231—252
§ 99. First conjugation (Anglo-Saxon)	231—240
§ 100. First conjugation (Old Norse, etc.)	240—242
§ 101. Second conjugation (Anglo-Saxon and other Germanic languages)	242—246
§ 102. Third conjugation (Anglo-Saxon)	246—248
§ 103. Verbs strong in Anglo-Saxon	248—250
§ 104. Romance verbs with syncopated preterites (*aspyde, caughte,* etc.)	250—251
§ 105. Romance verbs with unsyncopated preterites	251—252
§ 106. Preterite indicative, second person singular, of weak formations	252—253
§ 107. Preterite indicative, second person singular, of strong verbs	253—254
§ 108. Preterite indicative (first and third persons) singular of strong verbs	254
§ 109. Preterite indicative, plural of strong and of weak verbs	255—260
§§ 110, 111. Present subjunctive singular of strong and of weak verbs	260—266
§ 110. Ending in *-e*	260—265
§ 111. Exceptions to § 110	265—266
§ 112. Present subjunctive plural of strong and of weak verbs	266—268
§ 113. Preterite subjunctive singular	268—272
I. Strong verbs	268—270
II. Weak verbs	270—272
§ 114. Preterite subjunctive plural of strong and of weak verbs	272—273
§§ 115—117. Imperative second person singular	273—280
§ 115. Weak verbs (Germanic)	273—276
§ 116. Latin and Romance verbs	276—277
§ 117. Strong verbs	277—280

Table of Contents

	PAGE
§ 118. Imperative second person plural of strong and of weak verbs	280—286
§ 119. Infinitive	286—301
§ 120. Present participle	301—303
§ 121. Perfect participle of weak verbs	303—311
§ 122. Perfect participle of strong verbs	311—317
§ 123. Præterito-present verbs	317—331
I. *wot*	317—319
II. *not*	319—320
III. *oughte*	320—321
IV. *kan*	321—323
V. *dar*	323—324
VI. *thar*	324
VII. *shal*	324—326
VIII. *may*	326—329
IX. *mot*	329—331
§ 124. Other irregular verbs	331—345
I. *to be*	331—334
II. *will*	335—338
III. *nyl*	339—340
IV. *do*	340—341
V. *go*	341—343
VI. *haue*	343—345

II. METRICAL CHAPTER.

	PAGE
§ 125. Elision of weak -*e*	345—347
§ 126. Hiatus (exceptions to § 125)	347—352
§ 127. Elision before strong *h*	352—353
§ 128. Elision of weak -*e* in monosyllables (*thĕ, nĕ*)	353—355
§ 129. Elision of close -*e* (*me, we,* etc.)	355—359
§ 130. Elision (or slurring) of -*o* and -*a*	359—361
§ 131. Slurring of -*y* (-*ye*)	362—363
§ 132. Weak *e* in two successive syllables (syncope or apocope)	364—365
§ 133. Apocope or syncope of weak *e* after an unaccented syllable which is capable of bearing an accent	365—366
§ 134. Apocope of weak -*e* after a syllable bearing a secondary accent	366
§ 135. Apocope of weak -*e* immediately after the syllable bearing the main accent	366—372
§ 136. Syncope or slurring of *e* in final syllables when the noun-accent falls on the syllable immediately preceding	372—377
(*a*) -*es*	372
(*b*) -*est*	372—373

Table of Contents. xiii

	PAGE
(c) *-eth*	373
(d) *-de, -te, -ede, -ed*	373—374
(e) *-en*	374—375
(f) *-er, -ere, -re*	375—377
(g) *-el, -le*	377
(h) *-em (-me)*	377
§ 137. Interior weak *-e-*	377—378
§ 138. Other instances of syncope	378—381
1-5. Vowels (not weak *e*)	378—380
6. *whether, wher; other, or*	380—381
7. *euere, neuere*	381
8. *benedicite*	381
9. *comprehende*	381
10. *desespeir, despeir*, etc.	381
§ 139. Apocope of consonants	381—384
I. *-n* in verb-forms	381—382
II. *-eth* in imperative	382
III. *-s* in proper names	382—384
§ 140. Synæresis	384
§ 141. Diæresis	384
§ 142. Synizesis	384—387
§ 143. Miscellaneous slurs and contractions	387—389
§§ 144-145. The "extra syllable" before the cæsura	389—405
§ 144. I. Cases of *-e*	389—398
II. Cases of unaccented terminations ending in a consonant	398—400
§ 145. Certain final syllables before the cæsura	401—405
I. Consonant + *-le, -me, -ne, -re*	402
II. *-ene, -ere*	403
III. *-el, -en, -er*	403—404
IV. *-we*, etc.	404
V. *-y, -ye*	404—405
§ 146. "Nine-syllable" verses	405—421
ADDITIONS AND CORRECTIONS	422—426

INTRODUCTORY NOTE.

The following Observations on the Language of Chaucer's *Troilus* are based on four MSS. A (Campsall), B (Harl. 2280), C (Camb. Gg. 4. 27), and D (Harl. 3943), as edited by Dr. Furnivall for the Chaucer Society.[1] When there is no indication to the contrary, the forms quoted rest on a consensus of these four MSS. in the verse referred to. Indications to the contrary are of several kinds: (*a*) an express note, either at the foot of the page or in parentheses immediately after the verse-number; (*b*) a general note as to disregard of variants; (*c*) the abbreviation "cf.", which signifies that in the references that follow variants are mostly or altogether neglected; (*d*) a list of variant spellings (marked "Var.").[2] In case some word not immediately under discussion has to be emended in order that the line referred to may afford the form registered, the necessary emendation is indicated in a foot-note or elsewhere.[3] In case a line falls within a gap or omission of a stanza or more in B, C, or D, the fact is not noted. The following is a list of gaps in B, C, D.

In B one leaf containing (vv. 7708—91) is missing; 5370—6 not in A.

In C the following passages of a stanza or more in length are wanting 1—70 (*cut out*), 1037—1169 (cut out), 2843—98 (cut out), 4649—4774 (cut out), 5468—95 (omitted), 5615—5740 (omitted), 6329—98 (cut out), 7076—82 (omitted; two stanzas run together), 8065—*end* (cut out). The following single lines are omitted in C; 86 (no gap in MS.), 1701, 2231 (no gap), 2707 (blank line in MS.), 3799 (blank line), 5752 (blank line), 6550 (no gap), 6557 (blank line), 7244 (no gap), 7285 (blank line after 7286).

After 890 D has a stanza not in ABC.

---

[1] A, B, and C in *A Parallel-Text Print of Chaucer's Troilus and Criseyde* (1881-82); D in *Chaucer's Troylus and Cryseyde (from the Harl. MS. 3943) compared with Boccaccio's Filostrato translated by* Wm. Michael Rossetti (1873—83).

[2] See, for example, *wrecche* (p. 5, l. 3), note at the end of article *sonne* (p. 7), *tonge* (p. 7, l. ult.), *lady*, (p. 9), *wyfe* (p. 11).

[3] Thus foot-note 1, p. 33, indicates that in 3074 C has *wyȝt was woyd*, but that, after the last word has been changed to *woyded*, the line affords evidence for the form *woyght*. It will be seen that this is in effect but a means of registering corruptions that are easily emended.

Introductory Note.

In D the following passages of a stanza or more in length are wanting: 484—490, 4131—4270 (two leaves gone), 4586—4613 (omitted), 8170—90 (omitted). The following single lines are omitted in D: 148, 1594 (blank line). Vv. 1—70, 498—567, 4859—end, are in a late hand.

Other MSS. than ABCD have been used for purposes of comparison. Those used most were Cp. (Corpus 61) and John's, a collation of both of which by Mr. Thomas Austin was furnished me by the kindness of Dr. Furnivall, and G (Additional MS. 12044), of which Dr. Furnivall lent me a copy. Harleian 1239 (E), 2392, 4912, of which I have had specimens and partial collations, and Durham II. 13, Digby 281, Selden B, 24, Phillipps 8252, of which I have had specimens, have been compared occasionally. For all these collations and specimens I am indebted to Dr. Furnivall.

Rhyme-words are given in the form in which they occur in A, without variants. Exceptions to this practice are signified when they occur.

In citing words from Anglo-Saxon and Middle English in illustration of words or forms from the *Troilus*, no attempt has been made at anything more than a brief and handy reference, and no implication is intended as to the particular dialect of Anglo-Saxon or Middle English of which Chaucer's word is the descendant or representative. In these references *L.* means the *A-text of Laȝamon*, and does not necessarily imply that the *B-text* has the same form.

In marking elision, apocope, and syncope in the Grammatical Chapter, it has been assumed that ten syllables (or eleven, when the rhyme is feminine) are the normal number, and elision, syncope, etc., have been taken for granted when the preservation of a final or an interior *e* would make a trisyllabic foot or an "extra syllable before a pause." This is merely for conciseness. There is no intention of maintaining that Chaucer never used a trisyllabic foot or that different slurs do not differ in the degree in which a sound is suppressed or modified. Special sections (§§ 144—5) in the Metrical Chapter deals with the so-called "extra syllable before the cæsura." This renders the marking of the cæsura in the grammatical part unnecessary; yet the sign ‖ has often been added to a form when occasion seemed to require.

In registering forms, the following signs, etc., are made use of to indicate the presence or absence of the final *e* in writing or in sound.

-e (Roman, without a diacritic sign) indicates a final -e pronounced before a consonant (not *h*) or -e in rhyme.[1] In the latter case an *f* is

---

[1] This statement applies, of course, to -e in the word immediately under discussion in any instance. If a fragment of context is quoted, I have not always taken the superfluous trouble to mark what happens to all the -e's.

Introductory Note. xvii

attached to the verse number. In a considerable number of cases a faulty final *e* in rhyme is registered without remark if the rhyme-word makes it clear that the -e is not pronounced.

-ĕ indicates a final *e* pronounced either (1) before a vowel or *h* (in which case the fact that a vowel or *h* follows is always made clear), or (2) before a consonant (in which case -e is used merely for emphasis or out of caution). In the interior of a word the diæresis indicates that the vowel over which it is placed is pronounced.

-*e* (Italic) indicates a final *e* written but elided before a vowel or *h* (the former unless the contrary is indicated). Hiatus is always carefully and unmistakably marked.

-ę indicates a final *e* written but not sounded before a consonant (not *h*). When not final, ę indicates syncopated *e* (and so of other vowels).

-(e) indicates an erroneous final *e* written but not pronounced. When necessary this is distinguished as -(e),—*i. e.* before a word beginning with a vowel or *h*,—and -(ę),—before a word beginning with a consonant (not *h*); but this distinction is usually superfluous.

-[e] indicates that the metre requires an -e (pronounced) at the end of a word which is written without -e in the MS.

-[*e*] indicates that a grammatically justifiable -e is elided before a vowel or *h*, and is actually not written. This sign is seldom used.

-[ę] indicates that a grammatically justifiable -e is not pronounced before a consonant (not *h*) and is actually not written. This sign is seldom used.

When the fact that a word ends in a consonant or any vowel but -e renders it impossible to indicate by any of the signs just explained whether the word that follows begins with a vowel or a consonant, the necessary information is given either in plain terms or by means of the signs (i.) and (ii.). (i.) indicates that the forms that follow occur before a consonant (not *h*); (ii.) indicates that they occur before a vowel or *h* (the former, unless the contrary is mentioned). When neither of these signs is used, the forms that follow occur before consonants (not *h*) or in rhyme (indicated by *f*) in the places cited. (i.) (ii.) indicates that no distinction as to following vowel or consonant is made in registering the forms. These conventions are used especially in the case of nouns and adjectives that properly or regularly end in a consonant (see §§ 11, 18, 19, 34, 49), and of adverbs without -e (see §§ 85, 86, 88, 91): see also § 14. In the case of forms as to which there is no possible interest in knowing whether a vowel or a consonant follows, no such signs are used (see §§ 35—42, 44, 93, 94, etc.).

b

Introductory Note.

The relations of the *Troilus* MSS. are complicated. In general the MSS. seem to fall into two groups, the first represented by ABCpG, the second by CEJ. D_1 (the old hand of D)[1] is closely related to C, D_2 (the late hand of D) has much in common with group i., but shows also some relation to C. Phillipps is closely related to D_1. H has close relations with both D_1 Ph. and D_2. There is excellent evidence for contamination in the case of H, and, in general, it must be said that no genealogy for the MSS. of group ii. can be made out that is free from difficulties. I have made many notes on the relations of the MSS., and have even constructed a scheme which seems to satisfy most of the phenomena; but the material in my possession, though considerable, is not sufficient to warrant definite conclusions. I hope to return to the subject later, when opportunity for a complete collation of the MSS. concerned shall offer.

Of the MSS. of group i., Corpus is the best, though it makes some serious omissions. B is often better than A, but the grammatical forms of A usually deserve the preference. Of group ii., J seems to be the best. C is copied from a bad MS., and is full of errors and of corrections. D_1 and Phillipps have an extraordinary number of corruptions, and were evidently written by scribes who had no feeling for Chaucer's verse. Harl. 2392 is a poor MS. and E is apparently but indifferent. Selden, Durham, and Digby are all poor, and Harl. 4912 is far from good.

---

[1] There are three hands in D : a late hand (1—70, 498—567, 4859—end), and two earlier hands (one writing 3921—4480, the other writing the rest)

COMPARATIVE TABLE OF LINE-NUMBERS IN THE *TROILUS*.

REFERENCES are made by *verses*, and for this purpose the lines have been numbered throughout the poem from 1 to 8232 without regard to the division into books. The following table exhibits, in parallel columns, the numbering here used and the corresponding book, stanza, and verse numbers in Furnivall (Campsall MS.)[1] and Morris (Aldine ed.).

1—1085 = book i. The numbering used in the *Observations* follows Furnivall's numbering (Campsall MS.) exactly. Morris inserts a stanza (not found in A) after st. 127 (*i.e.* after v. 889). Hence, beginning with v. 890, one must add 7 to Furnivall's verse-numbers (beginning with st. 128, 1 to his stanza-numbers) to reduce them to Morris's numbering.

	FURNIVALL				MORRIS
	Book	Stanza	Verse of Stanza	Verse	Agrees with Furnivall throughout this book.
1086	II,	1,	1	II, 1	
1100		3,	1	15	
1150		10,	2	65	
1200		17,	3	115	
1250		24,	4	165	
1300		31,	5	215	
1350		38,	6	265	
1400		45,	7	315	
1450		52,	1	365	
1500		60,	2	415	
1550		67,	3	465	
1600		74,	4	515	
1650		81,	5	565	
1700		88,	6	615	
1750		95,	7	665	
1800		103,	1	715	
1850		110,	2	765	
1900		117,	3	815	
1950		124,	4	865	
2000		131,	5	915	
2050		138,	6	965	
2100		145,	7	1015	
2150		153,	1	1065	
2200		160,	2	1115	
2250		167,	3	1165	
2300		174,	4	1215	
2350		181,	5	1265	
2400		188,	6	1315	
2450		195,	7	1365	
2500		203,	1	1415	
2550		210,	2	1465	
2600		217,	3	1515	
2650		224,	4	1565	
2700		231,	5	1615	
2750		238,	6	1665	
2800		245,	7	1715	
2842		251,	7	1757	

[1] Bk. iv, st. 102 [= iv. 98, vv. 680—686 in Morris], though not in AB, is included by Furnivall in his numbering, and accordingly in the numbering adopted for these Observations (vv. 5370—76).

Comparative Table of Line-Numbers.

	FURNIVALL					MORRIS			
	Book	Stanza	Verse of Stanza	Verse		Book	Stanza	Verse of Stanza	Verse
2843	III,	1,	1	III,	1	Proem to III,	1,	1	Proem 1
2891		7,	7		49		7,	7	49
2892		8,	1		50		1,	1	III, 1
2900		9,	2		58		2,	2	9
2950		16,	3		108		9,	3	59
3000		23,	4		158		16,	4	109
3050		30,	5		208		23,	5	159
3100		37,	6		258		30,	6	209
3150		44,	7		308		37,	7	259
3200		52,	1		358		45,	1	309
3250		59,	2		408		52,	2	359
3300		66,	3		458		59,	3	409
3350		73,	4		508		66,	4	459
3400		80,	5		558		73,	5	509
3450		87,	6		608		80,	6	559
3500		94,	7		658		87,	7	609
3550		102,	1		708		95,	1	659
3600		109,	2		758		102,	2	709
3650		116,	3		808		109,	3	759
3700		123,	4		858		116,	4	809
3750		130,	5		908		123,	5	859
3800		137,	6		958		130,	6	909
3850		144,	7		1008		137,	7	959
3900		152,	1		1058		145,	1	1009
3950		159,	2		1108		152,	2	1059
4000		166,	3		1158		159,	3	1109
4050		173,	4		1208		166,	4	1159
4100		180,	5		1258		173,	5	1209
4150		187,	6		1308		180,	6	1259
4200		194,	7		1358		187,	7	1309
4250		202,	1		1408		195,	1	1359
4300		209,	2		1458		202,	2	1409
4350		216,	3		1508		209,	3	[1]1459
4400		223,	4		1558		216,	4	1509
4450		230,	5		1608		223,	5	1559
4500		237,	6		1658		230,	6	1609
4550		244,	7		1708		237,	7	1659
4600		252,	1		1758		245,	1	1709
4650		259,	2		1808		252,	2	1759
4662		260,	7		1820		253,	7	1771
4663	IV,	1,	1	IV,	1		254,	1	1772
4690		4,	7		28		257,	7	1799
4691		5,	1		29	IV,	1,	1	IV, 1
4700		6,	3		38		2,	3	10
4750		13,	4		88		9,	4	60
4800		20,	5		138		16,	5	100
4850		27,	6		188		23,	6	160
4900		34,	7		238		30,	7	210
4950		42,	1		288		38,	1	260
5000		49,	2		338		45,	2	310
5050		56,	3		388		52,	3	360
5100		63,	4		438		59,	4	410
5150		70,	5		488		66,	5	460
5200		77,	6		538		73,	6	510

[1] Marked 1460 in Morris, but the error is not continued. Morris's 1470 is right again.

Comparative Table of Line-Numbers.

	FURNIVALL.			MORRIS.		
	Book Stanza	Verse of Stanza	Verse	Book Stanza	Verse of Stanza	Verse
5250 ...	IV, 84,	7	IV, 588	IV, 80,	7	IV, 560
5300 ...	92,	1	638	88,	1	610
5350 ...	99,	2	688	95,	2	660
5400 ...	106,	3	738	102,	3	710
5450 ...	113,	4	788	109,	4	760
5500 ...	120,	5	838	116,	5	810
5550 ...	127,	6	888	123,	6	860
5600 ...	134,	7	938	130,	7	910
5650 ...	142,	1	988	138,	1	960
5700 ...	149,	2	1038	145,	2	1010
5750 ...	156,	3	1088	152,	3	1060
5800 ...	163,	4	1138	159,	4	1110
5850 ...	170,	5	1188	166,	5	1160
5900 ...	177,	6	1238	173,	6	1210
5950 ...	184,	7	1288	180,	7	1260
6000 ...	192,	1	1338	188,	1	1310
6050 ...	199,	2	1388	195,	2	1360
6100 ...	206,	3	1438	202,	3	1410
6150 ...	213,	4	1488	209,	4	1460
6200 ...	220,	5	1538	216,	5	1510
6250 ...	227,	6	1588	223,	6	1560
6300 ...	234,	7	1638	230,	7	1610
6350 ...	242,	1	1688	238,	1	1660
6363 ...	243,	7	1701	239,	7	1673
6364 ...	V, 1,	1	V, 1	V, 1,	1	V, 1
6400 ...	6,	2	37	6,	2	37
6450 ...	13,	3	87	13,	3	87
6500 ...	20,	4	137	20,	4	137
6550 ...	27,	5	187	27,	5	187
6600 ...	34,	6	237	34,	6	237
6650 ...	41,	7	287	41,	7	287
6700 ...	49,	1	337	49,	1	337
6750 ...	56,	2	387	56,	2	387
6800 ...	63,	3	437	63,	3	437
6850 ...	70,	4	487	70,	4	487
6900 ...	77,	5	537	77,	5	537
6950 ...	84,	6	587	84,	6	587
7000 ...	91,	7	637	91,	7	637
7050 ...	99,	1	687	99,	1	687
7100 ...	106,	2	737	106,	2	737
7150 ...	113,	3	787	113,	3	787
7200 ...	120,	4	837	120,	4	837
7250 ...	127,	5	887	127,	5	887
7300 ...	134,	6	937	134,	6	937
7350 ...	141,	7	987	141,	7	987
7400 ...	149,	1	1037	149,	1	1037
7450 ...	156,	2	1087	156,	2	1087
7500 ...	163,	3	1137	163,	3	1137
7550 ...	170,	4	1187	170,	4	1187
7600 ...	177,	5	1237	177,	5	1237
7650 ...	184,	6	1287	184,	6	1287
7700 ...	191,	7	1337	191,	7	1337
7750 ...	199,	1	1387	199,	1	1387
7800 ...	206,	2	1437	206,	2	[1]1438
7850 ...	213,	3	1487	213,	3	1488
7861 ...	214,	7	1498	214,	7	1499

[1] Morris counts the signature *Le vostre T.* as v. 1422; hence the verse-numbers increase by one, as indicated.

Comparative Table of Line-Numbers.

Latin Thebaid argument following v 7861 is not counted.			not counted.	Here Morris inserts the Latin Thebaid argument as st. 215, vv. 1500—1511.			
7862	.. V,	215, 1	V, 1499	V, 216,	1	V,	1512
7900	...	220, 4	1537	221,	4		1550
7950	..	227, 5	1587	228,	5		1600
8000	.	234, 6	1637	235,	6	[1]	1651
8050	..	241, 7	1687	242,	7		1701
8100	..	249, 1	1737	250,	1		1751
8150	..	256, 2	1787	257,	2		1801
8200	..	263, 3	1837	264,	3		1851
8232	.	267, 7	1869	268,	7		1883

[1] Morris counts the signature *La vostre C.* after v. 7994 (his v. 1644) as v. 1645; hence his verse-numbers after 1644 increase by one.

[Professor Skeat's edition of the *Troilus* did not appear until this table had been sent to the printers. His numbering corresponds with Dr. Morris's for Book I., and with Dr. Furnivall's for the other books.]

ABBREVIATIONS AND SIGNS.

The Manuscripts.

A : Campsall MS.
B : Harleian MS. 2280.
C : Cambridge University Library MS. Gg. 4. 27.
Cp. : Corpus MS., Cambridge, 61.
D : Harleian MS. 3943.
Digby : Digby MS. 281, Bodleian Library.
Durh. : Durham MS. II. 13.
E : Harleian MS. 1239.
G : Additional MS. 12,044, British Museum.
Hl. (*Harl.*) 2392 : Harleian MS. 2392.
Hl. (*Harl.*) 4912 : Harleian MS. 4912.
John's : St. John's MS., Cambridge.
Phillipps : Phillipps MS. 8252.
Selden : Selden MS. B. 24, Bodleian Library.

Miscellaneous.

c (after the abbreviation for a MS. : as, C^c, D^c) : by the corrector.
def. adj. : adjective in the definite construction.
-*e*, -e̥, -(e), etc. : see explanation, pp. xvi, xvii, above.
f (*as in* 1643 f) : in rhyme.
L. : Layamon (A text). L^b. : Layamon (B-text).
n. : neuter *in the etymological notes; elsewhere usually* nominative.
O. : Ormulum.
P. Pl. : Piers Plowman.
rh. : rhymes with (*but a colon is usually employed*).
Var. : variant spellings.
9-*syl.* : a nine-syllable verse (*i. e.* a verse lacking the unaccented part of the first foot).
(i.), (ii.), (iii.) : see explanation, p. xvii, above.
ˈ indicates the ictus.
‖ indicates cæsura.
: indicates *rhymes with.*
† indicates a word or a verse certainly wrong, either in sense or metre.
‡ indicates a word or a verse that may be scanned and makes sense but that is shown by comparison of MSS. to be wrong.
A dot under a vowel indicates that it is suppressed in pronunciation by syncope or apocope.
[ ] indicates that something which is omitted in the MS. should be supplied.
( ) indicates that something which is written in the MS. should be omitted.
A slur or ellipsis different from the ordinary ellipsis of final weak *e* is often indicated by italicizing the final vowel of the first word and the initial vowel of the second. Thus,—lad*y* v̥nto (p. 9), pit*e* on (p. 89), stor*ye* it (p. 87).

OBSERVATIONS ON THE LANGUAGE OF
Chaucer's Troilus.

A = Campsall MS.   B = Harl. 2280.   C = Camb. Gg. 4.27.
D = Harl. 3943.   E = Harl. 1239.   G = Addit. MS. 12044.
                   Cp. = Corpus 61.

§ 1. Masculine, feminine, and neuter nouns of the *n*-declension in Anglo-Saxon end in the *Troilus* in -*e*.

§ 2. I. Masculine nouns of the *n*- declension (Child, § 3).

ape (A.S. apa), 2127 f (: iape *n.*).
asse (A.S. assa, O. asse), 731 (-*e* D).
bane (A.S. bona, baua, L. bone, L⁰. bane), 1405 (-ë ‡ it C), 4995, 5436, 5569, 6965 f (ban C) (: the blood Thebàne, -bàn C).
bere, beere (A.S. bera), 6115 f (: stere *inf.* : ledère); -*e*, 4622 (-ë ‡ or D).
byleeue (A.S. ge-léafa, L. i-læfe, O. læfe), 6956 f (beleue BCD) (: greúe *inf.* : leeue *adj. pl.*).
bowe (A.S. boga, L. boʒe, bowe), 208 (-[e] B, bow ‡ D), 1946 f (bow D) (: knowe *ind.* 3 *pl.*), 2620.
crede (A.S. créda), 6452 f (: Diomede : hede *n.* heed).
drope (A.S. dropa, L. drope), 934 f (: hope *ind.* 1 *sg.*); -*e*, 23.
drynke (A.S. drinca; but also drinc, *m.*, i-stem; L. ᵃᵇ drench, ᵃ drinc, ᵇ drinke, O. drinnc, drinnch, drinnke), 1736 f (: synke *inf.*); -[e], 5437 (-e D); drynk and, 4057 (-*e* BD). [Cf. drynk[e]lees, § 49, n. 5.]
fere, feere (A.S. ge-féra, L. i-vere, O. fere), 13 f, 4133 f ‡ B, 4338 f, 5453 f (fer D).
   Rhyme words.—cheere (13), dere *adj.* (4133 B, 4338), spere *sphæra* (4338), y-fere (5453).
galle (A.S. gealla, galla, O. galle), 5799 f (gaH D) (: falle *inf.*); -*e* ys, 7095 f (galles = gall is D) (: halles : wallys).
grame (A.S. grama, L. grame), 372 f (gaine † C, game † D) (: shame), 3870 f (: name), 5191 f (game † D) (: blame *inf.* : shame).

B

hawe (A.S. haga), 3696 f (haue C) (: i-drawe *p.p.*).
hele (A.S. héla), 5390 f (heele B) (: fele *inf.*).
hope (A.S. hopa, L O. hope), -*e*, 391 (-*e* he), 1895, 2392, 2408, 2414, 2418 (hoop D), 2425, 3257, 3268, 5240, 6092 (hep*e* † B, hoope D), 6993, 7048, 7276, 7558, 7561, 7570, 7761 (lou*e* ‡ C), 7763, 7801 (hoop*e* D).—hop*e* || the, 1092 ; -*e* halt, 6711. [hope †, 2357 D.]
hosbònde (A.S. húsbónda, L. husbonde, L^b. hosebonde, P. Pl. hosebonde), 1839 (hous*e*bonde B, husbonde C, husbond[e] ? D).—housbond*e* was, 7893 (hosband*e* C, husbond*e* D). [Cf. bonde, *adj.*, § 67, n. 2.]
knaue (A.S. cnafa, cnapa, L. cnaue, O. cnape-child), 3233 AC (sclaue B, own[e] D, felawē G).
knotte (A.S. cnotta), -*e*, 4574 B (knot ACD).
lappe (A.S. læppa, L^b. lappe (= L^a. bærm), P. Pl. lappe), 1533 (lape D), 2901 f (lape C) (: quappe *inf.*), 3584 f (: trappe *n.*).
mone, moone (A.S. móna, L.O. mone), 524 f, 1017 f, 1159 f, 2005, 2397 f, 3391 f, 3466, 6638 f, 6740 f, 7011, 7012 ; -*e* hath, 4598 ; -*e* o, 7552.
 Rhyme words.—to done (1017, 1159, 3391, 6638, 6740), soone (524, 1159, 2397, 6638), bone *boon* (1017).
name (A.S. noma, nama, L. nome, name, O. name), 251 f, 542 (Crisseide ‡ D), 870, 876, 880 CD, 895 f, 1069 † D, 1847 f, 3108 f, 3109 CD, 3160 f, 3871 f, 5226 f, 6129 f, 6228 f, 6243 ; -*e*, 99, 878, 880 AB, 3109 AB, 5819, 7418 (I men*e* † C), 7458, 8049.
 Rhyme words.—shame (251, 895, 1847, 6129, 6228), blame *n.* (3108), to blame (3160), grame (3871), game (5226, 6129, 6228), defame *inf.* (5226).
nekke (A.S. hnecca, L. necke), 2071 (nek ‡ D), 5767 ; -*e*, 4417 (nek D).
oxe (A.S. oxa, O. oxe), -*e*, 7832 (ox B).
shawe (A.S. scaga), 3562 f (schawe C, sawe † D) (: slawe *p.p.*).
skathe (O.N. skaði, cf. A.S. sceaða, scaða, L. scaðe, O. skaþe-læss), 4869 f (schathe C) (: rathe *adv.* : bathe *inf.*), 7301 f (: rathe *adv.*).
stede, steede (A.S. stéda, stǽda, L. stede), 1066, 1709 f (: blede *inf.*), 6669 f (sted D) (: to glede *n.* : hede *n. heed*), 7401 f (: nede *n.* : Diomede). [stedé † ire, 4545 C.]
stere (A.S. stéora *gubernator*, stéor *gubernaculum*), 4133 f (fere ‡ B) (: dere); -*e*, 7004 (-ee- B, ster(id) C, ster D). [Cf. ster[e]les, § 49, n. 5.]
 Note.—In 4133 *stere* = pilot; in 7004 *in stere* = astern.
sterre (A.S. steorra, L. steorre, sterre, O. sterrne), 175 f (: derre *comp.*); -*e*, 7001.—lodè-sterre, 6595 f (lodis s. C, lode-sterr D) (: werre *n.*), 7755 f (loode sterr D) (: werre *n.*).

tene, teene (A.S. téona, L. teone, O. tene), 814 f, 1146 f, 4068 f, 5458 f (teen B), 6267 f, 6603 f, 8077 f.
  Rhyme words.—grene (814, 1146, 6603), queene (814), kene *adj. pl.* (1146), to sene (4068), I wene *ind.* (5458), sustene *inf.* (5458, 6603), i-sene, sene *adj.* (6267, 8077), shene *def. adj.* (6267).

tyme (A.S. tíma, L.O. time), 155 f (: pryme), 351 f (: lyme *inf.*), 2074 f (: by me : pryme), 2178 f (: pryme), 2640 f (: pryme), 6833 f (: pryme).—tymë (*before consonants*), 703, 1057, 1075, 1877 ‡ CD, 2278 AC, 2682, 2806 BC (tyme y-se A, -ë se BC; D†), 3050 ‡ A (?), 3350, 3360, 3450, 3738 C (-e ylost ABD, -ë lost C; cf. 5945), 4321, 4423, 4437, 4510, 4556, 4917, 4996 (-e † D), 5013, 5786, 5922, 6178, 6274, 6470 CD, 6584, 6713, 6757, 6758, 6767, 7109 BCD (tyme ypassed A, -ë passid C (presente † B) D).— tymẹ, 1228 (t. that AB, tydẹ C, tymë ‡ that D), 2296 (t. my AB, tydẹ by C, tydẹ my D), 2834 D (t. ‡ be), 3146 ‡ D, 3337 ‡ C, 5986 AB (t. ther), 7111 † C.—tymë (*with hiatus*), 1305 ‡ AB, 2386 ‡ D, 3472 † D, 7110 ‡ CD; tymë (*before h*), 1877 ‡ A, 3671 † A, 4501 † D.—tyme (*before vowels*), 474 ABC, 564, 1305 CD, 1807, 2068, 2278 BD, 2386 ABC, 2537, 2582, 2606, 2806 A, 2828, 2834, 3050 BCD, 3472 ABC, 3697, 3738 ABD, 3914, 4244, 4621 ABC, 4720, 4761, 4996 † D, 5576, 5593, 5945, 6274, 6349 (B†), 6712, 6987, 7109 A, 7110 AB, 7111 ABD, 7199, 7688, 8062, 8167.—tyme he, 2841, 3671 BCD, 4501, 6625, 7043, 7581; t. hem, 6713; by tyme his, 5767 (be t. CD).

somtyme[1], 747 AB (-ẹ C ‡ D ‡),[2] 1367 (B †), 2586, 3293 (-e [and] A), 4037, 5315, 6273; -e he, 314; -e han, 5967 (-ẹ (to) haue CD); -ẹ, 508 ‡ D, 2972 AB (-e CD).[3]

tyme *in the phrase* ofte tyme, 1877 CD, 6833 f ‡ C, 7172 (tymes D); -e, 913, 7946 (-ẹs D), 8121 A (oft[e] t. B, ofte tymẹs D); -e (*before he, his, hym, here* = her, *hath*), 1850, 1877 B, 3971, 5823 (-ẹs D), 7939 (-ẹs D); tymẹ that, 5986 AB (*reading doubtful*); tymë ‡ hath, 1877 A.

a thousand tyme, 531 f (: ryme *inf.*); a thowsand tyme he, 457 BD (-ẹs A, sythis seyde C); a th. t. here (*eam*), 4094 (sithis C, tymẹs D); sixty tyme a day, 441; a hunderid tyme, 4437 C (-ẹs D, sithe A, sithe he B); tweynty tyme he, 6554 (-ẹs D).—an hundred tymës gan, 4202 (-ys C); a thousand tymës selle, 4443 (-ë CD); a

---
[1] In this compound *som* is variously spelt, but always monosyllabic.
[2] Apparently we should read: Ek som tyme it is (i. e. it's) a craft to semë fle.
[3] Or, Ye woldẹ som tymë, etc.

th. tymés more, 5488 A (-e B, -eʒ D); a th. tymès mercy, 6162 (-e B, -ys C); a th. tymes (*before vowels*), 2174 (-ys C), 3231 (-ys C), *so* twenty th. t., 3315 (-ys C, -es D).—Compare, tymés twyés twelue, 6460 (-e D, B ‡ (?), C ‡ (?)). [Cf. sithe, § 14.]

welcome¹ (A.S. wilcuma, L. wilcume, wulcume, L.ᵇ wil-, wel-, wol-come, P. Pl. welcome, welcomen), he was wel-come, 6436 f (: i-come *p.p.*); wel come (*as interj.*), 6555 f (: nome *p p.*); wher shal I seyę to yow wel come or no, 5493 A (wel com B, wheider shal I sey welcome ‡ or no D).—wel-comę my knyght, 4151 (w. myn peʒ † C). [Var. wolcome, C 6436 and 6555.]

wele (A.S. wela), 5145 (welè knowe A, welę y-knowe BC, wel I knowe D †); -e, 4, 1951 (D †), 3662, 3678, 4314 (wel B; D †), 5144 (wel BD), 7693 (wel D). [welę for welę, 335 D (wel for wel AB), = well *adv.*]

welle (A.S. wella; but also wiell, *m.*, i-stem; L. welle, L.ᵇ wel, O. welle), 873 f, 1263 f, 1593 f, 5807 f, 6215 f, 7693 f (weH D), 7860 f (weH D), 7928 f (weH D); -e, 1926 (wel B), 4315.

Rhyme words.—telle *inf.* (873, 1263, 1593, 7928), dwelle *inf.* (1593, 5807, 7693, 7928), vnswelle *inf.* (5807), helle (873, 6215)

wille, wylle. (A.S. willa, L. wille, ıwille, O. wille), ·125 f, 1316 f, 2687 (wıl[le] D),² 2773 (wil[le] D), 4769 (willes B, wil[le] D), 6950 f (wiH D), 8168 f (wiH D) [His wille hath, 7905 C, is an error.]

Rhyme words.—stille *adj.* (125), stille *inf.* (1316), spille *inf.* (6950) Achille (8186).

The form *wil* (A.S. ge-will, *n.*, quasi jo-stem, common instead of gewile, *n.* (prob.), i-stem, see Siev. § 262. 2 and n. 3, Cosijn, Aws. Gr. II, 12; L. i-wil, O. will, P. Pl. wil) is common. Sometimes it is impossible to decide between *wil* and *wille*).—wil, wyl, (i.) 228 (willę B, will CD), 861 (willę B, wil [sche] C), 1355 (wyH A), 1564 (willę D), 3465 (wiH D), 4362 (willę BD), 7720 (wille C, wil [it] A), 8000. (ii.) 1939, 2294, 5175 (wiH D).

wone (A.S. ge-wuna, L. wune, i-wune, L.ᵇ wone), 1403 f (: sone *filius*); wonę to, 7010 (he was ‡ wont(e) D).

wrecche (A.S. wrecc(e)a, L. wræche, L.ᵇ wrecche, wrech, O. wrecche), 798 f, 889 f, 1425 f, 1518 f, 1975, 4215 f, 5238, 5291 f, 6106 f, 6251 f, 6684 f; -e, 708, 777 (wrecch D, -e ‡ be A), 805, 4933 (wrich B), 5406 (wrech D), 5500 (-e se CD), 7068 (wrech D).

---

[1] Confused, as is well known, with *wel, adv.*, and *come, p.p.*: cf. Icel velkomınn.
[2] ABG seem to have *yourě willě be*; CD read "ʒif (If) it ʒourę (ʒour) wille (wıl[le]) be (were)."

Rhyme words.—recche *inf.* (798, 1425, 1518, 6251), recche *subj.* 3 *sg.* (5291), strecche *inf.* (889, 1425), kecche *inf.* (4215), drecche 2 *pl.* (6106), fecche *inv.* (6684) [Var. BCD wreche; B wriche; D wretche]

Note.—For *awe, bole, felawe*, see § 15. For *make-les*, see § 49, n. 5.

§ 3. II. Feminine nouns of the *n*- declension (Child, § 4).

arwe (A.S. arwe, arewe (mid arewan *Chron.* 1083; arwan *catapultas* Aldh. Gl.; see Sweet, p. 281), *earlier* ærig, carh, L. arwe, L^b. arewe), an arwe, 1726 (a narwe B), 6210.

asce (A.S. asce), 1624 (asshen B, asschin C, asshyn D).

belle (A.S. belle, L.O. belle), 2700 f (: telle *inf.* : dwelle *inf.*), 3031, 3040 f (bell D) (: telle *inf.* : dwelle *inf.*), 7425 (bel[le] B).

blase (A.S. blǽse, L P. Pl. blase), -e, 4846.

cheke, cheeke (A S. céace, céce), 4792 f (: cke : byseche *inf.* A, by-seke BD, beseke C).

dokke (A.S. docce), -e, 5123.

erthe (A.S. eorðe, L.O. eorðe, L.^b O. erþe), -e, 2850 (erhte B), 2863 (erthe and [whom] B), 4586 (eriþth B, erthe ‡ hath E), 4603 (erth B).—erthe that, 8178 A (erth B). [Cf. ertheles, § 49, n. 5.]

harpe (A.S. hearpe, L. harpe), 731 f (: sharpe *adv.*), 2116 f (hare † B) (: harpe *inf.* : sharpe *adv.*).

herte (A.S. heorte, L. heorte, O. heorrte, herrte), 307 f, 792 f, 1987 f, 2016 f, 2064 f, 2181 f, 2372 f, 2717 f, 2940 f, 2989 f, 3578 f, 3746 f, 3789 f, 3843 f (C †), 3913 f, 3940 f, 4025 f, 4213 f, 4340 f (-t C), 4757 f, 4902 f, 4908 f, 5089 f, 5802 f, 5846 f, 6071 f (C †), 6111 f, 6161 f, 6282 f, 6426 f (-t C), 6496 f (-t C), 6564 f (-t C), 6618 f, 7085 f, 7413 f, 7588 f (-t C), 7687 f, 7707 f, 7783 f (-t C), 7857 f, 7897 f. (In many of the above cases D has *hert.*)—herte (*before consonants*), 367 (-[e] BD), 1693 (-[e] BD), 2389 (-[e] D), 3881 (-[e] BD), 4052, 5338, 6149 (-[e] B), 7371, 7563 (-[e] B), 7570 (-[e] B), 7682; cf. also 228, 502, 599, 606, 749, 1006, 1063, 1664, 1783, 1845, 1894, 1985, 2007, 2016, 2035, 2067, 2193, 2326, 2406, 2411, 2442, 2677, 2885, 2899, 2952, 2969, 3198, 3453 B, 3616, 3642, 3645, 3685, 3730, 3750, 3752, 3830, 3845, 3885, 3911, 3928, 4023, 4120, 4123, 4146, 4191, 4263, 4330, 4391, 4407, 4433, 4486, 4536, 4674, 4981, 5242, 5269, 5361 A, 5871, 5936, 5973, 6079, 6190, 6214, 6252, 6591, 6808, 6816, 7275, 7490, 7552, 7676, 7684, 7694, 7746, 7931, 7934, 8022, 8060. (In some of these cases *hert[e]* is found in B or D or both. Even A occasionally has *hert[e]*, as in 229, 453, 1652.) [Cf. herteles, § 49, n. 5.]

herte is occasionally found, but in nearly every case a comparison of MSS disposes of this apocopated form (so in 1759 C, 1941 C, 3189 C, 8022 C). The same is true of *hert* before a consonant (see, e.g., D in vv. 599, 2193, 2442, 3750, 4391, 5269; cf. also 278 A). The following lines seem to admit of two scansions :

As muche ioie as hertę (hert D) may (myght D) comprehende (herte ... complende A), 4529 (-e may comprende Cp.).

A kynges hertę (hert D) semeth bi hiręs a wreche, 889 (or, hertë semęth). (Cf. 4674, especially CD.)

There are no cases of hiatus except such as a comparison of MSS easily corrects. Thus,—hertë ‡ is, 1957 A; hertë ‡ alle, 1956 B.

herte, 2456 (-t BD), 2911 (-t D), 2956 (-t D), 3849 (-t BD); cf. 250, 461, 1561, 2186, 2310, 2951, 2987, 3018, 3235, 3475, 3729, 3835, 3838, 4330 B, 4367 A, 5873, 6672, 6711, 6749, 8209. The spelling *hert* before a vowel is found in all MSS to some extent: see the above list and cf. the following lines, in which A has *hert*,— 535, 928, 1954, 2014 (C herte).—herte he, 2013 AB[1]; 3645 ‡ C, 5572 AB, 7141, 7937; -e hym, 3857 A; -e hath, 6501 (-t D), 7880.—hertë happe, 7159 (D?).

> Rhyme words.—conuerte *inf.* (307, 1987, 6071), peynes, sorwes smerte (792, 3789, 4938, 5089, 5802, 6161, 6564, 7085, 7687, 7783), smerte *adv.* (4902), smerte *prcs. and pret. subj.* 3 *sg.* (2181, 2989, 3746, 3843, 5846, 6426, 6496, 7588), *pret. ind.* 3 *sg. inf.* (2016) *inf.* (2372, 4025, 6111, 6282), asterte *pres subj.* 3 *sg* (7707), sterte, asterte *pret. ind.* 1, 3 *sg.* (2181, 2940, 3913, 4757, 6071, 6564, 7857, 7897), sterte *inf.* (2717, 3789, 4340, 4902, 6618), to-sterte *inf.* (2064), sherte *n* (3578, 3940, 4213, 4757).

howue (A.S. húfe, P. Pl. howue, houue, houe), -e, 3617 (houe C, howe D), 6832.[2]

larke (A.S. láwerce, P. Pl. larke), 4033 (- [e] B).

[lilie (A.S. lilie), the lilie ‡ (*dissyl.*) wexith, 942 D (rose ABC).]

lyne (A.S. líne, P. Pl. lyne), 2262 f (: dyne *inf.*), 2546 f (: dyne *inf.*: fyne *inf.*), 3070 (blyve ‡ D), 7140 f (: fyne *inf.*); -e, 1061, 3346 (lynę C).

> Note —In 2262 and 3346 a *line of writing* is meant ; in the other instances, a *word* or the like. In 7844, where *lineage* is intended, A and B have *ligne*, D has *lyne* (*lyue* † C).

masse (A.S. mæsse, O. messe, P. Pl. masse), 2930 f (: neuere the lasse : passe *inf.*) [mes : les : passe D].

more, moore (A.S. more ; also moru, *f.*, see Sievers, § 278, n. 1; P. Pl. more), 6388 f (moor D) (: forlore *p.p.* : eueręmore).

myte (A.S. míte, P. Pl. myte), 3674 f (: lyte), 3742 f (: lyte : white

---

[1] *herte rente* C is doubtless for *herte he r.* In D, read *hert[e] r.* (?). But cf. 5572, where *hertë* seems to have given rise to *herte he* in AB.

[2] A alone preserves the right reading. B has *howen*, C *enmy entendit*, D *ougne*, G *honde*. See Skeat's n. on P. Pl. xxiii, 172, ed. 1886, II, 280.

§ 3.]   *of Chaucer's Troilus.*   7

adj. pl.), 5346 f (: visite *inf.* : delite *inf.*). . [For *mytę,* 4445 D, read *mot* (A.S. mot) with A (moote B, mote C).]

netle (A.S. netele, netle), 941 (nettyl C, nettle D); netle in dokke out, 5123 (nettle B, nettil C, netill D).

nyghtyngale (A.S. nihtegale, nehtegale), 4075 f (: tale *n.*); -e, 2003.

owle (A.S. úle), -e, 6682.

✓ pride (A.S. pryte; also pryt, *f.*; L. prude, prute), -e, 230, 4643, 4647 (?).

rose (A.S. róse), 942 (lilie ‡ *dissyl.* D), 2341 f (: suppose *ind.* 1 *sg.*); -e ‡, 7207 C.

shete (A.S. scéte (M.), scyte (L.W.S.), P. Pl. schete), -e, 3898 (-e hit = it D), 4412 (9-syl.). [Var. B shette; CD schete.]

✓ side, syde (A.S. síde, L.O. side, P. Pl. syde-borde, sydbenche, sydtable), 185 f, 321 f, 3818 (-e BCD), 4308 f (biside D), 4577 f, 4826 f, 5354 f, 5486 f, 5740 f, 6012 f, 6053 f, 6128 f (s(e)yde B), 6947 f, 7062 f, 7115 f; -e, 4896, 7050; -e hym, 3078, 4431; -e here (*eam*), 3524 (-e [her] D).

Rhyme words.—I. Infinitives: gyde (185), hide (321, 5486), chyde (4308), betide (4577, 6128), byde (4826), abyde (5486, 6012). II. Subjunctives: gyde 3 *sg.* (5354), bytyde 3 *sg.* (6053, 7115), aspiede (aspie † A, aspied B, espied D) *pret.* 3 *pl.* (*sg.* ‡ C) (6053). III. Nouns: tyde (5740, 7062), Cupide (6947). [The rhyme with *seyde* (dixit) in 321 C counts for nothing; *seyde* is wrong.] (For *aside, beside*, see § 88.)

sonne (A.S. sunne, L. sunne, Lb. sonne, O. sunne), 1259 f, 1849, 1866 f, 1947, 1990 f, 2054, 2322 f, 2671 f, 3220 f, 3610, 4306 (sonnę Tytàn A, *but omit* to *and read* sonnë Tytan), 4446, 5029 ABD, 7024, 7648; -e, 1852, 3950, 5901, 6094, 6105 ABD, 6911 (forme ‡ C), 7249; -e hym, 4549 (-e ‡ hastith D). [sunnę, 5029 ‡ C, 6105 ‡ C.]

Rhyme words.—konne *ind.* 1, 3 *pl.* (1259, 1866, 2671), *inf.* (3220), bygonne *p.p.* (1866, 2322, 2671), y-ronne (1990), y-wonne (2322), donne *pred. adj. pl.* (1990).

Note.—*Sonne* is the spelling of AB, *sunne* the usual form in C. D has both forms and also *sun* (2671 f, 3220 f).

swalwe (A.S. swealwe, swalwe), 1149 (-ow † D).

throte (A.S. þrote; also þrotu, *f.*, see Sievers, § 278, n. 1), 1410 (-ę ‡ A); -e here (*poss. sg.*), 4092.

tonge, tunge (A.S. tunge, L.O. tunge), 1315 (-[e] D), 1889 f (-g D, tunge(n) A), 3136 f, 5183, 5463 f, 5543, 6358, 6808, 7167 (C †), 7424 f, 7684 (-ę (?) D †), 8157 f, 8159 f; tonge, 1099 AB, 2766 (tung D), 3144 (tong B, tung D), 7926 BD (-ë may C, -ę ‡ A). [tung[ë] it ‡, 1099 D.]

Rhyme words.—ronge *p.p.* (1889 [runge(n) A], 7424), songe, y-songe *p.p.* (5463, 7424, 8157, 8159), to vs yonge (3136), tonge (8157). [AB have usually the spelling *tonge*; C has usually *tunge*, D usually *tunge* or *tung*.]

trappe (A.S. træppe, O. trapp), 3583 f (: lappe *n.*); trappë dorę, 3601 (trap[pe] D).

wodë-bynde (A.S. wudebinde), 4073 f AC (wonbynde † B, woodbynde D) (: wynde *inf.*).

wyke, wowke, see § 8, p. 15.

wyse (A.S. wíse, L.O. wise, L.ᵇ wis, guyse), 81 f, 159 CD (*pl.* AB), 162 f, 275 f, 336 f, 363 f, 697 f, 952 f, 957 f, 985 f, 1114 f, 1359 f, 1471 f, 1764 f, 1806 f, 2001 f (gyse C), 2149 f, 2548 f, 2631 f, 2752 f, 2785 f, 2897 f, 2912 f, 2974 f, 3079 f, 3298 f, 3618 † f C, 3693 f, 3785 f, 3811 f, 3889, 4129 f, 4310 f, 4390 f, 4436 f, 4516 f, 4639 f, 4660 f (wys A), 4740 f, 4899 f, 5056 f, 5174 f, 5472 f, 5495 f, 5551 f, 6000 f, 6189 f, 7460 f, 7683 f, 7831 f; wyse, 61, 285, 440 ABC, 2006, 2154, 3336 † D, 6427 (guise D); -e his, 3797; -e he, 8197.— wysę ‖ soth, 3197 AB (-ë CD).

>   Rhyme words.—this wyse *sapiens* (81), wyse *adj. pl.* (697, 957, 985, 2001, 3693, 3785, 4390), seruice,-ise,-yse (81, 162, 336, 952, 957, 985, 1764, 2974, 4129, 4639, 4660, 5056, 5174, 5472, 5495, 7683), sacrifice *n.* (7831), deuyse *inf.* (275, 1114, 1471, 2149, 2631, 2897, 3079, 3298, 4436, 4516, 4639, 4660, 4740, 4899, 5472, 5551, 7460, 7683), deuyse *ind.* 2 *pl.* (6189), ryse *inf.* (275, 697, 2912, 3811, 4310), aryse *inf.* (2752, 3785), aryse *p.p.* (2548), auyse *inf.* (363, 2785, 4436), auyse *ind.* 3 *pl.* (1359), des-, dispise *inf.* (1806, 4310, 7381), dispise *subj.* 3 *pl.* (6000), suffise *inf.* (3693, 5056, 7460). [wyse ‡ *n.* (81 D).]

wydowe (A.S. wiodu (*old and rare*), widuwe, weoduwe, wuduwe, Ps. widwe, N. widua, Sievers, §§ 71 and n. 1, 156.4, L. widewe, O. widewe, widdwe), wydowe (*dissyl.*) was, 97 AD (wydew B, wedęwe C).

>   Note.—For *loue*, see § 8; for *rynde, rysshe, sleue*, § 9; for *bore, sherte*, § 15.

§ 4. III. Neuters of the *n*- declension (Child, § 2).

ere, eerę (A.S. éare, O. ære), 106 f, 725 f, 767 f, 1280 f, 1536 f, 2722 f, 3301 f, 3408 f, 3596 f, 3951 f, 4725 f, 5306 f; ere, 5096.

>   Rhyme words.—fere *timor* (106, 725, 767, 1536, 3301, 3596), were *pret. subj.* 3 *sg.* (725, 767, 3301, 3408, 3951), there (1280, 3596, 5306), bere *feretrum* (2722), euery where (4725).

eye, yë (A.S. éage, L.ᵇ eʒe, O. eʒhe), 272, 453 f, 1386 f, 1488 f, 1989 f, 4188 ‡ E, 4972 ‡ f C, 5060 f, 6318 f, 6811 f, 6917 f, 7264 f; eye, 6442 (eyʒyn C).

>   Note.—*Eye* is the prevailing spelling; *yę*, which is shown by the rhyme to be Chaucer's form, is found in 7264 (ABD), 6917 B, 6811 D, 4972 C. Other forms are: in B, *eyghe*, 272; *eighe*, 1386; *eigh*, 1488; *heye*, 1989; in C, *eyʒe*, 453, 1386; in D, *ey*, 1488, 5060; *yhe*, 6318, 6442; *yee*, 6917. *Heighe*, 1989 A, is an error. *Eyę* occurs in 272 D.

>   Rhyme words.—companye (453, 6811), folye (453), lye (1386, 5060, 6318, 7264), heighe (*l.* hye) (1488), prye (1488), wrye *inf.* (1989), y-wrye *p.p.* (6318), aspye *inf.* (6917), sl(e)ye *adj. pl.* (7264). [In 4972 C the rhyme is false,—twye : yë : awcye.]

§ 5. In *lady* (A.S. hlǽfdige, *f.*) and *pley* (A.S. plega, *m.*), the final vowel disappears, and in *pley* the *g* unites with the preceding vowel to form a diphthong (Child, § 5; ten Brink, § 211). In *fo, foo* (A.S. ge-fá, *m.*) an old (A.S.) contraction is preserved (ten Brink, § 211; Sievers, § 277, n. 2).

lady (A.S. hlǽfdige, L. læfdi, O. laffdiȝ), làdy (*before vowels and consonants*), 106, 166 ABC, 346, 434, 493, 524 (bodıe † D), 1025, 1093, 1164 BD, 1510, 2150, 2177, 2501, 2718, 2799, 3797, 3910, 4131, 4327, 5265, 5863, 6112, 6507 (laydy B), 6525, 6581, 6592, 6815, 6820, 6939, 7032, 7235, 7678, 8029, etc.; lad̄y̆ (*before vowels and consonants*), 166 ‡ D, 269, 7879; làdy vntò, 1164 A. [*ladi* is common in C.]

pley (A S. plega, *m.*, L. plæȝe), 6291 f (pleye B, play. C) (ˊ weye *acc.* (way BD, alway ‡ C): away); pley and, 1790 (*-e* B, play C †); pleye the, 5528 (pley CD).

fo, foo (A.S. ge-fá, *sbst.* (fáh, fá, *adj*), Lᵃ. ifa, Lᵇ. fo, ifo), 837 f (wo † B), 1573 f, 1769 f, 2567 f, 2701 (for † C), 4828 f, 5751 f, 6522 f, 6591 f (soo † D); *before vouels*, 485, 1990.

feldefare, 3703 f BC (feld[e] fare BC, feldyfare D) (: fare 3 *pl.*) (cf. Parl. F., 364) is referred to *felofor, m.*, though Bosworth Toller questioningly recognizes a weak feminine *feldefare* on the strength of the eleventh-century gloss *clodhamer and feldeware*, Wright-Wülck., p. 287, 17. The M.-Eng. form has perhaps been influenced by popular etymology (quási *feld-gefara*).

Note.—For *wyndowe*, see § 15.

§ 6. Anglo-Saxon masculine and neuter vowel-stems that have a final vowel (-e or -u) in the nominative singular, preserve this vowel as -e in the *Troilus*.

For convenience the following nouns are thrown together in a single alphabetical list : (i.) masculine jo- (ja-) stems with long stem-syllable,—*ende, leche*; (ii.) neuter jo- (ja-) stems with long stem-syllable,—*wede, wyte* (for *ernde*, see § 7); (iii.) neuter wo-stem,—*bale*; (iv.) masculine i-stems with short stem-syllable,—*ache, hate, hegge, lye, mete, pilwe*; (v.) neuter i-stem with short stem-syll ble,—*spere*; (vi.) masculine u-stems with short stem-syllable,—*sunu, wudu*. Masculine nomina agentis in *-ere* (which properly belong under i.) and abstract nouns in *-scipe* (which properly belong under iv.) seldom (nouns in *-scipe* perhaps never) retain -e : see § 7. For *wil, wille*, see § 2. For *awe*, see § 15.

ache (A.S. ece, *m.*), *-e*, 5390 (ach B, eche C).

bale (A.S. bealu, *n.*, L. balu, bale), 5401 f (: fyngres . . . smale : pale *pred. adj. sg.*).

ende (A.S. ende, *m.*, L.O. ende), 966 f, 1303 f, 1876 f, 2320, 2333 f, 2580 f, 2960 f, 3047 f, 3234 f, 3304 f, 3457 f, 3544 f, 3611 f, 3773 f, 4601, 4655 f, 5777 f, 6062 f, 6242 f, 6838 f, 7257 f, 7421 f, 7636 f, 7917 f, 8032 f ; end*e*, 1345, 5498, 7756 ; end[e], 6862 f AB (-e CD). [Cf. endeles, § 85.]

> Rhyme words.—I. Infinitives: bende (2333), wende (2333, 2580, 3457, 3544, 3611, 4655, 5777, 6242, 6838, 6862, 7917), blende, blynde, *carcare* (2580, 3047, 6062), sende (3304, 5777, 8032), shende (6242, 7257, 7421) ; II. shende *ind.* 1 *sg.* (7636), *subj.* 3 *sg.* (966), wende *eam* (1303), *cas* (3234), *camus* (3047, 7257), *eatis* (2960 ABC), to-rende *subj.* 3 *pl.* (1876), sende *mittas* (3544), *mittat* (3773, 6862).

-ere : see § 7.

ernde. The best MSS. have *erand*. See § 7.

hate (A.S. hete, *m.* (cf. hatian), L. hæte, hete, O. hete), 1798 ; *-e*, 3870 ; *-e* he, 477.

hegge (A.S. hege, *m.*, cf. hecg, *f.* (?), hecc), He loketh forth by *hegge* by tre by greue, 7507 (hegg B, hegis ‡ C, hegges ‡ D, hege G).

leche (A.S. léce, léce, *m.*, L. lecho, læcho, O. læche), 857 f (: I beseche), 1656 f (: preche *inf.* : speche), 2151 f (lece A) (: seche *petunt* : speche), 2667 f (: techo *inf.*), 7900 f (: speche : seche *inf.*) ; *-e*, 2664. —lechëcraft, 5098.

lye (A.S. lyge, *m.*, N. lyg) ; And for a soth they telle that lyie is, 6069 C° (: amphibologyis), *but read* twenty lyes *with ABD*.

mete (A.S. mete, *m.*, N. met(t), L.O. mete), *-e*, 907 (mone † C, brede ‡ D); 5437 ABD[1] (-e C) ; *-e* his, 485.

pilwe (A.S. pyle, pylwe, *m.*), Saue a pilwe (pilwo B, pillowe D, pilowe G) I (*om.* C) fynde nought (G *inserts* elles) tenbrace (to embrase CG, to enbrace D), 6587.

-shipe (A.S. -scipe) : see § 7.

sone (A.S. sunu, *m.*, L. sune, sone, O. sune), 226, 1401 f (: wone *custom*), 7027 ABC ; son*e*, 2, 261, 1187, 1793, 3012 (some † B, sone ‡ thogh D), 4650 (son D †), 6375, 6451, 7953, 8109.—Tydeus sone that doun descended is, 7877 ABDG. (sone †, 7027 D.)

> Note.—Verses 226, 7027 disprove ten Brink's remark (Chaucers Sprache und Verskunst, §§ 260, 261) that *sone* never occurs as a dissyllable in the interior of a verse in Chaucer. Further examples of dissyllabic *sone* will be given from the *Legend of Good Women* in an article by Professor J M. Manly, which is soon to appear. (Cf. also Child, § 12.)

[1] Later in the line read *drynk*[*e*] ABC (drynke D).

spere (A.S. spere, *n.*, L. spere, sper, P. Pl. spere, sper), 3216 f (speere
B) (: swere *juro*); spere, 2512 (spore A), 4702; sperę ‡ for, 1286 C.
wede (A.S. (ge)wǽde, *n.*, L.ª iwede, ᵇ wede, O. wæde), 177 f, 4273 f
(-ee- D, wode † B), 4561 f.

> Rhyme words.—drede *n.* (*all*), brede *n.* (177), rede *ind.* 3 *pl.* (4273, 4561).

wil, wille : see § 2.

wode (A.S. wudu, *m.*, L. wude, wode, O. wude), haselwodé thoughte,
6868 (hastow † B); from haselwodę ‖ there, 7537; haselwodés
shaken, 3732 AB (*-e* is CD); *-e*, 2417. [Var. B -wodde; D -woode.]

wyte (A.S. wíte, *n.*, L.O. wite), 2733 f (: lite *adj.*), 3581 f (: byte *inf.* :
a lyte). [Var. C wite, wy3te.]

§ 7. Exceptions to § 6.

A.S. *ǽrende* and *stéle*, neuter jo-stems, lose their -e in the *Troilus*.
The final -e of the termination -*shipe* (A.S. -scipe, masc. i-stem) is
not sounded and sometimes not written. The final -e of the termination -*ere* (A.S. -ere, jo-stem) is not sounded except in rhyme.

ernde. Instead of *ernde* (A.S. ǽrende, *n.*, jo-stem, L. ærnde, ernde, O.
errnde), the best MSS. have (*h*)*erand* in the only place where this
word occurs,—erand was, 1157 (herand B, erndé D).

stel (A.S. stéle, stýle, *n.*, L. stel, dat. stele) shows no -e,—of stel,
1678 f (-e BD) (: euęry del : wel(e) *adv.*), 4987 f (stiel B, stele D)
(: vpon the whiel)¹; of stel and, 3322 (stiel B, stele D); trewë as
stel in, 7194 (steele B, stele D).

-ere (A.S. -ere, L.W.S. also -re, *m.*, forming nomina agentis) :
èndere, 5163 (-er C, yendir D).
fýndere, 1929 (-er BD, fingir † C). [-ère (?).]
hàrpour (A.S. hearpere), *before vowel*, 2115 (ha[r]ppour B).
hòldere, 1729 (-er D, -yn † C).
ledère (A.S. lǽdere ?), 6116 f (-dèr D) (: yfere : bere *ursus*).
lòuére, 510 (-er D), 512 (-er AB), 2431 (-er BD), 4634 (-er BD),
4640 (-er BD), 5862 (-er BD); lòuere, 20 (-er D †), 1115 (-er BD),
4228 (-er E), 4570, 5233 (-er D, -ers B); -ëre hastow, 4301
(-er B, oone † D); lòuere I, 1097 (-er BD); -ere he, 2130 (-ëię
seyde C, -er he D).
lyere (A.S. léogere), 3151 (-er BD); lyerę, 3157 (accent uncertain
A ; -er BD, h[e]ie C).
màkere, 741 (-er BD ; *in* A *read* [y]beten), 4279 (-er BD)² ; -erę
yet, 8150 (-er BD).

---

¹ C ‡ om. *of*.   ² Thow rakel nyght there God makere of kynde.

mòrter (A.S. mortere, *m.*, from Lat. mortarium, cf. Pogatscher, §§ 259, 287), m. that, 5907 (percher C).

rèdere (A.S. rédere), 6633 (-er D).

> Note.—The following verses, though they prove little or nothing, are curiously illustrative of the ending *-ere* in the fourteenth century:—
> Jak Chep, Tronche, Jon Wrau, Thom Myllere, Tyler, Jak Strawe, Erle of the Plo, Rak to, Deer, et Hob Carter, Rakstrawe;
> Isti ductores in plebe fuere priores.—Versus de tempore Johannis Straw. Wright, *Political Poems*, I, 230.

-shipe, -ship (A.S. -scipe), termination forming abstract nouns:

felawship. And wher that (*om.* BCD) hym lyst (liste B, leste C) best felawship (felaweschipe B, felauschepe C) kan, 1291.— felawshipe, 3245 (-shyp B, -ship D †, felauschepe C).

frendship (A.S. fréondscipe, L. freonscipe), (i.) 2872 (-schipe B, -shipe D). (ii.) frenship, 1456 (-shippe B, -schepe C, frendship D); frendship, 6498 (frendeschipe B, frenschepe C, frensshipe D), 7985 (-e D, -schip B, frenschep C); frendship haue, 1325 (-e D, frenschepe C), 2047 (frenship B, frenschepe C, frendship to D); frendship-here (*dat.*), 6548 (frenchep B, frenschepe C, frensshipe ‡ to D).

lordship (A.S. hláfordscipe), lordship yow, 2505 (-chip B, -schepe (I) ȝow C); -ship hym, 2921 (-schepe C, -ship was ‡ D); -ship ouer, 4598 (lorchip B, lorschepe C, lord(e)schipe E).

worship (A.S. weorðscipe, L. wurðscipe, worðschepe, O. wurrþshipe), w. and, 46 (-schip B, -shipp D), 82 (-schipp B, -schepe C).

§ 8. Anglo-Saxon feminine nouns that have -u in the nominative, end in the *Troilus* in -e throughout the singular (except in the genitive).

The following list includes (i.) -ā- (-ō-) stems with short stem-syllable: *an-swere, care, fare, lawe, love, sawe, shame, tale, wyke* (originally n-stem); (ii.) abstract nouns in *-u*, *-o*, corresponding to Gothic abstracts in *-ei* and usually indeclinable in the singular: *brede, elde, hele, hete*; (iii.) feminine u-stem with short stem-syllable: *dore*. For *more, throte*, see § 3. [For *gere*, see § 43, n. 3.]

answere (A.S. andswaru, Durh. ondsuere *acc.*, L. æn(d)-swere, answare, O. anndsware, -swere); answere, 69 (-er B, aunswer D), 72 (-er B), 2245 (-er B), 7786 A (C (?); -er D) [1]; answere yow, 2210 (answère † ȝow CD); answere hym, 5556 (answer to ? B, answère

---

[1] Of wich in effect hire answere was this C.

him C, answèr him D); answère, 2139 (ans(e)wère B, answèr(d) D), 5820 (-èr D).[1]

brede (A.S. brǽdu, L[a]. brǽde, L[b]. brede), 179 f (: wede n. : drede n.), 530 f (: lede inf. : drede n.), 8020 f (: Diomede : hede n. heed).

care (A.S. caru, L O. care), 505 f, 550 f, 587 f, 612 f, 660 f, 1016 f, 1192 f, 2085 f, 4407 f, 4891 f, 5124 (?) f AB (vb. CD), 5194 ‡ f (fare AB), 5241 f, 6230 f, 6383 f, 6417 f, 6600 f, 6698 ‡ f B, 6699 f AC[c]D (fare B), 7112 f, 7321 f, 7511 f, 7731 f (càr D); care, 1862 ‡ D; care hym, 3908.

Rhyme words :—in the snare (505, 7112), Pandare (550, 587, 612, 5124 (?) AB, 5241, 7511), fare n. (550, 1016, 2085, 4407, 6230, 6417, 6698 B, 6699 AC[c]D, 7731), wel-fare (4891), ye fare ind 2 pl. (1192, 6600, 7321), inf. (4407, 5194 CD, 5241, 6383, 7321), bare adj (660, 1192, 4891), spare inf. (6417).

dore (A.S. duru; cf. dor, n.; L.O. dore, dure), -e, 180 (-è ‡ vndir C), 3540, 3590, 5014 (C †); -e he, 4894; -e hym, 2033.—dorę (before a pause), 3526, 3587 (dere † C)[2], 3601 (trap[pe] dore D).

elde (A.S. ieldu; also ield; L. ælde, æld, O. P. Pl. elde), 1478 (-[e], C), 1484 (-[e] D, olde C); -e, 6031 (age D).

fare (A.S. faru, L. fare, fære, uore, P. Pl. fare), 551 f, 1018 f, 2086 f, 2229 f, 3447 f, 3595 † f B, 3948 f, 4408 f, 5194 f AB, 6229 f, 6416 f, 6698 ACD, 6699 ‡ f B, 6870 f, 7729 f (far D); welfàre, 4890 f; a faré carte, 7525 f (a soory ‡ c. D); welfàre, 7722 AD (wèl-farè ‡ and C); fare he, 5582.

Rhyme words.—stare inf. (2229), Pandare (3447, 3948, 6870), fare inf. (5194 AB)   For the other cases, see care, above.

hele (A.S. hǽlu; also hǽl, -e, f.; L. hele; O. hæle), 1792 f, 2835 f, 3163 f, 7959 f (all four : dele inf.); -e, 461, 2848, 7722 (ese ‡ C), 7766.—hele honour, 6104 ABD. [Cf. helelcs, § 49, n. 5.]

With helé swych that but ye yeuen me
The same hele I shal noon hele haue, 7778-9.

hete (A.S. hǽtu; also hǽte, -an, f.; L. hate, O. hæte), 971 f, 2027 f (herte † C), 5173 (heete B, herte † C), 6245 f, 7470 f, 7602 f, 8124 f.—For hete (hote B) of cold for cold of hete I deye, 420 (ffor cold of hetę for hetę, etc. C).

Rhyme words.—trete inf. (971), lete inf. (6245), bete inf. (8124), bygete p.p. (971), ybete p p. (2027), swete pres. ind. 2 pl. (2027), wete adj. pl. (7470), grete adj pl. (7602, 8124).

lawe (A.S. lagu; also lah, n. (?) and laga, -an; L[ab]. laȝe,[b] lawe, O. laȝhe), 223 f (: drawe inf.), 996 f (: drawe inf. : awe), 5280 f (: awe : gnawe inf.); -e, 238, 4590 (law B; E †); -e han, 2878 (-e haue D).

---

[1] Answęre and is possible in AB, answęr and in D.
[2] In A read lay[en].

loue (A.S. lufu; also lufe (nom. not W.S.), -an, *weak fem.*, see
Sievers, § 278, n. 1, Cosijn, Altws. Gr., II, § 33, Platt, *Anglia*, VI,
176; L.ᵃ lufe,ᵇ loue, O. lufe), 231 f (: aboue), 925 f (: louc *amo*),
1933 f (alone † C) (: loue *amo*), 3718 f (: aboue), 3866 f (: shoue *p.p.*
: aboue), 8191 f (: aboue), 8205 f (: aboue).

Of *loue* (dissyllabic) in the interior of the verse there are but four
certain examples :

Han felt that *loue* dorst[e] yow displese, 27 (dorste B ; D ?).
It semeth not that *loue* doth yow [1] longe, 1631 (semyth me not C).
Love that with an holsom alliaunce, 4588.
Loue that knetteth lawe of companye, 4590 (D (?) ; loue that en-
dytyth ‡ C).

To which is probably to be added

And to the God of *loue* thus seyde he, 421 (seyd he D).

In 8132 we have apparently a verse of nine syllables, though a very
disagreeable one :

Of his *loue* I haue seyd (seyd(e) B) as (that D) I kan. (Of course
it is possible to read 4588 and 4590 as 9-syl. lines; cf. 1585.)

In

Loue ayens the (om. C) which (-e C) who-so defendeth, 603, and
Loue hym made al prest to don hire byde, 4824,

we have to choose between nine syllables and hiatus.

Note.—The other cases of *loue* (dissyllabic) in the interior of the verse are
without doubt scribal errors. Thus,—196 ‡ AD (-e of), 200 ‡ D (-e and),
234 C, 242 ‡ C (-e hath), 249 (?) ‡ D (-e have), 400 † AD (-e is), 436 ‡ Cᶜ,
500 † D, 663 ‡ D (-e hym), 677 ‡ CD, 991 † D (-e of), 1144 ‡ D, 1182 ‡
A, 1542 ‡ D (-e in), 1588 ‡ C (-e I), 1607 ‡ D (-e he), 1976 ‡ CD, 2007 ‡
CD, 2182 ‡ C (D ?), 2593 † D (-e is), 3014 ‡ D, 3359 ‡ D, 4170 ‡ E, 4604 †
E (-e oug(u)ht), 4987 ‡ C, 5147 ‡ CD, 6234 ‡ D, 6296 ‡ C, 6314 ‡ C,
6844 ‡ D, 7930 ‡ AD.

loue (before vowels), 196 BC, 200 ABC, 237, 400 BC, 401, 571, 584,
612, 698, 899 ABD, 902, 972, 991 ABC, 1005, 1020, 1104, 1111,
1112, 1124, 1182 BC, 1208, 1331, 1394, 1456, 1464, 1477, 1542
ABC, 1635, 1662, 1764, 1827, 2160, 3564, 4608 ABC, 4987, 5077,
5147, 5243 ‡ CD, 5340, 8232, etc.—loue he, 353 ‡ C, 388 (B †),
1607 AB; -e his, 484 ABC; -e hem, 31 B (him A = hem), 1875 ;
-e hath, 879 AB, 960 ABC (D ?); -e hadde, 304, 663; -e how,
1752 ; -e halt, 4606 ; -e hire (?), 1986 A.

loue, 206, 255, 308, 353 ABD, 384, 402, 436 AB, 443 ‡ C, 518, 523
ABC, 622, 646 [2], 711, 744, 810, 864, 1118, 1129, 1147, 1181,
1182 † D, 1477, 1588 AB, 1759, 1789 (-e ‡ D), 1823 AB, 1866,

---

[1] Cp. inserts *nat* here.   9-syl. verse in ABC(D ?).

[§§ 8, 9.] *of Chaucer's Troilus.* 15

1912, 1950, 2007 ABC, 2251 ABC, 2285, 2309, 3014 AB, 4103, 4433, 4586, 4587, 4590 ‡ C, 5243 AB, 6234 ABC, 6296 AB, 6314 ABD, 6844 ABC, 7418 AB, 8039, 8052. The old-face figures indicate lines in which *loue* may be read if one chooses to admit the extra syllable before a pause (usually the principal caesura). Thus,—Blyssyd be *loue* / that kan thus folk conuerte, 308; In *loue* / for which in wo to bedde he wente, 1147.

luf occurs once;—Of vertu rote of *luf* fyndere and hed, 1929 A (lust BC, fynder of lyst D). [Cf. lufsom, 6828 AB (loue- D), 7274 (loue- CD).]

sawe (A.S. sagu, L. saʒe, sœʒe, P. Pl. sawe), 6401 f (: gnawe *inf.*). [sawe †; 3562 f D, *see* shawe.]

shame (A.S. scamu, sceomu, sceamu, O. shame), 252 f, 374 f, 868 f, 896 f, 1440, 1730 f, 1848 f, 2922, 2931, 3479 f, 3969 f, 5192 f, 5258 (-e B, iape † in C), 6130 f, 6227 f; -e, 642 (-ë by † D), 2370, 2376 (speche CD), 2585, 2867, 3091, 3619, 4412 (schame red D); -e his, 107 (-ë falsenesse C).

    Rhyme words.—name *n.* (252, 896, 1848, 3479, 6130, 6227), game (868, 1730, 3969, 5192 D, 6130, 6227), grame (374, 5192 ABC), blame *inf.* (5192).

tale (A.S. talu, L.O. tale), 263[1], 1393 ‡ C (*pl.* ABD), 2278 f (: smale *adj. pl.*), 2651 C, 2707 (*line om.*, C), 4036, 4077 f (: nyghtyngale), 4245 (take † C), 7395 CD (tales A; B †); -e, 14, 1303 (talk ‡ was C, tale ‡ was D), 1344 BCD (tales † is A), 1390 ABC, 2690, 3456 (-es ‡ A), 3611 A (-ë brought BC, -é ‡ is D), 4507 (-é was D), 4789, 5324 AB (-ë newe C, thes ‡ tidinges D), 5328. [tale ‡ to, 1390 D.]

wyke, wowke (A.S. nom. wicu, wucu, orig. a fem. *n*-stem; oblique cases in *-an* occur, see Siev., § 278, n. 1, Cosijn, *Altws. Gr.*, II, § 33; L. wike, O. wuke, P. Pl. woke, weke, wyke), wyke, 1515 f (: syke *inf.*), 2358 f (weke BD, weyke C) (: pyke *inf.*); wowke, 5940 (wouke C, wooke D), 6855 (wouke C, wooke D). [Cf. ten Brink, § 35. A.]

§ 9. Monosyllabic feminine nouns with long stem-syllable take in the *Troilus* a final *-e* (perhaps derived from the oblique cases) throughout the singular, except in the genitive (cf. Child, § 16; ten Brink, § 207).

    The following list includes: (i.) pure ā- (ō-) stems,—(a) *bene, bere, bote, browe, chyste, gloue, halle, halue, helpe, leue, lode, mede*

---

[1] Supply [*for*] in C.

(A.S. mǽd), myle, reste, rinde, rode, salue, scole, snare, sorwe, soule, steuene, stounde, strete, throwe, while, wounde, youthe (originally i-stem); (b) filthe, highte, lengthe, murthe, [routhe,] sleyghte (O.N. slǽgð), slouthe, strengthe, trouthe, wrathe, (ii.) jā- (jō-) stems,—blysse, egge, helle, hire, keye, lysse, -nesse, shethe, speche,[1] synne, wreche,[1] yerde; (iii.) wā- (wō-) stems,—mede (A.S. mǽd), rowe, trewe; (iv.) i-stems,—bone (O.N. bón), [byrthe,] dede, glede, hyue, mynde, nede, quene, sighte, tyde, wene. Sleue (A S. sléf, slýf) belongs either to the jā- or to the i- declension; the history of rysshe (A.S. risc, etc) is not satisfactorily determined.

> Note.—For convenience soule and steuene are included in this list. Some of the nouns under i. b show in Anglo-Saxon a by-form in -u (cf. also scole). For pryde, see § 3. For hegge, see § 6.

bene (A.S. béan, P. Pl.ᶜ bene), 4009 f (: mene ind, 1 sg. : clene adj.), 6726 f (: mene 3 pl.). [Var. B beene.]

bere (A.S. bǽr, bér, L.O. bære), 2723 f (: ere), 5525, 5845 f (ber D) (: manere), 5870 f (C †, ber D †) (: yfere adv. : dere adj.). [Var. B beere.]

blysse, blisse (A.S. blíðs, bliss, L.O. blisse), 623 f, 3023 f, 3184 f, 3546 (-[se]? D),[2] 4063, 4114 (-[se] D), 4164 (-[se] C, blyssyd ‡ A), 4465 f, 4499 (-[se] D), 4870 (D †),[3] 5985 (ioye C), 6759, 6911 f (blys C), 6913 f (blys C, hisse † D), 7021; blysse, blisse, 1934 (blis C, blys[se] which? D), 1970 (D †), 1974, 1976, 2152 (blis C), 4026, 4248, 4558 (blis C), 5497 (ioye C), 5498 (blys C), 5912 (ioyis C †), 6969 (blys C). [Var. D blis or blys in the lines marked by old-style figures.]

> Rhyme words.—wysse inf. (623), kysse inf. (3023, 6911, 6913), lysse n. (3184), mysse inf. (4465), blysse n. (6911, 6913).

bone (O.N. bón, bœn, f., A.S. bén, O. bene, L. bone), 1020 f, 4730 f, 6957 f.

> Rhyme words —mone moon (1020), to done (1020, 4730), soone (4730, 6957). [Var. B boone.]

bote (A.S. bót, L.O. bote), 763, 1430 f (boot D), 2464 f (bete ‡ C, boot D), 7035 f, 7609 f, 7690 (but † C); -e, 832, 2903, 4050 (boot B), 5276, 5401 (-é ‡ on C), 5921 ; -e hym, 352. [Cf. boteles, § 49, n. 5.]

> Rhyme words —vnderfote (1430), rote (1430, 2464, 7609), soote adj. (7035). [Var. BD boote.]

browe (A.S. brú, gen. brúwe), 204 f (: to loken rowe).

byrthe, birthe, burthe (cf. A.S. ge-byrd, f., n., ge-byrdu, f., Siev.,

---

[1] See Kluge, Nominale Stammbildungslehre, § 113.
[2] Supply [For] in A, [in] in D.   [3] Supply [in] in D.

§ 267, n. 4, O. birde, P. Pl.[b] burth,[c] burthe), byrthe, 3559 f (-th B, burthe C, birthe D) (: murthe AC, myrthe B, mirthe D); birthe, 5501 A (birth D, [my] burthe B); burthe hym, 6572 (byrthe B, bur[t]h C, birthe D).

chyste (A.S. cest, W.S. ciest, cyst, P. Pl.[c] cheste), -e, 7731 (cheste CD).

dede (A.S. dǽd, déd, L. dede, O. dede, dæd-bote), 93 f, 1187 f, 1427 f, 3133 f, 4143 f, 5286 f (nede A), 5641 f, 5893 f (drede ‡ C), 6003 f, 6234 f, 6413 f, 6837 f; -e, 3271, 3895 (drede † C), 5643. [dede, 4615 f C, *is an error; read* dy3t.]

> Rhyme words.—rede *ind.* 1 *pl.* (1187), 3 *pl.* (3133, 5641), *inf.* (93, 1187, 6837), arede *inf.* (6234), nede *n.* (1427), dede *pred. adj. pl.* (3133, 5286, 5893), drede *n.* (93, 6003, 6234, 6413), lede 1 *sg.* (6003), womanhede (4143, 6837)

egge (A.S. ecg, L. mid egge), 5589 f (: abregge *inf.*).

filthe (A.S. fýlð), -e, 3223 (-e ‡ and B, felthe C), 6240 (folye *it* ‡ C, filth D).

glede (A.S. gléd, P. Pl.[e] glede), 4999 f (· fede *inf.*), 6666 f ABC (: hede *n. heed* : stede *steed*).

gloue (A.S. glóf, but also foxes glófa, *weak*), -e he, 7376.

halle (A.S. heall, hall, L. halle), 2255 f (hıH D) (: calle *inf.*), 3698 f haH D) (: alle *pl.* : falle *p.p.*), 5394 f (. alle *pl.* : falle *inf.*).

halue (A.S. healf), in *byhalue* and *on .. halue*. (*q*) byhalue (A.S. be healfe), on myn (my BD) byhalue, 2543 (bi- B, be- C); on his byhalue which, 2819 (on his half † with C, on his halue that C, on his half which D).[1] (*b*) on ... halue (A.S. on healfe, O. o ... hallfe, cf. L. an his halue), on myn h., 5607 f (vn niy behalue D) (: salue *n.*).

> Note.—The adjective *half* may be seen in 3186, 3345, 3481, 4921, 5927, 5970 (hal † C, halfe D), in phrases with *a*, *tho*, and *this*. The plural appears in *halue goddes* (= demigods), 6207 (half[e] C, halfe D).

helle (A.S. hell, L. (*obl.*) O. helle), 786 f, 872 f, 1190 f (heH D), 1981 f (-H D), 3434 f, 4300 f, 4442 f, 5374 f C (-H D), 6202 f, 6216 f, 6360 f, 6575 f (-H D), 7759 f, 7895 f; -e, 859 (-H D); 1521 (-H D), 2850 (-H D), 7739.

> Rhyme words.—welle *n.* (872, 6216), *inf.* (5374, 6575), telle *inf.* (872, 1190, 1981, 3434, 4442, 6360), *ind.* 3 *pl.* (786, 7895), dwelle *inf.* (4300, 5374, 6202, 6360, 7759), *ind.* 3 *pl.* (3434), *subj* 2 *sg.* (786), selle *inf.* (4300, 4442), vnswelle *inf.* (6575). [Var. holle, 786 B.]

helpe (A.S. help, L. help, dat. -e, O. hellpe), helpe to, 695 AC (help D, -e? B); -e the, 5954 (help B); help to, 2531 (-e C, he[l]pe B, help ‡ of D); help yet, 672 (-e ‡ sumwhat C); help do, 795 (-[e] ‡

---

[1] Line 2819 is unmetrical in D and a poor 9-syl. verse in C. B is nonsense. C and Cp. read : On his half whiche (which Cp.) that soule vs alle sende.

D, helę C); helpe, 2709 A (-p B); help (*bef. vowels*), 18 (-e BD), 1003 (-e C), 4455 (-e CD), 4765 AD (-e B)¹, 6221 (-e CD), 7390 (-e CD). [helpë ‡ more, 2540 C (-es ABG, help to D).]

> Note.—The interjectional *help!* (see 1047) was no doubt originally an imperative, though such passages as "*Gentleman.* Help, help, O, help! *Edgar.* What kind of help?" (*King Lear*, v. 3, 222) show that our modern feeling that this *help* is a substantive is of long standing.

highte (A.S. héahðu, héhðu, híehðu), 7190 f (heighte B, hy3te C, hight D) (: myghte, myght, my3t, might *pret.* 3 *sg.*).

hire (A.S. hýr, L. hure, P. Pl.ᵃᵇ huire,ᶜ hure, huyre), 4787 f (here C), 5168 f (here AC, hir D); -e, 334 (C †).

> Rhyme words.—on fire, a fire (on fere C) (4787, 5168), desire *ind.* 1 *sg.* (5168).

hyue (A.S. hýf), 6018 f (heue C) (: dryue *inf*: blyue *adv.*).

keye (A.S. cǽg; also (rarely) cǽge, -an, Pet. Chron. keie, P. Pl.ᵇ keye), 6823 f (kay C, key D) (: aweye : pleye *inf.*).

kynde (A.S. cynd, *n.*, but usually ge-cynd, *f.* (later *n.*); late A.S. ge-cynde, *n.*, ge-cyndu, -o, *f.*, see Sievers, § 267. b and n. 4; L. icunde, dat. cunde, O. kinde), nom., 2459 (-[e] D), 4572 f; of, 238 f, 972 f, 1455 f, 1947 (-[e] D), 2528 f, 3150 (-[e] D, kyng † A), 4279 f, 4563 f, 4607 f, 5080 (be kyndë C), 7825 f; out of, 5798 f; in, 254 f (*adj.* ‡ C), 3176 f, 3745 f, 5527 f; by, 5113 f, 6739 f.—kynde, nom., 4468, 7192.—kyndę the, nom., 5758 AB (-ë ‡ wrou3t C, nature † D).

> Rhyme words.—bynde *inf.* (238, 254, 4279, 4607), *ind.* 3 *pl.* (5527), vnbynde *inf.* (4572), wynde *inf.* (254), *subj.* 2 *sg.* (4279), fynde *inf.* (972, 2528, 3176, 3745, 4563, 5113, 5527, 6739), *ind.* 1 *sg.* (5798), *ind.* 3 *pl.* (7825), mynde *n.* (1455 [mende C], 3176, 6739), rynde (5798). [Var. C kende, 1455; D kynd, *in the lines marked by old-style figures.*]

lengthe (A.S. on lengðe; also, lengu, -o, *f.*), 1347 f BD (lenghthe A, lenthe C), 7854 f (lenthe C, length D); -e, 4917 (lenghe B, lenthe C), 5807 (lenthe A, lenghthe B, leue ‡ C, length D), 6343 (lenght B, length D), 8020 (lenghte B, lenths C, [of] the lengh D). (Rhymes only with *strengthe.*)

leue, leeue (A.S. léaf, L. leue, leaf, O. lefe), 1819 f AB, 2387 f, 2621 (-e BCD), 2743 f, 2806 f, 3067 (-e D), 3401 f, 3436 f, 3464 f, 6020 f, 6441, 6843 f, 6845, 6856 f, 6863, 6974 f, 7378 f, 7448 f; -e, 1294, 1681, 2545, 2719 (loue † B), 2774, 3051, 3458, 3525, 5392; leuë home, 126 A (-e and BCG Cp.). [leuę ‡ went, 126 D.]

> Rhyme words.—byleue, bleue *manere* (1819 AB, 3464, 6020, 6843, 6856), reue *inf.* (2743), reue (by-reue) *subj.* 1 *pl.* (2806), to-cleue *inf.* (6974), leue *relinquo* (7448), eue, eeue (2387, 3401, 3436, 6843, 6974, 7378).

---

¹ Read *among*[es] AD, *amonge*[s] B.

§ 9.] *of Chaucer's Troilus.* 19

lode (A.S. lád, L. lod-cniht, O. lade), lodë-sterre, 6595 f (lodis C), 7755 f (loode D).

lore (A.S. lár, L.ᵃ lære, lare, leore,ᵇ lore, O. lare) 645 f, 754 f, 1083 f, 1650 f, 2426 f, 3085 f, 6385 f, 6690 f, 7099 f; -e, 1482..

    Rhyme words.—more *adv* (1083), the more *advl.* (645), no more *adv.* (754), I kan nomore (6690), routhe more (1650), more *n. acc.* (2426), *pred. adj. sg* (3085), eueremore *adv.* (6385), sore *adv* (754, 1083, 1650, 3085, 7099), sorwes sore (2426), yore *adv.* (6690). [Var. B loore.]

lysse (A.S. líðs, liss, L. (*obl.*) P. Pl.ᵃᶜ lisse), 3185 f (lesse B, lisse C) (: yn blysse).

mede (A.S. méd, L. O. P. Pl. mede), 3257 f (: nede *n.* : drede *n.*); -e, 1508.

mede (A.S. mǽd, méd, gen. mǽde, mǽdwe, L. (dat.) medewe), 156 f (: rede *adj. pl.* : rede *lego*), 1138 f (: rede *adj. pl.* : sprede *inf.*).

murthe (A.S. myrgð, myrð, L. murðe), 3557 f (: byrthe A, byrth B, burthe C, birthe D); myrthe ‡, 7740 C. [Var. B myrthe; D mirthe.]

➤ myle (A.S. míl, L. O. mile), 6766 f (: while : bygile *inf.*).

mynde (A.S. ge-mynd, *f, n.*, O. minde), of, 365 f; yn, 1456 f (-d D), 3173 f, 4348 f, 4385 f, 4680 f, 6736 f; to, 1606 f (-d D), 1687 f (-d D); out of, 5579 f, 5963 f, 6099 f, 7805 f, 8058 f; acc., 5335 f, 3772 ABC; -e, acc., 3963; yn mynde he, 733 (-d D), 3914 (-d D).

    Rhyme words.—fynde *inf.* (365, 3173, 4348, 4680, 5963, 6099, 8058), *subj. 3 sg.* (5579), *ind. 3 pl.* (6736), wynde *inf.* (1687, 4385), vnbynde *inf.* (5335), kynde *n.* (1456, 3173, 6736), vnkynde (4680, 6099, 7805), by-hynde (1606). [Var. C mende.]

nede (A.S. néd, níed, nýd, néad, néod, L. ned, ncode, O. ned, acc. dat. nede), 772 f, 863 f, 1428 f, 3259 f, 3296 f, 3308 f, 3331 f, 3388 f, 3548 f, 3570 f, 4067 f, 4736 f, 4808 f, 5286 f, 5768 f, 6194 f, 6220 f, 7389 f, 7403 f; nede (*before consonants*), 128 AC (-ed ‡ B), 2617 (A † B †), 2638 (-e C), 3266 ‡ C (-es AB, -is D), 3984; -e, 4480, 5696, 5697 (A †), 6699 ABD, 6949 ABD, 8221.—nede to, 886, 4853 A (-e CD; B †); -e‖ there, 1799 (-e wher D); -e‖ sestow, 2888; -e was, 4630; -e ful, 4797 ‡ C (-e he (?) D†); -e were, 6170 ‡ A (?).—nede were it (=wer't), or nede were it, 4773 AB (cf. 6170 A). [2891 ?] [Cf. nedeles, § 85; nede, -es, § 91.]

    Rhyme words.—spede *inf.* (772, 863, 4736), blede *inf.* (863), procede *inf.* (3296), *ind 3 pl.* (*inf.* ‡ D) (4808), for-bede *inf.* (3308), *subj. 3 sg.* (3388, 6220), bede *inf.* (5768), brede *inf.* (7389), drede *n.* (772, 3259, 3331, 3548, 3570, 4736, 6194), dede *n.* (1428), dede *pred. adj. pl.* (5286), mede *meed* (3259), hede *n. head* (3308, 4067, 6220), Diomede (7389, 7403), stede *steed* (7403).

-nesse, termination (A.S. -nes, -nis, -nys, *late* -nisse, L. O. P.Pl. -nesse).

 besynesse, bysynesse, 795 f[1], 1035 f, 2259 (-nes[se] D)[2], 2401 f, 3007 f, 3086 f, 3205 f, 4241 ‡ f E, 4255 f (bes!nes C), 4452 f (besynes C,) 6150 f (buxsomnes ‡ C).

- bitternesse, 639 f (bet- B, bittyr- C), 3657 f, 5506 f; -e, 4062.
 brotelnesse, 8195 f (bri3tilnes D).
 corsednesse, 5656 B (cursed- D, wykkednesse A).
 derknèsse, 18 f (derke- BD)[3], 3668 f (distresse † B), 4962 f (derkenesse B, derknes C).
 drerynesse, 701 f, 964 f, 5563 ‡ C f.
 dronkénesse, 1801 f (dronkenes C, drunkenesse D).
 fàlsnesse, 107 (fàlsenesse BC).
 fièblenèsse, 1948 B (febjluisse C, fèblenès D, fèblesse A).
- gentilnesse, 7980 f D (gentilesse ABC). (Cf. variants under *gentilesse*, § 25.)
 gladnèsse, 19 f 22 f (gladde- B), 615 f, 1790 f, 2848 f (gladde- B), 2889 f, 3008 f (gladde- B), 3022 f, 4038 f, 4057 f, 4086 f (-nes C), 4242 f (-nes C), 4289 f, 4357 f (-nes C), 4568 f, 7956 f; glàdnesse, 640 C; -nèsse, 4155 (-e 3if C, -e yif D).
 goodnèsse, 991 f, 2849 f (goode- B); -nèsse he, 116 (gòde- B).
 hardnèsse, 2330 f.
 hardi-, hardynesse, 566 f, 1719 f; -e, 4618.
 heuynesse, 24 f, 655 f, 963 f, 3849 f, 4039 f, 4241 f (-nes C, besinesse E), 4288 f, 4767 f (wrecchidnes ‡ D), 5025 f, 5464 f, 5563 f (drerynesse ‡ C), 5745 f, 5929 f, 6503 f, 6984 f, 7154 f (-nes C), 7577 f.
 holynesse, 560 f.
 hòlwghnesse, 8172 ([the] hòlugh- B).
 kyndénesse, 5382 f.
 lustynesse, 3019 f
 rudènesse, 6151 f (reudënes C, rud[è]nesse D); -e, 6339.
 secrenesse, 1928 (sekyrnes C, sikernesse D, sekirnesse G).
 selynesse, 3655 f, 3667 f, 3673 (-[se] D).
 shrewëdnesse, 1943 f (sh(e)rewed- B, schrewed(e)nes C, shrewdënesse D).
 sike-, sykenèsse, 2661 f (sik- CD), 5507 f (seke- B, sek- C); syknesse lest, 489 (sike- B, sek- C); syknèsse, 4055 f (sek- C, sijk- D).
 siker-, sykernesse, 3824 f (sekir- C), 4085 f (sekirnes C), 4157 f,

---

[1] Old-style figures indicate that D has -nes.
[2] But of hire bysynesse (-es Cp.) this was on. [3] Scansion uncertain.

§ 9.]   *of Chaucer's Troilus.*   21

4355 f; -nesse, 1858 (sekirnes C), 6174 (sekirnes C). [Cf. *secrenesse.*]

sothfastnesse, 5742 f (soth(e)- D).

swetnèsse, 1036 f (swett(e)nesse B), 2886 f (swenienessé † B), 3021 f (swett(e)- B); -nessĕ, 4061 (*perh.* -nèssę *in* A); swètnesse haue, 638 (swèt(e)nesse han B, swètnesse a C).

vnliklynesse, 16 f.

wikked-, wykkednesse, 992 f (-yd- BD, weked- C), 5656 f A (corsed- B, cursed- D).

wildernesse, 6207 f.

wilfulnesse, 793 f.

witt(e)nesse, 6212 (witnesse BCD); wytnèsse, 3102 f (witt(e)- B).

wodnèsse, 3636 f (wod(e)- B); woòdnesse, 4224 (woo(n)d(e)nes B, wod(e)nessę ‡ E); -nèsse, 4900 (wod(e)- B, distreste † C, wood(e)- D).

worthi-, worthynesse, 567 f, 642 f, 961 f (-nes C),[1] 1246 f, 1263 (-[se] D), 1789 f, 1926 f (-nes C), 4158 f, 4451 f (-nes C), 4631 f (-nes C), 6148 f (-nes C), 6330 f, 7080 f, 7928 (-[se] D, -ę the C), 8192 f; -nesse his, 4392; vnworthynesse he, 2166 (on- C).

wrecchednesse, 1371 f (-nes C), 4629 f (-nes C), 6402 f (wreched(e)- B, wreched(e)nes C); -nesse, 3223 (wreched(e)- C); wrecchidnes ‡; 4767 f D (heuynesse AB).

But:—

buxsomnes ‡, 6150 f C; gladnès ‡ ho, 2891 D; goòdnes ‡ herye, 4514 D; noblènes ‡, 8194 f D (noblèsse AB); witnes of, 5403 A (-nesse BCD).[2]

See also the variants in the preceding list.

A.S. bieternes, biternys; dréorinys; druncennes; glædnes; gódnes; hálignes; heardnes; hefignes; séocnes; swétnes; ge-witnes; wódnys [; búhsomnes Bosw.- T. *without authority*].

Rhyme words.—Nouns in -nesse rhyme principally with each other; but the following rhymes also occur,—distresse (615, 639, 641, 1801, 1943, 2330, 2886, 3086, 3102, 3205, 3824, 4055, 4057, 4288, 4289, 4629, 4631, 4767, 4962, 5025, 5382, 5464, 5506, 5563, 5742, 5745, 6330, 7080, 7956), accesse (2401, 2661), gentilesse (1246, 1789, 1790, 3007, 3008, 4255, 7956), largesse (4568), prowesse (1719), richesse (6330), noblesse (8192), goddesse (6207), hierdesse (655), presse *n.* (560), lesse, lasse *adj. sg.* (701, 793, 5464, 6984), *plu.* (6207), 1 gesse *ind.* (655, 991, 992, 1371, 1801, 1943, 4568, 5563), gesse, gysse *inf.* (3824, 4085, 4086, 5656, 6984), dresse *inf.* (1719, 6402), redresse *inf.* (3849, 5929, 6402, 6503), expresse *ind.* 3. *pl.* (7154), blesse *subj.* 3 *sg.* (7577).

queene, quene (A.S. cwén, cwǽn, L. quen, quene, O. cwen), 699 f,

---

[1] In C read *worth[y]nesse.*   [2] In A supply [*herę*].

759, 817 f, 2772 f (the quene ‡ elyne C ?), 2788 f, 5900 f, 6256 f, 6375 f, 7258 f; -e, 2641 (quen C), 2799, 6009 (quen C).

Rhyme words.—y-seene *adj* (699), sene *adj.* (7258), tene (817), grene (817, 2788, 6375), susteyne (-tene) *inf.* (2772), shene *adv. ?* (5900), shene *adj. def.* (6256), wene *n.* (6256), ? clene[1] *adv.* (6375). [Var. D qwene.]

reste (A.S. rǽst, rest, L. dat. reste, O. ressté), 188 f,[2] *600 f, 1845 f, *1996 f, *2029 f, *3066 f, 3767 f, *3808 f, 3887 f, *3973 f, 4277 f, *4360 f, *4441 f, *4522 f, *5243 f (rest B); 5781 f (prest † C), *5949 f, 6107 (-[e] D), *6264 f, 6299 f, 6881 f, 7370 f, 7384 C (-[e] D, bedde AB), 7468 f, 8098 f ([vn]to r. A), 8112 f; -e, 4274 (-t B, nest † D); -e hym, 8036 (-t B). [rest ‡, 330 f C[c] (lyst AD, lest B).]—vnreste, 5541 f, *7930 f, *7967 f. [Cf. resteles, § 49, n. 5.]

Rhyme words —the beste (3767, 3887, 5541, 5781, 5949, 6264, 7967, 8112), the alderbeste (4441), my beste (600), breste *subj.* 3 *sg* (600), breste *inf.* (4277, 5243, 6299, 7370, 7930), moleste *inf.* (5541), keste (kyste) *prct. ind.* 3 *sg.* (3973, 4360), leste (lyste) *pret. ind.* 3 *sg.* (188[3], 1996[3], 3066[3], 3973, 4522, 6881, 7468, 8098), lyste *pres. subj.* 3 *sg.* (1845[4], 2029, 3808, 3887), the worthieste (1845). [best *adv.* (330 C[5]).]

rode (A.S. ród, L.O. rode), 8223 f (roode BD) (: Strode *nom. pr.*: good[e] *pl.*, garde † A).

rote, roote (A.S. rót, O. rote), 1433 f, 2463 f (a root? D), 7608 f; -e, 1929 (root(a) B, rotę ‡ fynder D). [Cf. roteles, § 49, n. 5.]

Rhyme words.—bote *A S. bót* (1433, 2463, 7608), vnderfote (1433).

routhe, ruthe (2441), reuthe (4924) (not in A.S.; formed from the vb. reouwen, rewen, A.S. hréowan, on the analogy of other abstract nouns in -th; cf. O.N. hrygð and hryggva; L. reouðe; P. Pl.[b] routhe, reuth,[c] reuthe), 582 f, 769 f, 1434 f, 1574 f, 1649[6], 1749 f (rowihte † B), 2092 f, 2224 f, 2365 f, 2441 AB, 2587 f, 2964 f, 3737 f, 4353 f, 4924 (ruth † D), 6138 f,[7] 6152 f, 6271 f, 6335 f, 7363 f, 7462 f, 7748 f, 7950 f, 8050 f; -e, 1608 BD, 2355, 2460 (-th B), 6244, 6989. [-e ‡ on, 1608 A, *l.* -e vpon (mercy ‡ C).] [Cf. routhelees, § 49, n. 5.]

Rhyme words.—slouthe (2092, 2224, 2587, 3737, 7950), vntrouthe (7462), trouthe (*all the rest*). [Var. B rowthe; BC rewthe; C reuthe.]

rowe (A S. ráw, réw, P. Pl.[c] rewe, by rewe), by r., 2055 f (row D) (: lowe *adv.*: throwe *inf.*).

---

[1] clere ABG Cp Durham MS, clene Phillipps MS. 8252, cleene John's MS., shene D Selden MS.B. 24. (C cut out.)
[2] The asterisk indicates that C has no -e, old-style figures indicate that D has none   [3] Perh. subjunctive.   [4] lyst A (: the worthieste).
[5] "In rest," the reading of C, is clearly wrong.   [6] Supply [*ne*] in D.
[7] Old-style figures indicate that D has *trouth*.

§ 9]   *of Chaucer's Troilus.*   23

rynde (A.S. rind, but a pl. rindan occurs), 1727 f (rynd D) (: byhynde : fynde *inf.*), 5801 f (: kynde *n.* : fynde *ind.* 1 *sg.*).

rysshe (A.S. risc, *f.*, weak forms also occur; P. Pl. rusche, ruysshe), 4003 f (ryshe B, rische D, reche † C) (: fysshe *inf.*).

salue (A.S sealf, O. sallfe), 5606 f (: on myn halue).

scole (A.S. scól, see Sievers, *Beitr.*, I, 488, but scólu, Chron. 816; L. in scole, P. Pl. scole), *-e* is, 634 (: tolys : folys).

shethe (A.S. scǽð, L. dat. scæðe, scaðe, O. dat. shæþe), out of . . . . shethe he, 5847 (sheth D, schede anon C).

sighte, syght[e] (A.S. gesihð, L. siht, dat. sehte, i-sihðe, etc., Q. sihlþe), nom., -[e] trewely, 1713 AD (-e BC); acc., -[e] fle, 1795 ACD (-e B); acc., sighte, 294 f (syȝth C, sight D) (: lyghte *inf.*); acc., -[e], 4974 f AD (-e B) (: eyen bryght[e] (-e D) : lyght[e] *inf.* (-e BD)); for, -[e] ye¹, 1754 ABC (D †); from . . . sighte, 6998 f (-t CD) (: myghte *pret. ind.* 3 *sg.* : lyghte *inf.*); with sighte, 2380 f (-t CD) (: myglite *pret. subj.* 3 *sg.*).

sight, (i.) acc., 5375 f CD² (: knyȝt C, sighte *pret. ind.* 3 *sg.* D). (ii.) by, 1787 (acc. D, seyth C); vpon, 7735; in, 5603; nom., forsight, 5623. [of that sight † that, D 3338.] [Var. C syȝt, siȝt, syȝte ; D siȝt.]

sleue (A.S. sléf, L.W.S. slýf, but slýfan pl. occurs as a variant in Benedict.-r., ed. Schroer, p. 89), 6065 f (: preue *inf.*), 7406 f (: releue *inf*).

sleyghte, sleighte (O.N. slǽgð, Lb. slehþe, P. Pl.b sleighte,c sleithe), 2597 (-[e] BC, -[e for] D), 6158 (sleyt[e] C, sleyghtes D) ; -e, 6121 (-t D, flyȝt † C), 6123 AB (sleyȝt C), 7136 (sleight D). [Var. B sleughte ; C sleyȝte.]

slouthe (A.S. slǽwð, L. slauðe), 2044 f, 2093 f, 2221 f, 2585 f, 3738 f, 7947 f (-th D) ; -e, 1371, 3777 (th D).

 Rhyme words —routhe (2093, 2221, 2585, 3738, 7947), trouthe (2044, 2221, 2585, 7947).

snare (A.S. snearh, but also sneare, Sweet, 4), 507 f (sware † B) (: care *n.*), 663 f (: care *n.* : bare *pred. adj. sg.*), 7111 f (: care *n*).

sonde (A.S. sand, sond, L. sonde), 7735 f (: in honde); -e, 3334 (-d BD, [or] soun C). [in goddes sonde, 4207 D, *is error for* hond.]

sorwe³ (A.S. sorg, sorh, L. sorhȝe, seorwe, O. serrȝhe), 390 (C †),

---

[1] "Right for the firste syght[e] ye parde."
[2] This stanza is not in AB.
[3] Old-style figures indicate that D has *sorow* (before vowels, *sorqw*) ; an asterisk indicates that B has *sorw*.

485 f ABC, 527 (-ow B), 563 C, 665 (*pl.* BD), 706 (sorǫwe B), 860 f, 945 f, *1491 f, 1930¹, 1951, 2049 f, 2184 f, 2594, 2608 f (sorwyn C), 2694, 2955, 3147 (-es AB), 3189 † A, 3715 (-[e] B), 3730 f, 3900 f, 3928 (sorwȝ *dissyl.* D), 3935 (-[e] D), 4312 f, 4369 (-[e] B), 4760 f, 4816 C (*pl.* ABD), 5033 (-[e] B), 5091, 5094 (-[e] B), 5133 (-[e] B), 5199 C, 5422 (-[e] B), 5446 (-[e] B, -yn C), 5465 (-ę ‡ to C), 5568 ABD, 5587 (-[e] B), 5590 BC (*pl.* AD), 6107 f, 6278 f, 6376 f, 6499 C (*pl.* ABD), 6567 D (*pl.* ABC), 6628 ‡ C, 6629 C (*pl.* ABD), 6652 (-[e] B), 6658 f, 6769 f, 6813, 6923 ACD (-es B), 7017 f, 7049 f, 7070, 7086 f (destresse † B), 7238 f, 7308 f, 7649 (C †), 7695, 7888 f, 8026 f.—sorwe, 1 (sorǫwe B), *108 AC, 530 (-ǫwe BD),² *579, 582 ‡ A, 641 (-ow ne D, -we or ‡ in C), *712, 3640, 3742 (so[r]w B, sorw(is) C, sorow at D), *3810 (-e hirę C), 3932 (sorwȝ D), 4527, 4759, 5021 AB (-ǫwe D), *5171, 5436 (-ě ‡ of C), 5438 † C, *5458, 5482, *5498, 5503 (sorw D), *5541 (wo C), 5561, 5586 (-ę ‡ for D), 5743, 6226 (-ę ȝe B, -é that C), 6380, 6480, (-ě pese ? C, D *dub.*), 6540, 6561, 6712, 6821 (-yn ‡ C, -ě † vpon D), 6895 (-ě doun C), 6921, 6976, 7559 (-ęs ‡ and B), *7605³, 7927 (-yn ‡ of C), 7930 A(?)BC (-ę ‡ for D), 8102, 8107, 8144, sorwe he, 7012 (-e ‡ on-to C), 8089 ; -e hym, *7405 AD (C ?).—sorw[e] doubleth, 5565 AB (-é CD): [sorwę ‡ to, 5092 AC, 5465 C (-ě AB) ; sorwę gan, 546 C (-ǫwę D), *read* wo ; sorow, 705 † D (*pl.* AC, -[es] ? B), 3747 ‡ D (*pl.* ABC) ; sorwë † of, 5791 C ; sorwyn † brynge, 3768 C.] [Cf. sorwful, -w[e]ful, § 49, n. 3.]

Rhyme words.—moiwe (*everywhere*), tó borne n. (2049, 2608, 8026), borwe *inf.* (485, 7086).

soule, sowle (A.S. sáwol, gen. sáwle, sáule, L. saule, O. sawle), 47, (B †), 1853 (hert[e] ‡ D), 2944 (D †), 3768 AB (-[e] D), 4343 (D †), 4967, 4979⁴, 5134, 5361, (-ę ful C, hertě A), 5836, 6026, 6061, 6155, 6216 (-ę synke CD), 6685, 6942 (-ę ‡ me ? D), 7913.— So that his sowle here sow[l]é (soule BC, sowle D) folwen myghte, 5849.—soul*e*, 2723 (soul D, -é brouȝt C),⁵ 3187 (soul D ; C ?), 3433 (soul D), 4161 (-ě brought E ; C †), 4441 (-ę ‡ to D), 5438 (sorwe † C), 6058 (soul B, -ě ‡ schal CD),⁶ 6362, 7035, 7386 (-e ‡ vp C). [sowlę ‡ she, 7079 D.] [2819 (?), see p. 17, foot-note.]

speche (A.S. spréc, spréc, L.W.S. spéc, L. spæche, speche, O. spæche), 702 f, 884 f, 1142 f, 1333 f, 1582 f, 1657 f, 2154 f, 2506 f, 3237 f,

---

[1] All four MSS. defective (sor C).   [2] AC corrupt
[3] In B supply [u].   [4] AB too short ; C † ; D apparently right.
[5] soule I-brought AB, soul y-broght D (cf. 4161).   [6] sowle-is A, soul-is B.

3352 C, 3426 f, 3598 f, 4179 f, 4352 f, 4552 (D †), 4628 f, 5117 f, 5813 f, 6136 f, 6470 f, 6751 f, 7161 f, 7218 f (spech D), 7494 f, 7898 f, 7973 f, 8079 f (spech D), 8162 f, 8217 f; -e, 327, 1107, 1119, 2276, 2376 (shame AB), 2685, 3138, 3301 CD, 3304 (spech C; D †), 4477, 4790 (D †), 7185, 7289 (-é ‡ a ? C); -e hym, 4911 (spech B). [Cf. specheles, § 49, n. 5.]

    Rhyme words.—seche *inf.* (702, 884, 7161, 7494, 7898, 8079), *ind 3 pl.* (2154), *subj. 2 pl.* (8217), eche *inf.* (702, 884, 4352, 6470), preche *inf.* (1142, 1582, 1657, 6136), beseche *in l 1 sg.* (1333, 2506, 3237, 3598, 4179, 4352, 5117, 5813, 6751, 7494, 7973), *inf.* (3426, 4628, 6470, 7218), *imv. sg.* (8162), teche *inf.* (6136), leche (1657, 2154, 7898). [Var. BC speeche.]

steuene. (A.S. stefn, stemn, L. stef(e)ne, steuene, O. steffne), 4565 f (neuene B) (: heuene),

stounde (A.S. stund, L. stunde, O. stunnd), 1060 f (-d D), 1079 f (-d D), 4537 f (-d D), 4738 f (-d D), 5287 f, 7818 f, 7865 f (7866 f C); stoundemele (A.S. stundmælum), *adv.*, -e, 7037 ABD (stormyal † C) [stound, 5256 ‡ D.]

    Rhyme words.—founde *inf.* (1060), found *p.p.* (5287), wounde *n.* (1079, 4537, [5256 D,] 5287, 7865), grounde (4738, 7865), expounde *inf.* (7818). [Var. A stonde (5287); B stownde.]

strengthe (A.S. strengðu, strengð, L. strengþe, strenðe, O. strenncþe), 1345 f (strenghte B, strenthe C); strenghthe, 7853 f (strenthe C, strength D). (Both rhyme with *lengthe, lenghthe*.)

strete (A.S. strǽt, strét, L.ᵃ stræte, stret,ᵇ stræt, O. stræte), 2271 f, 2312 f, 4723 f, 5591 f; -e, 5288; -e he, 1701 (*line om.* C).—strete se, 1697 (e ‡ tho D); -e lokynge, 2100.

    Rhyme words.—ete *pret ind. 3 pl.* (*inf.* D) (2271), y-bete *p p* (2312), grete *def. adj.* (2312), grete *adj. pl.* (4723), trete *inf.* (4723), swete *voc.* (5591), bete *imr. pl.* (5591).

synne (A.S. synn, L. dat. acc. sunne, O. sinne), 824 f (-n D), 1937 f (-n C), 3755 f (-n CD), 5423 f, 6244 f (-n C); -e, 556.

    Rhyme words —inne *in* (824, 1937, 3755, 5423), wynne *inf.* (824, 6244), I gynne *ind.* (1937), twynne *subj.* 1 *sg.* (5423).

throwe (A.S. þrág, L. prowe, O. þraȝhe), 1772 f (throw D), 2740 f, 5046 f, 7824 f (trowe B).

    Rhyme words —lowe *adv.* (1772), knowe *inf.* (2740, 7824), ouerthrowe *inf.* (5046), *p p* (7824).

trouthe, trowthe (A.S. tréowð, tréowðu, L. treouðe, O. trowwþe), 450 ‡ D, 584 f, 770 f, 1409 (-[e] B), 1435 f, 1575 f, 1750 f, 1927, 2043 f, 2223 f, 2366 f, 2588 f (-th B), 2962 f, 3624[1], 3805 (-e † y D), 4354 f, 6139 f, 6153 f, 6272 f, 6334 f, 7364 f, 7749 f, 7949 f, 8042 (-[e] ? D), 8049 f; -e, 676, 691 (-e † wolde C), 899

[1] trouthe plyght A, -e I plighte (i. e. i-plight) B, -e y-plight D, treuthe plyȝt C.

(-th B),[1] 988, 1047, 1054 (D †), 1245,[2] 1364, 1591, 2168 (-th B), 2282, 2447, 2975 (-th B), 3005, 3478 (-th B), 3834, 3953, 4071, 4139, 4228, 6311 ABC,[2] 7418 ACD, 7521, 7777 (hertes † pete C), 7798, 7980, 8034 (-th B), 8070, 8141; -e here (*pass. sg.*), 2771 (-th B); -e here (*dat.*), 5107 ABD; -e he, 8039; trouth ‡ hold, 2168 D; trouthę the, 1255 (heed D); -ę but, 831 (-e C) (cf. 2771 † B, 6311 † D, 7418 † C).—vntrouthe, 7461 f (ontreuthe C, vntrought D); -e, 3826 (-th BD, ontreuthe C); -trothe, 7811 (-trouth BD, ontreuthe C). (Old-style figures indicate that D. omits -e)

 Rhyme words.—routhe (*all but* 2043), slouthe (2043, 2223, 2588, 7949). [Var. BC treuthe ; B trouhte, throuth ; D trongth.]

truwe, trewe (A.S. trèow, cf. also trúwa), truwe, 5974 f (trewe CD) (: in muwe (mewe CD)); truwe, 5976 (trewe C, treus ‡ be D); trewe, 4621 ABC, 4720 (trew B, trews D).

tyde (A.S. tíd, L. dat. tide, O. tid), 947 f ([t]yde C) (: abyde *inf.*: hide *imv. sg.*), 5739 f (: syde), 7063 f (: side).—meltid ‖ that, 2641 (meel(i)-ted B, mele ‡ that C, *om.* † D); tid but, 2824 AC (tyd B, -ë ‡ lost D); tyd that, 1228 C (tymę A, tymë BD).

wene (A.S. wén, *f.*; also wóna, -an, *m.*, Gn.; L. wene, buten (wihuten) wene, O. wen, wiþuten wen), withouten ony wene, 6255 f (: shene *adj. def.*: queene).

while, whyle (A.S. hwíl, L. while, O. whil, whle), 328 f, 718 f, 1353 f, 1592 f, 2768 f, 2892, 3618 f (wyse † C), [3919 † f CD,] 3920 f, 4663 f, 4922 f, 5366, 6764 f, 7245 f, 7638 f; -e, 2684, 2941 (whil(y) and A), 3292 (whiche † B), 3336 (wise ‡ D), 5781, 7291; -e he, 3380 (Ther while he AB, The while he CD) [, 7289 D (*l.* wight)]; whilę ‖ which(e), 3277 AB (-e which C, - [ę] that D).

 Rhyme words.—smyle *inf.* (328, 1592), bygyle *inf.* (718, 1353, 4663, 4922, 6764, 7245), *ind.* 3 *pl.* (7638), wyle (718, 1353, 3920), gyle (3618), affyle *inf.* (2768), myle (6764). [Var. B. qwhile, 5781, qwyle, 6764.]
 Note.—As adverb,—*whil* (without sounded -e) (O. whil) · cf. 468, 536, 3016, 5167, 5339, 5745, 5925, 6048, 6326; for *while*, cf. 315 AB (whilys ? C), 536 D, 5167 D, 5339 D, 6326 D; while he, 5745 BD —536 C, 6048 D, 6326 A, should be emended so as to keep *whil*.

wounde (A S. wund, L. O. (*obl*) wunde), 858 f (-d D), 1081 f (-d BD), 1241 f (-d D), 4539 f (-d D), 5257 f, 5289 f, 7866 f (D †; 7865 † f C).

 Rhyme words.—grounde *n.* (858, 7866), stounde (1081, 4539, 5257 + D, 5289, 7866), bounde *p.p.* (858), y-founde, founde *p.p.* (5257 ABC, 5289), the secunde (-ou-) (1241), abounde *inf.* (1241). [Var. C. wonde.]

wrathe, wratthe, wraththe (A.S. (N.) wrǽð(ð)o, L. wraððe, wræððe, O. wrappe), 6054 (wreth[e] B, wrethe C), 6510 (wreth[e] BD,

---

[1] In C insert [*by*].   [2] Read *al*[*le*] (*att*[*e*]) in 1245 CD, 6311 ABC.

wrethe C)[1]; -e, 7323 (wrath B, wrethe C, wreth D), 7619 (wrethe C, wrath D), 8163 (wrath BD); -e hast, 933 (wrothe D, wrethe ‡ C). [wrethe, 2952 ‡ C.]

wreche (A.S. wréec *ultio, miseria*, L. wreche, O. wrœche), -e, 1869 (-ë ‡ is D), 7253 (wrech D; C †), 7259.

Note.—In 1869 *wreche* = misery; in the other two cases it = veugeance.

yerde (A.S. gerd, W.S. gierd, gyrd, L. ȝerd, ȝeord, O. ȝerrde), 740 f (yerd D), 1239 f (-d D), 2512 f (ȝerd D), 3909 f (ȝerd D); -e, 257 (wand ‡ that D), 2979 (-ë † eke D).

Rhyme words —answer(e)de *ind.* 3 *sg.* (740), ferde *subj.* 3 *sg.* (740, 1239), herde *ind.* 3 *sg.* (8909), *subj.* 3 *pl.* (2512). [Vai. BCD ȝeide.]

youthe (A.S. geoguð, Ps. iuguð, L. ȝuȝeðe), 975 f (ȝouthe BCD) (: kouthe *subj.* 3 *sg.* : nowthe).

§ 10. Nouns in -yng, -ynge.

I. The following list includes such nouns (including "gerunds?") in -*ynge* as rhyme with an infinitive in the *Troilus*. All the rhyme-words are recorded in each case. D almost always lacks -e in this ending, but I have not taken the superfluous trouble to register this lack of -e. Minute varieties of spelling are also disregarded.

calkulynge (kalkelyng C, calkelyng D), 71 (: brynge).
compleynynge, 4903 (. sprynge).
comynge, 3801 (: brynge), 6866 (-g C) (: synge).
helpynge, 853 (he[l]pynge A) (. synge).
konnynge, 2943 (: brynge).
sobbynge, 5796 (wepynge C) (: brynge).
taryinge, 7137 (: brynge : arguynge *ptc.*)
tellyng (-e B), 743 (in his counseyl tellyng) (: sprynge).
tydynge, 2036 (: synge).
wytynge, 1321 (wet- C) (: rynge : lyuyng *ptc.*).

II. Here follow all the other cases of nouns in -*ynge* in rhyme. Where no note is added, the rhyme-words are other nouns in -*ynge*; an asterisk indicates that the rhyme-word is a present participle (or participial adjective) in -*ynge*; an asterisk and an old-style verse-number indicate that one rhyme-word is a noun in -*ynge*, the other a present participle.

byfallyng (-e B), 5680 f.
cherysshynge (cherisynge B, -isyng C, -isshing D), 6196 f.
cheterynge (chit- B), 1153 f.
compleynynge, *1645 f.

---

[1] That half so loth yowre wraththe (wreth BD, wrethe C) wolde (wold B) descrue.

comynge, 3038 f.
deyinge, 572 f (de[y]inge B).
doyng (-e B), 1119 f (: thyng D).
dwellynge, *304 f.
festenynge, *6818 f (feestynge B, festyng C, noon ‡ thing D).[1]
forsẅynge, 5651 f.
guerdonynge, 1477 f (-g CD).
gynnynge, *377 f ((by)gynnyng D).
langwysshynge, 569 f (-guyssinge B, -guissyng C).
louynge, 1476 f (-g CD).
lyuynge, 197 f.
meuynge, *285 f (-n- B, menyng C, mevyng D).
preyinge, 571 f (-g C).
purueyinge, *5648 f (-ueÿnge B, -uy[i]nge D), *5677 f.
semynge, *284 f.
shewynge, 5678 f (sh[e]w- B).
slomerynge, 1152 f (-berrynge B, slombryng ? D).
taryinge, *7938 f (-g CD).
warnynge, 3037 f.
weddynge, 6198 f (-g CD).
wenynge, 5654 f.
weymentynge, 1150 f.
wityuge, 5653 f (wet- B, wetıng D).
wonderynge, 1120 f (-[e]rynge B, wondur ‡ thyng D).
wynnynge, 199 f.

goynge, 5596 f (: whan I hym brynge).
heriynge, 2890 f (-y[ı]nge B) (: brynge *subj.* 3 *sg.*).
in-comynge, 2393 f (: brynge *ind.* 1 *sg.*).
rekenynge, 2725 f (-g CD) (: brynge *subj.* 2 *pl.*).
taryinge, 2727 f (-g CD) (: brynge *subj.* 2 *pl.*).

Note the exceptional rhyme in,—
hyfallyng, 5738 f (-e B) (: thing : comynge *ptc.*).

III. Nouns in *-ynge, -yng,* before consonants. (D has almost always *-yng.*)

[abettyng, 1442 D (*l.* abet).]
bygẏnnynge, 1876 (begınnyng ‡ oftyn C).
comẏnge, 4803 (-ę [the] C).
dȯıryng, 7200 (duryng B, dorynge (to) C, doyng † D).

---

[1] BC one syllable short: *l.* festenynge.

fȧllyng, 5683 (-ẹ BD).
faẏlyng, 921 (-ẹ B, D †).
gòyngẹ, 5959; gȯlngẹ, 6006 ‡ C (gȯing ‡ D, wèndyng A, wèndyngẹ B).
haùkyngẹ, 4621.
kèpyng, 200 (-ẹ BC, D †).
kònnyngẹ, 662 (cùnnyng D, cùnnyng is ‡ C); connỳng, 1089 G (con(ı)ẏngẹ B, C *cut out*, comỳngẹ † A, comỳng † D).[1]
làngurỳngẹ, 6405 ‡ C.
lèsyng, 3672 (-ẹ B, lesyng(is) C).
likìngẹ, 4315 † C.
lòkyng, 173, 293 (-ẹ BC), 8183 (-ẹ B).
lòuyngẹ, 1144 B (A † *om.*, of loue so ‡ D).
màkyng, 8152 (-ẹ B).
mènyngẹ, 7510 (-g [now] C).
preẏsyng, 2674 (-ẹ B).
ràueshỳng, 62 (ràuysỳngẹ B, ràvysshỳng D).
slttyng, 5700 (-ẹ B), 5704 (-ẹ BD).
tùrnyng 856 (-ẹ C, tornyngẹ B).
wèndyng, 6006 (-ẹ B, gȯlngẹ ‡ C, gȯing ‡ D).
wòpyngẹ, 5199 (sòrwè ‡ C), 5548 (-ẹ B, -e hym ‡ C).
  The cause of his comynge (-yng D) thus answèrede, 2187 (cause ?).

  IV. Before vowels and -h (vowel, unless otherwise noted).
àkyngẹ, 1081.
auỳsyng here, 2999 (-e B, avisid ‡ D, and send † C).
bùryngẹ (*dissyl.*), 7862 (brennyngẹ C, burying (*dissyl.*) D).
callkulỳngẹ, 6060 (kakelyng ‡ C, calkelyng D).
chaùngyng, 3391 (-e B, schaungyng C); -e, 4893 (eschaungé of ? D); schaungyng, 5060 C ‡ (lòkyng AD, lòkyngẹ B).
còmyng, 3763; -e is, 5169; -ỳng, 3754 (-e B); còmyngẹ hom, 7743 (-e à-ʒen † C); còmyng into, 4294 (-e BC).
dàwyng, 4308 (dawnyngẹ BD).
dissimulyngẹ, 7976 (dishomblyngẹ † C).
dòyng, 1125 (-e B, dèlyng D).
drècchyng, 3695 (-e B).
èsyng, 2372 (-e BC).
fàllyngẹ, 5723.
fòcchyng, 7253 (-e B, fechyng hom † C, fètting of D).
fèlyng, 3932 (-e BD, fỳllyng † C); fèlyng han, 4175 (-e B, -g haue E).

[1] connyng Digby Hl. 4912, konnyng E, commyng Cp. Durh., comyngẹ John's, comyng Phillpps MS.

flòmyng, 3775 (-e B).
gòynge how, 5764.
gỳdyng, 7006 (-e BC, guiding D).
gỳnnyng hath, 1756 (bygynnyng † D).
hàrmyng, 2225 (-e BC).
hèlpyng, 857 (hèlynge B, hèlyng D).
konnỳng, 2164 (-e B, cunnỳnge C, cunnỳng D); kònnynge, 3841 (knòwynge C, kùnnyng D); kònnyng hem, 83 (knòwynge him B, knòwynge hem C, kunnyng[e] hem ‡ D); kònnynge hadde, 7229 (knòwynge C, konnỳng ‡ and ? D).
kỳssyng, 4245 (-e BC).
làngwysshỳng, 529 (-e B, -guissyng C, -guysshyng D).
lòkyng, 182 (-e B, -ỳng and ? D), 1619 (-e B), 5020 (-e B), 5060 (-e B, schaùngyng C); -e, 4790 (tèllynge † C, lòkyng † D).
lòuyng, 55 (-e B), 1003 (-e BC); -e, 8196; -e how, 3.
màkynge, 3131 (-g [of] avaunt[es] D).
mèd[e]lyng, 4829 ‡ A (mèdlynge B, mèdelyng C, mèdlyng D).
mètyng, 4554.
pàrtyng here (eam), 4370 (-e BC).
poùring, 4302 (-e B, -e [in] D).
prèỳsyng, 3057 (-e B, -g [of] D, [in] preisyng C).
pursùing, 2829 ‡ C.
ràuesshynge, 7258 (to rauysshen any B, to rauych ony C, to rauissh any D)[1]; ràuysshỳng, 5210 (rauaschyng C).
[rehètyng †, 3191 D.]
rèsonỳnge, 5708.
scòmyng, 105 (-e C, scornë ‡ of D).
sèỳnge, 5085.
shrỳkyng, 6745 (schrychynge B, strichinge C, shrikyng D).
sìkynge he, 724 (sighyng D).
slòmberỳng, 6609 ‡ C (pl. ABD).
slỳnging of ‡, 2026 C.
sỳttyng, 5696 (-e B).
tàryinge (dissyl.) of, 7800 AC (tàrrynge B, tàriyng (dissyl.) D).
tèllynge, 4790 † C.
titerỳng, 2829 (-e B, tìteryng C) [perh. tìterỳng in AD, -erỳnge in C].
tòkenynge, 5532 (-g CD, tòknynge B); -e herte, 5441.
twỳnnynge, 5965 (-g CD).
vỳsitỳnge, 1126.

[1] Read hen[ne]s forth in AD.

wàggynge, 2830.
wàlyng, 408 (wailynge B, wele † and C, weylyng D).
wèndyng, 6098 (-e B, wỳndyng C), 6292 (-e B).
wèpyng, 701 (-e BC), 5603 (-e BCD); -e, 6439 (-ing ? D), 7872 (C †).
whỳsprynge, 2838 (whisperyngis ‡ C, whistryng † D).
wrìtynge, 7732 (at (the) writyng C); wrỳtyng, 8157 (-e B).
Observe,—
comỳngë ànd, 4517 AB (-e & ek C, -g and eke D). And compare,—
comỳngë ‖ thus, 2187 ABC (-[e] D); òr, the causè of his còmyngę (?).

§ 11. The following feminine nouns with long stem-syllables do not take -e in the *Troilus* (cf. Child, § 17):

(i.) à- stem,—*forward;* (ii.) i- stems,—*bench, might, plit, sped, thrift, wight, won, world;* (iii.) consonant stems,—*bok, nyght, ok.* In the case of *bench*, the example is not decisive.

> Note.—*Candels* (A.S. *candel, condel,* f.) is always dissyllabic,—candele to, 3983 (-del D, cardele † C); -dele in, 3701 (-deł D). For *sholder* (A.S. *sculdor,* f., m., -ru, n. pl., see R. von Fleischhacker, *Trans. Philol. Soc.* for 1888-90, p. 241), cf. 2756. For *cedre*, see § 29; for *hond,* see § 13; for *helpe,* see § 9. *Mylk*, 2011 f C, is an error for *bon.*

bench (A.S. benc), on bench hym, 1176.
bok, book (A.S. bóc), 4679 f (-e D) (: forsook *pret. ind. 3 sg.*), 6654 f (-e BD) (: wook : took *both pret. ind. 3 sg.*). Before consonants,—1095, 1180, 1189 (*metre ?*), 1196, 4660 (-ę D), 4688, 6948 (bouę † D); 8149 (-ę D), 8152 (-ę D); before vowels,—1171 (AB *too long*), 3345 (-e B, -e D †). O moral Gower this boke I directe, 8219 ABD.
forward (A.S. foreweard), 6860.
might, myght, (A.S. mi(e)ht, meht, L. mihte, O. mihht, acc. dat. mihhte); (i.) nom., 2058 [,4599 † C (pl. ACE)], 7782 AD, 7801 f, 8117 f (-e B); acc., 33 (-ę D), 227 f, 1264 f, 1718 f, 2425 f (-e B), 3354 f, 3496 f, 4247, 5148 f (-e B), 5281 f, 5602, 6478 f, 7046 f, 7229 f, 7284 f, 7464 f; with, 1419 f, 1954 f, 2083 f, 2637 f, 2770 (-t alone † D), 3020 f, 3278 f (-e B), [3843 † f C,] 6149 f, 6438 f (-e B); by, 5210 f (nyght B)[1]; of, 4618 f, 6435, 7201 f; to, 6491 f (-e B); for, 7322; through, 6200 f (-e B), 7613 f (-e B); emforth, 3841 f (emfor[th] C, after ‡ D). (ii.) nom., 1260, 2849, 2851, 2870 (-t † hym D); acc., 8067 (-e B); with, 3085, 8084 (m. [y]serued B, herte D); by, 6708[2]; on, 5857 (miʒt(es) D); thorugh, 2402; acc., myght hire, 45 (m. their D).—thourgh myghte, 5778 f AB (-t CD) (: nyght *nom.*).

[1] In A read *by* for *my.* [2] Dele (*&*) in C; insert [*it*] in B.

32   *Observations on the Language*   [§ 11.

Rhyme words.—knyght (227, 1264, 1419, 1718, 1954, 3020, 3278, 3841, 5281, 6149, 6200, 6478, 7201, 7229, 8117), nyght (2083, 2425, 2637, 3278, 3354, 5778, 6491, 7046, 7284, 7464, 7801, 8117), wyght *n.* (1264, 4618, 5210, 6200, 6438, 6491, 7201, 7229, 7613), dight *p.p.* (4618), vpright (1419), aryght (2083, 3496), a-noon right (2637), vnright *n.* (5210), right *pred. adj. sg.* (3841), right *adv.* (7613), lyght *pred. adj. sg.* (5148, 6438, 7046), bryght *adj. post.-pos.* (7284), byhight *p.p.* (7464). [Var. B 33 mygth; C myʒt, myth 1954; D miʒt.]

nyght (A.S. neht, Midl. also næht, E.W.S. nieht, L.W.S. niht, L. niht, dat. nihte, O. nihht), (i.) nom., 2075, 3640, 4253, 4508, 5776 f, 6907 f, 7044 f, 7282 f (C †); *time*, 1174 (D †), 2423 f (-e B), 3071 f, 3281 f, 3356 f (-e B), 3476, 3552, 3756 f (-e B), 4157, 4399, 5175 f (-e B), 5315, 6494 f, 7466 f, 7543,[1] 8118 f (-e B); acc., 7022 f (nygh(t) B); nyght by nyght, 7003 f (n. & n. D); next, 944; to, 2081 f (into, D), 3511, 7532,[2] 7799 f; on, 4021 (lyght † B; of, C); vpon, 7148 f; in, 6826 f (-e B); ouer, 2634 f; of, 2052 f (thour, C), 4488 f; after, 5083 f; a fourtënyght, 6697 f (-e B, fortenyʒt C); in fourtënyght, 5989 (in † fortune nyʒt C); syn mydnyght,[3] 3444 (tul, D).—(ii.) nom., 1983; acc., 3183; voc., 4271; *time*, 3379, 3392, 7156; at, 7559 (at n. with C); by, 452; ouer, 2598 (to ‡, D [2]); at n. he, 2625; at n. homward, 4711 (at n. ‡ thei D).—by nyghte, 7065 (-t BCD), 7517 (-t BCD).

Rhyme words.—myght, myghte *n.* (2081, 2423, 2634, 3281, 3356, 5776, 6494, 7044, 7282, 7466, 7799, 8118), wyght (3071, 3756, 5083, 5175, 6494, 6697, 7148), knyght (3281, 3756, 4488, 6697, 8118), light *n.* (6907, 7003), *pred. adj. sg.* (7044), bryght *adj. post.-pos.* (2052, 6826, 7282), right *acc.* (5175), aryght (2081), anoon right (2634), as lyne right (3071), vnright *adv.* (7022) yhight *p.p.* (6907), byhight *p.p.* (7466). [Var. C nyʒt (nyʒ, 4167); D night, niʒt.]

ok (A.S. ác), 2465 f (ooke B, okes † D) (: strok *n.*); 2420 (okę D), 2474 (okę D). [Var. B ook].

plit, plyt (A.S. pliht, *m. f.*, L. pliht, plihte, O. plihht; influenced by O. Fr. plite), (i.) 1159 (-ę BD), 1797 f (-e BD), 3881 f, (-e BCD), 3981 (-ę B), 4219 f (-e BE), 4396. (ii.) 2816 (-e D), 3088, 4322 (place ‡ D); plyt he, 2823 (-e he D).

Rhyme words.—delit (delite) *n.* (1797, 4219), despit (despite) (1797, 3881, 4219). [Var. BCDE plit(e); BD plyt(e); C plyʒt, pliʒt; D pliʒt.]

sped, speed (A.S. spéd spǿd, L.ᵃ ispede, ᵇ spede, O. sped), s. be, 1036 (speedę B, spedę D); s. fro, 1094 (-ę B, -e herafter D); s. al, 17 (spedë ‡ though D).

thryft (O.N. þrift), (i.) 3713 (-ę B), 4091 (-ę BD, thrif C), 6292 (-ę BD). (ii.) 1667, 3789 ([good] th. A); th. haue, 1932 (C †)[4], 2772

---

[1] C, metre ?
[2] D, metre ?
[3] Supply [*in*] in A.
[4] In A supply [*so*].

(C †); th. he, 2568.—vnthrift that he, 5093 BC (vnthryf [that].
he A). [Var. BCD thrift, BD thrifte.]
wight, wyght (A.S. wiht, wuht, wyht, *f., n.* (Siev. § 267, n. 3), L.
wiht, whit, O. wihht, P. PL.ᵇ wyght,ᶜ wight, wiht, wiʒt), 101 f,
163 f, 1072 f, 1265 f ABC, 1535 f, 3068 f, 3621 f (-e B), 3754 f,
4126 f, 4617 f, 4635 f, 5070 f, 5085 f, 5108 f, 5178 f, 5213 f, 5406 f,
6197 f, 6287 f, 6435 f, 6493 f, 6527 f, 6694 f, 6718 f, 7150 f, 7198 f,
7226 f (-e B), 7478 f, 7611 f (-e B), 7710 f, 7918 f. *Before
consonants:* 13 (-e a ‡ D), 534 (-e D), 685 (wygh A, thinge B), 692,
1031 (nonwyt ‡ C), 1058, 1121 AB (D †), 1273, 1432, 1613, 1655,
1881, 1916, ABC (D †), 2079, 2120, 2663, 2945, 3074 (man D¹),
3213, 3300, 3338 (wit † C, sight † D), 3445, 3517 (-e B), 3534
(man CD), 3598 (hem not ‡ C), 3602, 3631 (whit C²), 4633,
4947 (-e D, which † C), 5027, 5053 (wit † C), 5914, 6825, 6923,
6988, 7242 (-e B), 7730, 7798, 8208.—*Before vowels :* 268, 382,³
690,⁴ 1372,⁵ 1481, 2033, 2739,⁶ 2869; 3275 (iche in ‡ CD), 3586,
5917 (wyʒt his? C, wight his D), 6851, 7290 (w. his BD, with ‡
C.—*Before* h : w. hadde, 500 (D †); w. hath, 2669 (men. have ‡
D), 6736 ; w. he, 7289 (C om. ‡ (*hiatus*), while † he D).
  Rhyme words.—knyght (163, 1072, 1265, 1535, 3621, 3754, 5406, 6197,
6694, 7198, 7226, 7918), nyght (3068, 3754, 5085, 5178, 6493, 7150),
fourtenyght (6694), myght (1265, 4617, 5213, 6197, 6435, 6493, 7198,
7226, 7611), ryght *n.* (4126, 4635, 5108, 5178, 7710), *adv.* (101, 7611),
as lyne right (3068), aright (5070, 7478), vnright *n.* (1535, 5213), light
n. (5406), *pred. adj. sg.* (5070, 6435, 6718, 7478), bright *adj. indef.* (163,
6527), plyght *p.p.* (3621), hight *p.p.* (5108, 6287), dight *p.p.* (4617),
byhyght *p.p.* (6718). [Var. B wyʒt, witht, wygth, wyth ; C wyʒt, wiʒt ;
Cᶜ whiʒt ; D whiʒt.]
won (O.N. vǎn), ther was non other won, 5843 f (-e BD) (: noon *pron.* :
agon *p. p.*).
world (A.S. woruld, W.S. weorold, L. weorld, weorlde, O. weorelld), (i.)
nom., 3264 (w. hit D), 3302 (wor[l]d C), 3318, 3481, 5052 (-e D),
5985 (-e BD, w. [ne] C), 7014 (-e D), 7196 (-e D),⁷ 8111 (-e D), 8204
(-e B) ; voc., 4868 AB (-e D) ; acc., 504 (-e D), 3215, 4272, 4593 (e ?
E), 5177 (C †, -e D), 5860 (-e D †)⁸ ; in, 1262, 1320, 2855 (wor[l]d
A, wirk † D), 3132 (-e B),⁹ 5048 (-e BD), 5802 (-e D); 6308 (-e
BD), 6805 (-e D), 7085 (-e D); out of, 41 (-e D), 5613 (-e BD); of,
1495 ; for, 1214 (-e B, wor[l]d C), 6099 (-e D), 8060 (-e D);
thorough-out, 7425 (-e D, wo[r]ld B). (ii). nom., 1573, 3370,

---

¹ Read in C, *wyʒt was woyd[ed]*.   ² =person.
³ Supply [y] in D (*y-born*).   ⁴ Supply [*for*] in AD.
⁵ Supply [a] in A, [*for*] in D.   ⁶ D unmetrical.
⁷ Supply [*that*] in D.   ⁸ CD read *in* †.   ⁹ AC defective.

3392; voc., 211; acc., 1505, 4563, 5284 (-e D), 8180; in, 1378, 1383, 3167 (w. ‡ now D); out of, 5442 (-é gon D)¹; fro, 5831 (-e BD, wor[l]d was C); for, 4086 (wor[l]d A), 5961 (-e D), 5998 (-e D); in ... w. here, 3678.—on of this world [the] beste y-preysed, 7836 A (worldę the best [ı-]preysed B, world (-ę DG) the (*om.* D) beste (best D) i-preysed(e) C).— world(ę) (*acc.*) may, 4446 A (world BCD).

§ 12. Apocope of A.S. -n in nouns is found in the *Troilus* in the following words (cf. Child, § 15; ten Brink, §§ 203, 207):

morwe (A.S. morgen, *m.*, o-stem), *eue* (A.S. æfen, *n.*, *m.*, jo-stem), *game* (A.S. gamen, *n.*, o-stem), *mayde* (A.S. mægden, *n.*, o-stem), *kynrede* (A.S. cyn(n) + ræden, *f.*, jā-stem). Compare also *melle* (*mylle*) (A.S. mylen, myln, *m.*) and *fast* (A.S. fæsten, *n.*, jo-stem).

eue, eeve (A.S. æfen, éfen, *n.*, *m.*, L.ᵃ æuen,ᵇ heue, O. efenn), 2386 f (euen : leue B), 3437 f, 6977 f, 7377 f, 7505 f (euene C : grene (*l.* -ue)); at, 3402 f, 6844 f; it wol neygh euen bė, 7500 (euyn CD); *time*, eue, 7088; euęn and, 487 (eue BD, euyn (?) C).

Rhyme words.—leue *noun* (2386, 3402, 3437, 6844, 6977, 7377), bleue *inf.* (6844), to-cleue *inf.* (6977), by greue (7505).

game (A.S. gamen, gomen, *n.*, L. gomen, gome, game), nom., [372 † f D,²] 868 f, 1123 (-en B, -e D),³ 1732 f, 3968 f, 6225 f; acc., 5224 f; for, 3478 f (a-game BD, on g. C), 6127 f; of, 3926 f, 6783 f (fame † C); lettė-game, from, 3369 f (of, BC, of ... let[tė]-game D).— gamę, acc., g. bygonne ‡, 3092 A (gamėn pleye B, -ė pleye C, gamę ‡ to D).—game, nom., 4336 (gam B); acc., 2195 (gamyn in C); bytwene, 3096 (gam B); a game, 3490 (on g. C, a-gamę ‡ that D), 3492 (on g. C)⁴ (cf. 3478 f).

Rhyme words.—shame *n.* ([372 D], 868, 1732, 3478, 3968, 5224, 6127, 6225), name *n.* (6127, 6225), tame *adj.* (3369), frame *inf.* (3369), to blame (3926, 6783), defame *inf.* (5224).

kynrede (A.S. cyn(n), *n.*, + ræden, *f.*, cf. hús-ræden, mǽg-ræden, etc., P. Pl.ᶜ of kynredene, ᵇ kynrede), 7342 f (ken- C, kynred D) (: out of drede).

mayde (A.S. mægden, L W.S. mǽden, *n*, L. maiden, maide, O. maȝȝdenn, P.Pl. mayden, mayde), nom., 1965 f (: Criseyde : seyde

---

¹ world a-gon A; worlde gon B (*defective*); world i-gone C; worlde gon D.
² L *grame* (AB; C gaine †).
³ game shent A, -en shente B, -e y-shent D.
⁴ In the last two examples the MSS. have no hyphens; 3490 ABD may then (possibly) be acc., 3492 ABD may (not improbably) be nom.

[§§ 12, 13.] *of Chaucer's Troilus.* 35.

ind. 3 *sg.*); acc., maydë fre, 7838 (-en B); -e, nom., 7836 A(?)
BCD; -e, of, 8232.—cf. mayden bright, nom., 166; mayden, acc.,
1168.[1] [Var. BD maide; BCD maydyn.]

morwe, morwen (A.S. morgen, *m.*, tó morgen, dat. morne, L. morȝen,
morȝe, morwe, P. Pl. morwe, morwen), I. morwe, (i.) nom., 944 f[2],
1150, 4311 f.(-owe D *late hand*), 7393 (-ën B); *time indicated*,
487 f (on, C), 2183 f, 4405, 7048 f, 7088 f, 8024 f; tò, 861 f, 2518,
3227, 3731 f, 4759 [3] f, 6660 f, 7307 f, 7889 f; vnto, 6768 f; til,
6279 f (to = til C, til (to) m. D); on, o-, a-, 1490 f, 2573, 2606 f,
3265 (-ën B) [4], 4397 (-[e] B), 6105 f, 6377 f, 7467; on half a m.,
5970 f (morowe D); by, 2046 f, 7015 f (-owe D), 7237 f; of, 3903 f.
[to morwe ‡ wele, 7358 C (-e ABD).] (ii.) morwe, to, 2583, 3651.
(to more A), 3690, 3692 (-(yn) C), 7114 (D †), 7358 ABD; on, a-,
o-, 2179, 3394, 6882, 7555 (-(yn) C); on the -e he, 6649.—II.
morwën,—the m. com, 2640 (-yn C), in a m. sterue, 3231 (on a m.
B, on a morwyn C).

Rhyme words.—borwe *inf.* (487, 7088), to borwe *dat.* (2046, 2606, 8024),
sorwe (*everywhere*). [Var. morw, B 1490, 3651, 3690, 4311, 6768, 6882,
7015, 7114, C 2583, 4311.]

mylle? (A.S. mylen, myln, *m.*), myl[lë]-stones, 2469 AD (mylnë stones
B, mellë stonys C[c], melnë stones G, milnë stones Cp.). [melle, C.T.
3921 f, 4240 f; mylle, 4019; millen, 4039: *Child*, § 16. So melle
nom. (: the coldë welle, *The Former Age*, 6, Skeat, *Minor Poems*, p.
186. A.S. mylen-stán, P. Pl.[c] mulle-stones.]

fast (A.S. fæsten, *n.*, O. fasste), of, (*bef. vowel*) fast, 6733 (-e D).

Note.—With these may be compared *a-swowne*, 3934 f (on s. C, in a
swoun D) (: out of towne) (L. iswowen, iswoȝen, AS. geswógen *p.p.*).

§ 13. *Hond* (A.S. hond, *fem.* u-*stem*) takes -e in the
dative phrases *on honde, yn honde*.

Note.—"Dativ auf -*e* bei consonantisch auslautendem Nom. liegt vor in
honde, woneben *hond* gilt (A.E. *honda hond*):" ten Brink, § 209. It
will be observed, however, that the dative in -*e* is used only in certain
idiomatic phrases which had an existence independent in some measure
of that of the noun (cf. infra. § 14).

honde (A.S. hand, hond, *f.*, L. hand, hond, dat. -e, O. hand, wiþþ
hannd, wiþþe hande), on h., 3779 f (in hond D), 3996 f, 6066 f;
yn h., 1288 f (hond D), 1302 f (on hende C, on hond D), 1562 f
(-d D), 2307 f (holde † C), 3615 f (hand D), 7734 f; 7978 f, 8043 f.
[acc., hondë ‡ yp, 2287 A (*pl.* BCD); -ë † wrong, 5833 A (*pl.* BCD).]

[1] A remarkable succession of -*en*'s: "herden a mayden reden."
[2] Old-style figures indicate that D has *morow* (before vowels, -*ow*).
[3] to = till.   [4] morow whan D.

hond, (i.) acc., 1378 (-ę D); by the h., [2266 f † C (hood AD, hoode B),] 4579 (-ę D); of otheres h., 8127 (-ę B), cf. 2090; with rakel h., 1060; withouten h., 3030 (-ę B).—(ii.) [voc., 4103 † B (bond AC, god † D);] acc., 6515 (-e BC), 7236 (-e B, haue † D); into hire h., 433; of here h., 2140 (-e B)[1]; yn thyn h., 1046 (-e B); in goddes h., 4027 (-e B, sonde ‡ D); on h., 4702 ‡ A (in honde B, in hond D), 6428 AB (-e D); by the h., 1173, 6444 (-e B, -e ‡ sobirly D); by the h. here, 2689 (-e B).

Rhyme words.—stonde *inf.* (1302, 8043), vnderstonde *inf.* (2307, 3615), *p.p.* (6066, 7978), withstonde *inf.* (1288, 3780), ystonde *p.p.* (7978), fonde *inf.* (1582, 3996, 6066), bonde *p p.* (2307), sonde *n.* (7734). [Var. D hand.]

§ 14. The following masculine and neuter nouns which in Anglo-Saxon end in a consonant in the nominative sometimes or always take an -e in one or more cases in the *Troilus:*

(i.) masculine o- stems,—*borh, botm, clúd, déað, fǽr (fér), grǽf (graf), grund, -hád, héap, heofon, pin* (m. ?), *prím* (m. ?), *scrín, síð, stǽger, steal(l), téar, tún, -twist, weg, wer*, (ii.) neuter o-stems,—*crǽt, fýr, gǽt (geat), géar (gér), gód, hors, líf, los, sǿð, tempel, -wíl, wolcen;* (iii.) neuter jo-stems,—*bed(d), hiew;* (iv.) neuter wo-stem,—*cnéow;* (v.) masculine i-stem,—*flyht;* (vi.) neuter i-stems,—*ge-fér, (ge)wiht;* (vii.) masculine consonant-stem,—*fót.* For *stere* gubernaculum, see § 2.

(a)[2] In some of these words the Chaucerian -e is clearly the Anglo-Saxon dative singular ending. So in *bedde, borwe, dethe, fere* (in *yfere*, see § 88), *fyre, hepe, horse, knowe, lyue, towne, yere.* For most of these a nominative or accusative in a consonant is found in the *Troilus* (thus, *bed, borw, bourgh, deth*, etc.), and in all of them the -e is confined to dative phrases with a preposition. Some of the words, to be sure, exhibit also forms without -e after prepositions that in Anglo-Saxon require the dative; but it will usually be found that such phrases as preserve -e are idioms in which the preposition has come to be very closely associated with the noun, whereas in the (presumably dative) phrases that show no -e the collocation of noun and preposition may be regarded as accidental or occasional. The distinction may be seen by comparing such

---

[1] Metre in AB ? In D supply [*that*].
[2] The following paragraph was in type before Kluge's note in Paul's *Grundriss*, I, 900, met my eye.

idioms as *to bedde, abedde, to towne, on horse,* on the one hand, with *in his bed, on the bed, on here hors,* on the other. In the first class of examples there is no article or other word between the preposition and the noun: the phrases are units, and as such have an existence more or less independent of the individual history of their component parts (in *abedde, afyre, alyue, yfere,* we have actual compound words). It is easy to see how the Anglo-Saxon dative -e might be lost elsewhere but preserved in these petrifactions. In the second class, on the contrary, we have no such unified phrase, and consequently no -e. The difference is well illustrated by *to dethe* (A.S. tó déaðe) and *to the deth.* In other words, *bed, deth,* etc., were not inflected in the dative by Chaucer. When he appears thus to inflect one of them, he is merely using an inherited petrifaction containing a dative (compare our use of *alive, whilom*). In a few cases, however, an article or pronoun is inserted between the preposition and the noun in these phrases, and the -e still preserved,—by analogy, no doubt. The following list of the phrases included under this present sub-head *a* will make this clear: *abedde, to (unto) bedde, vnto here bedde, to borwe, to dethe, afyre, on fyre, in the fyre, to the fyre, to hepe, on hors[e], on knowe, on (vpon) lyue, alyue, yn al his lyue,*[1] *in towne, to towne, out of towne, in the towne*[2], *to yere, of fern[e]yere. On grounde* seems to be a similar survival, and stands over against *on a ground* (i.e. on a foundation): cf. *on the grounde, to grounde, to the grounde, through the grounde* (but *through the ground, vnder the ground*). *Gode* in *to gode* (A.S. tó góde) and the analogous phrases *sowuen ynto gode, for gode, for the townes gode,* probably belongs here. (Cf. *on, yn honde,* § 13.)

(*b*) One is tempted to refer to *a* the following phrases: *yn stalle* (but cf. *into a litel oxes stalle,* C. T., E 207, *in an oxe stalle,* id., 398, and see Child § 14, ten Brink § 199 Anm.), *put to flyght[e]* (but cf. *to the flyghte*), *to were* (but cf. *to the sorwful were,* Parl. F. 138). In *on the stayre, adoun the stayre, downward a stayre,* we probably have to do with an inorganic -e, not with a dative-ending (cf. *He passeth but oo stayre in dayes two,* Compl. Mars, 129); and so perhaps in *with many a twyste* and *of wighte.* For *vpon a rore,* see § 15.

(*c*) The Chaucerian -e represents an Anglo-Saxon dative plural ending (-um, later -an, L. -en) in *sithe* (as, *an hundred sithe,* cf. *tyme*

---

[1] *Lyue* is also used in the adverbial phrases *my (his, al my) lyue* = during my (etc.) life (but see 4140). Cf. also the adverb *blyue.* [2] But,—*in to town,* 4624 f.

and *tymes* in similar phrases, § 2, p. 3, above). So perhaps in *vnder fote* (see Zupitza, Guy, note on v. 598).

(*d*) Unmistakable inorganic -e's appear in the following words, in which -e appears in nominative, accusative, or vocative,—*clowde, feere, graue, hewe, pryme* (French influence), *pyne, tere* (but also *teer*),[1] *weye* (but also *wey*), *wyle, yate.* So also in the suffix *-hede* (but also *-hod*). Cf. also *carte, shryne.* In *botme, -me* represents Anglo-Saxon syllabic *m* (A.S. botm) (cf. ten Brink, § 199 Anm.). *Temple* represents A.S. *tempel*. In *heuene* (dissyllabic in all cases; before vowels, *heuẹne*) the MSS. vary between *-ne* and *-en* (*-yn*); for *walkene* (A) there are the variants *walken* (B) and *walkyn* (CD) : ten Brink decides for *heven* and *welkne*, but admits *hevne* (§ § 199. 1, 203. 5, 219); but it cannot be regarded as settled whether Chaucer in such cases said *-nẹ, -ën*, or *-n*, whatever he may have *written*.

(*e*) The -ẹ in *the sothe* seems the result of an adjective analogy. But we find also *forsothe* (A.S. *forsóð*,—but *tó sóðe, tó sóðon, -um*) ; cf. *for a soth.*

Note 1.—Ten Brink's dictum that the nominative and accusative of neuter vowel stems have "tonloses e durch Analogiewirkung in der Mehrzahl der kurzsilbigen und einigen mehrsilbigen o- Stämmen" (§ 203. 5) gets slight support from the *Troilus*. See the evidence under *bak, col, god, gres, los, mot, path, ship* (§ 18, below). *Holë of*, 3443 C (holë D) is an error, and *lossẹ, losse* are hardly significant. As to *col* (*cole*), *cols* is the only form recognized by ten Brink, except in composition, but *col* occurs.

Note 2.—For instances of an erroneous -e written, but not pronounced, see especially § 18 under *bor, brest, cold*(*e*), *dom, fond*(*e*), *flood, foul*(*e*), *frend, gold, harm, hed, hom, knyght, kyng, lord, noon, reed, ryng, thing, work, wynd*. The following apparently sounded -e's are due to copyists' errors, and are easily corrected by a comparison of MSS.—*lodẹ* (A.S. léad), 1624 f D (: *rede adj. pl.*); *rymë holde*, acc., 2932 C (rimes ABD); *with the stremë of*, 2971 D; *lossë me*, 4751 D. For *geste* (?) see § 18.

Note 3.—For *thondre* see *thonder* (§ 18). For *angre* see § 19 ; for *shyvre, slyvre*, see § 15, n. 1. On the confusion between *-er* and *-re* cf. Child § 84 and infra §§ 15, note 1, 29. For *feuere, feuer*, see § 18.

bedde (A.S bed(d), *n.*, L. bed, dat. bedde, O. bedd, i min bedd, o bedde), to bedde, 3497 (-[de] D), 3533 (-[de] D), 5905; vnto bedde, 2032 f (& ‡ to bedde C; to her bed D) (: spedde *pret. ind.* 3 *sg.*); vnto here bedde wente, 7384 (reste C, rest[e] D); a-bedde, 2390 f (in b. C, a bed D) (: spedde *pret. ind.* 3 *sg.*), 3531 (-[de] D), 3535 (-[de] D), 4426 (in b. D), 4521 (-[de] D ?).—to bedde he, 1147 (bed B), 6574; a bedde, 908 B (in b. C, in bed D, a bedde and [make] A) ; a beddẹ half, 1152.[2]

bed : (i.) vpon his b., 1642 (beddẹ B); in his, thi, the b., 2395

---

[1] " Wie es scheint gilt *tere* statt *teer :*" ten Brink, § 199 Anm. But *teer* occurs.
[2] Pandarẹ a-bedde (*so in* ABCp. ; a bed DG) ∥ half yn a (*om.* DG) slomeryngẹ (slomberyngẹ B, slombryng DGCp.). Leaf cut out in C.

§ 14.]   *of Chaucer's Troilus.*   39

(-de C), 2602 (-de B), 3897 BCD (*line too long in A*), 6772 (-de D); into his b., 4377 (-de A); on here, the b., 5395 (-de D), 6657 (-de D); toward the b., 5017 (-de ? B, D).—(ii.) from his b., 7899 (-de D); in here b., 5909 (-de BCD), 6709 (-de D, in . . . bed ben ‡ C); in . . . bed he, 4457 (on his bedde he D); vpon . . . bed he, 4918 (-de BD); into bed hym, 3939 [1] B (-de C, D ?); vpon . . . bed hym, 4886 (-de D); in . . . bed hym, 7802 (-de D).

Note.—vpon his beddë side, 4896 D, is merely haplography for *beddës sidë* (AB, beddys s. C).

borwe (A.S. borh, *m.*, L borh), to, 2048 f (: morwe : sorwe), 2609 f (: morwe : sorwe), 8027 f (: morwe : sorwe).—And I thi borw (borugh B, borow D) fy (*om.* C) no wyght doth but so, 1031.— And I youre bourgh ne neuere shal for me, 1219 (borugh B, borw C, borow D. [borow 2048 f D, 2609 f D.]

botme (A.S botm, *m.*), in . . . b., 297 (boteme C, botme ‡ hit D); to . . . -e, 1620 (botëme ‡ C, botmë ‡ it D). [Cf. botmeles, § 48, n. 5.]

carte (A.S. cræt, *n.*, L. carte, O. karrte, P. Pl. cart-whel), with, 6641 ABC; nom., farë carte, 7525 f (soory ‡ carte D) (: arte = *art thou*); cart a-myś, acc., 7028 (-e BCD); carte, acc., 4597 ‡ B.

clowde (A.S. clúd, *m., rock*, L. clude, *rock*), nom., 3275 f (cloude BCD) (: kowde *potuit*).—cloud, (ii.) nom., 1851 (-e BC, c. that † D), 1866 (-e BC, cloudis ‡ in D), 4862 (-e BC, D †).—vnder cloud[ë] blak, 175 (-ë BC, vndur blak cloud so D †).

dethe (A.S. déað, *m.*, L. dæð, deð, etc., dat. deaþe, deðe, O. dæþ, dat. dæþ, dæþe). A dative in -e is preserved only in the phrase *to dethe* (A.S. tó déaðe),—do to dethe, 5439 f ABG (to the dethe D, don to deye C) (: til I vnshethe (conueye C †)); to dethë mote I smete be, 2230 CD (-[e] BG, to deth[ë] mot I be smet[ë] A). But in *to the deth* no -e is preserved,—to the deth myn herte (= until death, etc.), 6937; vnto the deth myn, 606; vnto my deth to, 7348. [to deth ‡ or, 2840 C (-e D), *and* into myn deth ‡ in, 4934 C, of course prove nothing].—A doubtful line (in which however, we should no doubt read *deth*) is: That of his deth (-e D) ye be nought (not C, no thing D) to (for to CGCp.) wyte, 1470. In 4082 C, read *deth* (acc.) [*y*-]*schape* (deth is shapen A, deth y-shapen BD).

deth, everywhere else, whether before vowels or consonants (though D often adds -e, which, however, is never sounded, for

---

[1] A reads "he hym (i. e. he'm) into beddë caste."

40 *Observations on the Language,* [§ 14.

3185 D should be corrected). Thus,—nom., 1286 (-e D), 2905 (-ę D), 3913 ‡ C, 5132, 5165, 5444 (-ę D, they † C),[1] 5518 (day † C), 5571, 5859, 6257,[2] 7756; acc., 1046, 2980 (D †), 3185 (-ë ‡ sono D), 4419, 7750, 7776, 7920 (day ‡ C), 8081; voc. and exclam., 4912, 5163 (-ę D), 6568 (loude ‡ he C); of (NOT = ex), 527,[3] 799 f (-e D) (breth *acc.*), 825 (-e his D), 1423 (-ę D), 1518 (-e D), 2364 (-ę D), 3913 (*nom.* ‡ C), 4903 (C †), 5481 (-ę D), 6109; from the, his d., 469 (D †; dethes = deth his C), 536,[4] 1651 (-e hym D), 4085, with my, his, the d., 2952 (-e D), 3747 (-e he D), 5401[5]; neigh the d., 3204 (-ę D); after the, youre, my d., 5415, 5900, 7054 (day ‡ C), 8035 (day † C); toward my d., 7004 (C ‡); thorugh my d., 7636; for his d., 8185 AB. [Var. BD deeth.]

feie, in *yfere* (var. *in fere*), see §88.

fere, feere (A.S. faér, fér, *m.*), nom., 3425 f, 3986 f, 4183 f, 4527 f; acc., 3414 f, 3470 f, 3595 f, 4240 f; voc., 4163 f; for fere, 108 f, 768 f, 1388 (-[e] B), 1534 f (fer C), 5334 f, 5863 (B † om., fer[e] D), 5887 (fer ‡ to D), 6025 f, 7272 f, 7966 f; in f., 726 f; yn this f., 1399 (-[e] B); in swych f., 3299 f; of (= gen.), 3932 f.— for fere, 801, 1855 (fer C), 6744 (fer D); for fere he, 875 (fer C); of the feer his, 6619 (fere BD, fer ‡ the C).

Rhyme words.—were *cras* (4163) *crant* (3425, 3470, 3932, 4240), *esset* 726, 768, 3299, 3414, 3986, 4183, 6025, 7966), *essent* (4527, 5334), nere 3 *sing.* (4183), enquere *t.if.* (4527), ere, eere (108, 726, 768, 1534, 3299, 3595), tere *n.* (3932), there (3414, 3425, 3470, 3595, 4163, 6025, 7272), where (4240).

flyghte (A.S. flyht, *m.*, L.[a] fluht, dat. -e [b] fliht, dat. -e, O. flihht), to the flyghte, 2324 f (fly3t C, flight D) (: lyghte *adj. pl.*); is put .... to flyght[e], 1851 f (: the sonne shyneth bright (-e B)); put to flyght the, 1698 (fleyht C). [in fly3t as, 6121 † C.]

fote (A.S. fót, L. fot, dat. -e, O. fot, o fot, with fote), vnderfote, 1432 f (foot D) (: bote : rote); in his fot(e), 4034 f (foot B) (: sot : I mot); nom., fot is, 2049 (-e C).

fyre, fire (A.S. fýr, *n.*, L. fur, dat. -e, O. fir), in the fyre, 3553 f (fyr C); to the f., 3820 f (fere BCD); afyre, on fire, 2866 f, 4788 f (fere C), 4846 f (in f. A, on fere C), 5171 f (fere C), 7083 f, 7829 f; a fere, 229 f (a feere B, al fere C, ful † fere D).[6] fyr, fir, (i.) nom., 4475 f (-e BCD), 5080 (-ę BCD); acc., 445 (-ę C, fere D), 2417 f (-e B, fere CD), 3326 f (-e BCD); the ner the fyr the, 449 (fere D).

---

[1] In 5444 D dele (*the*).
[2] but [if] deth me D.
[3] In C read *to* for *the*.
[4] In C supply [*that*].
[5] In C supply [*to*].
[6] In B insert [*herte*].

§ 14.]   *of Chaucer's Troilus.*   41

(ii.) nom., 436 (fere D †), 490 (-e B), 4780 (fer C, fere D); a-fyr, 3698 (-e BD, à ‡ fere C); of, 6665 (-e D); nom., fyr he, 3267 (-e BD, fyr [he] C).

    Rhyme words.—ire (2866, 7829), hire, here *n.* (4788, 5171), desire *inf.* (3553, 4846, 7083), *ind.* 1 *sg.* (5171), enspire *inf.* (4846), *imv.* 2 *sg.* (3553); desir *n.* (2417, 3326, 4475), spir (-e BCD) *A.S.* spir (2417), wir (-e BD) *A.S. wir* (4475).
    ☞ fyre (fere BCD) : dere *adj.* : here *inf.* (3820); a fere : were *asset* : dere *inf.* (229). [Var. C 490 fuyr; C 449 fyer.]

gode, goode (A.S. gód, *n.*, O. god, inn gode, forr go.le), sownen yn-to g.; 1029 f (good D) (: vnderstode *subj.* 3 *sg.*); for g., 3766 f (good D) (: stode *ind.* 3 *pl.*); for the townes g., 5215 f (: withstode *subj.* 1 *sg.*); to good[e] mot it turne, 1175 (-ë BC).

    good, (i.) nom., 3950; acc., 1182 A (?) D (-e B; of, CG, *a doubtful line*)¹, 2263 f (-e B) (: stood *ind.* 3 *sg.*), 3480 f (-e B) (: on a flode, flood D), 3724 ‡ D, 6469 f (-e B) (: stood *ind.* 3 *sg.*), 7512 f (: hood, -e BD); for al the good, 3220 (-e B), 5583, 7249 ‡ C.—(ii.) nom., 7739; acc., 4749 (-e B), 5073 AD (-e B); ayen som g., 7529 (-e C).

grave (A.S. græf, graf, *m., n.,* O.N. grǫf, *f.*), nom., 7781 f (: haue *inf.* : saue *inf.*); vnto, 7105 (B † C †).

grounde (A.S. grund, *m.,* L.ᵃ grund,ᵇ -e,ᵃᵇ dat. -e, O. grund, to grund, to grunde), to the g., 856 f (-d CD), 4906 f; to g., 4707 f (-d D), 4739 f (-d D); on g., 4966; on the g., 7650 f; through the g., 7863 f.

    ground, (i.) nom., 939 (-e B), 1927; through the g., 1190 (-e B, -d † of D); vnder the g., 4282 (-e BD). (ii.) voc., 4146 (-e BE); on a g., 3824 (-e B); to the ground his, 5184 (-e B, -ë doune D).

    Rhyme words.—wounde *n.* (856, 7863), stounde (4739, 7863), bounde *p.p.* (856), y-grounde (4707), expounde *inf.* (7650), confounde *inf.* (4906). [Var. BD grownde; C. gronde.]

-hede (suffix, A.S. -hád, *m.* ; wreccehed *Pet. Chron.* ; L.ᵇ child-hode, man-ede; O. maʒʒdenn-had, maʒʒþ-had; P.Pl. maiden-hod, man-hede, man-hod, knyght-hod).

    goodlihede (-hed D), of, 7953 f (: in drede); -hed, of, 1927 f (-hede BD), (: hed *caput* : ded *adj. sing.*); nom., -hede, 4572 (-hed, -hid, -heed).

    knyghthod (A.S. cnihthád), of, 7954 (knythod C); nom., -hod and, 8117 (-e² D).

    manhod, (i.) nom., 6336 (-e B); with, 3270 (-e B), 5191. (ii.) nom., 1761; with, 7839 (-e B); acc. vnmanhod, 824 (-e BD³, òn-manhòd ‡ C).

¹ Cp. has the right reading: Is it of loue o som good ʒe me lere. B and the John's MS. also insert *o.*
² Supply [grete].   ³ D is hopeless as to metre ; in A supply [*a*].

womanhede, to (vnto BCD), 4144 f; of, 4582 f; fór, 6124 f (-hed CD); acc., 6836 f; to womanhode that, 283.

<small>Rhyme words.—dede *n.* (4144, 6836), drede *n.* (4582, 6124), lede *inf.* (4582), rede *inf.* (6836).</small>

hepe (A.S. héap, *m.*, L. hæp, hep, dat. -e), to hepe, 4606 f ABC (: lepe *inf.*).—acc., hep of, 5943 (-e D, heepe B).

heuene (A.S. heofon, *m.*: also, L.W.S. heofone, *f.*, cf. eorðe, *f;* L. heovene, heofne, O. heoffne, heffne), in, 878 f; to, 4046 f (in ‡. h. B), 5285 f (heuen D), of, 4567 f.—heuene, *before consonants*, always dissyllabic,—nom., 1911 (-yn D †)[1]; acc., 2844 (-yn D); in, 31 (-yn C), 1980 (-en B, -yn C), 3432 (-yn D), 4441 ‡ CD; of, 1766 (-en C, -yn D); to, 3026 (-yn D); from, 3468 (heue † C, -yn avale D), 5508 AC (en D; B †); on, 6637, 8188.— heuene, nom., 1722 (-en B, -yn ‡ on D); in, 2850 (-yn D), 4441 AB, 8182, 8207 (-en BD); from, 5374 (-en D); in . . . h. he, 4093 B (-yn ‡ he D)[2]; in h. his, 6058 (-en D); nom., h. his, 4584 (-yn D); in heuëne hye, 4587. [heuene † egle, 4338 D.]

<small>Rhyme words.—neuene *inf.* (878), neuene ‡ *n.* (4567 B), steuene (4567 ACD), seuene (4046, 5285).</small>

hewe (A.S. héow, *n.*, W.S. híew, híw, N. híu, see Siev. § 247, n. 3, Sweet, 1789; L heowe, O. hew, inn hewe), nom., 461 f, 4540 f (hew B), 5402 (-[e] BCD); acc., 441 f, 1388 f, 2555 f, 7766 f; of, 3145 f, 5041 f (-w C), 5398 f (-w D), 7936 f, 8135 f; with, 5325 f, 6922 f.—hewe, nom., 2936 ‡ D; acc., 1145 (D †).—in his hewe bothe, 487 (-e C ‡).

<small>Rhyme words.—newe *adv.* (441, 4540), *adj* (1388, 2555, 5325 [òf newe A], 7936 [anewe C]), newe *inf.* (3145), trewe *adj.* (5041, 5325), vntrewe 3145, 7936, 8135), rewe *inf.* (461 [rew A, rewe *pres. subj.* 2 *pl.* † CD], 5398, 6922), knewe *ind.* 3 *pl.* (4540).</small>

horse (A.S. hors, *n.*, L. hors, an horse, to horse, O. horrs), on hors[e] gan, 6400 AB (-e CD).—hors, (i.) on here h., 6545 (of = down from, BCD); from hire h., 6552 (-e D, C †). (ii.) nom., 223, 1711; acc., 4707, 7381 (-e D); on his h., 2346, 6398 (h. he D); of (= from) hors, 6876 B (of here h. AC (*plu.*), of horse light D); from his h. he, 6563 (-e D; C †).

knowe (A.S. cnéo(w), *n.*, N. cnéw, cnéo, Merc. cnéu, L.ª on cneowe, L.ᵇ a cnowe, O. o cnewwe), sat (fel C) on knowe, 2287 f (know D) (: I trowe *ind.* : sowe *inf.*).

losse, see § 18.

lyue (A.S. líf. *n.*, L. lıf, on liue, bı life, bi líue, O. líf, dat. líf, -e), acc

---

[1] it an heuene (it) was C.   [2] *heuene* om. in A.

of time (my lyue, his l., al my. l.), 594 f (lyf C), 1290 f (in ‡ my l. D), 2141 f, 4929 f (liff D), 6528 f (in ‡ his l. C); euere his l. and, 6799 (lyf C, liff D); on lyue, 1223 f, 1973 f, 5156 f (lyf C), 5425 f (onlef C), 6632 f (a lyue D), 7027 f, 7251 f, 7732 f, 8226 f; alyuë maken, 3734; on lyuë come, 7248; on lyue, 4958 ABD; on lyue han (haue), 5899 (o l. B, a-lyue a be C); vpon lyue, 2115 f; yn al his lyue, 2623 f ([in] C); yn lyue, 899 † C; of (= out of) lyue, 2693 f (on † l. C), 7924 f. [Cf. blyue adv., § 88.]

> Rhyme words.—blyue adv. (594, 1223, 1290, 2623, 2693, 5153, 6528), fyue (2115, 7251), Argyue nom. pr. (5425), thryue inf. (1223, 1290, 2141, 2693), dryue inf. (2623, 5156, 7732), dryue subj. 3 sg. (7027), depryue inf. (4929), dyscriue inf. (1973, 6632, 7732), ryue inf. (7924), stryue inf. (6528), circumscryue inf. (8226).

lyf, lif, nom. (i.) 1863 f, 536 (-[e] ‡ C), 772 (-ę B), 1041, 1199, 1286 B (of lyf D), 1447 (lyue B), 1551 ‡ A (lyf is B, l. in C, -ë ‡ in D), 1826 CD, 1936, 4952, [5273 † f C,] 5339 (C †), 6516, 7741 ‡ D, 7581, 7986¹; voc., 4264; nom. (ii.) 462 ABC, 1286 A, 1826 AB, 3217 (-e B), 4319 (acc. ‡ D, nom. -e B), 4936 (-e B); acc. (i.) 1046, 1557, 1915 ‡ D, 1917, 1920 f, 3257, 4447, 4559, 5229, 6703 f (-e B), 6720, 6992 (-[e] ‡ C), 7077, 7532 (-ę B, lyf ‡ I C, lif[e] ‡ D); acc. (ii.) 469, 1554, 1660, 4318 BD (lyf saue? AC)², 4444, 4963 (lyf ‡ wele C), 6004, 7741 AC, 7747 (-e D), 7770 AD, 7776; acc., lyf his, 2151; of (not = ex) (i.) 4323, 5610 (-[e] ‡ C, D?), 5826, (ii.) 4689, 4775 ABD; with (i.), 7637, 7682; by lyf be, 2103.—wreke vpon myn ownë lyf, 2950 f.—In 4140 f, al my lyfe (lyue BC, life? D), acc. of time, rhymes with wyf, voc.

> Rhyme words.—stryf n. (1863, 1920, 6703), wyf (2950, 4140, 6703), en tentyf adj. (1920).

pryme (A.S. prím, m. ?) seems to owe -e to the influence of Fr. prime.— pryme, nom., 2180 f; at, 2077 f, 6378; after, 2642 f; atwixen, 6835 f. (Cf., of lusty ver the pryme, 157 f.)

> Rhyme words.—tyme (everywhere), by me (2077). [Var. BCD prime.]

pyne (A.S. pín, m. (?), L.O. pine), nom., 1761 f; acc., 2250 f, 6631 f (peyne † A), 6653 f (peyne † A), 7490 f; in, 4685 f, 5136 f (peyne † C), 6369 f (peyne † B); of, 7255 f † B (l. peyna with ACD); -e, nom., 4300 (-es ‡ D).

> Rhyme words.—enclyne inf. (1761), myne inf. (1761), 5136), dyne inf. (2250, 7490), fyne inf. (4685), deuyne inf. (6631, 6653), defyne inf. (6631), twyne subj. 3 sg. (6369), Quyryne (4685), Proserpyne (5136). [Var. D pine.]

shryne (A.S. scrín, n., see Pogatscher, p. 161), voc., -e, 6916.

sithe (A.S. síð, m., L. síð, dat. -e, O. ann siþe, oþerr siþe, offte siþe,

---

¹ Supply [that] in A. ² Read my lyf an houre saue (so Cp.).

siþess), a hondred sithe, 4437 (-e he B, tyme and C, tymęs D); a thousand sithe, 5415 f (: swythe : lythe *inf.*); an hundred sithe, 6835 (-ę C, -ęs D); a thousand sithe, 7744 f (sith D) (: blythe : swythe). [Dat. pl. in A. S. : as, seofon sīðum.]

sothe (A.S. sóð, *n*, L. soð, soðe, O. soþ, to sʋþe). In the Middle English uses of this word there seems to be some confusion between sóð *sbst.* and sóð *adj.* The substantive phrase *the sothe* is perhaps due to the influence of the definite adjective form. *Forsothe* instead of A.S. *forsóð* (cf. *tó sóðon*) is noteworthy. See also *in soth*. In the examples that follow *soth* (*sothe*) seems to have been felt as a substantive. In *ye sey right soth ywys*, 1275 AB, perhaps *soth*[e] is an adverb.

the sothe, acc., 12, 1605, 4440 (-[e] B), 5615, 6983 (-[e] B), 7375, (-[e] BD), 7391 (-[e] B, [the] soth[e] C), 7398, 8003 (-[e] B, the soth † D); forsothe, 5697 f (for soth BD) (: in yow bothe); forsothé so it semeth by hirę song, 1968 ABCD (-[e] G), but cf. for a soth, 6069.—the sothe is, 5965 (B † D †; the s. (this) is C).

soth, sooth, (i.) nom., that is s., 1268 f (-(e) D) (: doth 3 *sg.*); acc. (in *soth to seyn, soth for to telle,* and similar phrases,—no def. or indef. article), 343, 591 (*om.* D), 712 (the sothę D), 822 A, 1706 (-(e) B; D †), 1769, 2071 (the sothę D), 2367 f (ful sothe, *as if adv.*, D, *but the rhyme* doth 3 *sg.* (doth(e) D) *condemns the form*), 2441 (the sothe [for] D; C †), 2601 (the sothę D), 3197 (-(e) D), 3272, 3492 (the sothę D), 3835, 4372, 4635 (-(e) D), 4709 (the sothę D), 5165 (soft † B), 7531 C (-(e) D), 7712, 7883; seye a soth, 1316 (-(e) D), 2222 (-(e) BD); homly s. to seyne, 2644 BC ((the) soth(e) D); in soth, 6506 (-ę D), 6734; for a s., 6069 (cf. *forsothe*). (ii.) nom. (in the phrase *soth is*), 3461, 4166 AC (-(e) B), 5930 (so[th] C, -(e) D), 6392 (-(e) D); acc., seyde . . . soth, 3420 (-(e) D); soth hym seyde, 822 C (-e BD); a soth, acc., 7821 (-(e) CD), 7902, 8087; a soth(e), acc., 7672 ABD (asay ‡ C); lyk a soth, 3761; cause of soth, 5703.

staire, steyre (A.S. stǽger, *m.*), on the s., 215 f (starre † B) (: contraire : debonaire); adoun the steyre, 1898 (steyȝęre C, stairé anon D †); downward a steyre, 2790 (steięre B, stair D).

stalle (A.S. steall, stall, *m.*, O. stall), oxe yn stalle, 7832 f (staH D) (: vynes alle).

temple (A.S. tempel, *n.*), 323 CD (*disordered*), 1458, 6728 (tempęle C), 6929; temple, 162 (AB *too long*, tomple B), 185 (D ?), 317, 363,

§ 14.] *of Chaucer's Troilus.* 45

3382 .(tempęle C); temple he, 267 (-ę̈ went D); templé he, 5609.[1]

tere (A.S. téar, tǽr, tœher, *m*), nom., 3929 f; acc., 6585 f, 7409 f, 7945 f; of, 7243 f; with, 7544 f (ter D); for . . . teer which, 3912 (terę BD, ter C).

    Rhyme words.—wer*e* erant (3929, 6585, 7544), *esset* (7243, 7945), of his fere (3929), where (6585), ellys where (7409), there (7243, 7544) [Val. BD teere.]

towne (A.S. tún, *m*, L. tun, dat. -e, O. tun, to tune, i, off tune, P. Pl.[ab] to toune), in the t., 3030 f[2]; in t, 5250 f, 6890 (-[e] D, in(to) toune for,C); to t., 4871 f; out of t, 3412 f (-n B), 3933 f, 5193 (-[e] B, of (=ex) the toun[e] C).—town*e*, of t., 270 (-[ë] ‡ or D, in toune † or C); into t., 2196; in t., 4724 (-n B), 5342 (-n B, tounnys ‡ C). —nom., townë start, 6048 D (*but supply* [thus]).

    Rhyme words.—sown*e inf.* (3030), rown*e inf.* (3412, 5250), a-swowne (3933), howne *n.* (4871).

town, toun, (i.) nom., 141, 1463, 5247 (-ę D), 6048 ABC, 7131 f, 7873 (-ę D); voc., 7369 f; acc., 558 f, 1464 f, 4741 (t. [to] B, *nom.* t. is ‡ D); in the t., in this t., in al this t., 64, 2501 f, 6002 AB (C(?), -e ‡ (?) D), 6042 f (-e CD), 6792 f, 7353 f; of (*not* = ex but equivalent to a genitive[3]), 186 f, 478 f, 1822, 3225 f, 4783 f, 4854 f ((s)town A), 6926 f (-e D), 7040, 7219 f, 7388 f (-e D), 7475 (-ę D); out of the t., 75, 6368 f-(-e BD); out of a t., 6384 (-ę D, [a] town A); into t., 4624 f (to, D); into this t., 7486 (-ę D); into the t., 7517; aboute Troye t., 4692 f, on al the t., 4780; traytor to the t., 4866 f; withinne Troyé t., 7332 f (-e D); thorughout Troye t., 8012 f (-e C).—(ii.) nom., 804, 6763 (-e D); yn al the t., 1224, 1833 (thour, C), 1966; yn the t., 3716; out of t., 3419; nom., t. hath, 5209 (-e D); in t. his, 1069.

    Rhyme words.—For *town,*—doun, down *adv.* (186, 4624, 6792, 6926, 7219, 7369, 7388, 8012), Sarpedoun (6792), attricioun (558), baroun (4692, 4854), conclusioun, -ion (478, 7131, 7369), condicion (7332), confusioun (4783), deuocioun (186, 558), dyscression (4866), disposicioun (6368), entencion (7131), execucion (6368), Lameadoun (4783), lyoun (4624, 4692), opynyoun (7219), oppressioun (2501), possessioun (2501), renoun (478), saluacioun, sauacion (1464, 6042), suspecion (8012), tribulacion (7353).

twyste (A.S. mæst-twist, *m.*?), with many a t., 4072 f (-t C) (: tryste *inf.* : wyste *ind.* 3 *sg*).

walkene (A.S. wolceu, wolcn, *n.*, pl. wolcnu, *Pet. Chron.* se wolcne; L. weolcne, wolćne, *pl.* (?); P. Pl.[b] walkene, welkne,[c] wolkene),

---

[1] A disagreeable line, but identical in ABCDG : "Til in a temple he fond hym allone." Cp. reads : "Til in a temple he fonde hym al allone."
[2] Old-style figures denote that D has no -e.
[3] Always with some word or words (as, *the, this, al this*) between *of* and *town*.

the walkene shop hym, 3393 A (walken B, walkyn CG, welkyn D, wolken Cp.).

were (A.S. wer, *m.*), to were, 2877 f (to the ‡ w. D) (: here *eam*). [Cf. This streme you ledeth to the sorwful were, *Parl. F.*, 138 (: spere : bere *inf.*).]

weye (A.S. weg, *m.*, L. weie, wai, dat. wei, weie, etc., O. weȝȝe), acc., 5954 f[1] (wey C), 6288 f (way B, alway † C), 6459 f, 6719 f (way C); by, 495 f, 6988 f (wey C); vpon, 2576 f (forth his w. C); in, 3089 f; adverbial, what w., 4821 f.—weye, acc., -e to, 1862 A (way B, why C); -e for, 6131 A (wey BD, om. C)[2]; which weye be, 3599 (way BC).—weye, acc., 4610 (wey B, wey ‡ no E); nom., weye is, 1702 (-e is C, way is B, wey is D); on . . . weye he, 1532 (way B). (Cf. aweye, awey, *adv.*, § 89.)

way, wey, (i.) nom., 2336, 7432 f; acc., 1160 BD (-e † A), 4851 (-e C); 5964 (-e C), 6180 AB, 6877 (woye (?) ‡ haue C, wey ‡ haue D ?), 7380; out of, 219 (-e C); on, 2388, 6864 (-e BC); by, 7025 (-e BC); went his wey, 1055; do wey do wey, 1978 (D †). (ii.) vpon . . . wey he, 2034 (-e him C, wey hym D); on . . . w. hym, 4365 (-e CD); a forlong wey on, 5899 (woy C).

Rhyme words.—seye *inf.* (495, 3089, 4821, 5954, 6459), obeye *inf.* (2576), pleye *inf.* (3089), deye *inf* (6988), leye = wager *inf.* (6719), preye *ind.* 1 *sg.* (5954), tweye (495, 4821, 6988), aweye (6288, 6459), awey (7432), pley *n.* (6288), weylawey (7432). [Var. BCD way; C waye, woye; D weie.]

wighte (A.S. ge-wiht, *n* , also -e, L.ª wiht,ᵇ weht, O. wiþþ fife wehhte off sillferr), of w., 2470 f (wyghte B, weight D, on † weyghte C) (: thynges lyghte).

wyle (A.S. wil *or* wile, *n.* (*Chron.* 1128), flygewilum *instr. pl.* (Mód. 27)), nom., 1356 f, 3919 f (w(h)ile CD); for, 719 f (gyle C).

Rhyme words.—while *n.* (719, 1356, 3919), bygyle *inf.* (719, 1356). [Var. BC wile.]

yate (A.S. gæt, W.S. geat, Ps. get, *n.*, *Pet. Chron.* iate-ward, L. ȝæt, dat. -e, O. gate *way*, P. Pl. gateward), acc., 3311 f (: late *adv.*), 7503 f (: late *adv.*); to the y., 1702 AB; vnto, 7501. But,—At the yate there she sholde oute ryde, 6395.—into the yate, 4567 (vnto BD, to C); vnto the yate he, 7555 (-is ‡ C); on to the gate he, 6966 C (*pl.* ABDG).

A and D write always *yate*; B and C, always ȝate (except in 6966 C).

yere (A.S. géar, gǽr, gér, *n.*, L. ȝer, dat. -e, O. ȝer) to yere, 3083 f (yeer D) (: dere); of fern[ë] yere, 7539 f (ferné[ye]re C, feuerèr ‡

---

[1] Old-style figures indicate that D has no -e.
[2] Obj. of *trusten to* (*on* BD); or, perhaps, nominative.

[§§ 14, 15]   *of Chaucer's Troilus.*   47

D) (: here *adv.*).—yer, (i.) of time, 1178 (ȝerę B), 4037 (ȝeerę D), 5755 AD (-ę B); of the yer (=gen.), 6739 (-ę B)[1]. (ii.) of time, yer or, 7982 (-*e* B). [Var. BC ȝere; C ȝer, ȝyr, ȝir; D yeer, ȝeer, ȝeere.]

§ 15. The following Germanic nouns, for which no corresponding Anglo-Saxon etymons can be cited, sometimes or always end in the *Troilus* in -e:

(A.) Suspicious or uncertified Anglo-Saxon words,—*crampe* (cf. A.S. *crompeht* adj.), *mone* (A.S. * *mán*, inferred from *ménan*), *werre* (see the word), *whippe* (A.S. *hweop* Somner). (B.) Words from the Old Norse : (i.) masculine n-stems, *awe*, *bole* (-ę, -*e*, never -*ë*) (but cf. A.S. *bulluc*), *felawe* (but cf. A.S. *féolaga*, itself from O.N.); (ii.) feminine n-stems,—*bore*, *sherte*; (iii.) neuter n-stem,—*wyndowe*; (iv.) neuter o-stems,—*on lofte, o lofte, a-lofte* (O. Norw. *á loft, á lofti*, originally u-stem), *at thy tryste* (but also *tryst, trust*). (C.) Probable Middle English formations from Anglo-Saxon words : (i) nouns from verbs,—*drede, hede, hye, lette,* and perhaps *ferde, mase, slynge*; (ii.) diminutive,—*stalke* (A.S. *stœl*); (iii.) *heste* (-*t*-formation from A.S. *hǽs*, f.), *beheste, wente* (cf. A.S. *wend,* f.). (D.) Borrowed from Middle Low German,—*grote, rore*. (E.) Miscellaneous words of more or less doubtful etymology,—*greue, haste, labbe* (var. *blabbe*), *were* (?).

For *hosbonde, skathe,* see § 2 ; for *arwe, wodebynde,* see § 3 ; for *feldefare,* see § 5 ; for *bone, byrthe, routhe, sleyghte,* see § 9.

awe (O.N. agi, *m.*, n-stem; cf. A.S. ege, *m.*, L. eiȝe, æie, O. eȝȝe, aȝhe), 999 f (: lawe : drawe *inf.*), 5282 f (: lawe : gnawe *inf.*).

blabbe, see *labbe*.

bole (O.N. boli, *m.*, n-stem; but cf. A.S. bulluc; L.O. bule), -ę, nom., 4901 (lole † C, bullę D); -ę, yn, 1140 (bullę D[e], bool it B); -*e*, of, 3565 (bool B, bok † C).

bore (O.N. bora *foramen*, f., n-stem, cf. Matzner), nom., -*e* hath, 4295 (hourre † C).

crampe (cf. O.S. cramp, *f.*, O.H.G. krampf, *m*, M.L.G., M.Du. krampe; Sweet, 269, assumes A.S. cramp from the adj. crompeht; P. Pl. crampe), -*e*, acc , 3913 (nom. ‡ C, craumpe, acc., B).

drede[2] (L. dred, drede, P. Pl. dre(e)de, cf. A.S. drǽdan, *vb.*), 95 f, 180 f, 499 f, 529 f, 575 f, 775 f, 1757 f, 1831 f, 1918 f, 2260 f, 2408 f,

[1] Supply [*the*] in C.
[2] A.S. drǽd *sbst.*, given in Bósworth, is rejected by Bosworth-Toller, the only evidence for its existence being Matth. xxv. 25 misunderstood (see Matzner).

2589 f, 2934 f, 3260 f, 3332 f, 3549 f, 3569 f,[1] 4080 (-[e] C), 4223 f,
4562 f, 4583 f, 4734 f, 4817 f, 5269 ‡ D, 5340 f, 5507 (-[e] C),
5753 f, 5775 f, 6001 f, 6070 (-[e] C), 6117 f, 6125 f (dred C), 6179 f,
6195 f, 6235 f, 6307 f (dred D), 6415 f, 6566 f, 6627,[2] 6993 f,
7122 f, 7343 f, 7453 f, 7643 f (dred D), 7955 f, 8144 f; drede, 2585
(-d C), 3672 (-d C), 4676, 6197 (-d C); -e his, 7570 (-d C); dred
awaketh, 1895 (-e BD).—drede is = dred's, 4400 ‡ A (dred is C, -e
is BD).—drede ‡ out, 6073 D. [Cf. dredful, § 49, n. 3.]

    Rhyme words.—dede n. (95, 6001, 6235, 6415), dede pred. adj. pl. (5753, 6179), wede A.S. wǽd (180, 4562), brede A.S. brǽdu (180, 529), hede heed n. (499, 575, 1831, 6566, 7122, 7453), nede n. (775, 1757, 3260, 3332, 3549, 3569, 4734, 6195), mede (3260), the rede red (4223), rede adj. pl. (2934), rede inf. (95, 2260, 2408, 2589 CD, 4223, 5340, 7643), arede inf. (2589 AB, 5775, 6235), atrede inf. (6117), rede ind. 3 pl. (6307, 8114), kynrede (7343), womanhede (4583, 6125), goodlihede (7955), Diomede (7453), blede inf. (499), lede inf. (529, 1918, 4562, 4583, 6179, 6993), I lede 1 sg. (6001), spede inf. (775, 4734), spede subj. 3 sg. (1831), forbede subj. 3 sg. (4817).

felawe (O.N. félagi, m., but A.S. féolaga, from the Norse, occurs in
    Chron. D, 1016, see Kluge in Paul's Grundriss, I, 786), for his
    felàwë daun, 7851 (fa- C, felowe D); nom., felàwe resteth, 4990
    (-owe B, -ow D); nom., felàwe deye, 5186 (fellawe D); felawe, acc.,
    709 (-aw BD).

ferde (A.S. vb. fǽran; cf. M.H.G. ge-vǽrde, f., n., 'betrug'), for ferd[e]
    caught, 557 (-ë BD); of fered thyn, 5269 (ferd C, ferde G, drede ‡
    D); for fered out, 6073 (-ë out BG, l. ferde out of [his][3]; fer C †,
    dredë ‡ out D). [For ferdë, and myn hewe al pale, B. Duch. 1214;
    And he for ferdë lost his wit, Hous F. ii, 442 (950).]

greue (cf. A.S. grǽfe, grǽfa, 'pit,' and the confused glosses in Wright-
    Wülcker, 225, 23-24), by, 7507 f (grene † C) (: eeue).

grote (O. Dutch groote, cf. L.G. (Bremen) grote; P. Pl.[c] grote), 5248 f
    (: hote adv. : note).

haste (cf. Dutch haast, O. Fris. hast, Dan. Sw. hast. A.S. hǽst and O.
    Fr. haste have also been compared), with hastë goodly, 2031 (-[e] D,
    laste † C); nom., ouer-haste, 965 (-t D, for euere † hast vb. C);
    nom., haste, 7968 (hast D); for . . . hast and, 4280 (-e BC); in al
    the haste he, 4428 (-t BD).

hede (cf. O. Fris. hûde, hôde, O.H.G. huota, f.; P. Pl.[b] hede), 501 f,
    577 f, 820 AB? (-[e] CD), 1832 f, 3306 f, 4066 f, 4389 f, 4671 f,
    5514 AB (-e ‡ therto C), 6221 f, 6451 f, 6565 f, 6668 f (hed D),
    7120 f (hed C), 7234 f, 7411 f, 7452 f, 8019 f, 8069 f; hede ther-

---

[1] Written for-drede.   [2] Supply [to] in D.
[3] A also has his. Perhaps, however, ferde out is right (hiatus in cæsura). Cp. has no his.

§ 15.] of Chaucer's Troilus. 49

of, 1666; heed for, 7266 (hede, BD, hed C); hede, 3481 (hed C), 5095 (hed AC), 5769 (hed D, -[e] ‡ what C).

Rhyme words.—drede n. (501, 577, 1832, 6565, 7120, 7452), nede n. (3306, 4066, 6221), Diomede (4671, 6451, 7234, 7411, 7452, 8019, 8069), the crede (6451), glede (6668), stede *steed* (6668), brede *A.S. brǽdu* (8019), blede *inf.* (501, 4671, 7411, 8069), forbede *inf.* (3306), *prcs. subj.* 3 *sg.* (6221), brede *inf.* (4389), spede *subj.* 3 *sg.* (1832). [Var C^c heede; D heed.]

heste, byheste (A.S. hǽs, *f.*, behǽsa *gen. pl.*, L. heste, bihǽste, O. hǽse), (*a*) heste, 3999 f (liste † B, heest D), 6718 (-es ‡ A, hest[e] B, beheste ‡ D); heste he, 6101 (-t C); heste hath, 4587 (*pl.* BCE). (*b*) byheste, 3157 BC (heste ‡ A, hest ‡ D), 3188 f (-t CD), 7554 f (-t D, heste C), 8038 f (-t D); behest, byhest, 1444 f (-e BCD), 1508 f (-e BC), 2414 f (-e B). [biheste, 7794 B, *should be plural.*]

Rhyme words.—feste n. (1444, 1508, 3999, 8038), at the leste (1444, 2414, 3157, 3999, 8038), by este (7554). [Var. BCD beheste, B bi-.]

hye (A.S. higian, *to hasten*), in hye, 1173 f (hy D) (: companye : thrie *adv.*), 2797 f (hy C) (: prye *inf.*: companye), 6047 f (heye B, hie D) (: iupartie). [5861 f ‡ C (: deye *inf.*: cumpanye).]

labbe (*Prompt. Parv.* blabbe, or labbe, wreyare of cownselle, *futilis, anubicus*), nom., 3142 f (blabbe D) (: gabbe *ind.* 3 *pl.*, *inf.* ‡ D).

lette (A.S. vb. lettan, O.L.G. *sbst.* lette, M.H.G. letze, *f.*, L.^b lette), withouten, 361 f (let D), 3077 f, 3541 f (let D), 3590 f, 4703 f (let D), 7214 f (lett D) —lettëgame, 3369 f (let[te]-game D).

Rhyme words.—sette *pret. ind.* 3 *sg.* (361, 3077, 3541, 7214), mette *somniavit* (361), mette *congressi sunt* (4703), dores were y-shette (3077), shette *pret. ind.* 3 *sg.* (3590), fette *pret. ind.* 3 *pl.* (7214).

lofte (O. Norw. O. Icel. loft, *n.*, á loft, á lofti, later Icel. lopt, etc., A.S. on loft *from the Scand.*, see Napier, *Mod. Lang. Notes*, 1889, col. 278, Kluge in Paul's *Grundriss*, I, 786; O. o lofft, P. Pl.^a on lofte, ^bbi loft, ^con loft), on lofte, alofte, o lofte, 138 f (-t BD, onloste † C), 915 f (-t D), 943 f (-t D), 3512 f, 5883 f (-t C), 6371 f, 6711 f (-t B); a-lofte, 6622 (of ‡ loft B, on loft C).

Rhyme words.—ofte (138, 915, 943, 3512, 5883, 6371, 6711), softe *adj.* and *adv.* (138, 915, 943, 3512, 6711).

maze (cf. A.S. amasod, *p. p.*), 6831 f (mase CD) (: glaze *inf.*).

mone, moone (quasi A.S. *mán, cf. mǽnan *vb.*; P. Pl.^c mone), nom., 1643 f; acc., 98 ‡ f A (*l.* mone *inf., with* BCD), 696 f, 5612 f, 6613 f; -e †, acc., 907 C.

Rhyme words.—allone (696, 1643, 5612, 6613), euerychone (5612), grone *inf.* (1643, 6613).

rore (cf. O.L.G. hrôra, O.H.G. ruora, *f.*, Ger. aufruhr 'uproar'; see, however, Murray s.v. *aroar*, where perhaps the quotation from the

E

Paston Letters is not in place. Confusion with *roar*, A.S. ge-rár (ἅπαξ), is prob. for Chaucer's time), sette al Troye vpon a rore, 6408 f ([a] roore D) (: pore *adj. pl.*).

sherte (O.N. skyrta, *f.*, n-stem, L. scurte, P. Pl.ᵉ sherte), aboue (vpon BC, [vp]on D), 3580 f (-t D); to, 3941 f; on, 4214 f; in, 4758 f (-t D), 6184 f (schert C).

 Rhyme words.—herte (3580, 3941, 4214, 4758), pouerte (-t C) (6184), sterte *effugi* (4758). [Var. C scherte; D schirte, shirte.]

slynge (O. Du. slinge, O.H.G. slinga, P. Pl.ᵇᵒ slinge), with slyng[e] stones, 2026 f (sleynge s. B, slynging ‡ of [*slurred*] stonys C).

stalke (dimin. of A.S. stæl, stel; P. Pl.ᵉ stalke), on stalk[e] lowe, 2053 AB (stalke C; -ys D, *supply* [on]).

tryste (O.N. traust, *n.*), Lo holde the at thi tryste clos and I, 2619 (-[e] C, tristre † D).

 tryst, trist, (i.) nom., 3783 f (-e B) (: lyst *lubet*), 4147 f (-e B, trust C, truste D) (: lyst *voc.*); acc., 3245 f (truste B) (: lyst *lubet*: wyst *p.p.*). (ii.) nom., 154 (trost C, trust D); voc., 4264 (-e B, trust CE) (cf. 7622); for, 6044 (-e B).—trust, (i.) in t., 83 AC (-e B); for wàntrust, 794 (-e B, -trost C, wantrowist † D). (ii.) nom., mystrùst, 1865 (-e B; C †); for m., 3165 (-e B, -trost C).

wente (cf. A.S. wend, *f.*?), acc., 1148 f (-t AD), 1900 f (-t Cᶜ D), 6968 f (-t ACD), 7557 f (-t CD); by, 3629 f (-t CD).

 Rhyme words.—wente *pret. ind.* 1, 3 *sg.* (1148, 1900, 3629, 6968, 7557), blente *pret. ind.* 3 *sg.* (7557).

were (= doubt, perplexity, Scotch weir, cf. Skeat, *Minor Poems, Glossary*); ffrom day to day til they be *in* were of ioye, 7910 C, but read *ben bare of ioye* (with ABD).

werre (cf. A.S. war-scot; wyrre, uuerre, in the *Chron.* 1119, 1140, are doubtless from French (see Behrens, p. 55); cf. O.H.G. werra, *f.*; L.ᵃ weorra,ᵇ werre), 134 f, 1953 f, 4614 f, 5209 f (werr D), 6597 f, 7756 f (werr D); -e, 6331 (guerre D), 7218 (werr D).

 Rhyme words.—derre *adv. compar.* (134), verre (1953), erre *pres.* 3 *pl.* (4614), *inf.* (5209), sterre (6597, 7756).

whippe (A.S. hweop, still given by Bosworth-Toller on the authority of Somner, but not yet found; cf. M. Du. wippe), of, 220 f (wyppe C, whip D) (: skyppe *inf.*).

wyndowe (O.N. vindauga, *n.*, P. Pl. windowe), to the wỳndowe nexst, 2271 (-ow BCD); yn the wỳndowe bothe, 2277 (-ow D); from hire wỳndow down, 4625 (-e C).—Before vowels, wỳndowe,—nom., 6897 (-ow B); acc., 4895 (-ow BD, wỳndowe [ek] C); thurgh out, 3443 AB, at. . . wyndòwe, 2100 (-òw BD, in. . . wyndòwe C).

Note 1.—For *angre*, see *anger* (§ 19). *-re* is also found in *slyuere* (cf. A.S. *slifan*, 'to split'), 3855 f ABC (shyvre ‡ D) (: wyuere (O. Fr. vivre, guivre, wivre) : delyuere *inf.*).

Note 2.—*A-wep* (for *a-wepe* ?) occurs once,—*and she bygan to brest a wep a-noon*, 1493 (a wepe B, to breste and † wepe C, to wepe ‡ right D). The substantive *wep* seems to be formed from the verb *wepen* (cf. A.S. *wóp, m.*).

Note 3.—*Here* and *howne* in *thus seyden here and howns*), 4872 (*h. and howns* C, *her and hown* D, *heer and houn* G, *here hownis* Cp.)·(: *hom to towne ; in to toune* C, *hom(e) to toun* D, [*hom*] *to toun* G), are unsolved riddles. The usual interpretation *hare and hound*, i. e. *everybody, of whatever estate*, is not satisfactory.

§ 16. Four monosyllables in -e may be here put together: *gle* (neut. jo-stem), *se* (i-stem m., f.) *stre* (masc. wo-stem), *tre* (neut. wo-stem).

gle (A.S. (poet.) gléo, W.S. *glíeg, glíg, Ep. glíu, see Sievers, § 247, n. 3 ; L. gleo), gle and, 2121 (glee B).

se, see (A.S. sǽ, inflected partly as m., partly as f., Siev. § 266, n. 3 ; L. sæ, sé, O. sæ), 417, 1088, 1090, 1528 f (: se *inf.* : he), 2850 f (: tre), 4600, 5685 f (: be *sit*), 6211 f (: be *sim* : free), 7249 f (: see *ind.* 2 *pl.* : me), 8178 f (: vanite : felicite) ; se hath, 4586.

stre, straw (A.S. stréaw, stráw-berie, stréa(w)berie, North. stré, Rush. stréu, Sievers, §§ 112. n. 1 and 3, 250. n. 1 ; P. Pl.[bc] strawe), stre, 2830 f (: she : he) ; straw is, 3701 (strow B, straw yfall D) ; straw yset, 4846 (-e C) ; a straw for, 6725 (-e D).

tre, tree (A.S. tréo(w), n., North. tré, tréo, tréu(o), Siev., § 250. 2 ; L. treo, dat. treowe, O. treo, tre), 2852 f (: se n.), 3385 f (: be *inf.* : fle *inf.*).—*Bef. csts.*, tre, 4072, 4888, 7507 (treis ‡ C) ; *bef. vowels*, 957.

Note 1. For *snow* (A.S. snáw, m., wo-stem), cf. 525 (-e B), 5029, 7539 (snowgh B).

Note 2.—For *wo, woo,* sbst., from A.S. *wá*, interj., cf. 4, 34, 248 f, 322, 378, 503, 546 AB, 582 f BCD, 1004, 1147, 1468 f, 2445 f, 3034, 4249, 4921, etc. ; cf. also *wher me be wo*, 2908 ; *wo is me*, 3113 ; *me is wo*, 4265 f ; *wo hym*, 694 (*wo is hym* CD) ; *me is for hym wo*, 3768 f ; *vs is wo*, 1868 ; *wo was hym*, 356, 6432 ; *hym was wo*, 5824, 6356 AD (*he was wo* B) ; *so wo was hem*, 4540. In "But lord this sely *Troylus was wo,*" 6892, the construction is ambiguous. Cf. *ful wo to bed he went*, 1147 D (*yn wo* AB).—The interjection *ho* is also used substantively in the phrase *withouten ho*, 2168 f AG (hoo BCp., for ay and o C John's MS., for Ay and oo D *added in later hand*) ; cf. "But *ho* no more now of this matere," 3032 ; "But *ho* (*hoo* BD) for we han right ynow of this," 5904.

§ 17. In the following nouns final *-y* comes from the vocalization of an Anglo-Saxon *-g*. Cf. also *wey* (§ 14), *lady, pley* (§ 5).

52 *Observations on the Language* [§§ 17, 18.

bodig (A.S. bodig, *n.*), cf. 122, 1718, 4906, 4920, 4966, 4984, 5425 C, 5505, 6216 (*slur*), 6616, 6666, 7682, 7923, etc., etc.
day (A.S. dæg, *m.*), cf. 442, 456, 482, 1068 f (: bay *adj.* : ay *adv.*), 1145, 1146, 1271, 1287, etc., etc. (Cf. ten Brink, § 199.2.)
iuy (A.S. ífig, *n.*), pype yn an iuy lef, 7796 (yuy C) (A.S. ífigléaf).
wery (A.S. wérig, *adj.*), for wo and wery of that companye, 5369.

Note.—*May* 'maiden' is perhaps from O.N. *mǽr* (stem *mǫyjō-*), late *mey*: see 7775 f (: may *possum* : day), 8083 f (*same rhymes*).

§ 18. The following masculine and neuter nouns, which in Anglo-Saxon end in a consonant in the nominative, take no -e in the *Troilus*, even in the dative.

(i) Pure masculine o-stems,[1]—(*a*) monosyllabic, *arm, bark* (gender?), *berd, blast, bor, bot, breth, chep, cherl, clerk, cloth, crop, dom* (and compounds), *drem, em, fissh, flod* (m., n.), *foul, fox, frost, gnat, god, gost, harm, hat, hauk, helm, hod, hom, hook, horn, hound, knyf, knyght, kok, kyng, lord, lust, mouth, non, oth, path, port, post, pyk* (gender?), *qualm, rēd, rēs, reyn, ryng, sheld, shour, slep, song, spir* (gender?), *ston* (*wheston*), *swarm, thank* (m., n.), *thef, thorn, thought, thral, thred, top, wal, wir, wynd, yerd;* (*b*) dissyllabic, *bisshop, bosom, bridel, crepul, epistol, ernest* (also *f.*), *feuer* (-*ere*), *laughter, martir, thonder, wimpil;* (ii.) pure neuter o-stems,—(*a*) monosyllabic, *bak, blood, bon, bond, brayn, brest, col, cold, corn, der, fel, folk, gold, gres, hed, heer, hous, lef, light, lond, loss(e), mel, mot, right, seed, shap, ship, sor, swerd, thing, vers, werk, wex, whiel, word, wrong, wyf, wyn;* (*b*) dissyllabic, *dewel* (m., n.), *forlong, gospel, iren, ordel* (q. v.), *timber, water, weder, wonder, yuel.* (iii.) masculine jo-stem,—*bryd;* (iv.) neuter jo-stems,—*kyn, net, wit;* (v.) masculine i-stems,—*craft, del, dynt, gest, gylt, hil, streng,* cf. *Grek;* (vi.) masculine u-stems,—*feld, wynter;* (vii.) masculine consonant stems,—*fend, frend, man;* (viii.) neuter consonant stems,—*bred, child.* For *fader,* etc., see end of list; for *cros,* see § 19.

In the following list MS. D has usually been disregarded, and insignificant variations in spelling have not been registered. For erroneous final -e's, not sounded, and due simply to the whim of the scribe, see especially *bor, brest, cold(e), dom, fend(e), flood, foul(e), frend, gold, harm, hed, hom, knyght, kyng, lord, noon, reed, ryng, thing, werk, wynd* (cf. § 14, note 2).

arm (A.S. earm, *m.*), (i.) acc., 2756; for, 2735 f. (ii.) acc., 3970, 4416

[1] U-stems that have in A.S. identified themselves with the o-declension are not distinguished.

[§ 18.] *of Chaucer's Troilus.* 53

(armęs ‡ B); yn his a. he, 1241 (-e B).—arm yn arm, (i.) 1908;
(ii.) 2201, 2810.

bak (A.S. bæc, n.), (i.) his b. byhynde, 1724; at herę b. byhynde,
7174 AB; (ii.) acc., 4089; by, 7174 ‡ C.

bark (A.S. bark, Leechd., I, 378, O.N. bǫrkr, m.), (ii.) vnder, 3569;
ther nys but b., 4889; thorwgh the b., 5801 (-e B, om. ‡ C).

berd (A.S. beard, m.), in the b., 4703 (-ę B).

bisshop (A.S. biscop, m.), (ii.) nom., 1189 (9-syl. verse).

blast (A.S. blǽst, blést, m.), for, 2472 f (-e B).

blood, blod (A.S. blód, n.), (i.) voc., 1679; acc., 435, 1530; of
(source), 4642; vnto, 6964. (ii.) ther nas but Grekes b., 1283;
vnto, 6963. [Var. B -ę, -e; C blud.]

bon (A.S. bán, n.), nom., 2011 f (-e B, mylk † C).

bond (A.S. band, n. (bande, pl., Pet. Chron.), Sweet, 254; but the
regular A.S. form is bend, m., f., see Sievers, § 266, n. 2), (i.) acc.,
4596 (in ‡ a boundę C); withouten, 4200 (-ę B); with, 4608
(boundę C); from, 4610 (-ę B, hond ‡ C). (ii.) voc., 4103
(hond † B).

bor, boor (A.S. bár, m.); bore, boorę, nom. 7812 D, acc., 4622 AB
(-ę ‡ D), 7601 D, 7834 D; with, 3563 BD; of, 7645 D (: hoore
adj. sg., A.S. hár; bor : hor AC; boor : hoor B).—boore he, acc.,
7840 D. Everywhere else written *bor, boor*; cf., besides the places
just cited, 7603, 7817, 7825, 7832, 7835, 7876, 7878.

bosom (A.S. bósm, m.), And yn herę bosǫm the lettre doun he thraste,
2240 ABC (bosom doun D).

bot (A.S. bát, m.), (ii.) withinne, 416; nom., the b. hath, 1088.
[Var. B boot.]

brayn (A.S. brægen, n.), yn 4346 (breynę B).

bred (A.S. bréad, n.), acc., 1529 f (: ded *adj. sg. pred.*). (Cf. 907 ‡ D.)

brest (A.S. bréost, n.), (i.) nom., 6582 (-ę B); acc., 5414, 5834
(bryst C); in, 4898 (-ę B); on, 4258 (-ę B); vpon, 5813 (-ę B);
out of, 5132; into, 2014 (-ę B). (ii.) acc., 4905; vpon, 4694 (-e
B); out of, 5000 (-e B, bryst C); fro, 6155 (-e B); nom., b. here,
5477 (-e B); vnder hire b. his, 2012 (-e B). [Var. B -ee-.] out of
my breste, 5438 AB (brest ‡ conueye C).

breth (A.S. brǽð, m.), nom., 801 f (-e B), 4935; acc., 3961, 5840.

bryd (A.S. brid, m.), nom., 2852.

brydel, bridel (A.S. brídel, m.), nom., 946 f (: on ydel); acc., 4604;
by, 6455 f (: on ydel); on, 7236. [Var. C -il.]

chep (A.S. céap, m.), as good chep, 3483 (schep C).

cherl (A.S. ceorl, *m.*), nom., 1017.
child (A.S. cild, *n.*), nom., 4770 D (-ẹ B, chy[l]d A).
clerk (A.S. cléric, clerc, *m.*, coincident with O.F. clerc); (ii.) nom., 2883 (clerc B).
cloth (A.S. cláð, *m.*), nom., 3575 f.
col (A.S. col, *n.*), thorugh, 2417 (-ẹ C, -ẹ [the] morẽ B).
cold(e) (A.S. ceald, cald, *n.*), for, 911 f (-d CD) (; told(e) (told CD) *p.p.*); through, -e, 2052 (-d B, D (?); the coldé nyȝt C), For hete of cold for cold of hete I deye, 420 (ffor cold of hetẹ for hete of cold, etc. C).
corn (A.S. corn, *n.*), nom., 219 f (-e B) (: by-forn *adv.* : shorn *p.p.*).
craft (A.S. cræft, *m.*), (i.) nom., 665, 747; acc., 379.; on (acc. BC), 6120 f. (ii.) nom., 4476; in, 6453; nom., lechẽcraft, 5098.
crepul (A.S. crypel, *m.*), by-fore, 6120 (-ıl C).
crop (A.S. crop(p), *m.*), nom., crop and rote, 1433, 7608 f (-e B); crop and more, 6388.
del (A S. dǽl, *m.*), ye shenden euẹry del, 1675 f (-e BD); ony del, 2299 f (-e BD); eche a del, 3536 f (-e BD); neuẹre a del, 3550 f (-e BD); no del, 1082 A (-(ẹ) D); euẹry del, 5721 f (-e B, -dell D); acc., haluendel the drede, 3549 (*nom.*, ‡ C). Cf. somdel, *adv.*, (i.) 290 (-(ẹ) B); (ii.) 1081 AD (somẹ deel B), 1688 (-ẹ BD).

Rhyme words.—wel *adv.* (*everywhere but* 5721); temporel, eternel (5721), stel *n.* (1675). [Var. B deele, decl.]

der (A.S. déor, *n.*), (ii.) acc., 2620 (deere B).
deuel (A.S. déofol, *m.*, *n.*), (i.) nom., 5292 (-yl haue ‡ C); voc., 2822 (-il C). (ii.) nom., the d. haue, 805 (-yl C). *As expletive*,—How deuel maystow bryngen me to blysse, 623 (de[ue]l C).
dom (A.S. dóm, *m.*), (i.) to my d., 5049 (-ẹ B), 5064; in myn d.‡, 5258 C (*supply* [no]). (ii.) nom., 5850 ([the] domẹ B; dom C †). [Var. B doom.]—to my dome, 100 (doom B, dom C).

Compounds.—frèdom, (ii.) acc., 235 (-dam C).—kỳngdom, (ii.) acc., 7850 (kyndom C, kingdham D).—thràldom, nom., 1941.— wỳsdom, wìsdom, (i.) with, 5590 (wisdhum D). (ii.) of, 1299; for, 452 (be wisdem C †).[1]

drem (A.S. dréam, *m*), (i.) acc., 6741 ((-en) B); for 7643 (-ẹ B); in, 7615. (ii.) nom., 7806 (-e B); acc., 7651 (-e B, -ys C), 7819 (-e B; C †); in, 7614 (drem [y]schewid C); by, 8078 (-e B ?); acc., d. he, 7815 (-e B).
dynt (A.S. dynt, *m.*), with, 7868 (-ẹ D, dent C).

[1] In B 452 dele the second (*for*).

em (A.S. éam, *m.*), (i.) nom., 1440, etc.; voc., 1394, etc.; of (=from), 1015. (ii.) nom., 3115, etc.; voc., 2244.

epistol (A.S. epistol, pistol, *m.*), e. hem, 3343 ([e]pistil C, lettre ‡ D).

ernest (A.S. eornest, -ost, *m., f.*), (i.) in, 2614, 2788; bytwene, 3096. (ii.) acc., 1537 (hernest B). [Cf. ernestful, § 49, n. 3.]

fel (A.S. fell, *n.*), (ii.) nom., 91.

feld, field (A.S. feld, *m.*), (ii.) in, 4704 (-e B), 5451 (-e D); through, 1280 (-e B)[1]; yn the feld he, 1067 (feelde B). (Cf. *feldefare*, § 5.)

fend(e) (A.S. féond, *m.*), 5099 f AD (fend B, frend † C) (: frend *voc.*).

fèuer, -ere (A.S. fefer, féfer, *m.*, Pogatscher, p. 164), feuere, 909 f (: keuere *inf.*); feuer and, 491 (-yr B, -ere CD)[2]; -er is, 2605 (-ere B, -ere D, [thi] feuere C); -ere or, 4055 (fyuer D).

fissh, fyssh (A.S. fisc, *m.*), (i.) nom., 5427. (ii.) nom., 2877; nom., f. herbe, 2852.

flood (A.S. flód, *m., n.*), on a flod(e), 3482 f (flood D) (: as muchë good); fro . . . flood of, 4442 (floode B, flod C, feende † D).

folk, see § 43.

forlong (A.S. furlong, -lang, *n.*), a f. wey, 5899 (forlonge B, furlong CD).

foul(e) (A.S. fugol, *m.*), nom., foule, 6788 A (fowl B, foul C^c).

fox (A.S. fox, *m.*), fox that ye ben, 4407 (ffor that ‡ C).

frend (A.S. fréond, *m.*), (i.) nom., 1348 (-e B), 2488, etc.; voc., 584 (-e B), 610, etc.; acc., 627 (-e B), 1052, etc.; of (=gen.), 98. (ii.) nom., 548 (-e B); voc., 2444 (-e B), etc.; acc., 550 (freende B); for, 1497 (-ee- B); of (=by), 3638 (-e B).—voc., frende, 602 AB (-d C), 5294 AB (-d C).

frost (A.S. forst, *m.*), (ii.) nom., 524 (froost B), f. hym, 6898.

gest (A.S. gest, giest, gyst, *m.*), nom., 2196 f BCDG (geste A) (: it thought here herte brest AC, breste BG, as thogh her hert to-brest D : yf yow lest CG, leste AB, list D). The collation of Cp. and John's records no variations from A in these three lines.

gilt, gylt (A.S. gylt, *m.*), (i.) withouten, 2365 (-e B); in, 4483; of, 4019 (-e B); for, 8138. (ii.) nom., 7620 (-e B); yn, 1329; for, 7459 (-e B); nom., g. hath, 7750. [Cf. giltles, gilteles, §§ 49, n. 5, and 85.]

gnat (A.S. gnæt, *m.*), nom., 5257 (gnatte C).

god (A.S. god, *m., n.*), (i.) nom., 195, 4607, etc.; voc., 400, etc.; acc., 40; to, 32; by, 1200 (be ‡ iouys C), 1222 (by g. he C); of (=gen.),

---

[1] A happens to read *field*. [2] In O dele (*al*).

69, 612, 1310, etc.; dat., I thankë god, 1240. (ii.) nom., 206, etc.; voc., 2145 (B †), etc.; to, 421, 925; by, 2043, 2322, 2962, 3214; of (=gen.), 571, 2402; to g. haue, 1667; to g. hope, 2357; I thanke it g.; 1836.

gold (A.S. gold, *n.*), (i.) of, 6061, 7175; with, 6039; for, 7249 A. (ii.) of, 6675; for, 3242, 7249 B; vpon a quysshon gold y-bete, 2314.— goldę, nom., 6185 ABD (gold. *acc.* ‡ C).

gospel (A.S. godspell, *n.*), nom., 7628.

gost (A.S. gást, *m.*), (i.) nom., 2462 (C †), 3306 (C †), 4849, 5572, 5883 (-ę B), 8171; voc., 4964; acc., 1616, 5447, 7733. (ii.) with, 7884. [Var. B goost.]

Grek (A.S. Gréc, Créc), 1068.

gres (A.S. græs, W.S. gærs, *n.*), (ii.) on, 1600 (gras D).

harm (A.S. hearm *m.*), (i.) nom., 75 (-ę B), 3755, 4006, 5505, 7588 (-ę B); acc., 839 (-ę B)[1], 2734 f, 3647 (-ę B); for, 1539 (-ę B), 3167 (-ę B), 4717 (-ę B); with, 1925 (-ę B, C †); by, 3171 BC (*om.* † A). (ii.) nom., 1874, etc.; acc., 347 (-e B, h.‡ by C), etc.; to, 1661 (-e B),[2] 2233; for . . . h. he, 4000.—harmę, nom., 333 (harm C); voc., 411 (harm C); acc., 3560 (harm C); yn, 7739 (in(to) harm C); harme, nom., 409 (harm C).

hat (A.S. hæt(t), *m.*), nom., 3162 f (hattę B) (: what : that).

hauk (A.S. hafoc, *m.*), (i.) nom., 671. (ii.) with h., 6428 (-e B).—goshauk, (i.) nom., 5075 C°.—sparhauk hath, nom., 4034 (speręhauk C).

hed (A.S. héafod, *n.*), (i.) nom., 1929 f (-e D); acc., 1492 f (hede D), 1742 (-é ‡ D), 1774, 2923 f (-e D), 3799 f AB, 3897 (A †), 3921 f (-e D), 4906 (-ę D), 7290 f (with . . . ‡ hed C); at, 2781 f (-e D); to, 5821 f (-e D); by, 530 A † C †, 1255 ‡ D, 5255 (hod C); in, 5754; of, 5390; saue, 1710. (ii.) nom., 6357; acc., 1625, 1952 (-e D); out of, 3736 (heuid C, hédę ‡ gone D); on, 6646 (in his hed he ‡ D); acc., hed he, 7840. hede, acc., 4415 f (hed BCD); by herę beddes hede, 3796 f (hed B).

<small>Rhyme words.—ded *adj. sg.* (1492, 1929, 2781, 2923, [3796 D (dede),] 3921, 4415, 5821), goodlyhed (1929), hed, hede *head* (3796, 3799), red *n.* (2781, 5821), red *adj.* (2923, 3796, 3799, 4415, 7290). [Var. heuęd, heuyd, heuid C 1710, 1952, 3736, 5821 f, 5390, 5754, 6646; heed, heede D.]</small>

hoer (A.S. hǽr, hér, *n.*), (i.) acc., 5398 (herę B, her CD). [*here* in 5478 f B, 7173 C, 7362 D, is an error for *heres*, pl.]

helm (A.S. helm, *m.*), (i.) nom., 1723 (-ę B); vpon, 8125 (*in B supply* [*to*]). (ii.) acc., 6670 (-e B).

---

[1] In C supply [*crucl*].   [2] In C supply [*am*].

hil, hill (A.S. hyll, *m.*), (i.) to, 6973 (C?); i[n] hil Parnaso, 4652. (ii.) nom., 943 (hille B).

hod, hood (A.S. hód, *m.*), by, 2266 f (-e B, hond † C) (: good *n.* : stood ind. 3. *sg*), 5255 ‡ C, 7514 f (-e BD), (: good *n.*); acc., 2039 (-ę B); in, 2195.

hom (A.S. hám, *m.*), (i.) as limit of motion, as in A.S. (=domum), 1995 ‡ C, 3068, 3486, 4423 (-ę D), 4871 AB, 5392, etc.; at hom, 4755 (-ę B); homward, 3463 (hom C). (ii.) = domum, 6848, etc.; home, 126 A (hoom B, hom C), home he, 1681 AB (hom C).

hook (A.S. hóc, *m.*), (ii.) acc., 7140.

horn (A.S. horn, *m.*), (ii.) acc., 1727 (hed ‡ C).

hound (A.S. hund, *m.*), (i.) acc., 3606 (-ę B). (ii.) with, 6428 ‡ C. (Cf. § 15, n. 3, p. 51.)

hous, hows (A.S. hús, *n.*), (i.) nom., 3477; acc., 1058 (-ę B), etc.; in, 3042, 6938 f (place † B) (: melodious); out of, 1522 (-ę B); at, 3037; to, 3356, 6891 (C †). (ii.) voc., 6904; acc., 2871; in, 1766, 3506; to, 2546 (-e B; C †), 2625; vnto, 2599 (-e B); in the h. he, 5485.

iren (A.S. íren, *n.*), acc., felt iren hot, 2361 (the thorn † C).

knyf (A.S. cníf, *m.*), with this k., 1410.

knyght (A.S. cniht, *m.*), (i.) nom., 165 f, 1074 f, 1262 f, 1416 f, 3280 f (-e B), 3757 f, 4329 f, 4490 f, 5013, 5231 f, 5279 f (kynght A), etc.; voc., 3018 f (-e B), 3838 f, 4151 (-ę B, *om.* ‡ C), 6199 f; acc., 979, 1956 f, 2679 (A †), 5376 f C (: sy3t *n.*), 6147 f; by, 225 f; vpon, 1846; lyk, 1716 f, 2348 f (-e B); to, 3623 f (-e B), 7200 f (-e B), 6696 f. (ii.) nom., 191; of (= gen.), 1537 f, 7228 f (-e B), 8115 f (-e B); fro, 5408 f, 6696 f; knyghte, nom., 3825 f AB (-t C).

kok (A.S. coc(c), *m.*), nom., 4257 (C †); pekok, acc., 210 (pakoc B).

kyn (A.S. cyn(n), *n.*), (ii.) nom., 5287, 5993; acc., 6183.

kyng (A.S. cyning, cyng, *m.*), (i.) nom., 1186 (-ę B), 5539 (-ę B), 7297; voc., 4856 (-ę B); acc., 4800 (-ę B), etc.; to, 5308 (-ę B); with, 6647 (-ę B), 6794 (-ę B); of, 4786 (-ę.B). (ii.) acc., 4938; to, 3224 (-e B); with, 3434 (-e B). of the kynge, 664 AB (of [the] kyng C).

laughter (A.S. hleahtor, *m.*), for l. wende, 2254 (-tere BC, -tir D); nom., laughtre men, 5528 (-ter CD).

lef (A.S. léaf, *n.*), (i.) nom., 4042 (leef B). (ii.) yn, 7796 (leefe B).

light, lyght (A.S. leoht, *n.*), (i.) nom., 3978 (C?), 6906 f; acc., 4298, 4543, 7001 f (-e B); wo worth ... l., 5409 f (ny3t ‡ C). (ii.) nom., 3979; voc., 2843; acc., 2105 (lettere ‡ C), 3821, cf. 4962 ‡

C; of, 1994; acc., l. here (*hic*), 4303 (lyth C). [Cf. lyghtles, § 49, n. 5.]

lond (A.S. land, lond, *n.*), yn somę l., 1123 (-ę B).

lord (A.S. hláford, *m.*), (i.) nom., 1415, 1524; voc. and excl., 330 (-ę B), 350 (now ‡ C), 422, 528, 2924, 6945 (-ę C), etc.; with, 1791; by, 2138 BC. (ii.) nom., 65, 2488; voc. and excl., 2406 ‡ C, 2444 (-*e* B), 6952 (*om.* † B); acc., 903 (-*e* B; C †). lordę, voc., 6962 ABD (lord C).

loss(e) (A.S. los, *n*, L. to lose, P. Pl.^e los, loos), nom., -*e*, 4689 (los B, loos D); -ę ne, 4751 (los B, lossé ‡ me D).

lust (A.S. lust, *m.*), (i.) nom., 4388 (lest D †), 6235, 7618 (C †; -ę B, listę D), 8194 (-ę B, list D); acc., 1915 (lyf D), 4741 (-ę B, *nom.* lust D), 5751 (-ę B, wil C), 8187 A (-ę B); ayens, 1561 (listę B, lyst D), 2142 (list D); for, 443 (louę C, list D); of (=gen.), 1929 (luf A, lyst and D); with, 7682; yn, 326; to, 2219. (ii.) acc., 2083 (-*e* B, list D), 3118 (-*e* B, lyst D), 4532 (-*e* B); of, 6389; at, 407; yn, 4661 (-*e* B, lyst D), 5155 (-*e* B, louę C); acc., l. his, 2151 (list D), 4392 (list D).

lest, lyst (cf. A.S. lystan),—lest, nom., 1872 f (-ę B) (: prest *pred. adj. pl.*). lyst, voc., 4145 f (listę B, lust C, trustę ‡ D) (: trist *n.*); yn, 330 f (lestę B, rest C^e, lyst D) (: best *adv.*).

man (A.S. man, *m.*) 232 f, 1633 f, 3805 f, etc., etc.

martir (A.S. martyr, *m.*; also, martyre), nom., 5285 (-tyr BC).

mel (A.S. mǽl, *n.*), see *tyde*, p. 26.

mot (A.S. mot, *n.*), (ii.) acc., 4445 (mootę B, mote C, mytę D).

mouth (A.S. múð, *m.*), (ii.) acc., m. he, 812 BC (m. yet ‡ A), 5823 (-*e* B, mout C).

net (A.S. net(t), *n.*), of, 4575 f (nette C); withoute, 1668 f, 6033 (C †); into, 7138. (Rhyme-words all *p.p.*,—set, yset, yknet, imet.)

noon, non(e), noon(e) (A.S. nón, *m.*), (i.) nom., noonę, 7477 (non C); after noonę, 2270 (-n BC); after noon, 7493 (and at ‡ after nonę D); byfor noon, 7485 (-ę D). (ii.) a-twixen noon, 6835 (-*e* BCD).

ordal (A.S. ordál, ordél, *n.*), (ii.) by, 3888 (ordel C, ordinal † D).

oth (A.S. áð, *m.*), acc., 3953 f (ath B); by, 3888 f (ooth B).

path (A.S. pæð, *m.*), (ii.) acc., 1122; gon som by-path, 4547.

port (A.S. port, *m.*, cf. O. Fr. port), to good port hastow rowed, 962 [1].

post (A.S. post, *m.*), (ii.) nom., 993.

pyk (A.S. pic, *m.* (?), cf. Fr. pique), acc., 2126 f (pik C).

---

[1] In ABD read *fasté* for *fast*.

qualm (A.S. cwealm, cwalm, *m*), (ii.) nom., 6745 (*-e* C).

red, reed (A.S. rǽd, rēd, *m*.), (i.) nom., 5160 f (*-e* BD), 6791 (counselll ‡ D); acc. 661 (*-ę* BD), 2783 f (*-e* D), 5822 f (*-e* BD), 6075 (*-ę* BD), 6690 C (redę ABD); to, 2624 (*-ę* BD); by, 2780 (*-ę* BD). (ii.) nom.; 1474 [1] (*-e* BD), 1507 AC (*-e* B), 7655 (*-e* B,[2] counseill ‡ is D); of, 2439 (*-e* BD); withouten, 6385 (*-e* D). [*redę* once in A, 6690.]

    Rhyme words.—ded *mortuus* (2783, 5160), she lay as for ded (5822), at his beddes hed (2783), to here hed (5822).

res (A.S. rés, *m*.), yn a r., 5012 (rees B).

reyn, rayn (A.S. regn, rén, *m*.), (i.) nom., 3468 (*-ę* B), 3498 f (*-e* B) (: agayn : fayn), 4402 (*in B supply* [me]); in, 3630 f (: to seyn: certeyn). (ii.) of, 3470.

right, ryght (A.S. riht, *n*.), (i.) nom., 591, 3840 f (perh. adj.); acc., 4124 f, 5177 f; by r., 3758, 5105 f (thour r. C); of r., 3826, 4637 f, 5233 f (*-e* B, on ryȝt C), 7708 f. (ii.) by r., 1848, 5058.—vnright, acc., 1538 f, 5212 f.

ryng (A.S. hring, *m*.), (i.) nom., 3732 (*-ę* B), 5531 f (*-e* B, ryngis † C); voc., 6912 (*-ę* B, r. of C); acc., 3735 C (*-ę* B, ryng I A); yn, 1670 (*-ę* B).—ryng(e), acc., 3727 f AB (ryng C) (: thing *acc.*).

seed (A.S. sǽd, *n*.), nom., 385 C (sedę BD, *om.* † A).

shap (A.S. ge-sceap, *n*.), (ii.) acc., 1747 (shappe B, *in A supply* [his]), 6836 (shap hire BC)

sheld (A.S. scield, scyld, sceld, *m*.), (i.) nom., 1286 (sheeld and B, schild & C), 1617 (*-ę* B, schild C), 1725 (*-ę* B, scheld C), 3322 (shield B, schild C); acc., 6671 (*-ę* B, child C); vnder sheld, 2412 f (*-e* B, schild C) (: byheld *pret. ind. 3. sg.* : held *pret. ind. 3 sg.*)

ship (A.S. scip, *n*.), (ii.) acc., 7007 (*-e* D).

shour (A.S. scúr, *m*.), (i.) in, 4709 (*-ę* B). (ii.) Doun fille as shour in aperill (aperil B) swythe, 5413 (Out ran as schour of aprille ful swythe C).

slep, sleep (A.S. slǽp, *m*.), (i) nom., 4380 (*-ę* C); acc., 484 f (: keep *n*.), 7810 (*-ę* B, C †); of (= concerning), 4250 f (shep † A, on slepe C) (: kepe *n*.); of (= out of), 6883 (*-ę* B). (ii.) in, 6724 (*-e* B), 8078 (*-e* B); yn his s. hym, 7597 (*-e* B); out of his s. he, 7606 (*-e* B); nom., s. hire, 2009 (*-e* B).

song (A.S. sang, song, *m*.), (i.) nom., 5828 (*-ę* B, song is C); acc., 7008 (*-ę* B); of, 393 (*-ę* B), 1961 (*-ę* B); in, 397 (*-ę* B), 4656 f

---

[1] *red*[*e*] *I shal* A (emend to, *red I sholde*).
[2] Supply [*this*] in C.

(-e B); on, 1910 (-ę B, lay C); by, 1968 f (-e BC). (ii.) nom., 7738; acc., 4666, 6996; on, 389 (-e B); in, 6095 (-e B).

sor (A.S. sár, n., f.), (i.) to his s., 5606 (soor B).

spir (A.S. spír, *inc. gen.*), an ok cometh of a litel spir, 2420 f (-ę BCD) (: fyr : desir n.).

ston (A.S. stán, m.), (i) 1685 f (-e B), 2579 f (stoone B), 3541 (-ę B), 5016 f (-e B); acc., 3733 f (stoone B); on, 2313 f (-e B); of, 2956 (-ę B); in (=into), 5129 f (stoon B, into a ston C). (ii.) nom., 1928 (A †), 8092 (-e B).

streng (A.S. streng, m.), (ii.) acc., 2118 (-e B).

swarm (A.S. swearm, m.), (ii.) nom., 1278.

swerd (A.S. sweord, n.), (i.) acc., 5433 (-ę B), 5877 (-ę B), 6670; with this . . . s., 5902 (-ę B). (ii.) acc., 4415, 5886 (-e B; C †); with s., 5873.

thank (A.S. þanc, þonc, m.), (i.) acc., 803, 1008 (-ę B), 1100 (-ę B). (ii.) acc., 3485, etc.; t. him, 1461 (-e B).—vnthànk, (ii.) acc., 7062 (-thonke B).

thef (A.S. þéof, m.), (i.) voc., 870 (theef B, if † C). (ii.) voc., 3940.

thing, thyng (A.S. þing, n), (i.) nom., 174, 217 (-ę B, thyngys C), 254 (-ę B), 5533 f (-e B), 5735 f (-e B), etc.; acc., 1229 (-ę B), 3725 f (-e B), etc.; on, 5247 (-ę B); in, 5070 (-ę B); to, 5684 (-ę B); fro, 748 (-ę B, for ‡ th. C); ayeyns, 2499 (-ę B); of, 511, 673 (thy(i)ngę B), etc.; any thyng, any thing, *adv'l.*, 848 (-ę B), 3474 (-ę B).—(ii.) nom., 401 (-e B), 5358 f (-ęs B), etc.; acc., 1719 (-e B); in, 1800 (-e B); on, 2860 (-e B); of, 2960; lyk, 103 (-e B); for that thyng hym, 1805.—no thing, no thyng, (i.) nom., 2135; acc., 1460 (-ę B), etc.; for, 7057 (-ę B); with, 2380 (-ę B); of, 797 (-ę B), etc.; adv'l., 137 (-ę B), etc. (ii.) nom., 339 (-e B), etc.; acc., 1558 (-e B), etc.; in, 5827 (-e B); no manerę thyng, adv'l., 5939 (-e B). thingę, acc., 2791 A (thyngę B, thyng C).

thonder, thondre (A.S. þunor, m., L. þunre), of thondre, 3504 f (thonder B, thundyr C, thundre D) (: a-sonder: yonder); with thonder dynt, 7868 (-dir C, thuhder D); with thonder, 2230 f (-ir C, -re D) (: wonder: yonder); acc., the thonder rynge, 1318 (thundir D, thondyr (to) rynge C).

thorn (A.S. þorn, m.), acc., 2357 f (-e BC), 3946 f (-e B).

thought (A.S. ge-þóht, m.), (i.) nom., 442 f, 1853, 5643 (-ę B) (cf. 1856, 1891); acc., 3981 f, 4951 f, 5727 f, 7529 f, 7644; for . . . th., 579 f; yn th., 1779 (in hirę th. argue BC); yn herę th., 1688 f, 6465 f (-ę B); in his th., 4383; out of my th., 4342 f; of herę . . .

§ 18.] *of Chaucer's Troilus.* 61

.th., 1737 ; of this th., 1830 f (-e B); with that th., 1741. (ii.) nom., 6316 ‡ C; acc., 5641; with, 7682; in his th. he, 3285; withinne hire th. his, 1745; with that th. he, 827; with . . . th. hire, 1894.

thral (A.S. þræl, *m.*), acc., 439 (thralle B).

thred, threed (A.S. þræd, þréd, *m.*), (ii.) acc., 6208, 6370 ; with, 7175 (-e B).

top (A.S. top(p), *m.*), acc., 5658.

tymber (A.S. timber, *n.*), (ii.) nom., 3372 (-yr B, -ir C, -re D).

vers (A.S., fers, *n.*, cf. O.F. vers), nexst this vers he, 399.

wal (A.S. weal(l), wal(l), *m.*), (i.) nom., 3321 f (: in al); in, 1132 f (walle B) (: yn al : shal 3 *sg. ind.*). (ii.) nom., 1239 ; to . . . w. his, 4906 (walle B); ouer . . . w. he, 7508 (walle B, waH.‡ his C). [Var. C waH.]

water, watre (A.S. wæter, *n.*), (i.) to watre, 2957 (-er B, -yr C); withoute water, 5427 (-yr C).

weder (A.S. weder, *n.*), (i.) nom., 1087, 3499 (-ir C). (ii.) nom., 3512 (-ir C).

werk (A.S. weorc, *n.*), (i.) acc., 1059, 8186; for, 2078, 4828 (-e B); of, 1101, 8021 (-e B); on (vpon BC), 3539 ; to, 3577. (ii.) acc., 265, 3313, 5514 (wek † A); of . . . w. he, 3544.—woike, acc., 2045 AB (werke C).

wex (A.S. wæx, weahs, *n.*), vpon, 2173.

wheston (A.S. hwetstán, *m.*), (ii.) nom., 631 (weston C). (Cf. *ston.*)

whiel (A.S. hwéol, *n.*). (i.) nom., 848 (whelys ‡ C); on, 4673 ; vpon the w., 4985 f (: of stel); of (=gen.), 839. (ii.) from, 4668. [Var. C whel.]

wimpil (A.S. wimpel, *inc. gen.*), acc. wimpil and, 1195 C (*read* barbe).

wir (A.S. wír, *m.*), by, 4478 f (wyr B) (: fir *ignis :* desir *n.*).

wit, wyt (A.S. gewit(t), *n.*), (i.) nom., 5553 (C¶), 5599, 6273 f, etc. ; acc., 241 f (witte B), 1358 (witte B), 3839 f (witte B, wite C), 5766 f, etc.; out of, 108, 4892, 5010; emforth, 1328 f, 2082 f (euene with my w. C); with, 2757 ; to, 4153 (*om.* † C); by, 7121 f (: yit ; it). (ii.) nom., 1217 (B †), etc.; acc., 7706 ; yn, 989; of, 1928 (A †, wight C), 3058; out of, 7625; with, 2977 (B †), 3007, 3085 C, 6149, 8145 ; thurgh, 2926 (C° †).

wonder (A.S. wundor, *n.*), (i.) nom., 403 (-yr C), 2228 f (-ir C) (: with thonder : yonder), 5250 (-yr C), 5762 (-ir C); acc., 7344 f (-ir C, wonnder B) (: asonder). (ii.) nom., 955 (-yr C), 959 (-yr C), 1105, 1828 (-ir C), 1834 (-ir C) (cf. 4920, 6425, 6484). (Cf. the adverbial and adjectival uses of *wonder,* § 85, note 2.)

word (A.S. word, *n.*), (i.) nom., 1102 (-ę B), etc.; acc., 397, etc.; of, 820 (-ę B); with, 875 (-ę B), 1176 (-ę B), 1293 (-ę B), 1961 (-ę B), 2777 (-ę B), 3000, 3752 (-ę B); withouten w., 3308[1]; at, 4150 (-ę B). (ii.) nom., 2896 (-e B); acc., 737, 2113 (-e B), etc.; word by word, 2262 (C †); by, 3273 (by w. ne ‡ C); withouten w., 5362 (-e B; C †); with that w. he, 204 (-e B), 869 (-e B), 1349, 3583, 3806 (-e B), 3820; with that w. here (*poss. sg.*), 1335; withouten w. he, 6900; word and ende, 2580, 3544 (-e B).—acc., by-word here (*hic*), 5431 (-e B).

wrong (A.S. wrang, see Kluge in Paul's *Grundriss*, I, 787), (i.) acc., 2557 (-ę B), 3850 (-ę B). (ii.) nom., 4017 (-e B); acc., 2764; in w., 594 (-e B); acc., wrongé ‡ to D (-ës AB).

— wyf (A.S. wíf, *n.*), (i.) voc., 2948 f (: lyf), 4138 f (: al my lyfe A, lyue BC); from 6701 f (: lif : stryf). (ii.) nom., 678, 6134 (-e B).

wyn (A.S. wín, *n.*), acc., (i.) 7215, (ii.) 3513.

wynd (A.S. wind, *m.*), (i.) 3585 (-ę B), 7036 (-ę B); acc., 7041 (-ę B); with w., 1851 (-ę B); in the w., 3368 f (-e BC) (: blynd *pred. adj. sg.*); o wynd o wynd, 1087 (-e . . . -ę B). (ii.) thorugh, 6806 (-e B); with w., 7004 (-e B); wynde, nom., 2473 AB (wynd C).

wynter (A.S. winter, *m.*), (i.) nom., 1137; in, 3194 (-ir C), 4887 (-yr C); after, 3904 (-yr C); yn wynter mone, 524 (-yr C).

yerd (A.S. geard, *m.*), nom., ȝerd, 1905 D (yérdę B, gardeyn (*slurred*) ‡ A, ȝerd [was] C).

yuël (A.S. yfel, *n.*), (i.) acc., 1666 (euel B, euyl C, evil D), 4006 (euelę B, euyl C); for, 5268 (euel B, grif † C); an yuyl that ye ne take, 7988 (an euyl ȝe B, on euyl ȝe C, on yuęłł that D).[2] (ii.) nom., 782 (enyl C); acc., iuyl and, 6780 C (harm AB, harme D).

The five Anglo-Saxon kinship nouns *fæder, módor, bróðor, sweostor, dohtor* (r-stems):—

fader, (i.) 5994 (fadıdyr † C, fadir D †), 6043 (-ir D, -ir I C), 7499 (-yr C); cf. 121, 4756, 4938, 5329. (ii.) cf. 4687, 5217, 5220.

moder, (i.) 5424 AB (-ir D), 7589 (-ir C), 8232; cf. 5869. (ii.) cf. 1135, 4097.

brother, (i.) 653 (-er(e) D), 3094 f (-ir D), 6670, 6884; cf. 51, 1242, 2131, 2444, 2481, 2483, 2496, 2535 f, 2705 f (-er(e) D), 2711, 5067 f, 5120 f, 5203, 5270 f, 6497, 7869 f. (ii.) brother ‖ I, 8094 A (-er deere BD); brother holdere, 1729.

---

[1] In B insert [*it*].   [2] In B read *ne* for *it*.

suster, (i.) 6253 (systyr C), 7813 (systyr he ‡ C); cf. 1154, 2778, 5510. (ii.) cf. 860, 2309, 2644.

doughter, douhter, (i.) 6200 (douȝtyr C), 7473 (douȝtyr C); cf. 94, 2845, 4649, 4754, 5325. (ii.) cf. 664.

§ 19. The following nouns of Germanic origin, which have no substantives to represent them in Anglo-Saxon, end in the *Troilus* in a consonant.

For erroneous -e (not sounded), see *fold(e) lok, skil.*

abod (cf. A.S. ábídan), nom., 7670 (abood B; C †).

anger, angre (O.N. angr, *m.*), with an angre don, 563 (-yr C, -re to D)[1]; after anger game, 6225 (-ir C); ffor angrë of, 7898 (-ir CD).

bark, see § 18.

bost (etym. dub.), for b., 3090 f (-e B) (: wost *scis*); thorugh, 3140 f (: almost : wost).

cast (cf. O.N. kasta *vb.*, kǫstr, *m.*), (ii.) fro, 1953 (-e B).

cros (O.N. kross, *m.*; A.S. Normannes cros, Birch, *Cart. Sax.*, III, 367, see Skeat, *Trans. Philol. Soc.* for 1888-90, p. 286) is of Romance origin, but its precise history is doubtful, see p. 92.

flat (cf. O.N. flatr, *adj.*), of, 5589 B (A † C †).

fold(e) (cf. O.N. faldr, *m.*, O.H.G. falt, *m.*), in many fold(e), 1782 f (-d CD) (: told *p.p.* : cold).

Note.—For *-fold* (A.S. -feald) in the adverbial phrase *a thousand fold*, see (i.) 2088, 2671, 3094, 3416 (-e ‡ dye B), 4382, 4526 (-e B); (ii.) 1227 (-e B); a th. f. his, 546 (-e B); a thowsand foldę more, 819 (-d C).

hap (O.N. happ, *n.*), nom., 2781; acc., 2539; with, 4088 (B †).—vnhap, acc., 552.

keep (cf. A.S. cépan), acc., 486 f (-e B) (: sleep); kep(e), acc., 4252 f (kep BC) (: of slep).

lak (O.N. lakr, *adj.*), (i.) nom., 2263 (lakke B). (ii.) nom., 2044 CD (lat † A, lokke † B)[2], 7.177 (lakke BD); for, 1994 (lakke B), 2365 CD.

lasch (cf. Dutch lasch), acc., L haue, 220 (lasche C⁰).[3]

lok, look (cf. A.S. lócian), (i.) nom., 2352, etc.; acc., 2344, 7292 f (-(e) B), etc.; with, 307 (-(e) B), 325 (-(e) B), 538 (-(e) B), etc. (ii.) acc., 291 (-(e) B), etc.; of, 295 (-(e) B); with al his l., 229.—of hirę lok(e), 364 AB (lok C).

skil (O.N. skil, *n.*), nom., it skil(e) is, 3488 (skyl BC, skil hit D), skyl ywys, 1450 (-(e) D).

---

[1] In A supply [to].   [2] Verse too long in C.   [3] In C supply [hc].

smert (cf. A.S. smeortan ; Dutch smart, O.H.G. smerzo, *m.*, smerza, *f.*), (i.) nom., 5507 (-ę D); for s., 5035 (-ę BD). (ii.) on s., 5128 (*e* B, smerthe D).—smert (-*e* D), 6780, is perhaps a verb (= smerteth). [On the supposed sbst. *smerte*, see § 67, s. v. smerte, *adj. pl.*]
stert (cf. Dutch storten ; cf. A.S. steort *tail*), (ii.) with, 6617 (-(*e*) B).
strok (cf. A.S. strícan), acc., 2467 f (-(e) B) (: ok); with s., 5173 (strook(ę) B).
sweigh (= impetus ; cf. O.N. sveigr, *m.*), nom., 2468 (swough B, swey C, sweyf D).
swough (= swoon ; cf. A.S. swógan), of (= out of), 3962 (swouʒ C, swoun D), 5874 (swów C, swogh D).
syk (cf. A.S. sícan), with, 1230 (-(ę) D), 1548 (sikë † seide B, syk(ę) she D), 3643 (-(ę) D), 3965 (-ë ‡ whan B), 4335, 6189. [Var. B syhg; BC sik; D sike, siʒ, sigh.]
walk (cf. A.S. wealcan), in his w., 190 (C?).

Note 1.—For *thryft* (O.N. þryft, f.) and *won* (O.N. ván, f.), see §11; for *shyvre, slyvre*, see §19, n.
Note 2.—For *kankedort*, of very doubtful etymology, see 2837 f (*cankedort* C, *kankerdorte* D).

§ 20. In Romance nouns final -e (-e mute) is usually retained, both in writing and in sound, except for the regular elision. But there are a good many exceptions, in some of which the -e is preserved in writing but loses its value as a syllable, in others of which the -e is neither written nor pronounced. (Cf. Child, §19; ten Brink, §§ 222, 223.)

For details see the following sections (§§ 21—31).—§ 21. Miscellaneous Romance nouns in -e which sometimes or always retain -e in the *Troilus*. § 22. Exceptions to §21. § 23. *-aunce*. § 24. *-ence*. § 25 *-esse*. § 26. *-ice*. § 27. *-ure*. § 28. *-ere*. § 29. *disclaundre, lettre*, etc. § 30. *-ye, -ie*. § 31. *comèdye, augùrye, fùrye, stòrie*, etc.

§ 21. Miscellaneous Romance nouns in -e (-e mute) which sometimes or always retain -e in the *Troilus*.

This list contains the following words: *age, Ariète, assège, batayle (bátayle), baúde, baẁme, bille, blame, calle, cáuse, caue, charge, charme, cháunge, cheyne, clause, compleýnte (cómpleynt*[e]); *constreýnte (cònstreynt*[e]), *cope, coràge (còrage), corde, demaunde, descènte, disese, doute, egle, ensàmple, entènte, eschaunge, ese, executrice, fáce, faile,*

§ 21.] *of Chaucer's Troilus.* 65

fame, fate, fayre, feste, flaumbe, force (*fors*), *fortùne* (-e; *fòrtunę*, -e), *frape, garde, gaude, gemme, gestè* (*gest*[e]), *grace* (*gracę*), *gyle, gyse, herbe, houre, infortùne, inpossible, inke, ire, ìapę, ioyę* (*ioyę* ‡), *lessę, ligne, ma dàme, martire, mayle, mèdecỳne, meruaỳle, messàge, mewe* (*muwe*), *moble, mowe, muse, nysèricòrde, nece* (*necę*), *note, noyse, orisonte, pennè, peple, persòne* (*pèrsono his*), *peyne, place, planète, pleynte, pompe, potèntę, pouèrte, preue, prològe, prouèrbe, pùrsuyte* (-ę), *quiètè* (*quiètè*), *ragę, rascaỳlle, regnę, rèntę, reprèue, requèste* (-*i*?), *reynę, roche, route, ruỳne, sauegarde, sege, signe, sirè, space, stewe* (*stuwe*), *table, tente, terme, title, trone, vncle, vniuerse, vrne, vsàge, vermìne, verre, veyne, viàge* (*viagę*), *visàge, ymàge*.

Note 1. The Romance words in this list are all French except *Ariete* (Ital. *ariete*)[1] and *orisonte* (Ital. *orizzonte*). *Poverte* (O. Fr. *poverté*), and *stuwe* (O. Fr. *estuwe*) exhibit peculiarities of formation. *Potente* has no direct French etymon (cf. O. Fr. *potence*), and may be imitated from Latin. The four words *fate* (Lat. *fatum*), *medecyne* (Lat. *medecina*, cf. Fr. *médecine*), *quiete* (Lat. *quietem*, or, perhaps, Ital. *quiete*)[1], *vniuerse* (Lat. *universum*; cf. Fr. *univers*), *vrne* (Lat. *urna*, see p. 74, footnote 1), are included in this section for convenience. For *chimenay*[e], see § 33, note.

Note 2. Ten Brink's rule, "Nach tonloser Silbe verliert -e regelmässig seinen Silbenwerth" (§ 223), is illustrated by *fortunę, pùrsuytę*. In all other cases in point the word that follows begins with a vowel or a weak *h*, except those in § 22.

Note 3. Other instances of apocope may be seen in *gracę, ioyę* ‡, *necę, sirę*. For irresponsibly omitted -*e*'s (scribes' errors), see especially *entente, gestę, requeste*.

Note 4. *Egle, ensample, inpossible, moble, peple, table, title, vncle* illustrate the treatment of consonant + *le*. But cf. *marbel* (O. Fr. *marble, marbre*), 700 (infra), *werbal* (infra).

Note 5. *Werre* bellum, might fairly have been included in § 21; but it seemed better, on the whole, to give it a place in § 15.

age, 1480[2], 7189 f (: corage), 8199 f (: visage : ymage).

Ariëte (Ital. ariete), 6254 f (aryëte C) (: herte swete), 7553 f (aryëte C) (: swete).

assege; thassege, 6142 (thassage B, the sege CD). [Cf. *sege*.]

batàyle, 1715 f (: withouten faile); bàtayle, 8114 (-H D)

baude, 1438 f (: gaude).

bawme, -e is, 1138.

bille (Anglo-Norm. bille, L. Lat. billa), 2215 f ABC (: stonde stille).

blame, 1100 f (: lame *pred. adj.*), 3107 f (: name); -*e*, 5213, 5256, 7431; -*e* haue, 1295 (-ë ‡ haue BD[3]).

calle, 3617 f (calł D) (: alle *pl.* : calle *inf.*).

cause, 854, 1812 f (: clause), 2492, 2524, 2718, 2771 (D †), 3607,

---

[1] Cf. ten Brink, § 222 Anm., who is inclined to regard *Ariete* and *quiete* as "romanisirende Abklatsche lateinischer Wörter." He says nothing about *orisonte*.
[2] AD defective. Supply [*that*].
[3] Read in BD, blame haue. I [myn] vncle.

F

3637, 3993, 4004, 4421, 4681, 5379,[1] 5491, 5677, 5889 (-e hire BD), 5932, 6313, 6443 (-es † D), 7239, 7391 (-is wich † C), 7593, 7665 f (: clause), 7668, 7757 C (-e AD); cause, 20 (D †), 579, 670[2], 1568, 1580, 1917, 2187[3], 2848, 2872, 3206, 3378, 3462 CD, 3828,[4] 3833, 3874, 3987, 4761, 4803, 5350, 5589 (A †; -ę to C), 5672, 5674 (-e. of [the] D), 5703, 5724, 6003, 6316 (thouʒt ‡ C), 6335, 6490 ([the] cause D ; B †), 6769, 6783, 7017 (-ë is ‡ D), 7592 (C †; -e ‡ of D), 7705[5] (D †), 7757 (-e doth C), 8055.— -e (before h), (he) 4787, 4885, 6890, 7578 (-e of C, -e he? D); (haue) 7619; (hadde) 4069.—O cause of wo that cause hast (hath † C) ben of blysse, 6913. [Cf. causeles, § 85.]

cauo, 1202 f (: saue *subj.* 3 *sg.* : raue 2 *pl.*).

charge, 2079, 4096 † f B, 4842[6]; -e, 651 (charg C); -e he, 444.

charme, 2399 (-[e] C) ; -e, 2665 (charm C).

chaunge, 1107 f (: straunge), 7997 f (: straunge) (chung C : strong); -e, 5327 (-g ‡ for C). [Cf. eschaunge.]

cheyne (O. Fr. chaaine), 509 f (cheyn D) (: pleyne *inf.* : peyne *n.*), 1703 f (: tweyne : to seyne).

clause, 1813 f (: cause), 7664 f (: cause).

compleỳnte (O. Fr. complainte, -nt), 541 f (-t D) (: dreynte *pret. ind.* 3 *sg.* : pleynte), 5404 f (: constreynte); -e, 5446 (-t CD), 5467 (pleynt C, compleinte † D); compleỳnt hym, 2668 (-e B); còmpleynt of, 655. [Cf. pleynte.]

constreỳnte, 5403 f (: compleynte); cònstreynt and, 1861 (D †; -e B, constaunt ‡ C).

cope, 3566 f (: Euròpe).

coràge, 3739 f (: rage *n.*), 7188 f (: age); còrage, 564 (couràgë ‡ wake D), 5281 (cùrage B).

corde, 6806 f (: recorde *inf.* : accorde *inf.*).

demaunde, 5957 f (: comaunde *pres. pl.*), 6356 f (: recomaunde *inf.*); -e he 7222 (-é ‡ he D).

descente, 319 f (dissent D) (: wente *iit* : mente *pret.* 3 *sg.*).

disese, dishese, 1232 f, 2445,[7] 3726 f, 4118 f, 4751 f, 5759 f; -e, 2072, 3885, 4658, 6472 (desese A, de-sese C, di[s]ease D), 7783 (*pl.* ‡ C).
    Rhyme words.—displese *inf.* (1232), plese *inf.* (3726, 4118, 4751, 5759), apese *inf.* (3726), ese *n.* (4118, 4751, 5759). [Var. D dissese, disease]

---

[1] AB defective. [2] Supply [*for*] in D.
[3] "The cause of his comynge (-yng DG) thus answer(e)de." The choice lies between *cause* and *comynge*. The collection of Cp. and John's MS. notes no variants.
[4] Supply [*in*] in C. [5] Supply [*my*] in A.
[6] Supply [*that*] in AD. [7] Supply [*that*] in D.

§ 21.]   *of Chaucer's Troilus.*   67

doute, 152 f (-t D), 1820 f ‡ C (-t ‡ D), 2477 f (-t D), 5066 f, 5939 f,
6233 f (dought D), 6431 f, 7658 f, 7816 f, 7881 f, 8007 f; -e, 1451
(-t D), 3360. [Cf. douteles, § 85.]

    Rhyme words.—aboute (152, 1820 CD, 2477, 5066, 5939, 6233, 7658, 7816, 8007), oute (7881), withoute (6431), route (5066, 6431), deuoute (152), tuskes stoute (7816).

egle, 2011 (egęle C), 4338 (egęle C, egle ? D).

ensàmple, *trisyll. bef. csts.*, 232 (-saumple BCD), 995 (-saumple B, on-saumpęle C).—ensàmplę, 3714 (-sampęlę by C),[1] 4863 (-saumpęle C), 7953 (-saumpęle C). [Var. B ensaumple.]

entènte (O. Fr. entente); 61 f, 738 f, 928 f, 1448 f, 1609 f, 1913 f,
1963 f, 2008 f, 2145 f, 2304 f (-t B), 2531 f, 2645 f (-t B), 2808 f,
2967 f, 3395 f, 4030 f, 4081 f, 4424 f, 4835 f, 5297 f, 5515[2] f, 5882 f,
6187 f, 6513 f, 7230 f, 7473 f, 7668 f, 8057 f. [In the above list
D has *entent* throughout (*intent*, 61), and C has *entent* except in 61
(where a part of the MS. is cut out) and in 1448, 1963, 3395,
4081, 4835, 5297 (in which lines it has *entente*.)]—entèntë (*bef. cst.*),
4008 (-[e] C, -t ‡ is D)[3]; entènt[ë] (*bef. cst.*), 4071 AC (-e B,
èntent ‡ clene D).—entènte, 5319 (-t BCD)[4]; entènt' (*bef. vowels*),
2378 (-e B), 7993 (-e B, cèntence is ‡ C)[5]; entènt he, 7139 (-e B).—
entènt, 2750 f ACD (-e B) (: went *ierunt*), 6078 f ABCD (: mente
pret. ind. 3 sg. : wente *iit*).

    Rhyme words.—wente *iit* (2808, 3395, 4424, 5882, 6078, 7473, 7668), wente, went *ierunt* (61, 2750), wente *pret. subj. 3 sg* (4835), stente, stynte *pret. ind. 3 sg.* (738, 1963, 4081), stente *pret. ind. 3 pl.* (61), repente *pres. ind. 1 sg.* (928, 1609), consente *pres. ind. 1 sg.* (928), *inf.* (2531), mente *pret. ind.* 1, 3 *sg.* (1448, 2304, 2645, 2967, 4030, 6078, 7230), 2 *pl.* (8057), 3 *pl.* (4835), rente n. (1913), sente *misit* (1913, 5515, 7473), *pret. subj.* 3 *sg.* (2531), hente *pret. ind.* 3 *sg.* (2008, 4030), assente *pres. ind.* 1 *sg.* (2145, 5297), *inf.* (6187), tormente *inf.* (5297), glente *pret. ind.* 3 *pl.* (5882), tente *n.* (6513).

    Note.—A consideration of the above data shows that the only form that Chaucer uses in the *Troilus* is *entente*, never *entent* except when a final -e would disappear by the regular operation of the rules for elision. The scribes sometimes omit -e where we must supply it, not only in *entente*, but in the rhyme words; but Chaucer in the *Troilus* never rhymes *entente* with a word that has no right to a final -e and never apocopates the -e in the middle of a verse.

eschaungè (cf. chaunge); -e 4808 (chaunge CD), 5221 ([es]chaunge C), 5540 (chaunge D, eschaung ‡ for C).—eschaungë ‡ of, 4893 D (chaungynge ABC).

ese, 28 f, 43 f, 1835 f, 2310 f, 2951 f, 3475 f, 4121 f (ateste † B), 4248 f, 4570 f, 4748 f, 5365 f, 5756 f, 6479 f.—Before consonants,

---

[1] In 3714 C read, *ensampęle of* for *e. by*.
[2] In CD the rhyme word is spelled *sent*; but this is not *sent* = *mittit*.
[3] In BD read *a*[*te*].   [4] In C supply [*e*].   [5] In B supply [*the*].

2746, 3453, 5388, 6474.—ese, 2861, 4146, 5142 (-e and [in] D), 7742 (B †; crese † D), etc.; ese hym, 2744. [7722 ‡ C (?).] (Cf. disese.) [Var. D ease.]

    Rhyme words.—displese *inf.* (28), *pres. subj.* 3 *sg.* (2951), plese *inf.* (43, 2310, 3475, 4121, 4570, 4748, 5365, 5756, 6479), apese *inf.* (2951, 6479), countrepeyse (-pese BCD) *inf.* (4248), dishese *n.* (4121, 4748, 5756), lese, *O. Fr. lesse* (1835). [Var. D eese, ease.]

exècutrìce, 3459.

face, 1071 f, 1195, 1350 f, 1850 f, 4188 f, 4411 (D †), 4670 f, 4812 f, 5526 (C †), 5812 f, 5999 f, 6449 (C †), 6562 (*om.* A), 6607 f, 6899 f, 7037 f, 7071 f, 7277 f; -e, 1490, 5477, 5483, 6918, 7170[1]; -e he, 5023 (fate ‡ D); -e hem, 4730 (-e he D).—at prymé face, 3761 f (: place : grace).

    Rhyme words.—grace *n.* (1071, 1350, 3761, 4188, 4670), space (1850, 5999, 7037 CD), pace *inf.* (1850, 5812, 6899, 7277), place (4188, 4812, 5812, 6607, 6899, 7037 AB, 7071), deface *ind.* 2 *pl.* (7277). [Var. C fase.]

faile, fayle, 1714 f (: batayle), 6258 f (: assayle *subj.* 3 *sg*).

fame, 5321 (fane † C), 6783 f C †.

fate (Lat. fatum), 7913 (face † C); -ë helpeth, 7915 (-e hym BD, face † C); -e, 6572 (stat ‡ C); -e he, 5023 D †.

fayre (O. Fr. feire), 8203 f (faire B, feir D) (: floures fayre (faire B, fair D)); To morwe? allas! that were a fayre! quod he, 3692 (fair B, fayr C, [a] fair D).

feste, 161 (-[e] C, -t ‡ D), 168 f (feest D), 1446 f (festis † C), 1506 f (fest D), 2992 f (-t CD), 3186 f (-t BD), 4001 f (-t D), 4154 f, 6440 f, 6804 f, 6819, 6887 f, 8040 f; -e, 3495 (-t BD), 4070 (-è ioye? D), 4581 (-t D),[2] 6667, 6809 (ferste † C).

    Rhyme words.—leste *adj. pl.* (168), behest, -e (1446, 1506, 3186), heste (4001), the leste (1446, 4001, 4154, 6440, 6804 *pl.*, 6887, 8040), request (-e B) (2992). [Var. B feest, feeste; D feest.]

flaumbè funeral, 6665 (flambe C, flawme D); -e, 4780 (flaumme C, flaume D).

force, 6137 (fors C), 6784.—fors, (i.) what fors, 1463. (ii.) In *no fors*, 2562, 4984 (-*ce* D, fors whan C), 7118, 7979 (-*ce* D); no fors hardyly, 2802.

fortùne, 841 f (: commune *pred. adj.*), 4664 f (: entune *inf.* : comune *adj.*), 5053 f (: comune *pred. adj. pl.*), 7904.—fortùne, 138, 849 AB (-tùne ‡ to C, -e † for D), 3459, 4509, 4556 (D †), 4922 (fòrtune allas ‡ D), 4936 (-e ȝif C, -e yif D), 5047, 5262, 5854, 8108 (-è ‡ ay D), 8126 (-ë ‡ it D); -e his, 6832; -e hem, 7497.—fòrtune, 837,

---

[1] Supply [*of*] in B.
[2] B, apparently, "swich a festè and swichè proces," where *swichè* seems to be written, by error of ear, for *swich a*.

843, 4986, 5851, 6250, 7283; -e hym, 1370.—Ne remuable fortunë
deface, 6344¹. fortunę wole, 1420 AD (-tùne B; D †). [Cf.
infortune.]

frape, 3252 f (: iape : i-shape *p.p.*).

garde,—sauë-gard[e], 4801 (-ë B, saf cundwyt hem C, safę conduyt
hem D ‡).

gaude, 1436 f (: baude).

gemme, 1429 (comme † B, gom[me] ‡ C).

geste, 3292 f (geest D) (: leste *pret. sg.* : the beste).—gest[e], 1168 f
(geeste B, geest D) (: leste *pret. ind. 3 sg.*).

grace, 42 f, 370 f, 713 f, 900 f, 926, 955 f, 1056 f, 1070 f, 1117 f,
1351 f, 1799 f, 1916 (D †), 2155 f, 2207 f, 2450 f, 2611, 3303 (spase
CD), 3314 f, 3547, 3764 f, 4018 f, 4109, 4111 f, 4191 f, 4298 f,
4646 f, 4672 f, 5217 f, 5614 f, 5895, 6055 f, 6346 f, 6534 f, 6535
(-ę ‡ befalle D), 6865, 6944 f, 6955 (-ę ‡ C), 7057 f, 7303 f, 7320 f,
7686 f, 7994 f, 8065 f, 8231 (mercy BD); grace, 973, 998, 1328
(D †), 2058, 4925, 4955.—gracę for, 3770 (-ë had B, -ë to D, *om.* †
C). [Cf. graceles, § 49, n. 5.]

    Rhyme words.—pace, passe *inf.* (42, 370, 3314, 4111, 5614, 6055), passe
subj. 1 sg. (7057), trespace *inf.* (4018), purchace *inf.* (900, 1117, 1799,
5217), *imv. pl.* (2207), chase *inf.* (4646), face (1070, 1351, 4191), at prymë
face (3764), space (713, 2155, 2207, 7303, 7994, 8065), place (900, 955,
1056, 1117, 2450, 3764, 4111, 4191, 4298, 4646, 5217, 6346, 6534, 6944,
7303, 7320, 7686), deface *inf.* (6346), arace *inf.* (7320). [Var. C grase;
C 4018 gras; D 42 gras.]

gyle, 719 f C (wyle AD, wile B) (: begile *inf.* : while); 3619 f (gile C)
(: while).

gyse, see § 26.

herbe, -e, 957 (erb B), 1430 (herb B, erbe † C), 2852. [Var. C erbe.]

houre, oure, owre, 456 f (hour D), 1478 f, 1673 f (-is † D), 2792 f
(hour D), 2982 f (our C), 4318², 5200 f (hour D), 7006 f; -e, 2642
(hoür ‡ aftir D), 3374 (-r CD)³, 6826 (-r D)⁴, 7696 (-r CD).
[hourre † hath, 4295 C.]

    Rhyme words.—laboure *laboro* (456), deuoure *inf.* (7006), *subj. 3 sg.* (1478),
powre *inf.* (2792), honoure *inf.* (2982), he is youre (ʒoures ‡ D) (1673),
oure *ours* (5200).

Infortùnë wolde, 4847 (-e it AB); -e, 4468, 4959. [Cf. *fortune.*]

inke, 4535 f (ynke C, ynk D) (: bythenke (bithynke) *inf.*).

---

[1] So in ABECp. John's Phillipps 8252 (with *remewable*) G (with *remeweable*) Harl.
2392 (with *nor* for *ne*) Selden B 24 (with *It* after *fortune*). Cut out in C. No
resonable † fortune to deface D ; No remuable fortune for to deface Durham II 13.

[2] For how sholde (shold[e] B) I my lyf an hourë (ourë B, our[e] D) saue, 4318 Cp.,
is apparently the correct reading. A, hour[e] my lyf (?) ; C, our[e] myn lyf (?).

[3] Supply [*she*] in C.   [4] Supply [*nas*] in D.

inpossible, an inpossible were, 3367 (im- B, & † inpossibele C; D?).

ire, 11re, yre, 2864 f, 6952 f, 7827 f, 8118; ire, 793; ire he, 6399, 7586.

    Rhyme words —a-fyre (2864, 7827), I desire *ind.* (6952).

iape, 2128 f (: ape), 3250 f (: frape : i-shape *p.p.*); -e, 1215. [-ë ‡ in, 5258 C.]

ioye, 4 f, 118 f [1], 608 f, 1225 f, 1728 f, 1834 f, 1902 (-[e] D), 1967 f, 3059 (C † D †), 3190 (ioy ‡ to D?), 3198 f, 3632 f, 3717 f, 4070 (-e ‡ D), 4162, 4221, 4249, 4284 f, 4292 f, 4513 (ioy ‡ his D), 4556 f, 4718 f, 4752 f, 4931 (-[e] D), 4936 f (foye † C), 4997 f, 5004 (-[e] D ?, -ë ‡ or B), 5047 (-[e] D), 5968 f, 5985 ‡ C (blysse ABD), 6093 [2], 6104 f, 6293 f, 6390 f, 6481 f, 6790 f, 6971 f, 6978 f, 7094 f, 7144 f, 7293 f, 7745 f, 7910 f; ioye, 1918, 3662, 4520, 8077, etc.; -e he, 2389; -e hastow, 6951; -e hadde 3311; -e here *poss. pl.*, 1861 [3]; -e halt, 4478 (-e haldyth † C) —ioyë have (*inf.*), 2329 (-[e] D).—1oye and (*l.* ioye and [al]), 3495 C (-e AB).—ioye ‡ may, 4535 A (-ë BC, -[e] D).

    Rhyme words.—fro ye (4), anoye *inf.* (5968), acoye *inf.* (7144), Troye (*all the passages cited*). [Var. BD ioie; C 1728, 1918 Ioyʒe.]

lesse (O. Fr. lesse), 1837 f (leese B) (: ese *n.*).

ligne, see *lyne*, § 3, p. 6.

ma dàmë, 1170 (-[e] B); -e, 1965 (madàm B).

martire, see 5480 f (under *matere*, § 28).

mayle, 7922 f (: by-waylle *inf.* : auentaylle).

medecyne, 659 f (-[e]cine B, medicynys † C, medicine D) (: fyne).

meruaẏle, meruey̆le, 476 f (: trauayl, -e BCD); -e, 3031 (meràkele C, miràcle D).—mèrueyle, 6484 ‡ D (wonder AB, wondyr C).

messàge, 3243, 5474 f (: rage *n.*), 5552 f (: rage *n.*). [massàge ‡, 2021 C.] [5516 B, *extra metrum.*]

mewe, muwe (O. Fr. mue), 381 f, 3444 f, 4626 f, 5158 f (mew D), 5972 f.

    Rhyme words.—suwe *inf.* (381), saluwe *inf.* (4626), arguwe *inf.* (5158), stuwe *n.* (3444), truwe *truce* (5972).

miracle, see *meruayle*.

moble, moeble (*dissyl.*), 6042 (mobelé C), 6663; moeble is, 6122 (mooble B, mebil C, mobles ‡ ben(e) D).

mowe (Fr. moue), 4669 f (mow D) (: y-throwe *p p.*).

muse, 1094 f (: vse *inf.* : excuse *ind.* 1 *sg.*).

---

[1] Old-style figures indicate that D has no -e.

[2] Bygan for Ioye the amorouse (thamorouse Cp: John's, thamarouse B, the amerous[e] CD) daunce.

[3] Supply a third [her] in D.

[§ 21.] *of Chaucer's Troilus.* 71

mysèricòrde, 4019 f (-d B) (: recorde *imv. pl.*).

nece, 968 (-ẹ to D), 1177, 1334, 1559, 2288, 2550 (-e [myn] A, C *defect.*), 3051, 3594 (-ë ‡ he C, -ẹ quod D), 3788 (nece(ce) C, -ẹ dere ‡ ? D), 3817, 8075 (nees[e] D), etc., etc.—nece, 1409 (trowth[e] nece B), 1491. AB, 2338 (-ë lo ‡ C), 2502, 3117 (-ë put C, -ẹ ‡ put D), etc.; -e haue, 1373; -e hath, 8090 (nees D); -e how, 4405. [Var. C 2042 nese; D 4398 nice.]—necẹ who, 2272; necẹ se, 3804 (-e how CD)[1]; necẹ lo, 1340 (-e BC, -ë ‡ alwey D).

note, 5247 f (: hote *adv.* : grote).

noyse, 3586, 6620 ABD; -e 85 AB (C †), 1155, 3504 (D †), 4732, 4845 (voys ‡ D), 5248; -e he, 5036. [Var. BD noise.]

òrisònte (Ital. orizzonte), 6639 (-soùne B, oryʒonte C, orisent[e] D).

penne, -e, 4675.

peple, (i.) *dissyl. bef. csts.*, 73, 1728, 1743 (-il C), 3426 (-ës B, puples C †), 7515 (puple C, people D). (ii.) *elided before vowels*, 1731 (peplë on CD), 3110 (pepil ‖ as C), 4845 (peplë stert ‡ D), 6231 A (peplë al(le) B, pepẹle ek C; D †). [Var. C. pepelë.]

persòne, 1786 f, 2572 f, 4745 f (all rhyme with *to done*); -e, 1253.— pèrsone his, 2352 (person C, -e [his] D).

peyne, 9 f, 63 f[2], 508 f, 589 f, 674 f, 709 f, 1560 f, 1608 f, 1861 f ABC (peyn D1862), 2072 f, 2212 f, 2316 f, 2440 f, 2586 f, 2615 f, 2821 f, 2947 f, 3836 f, 3848 f, 3960 f, 4333 f, 4373 f, 4958 f, 4980 f, 5140 (pleyne † C, peyne † D), 5166 f (peyn C), 5296,[3] 5372 f CD, 5411 f (-n C), 5414 f C, 5451 f, 5509 f, 5532 f, 5565 f, 5604 f, 5803 ‡ (-es AB, -ys C), 5806 f, 5919 f, 5967 f, 6398 f (pyne B), 6653 † f A (pyne BCD), 6778 f (pyne † BD), 7041 f, 7090 f, 7255 f, (pyne † B), 7399 f (-n C), 7592 f (payn C), 7599 (-es AB), 7632 f, 7763 f.—peyne, 34, 497, 3634 (wo ‡ B), 4058 (-es ‡ B), 4060 (-e hath BCD), 4344 (pleyne † C), 5799, 6861; -e hym, 7563; -e hire (*pl.*), 5791 BD (-es † A, sorwe † of C).—peyn ‡ ther yn, 1960 D.

Rhyme words.—pleyne *inf.* (9, 508, 1608, 1861, 2440, 2615, 2947, 6398, 7592, 7763), pleyne *ind.* 1 *pl.* (709), compleyne *inf.* (4958, 5451, 5565, 7090, 7632), *imv.* (2586), querar (3848, 6778), queratur (5919), to seyne (to seyn 3848) (9, 589, 709, 1608, 2072, 2212, 2440, 3836, 3960, 4373, 5166, 7399), restreyne *inf.* (674, 5372 CD, 5532, 5604), constreyne *inf.* (1560), cogitis (2316), destreyne *inf.* (4373), feyne *simulem* (2615), reyne pluere (4958, 5532), reyne *ind.* 3 *pl.* (5509), freyne *inf.* A.S. *frignan* (7592), tweyne, tweyn (2821, 3960, 4333, 5411, 5414 C, 5451, 5806, 5919, 5967, 7041, 7632), Eleyne (63, 674, 7255), cheyne *n.* (508), souereyne *adj.* (4980), veyne *n.* (5604, 6778). [Var. CD peine; D payne.]

place, 898 f, 953 f, 961,[4] 1057 f (space D); 1115 f, 1128, 1163 f,

---

[1] Supply [*can*] in B.   [2] Old-style figures indicate that D has no -e.
[3] Supply [*ne*] in D.   [4] AB slightly defective.

2449 f, 2652 f, 3060 f, 3763 f, 3856 f, 4113 f, 4190 f, 4297 f, 4339, 4645 f, 4810 f, 5220 f, 5814 f, 6347 f, 6532 f, 6586 f, 6608 f, 6897 f, 6943 f, 7039 f (space CD), 7040 f (space AB), 7073 f, 7306 f, 7319 f, 7685 f, 7992 (spacë C).—place, 429, 2098, 3518 (-ę † gan D), 4322 ‡ D, 4435 (-ë rise ‡ D), 4970 (-ë ‡ is C°); -e his, 2455 (-ë ‡ his C ; D †); place horrìble, 6613 (plase oribęle C).

Rhyme words.—face and grace (q. v.), and the following:—purchace inf. (1115, 5220), pace, passe inf. (1163, 2652, 3060, 4113, 5814, 6897), chase, chace inf. (898, 4645), space (7039 AB, 7040 CD, 7306), enbrace inf. (6586), race (a-race C) radat (3856), arace inf. (7319), deface inf. (6347). [Var. C plase.]

planète, 4099 f (: the swete : the grete).

pleynte, 408 f[1] (: I feynte ind. : queynte), 544 f (compleÿnt D) (: compleynte : dreynte pret. ind. 3 sg.), 5001 ‡ D (pl. ABC), 5462 (-[e] C, còmpleintę that ‡ D), 5489 B (-[e] A, còmpleint ‡ thus D), 5593 f (-t C) (: dreynte pret. subj. 2 pl.)[2].—pleynte, 5522 (-t C), 5807 (-t C), 7738 (-t C); -e his, 6631 (-t BC). [5504 ?] [Var. D pleint, pleinte.]—pleynt of, 8107 (-e B).

pompe, 6332 (pomp B).

potènte (cf. O. Fr. potence), 7585 f (-t CD) (: wente : shente, both pret. ind. 3 sg.).

pouèrte (irregular formation, see ten Brink, § 221 ; O. Fr. poverté), 6182 f (-t C) (: sherte).

preue, 690 f, 3149 f, 3844 f, 6321 f. (preue, 470 f, is perhaps an adjective : "The shoures sharpe fille of armes preue.")

Rhyme words.—leue credere (690, 3149, 6321), remeue inf. (690), greue subj. 2 pl. (3844).

prològe, 5555 (prolong † CD).[3]

prouèrbe, 1482 (prouèrb B).

pùrsuyte, 2829 (pursute D, pursuing C); pùrsuyte[4] make, 2044 (purseut (?) C, pùrsute D).

quiète, quyète (Lat. quietem), 3348 f, 4661 f, 5152 f, 5167 f (qui[e]te B), 5443 f.—quiète, quyète, 4522 (quyètë and[5] A), 7370.

Rhyme words.—swete adj. indef. (all), mete meet inf. (3348), pres. subj. 3 sg. (5443).

rage, 3741 f, 4915 f, 5473 f, 5554 f.

Rhyme words.—corage, asswage inf., message (5473, 5554).

rascaÿlle, 8216 f (: auaylle inf. : trauayle n.).

regnë shal, 7907 ‡ B (-ës AC,-is D); regne and, 2871.

---

[1] Old-style figures indicate that D has no -e.
[2] A has drenche (C drenk) for dreynte.
[3] Dele the first as in A.
[4] Supply [thi] in A.   [5] But supply [thus] and read quyète.

rente, 1915 f (-t CD).(: entente *n.* : sente *misit*), 4747 f (-t D) (: wente *ivi*).

reprèue, 1504 f (reprefe D) (: leue *credere*), 2225 f (-oue † B, -efe D) (: leue *creditis*).

requèste, 4719 f (: leste *minimos*), 5176 (-[e] CD), 7312 f (-t D) (: at the meste : at the leste).—requèst, 2990 f (-e B) (: feste *n.*); requèst ‖ is, 1450 (-e B).

reyne (Cotgr. reine), -e herę, 6453 (-e he C, rene D).

roche (O. Fr. roche, roke), -e, 4339 (rok C, rock D).

route, rowte, 271 f (-t D), 1698 f (-t D), 1903 f, 5065 f, 5344 f, 5379 f, 6428 f, 6450 f (-t C), 6765 f, 6915 f, 7858 f.

    Rhyme words —aboute (all but 1698, 6428, 6915), withoute (271, 1698, 6428), oute (6915), shoute *inf.* (1698), doute *n.* (5065, 6428), knyghtes stoute (7858).

ruÿne, 5049 f (: deuyne *inf.* : defyne *pres.* 1 *sg.*).

saue-garde (O. Fr. sauvegarde), 4801 B (saue-gard[e] A, saf cundwÿt hem C, safę conduÿt hem D).

sege (cf. assege), 6142 CD (thassègë A, thassàge B); -e, 1169 (sege(e) B).

signe, 3994 ; -e of, 5826, 8015 (-e of [his] D).

sire, 2042 (-[e] BD)[1]; -e, 2501 (sere C, here ‡ D), 2544 (sir BD), 6117 (syre C, sir D); -e his, 2925 (sir D).—sirę come, 2917 (syr B, for † D).

space, 505, 714 f, 1852 f, 2156 f, 2209 f (sp[a]ce B), 3303 (gracë AB), 5998 f, 7039 f CD, 7040 f AB, 7305 f, 7992 C, 7993 f, 8067 f.

    Rhyme words.—*face, gracę,* and *place* (q.v.), also, chace *imv. pl.* (2209), pace *inf.* (1852).

stuwę, stewe (cf. O. Fr. estuve), 3443 f (: mewe); the stewe dore, 3540.

table, 6800 f (tabele C) (: honourable, honurabele C).

tente, 6511 f (-t C) (: entente), 7208 (-ę ther B), 7385 f (-t CD) (: wente *iit*).

terme, 7059, 7453 ; -ë holde, 7572 (-[e] D, hestis ‡ C).

title he, 488 (tytęle C, *stanza not in* D).

trone, 5741 f (: sone *adv.*), 5748 f (: to done), 5837 f (: sone *adv*).

vncle (*dissyl.*), 1172, 1183, 1207 (C †), 1221 (D †), 1231, 1324,[2] 1579, 1739, 2188, 2217, 2561, 2809, 3487, 3684 (vncle [myn] D), 4420,[3] 5601 ; vncle (*dissyl.*) herde, 2185; vncle, 1335 (-e hir D [4]). (C always spells the word with an interior e, vnkele, but never makes it a trisyllable.) [5]

---

[1] "Sire my nece wole do wel by the." (Hardly to be regarded as a 9-syl. verse.)
[2] Supply [*myn*] in AB.   [3] Dele (*for*) in A.
[4] In a rather later hand.   [5] In 2188 supply [*myn*] in C.

vniuerse (Lat. universum, cf. Fr. univers), 2878 f (vniuers(it)e A) (: the worse).

vrne[1] (Lat. urna, rather than Fr. urne), 6674 f (: torne (turne) *inf.*).

vsàge, 150.

vermìne, 3223 f (: determyne *inf.*).

verre, 1952 f (: werre).

veyne, 5605 f (: restreyne *inf.* : peyne), 6780 f (: peyne : pleyne *plorem*); -*e*, 866 (vayne D).

viàge, 3574[2]; -*e*, 1160 (A *too short*); vìage, 2146.

visàge, 5524 f (vesage C) (: ymage); 8201 f (: age : ymage).

ymàᵨe, 4897, 5526 f (: visage), 8202 f (: age : visage).

§ 22. Exceptions to § 21 (cf. § 21, note 2).

acòrd (O. Fr. acorde, acord), 4592 (-ę B; *l. om.* † E).

àngwyssh (O. Fr. anguisse, angoisse), (i.) 5506 (-guys C). (ii.) 4817 (-guys C, -gwisshe D).

aungel (O. Fr. angele, angle), 5306 ‡ C (Iouc AB; Iouę D (?))[3]. (Cf. ten Brink, § 221.)

bestę (O. Fr. beste), 2852 (best BD).

brochę, broch (O. Fr. broche), (i.) broch, 4212 (-ę BC, -e (of) gold (?) C), 8024 (-ę BD; C †); -ę ‖ yow, 8051 (broch B, -ę (?) D); -ę ‖ that, 8053 (broch B). (ii.) -*e*, 7403 (broch B, -*e* [and] that C); -*e* he, 8032.

còncord (O. Fr. concorde), còncord and, 3348.

cùrtyn (O. Fr. curtine, cortine), cùrtyn pyke, 2902 (-teyn C).[4]

marbel (O. Fr. marble, marbre), 700 (-il C, -le D) (cf. § 21, n. 4).

phisỳk (O. Fr. phisike), 2123 f (fisyk B, fysik C, physik D) (: lyk *pred. adj. sg.* : pyk *fish*).

pres, prees (O. Fr. presse), (i.) cf. 173 f, 2734, 2803, 4765 f. (ii.) pres he, 2728. [Var. D presę.] In all the above cases *pres* = throng; in the phrase *leye on presse, presse* occurs, 559 f (: holynesse).

ràket (O. Fr. rachete), ràket to, 5122 (rakett D).

rebel (O. Fr. rebelle, *noun* and *adj.*), Al haue I ben rebel yn myn ententę, 1609.

rèfuyt (O. Fr. refuite, refuit), (ii.) 3856 (-fut BC, -fute D).

rèlyk (O. Fr. relique), rèlyk ‖ hight, 153 (-ike C, -ique D).

---

[1] Apparently then a new word: "a vessel that men clepeth an vrne."
[2] Supply [*to*] in C.
[3] Cp. has *Iouc*; E. Harl. 4912 John's have *But any aungel*.
[4] Supply [*in*] in A.

rescoùs (O. Fr. rescous, rescousse), (i.) 4084 (rescousse D). rèscous, (ii.) 478.

skàrmyssh (O. Fr. escarmouche), s. al, 1696 (scarmich B, scharmus C, skarmisshe D †); s. of, 2019 (scarmich B, charmys B, scarmysshe D).[1]

sours (O. Fr. sourse), (ii.) 7954 (sors D, giound ‡ C).

text (O. Fr. texte), text ‖ ful, 4199 (tex B, tixite † E, tixt is C); text ‖ to (so C), 6072 (-ę D).

tràuers (O. Fr. traverse), 3516 (-eręs B, curtyns ‡ D). [Plural?]

ÿssuę (O. Fr. issue), 6568 (is- BD, isseu C).

Nobley (O. Fr. *nobleıe*, *noblée*) occurs once (before a vowel), see 6332. Cf. *chımeneye* (O. Fr. *chemınée*) and *valey* (O. Fr. *valée*) (§ 33, n. 2).

§ 23. Nouns in -*aunce*.

That -e counts as a syllable is clear not only from rhyme, but from the cases in which *mischaunce* occurs in the interior of the verse before a consonant (5332, 6024; cf. also 3132). For convenience, *balaunce*, *daunce*, *romaunce*, and *traunce* are included in this list. Interesting words are *asèuraùnce*, *desèsperaùnce*, *obèysaùnce*, *signi- fiaunce*, *suffisaunse* (var. *sufficiaunce*), *vengeaunce*.

In the following list all rhyme-words are given, except nouns in -*aunce* :—

ȧbundaùnce, 3884 (hab- A, ab- D †).

àlliaùnce, 4588 f.

aqueyntaunce, 6485 [2]; acqueÿntaunce, 6492 (-ns CD).

asèuraùnce, 7622 f (esèur- B, ass[è]ùr- C, ass[è]uraùns D).[3]

balaùnce, 1551 f, 6222 f (-auns D).

chaunce, 1549 f, 2432, ‡ f B (*pl.* ACD), 8031 f (chauns D).

còntenaùnce, 1637 f (. daunce *n.*), 2102 f, 3821 f, 4384 f. [Var. C cuntenaunce; D countyn-.] còntenaùnce, 6902 (cuntenauns C, countenauns D).

contìnuaùnce, 2919.

daunce, 517 f (: auaunce *inf.*), 1638 f (: contenaunce), 2191 f (: penaunce), 3375 ‡ f C° (: ordenaunce), 6093 f (dauns D) (: penaunce).— daunce, 3537 (C †), 6811 (dauns D).

delÿueraùnce, 4864 f (delib- C).

desèsperaùnce, 1615 f (des[es]p- CD), 2392 f (dis- C, des[es]p- D) (: daunce *inf.* : traunce *n.*).

---

[1] 9-syl. line in A.

[2] Thaqueyntaunce (The aqueyntau[n]se C, The acqueintauns D) of those (this BC, thes D) Troians (-yans B, -iaunes D, Troylus C) to (for to C) chaunge.

[3] If we read *dcye* before this word we can shun the -eu-.

dessèueraùnce, 4266 f (dis- BD).
disauenaunce, 1596 f C (l. disauaùnce inf.).
dìsplesaùnce, dysplesaunce, 3322 f, 4137 f.
doutaùnce, 5625 f (doughtauns D), 5706 f; cf. 200 f C.
gòuernaùnce, 1304 f (: daunce inf.: myschaunce n.), 1552 f, 2105 f, 2527 f (generaunce † B, sustenaunce ‡ D), 3269 f, 3323 f, 3787 f (gouerẹnaunce B), 4586 f.—gòuernaùnce hire (poss. sg.), 3058.
ìgnoraùnce, 4136 f, 5646 f, 5663 f, 5733 f; -e, 3668, cf. 2133 ‡ C.
instaùnce, 2526 f.
mischaùnce, myschaùnce, meschaùnce, 92 f, 1307 f (: gouernaunce.: daunce inf.), 2104 f, 3533 f (: ordenaunce: traunce inf.), 4227 f (mysschance D) (: auaunce subj. 3 sg.), 4865 f, 5153 f (-ns D), 6223 f (-ns D), 6722 f (-ns D), 7797 f (myschauns D, mys-schaunce C) (: auaunce inf.). myschaùncë (bef. csts.), 5332 (mes- B, mischauns[e] D), 6024 (mes- B, myschaunse C, mischauns[e] D).—myschauncé‖ in, 3132 (meschaunce B, myschauns[ë] C, mischéf ‡ yet D).—mischaùnce, 118 AB (-é‖ and B).[1]
moùntaunce, 2792 (mountẹnau[n]s C); moùntance, 4574 (moùntẹnans C).
obèÿsaùnce, 3320 f (obseruaunce † D).
òbseruaùnce, 1197 f (: daunce inf.), 3812 f; cf. 198 ‡ f D, 2430 ‡ f B, 3320 † f D.—òbseruaùnce, 5445 (-ns D).[2]
òrdenaùnce, 1595 f (: disauaunce inf.), 3377 f (puruyaunce ‡ C), 3530 f (: myschaunce n.: traunce inf.), 5626 f (ordinauns D), 7968 f (ordinauns D). [Var. BD ordinaunce; B orḍy-.]
penaùnce, pennaùnce, 94 f, 1614 f (pen[a]unce C), 2190 f (: daunce n.), 5004 f (: traunce n.), 6091 f (-ns D) (: daunce n.), 6724 f (-ns D), 8034 f (-ns D); cf. 201 f CD (-ès AB).
persèueraùnce, 44 f (: plesaunce: auaunce inf.).
plesaùnce, 46 f (: perseueraunce: auaunce inf.), 3268 f, 3786 f, 3813 f (displesaunce † C), 4264 f, 4374 f, 4386 f, 5069 f (-ns D) (: daunce inf.), 5081 f (-ns D), 5155 f (-ns D), 6177 f (-ns D), 6304 f (-ns D), 6677 f (-ns D), 6927 f (-ns D) (: remembraunce: daunce inf.), 7623 f (-ns D), 7971 f (-ns D); cf. 5761 f CD.—plèsaunce, 6324 (-ns D), 7094 (-ns D); plèsaunce or plesaùnce, 2846 (-ns D).
pùrueyaùnce, pùruyaùnce, poùrueyaùnce, 1612 f, 3375 f (daunce ‡ C°, pùrvëaùnce D), 5623 f (-ns D), 5644 f, 5662 f, 5708 f, 5732 f, 7809 f (-ns D).—pùrueyaùnce hath, 5639 (-ns D).

[1] But 118 B supply [ye] and read mischaunce in.
[2] In 5445 C dele (l).

rèmembraùnce, 3810 f (-ance C), 4375 f, 4387 f, 5082 f (-anĉe C, -auns D), 6305 f (-ns D), 6678 f (-ns D), 6925 f (-ns D) (: plesaunce: daunce *inf.*), 7807 f, 7970 f (-br[a]unce C, -brauns D).—rèmembraùnce, 7084 (-ns D), 8026 (-ns D), 8054 (-ns D).[1]
rèpentaùnce, 4150 f.
romɹùnce, 3822 f (-ance C).—ròmaunce, 1185 (-ns CD).
signi*fia*ùnce, 6725 f (signe*fya*unce C, significauns ‡ ? D); signy*fya*ùnce, 7810 f (-ni*fia*unce B, -ny*fia*unce C, -ni*fia*uns D). (Synæresis of the italicized vowels.)
substaùnce, 6175 f (-ns D).—sùbstaunce, 4879, 6167 (-ns D).
sùffisaùnce, 4151 f (sufficyaùnce C, soùffi*cia*ùnce E), 6302 f (sùffi*cia*ùnce C, -*ficia*uns D), 7126 f (sùffi*cia*ùnce C, -*ficia*ùns D).—sùffisaùnce, 4558 (-ns C). (Synæresis of the italicized vowels.)
sùstenaùnce, 2527 ‡ f D.
traunce, 2391 f (: daunce *inf.*: desesperɹunce), 5005 f (trau[n]ce C) (: penaunce).
vàriaùnce, 5647 f, 7125 f (-ns C), 8033 f (-ns D).
vèngeaunce, 8071 AB (-geauns D).

§ 24. Nouns in -*ence*.

This ending always rhymes with itself. In the few cases in which it occurs before a consonant in the middle of a verse, the -e does not count as a syllable (see under *prescience* (5683) and *science* (67)) (cf. ten Brink, § 223). For convenience, *defence* and *offence* are included in this list.
absènce, 513 f, 3056 f (-ns B), 4142 f, 5445 f (-ns BD), 6599 f (-se C, -ns BD); -e, 5089 (-ns BD)[2].—àbsence, 7759 (-ns D, -nce be C).
àbstinènce, 5446 f (-ns D).
àduertènce, 7621 f (-ns D); -e, 5360 (-ns BCD).
àudiènce, audyence, 4732 f, 5207 f (-ns D), 6598 f (-ns BD).
cònsciènce, 554 f (concience C).
defènce, 2980 f (A †), 4141 f (diff- B, defense D), 4949 f (diff- D).
dìfferènce, 395 f (-ns CD, deference A).
dìligence, deligence, 2977 f, 4139 f.
èxcellènce, 3057 f, 3830 f, 4116 f, 4167 f.
expèriènce, 7620 f (-ns D); -e, 4125.
ìnnocènce, 2133 (-ns D, ygnoraunce ‡ C).
offènce, 556 f, 2979 f (-nse C), 4861 f.
pàciènce, 7760 (-ns D).

---

[1] Supply [a] in D.   [2] Or, àbsenco (first word in the verse).

prèsciènce, 5726 f (-nt † D); -e, 5649 (prescient D); -e hath, 5660 (-nt D); -ę put, 5683 (-nt D).—prèscience, 5673 (prèscient D), 5724 (prèscient D). (Synæresis in 5673, 5724.)
presènce, 6596 f (-se C); -e, 1545 (presaunce B).
prudènce, 7107 (-ns BD).
rèsistènce, 3832 f.
rèuerènce, 516 f, 3054 f, 4115 f, 4170 f, 4731 f BD (reuęrence A); -e, 2882.
sàpiènce, 515 f.
sciènce, 7618 f (sience C, sciens D). —sciènçę so, 67.[1].
sentènce, 393 f, 4169 f, 4859 f, 5208 f (-ns D), 5725 f.
vìolènce, 4948 f; -e, 5224 (-ns D).

§ 25. (I.) Abstract nouns in -esse. (II.) Feminine nomina agentis in -esse.

(I.) For convenience *distresse, oppresse, presse,* and *redresse* are included in this list. Rhyme words are commonly nouns in *-esse* or in *-nesse*. All other rhyme-words are indicated. For *-essë* before a consonant, see *gentılessë* (3100). For *accèsse, èxcessę,* see § 32.
(II.) All the examples of this ending occur in rhyme or before a vowel.

I. distrèsse, dystrèsse, destrèsse, 439 f (-es D) (: blyssē *subj. 3 sg.*: prowesse), 616 f (-es D), 641 f (-es D), 1011 f (: lesse *pred. adj.*), 1748 f, 1804 f (: dronkenesse : gesse *ind.* 1 *sg.*), 1941 f (-es C) (: shrewednesse : gesse *ind.* 1 *sg.*), 2331 f (distrès D), 2355 f, 2457 f (: impresse *inf.*), 2888 f (-es D), 3087 f (disdresse † B), 3104 f, 3206 f (-es D), 3634 f, 3723 f, 3827 f (sykernesse : gesse *inf.*), 3877 f, 4058 f, 4286 f, 4438 f ABC (: blysse *inf.*), 4632 f (-es CD), 4766 f, 4963 f, 5026 f, 5188 f (-es D), 5383 f (-es D), 5462 f (-es D) (: heuynesse : lesse *pred. adj.*), 5504 f, 5560 f (: heuynesse : gesse *ind.* 1 *sg.*), 5744 f (detresse D), 6333 f, 7078 f, 7957 f.—distrèsse, 550 (-es D)[2].
durèsse, 6762 f.
èxcessę, see p. 87.
fèblesse, 1948 (fièblęnesse B, fèbịlnesse C, fèblenès D)[3].
gèntilèsse, gèntillèsse, 881 f (-nesse D) (: gesse *ind.* 1 *sg.*), 1245 f (ientilnesse D), 1747 f (gentilnesse BD), 1787 f (-nesse B, -nes D), 2353 f (-nesse CD), 3005 f (-nesse B, -nes D), 3244 f (-nesse BC,

---

[1] In D supply [*that*]. [2] Supply [*swich*] in C.
[3] Supply [*that*] in C.

ientilnesse D), 3724 f (-nesse BCD), 3878 f (-nesse C, -nès D), 3990 f (-nesse BCD) (: gesse *ind.* 1 *sg.*), 4256 f (-nesse B, -nes C), 7954 f (-les C, -lnes D), 7980 f (-nesse D) (: gesse *inf.*).—gèntilèsse triste, 3100 (gentileste † B, -nesse C, -nes to D).—gèntilèsse, 4393 (-nesse CD).

largèsse, 4566 f (: gladnesse : gesse *ind.* 1 *sg.*).

noblèsse, 287 f (: gesse *inf.*), 6802 f (nobęlesse C [1]), 8194 f (noble- nes ‡ D).

opprèsse, 6761 f.

presse, 559 f (: holynesse). Cf. *pres*, *prees*, § 22.

prowèsse, 438 f (: blysse *subj.* 3 *sg.* : distresse *n.*), 1717 f (: hardynesse : dresse *inf.*), 1745 f (pruesse C), 6799 f (largesse CD).

redrèsse, 5190 f (retresse B).

richèsse, 3242 f, 6332 f (rich[e]sse B), 6801 f.—rìchesse, 3191 (rechesse B, rehetyng † D).[2]

tendresse. For tendresse how shal she this sustene, 6605 A (tèndrenèsse B, tendirnesse CD).[3]

II. deùynerèsse, 7885 f (deuineresshc C) (: sorceresse).

goddèsse, 6204 f (goddès D) (: lesse *adj. pl.* : wıldernesse) ; For nece by the goddesse Mynerue, 1317 (-des[se] C) ; gòddesse, 8.

hierdèsse, 653 f (hye[r]desse D) (: heuynesse : gesse *ind.* 1 *sg*).

maỳstresse, 1183.

sòrcerèsse, 7883 f (sercheresse C) (: deuyneresse).

§ 26. **Nouns in -*yce*, -*yse*.** For apocope, see *seruise* (315). For *-ë* before a consonant, see *coueytise* (3103).

àuarỳce, 4647 f (aueryce C) (· vice).

còueytise, coueitise, 4231 f (: dispise *ind.* 3 *pl.*), 6031 f (: suffice *inf.* : gyse *n.*), 6040 f (: deuyse *inf.*). [Var. C couetyse ; D couetise.]— còueytise wroughte, 3103 (-e (I)wroughte B, còuetisę ‡ this D).

còwardise, -yse, 5264 f (: emprise), 6775 f (· ryse *inf.*).

emprìse, 1158 f (: ryse *inf.*), 2476 f (empresse † C) (: aryse *inf.* : for- byse *inf.*), 3258 f (: seruyce), 5263 f (: cowardise).

gyse, 2001 f C (wyse ABD) (: ʒe ben wise), 6032 f (: suffice *inf.* : coueytise) ; -e, 7224, 8013 (-ę ‡ C, guise D †) ; guise, 6427 D (wyse AB, wise C).

malice, 3168 f (maleys C) (: nice *adj. pl.* : vice).—malıs if, 3722 (-ice B, -ice ʒif (?) C, -ıce ‡ if D) [4].—màlys hir, 3997 (malice BD, -eys C).

[1] Dele (*a*) in B.   [2] Supply [*his*] in B.
[3] Dele (*the*) in D. Cp. has *tendernesse* ; John's has *tendrenesse*.
[4] In B read *yf* for *of*.

office, 4278 f (-yse C?) (: vice).

sàcrifice, 3381 f (: seruyse), 4550 f (: ryse *inf.*), 7828 f (: dispise *inf.*: wyse *n.*). [Var. BCD -ise.]

seruȳce, -ȳse, -ice, -ise, 82 f, 164 f, 335 f (servys D), 951 f, 956 f, 982 f, 1763 f, 2884 f, 2975 f, 3003 f, 3256 f, 3279 f, 3317 f, 3380 f, 4130 f, 4444 f, 4636 f, 4657 f, 5059 f, 5176 f, 5471 f, 5494 f, 7681 f. [Var. B ceruyse; C serwyse.]—seruìse, seruȳse, 430,[1] 3250, 4230[2].—sèruyse, 3834.—sèruise, 315.

> Rhyme words.—wyse *n.* (82, 164, 335, 951, 956, 982, 1763, 2975, 4130, 4636, 4657, 5059, 5176, 5471, 5494, 7681), wyse *adj. sg. and pl.* (82, 956, 982), deuyse *inf.* (2884, 3003, 3317, 4636, 4657, 5471, 7681), deuyse *ind.* 1 *sg* (3279), emprise (3256), sacrifice *n.* (3380), suffise *inf.* (4444, 5059).

vice, 980 f, 1810 f (nyse ‡ A), 1940 f, 3169 f, 4234 f, 4280 f, 4648 f, 5258 f, 8071 f. [Var. CD vise.]—vicé ‖ for, 3142 (vis[e] C; D †). —vice is, 689 (C † D †) (: vices *pl.*); vice, 252 (vys D), 1937[3], 2974.

> Rhyme words.—cherice *inf.* (980, 1810), nyse, nyce *adj. sg. and pl.* (1810, 1940, 3169, 4234, 5258), malice (3169), office (4280), auaryce (4648), punyce *inf.* (8071).

§ 27. Nouns in -*ure*. Except as indicated, nouns in the following list rhyme only with each other.

armure, cote arm[ùr]e, 8014 (c. armùr B, cote armùre CD).

asùre (O. Fr. azur, asur), see § 32.

àuentùre, 35 f (: endure *inf.*), 368 f, 568 f (mys- ‡ C), 784 f, 1085 f, 1309 f (: disfigure *inf.*), 1366 f, 1827 f, 2604 f (: endure *inf.*), 4059 f, 4209 f, 4986 f (: endure *inf.* : sepulture), 5050 f, 5991 f (: endure *inf.*), 6661 f (-tur D) (: endure *inf.* : sepulture), 7903 f.— disàuentùre, 1500 f, 4959 f (mys- C, disauentur D) (: dure *inf.*), 5417 f, 7811 f; mysàuentùre, 706 f.—àuentùre, 1373 (-ë ‡ bele CD). —mysaùnter[4] ayleth, 766 (mȳsauènture D ‡, mysau(e)ntur(e) B, auèntùrè mys-aylyth † C).—For *paraùnter* (var. C parauenture, perauenture, etc.; D perauntre, perauention, etc.), cf. 619, 668, 854, 1796, 2006, 2458, 3333, 5260, 7354 (perh. trisyl.), 7645, 7889.

crèatùre, 104 f, 115 f, 283 f, 570 f (cry- C), 1502 f, 1802 f, 2855 f (: endure *inf.*), 4914 f (crya- C), 5048 f (crya- C), 5418 f (-tur D), 5429 f (: dure *inf.* : noriture), 6341 f (: dure *inf.*), 6517 f (cria- C) (: dure *inf.*), 6573 f, 6604 f (crya- C, creatur D) (: endure *inf.*), 6747 f (-tur D), 7077 f (*l. om.* † C), 7171 f, 7195 f (cria- C, creatur D),

---

[1] In D supply [*my*].
[2] In 4230 the word stands first in the verse. Either accentuation is permissible. In 4230 C read a[*l*]s[*o*], and so too in Harl. 2392.
[3] In C read *fle*[*me*]*n* and in D *al*[*le*]. [4] Cf. paraunter. See ten Brink, § 263.

8064 f (-tur D) (: endure *inf.*).—crèatùrè (*bef. csts.*), 5110 (crya- C); -tùre, 1383 (crìatoùr C), 5113 (criateure C), 5156 (cryatour C).

cure, 369 f, 469 f (: dure *inf.*), 707 f, 783 f, 1084 f, 1368 f, 1826 f, 3884 f (: endure *inf.*), 4060 f, 6412 f (: endure *inf.*), 7076 f, 7902 f (cur D); -e, 5593 (care D, curẹ than C).

figùre, 366 f, 7812 f.

iniùre, 3860 f (D †).

mesùre, 1503 f, 1800 f.

natùre, 105 f, 113 f, 3858 f, 4913 f, 5430 f C †, 6572 f.—nàture, 6015.[1]

nòritùre, 5430 f (nòretùr D, natùre ‡ C) (: dure *inf.* : creature).

ordùre, 6748 f (-ur D).

scriptùre, 4211 f.

sèpultùre, 4989 f (: endure *inf.* : auenture), 6662 f (*same rhymes*).

statùre, 281 f, 7169 f (stàteùre ‡ C).

§ 28. Nouns in -*ère*.

In the following list are put together, for convenience, *chere, mànere, matere, preyere, ryuere, spere* (= *sphere*). Observe *mànerẹ, màner*. The spelling *èmyspèry* for *hemispere* (see *spere*) is interesting.

chere, cheere (14 A, and sometimes in B), 14 f, 124 f, 181 f, 280 f, 289 f, 433 f, 879 f (shere B), 1125 f, 1234 f, 1417 f, 1445 f, 1556 f, 2214 f, 2352 f, 2446 f, 2597 f, 2626 f, 2811 f, 2896 f, 2938 f, 3072 f, 3174 f, 3271 f, 3334 f, 3484 f, 3589 f (cher C), 4198 f, 4396 f, 4506 f (clere † A), 4552 f (D †), 5317 f (cher D), 6097 f ‡ B, 6298 f, 6394 f (cher D), 6547 f, 6779 f (cher D), 7170 f, 7276 f (shere B, cher D), 7591 f (cher D).—chere (*bef. csts.*), 2660 (-[e] C ; D †), 2592 D (-es AB, -is C).—cher*e*, 1006, 1734 (cher C), 2343 (C ? ‡), 5020, 5060 (cher CD); chere hym, 1663 (cher C); cher (*bef. vowel*), 327 A (-e B, chyr C, chere he D †).—He neither chere (schyr C) ne (*om.* BCD) made ne word (worde B, woord D) tolde, 312 (Shall we read : He neither chere madẹ ne word [ne] toldeʔ The Cp. collation makes no note.).

Rhyme words.—fere *comes* (14), manere (181, 289, 879, 1125, 2597, 2626, 2811, 2896, 2938, 3271, 4552, 5317, 6394, 6547, 7170), dere *adj.* (433, 879, 1417, 1556, 2214, 2446, 2811, 2896, 2938, 3174, 3334, 4198, 4396, 4506, 6547, 6779, 7276, 7591), here *hic* (124, 289, 1125, 3484, 6298), here *inf.* (124, 280, 3334, 3589, 5317), matere (1234, 2214, 3271, 4506), requere *ind.* 1 *sg.* (1445), 2 *pl.* (1556), yfere *adv.* (1234, 2352, 3072, 3589, 4552, 6097 B), preyere (3484, 6298), clere *adj. pl.* (4198, 7170).

manere : (1) manère, 33 f, 182 f, 291 f, 880 f, 1014 f, 1052 f, 1122 f,

---

[1] Supply [*the*] in C ; [*pcs*] in D.

2596 f (matere D), 2628 f, 2664 f, 2812 f, 2893 f, 2935 f, 3058 f, 3273 f, 3676 f (matere BD), 4254 f, 4291 f, 4555 f, 4585 f, 4946 f, 5315 f (-er D), 5580 f (-er D), 5844 f (-er D), 6392 f (-er D), 6549 f (-er D), 7172 f, 8170 f; manère, 1077 AB (-èr D).

(2) mànërẹ, màner, *bef. csts.*, (*a*) mànerẹ, 1333 (-er B)[1], 1542 (-er CD),[2] 1937 (-er C)[3], 2460 (-er BC), 2560 (-er D, *om.* † C), 3631 (-er D, -ẹr of C), 4577 (-er C), 4740, 5664 (-er D), 5939 (-er BCD), 6415 (-er C, -ẹr of D), 7115 (-er CD), 7124 (-er BD, -yr C), 7748 (-er CD), 7918 (-er CD), 8014 (C †; -er D).[4] (*b*) mànër, 313 (-ẹ BD),[5] 321 (-ẹ CD), 495 (-ẹ D), 844 (-ẹ D), 1944 (-ẹ D, -ẹr of C), 2189 (-ẹ CD),[6] 3159 (-ẹ BD), 3469 (-ẹ BD), 5822 CD (other AB), 7478 (-ẹ B), 7582,[7] 7640 (*om.* † C).—mànërẹ, *bef. vowels*, 742 B (-er CD, -erẹs A), 2001 (-er C), 2353 (-er C). (3) mànẹre ‡ vpon, 7751 A (more CD).

Rhyme words.—here *inf.* (33, 1014, 1052, 2664, 3058, 4585, 5315), dere *adj.* (33, 880, 2812, 2893, 2935, 4254, 4291, 4946, 6549), chere *n.* (182, 291, 880, 1122, 2596, 2628, 2812, 2893, 2935, 3273, 4555, 5315, 6392, 6549, 7172), here *hic* (291, 1122, 3676, 5580), matere (1052, 3273, 4254), lere *inf.* (2664), yfere *adv.* (4555), stere *inf.* (4946), bere *bier* (5844), clere *adj. pl.* (7172), spere *sphere* (8170).

Note.—In most of the cases under 2*a.* and 2*b.* above, *maner* is used in such phrases as *no manere routhe, som manere syde, swych maner folk, any manere syde, euery manere wyght, youre frendly* (L *fremde*) *maners speche*, etc. 313 is an exception, however.

matere : (1) matère, 53 f, 265 f, 1055 f, 1090 f, 1236 f, 1580 f, 2124 f, 2216 f (mat[e]re B), 2332 f, 2514 f, 2596 ‡ f D (manere ABC), 2711 f, 2779 f, 3032 f, 3128 f, 3212 f, 3274 f, 3358 f, 3676 f BD (manere AC), 3751 f, 4148 f, 4251 f, 4503 f, 5313 f (matier D), 5480 f AB (martìr D),[8] 5746 f (-er D), 7106 f (-er D), 7314 f (matier D), 7359 f (matier D), 7951 f (matier. D).—matèrë (*bef. csts.*), 968 (-[e] B, matyr[e] C), 3371. (2) matère, 144 (matyèr (*dissyl.*) and C), 1346 (-yr C, -er D), 1780 (-er C). (3) màtère, 4485 AB (thyng C, thing to D), 7685 (-er C, -er D ‡), 7735 (-er C, màtier *dissyl.* D).

Rhyme words.—dere, deere *adj.* (53, 1580, 2216, 2514, 2779, 4148, 4251, 4503, 5313), here *inf.* (53, 1055, 2711, 3212, 5746, 7314, 7951), *audio* (3032), refere *inf.* (265), manere (1055, 3274, 4251), clere *inf.* (1090), clere *adj. pl.* (7359), stere *guberno* (1090), *gubernare* (3751), chere *n.* (1236, 2216, 2596, 3274, 4503 (clere † A)), yfere *adv.* (1236, 2124, 2332, 3358), here *hic* (1580, 2711, 3358, 3676, 4148), 7106, 7359), preyere (3128), desire *inf.* (5480).

[1] Supply [*to me*] in A.   In all read *fremde* for *frendly* (etc.).
[2] Supply [*and*] in D.   [3] In C read *fle[me]n*; in D, *al[le]*.
[4] In A read *arm[ur]e* (with Furnivall).   [5] In D read [*a*]*far* for *ferre*.
[6] In C supply [*now*].   [7] In C read *defet* for *disfigured*.
[8] The correct reading seems to be *martire*. C omits the stanza. G has *matere*. No note in the Cp. collation.

preyere, (1) preyère, 2296 f (C ?), 3129 f, 3481 f, 6295 f (pràyèr D).
[Var. C preière; D prayère.] (2) preÿere, 4773 AB (prayer D †);
preÿere, 1538 (preÿers B, preleris C, praÿèr D). (3) preyere A
(preyer BC, prayer D), 2575 (bef. vowel), to be pronounced preyère
or prey'r (monosyl.), according as we read goodly (DGCp. John's)
or goodëly BC (A has good †).

Rhyme words —dere adj. (2296), matere (3129), here hic (3481, 6295), chere n. (3481, 6295).

ryuère, 5075 f (reuere C, ryuer D) (: dere adj.).

spere, sphaera, 4337 f (: dere adj. : fere comes), 7019 f (: dere adj. :
clere adj. def.), 8172 f (: manere).—hèmy-spère, 4281 (-sper(i)e B,
èmësper(i)e C, èmyspèry D).

Note.—O. Fr. gutiere becomes joter before a consonant in 3629 (gotur D); pere (masc.), shows an irrational -e : As he that was with-outen ony pere, 8166 (: boughten dere : here inf.), cf. ten Brink, § 222.

§ 29. Nouns in consonant +re (variants in -er and -ere).

cedre (O. Fr. cedre, cf. A.S. céder), 2003 (siderę C).

chaumbre, chambre, chaumber, (i.) dissyllabic before consonants, 2004
(-ir C), 2020 (-yr C), 2202 (-erę C, -ir D); cf. 358, 547, 2258,
3508, 3518, 3630, 4882, 4904, 5014, 5016 CD, 5394 CD, 6655.
(ii.) Slurred before vowels, chaumbre || and, 1641 (-ęr B, -ir C, -rë ‡
and D); chaumbęr afyr, 3698 (-ęre a B, -re a D ; C (?)); cf. 2797,
5016 AB, 5394 AB; chambre he, 6565 (-ęre he C) (cf. 6363,
6877). But,—But wel ye wot the chaumbrë is but lite, 2731 (-er B,
-ir C). [358 B, 547 D, 1641 D, are to be corrected.]

disclaùndre, 5226 (disclandre B, disclaundyr C, disclaunder D).[1]

iaspre : iaspre || vpon, 2314 (-ër on C, -ar on D, iapery † vpon B).

lettre, 2298 f (lettere C) (: bettre adv. : vnfettre inf.), 2782 f (lettere C)
(: bettre adv.). Before consonants (all forms dissyllabic): lettre,
656,[2] 1188 ‡ C, 2148, 2170 AB, 2175, 2205, 2240, 2246, 2261,
2281, 2286, 2303, 2403, 2421, 2787, 3034, 3062 (D †), 5222
(honour ‡ C), 7656,[3] 7704, 7758, 7785,[4] 7792, 7965.[5] [In 7995
B alone seems to have the correct reading.[6]]. Before vowels the last
syllable of lettre is slurred. Thus,—lettre I, 171 (-ęr C);[7] so in
2091, 2146, 2176 ABD, 2178 AB, 2232 (-ër to C, -rë to D), 7732,

---

[1] In C read mostë for mot.
[2] Old-style figures indicate that C has lettere (dissyllable). B has often lctre, which also occurs in A 2421.
[3] A needs transposition of thow and a lettre.   [4] In D read [vn]to.
[5] Supply [that] in AC and [why] in D.
[6] For This lettre this Troylus, Cp. and John's have Troilus this lettre. G agrees with B, reading This troilus this lettir thouht al strange.
[7] Metre defective in D.

7761, 7963, cf. 2405 ‡ C. (In this last list old-style figures indicate that C has lettẹre. As before, B sometimes omits one *t*,—*letre*.) lettre here (*hic*), 2208 (lettere *dissyl.* C)[1].—Towchyng thi lettre that thow art wys ynowh, 2108 A (*but omit* that, *with* BC; D *is hopeless*).[2]

ordre, ordre is, 336 (ordẹre C); ordre of, 5679; ordrë ay, 5444 (ordre ay D, orderẹ til C).

poudre, poudre in, 6672 (-ẹr D, -ir ‡ which C).

sucre, 4036 BGCp. (seukerẹ C, sugre D, sour A).

wỳuere (O. Fr. guivre, wyvre), 3852 f (wiuere C, wythir † D) (: delyuere *inf.* : slyuere *n.*).

Note.—*Feuere* (A.S. *fęfcr*, *fęfcr*) appears to have been influenced by the French. There are four examples of the word in the *Troilus* (see § 18).

§ 30. Nouns in -ỳe, -ie.

When the ending rhymes with itself, the rhyme-words are left unregistered. A remarkable verse is 4647, where we appear to have *enuỳe* ‖ *ire* (see under *enuye*). *Remedye* has the by-form *remède*.

armonye, 8175 f.

astronòmye, 4777 f (: lye *inf.*).

baùdery̌, 3239 f (-ye BC, bawdery D) (: folye : companye).

companie, companye, compaynye, 191 f (-y CD), 450 f, 1171 f (-y D), 2573 f (-y CD), 2798 f (-y C), 3238 f (-y D), 4590 f, 5369 f, 5864 f, 6429 f, 6810 f. [Var. B compaigniae, -ye; CD eumpanye, cumpany.]

compaignye he, 7580 (-paynye B, -panye C, -panie D).
Rhyme words.—aspie *inf.* (191), eye *n.* (450, 6810), hye *n.* (1171, 2798), thrie *adv.* (1171), denye *inf.* (2573), prye *inf.* (2798), hye *adj.* (4590), hye *adv.* (5864), gye *inf.* (4590), deye, dye *inf.* (5369, 5864).

còpye, 2782 (-ie BD, còpi C).

curtasie, -ye, 2571 f (-eysi C, -esy D) (: companye : denye *inf.*), 6427 f (-eysie B, -eysye C, -esie D).

enuye, 4937 f (: deye *inf.* : crye *ind.* 1 *sg.*), 7119 f, 7842 f (: lye *mentiuntur* : dye *inf.*).—That pride enuỳe ‖ ire and auaryce, 4647 ACD (That pride and ire enùye and auarice B).[3]

espie (cf. *spie*), esple, 2197 (aspie B, a spie C, a spye D).

[1] ABC we have *sent*, which the metre requires us to emend to *sent[e]* or *sendeth*. D reads *sent to*; Cp. *sente*.
[2] Cf. also 7702 C, where, however, we might read *lokyn* (which would still leave a hard line). 7702 is wrongly filled up by the corrector of C.
[3] Cp. = B; E Phillipps 8252 Harl. 2392 = ACD; G Selden B 24 John's read *That pride enuye and ire and auarice*; Durham II 13 reads *That ire enuy and auerice*.

fantasye, 1567 f (-y D), 3117 f, 3874 f (-y D), 4346 f, 6132 f (C †), 6624 f, 6692 f (-y C), 6721 f, 6824 f (-y C), 6986 f (-y C), 7886 f. [Var. BCD fantasie ; CD fantesie ; D fantesy.]

Rhyme words.—crye *inf.* (3117), dye *inf.* (4346), espye *inf.* (6132), drye *pati* (6624), lye *mentiri* (7886).

folỳe, 194 f (-y C), 452 f, 545 f (-y D), 1024 f (-y D), 1859 f (-y D), 2158 f (-y D), 2253 f (-y D), 2371 f (-y D), 2595 f (-y D), 3236 f (-y D), 3680 f, 3709 f (-y D), 3721 f (-y D), 3828 f (-y D), 4224 f (-y C), 6132 f CD †, 6173 f (-y C), 6626 f (-y D). [Var. BCD folie.] folỳe men, 532 (-ỳ C ; D ?).—fòlye for, 6688 (fòlie B, -y C). fòlye, 5919 (-y C, fooly D); fòlye he, 821 (-y CD); fòly ofte, 3168 (-ye BCD). fòly wroughte, 3604 (fòlye BC). The only case of elision with slur is *folye it*, 6240 C, where, however, the right reading is *filthe*.

Rhyme words.—aspye *inf.* (194, 1859, 2595, 3680), eye *n.* (452), multeplie *inf.* (545), dye *inf.* (1024, 2158, 2253, 2595), crye *inf.* (2158), lye *mentior* (2371), *mentiri* (3721), *mentiuntur* (4224), thrye *adv.* (2371), drye *pati* (6626).

frenesye, 727 f (-ie D) (: dye *inf.*).

glotonye, 6733 f (-enye CD) (: signifie *ind.* 3 *pl.*).

ialousye, -ie, ielousye, 1840 f, 3679 f (B †) (: espie *inf.* : folye), 3829 f (ielosy D), 3863 f (: crye *inf.*), 3872 f, 7576 f (: dye *inf.* : malencolye).—iàlousỳe, 1838 (ielosy D), 1922 (ielousy D), 3852 (ièlosỳe ‡ the D), 3866 (cf. 3867 ‡ D). [*ialousye (dissyl.*), 4010 A (ielousye D), should be *ialous* (as in B ; ielous C).] [Var. C ielusie ; CD ielousie, ielosye.]

ianglerye, 7118 f (iangelerye C, iangellarie D).

iupartie, 1550 f (: thrie *adv.*), 1857 f (-dy D) (: folye : aspie *inf.*), 3710 f (-dy D), 3719 f (-dy D ‡) (: folye : lye *inf.*), 6048 f (: in hye), 6174 f (-dy C), 7064 f (: spie *n.*), 7279 f (iupardi C), 7893 f (: lye *mentiuntur* : dye *inf.*). [Var. B iupartye ; C iupardie, -dye ; D iupardye, ieopardie. The divided form *iu-partye*, 6174 B, is interesting.]

lytargie, 730 f (litargye B, lytargye C, litargie D) (: plye *ind.* 3 *pl.* : melodye).

maladye, maledye, 419 f (: deye *morior*), 1568 f (-dy D), 6679 f (-dy CD) (: dye *inf.*), 7594 f (maledy C, malady D) (: dye *inf.*).— maladye awey, 2600 (-dy BCD).

malèncolỳe, 6723 f (-ly C, -lie D malycolye B), 6985 f (-ly C, -lie D), 7579 f (-ly C, -lie D, melencolye B) (: ialousye : dye *inf.*), 8009 f (-ly C, -lie D) (: dye *inf.*).

melodie,-ye, 733 f (-dy D) (: lytargie : plye *ind.* 3 *pl.*), 3029 f (: hye *adv.* : glorifie *inf.*), 6825 f, 8176 f.

nòuellerỳe, 1841 f (nouelrye BC, nouelry D).

pàrtie, 1479 (-tye B, -ti C).

poësye, 8153 f (-ie B, -y D) (: dye *moriatur* : enuye *imv. sg.*).

poetrie, 8218.[1]

prophesie, 7884 f (-cie BD, professye C) (: fantasye : lye *inf.*); -cỳ be, 7857 C (-cies B -sies AD).

pye, 3369 (pie B).

rèmedỳe, -le, 6285 f (: dye *inf.*), 6691 f (-y C), 7280 f (-y C), 7573 f (-y C) (: dye *inf.*).

    Remède and red by erbess she (*l.* he *as in* CD) knew fyrre,[2] 661 (remèd*ye and* C, remèdy *and* D).

    Remède in this yf ther were any wyse, 5551 (remèd*i in* C, remèd*ye in* D)[3].

    But what is thanne[4] a rèmede vnto this, 5934 (rèmade, remèdie vnto C, rèmedye vnto D).

    Ther nys non other rèmedye yn this cas, 6424 (C *has a spurious line*).

    Syn that ther is no rèmedye in this cas, 7633.

spie (= speculator), a spie, 7066 f (a spye BC, espie D) (: iupartie).[5] (Cf. *espie.*)

surquidrye, 213 (sur(i)quidrie A, sùrquidè and C, sùrquydè and D).

trecherye, 3120 f (-ie CD) (: crye *inf.* : fantasye).

vilonye, vilenye, vylonye, 1026 f (vilany D) (: folye : dye *inf.*), 1523 f (welany C, vilany D) (: crye *pres. ind.* 1 *sg.* : dye *inf.*)[6], 4683 f (: lye *mentiantur*), 6853 f (: hye *ind.* 3 *pl.*). [Var. BD vilanỳe; B vylenye, vilenye; C velenye.]

§ 31. Nouns in *-ye* unaccented.

    This list includes (i.) comèdye, tregèdie, paròdye, and (ii.) nine nouns in *-rye* (following an accented vowel).

augùrye,—By sort and by (*om.* D) augurye (augury D) ek (eke D) trewely (trewly B, truly D), 4778. And treweliche (truely D) ek (eke D, *om.* C) augurye (augery C, augurrye D) of this (thise B, thes D, these olde C) foweles (-is B, foulis C, foules D), 6743.

comèdye, 8151 f (: tregedie).

consistòrie, consistòrie *among*, 4727.

contràrye, in his contràrye, 7742 f (D †) (: wàrye *ind.* 1 *sg.*).

---

[1] In A supply [ye]. [2] In C read *he knew* for *he knyt*.
[3] In B supply [were]. In D omit the second (*in*). [4] C om. thanne.
[5] In A supply [*l*] [6] In AB dele *ony* (*any*) or *that* (?).

fùrye, fùrie,—fùrye *is*, 3879; fùrye *of*, 6091 (-ȳe‡ of 'D); fùrye *as*, 6575 (-y *as* D; C†); fùrye *and*, 4915 AD (fùr*ie* a*nd* BC); fùrie (*dissyl.*) ‖ sorwyng, 9 (wight ‡ that D).—Anoy smert drede (-[e] C) fùry *a*nd ek sikẹnesse, 5507 (*ye* and BD, *-ie* a*nd* C).

lètuàrye, 7104 f (lat- B, letewarye C) (: carye *ferunt*).

memòrie, 3671 f (-y D) (: transitorie), 6946 f (: storie : victorie).

mysèrie, mysòr*ie in*, 4934 (myn ‡ deth in C).

paròdye, 7911 f (paradie D) (: vnbodye *inf.*).

stòrie, stòrye, 6948 f (-y BD) (: memorie : victorie), 8014 f (: victorye); stòry, 3905 ‡ f D (storyes AB, storijs C).—stòrye (*dissyl.*), 3341 (-y CD; B†)[1].—stòry (*before consonants*), 1116, 7400 (-yẹ B)[2], 7414 (-yẹ B), 7457 (-iẹ B).—stòrye *it*, 7197 (*-y it* B, *-i as* C, *-y as* D).

tregèdie, 8149 f (tregeedie D) (: comedye).

victòrie, -ye, 6949 f (-y C) (: memorie : storie), 8015 f (: storye); victòry, 3906 ‡ f D (: story) (victories AB, -ijs C).

Note.—Compare the proper name *Mercurye*,—*Mercurye for the loue of Hiersc ek*, 3571 (Mercure B, -rie C, -ry D); *Ther as Mercurye sorted hym to dwelle*, 8190 A (-ie B). *Study*, 2265 (-ye B, -ie C, *dissyl.*), is perhaps rather from *studium* than from *estudie*.

§ 32. A few Romance words that end in a consonant in French take an *-e* in the *Troilus*.

accèsse (O. Fr. aces), 2400 f (: besynesse), 2663 f (axsesse C) (: sykenesse); *-e*, 2628 (acces C, actis † D).

asùre (O. Fr. asur, azur), 4212 f (: auenture *n*. : scripture).

auentaylle (cf. O. Fr. esventail), 7921 f (: by-waylle *inf*. : mayle).

darte (O. Fr. dart), 5433 f (: departe *pres.* 1 *sg.*); cf. 5134 f (§ 36, n. 2).

disioynte (cf. O. Fr. disjoint *p.p.*), 3338 f (-t D) (: poynte *inf*); disioynt[e], 7981 f (-e B) (: apoynte *inf*.).

excesse (rather from Lat. excessus than from Fr. excès), èxcessẹ dọth, 626 (-ces C).

mene, meene (O. Fr. meien), 3096 f, 6467 f (meane D); *-e*, 689 (C † D †), 7914 (-e † out D).

Rhyme words.—I **mene** (3096, 6467), clene *adj.* (3096).

pere (O. Fr. per), see note at end of § 28.

trauàȳle, trauàȳlle (O. Fr. travail), 21 f, 475 f, 1088 f, 2522 f, 3364 f, 8215 f. tràuayle, 6547.—trauaylle, 372 (-H D †)[3]; cf. tràuayl, 6457 ‡ C (*l.* labour).

[1] In C insert [*none*]. [2] In B read *telle*[*th*].

[3] A doubtful line. "Ymagynynge (-ing D) that (C *inserts* neyther) trauaylle (-uaille B, -uayle C, -uaile G, -vaiit D) nor (a*nd* D, ne G) grame (gaine C, game D)." Mr. Austin's collation gives *grace* for *grame* as the reading of Cp.E, but registers no other variants.

Rhyme words.—auayle *inf.* (21, 2522, 3364, 8215), sayle *inf.* (1088), fayle *inf.* (2522, 3364), rascaylle (8215), meruayle *n.* (475). [Var. B trauaille, trauelle (2522); BD trauaile.]

Note 1.—In 2817 Professor Child has suggested to me that we should read *by gynne* (dat. of *gyn* 'contrivance,' etc.) instead of *bygynne* (ABD) or *be-gyn* (C) (: with-inne). I find that G actually reads.—*And inwardly thus ful softely by gynne.* The Cp. collation shows no variants.

Note 2.—For *feuere, feuer*, see § 18.

Note 3.—April, etc. Of Aperil (Aperille C, apparaille D, Aprill G, April E) whan clothed is the mede, 156 (no variants in Cp. collation); And seyde (seid D) frend yn April (Aperil B, Aprille C) the laste, 3202 (not in G, no variants in Cp. collation); Donn fille (Out ran C, Out ronne John's) as shour (schoure G) in (of C) Aperill (Aprille C, Aprill DG) swythe (ful swythe C), 5413. *Aperil* seems to be certain for 156, 3202, and for 5413 C. In 5413 the other MSS. require *Aperillë*. On the forms of *April* in Chaucer, see Varnhagen's "Ueber die verschiedenen Formen des Namens des vierten Monats bei Chaucer," appendix to Freudenberger, Ueber das Fehlen des Auftakts, pp. 85 ff. (Erlanger Beiträge zur engl. Philol., IV). Varnhagen is inclined to believe that *Avril, April, Aperil (Averil), Aprillë* are all known to Chaucer. See also *Murray's Dictionary*, s.v. *March* (L. Martius) occurs in 1850 as *Marchę* AD (*March* BC).

§ 33. Words ending in Old French in -*é* and -*ée* end indiscriminately in -e in Chaucer. (See ten Brink, § 223 V.)

In the following list no variants are registered. Old-style figures indicate that a vowel follows without elision.

aduersité, 25 f, 404 f, 2861 f, 4467 f, 7446 f, 7738 f.

auctorité, 65 f.

beauté, 102 f, 1479 f.—beautë, 975, 1421, 1426, 1431, 1433, 1483, 4572, 4583, 7181, 7277, 7618, 7770.

benyguité, 40 f, 1617 f, 2881 f, 4127 f.

bestialité, 735 f.

bounté, 4771 f.—bountë, 2529, 3724, 4116, 4505; b. hem, 4106.

charité, 49 f, 4096 f.

cité, cyté, 100 f, 129 f, 149, 5867.—citë, 59, 2231, 5347, 6141, 7206, 7269, 7849, 7850, 7859.

contré, 7837 f.—còntrë, 7834; c. hath, 1127.

cruelté, 586 f, 1076 f, 5434 f.

degré, degree, 244 f, 437, 844 f, 6324 f, 7199, 7723 f.

dèité, 3859 f.—dèite *infernal*, 6205.

destené, destyné, 520 f, 2176 f, 3576, 5621 f, 5631, 6364 f.

deynté, 1249 f.—deÿntë, 3451, 6801 (adj. ?).

duëté, 3812.

dyuersité, 3247, 8156 f.

èntrë, 1162 (-ee B).

[§§ 33, 34.] *of Chaucer's Troilus.* 89

felicité, 3656 f, 4533, 5142 f, 7126, 8181 f.
honesté, 1791, 6238 f.
iolyté, 559.
liberté, 1858 f, 2377 f, 6019, 6648 f, 7663 f.
meyné, 127 f.—meÿnë, 1699, 6889.
mutabilité, 851 f.
natiuyté, 1770 f.
necessité, 1708 f, 5676, 5686, 5695, 5719 f, etc.
niceté, nyceté, 906, 2371 ‡ D, 2373.
pité, pyté, 522 f, 892 f, 1740 f, 3875 (plëté B),[1] 5030 f, 5393 f, 7187 f, 7961 f.—pĭte, pÿte, 23, 2662 (pĕte *it* C), 4908 (pi(e)ty D), 5451, 5509; pĭte *on*, 5486 A (-ë hadde B, -ë felte D); *-e and*, 7462 ‡ D. [7777 † C.] [Var. C pete; D pitee.]
possibilité, 1692 f, 3290 f.
predestĭné, 5628 f.
preuyté, preueté, 2482 f, 3125, 5773 f.
prolixité, 2649 (D †).
propreté hire, 5054 (properte B, properete C, prosperite † D).[2]
prosperité, 3659 f, 4469 f.
qualité, 2873 f, 4496 f.
quantité, 412 f, 6049 f.
soueraynté, 3013 f.
subtilté, -tée, 7617 f, 8145 f.
sùrẹtë, 1918 (seùrtë BCD); seùrté, 4520 (seurẹte C).
vnité, 2871 f, 8229 D.
vanité, -yté, 5198 f, 5365, 5391 f, 8180 f, 8200 f.

Note 1.—For *pardé*, cf. 717 f, 845 f, 1754 f, 1817 f, etc., etc. (pàrdë, cf. 2404, 5186, 5203, 5752, pàrdë harm, 3755) (see also § 34, VI.). For *benedicite* (*trisyllable*) see 780 f (bendistee B, ben(e)diste C), 3599 f, 3702.
Note 2.—For *chimeney*[*e*] (O. Fr. cheminée), see 3983 f (chymeneye B, chemeneye C, chymeny D) (: tweye). For *valey* (O. Fr. valée), see (i.) 6430 (-ẹ B), (ii.) 943 (valy C). For *nobley* (O Fr. nobleie, noblée) before a vowel, see 6332.

§ 34. Romance nouns which have no final -e in French show none in the *Troilus*. (A few Latin words are included in this section.)

In the following list of examples, variants are not regarded except as they concern *-e* (which some MSS. add sporadically, but which is never sounded). MS. D is usually disregarded altogether. The accent is recessive unless otherwise marked. For convenience the

---
[1] B alone of the four is metrical. Cp. also has *piëté*. [2] A has *his* †.

examples are classed as,—(I.) words in *-er*; (II.) words in *-our*; (III.) words in *-ent, -ment*; (IV.) words in *-aunt*; (V.) words in *-s*; (VI.) words in a vowel; (VII.) miscellaneous words. For nouns in *-ion, -ioun*, see the chapter on metre.

I. Words in *-er*:

astrologer, 4257 f (see note below).
auter (O. Fr. alter, autier), 7829.
auaùnter, cf. *auauntour*.
coler (O. Fr. colier), (i.) 8023. (ii.) 7174 (colèr ‡ be-hynde C).
corner (O. Fr. cornier, -e) (ii.) 6938.
courser (O. Fr. corsier), 6448 (curser B, coursir C).
daunger (O. Fr. dangier), (i.) 1469 (-(e) C †), 2328, 2461, (ii.) 1484, 4163 (daunder † A).
dyner (O. Fr. disner), (i.) 2574, 2682. (ii.) 2645.
herber (O. Fr. herbier), 2790 (erber BC).
heroner (O. Fr. haironnier), (ii.) 5075 (goshauk ‡ C^c).
laurer (O. Fr. laurier), 3384, 3569; cf. 7470.
leyser, layser (O. Fr. leisir), (i.) 1312,[1] 2454, 3042, 7308. (ii.) 3358; l. haue, 3352; l. had, 4401.
messager (O. Fr. messagier), 4259 f (massaugere C, messanger D).
papir (O. Fr. papier), (ii.) 7960 (-er ‡ ful C).
percher (quasi O. Fr. *perchier), 5907 C (*l.* morter).
power (O. Fr. poeir), (i.) 5120, 6529. (ii.) -èr, 1252.
presoner (O. Fr. prisonier), (ii.) p. he, 4841 (pris- BD).
quarter (O. Fr. quartier), (ii.) 7243, 8061.
soper, souper (O. Fr. soper), (i.) 3437 (A †), 3452. (ii.) 2032, 3449,[2] 6881.
squyer (O. Fr. escuyer), (ii.) 191 (swyer B).

Note.—In some of the words in this list the ending is doubtless the native *-er* (A.S. *-ere*). So also in *tapere*, 1425.

II. Words in *-our*:

accusour, (ii.) 4292 (C †; -er D).
auctor, (i.) 394 (autour BCD), 1103 (auter D), 1134 (-our B, autour D); cf. 3344, 3417, 4038, 7451. (ii.) cf. 3858, 4607.
auaùntour, (i.) 1809 (-er À). (ii.) 3150 (A †), 3151 (-e A), 3156.
conquerour, 7157 f (-e B).
errour, (ii.) 1001 (-(e) B), 5655 (-(e) B).
fauour, 1748, 2221.

---

[1] Insert [*this*] in A.   [2] Insert [*the*] in C.

flour, 7155 f (-e C).
hònour, (i.) 888, 1442, 1557, 1565, 1823, 2654, 3001, 3859, 4933, 5229, 5232, 6237, 7723, 8098. (ii.) 1382, 1847, 1989, 2912, 4566, 4821, 6177, 6771 (-ur B).—honoùr, (i.) 120, 1246, 1790 (C?), 2517, 2538, 3007, 3786, 6104, 6223, 6328. (ii.) 287, 1967, 2995 (-(e) B), 3005, 5991 [1].—dìshonoùr, 1816 ; dishònour, 7429 (-(e) B, -our & (*slur*) C).
làbour, 965 (-(e) AB), 4276, 6457 (-(e) B, trauayl C). (ii.) 948, 1035, 2289 ; làbour he, 3917 (l. (that) he C).—laboùr, (ii.) 5084, cf. 199.
langour, (i.) 5506 (-ur C, -or D), 6405 A (-(e) B, -or D). (ii.) 6608 (longyng CD), 6631 (-(e) B, -ur(e) C), 6760 (-ur C).
licour, 5182 (-quore D).[2]
myrrour, mirour, (i.) 1351 (-(e) B) ; (ii.) 365. myroùr of, 1927.
parlour, (ii.) 1167.
peyntour, 2126.
rumour, (ii.) 6416.
sauour, (ii.) s. han, 1354 (-aur A).
socour, (ii.) s. hem, 4793 (-(e) B, mercy CD).
tràytour, -or, (i.) 87, 4866. (ii.) 3115 (tractor B), 4542 (-ous A) ; traytoùr comune, 4667.
tremour, 6618 (-or A).
tresour, (i.) 4747, 6176 (-or(e) C). (ii.) 3716 (-or C).
vapoùr eterne, 2853.
vigoùr, (ii.) 3930.

Note.—*Harpour* for *harper* (A.S. héarpere) occurs, see 2115.

III. Words in *-ent, -ment*:
accident, (i.) 3760. (ii.) a. [h]is, 6167.
accusëment, 5218 f (-e B, acusament C).
argument, (i.) 5139, 5841 f. (ii.) 5618.
assènt, 5008 f (-e B), 5197 f (-e B, assen C), 5216 f (-e B), 5595 f.
auisement, auysement, (i.) 5598 f (-e B), 5962 f, 8174 f (-e B) (: went *p.p.*). (ii.) 1428 (-(e) B).
element, 8173 f (-e B) (: went *p.p.*).
entendement, 6358 (B †).
hardiment, 5195 f (-e B, hardy ‡ men C).
instrument, 10 f, 631 f (: myswent *p.p.*), 6805 f (-e B) (: ywent *p.p.*).
iuggëment, 5961 f.
pacient, 1083.

---

[1] Insert [*an*] in AC. BCp. John's have *an*.   [2] Insert [*out*] in A.

parlément, (i.) 4805, 4873 f (-e B), 5006 f, 5326, 5959 f. (ii.) 4880 (-men C); p. he, 5039, cf. 5221.

precident, 4875 f (president BCD).

sentement, 2885 f (-e B) (: present *adj.*), 5839 f (-e B). (ii.) 1098.

serpent, (i.) 3679. (ii.) 7860.

talènt, 2987 f.

tòrment, (i.) 6360, 7003 (-(e) B, tur(ne)ment C). (ii.) 6790 (-(e) B, turnent † C); cf. 404, 5473, 5554, 7017, 7955. tormènt, 8 f.

IV. Words in -*aunt*:

auaùnt, (i.) 1043 (-(e) B), 1812 (-(e) B)

geaùnt, 7201.

graunt, (ii.) 5214 (-(e) B).

remenaunt, 6038 (-(e) B).

scruaunt, (i.) 15 ‡ B, 6536, 7708. (ii.) 3825, 4329.

tyraunt, 2325.

V. Words in -*s*:

auỳs, (i.) 5078 f (-e C) (: wys *adj. sg.*). (ii.) 620, 3295.

burges, 5007 (borwis C, burgeys and A).

cas, (i.) 29 f, 271, 568, 836 f, 1370, 1507 f, 1510, 1542 f, 1689, 1814, 2153 A †, 2431 f, 2560 f, 2696, 2765 (B †), 3121, 3125 f, 3683 f, 4461, 4952 f, 5078, 5082, 5456 f, 5542, 6171, 6424 f, 7427, 7633 f, 8001. (ii.) 1843, 2741 (cause C), 3014, 5050, 5233, 5290; cas he, 5311.

choys, (ii.) 5633 (cloys † B), 5642, 5721.

conuers, 8173.

cors, (ii.) 7105 (C †).

cours (O. Fr. cours, course), (i.) 2055, 2470 (coures B), 8108. (ii.) 1992.

crois, (ii.) 8206 B (cros A, crosse D), cf. p. 63.

encrès, (ii.) 2418 (-ees B, encreseth ‡ hope C), 4618 (-ce D), 5919 (-cresse B).

paas, pas, 1705 (-ce B), 1712 (-e B), 2434 f, 3123 f, 6423 f, 6967 f (pace B).

pàlais, pàlays, -eys, paỳlays, (i.) 324, 1161, 1593, 1701 (*l. om.* † C), 2018, 2179, 2337 (to p. ward) (payleysseward B), 2622, 4371, 4376, 6564, 6875, 6903, 6907, 6910. (ii.) 6886, 6888, 6905.

paradys, 7180; cf. 5526.

pes, pees, (i.) 352, 3899, 4151, 4762 f, 5117, 5266 AC, 6014, 6021,

§ 34.] *of Chaucer's Troilus.* 93

6052 (C †), 6126. (ii.) 3937, 5354, 6008, 6127; p. herafter, 5266 B, 6224.

pows, (ii.) 3956 (pous B, pous(e) C).

pròces, (i.) 1509, 2700 (-cesse D),[1] 3176 (-cesse BD), 3312 (cesse D), 4581 (-cesse D), 5080 (-cesse BD). (ii.) 1353 (-cesse BD), 1377 (-cesse B, -cesse D), 1570 (-cesse B, mater C), 1763, 7854; cf. 6946 (before h*au*e).

prys, (ii.) 1266; p. hym, 2670; p. hath, 273.

purpos, (i.) 142, 379, 1062, 1130, 1982, 3172 (therto ‡ C), 3291, 3973, 5396, 5782, 6539, 6858, 7117, 7133, 7392, 7939. (ii.) 5, 4209, 4699, 6082, 8162; p. how, 7823.

remòrs, (ii.) 554.

recoùrs, 2437 f.

socoùrs, 2439 f.

solàs, 31 f, 1545 f, 6970 f.

surplus, 4722.

trays (Fr. traits, *pl.*), 222 (-(e) B).

tretis, -ys, 4726, 4798, 5332.

vòys, (i.) 1911, 2887, 2934, 6940, cf. 4565. (ii.) 111, 422 (-ce C), 2935, 4079, 4857 (acord C), 5809, 7164; v. he, 725 (-ce B), 6999.

Note.—For *ruby* (O Fr. *rubi, rubis*), see VI., note.

VI. Words ending in a vowel (not -e):

anoỳ, 5507.

araỳ, 2349 f, 3378 f, 4640, 6332; a. his, 2352.

assaỳ, 6170 f; cf. 7672 ‡ C.

ascrỳ aros, 1696 (the acry C, in the skye † D).

cry, 1281.

delàỳ, 3721.

dieù; a dieù, 5292 (adew C, and dey ‡ D); cf. 2170 CD. (Cf. pardieùx, 197; pàrdieux, 1844; depàrdieux, 2143, 2297; parde, § 33, n. 1.)

lay, 1149 f, 2006 f.

May, 1135, 1197, 3904 f, 6788 f, 7207 f.

mèrcy, (i.) (ii.) 535, 1503, 1676, 2161, 2940, 5811, etc., etc.; graunt mèrcy, (i.) (ii.) 3491, 4147, 5294, 6322; grant mercy, 1324 f.

prow (O. Fr. prou), 333 f (-e B), 2749 f, 7152 f.

tissew (O. Fr. tissu), t. heng, 1724 (-ewe D, C †).

tòrney, 6331.

---

[1] In AC supply [*out*]; in D supply [*hem*]. BECp. have *oute*; John's has *out*.

vèrtu, (i.) 429, 1078, 4591, etc. (ii.) 438 (-ue B), 4130, 4977, etc.—
vertuę, 896 AB (-u CD). [Cf. vertulès, § 49, n. 5.]

Note.—For *ruby* (O. Fr. *rubi, rubis*), see 1670 (rebe C), 2172 (-ye C), 4213 (-ię C), 6912.

VII. Miscellaneous.

Note.—Variants are usually not registered. In none of the following words is there a sounded -e, though -e is occasionally written, even in A. D very frequently adds such irrational -e's (-e, -ę), B not seldom (as *agrefe, appetite, arte, chare, conforte, conceyte, conseylle, cowarde, delite, dispaire, desire, deuoure (for deuoir), estate, fole, meschefe, ost, porte, poynte, refreyne, reporte, resorte, rewarde, scorne*, though in the case of most of these words the form without -e also occurs), and in C -e or -ę is sometimes found (e. g., *conscylę,* 985 ; *desirę,* 4324 ; *abitę,* 109 ; *partę,* 5087 ; *effectę,* 212, etc.).

abèt, 1442 (abek C).
agrief (a = on, O. Fr. gref, grief), 3704 f ([a]gref A), 4463 f, cf. 5275 f.
appetit (O. Fr. appetit, -te), 6339 f (-e BD).
art (O. Fr. art), (i.) (ii.) 659, 920 f, 1096, 4175 f, 5928 ; a. hire, 1342.
atỳr (ii.) 181.
awaỳt, (ii.) 3299 (*om.* † A).—awaỳtę, 3421 (-t BC).
baroùn, 4695 f, 4852 f.
bayard, 218.
busshel, 3867 (beschop † C, busshęll ‡ of D).
caytyf, (ii.) 4766.
char (O. Fr. char, cf. charre), 4546 f (-e BD) ; charhors, 7381 (-e h. D).
closet, 1684, 2300, 3505, 3529.
còmfort 845, 4736 (confert B), 4980 ; cònfort, 7531.—comfòrt, 528 f, 590 f, 2840 f, 2978 f. (Cf. discomfort.)
comparyson, 5112 f.
conceỳt, (ii.) 989.
cònseyl, coùnseyl (O. Fr. conseil), (i.) 985, 2129, 5101 (A?), 5547. (ii.) 5776, 6793 (-e B).—counseỳl, (i.) 743.
contek (etym. dub.), (ii.) 7842.
cost, 3364.
coward, *as adj.*, c. drede, 6235 (-ę B) ; coward(e) herte, 6071 (-d BD ; C †).
daun, (i.) (ii.) 70, 4851, 7851, 7852.
debàt, 1838 f (-e CD).
dèlit, delỳt, (i.) 1794 f, 4218 f, 6330, 6340 f, 6501 f (-yȝt C). (ii.) 762, 4152, 6198 (-yȝt C).
desdaỳn, 5853 f.

dèsespeìr, (i.) 605 (dis[es]pair D).—despeỳr, 813 f (dispaỳr B; D †); despeỳr that, 5616 (-(e) D, dispair(e) B). (Cf. also 779 A, 1091, 1615 f.)

desìr, (i.) 311, 374, 465, 607, 2419 f, 3328 f, 4105, 4324, 4373, 4477 f 4493, 5235. (ii.) 296, 381, 2422, 3268, 4388, 5057, 5234, 6061; d. hym, 4381.

despeyr, *see* desespeir.

des-, displt, (i.) 1796 f, 2134, 3879 f, 4216 f, 6337 f, 6498 f. (ii.) 207, 4547, 4786, 7606, 8056; d. hym, 902; d. hadde, 4629.

desport, 592 f, 4971 f.

denoir, (ii.) 3887.

deuỳn (O. Fr. devin), 66.

dìscomfòrt, 4973 f, 5510 f. (Cf. comfort.)

effèct (Lat. effectus, cf. O. Fr. effect), (i.) (ii.) 212, 2305, 2464, 2651, 3188 D (-*e* B), 3347, 4422, 4657, 5552, 5956, 6541, 6740, 7372, 7786, 7984, 7992, 8147.

engỳn, 1650, 3116 f.

estat, (i.) (ii.) 130, 287, 432 (estal † A), 884, 1290, 1304, 1550, 1746, 1792, 1836 f, 1966, 2223, 5246, 6198, 7388, 8112, etc.

eyr (O. Fr. air), 7034.

faucon, fawkon, (i.) 4626. (ii.) 5075.

feith, feyth (O. Fr. feid, feit, fei, apparently with Eng. abstract -*th*), (i.) 89 (feyt C), 336 (-(e) B, fay C), 1254, 2048, 2188 (fey B, fay † vnkele C), 4593, 8027. (ii.) 1247, 1495, 2588 (-(*e*) B), 7622 (feight D), etc.

fol, fool, (i.) (ii.) 532, 618, 630, 1455 (fel A), 1485, 2930, 3741, 4307, 6461, 7149, 7886.

fòrest, 7598, 7600.

fruyt, 385.

fyn, (i.) (ii.) 1510, 1612, 1842, 1879, 2681, 2967, 3355, 3395, 5139 f, 5584, 8191, 8192, 8193, 8194, 8195, 8215.

gardeyn, -yn, (i.) 1899, 2202, 4580. (ii.) 1904, 2199. [With slur, 1905 A.]

greyn (ii.) 3868.

grief, (ii.) 2717. (Cf. agrief.)

growel, (ii.) 3553 (gruwel B).

groyn, (ii.) 349.

guerdon, -oun, 6957, 7752, 8215 AB; g. hire (*eam*), 818.

habit, 109.

ìdỳòt, 903.

lambўc (O. Fr. alambic), As licour (-quore D) out (*om.* A) of a (*om.* D) lambyc (-bic B, -bik C, -bykę D) ful faste, 5182.
lessòn, (ii.) 2893.
mantel, (ii.) 1465.
mўschef, (i.) 755.——chèf, 5276 f; -chièf, 4464 f.
nerf, (ii.) 1727.
nўgard (O. N. hnogg-r + Romance -and), n. haue, 4221.
ost, (i.) (ii.) cf. 80, 4691, 5261 f, 6284 f, 6379, 6435, 7115, 7713 (hest(ę) C). [Var. B oost, ostę, oste.]
pailet, (ii.) 3071.
part, (i.) (ii.) cf. 918 f, 3148, 3281, 4173 f, 4718, 4843, 5087 (-(ę) C), 5665, 5690, 7681; p. he, 2413.
pencel (O. Fr. penoncel), (ii.) 7406 (-sel BC).
peril, (i.) (ii.) 84, 475, 1691, 1960, 3209, 3695, 4775, 7388; p. he, 3753.
port (O. Fr. port 'beaiing'), (ii.) 1077 (-e B).
poynt, (i.) 7648 (-(e) B). (ii.) 5320 (-(e) B).
preson, prison, 2302, 7247. presòn, -oùn, 3222 f, 4768 f.
pylgrym, 7940.
quysshon, 2314 (-en B, -yn C), 3806 (-en B, qwischin C).
refreўn, 2656 f (-e B).
refuyt (O. Fr. refuit, refuite), (ii.) 3856 (-fut BC).
renoùn, 481 f, 1382 f, 1746 f.
repòrt, 593 f, 5512 f (resport A).
reson, -oun, (i.) 796, 1451, 3693, 4250, 4826, 5234, 5236, 5710, 6340. (ii.) 764, 6245.
resòit, 2976 f.
rèspect, (ii.) 8181, cf. 4748.
respìt, 6500 f.
rewàrd, (ii.) 2218, 8099.
saf cundwўt hem, 4801 C (safę conduўt D, saue-gard[e] sente A, saue garde sente B).
scorn, skorn, (i.) 318, 335. (ii.) 514, 902.
scryt, 2215.
sermon, (ii.) 2050. sermòn, -oùn, 2200 f, 2384 f, 5499 f.
seson, (ii.) 168 (-on A).
seynt, (ii.) 6916.
signal, (ii.) 5480.
signet (O. Fr. signet, sinet). (ii.) 2172 (synet C).
sort (O. Fr. sort), (i.) 76 (soʒt † B, byfor ‡ D), 2839 f (: kankedort :

comfort n.). (ii.) 3889 ABC (D †), 4778 (D ?), 6063 (-e B, -ę ‡ to D), 6066 (-e D ?).
soun, sown, (i.) (ii.) 732, 1890, 2203 f, 6943.
spirit, (i.) (ii.) 362, 423, 3650, 4193, 4620, 4982, 5373, 5448, 5814, 5861, 5872, 6282, 7575.
> Note. The metre requires that *sprit* (7575 C), *spryȝt* (5448 C), and *spryt* (C in vv. 307, 4193, 5814, 5872) be expanded to *spirit*, and 423 C also needs correction; cf. 4620 C.

stomak, 787.
stryf, 1865 f (-ft A, -fe B), 1922 f, 6704 f.
subgit, 1913 (subiect C, suget D).
treson, 1878, 8101. tresoùn, 107 f.
venym, (ii.) 3867.
ver (Latin), 157 (veer B).
vessèl, 667 f.
wardeyn, (ii.) 3507, 7540.
werbul (from the verb, cf. O. Fr. werbler), w. harpe, 2118.

§ 35. The genitive singular of nouns, both Anglo-Saxon and Romance, ends in the *Troilus* for the most part in *-es*, irrespective of original gender and declension.

> Note.—CD usually have *-is* or *-ys*; B has *-is* in 453 (*brestis*), but regularly *-es*. In the following list trivial varieties in spelling are not registered.

Examples are,—

I. aspes, an a. lef, 4042 (-is C, auspen D).
asses, 2127.
beddes, 359, 3524.
brestes, 453.
bryddes, 2006.
dayes, 1989, 1992 (daijs C), 4543.
dethes wounde, 4539.
dowues, 4338.
emes, 1551, 1557.
horses, 223.
kynges, 226, 889, etc.
loues, 15, 34, 905, 2191, etc.
lyues creature, 4914 (C †), 5429 (other ‡ c. C); lyues ende, 7917 (last[e] ‡ D).
maydes, 3147 (maydenys C, -denes D).
mouses, 3578.
nyghtes, 1990, 4684.
shames, 180.
someres, 3903 (-eris C, somers D).
sonnes, 4546 (sunnys C, sunnis D), 7602 (sunnys C).
sorwes, 2151 (-owis D).
tales, 1345.
widewes, 109 (wedewys C, wydewys D), 170 (wedewys C); wydewes, 1199 (-owes B,

H

98   *Observations on the Language*   [§§ 35, 36.

-owis D, wedewis C); wydwes, 1307 (-owes B, -owis D, wedewis C).
wightes, wyghtes, 660, 1280, 7121.
wykes, 6862 (wekes B, woukis C, wookes D).
wittes, 3773.
worldes, 6242, 7257, 7421 (wor[l]des B), 8195, 8214.

> Note.—In the phrase *lyues creature* (see 4914, 5429), as well as in *that lyues body* (*Hous F.* 1063), Professor Skeat regards *lyues* as an adverb (A.S. *lyfes*) : see his notes, *Minor Poems*, p. 347, *Prioresses Tale*, etc., *Glossary*, s.v. *lyues*. The Anglo-Saxon adverbial *lifes* is, however, never used attributively, and one can hardly believe that *lyues* in *a lyues creature* was felt by Chaucer as very different in construction from *shames* in *shames deth* (*Leg. Good W.* 2064, 2072), or *dethes* in *dethes wounde* (*Troil.* 4539) or *dethes wo* (*Arthour and Merl.*, 2108), or *lyues* (undoubtedly a genitive pure and simple) in *lyues day* (*Leg. Good W.* 1624), or, especially, *mannes* in the line, *Ector or ony mannes creature* (*Troil.* 1502). For a rather late example of the construction, cf. "Whereby my hart may thinke, although I see not thee, That thou wilt come, thy word so aware, if thou *a liues man* be" : *Tottel's Miscellany*, Arber, p. 154. Professor Bright (*Modern Lang. Notes*, 1889, col. 363) explains *lyues* (gen.) *body* as "a living person's body," "a living man," taking *lyf* in the familiar Middle English sense of "a living person;" but this does not explain *lyues creature* or *lyues man* (unless we regard these phrases as due to analogy) and seems less likely than the interpretation of *lyues* in the sense of "of life"; cf. Byron's *a thing of life* (=a living thing = a lyues creature). On *Lyues* and *dethes* cf. Mätzner, s. vv.

II. disdayn[e]s prison, 2302(-ys C, disdeynous ‡ D).
fortunes, 4467.
Mayes day the thridde, 1141; a Mayes morwe, 2183.
neces, 1161, 1163, 2179, 2546, 2696.
spouses, 6709.
[doutës † wenynge, 5654 B (doutous AD).]
[furies (*dissyl.*) 1521 ‡ C.]

> Note 1. In one case the scribe of C has formed a genitive (to the destruction of the metre) by adding to a proper name *is* as if a separate word : *Nisus is dou3tyr*, 7473 (*nisus* ABD). Compare with this the form *herteis* (gen. sg.), which occurs at least three times in C (viz., 1620, 2482, 3887).

> Note 2.—*The goddesse wrethe*, 933 C, error for *goddes*, may serve as one more argument, in addition to those mentioned by ten Brink, § 109 a, that *s* in the genitive was unvoiced in Chaucer's pronunciation. Cf. also *heuynesse* for *heuenes*, 6256 B. It is a little odd that ten Brink should cite Mod. Eng. *else* as having a voiced *s* ("dagegen freilich *else* mit tönendem *s*=ME. *elles*").

§ 36. A few words make a genitive without change of form. Thus,—

his lady grace, 1117, 3314 (ladi C), 4672, 4619 ‡ D (ladyes thank AB, ladyis thank C).

this lady name, 99 ABD (ladyis C).

his lady mouth, 812 (ladyis C).

his lady heste, 3999 (his l. liste † B, his ladijs heste C, his ladies heest D).

his lady honour, 7440 (his [lady] h. B?, C; ladies D).
But,—
 my ladyes depe sikes, 7038 (ladys B, ladijs C, lady D).

any herdë tale, 4076 ACG (hard † B, heerdis D).
oure tongë deference, 395 A (tonges difference B, tungis differens C, spechis ‡ differens D).
hertë blod, 1530 (hertys B *later,* -[e] D).
myn hertë lust, 1915 (-es B, -is C, -is ‡ lyf D).
his hertë reste, 3973 B (-es A, -is CD).
hertë . . . suffisaunce, 6302 BC (-es AD).
hire hertë variaunce, 8033 (-es AD, -is C).
his hertë boteme, 297 C (-es AB, -is D). [Cf. 6816 C (?).]
But,—
for *hertes* cf. 1620 (-is BD, -eis C), 2482, 3887, 3973, 8103, 8112.

thi brother wyf, 678 B (brotheres A, brotheris CD).
his fader carte, 7028 B (fadres AD, fadiris C).
jour fadir tresoun, 117 D (fadres B, faderis C).
But,—
hire fadres shame, 107 (faderes B, faderys C, fadris D).
my fadres graunt, 5214 (faderis C).
youre faderes sleyghte, 6158 (faderys sleyt[e] C, fadres sleyghtes D).
here fadres . . . tente, 7385 (faderis C).

Note 1.—The following cases seem to be instances of *heuene* in composition, not genitives (cf. A.S. heofon-cyning, -dréam, -ríce, etc.):—*heuene blysse*, 3546 (hevyn blis[se] D),[1] 4164 BE (blyssyd ‡ A, blis[se] C, heven blisse D), 4499 (heuenes B, hevyn blis[se] D); *heuen quene*, 6256 CD (heuenes A, heu(y)nes(se) † B); *heuene* ‡ *egie*, 4838 D; cf. *the heuenes heighe*,[2] 1989 (the h. (h)eye B, [the] heuenis eye C, the hevenis eye D); *heuenys* † *lyst*, 4962 C. (*Heuene, -es*, etc., dissyllabic throughout.)
Note 2.—Compare also *peple speche*, 3426 AD (peples B, puple ? C[3]); *Criseyde darte*, 5134 A (-es BD -[e] C)[4]; *Criseydë hous*, 6891 A (-es BD, -is C). But,—*Criseydes net*, 4575 (-is D); *Criseydes eyen*, 4972 (-is D); *Criseydes herte*, 7138 (-is C).

§ 37. Many proper names in -s have the genitive identical in form with the nominative. Thus,—
the kyng Priàmus sone, 2 (Pryamys D).
Tròylùs vnsely auenture, 35.
Pandàrus voys, 725 (-ys C, -is D).

[1] Supply [*For*] in A; [*in*] in D. [2] Read *ye* (: wrye *inf.*). [3] C defective.
[4] In this verse perhaps the scribes of AC took *Criseyde* for a nom. and *darte* for an *inf.*, and this may be right. The Cp. collation has no note.

Tròylùs persone, 1786.
Pàndarùs byhest, 2414, 3188.
Pandàrus lore, 2426.
Deiphèbus hous, 2599 (dèiphèbus (?) D), 2625.
Pandàrus reed, 2624 (-is C).
Pàndarùs entente, 2808.
Venus heriynge, 2890.
Tròylùs seruyce, 4657 (cf. 7369 ‡ B).
Hèrculès lyoùn, 4694 (-is B).
Calkas ere, 4725.
Calkas doughter, 5325.
Saturnus doughter, 6200 (Saturnes BD, -ys C).
Phebus suster, 6253.
A broche . . . That Troÿlus (*dissyl.*) wàs, 7404 ABC (D defect.).
Nisus doughter, 7473 (nysus (is) douȝtyr C).
Àrchymòris buryngẹ, 7862 (archimoris B, arichmoure † C, Archemories D). [*Archimori bustum sexto ludique leguntur.*]
Tyḍeus (Tideus BD, Thedeus C) sone that doun descended is, 7877.

Some other genitives of proper names—
Ioues name, 878 (Iouues B, iouys C, Iovis D).
Ioues doughter, 2845 (Iovis D).
natal Ioues feste, 2992 (-is C, D †).
Ioues face, 5999 (iouys C; Ioue in his ‡ face D; = in 's ?).
Martes highẹ seruyse, 3279 (-is CD).
Cupìdes sone, 7953 (-is C, Cu(s)pìdes D).
Argẏues wepynge, 7872 (arthmes † C).
Penèlopeés trouthe, 8141 (-è[é]s B, Penàlopeés D).
Pallàdiòn[e]s feste, (161 Palladyon[e]s B, Palas † dionis C, Pallàdiòns ? D, Pallàdiònës G).
Troyes town, 7131 B (-ë AC); Troyès cyte, 100 (-yis C).
    Note.—The Latin genitive *aloes* may here be added—

        Tho woful teris that they leten falle
        As bittre weren out of teris kynde
        For peyne, as is *ligne aloes* or galle, 5797-9
        (lignum aloes C *one syl. over measure*).

§ 38. The plural of nouns (A.S. and Romance) ends regularly in *-ës* (*-is*, *-ys*) or (if the nominative ends in a weak *-e*) in *-s* (Child, § 22; ten Brink, § 202, 206, 210, 213, 225). Examples are :—

[§ 38.] *of Chaucer's Troilus.* 101

I. belles, 1890 (-e[s] C, -is D).
  foughles, 787 (fowles B, foulys C, foulis D); fowęles, 6743 f (-is B, foulis C, foules D) (: owlys : foul(e) is).
  soules, 5866 (-is C), 8206.
  tales, 2017 (-is C), etc., etc.
  walles, 7029 (waH = wallis C).
— bemes, 7006 (-ys C, -ęs (?) D).
  stremes, 305 (-ys CD).
  lymes, 282 (lemys C, lymys D), 5844 (lemys C, lymmes D), cf. 7164.
  pawmes, 3956 (paumys C).
  sones, 1255 (-ys C, -is D).
  stones, 1953 (-ys CD, stonnes B).
  sires, 4841 (serys C, sir[e]s D).
  shoures, 470 (-is C, -ys D).
  speres, 4705 (-is D), 8123.
  sterres, 1994 (-ys C, -is D), 6637 (-is C), 8175.
  auentures, 3 (-is D); cf. creatures, 7891.
  apes, 906 f (-is C, -ys D).
  iapes (-is CD), 904, 930, 2252 (D †).
  shippes, 58 (-is D).
  sobbes (-is CD), 4910, 5037.
  leues, 4887 (-ys C, -is D), 6095 (-ys C).
  loues, 6707 (-ys C), 8211.
  wyues, 6742 f (-ys C, vyues B, wiffes D) (: lyues *pl.*, -ys C, liffes D); cf. 1204 f.
  bokes, 788 (-ys C, -is D), etc., etc.
  sykes, 4999 (-ys C, -is D), etc.
  Grekes, 533 (-ys C, -is D), etc, etc.

rokkes, 2469 [1] (rochis C^c).
wrecches, 3775 f (wricħes B, wrechis C, wrecchis D).
tacches, 3777 f (tecches BD, techis C).
facches, 3778 f (fecches BD, fecchis C).
speches, 3352 (-ė ‡ C).
ages, 1112 f (: vsages *pl.*).
dogges, 5288 (-is C).
ymàges, 1458 (emagis C, ymagis D).
yates, 7540 (-is C).
nettes, 4197 (-is C).
nyghtes, 4598 f (nytyʒs C, om. † D) (: myghtes *pl.*).
routes, 1705 (-ys C).
rites, 8212 f (vyces † A, riʒtes † D) (: appetites *pl.*).
shotes, 1143 (shottis D).
festes, 7792 f (-is C) (: byhestes *pl.*, -e[s] B, -is C).
abodes, 3696 (abedes, abydis, abodis).
dedes, 4392 (-is CD), 7166 (-is C), 8133.
flodes, 4602 (-is C).[2]
gledes, 1623 (-en C, -is D).
goddes, 3226 (-ys C, -is D), 6068 (-is C), 8213, etc.
nedes, 355 (-is CD), etc.
hondes, 3956 f (-is C) (: bondes *pl.*).
clothes (-is C), 2629, 5440.
monęthes, 1135 (monthes B, D?); monthes, 7129 (monythis C, monęthes D), etc.
othes, 7626 (-is CD), etc.

[1] Read *myl[ne]-stones* at the end of the line in AD.   [2] Supply [*so*] in A.

II. dayes, 2831 f (daijs C) (: de-
layes, -is C); cf. notes 1, 2,
below.
weyes, 1907 f (: aleyes *pl.*,
aley[e]s C).
III. bowes (= boughs), 1906 (-is
CD).
bowes (=bows *arcus*), 4702 (-ys
D).
browes, 7176 (-is C).
clawes, 2012 (-is CD, clewes B).
hawes, 6060 f (-is C) (cf. *lawes*).
hewes, 2343 (-is D, -is C (?)),
2936 (-is C, -e is D), 5816
(-ys C, heweʒ D); hewys,
1106 f A (-is BD) (: newe
is). \
lawes, 1127 f (-is D) (: sawes *pl.*),
6059 f (-ys C) (: sawes *pl.* :
hawes *pl*).
sawes, 1126 f (-is D) (: lawes
pl.), 6057 f (-is C) (cf. *lawes*).
thewes, 1808 (-is C, -ys D).[1]
throwes, 6569 (-ys C), 7564 (-is
C).
trewes lasten, 6764 (treus[2] lestith
C).
wawes, 1086 (-is D), 7472 (waH
‡ C).
IV. arwes, 4706.
pylwes, 3286 (pilous B, pilwis
CD).
sorwes, 54 (sorǫwé D), 705 (-[es]
B, -ys C, sorow † D), 847
(-ys C, sorǫwes D), 2427 (-is C,
-ǫwis D (?)), 3147 (-e C, -ow
D), 3747 (-is C, sorow D),
3924 (dayès C, daies D), 3976

[1] Supply [*goode*] in D.
[2] Dissyllable needed.

(-is C), 4014 (-ys C), 4794
(-ys C, sorǫwis D, sorwues
dissyl. B), 4816 (-ė C, -ǫwis
D), 4910 (-is C, -ǫwis D),
5003 ‡ (peynes AB, teeris ‡
D), 5163 (-ıs C, -ǫwes D),
5590 (-e BC, -is D), 6499 (-e
C), 6561 (-is C), 6567 (-is C,
-ė D), 6628 (-è C, peynes D),
6629 (-ė C), 7718 (-is C †).
V. fethẹres, 353 (-ris D, federis C),
7909 (fedres D, federis C).
fyngres, 2117 (-geres B, -gerys
C, -gris D), 5399 (-geres B,
-geris C, -gers D).
chartres, 3182 (-teris C, -tris D,
charres † B).
lettres, 1188 (-teres B, *sg.* ‡ C),
3330 (-teris C), 6833 (letterys ‡
C), 7960 (letres B, letteris ‡ C),
7990 (letres B, letteris C;
D †).
candẹles, 7383 (-dels B, -delis C,
-deH D).
couples, 4591 (coupelys C).
ensaumples, 760 (examplys C,
ensaumplis D).
mobles, 6122 ‡ D.
peples, 4589 (pepelys C).
temples, 3225 (tempelis C, tem-
plis D), *so* 3957.
heuenes, 3460 (-ys C, -is (?) D).
swevenes, 6721 (*supply* [al] *in*
A; C †).
VI. aduòcacıes, 2554 AB (-catis ‡
C, -caries ‡ D).
àmphibòloglès, 6068 f (-gyis C)
(: lyes *pl.*).
fàntasỳës, 4855 (-sijs C, -sies.
D) ; cf. 6277.

§ 38.] *of Chaucer's Troilus.* 103

VII. Plurals with synizesis :—

àduersàries (-iē ‡ C), 2520.
contràries, 645 (-trarijs C).
ènemyis, 6615 C (ènemўs AB, ènnemyēs D).
fùryēs, 1521 (-ies B, furies ‡ *gen. pl.* C, furious † D), 7861 (-iēs B, -ies ‡ C, -iës ‡ D).
làdyes (*dissyl.*), 186, 1166, 2698, 5063, 6810, 6819 (laydyes AB, ladyis C, ladies D), 7887.

[Var. B ladys, ladis ; C ladijs, ladiis, ladyis ; D ladies].
pròphesiēs, 7857 (-ciēs B, pròfecỳ ‡ C).
stòryes (*dissyl.*), 3139 (-ies BD, -ijs C), 7407 (storyies C, -ies BD).[1] 3905 f (-ijs C, -y D) *rhyming with*
victòriēs, 3906 f (-ijs C, -y ‡ D), 7822 (-ies BD, -yis C).[2]

Note 1.—The usual ending of the plural in A is *-es*; but *-ys* (*-is*) occurs. Thus,—affectis, 4233 ACD (-os B); eris, 5479 f (eeres B, eres D); frendys, 2560 (-es B, -is CD); herys, 5478 f (-es D, here[s] B); heerys, 7173 (heres BD, here[s] C); hewys, 1106 (-is BD) (: newe(is); lordys, 2698 (-es B, -is CD); owlys, 6745 f (-is B, oules CD) (: foweles : foul(e) is); selys, 4304 (-es B, -is CD); tolys, 632 f (-is B, -es D) (: scole is : folys *pl.*); and in the plural of *tere*, -ys (*-is*) is the usual ending in A (cf. 700, 2112, 3893, 4287, 4791, 4919, 5002, 5172, 5412, 5746 f, 5508, 6578, 7089 (?), 7278, 7699, 7962, 8053; and for *teres* cf. 543, 1411, 2171, 7737). The indifference of some scribes to varieties of ending is shown by D in 4706,—*arwes dartis swerdus macys*. Instead of *-es*, *-eȝ* is written in *armeȝ*, 5881 D, 5909 D ; *besteȝ*, 3462 A. *Affectos*, 4233 B is doubtless a mere error for *-es*. Observe *vulturus*, 788 D (*volturis* AB, *wulturnus* C); *daỳs* (*dissyl.*), 2831 f C (*dayes* ABD) (: *delayis* C, *-es* ABD); *dais* (dissyl.), 2436 C, 6760 C ; *dayns*, 2447 C, 6602 C, 7569 C (cf. also the forms in 3924, 7022, 7713).

Note 2.—The following plurals are perhaps worth mentioning for their rhymes (cf other rhymes of the same kind in the lists above, I. ff.):—
tolys, 632 f (-is B, -es D) · folys *pl.* (-is BD) : scole is.
hewys, 1106 f (-is BD) : newe is.
hayes, 3193 f (-is B, halis † C) . may is.
owlys, 6745 f (-is B, oules CD) : foweles *pl.* ; foul(e) is.
halles, 7093 f (-is B, -es D, waꝉꝉ ‡ C) : wallys *pl.* (-is BC, -es D) : galle ys (galles D).
wellys, 7737 f (-is D, weꝉꝉ C) . helle ys : ellys.
stones, 2026 f (-ys CD) : at ones.
bones, 91 f (-ys CD) : onys (cf. 805 f, 2469 f).
desertes, 4109 f (-is CD) · certes
pleyes, 7862 f lord of Argeys (Argeyes B, Argeis D).

Note 3.—In some cases *s* only is written where *-es* (*-is*) should be pronounced. Thus—
answèr[i]s, 2435 D (-es A, -e[s] B, -is C).
bok[e]s, 7423 B (-es AD, [thes] bokys C). (Cf. 2933, 4041, 4271, 4616, 6382, 6738, 7153, 7162, 7452, 7826, 7841, 7844, 7896, 7925, 8218.)
dor[e]s, 6915 B (-es AD, -is C). (Cf. 3075, 6894.)
flour[e]s, 8204 B (-es AD). (Cf. 158, 1136, 2052.)

Note 4.—That the *s* in the plural ending *-es* was unvoiced is indicated by the formes *erbess* (661 A) and *kness*(e) (3922 B); cf. also *goddesse* for *goddes* (6067 C), and *dyce* for *des* (5760 D). Rhymes like *wellys · ellys, bones . onys,* are also significant (see note 2, above).

[1] Hiatus in ACD.   [2] Supply [*most*] in C.

§ 39. **Exceptions to § 38.** The following words ending in a consonant or an accented *-e* sometimes or always make their plural in *-s* (-ʒ, -z) or *-es* (cf. Child, § 22; ten Brink, § 226):

I. Words in *-aunt, -ent*:
argumentʒ, 466 (-tęs B, -tis CD), 4009 B (-tz A, -tis CD), 5189 B (-t[e]ʒ ‡ A, -t C, -tes D)[1]. But,—argument[e]ʒ, 5631 AB (-tes DGCp.); argumentus,[2] 2110 AB (-tis CD).
elementʒ, 4595 B (-tęs A, -tis C, -tus [2] ‡ E).
instrumentʒ, 6822 (-t CD).[3]
accidentęs, 6167 ‡ D (*sg.* ABC).
sèruauntʒ, 15 (-t[ʒ] B, -tis D), 48 (-tęs B, -tis C); sèruantʒ, 328 (-tęs B, -tys C, -tis D); sèruantz, 905 (-uauntʒ B, -uantis C, -uauntis D). But all these become *seruaùntes* if we read *louęs* instead of *louës*. Seruauntʒ, 371 (-tes B, -tis CD), may be read *sèruauntʒ* or *seruaùntës*, according as we read *èlles fòr* or *èllęs for*.
But,—auaùntes, 3131 (-is C; D †).

II. Words in *-ioun, -ion*:
affecions, 5086 (effèciounys *or* effèciounȳs C).
auysions, 6737 f (auisiounys C).
complexions, 6732 f (-iounnys C).
condicions, 1251 (condisciounys *or* condisciounȳs (?) C).[4]
illusions, 6731 f (-ys C).
impressions, 6735 f (enpressiounnys C).
reuelacions, 6729 f (-iouns CD).
But,—imprèssiòn[e]s, 2323 (-yon[e]s B, -iou[ne]s C).
pàssiòn[e]s, 5130 (-ioun[e]s B, pàsciouny̆s C).

III. Dissyllables in *-en, -on, -an*, with the accent on the penult:
maydens, 1204 (-ys C, màydenis ‡ D).
resonęs, 2932 (resons B, werkis ‡ C, wordis D †).
Tròians, 2062 (Troyés CD), 6152 (Troilus † C, Troian D), 6504 troyanys C, Troiauns D). Troiàns, 4769 (*or* Tròians). [6485 ?]

IV. Words in *-r*:—
lòuers, 11, 198 (AB *are defect.*), 376, 1971, 2836, 5233 ‡ B (*sg.* ACD); lòueręs, 45 B (loués AD), 331, 344, 516, 919, 2153, 2391, 2879, 4235, 4299, 4310, 7935; louèręs, 22, 4985. In all the above-

---

[1] Doubtless we should read *argumentʒ* in A, supplying [*to*] before *blame*.
[2] MS. *t* with sign of contraction for *us*.   [3] In A read *on*(*y*).
[4] Dele (*to*) in D.

[§ 39.] *of Chaucer's Troilus.* 105

cited passages B reads *louers* (except 45, 344, 2879, loueręs), C *loueris* (or -ys), D *louers* or *lovers* (except *louës*, 45), *lovyers* (dissyl.), 331, *faytours* 919, *loueris* 4310).

màneręs, 742 A (manere B, maner CD).

messàgers, 2021 ‡ D (messàgës AB, massagë C).

pòrterys, 7502 AC (portours B, porters D).

prèyers, 1538 B (preieris C, *sg. in* AD).

ambàssiatoùrs, 4802 (embàssadoùrs B, embàssatoùrys C); embàssadoùrs, 4807 (-tours B, -doùrys C, ambàssiatoùrs D).

prìsonèręs, 4721 (-èrs BD); prìsonèrs, 4808 (presoneris C).

> Note.—In 1321 *paramours* (-is C¹, -our † D) may be the plural of *paramour* = lover; but perhaps the phrase (*withouten paramours*) means "not taking the kind of loving that we call 'to love par amours' into account." In "I louede neuer womman here byforn *As paramours*," 6520-1 (-ęs B, paramour C), and in "Hath loved *paramours* as wel as thow," 6695 (paramour CD), we have this adverbial phrase *par amours*.

V. Monosyllables in -*e*:

des, dees, 2432 (deis C), 5760 (deth † C, dycę riʒt as [therę], D).

knes, knees (*monosyl.*), 110 (kneis C), 1037, 3025, (kneis C), 3795 (knowęs B, kneïs C, kneës D), 3922 (knes(se) B, kneïs C).² But,—

kneës, 4434 (knowës B, kneïs C, kneës D *defective*).

treis 7507 C (*sg.* ABD).

VI. benygnitees (*not* -teës), 8222 (-tes B).³

> Note 1.—Many apparent cases of -*es* (with syncope of -*e*-) disappear on comparison of MSS. Such are: folęs, 217 A (cf. 3171 D) (for *folēs*, *folys* *foolēs* cf. 635 f, 705, 762, 903, 3166, 4666, 5377); talęs, 1344 A; 3456 A⁴ (for *talēs* cf. 1234, 1342, 1393, 1588, etc.); whelys, 848 C; armęs, 4416 B, 6553 B (for *armēs* cf. 1038, 3024, 3448, 4029, 4043, etc.); dremys, 7651 C (cf. 6741 D) (for *dremēs* cf. 4184, 6680, 6727, 6729, 7640, etc.); amendes (?), 1427 A; effectis, 2305 C, 3188 C (cf. 2857, 7992 C); ʒatis, 7555 C (cf. 1700, 1702 CD, 6966, 7541); hertęs, 4955 D, 6711 D (cf. 235, 2865, 2959, 3039, 3453, 3808, 3982); londes, 5901 A (cf. 1113); miʒtes, 5857 D (cf. 4599); sykes, 7397 A, sikis, 7717 C (cf. 3191, 4203, 5037, etc.); tungis, 1870 C (cf. 39, 565); wordes, 5298 A (cf. 540, 561, 736, 754, 1108, etc., etc.); othęs, 1384 A (cf. 3985, 3988, 7626); hestes, 6718 A (cf. 3261, 4587, 7571 f, 7572 C); dayis, 6716 (?) C; aleys, 1905 f C; songis, 6994 C; tidingęs, 5324 D; whisperyngis, 2838 C; lesyngis, 3672 C (cf. syngyngęs, etc., 2198 f, 2653, 4558 f, 4560 f, 6609 f); peynes, 4058 B, 4300 D, 5791 A (cf. 303, 2984, 4046, 5003, etc.); Grekis, 1209 C, 1596 C, 3386 D (cf. 802, 1039, 4696, etc.); fendis, 1981 (?) CD; kalendes, 7997 D (-ës A, -as B, -is C), used as a singular (*a kalendes*) (cf. 1092); workis, -ys, 265 D, 5857 C; desesis, 7783 C. In 2820 B we may read *coròněs* or *còrones*, but it is better to omit *the* (with ACD) and *coroùnēs*. Forms like *hegis* (7507 ‡ C, cf. D) and *sorwes* (7559 B) are of course out of the question. In 4439 we should read *frendēs the alderbeste*,

---

¹ In C dele (*as*).   ² In D supply [*he*].   ³ In A read *goode* for *garde*.
⁴ This is the famous line about the "tale of Wade"—*he told[e] talēs of wade* A, *he told talēs of wade* Cp. (no other variants in Mr. Austin's collation), *he told[e] tale of wade* B, *he toldē tale of wade* C, *he tolds the tale of wade* D, *he toldē tale of wade* G.

not *frendes the alderbeste* (cf. 1237, 1464, 1888, 5343, 6213, 6706, 7217).
Influens (3460 D), *chauns* (5760 f D, *chaunce* C), and *plesauns* (5761 f,
-aunce C), seem meant for plurals, but need correction.
But there is good MS. authority for syncope in 264 (*ioyes* AC) (cf.,
however, 846, 2870, 3660, 4351, etc.), 1725 (*swerdes* AB) (cf., however,
2026, 4706), 2847 (*hertes* AB). For *sithes, tymes,* see §§ 2, 14 (but *tymes*,
2853, 4273, 6739). For *thynges,* see *thyng,* pl., below (§ 43). *Pens,* 4217
(*pans* BC, *peynes* † E), and *vers,* 7 (*wordes* ‡ D), deserve notice.
Note 2.—A few Latin plurals occur. These are *satyri* and *fauni* in

On *satiry* and *fawny* more and (*om.* A) lesse
That halue goddes ben of wildernesse, 6206-7

(*satury* B, *satary(e)* & *fany* C, *statery* † & *ferry* † D, *satiri* and *fawny* G);
and *manes,* 7255 (*mannes* C). But instead of *Parcae* we have *Parcas*
(6366). *Kalendas,* 7797 B, perhaps preserves a bit of the copyist's
learning. See also *vulturus* (etc.) for *vultures,* § 38, note 1.

§ 40. Plurals of the n-declension which preserve the
Anglo-Saxon ending (-*an*) in the form -*en*, are the
following:—

asshen (A.S. pl. ascan, L. on axen; O. asskess, P.Pl.ᶜ askes), 4781
asschyn C, asshyn D); asshen pale, 1624 B (asschin C, asshyn D,
asshë A).

ben (A.S. pl. béon, Ps. bían), 1278 f (: ben *p.p.*; flen *fugere*), 6018
(ben [flen] C). [Var. B been; D bene.]

eyen, eien (192), eyghen (2056, 5754), eighen (3929, 4194, 5412) (A.S.
pl. éagan, L. æʒen, eʒen, P. Pl.ᵃ eʒen, eiʒen, ᵇeyghen, eyghes, ᶜeyen),
191,¹ 305 f, 428, 726, 1227, 1338,² 1411 f, 1619 f, 1733 f, 1948 f,
2056 ³, 2971, 2997, 3025 f, 3894, 3929, 3979 f, 4194, 4195, 4295 f,
4908 (ey[e]n(e) two D), 4971 (eyen ‡ C corrector, ey[e]n D), 4972
(ey[e]n D), 4976 (seyn † C, ey[e]n D), 5184,⁴ 5410, 5412, 5531,
5535, 5754 (thy nenë semen B), 5821, 5885 (eyë B, ey[ën] (?) D),
6583, 6929, 7107 (ey[e]n B), 7178,⁵ 7180 f, 7362 C (eyyn ‡), 7368
(-[en] A (?)), 7522, 7699, 7701, 7736. [eyen (?), 3200 ‡ D; eyʒyn,
6442 ‡ C.] [eyen †, 3116 f B *is error for* engyn.]

Rhyme words.—dryen *patiuntur* (305), dryen *pati* (1948), dyen *mori* (*also
spelled* deyen) (305, 1411, 1619, 3025), spyen, aspien, espyen *inf.* (1733,
3979, 4295, 7180), lyen (lye) *mentiri* (1411), by-wryen *inf.* (1619), cryen
inf. (1733), *pres. subj.* 3 *pl.* (1948), ywryen *p. p.* (4295), syen *viderunt*
(7180). [Var. B eyen, yën, eyghen, eighen; C eyen, eyʒen, eyʒyn, eyʒin,
eyʒeyn, eynyn (2971); D eyen, yën, yhen, iʒen.]

foon (A.S. ge-fán), 8229 f (foone D) (: oon : eurychon). But,—foos,
994 (foes B, fois (to) C, foos [to] D), 2513 (fois C).

¹ In the following list all forms are dissyllabic unless the contrary is noted. No
distinction of *eyen* before consonants from *eyen* before vowels has been made.
² Supply [*to*] in D.   ³ eyen † D
⁴ Transpose in D.   ⁵ Supply [*her*] in D.

Note.—*Ere* forms its plural in -*s*. Thus,—eeres, 2107 (eris BCD); eerys, 4230 (erys B, eris C‡),[1] 6084 (eres BD, eris C); eris, 5479f (eeres B, eres D) (terys . herys). For *apes, belles, bowes, ladyes, sterres, wrecches*, see § 37.

§ 41. Plurals in -*en* by imitation (Child, § 24; ten Brink, §§ 215, 217).

bretheren (A.S. pl. bróðor, bróðru, Pet. Chron. bréðre, L. broþere, breþren, broþeres, O. breðre), 471 (brethyryn D †), 2523 brethern B, brethȩryn C, bretherin D), 4939 (bretheryn C, brethern(e) D), 5868 (brethern D). (Cf. *sustren*.)

doughtren (A.S. pl. dohtor, dohtru, dohtra, L. dohtere, dohtren, dohtres, P. Pl.ᵇ douȝtres, ᶜdouhtres), 4684 (doghtryn D).

sustren (A.S. pl. sweoster, L. sustren, sostres, P. Pl.ᶜ sustres, susteres, sustren), 3575 (-terin C, -trin D), 4651 (-tryn D), 6366. his bretheren and his sustren, 7590 (his(e) brètherèn ‡ his sisteren C, his bretheryn & his sisters D).

children (A.S. pl. cild, cildru, L. childere, children, childres, O. chilldre), 132 (schilderyn C, childryn D †).

housen (A.S. pl. hús), 6910 ‡ D (-es AB, -is C).

Note.—*Gamen* (1123 B), *gleden* (1623 C), *bonden* (2061 f A), *sorwyn* (3768 C), *dremen* (6741 B), *tenten* (7033 A), are merely errors of the scribe.

§ 42. Plurals with umlaut (Child, § 26; ten Brink, § 214).[2]

feet (A.S. fét), 359, 1488 (-(e)B), 2127. [Var. C fet.]

men (A.S. menn), 241, 279, 3438 f (: ten), 7105, etc., etc.; fomen, 4704:

wommen, women (2257) (A.S. wífmenn, Pet. Chron. wimmen), 1297 (wemen C, womman A, woman D), 1819 (women C, wymmen D, woman ‡ A), 1867 (wemen C, wymmen D), 1878 (women C, wymmen D, womman A), 2257 (women AC, wymmen D), 3097 (women C, wymmen D), 3164 (wemen C, women D, womman ‡ A), 3614 (wemen C, wymmen D), 4844 (wymmen D, woman C), 5210 (wemen C, women D), 5347 (wemen C, women D), 7051 (wemen C, women D). [Sing. (A.S. wífman, late wimman, see the forms cited by Sweet, *Hist. Eng. Sounds*, no—1879), womman, woman, 798, 807, 1486, etc.]

[1] In C read *also* for *as*.
[2] No distinction as to the word that follows the plurals cited in this section is attempted.

§ 43. In the following words plurals occur identical in
    form with the singular.
wynter (A.S. *n.* pl. wintru, winter), twenty wynter, 811 (-yr † C,
    -ir D).
yer (A.S. *n.* sg. pl. gḗr, gér, W.S. géar), 60, 1108 (ȝere B, ȝeer D).[1]
    yerës two, 2383; lengthe of yeres, 6343. [Var. B ȝeres, CD ȝeris.]
nyght (A.S. *f.* sg. pl. neaht, niht), a (ek B) wonder last but ix.
    nyght neuere in towne, 5250 AB (dayis ‡ C, nyghtes ‡ D). But,—
    ouer the nyghtes, 4598 f (: myghtes)[2]; lyk the nyghtes, 5910; er
    nyghtes ten, 6347; alle this nyghtes two, 6683. [Var. C nyȝtys,
    nyȝtis, nytyȝs, 4598; D nightes, niȝtes.]
folk often has a plural verb. Cf., e.g., 34, 199, 241, 243, 1888,
    1973, 2592, 2669, 2815, 2874, 3860, 3865, 4204, 4271, 4680, 4710,
    4864, 6707 (How don this (these C, thes D) folk (folkes D) that
    seen here loues wedded), 6778, 7124, 7541, 7641 (men A), 7942.
    Cf. also: Whi alle thes(e) folk assembledin in this place, 2652 C
        (al this folk assembled AD, al this f. assemlede B).
    If that I may and allë folk be trewe, 2695 (al[lë] f. BD, allë f.
        ben C).
    (Pandarus) Seyde alle folk for goddes lou*e* I preye
    Stynteth right here and softëly yow pleye, 2813-14 (D †).
    Swowneth not now lest more folk aryse, 4032 (cf. 6050).
    As (For BC) wys[e] (wyse B, wise C, thes D) folk (folke D)
        in bokes it expresse (expres C), 7153 (cf. 3169).
    The (ffor C) folk (folke D) of Troye as who seyth (wis sithe † C)
        alle and some In preson ben, 7246-7.
    If that I may and alle (al[le] BD) folk be (ben C) trewe, 2695.
    Note.—In general *folk* is apt, as a noun of multitude, to take plural
    constructions, and, of course, in many cases it is impossible to determine
    whether a singular or a plural is meant. A good case of a certain singular
    is: Whil (wilk † C) folk is blent lo al the tyme is wonne, 2828.
    For other examples of *folk* in various constructions cf. 26, 138, 160, 169,
    176, 179, 251, 308, 319, 354, 357, 560, 1164, 1704, 1860, 1995, 2242,
    2279, 2732, 4275, 4637, 6486, 6951, 6965, 7219, 7332, 8144. The word
    is regularly spelled *folk*, though *folke* or *folke* is occasionally found (as 160
    B, 169 B, 179 C, 319 B, 1704 B, 2242 B, and often in D), but not in A;
    fok is found in 26 A and 176 C.
    A plural in -*es* is also found,—folkes, 6002 (folk[es] C, folkë[s] D), 8198;
    folkis, 4275 D; folkes, 6707 D. *Folkes* is genitive in *good for syke folkes
    eyen*, 3979 (-[es] B, -is D, follys ‡ C).
thing. Chaucer sometimes uses *thing* as a plural; but it is not
    always easy or even perhaps possible to distinguish this use from

---

[1] Both cases before a vowel.
[2] Word omitted in D.

[§§ 43, 44.] *of Chaucer's Troilus.* 109

idioms in which the singular may be employed (note, e. g., variants in 3605, 5358).

Cf., however;—And letten other thing collateral, 262 (thing(e) B, thyngis C, thinges D).

And more thyng than thow deuysest (demys C †, demist D †) here, 5205 (thyng(e) B, thyng C, thing D).

Nece al[le] thing hath tyme I dar avowe, 3697 (alle thyng(e) BC).

But the ordinary plural is *thynges* (cf. 134, 1993, 2197 f,[1] 2260, 2276, 2350, 2471, 2858, 2874,[2] 3427, 3765, 4103 f,[3] 4208 f,[4] 4820, 5322, 5356 f,[5] 5667, 5669, 5681, 5995, 6499, 7905, 7975, 8086).

thynges seems to be right in 2453 A (-ës B, -is D; C †) (cf. 2001 ‡ D, 2319 ‡ C, 3248 ‡ C, 3605 ‡ C).

The phrase *all[e] thing* seems to deserve some special attention. Ouer al[le] thyng he stood [for] to byholde, 310 AD (alle thing(e) . . . for to BC[6])[7].
Considered all[e] thyng it may not be, 2375 (al[le] thyng(e) B, alle thyng(e) C, al thing wel(ë) D ‡).
Considered alle thingës as they stode, 3765 (alle thyngis C, al[le] thing[es] D).
That wost of alle thing(e) the sothfastnesse, 5742 AD (al this thyng(e) B, al this thyng C).
In alle thynge is myn ententë clene, 4008 (al[le] thynge B, alle thyng . . . entent[e] C, al[le] thing al myn entent D).
Whan that he sey that al[le] thyng was wel, 3538 (alle thyng(e) B, wostë alle thyng(e) was C, wist that al[le] thing (?) D).
The last cited example is particularly surprising. May we not, however, suppose that *alle thing*, originally plural, became a stock phrase, of which the syntax was forgotten or obscured, so that even when a singular was used the plural form *alle* might be retained?

Note 2.—*God* is used with a plural verb in 1919 ABC John's, *The blisful god han me so wel beset* (god have D, god hath G); but Cp. has *ȝe blisful god han*, which is no doubt right, *god* being vocative (cf. *lord* in the same stanza, 1922). For the regular plural *goddes* cf. 151, 3432, 4045, 4101, 4514, etc.

Note 3.—*Gere* is the A.S. fem. pl. *gearwe*: see 2097 f (: there : were *subj.* 3 *sg.*), 6185 f (ger D) (: elles where : there); gere him, 1720 (ger C). (Cf. ten Brink, § 210 Anm.)

§ 44. The genitive plural does not differ in form from the genitive singular.

seyntes lyues, 1203 (-is CD).
nayles poyntes, 2119 ‡ B.
foles bost, 3140 (-is CD).
foles harm, 3171 B (-ys C, A defect.).

the goddes wyl, 3465 (-is CD);
the goddes ordenaunce, 7968 (-is C).
tonges ianglerye, 7118 (-is C).
crowes feet, 1488.

[1] *rh.* tidynges. [2] A thing[es]. [3] *rh.* wynges.
[4] *rh.* rynges. [5] *rh.* thing is. [6] But C by accident omits [he].
[7] In 2001 the proper reading is certainly *al this thyng* (sing.) *thou*. D has *all the thinges*.

frendes gouernaunce (-is C, frendes generaunce † B, -is sustenaunce D), 2527; frendes myght, 6708 (fryndis C); frendes help (-is C), 7390.[1]

clerkes[2] lawes, 6059 (-is C, clerkysshe); clerkes speche, 8217.

the lettres space, 7993 ([the] B, letterys C).

teris[2] kynde, 5798 (-es BD).

Grekes ost, 80 ABD, 5261, 6284, 6379, 6435, 7030 AB; Grekes yerde, 1239; Grekes route, 1698; on the Grekes syde, 6128; Grekes gyse, 7224. [C usually -ys or -is; D -is, -ys, -es.] But, —at Grekes requeste, 4719 A (-ys D, a grek † requeste B).

payens corsed olde rites,[3] 8212 (paynymes D).

rauenes qualm, 6745 (-ys C).

sweuenes signifiaunce, 6725 (sweuenys C, sweuenys significauns D).

§ 45. Dative plural (Anglo-Saxon -*um*):

whilom (A.S. hwílum), 508 (whilhom C, somtyme D); cf. 5402, 5731, 5817, 6904, 6907, 6910, 6927.

sithe (A.S. síðum), see § 14.

fote (A.S. fótum), see § 14.

ADJECTIVES.

§ 46. Anglo-Saxon adjectives that end in -*e* or -*a* in the indefinite use preserve a vowel in Chaucer. (Child, § 29; ten Brink, § 230).

In the *Troylus* such are (i.) of the jo- declension, *blithe, breme, clene, dere, ethe, grene, kynde, lene, mylde, newe, shene, sterne, stille, swete, thikke, trewe*. To these may be added (ii.) *lame* (A.S. *lama*, regularly used in the weak form) and *allone* (A.S. *eall ána*), for which see § 47. (iii.) *smothe*, and *softe* (A.S. smóðe, sófte, adverbs, but also used as adjectives instead of sméðe and séfte, see Sweet, 2051, 2081, Sievers, § 299 Anm. 1), and *swote, soote* (A.S. swót *adv.*, swóte, *adj.* in comp.). For *merye, mery*, see the end of the list.

blithe, blythe (A.S. blíðe, L. O. blíðe), 7746 f (: a thousand sithe : swithe *adv.*); -*e*, 4160.[4]

breme (A.S. bréme, O. breme), -*e*, 4846.

clene (A.S. cléne, L. cléne), 1665 f, 3099 f, 4008 f. [4071 ‡ ? D.]

Rhyme words.—I mene *ind.* (1665, 3099, 4008), mene *n.* (3099), bene *A.S. bean* (4008).

---

[1] Perhaps singular, cf. *frendes loue*, 7443. [2] Possibly singular.
[3] vyces † A (. appetites). [4] Supply [*two*] in A.

§ 46,]   *of Chaucer's Troilus.*   111

dere, deere (A.S. déore, W.S. díere, dýre, L. deore, dure, O. deore, dere), 32 f, 51 f, 434 f, 877 f, 1336 f, 1415 f, 1559 f, 1579 f, 1679 f, 1893 f, 2057 f, 2188 f, 2217 f, 2295 f, 2444 f, 2516 f, 2561 f, 2778 f, 2809 f, 2845 f, 2895 f, 2937 f, 2969 f, 3081 f, 3114 f, 3172 f, 3336 f, 3487 f (drede † A), 3762 f, 3788 f, 3817 f, 4052 f, 4131 f, 4146 f, 4197 f, 4253 f, 4290 f, 4335 f, 4395 f, 4505 f, 4947 f, 4969 f, 5074 f, 5203 f, 5312 f, 5557 f, 5871 f, 5973 f, 6014 f,[1] 6112 f, 6236 f, 6507 † D, 6523 f, 6550 f, 6581 f, 6670 f, 6705 f, 6777 f (C †, D †), 6830 f, 6884 f, 6930 f, 6939 f, 6999 f, 7016 f, 7274 f, 7589 f, 7678 f, 7703 f, 7820 f.—Now uncle derë quod she tel it us, 1207 (C †).—al dere ynow a rysshe (C †), 4003 (cf. 5346).— -e, 8094 BD.

    Of these the following are in formulæ of address (as, for example, *frend so dere, gode nece dere, myn hertë dere*),—877, 1207, 1336, 1559, 1579, 1679, 2057, 2188, 2217, 2295, 2444, 2516, 2561, 2778, 2809, 2845, 2969, 3081, 3172, 3487, 3788, 3817, 4052, 4131, 4146, 4335, 5203, 5312, 5557, 5871, 5973, 6014, 6112, 6236, 6523, 6581, 6670, 6705, 6777, 6830, 7274, 7703, 7820.

    Rhyme words.—here *inf.* (32, 51, 2188, 3336, 3762, 3817, 5203, 6830, 6999, 7678, 7820), y-here *inf.* (5973), *ind.* 1 *sg.* (6939), here *adv.* (1336, 1579, 1679, 2057, 2188, 3487, 3788, 4052, 4146, 4969, 5203, 5557, 5973, 6830 BCD), there *adv.* (6830 A, here BCD), clere *inf.* (1893, 6884), clere *adj. sg. def.* (7016), *adj. pl.* (2845, 2969, 4197, 6581, 6930, 7703), *adv.* (6236, 6670, 6939), lere *inf.* (6523), requere *pl.* (1559), manere (32, 877, 2809, 2895, 2937, 4253, 4290, 4947, 6550), matere (51, 1579, 2217, 2516, 2778, 4146, 4253, 4505, 5312), ryuere (5074), preyere (2295), chere *n.* (434, 877, 1415, 1559, 2217, 2444, 2809, 2895, 2937, 3172, 3336, 4197, 4395, 4505 (4506 A has *clere* for *chere*), 6550, 6777, 7274, 7589), spere *sphere* (4335, 7016), fere *comes* (4335), y-fere *adv.* (2561, 3114, 5871, 6014, 6112, 6705), to yere (3081), to the fyre (fere BCD) (3817), stere *n.* (4131), *inf.* (4947), bere *feretrum* (5871).

ethe (A.S. éaðe, éðe, L. æðe, O. æþ), he was ethe ynowh to maken dwelle, 7213 (C †).

grene (A.S. gréne, grǿne, L. grene), 816 f, 1145 f, 2003 f, 2790 f, 2852, 3904, 6606 f.

    Rhyme words.—tene (816, 1145, 6606), queene (816, 2790), shotes kene (1145), the mone shene (2003), by-twene (2790), sustene *inf.* (6606).

grene *as sbst.*,—with newë grene, 157 ; in grenë when, 3195 ; roteles mot grenë sonë deye, 5432 (ertheles grenë ‡ mot C).

kynde (A.S. cynde, but usually ge-cynde), 6079 f, 6489 f, 7283 f ; -e, 8006 BC (trewe ‡ A, kynde as [that] D).—vnkynde, 4678 f, 4928 f, 7804 f. (Cf. if ye be vnkynde, 6102 f ; beth me not vnkynde, 6314 f).

    Rhyme words.—I fynde *ind.* (6079), fynde *inf.* (4678, 4928, 6489, 7283), mynde *n.* (4678, 7804). [Var. C on-kynde.]

---

[1] Old-style figures indicate that D has *der*.

lene (A.S. hlǽne, L. P.Pl. lene), 1217 f (leene B, C † D †) (: mene *pl.*);
  -e, 7584 (leen B).
mylde (A.S. milde, L.O. milde), And stod forth mewët (meuyth † D)
  myldë (-[ë] D) and mansuete, 6557 (*line om.* C, And stode forthe
  full mylde and manswete G).
newe (A.S. néowe, níowe, W.S. níewe, níwe, L. neowe, niwe, O.
  neowe, newe, P. Pl. newe, nywe), 157 (-[e] B), 1390 f, 1873 f (new
  D), 4246 (-[e] B, E †), 4496, 5084 (-[e] BD), 6484 f (new D), 7511
  (-[e] D, -[e] † is B, now † al C), 7618 (-[e] B, *om.* † C), 7632 (-[e]
  BD); span newe, 4507; And vpon newë (newe BC, new D) cas
  (cause ‡ D) lyth (lyëth D) newe (new D, a newe BC) auys, 5078.—
  newe is (new is BD)[1] (: hewys).—made this tale of newe, 5324 f
  (al newe B, this talë newe C, thes tidinges new D).
    Rhyme words.—hewe *n.* (1390, 5324), trewe *indef. adj. sg.* (1390, 6484),
    vntrewe *pred. adj. pl.* (1873), trewe *adj. pl.* (5324), rewe *subj.* 3 *sg.* (1873),
    knewe *ind.* 2 *pl.* (6484).
shene (A.S. scéne, scýne, scéone, L. sceone, scone, L.[b] scene, O. shene,
  scone), 6094 f (she[ne] A) (: bi-twene : leues grene), 6639 f (: sterres
  werë sene); ayen the monë shene, 2005 f (: grene *indef. adj. sg.*).
  [Var. B sheene, C schene.]
smothe (A.S. smóðe, *adv.*, but also used as *adj.* instead of sméðe,
  smœ́ðe (cf. Sweet, 2051), O. smeþe), -e, 942 ABD.
softe (A.S. sófte, *adv.*, but also used as *adj.* instead of séfte, scéfte
  (cf. Sweet, 2081), L. softe, O. soffte), 137 f (*perh. pl.* ?) (vnsoft ‡ D),
  942 f (-t D); he[r] streyght[e] bak and softe, 4089 f; with soft[ë]
  voys, 6999 (-e C, lofte † D).
    Rhyme words.—ofte (137, 942, 4089), on lofte, a-lofte (137, 942).
sterne (A.S. sterne, W.S. stierne, styrne; L. sterne, O. stirne), 7164
  (sticrne B); -e, 5846.
stille, stylle (A.S. stille, L. stille, O. stille, still), held hire s., 126 f
  (: wylle); -e, 723 (stil D),[2] 1685 (stil D †), 8092; stille, 7183 ‡ C.
swete (A.S. swéte, swǿte, O. swet), 385,[3] 3350 f, 4087 f, 4367 f CD,
  4400 f, 4510 f, 4662 f, 5151 f, 5169 f, 5441 f, 5588 f, 5936 f (B †),
  6252 f, 6554 f, 7552 f; -e, 4126; swet[e], 4061 f (-e BCD); swete ||
  how, 4120.
    Rhyme words.—mete *métan inf.* (3350, 4087, 4367, 4510, 5936, 6554), *subj.*
    1 *sg.* (5441), mete *métan inf.* (4400), grete *grétan inf.* (4400), flete *inf.*
    (4510), *ind.* 3. *pl.* (4061), ye his sorwes bete *subj.* (?) (5588), strete (5588),
    quiete (3350, 4662, 5151, 5169, 5441), Ariëte (6252, 7552), mansuete,
    (6554). [Var. D suete, swette.]

[1] Supply [it] in D.   [2] Supply [as] in AD.
[3] Supply [seed] in A.

Note.—Of the above the following occur in forms of address (*herte swete, my dere herte swete*, and the like): 4120, 4367, 4400, 5441, 5588, 5936, 6252, 7552.

soote, 7034 f (soot B, swote CD) (: bote *A.S. bót*); sot, 4036 f (soot B, sote CD) (: in his fote (foot B) : I mot *ind.* (-e BCD)).[1]— swote, 942 AB (swetę ‡ ? C).

thikke (A.S. þicce, L. thicke), 941 f (thekke C, thik D) (: the wedys wykke); -e, 1278 (thik D).

trewe (A.S. tréowe, W.S. tríewe, trýwe, L. treowe, O. trowwe), 1391 f, 3175 (-[e] B), 4490, 5043 f, 6079 (-[e] ? D), 6082 f (true D), 6101 (-[e] D), 6190 f, 6487 f (trew B), 7014 f (true D), 7069 f, 7434 f, 7694 f (drewe † C), 7728 f, 7764 f (myn owęnë hertë trewe), 7948 f.—Trewë as stel in ech condicion, 7194 (-[e] B), *if not a 9-syl. line.*—vntrewe, 3148 f, 3895 f, 5108 (-trow[e] B), 6213, 7660 (vntruë D), 7933 f, 8137 f.—trewe, 593 (-w BD, trowe C), 950 (-w D), 1424 (-w D), 1913 (-w D), 3843 (-w B, trew † with D), 4859 (soth C, sothe D), 5100 (trowis † C), 6272 (-w B, -e I [hauę] D), 8006 A, 8075 (-w B, true D).

Rhyme-words.—hewe *n.* (1391, 3148, 5043, 7764, 7933, 8137), newe *adj.* (1391, 3895, 6190, 6487, 7696 *perh. adv.*), *adv.* (7014, 7933, 7948), *inf.* (3148), knewe *ind.* 2 *pl.* (6487), *ind.* 3 *pl.* (6082), rewe *inf.* (6190, 7434), thou rewe (7069), rewe *subj.* 2 *pl.* (7728). [Var. C ontrewe.]

merye, mery (A.S. mirige, mirg), a merye somęres day, 3903 (merie C, mery D); merye, *pred. sg.*, 4515 f (: herye *inf.*); with mery chere, 1234 (merie C), 3072 AB; this murye morwe, 4405 (merie C, me[r]y D); we shullę ben alle merye, 3794 f (merie C) (: herye *laudo*); merye dayes, 2831 (merie C, mery D). (*All forms dissyllabic.*)

Note 1.—*fremde* (A.S. fremðe, freinde) occurs only in the definite use and in the plural,—*yourę frendly manerę speche*, 1333 f (frende BCp., frendely C, frend D, fremde G, friende John's), where *fremde* alone makes sense; *In this matere bothe (with B) fremed and lame*, 3371 ABG (frend C, frende D), where we should read *fremde*. *Dreye* (A.S. drýge) occurs only in the plural,—*Haue . . . ded[e] ben and dreye*, 3194 f (drye BCD) (: pleye *inf.* : to seye); *He gan the teris wypen of ful dreye*, 5835 (drye D, dreye *inf.* ‡ C) (: seye *inf.* : preye *inf.*).

Note 2.—In *fawe*, which occurs once,—*he desireth fawe*, 5549 f (: slawe *p.p.* : with-drawe *p.p.*),—a final -n has been lost (cf. O.L.G. *fagan*, -*in*, A.S. *fægen*, and see ten Brink, § 44. *a*).

Note 3.—For the adj. *fre, free* (A.S. fréo), invariable in form, cf., for examples of all sorts, 840, 1073 f, 1402 f, 1856 f, 2206 f, 2970 f, 4364 f, 5633, 5642, 5721, 6214 f, 6507 f, 7032 f, 7186 f, 7725 f, 7753 f, 7768 f, 7838 f.

§ 47. In *allone, lame*, -e goes back to the Anglo-Saxon weak ("definite") ending -a.

---

[1] The right reading is *soot*, noun, which A mistook for the adj.

I

allone, alone [1] (A.S. eall ána), 97 f, 178 f, 358 f (allon B), 547 f, 694 f (allon B), 907 f (alon CD), 1602 f, 1640 f, 3255 f (alon CD), 3382 (aboue † C), 3506 f, 4882 f (alon C), 4943 (D?), 5530 f (alon C), 5609 f, 5770 ‡ C, 6585, 6612 f, 6834 (alle one C); -e, 1021 (-n B), 1695 (-n B), 1775, 2301 (*om.* D), 2486, 4960 (allas † A), 7389 (-n B); allone here (*hic*), 806. (All singular except 907.)

Rhyme words.—mone *moan n.* (97, 694, 1640, 5609, 6612), euerichone (178, 907, 3255, 3506, 5530, 5609), echone (4882), grone *inf.* (358, 547, 907, 1602, 1640, 6612).

lame (A.S. lama, L. lome, lame), 1102 f (: blame *n.*).

§ 48. *Lyte, muche* belong in a category by themselves. On their relations to A.S. *lýt, lýtel, micel, mycel,* see especially Bright, *American Journal of Philology,* IX, 219.

lyte (A.S. lýt, *adv.*, lýtel, *adj.*) is said by ten Brink, § 231, to be "im Sing. wohl nur substantivisch gebraucht," but this is shown to be an error by two places in the *Troilus*: *the chaumbre is but lite,* 2731 f (: *wyte blame* acc.), and *yn place lite,* 7992 f (light † D) (: *write scribo* : *endite inf.*); compare also 2288 f and 7653 f, though in these two cases the word may well enough be substantive. In the definite use AB have *my lite closet* in 3505 AB (litil CD). In 826 f, 1339 f, 1354 f (lite(l), A), 1469 f, 2112 f, 2302 f, 2363 f, 2731 f, 3582 f, 3675 f, 3740 f, 7653 f, -e, 291 (lytil C † D), 1517 (D?), 5992 B, 6539 B, *lite, lyte* is apparently substantive. Old-style figures indicate that the reading is *a lite*,—a phrase sometimes used adverbially.—*That is lite fors,* 7290 C, is a wrong reading for *my birthe accurse.* In 7290 C reads *a lite with,* doubtless for *a lite wight* (litel wight AB, littel wight D). *lite,* 4410 f (a ‡ lite D) (: wordes white), is adverbial; *lyte,* 4092 f, is plural (: white *pl.* : delyte *inf.*).

Rhyme words.—wyte *blame inf.* (826, 1469, 2363), *noun* (2731, 3582), delite *ind.* 3 *pl.* (1339), endite *subj.* 1 *sg.* (1354), *inf.* (1339, 2112, 7653, 7992), plyte *inf.* (2288), smyte *inf.* (2363), byte *inf.* (3582), write *ind.* 1 *sg.* (7992), *subj.* 2 *sg.* (2112, 7653), *inf.* (2302), myte (3675, 3740), white *pl* (3740).

Note.—For *lytel, litel* [Var. B litil; C lityl, litil, lytil, lytyl; D litle, litell, litrl; litill, liteell (5256)], adjectival, adverbial, and substantive, cf. (i') 179, 216, 1241, 1327, 1730, 1590 BCD, 2163, 2165, 2420, 3389, 3443, 3935, 4252, 4401, 4453, 4487, 4530, 4663, 4860, 5243, 5385, 5546, 6109, 7289, 7403, 7468, 7818, 7865; (ii.) lytel, litel, cf. 5046, 5256, 5992 (lite B), 6539 (lite C); litel hed, 5095; litel hertes reste, 8112 (cf. 5243 C); litel hath, 5352; a litel here (*acc. sg.*), 5265 (a lite B, a ‡ litèll D); a lytel his, 6577 (a lite vnswelle B).

[1] A almost always has *allone* (*alone,* 2390).

muche (A.S. micel), 386 (muchel B, meche C, myche D), 442 (-el B, mechil C, mych[e] D), 1313 (nuch † B, meche C, D †), 2156 (muchel B, meche C, mychil D), 3480 (B †, meche C, mich[e] D), 4529 (meche C, miche D), 5561 (-el B, meche C, moche D); thow hast so meche don, 3228 (much i·do B, myche ‡ for D); meche knowe, 1260 C.—muche,—as m. as, 796 (meche AC, mych D),3840 (meche C, mich D), 5156 (meche C, moch D); as meche as, 5998 C (wyd A, wyde BD); thus muche, 2948 (meche C, mych D), 7361 (meche C, much D); in as m. as, 7428 (meche C, much † D); so m. as, 1327 (meche C, mych D); for as m. as, 7715 (meche C, much D);[1] so muche honoure, 2981 (muchel B, mechil C, D om. †).—so mych ‡ grace, 1070 D (?).—mechel of 2744 (muchel B, meche C, mychil D). (Non-adjectival uses, substantive or adverbial, are indicated in the above list by old-style verse-numbers.)

§ 49. Several adjectives which in Anglo-Saxon end in a consonant, sometimes or always take -e in the *Troilus*. (Child, § 30 ; ten Brink § 231.)

Some of the -e's in the following list are perhaps to be explained on grammatical grounds. In *brode Phebus, false Poliphete, proude Bayard, heighe God, heyghe Ioue*, we perhaps have a petrified vocative like that recognized by ten Brink (§ 236. Anm.) in *goode fayre Whyt she heet* (B. Duch., 948), cf. *fierse Mars*, 2864 (-[e] D). (Cf., however, Zupitza, *Deutsche Litteratur-Zeitung*, 1885, col. 613, and Freudenberger, *Ueber das Fehlen des Auftakts in Chaucer's heroischem Verse, Erlanger Beiträge zur Engl. Philol.*, Heft iv, pp. 37-39.) Is it not possible that *salte se, false worldes brotelnesse*, and *wode ialousie* (or read *the wode*?) are to be referred to the same idiom? The relation between a vocative and a constant epithet is in some respects sufficiently close. The exclamatory form *goode grace* may also be of the same vocative nature, but *harde grace* has nothing to do with address or with constant epithets. Observe *gon sithen longe while*, etc. (see *longe*) and *of olde tyme*.

bare (A.S. bær, L. bare, bar, P. Pl.ᶜ bar,ᵇᶜ bare), 662 f (: care n. : snare n.), 1195 f (: care n. : fare pl.), 4888 f (: wel-fare : care n.), 5830 f (: yfare p.p.); -e, 5887. [For definite form, cf. 3941, 6184.]

brode (A.S. brád, L. brad, brod, O. brad, P.Pl.ᵃᵇᶜ brod), brode Phebus, 7380 (broode D, the ‡ brode Phebus C).

---

[1] Supply [me] in D.

faire, fayre (A.S. fæger, L. fæir, fæire, O. faʒʒerr, P. Pl. fayre), the thriddë hëuene faire, 2844 f. (: debonaire : repaire *inf.*); in a ful fairë ‡ wyse, 5472 B (seerë † A, sècret(e) D, sècrë G).¹—faire, 1309 (glad CD), 3253 (-r D, fayr nor C), 3564 (fair D).—fairę, 101 (fayr C), 1669 (-r BCD).

fair, fayr, feyr, (i.) 815 f (-e BCD) (: despeyr *n.*), 882 (-ę B); (ii.) 115 (-e BD), 277; 294 (goode B, good CD), 900 (-e B), 4448 (-e B, -ę ‡ so D), 5073 (fayr ‡ sche C), 6535 (-e B), 6810 (-e BD). [faire *extra metr.*, 1171 AB.] [In address : goodly fayrë fresshë may, 7775 f.]

false (A.S. fals, *late*, P. Pl. fals), falsë worldës brotelnesse, 8195 (-[e] B, -ę D); falsë Poliphete, 2552 C (that fals ‡ polyfete D, fals[e] AB).²

fals, sg., 87 AB, 593, 3656, 5278 (-ę D), 5725 (-ę D); cf. 6199, 6209, 6319, 7642, 7889)³; false, pl., 5321 (-[e] B, C †), 8144 (-[e] B).

ferne (A.S. fyrn, *adj.*, fyrn-gear, *n.*, fyrn-géara, *adv.*, O. Sax. fernum gêre, P. Pl. fernyere), Ye fare-wel al the snow of fern[ë] yere, 7539 (fern[ë]yere B, fern[ë]yere C, feuerer ‡ D) (: here *hic*).⁴

fresche (A.S. fersc, L. freche, frech, O. fressh), Yong freschë (fresshë B, frosch † C, freisshë D) strong and hardy as lyon, 7193.

fressh, fresch, (i.) 1721 (-ę D); (ii.) 166 (-e B, frosch C, fressh ‡ lady D), 816 (-e CD), 1637 (-e BD), 1972 (-e BC), 2007 A (-e B), 2182 (-e B), 4626 (-e D), 5817 (frosche ‡ *pl.* C), 7207, 7473.

In address,—o goodly fresshë fre, 2970 (-[e] B, fressh and D(?)); fresshë wommanlichë wyf, 4138; cf. 7680, 7775.

Var. B fresh; C frosche, frossche ; D freissh, -e.

goode (A.S. gód, L.O. god), And seyde On suche a mirour good[e] grace, 1351, (goodë B Cp., gode E, good[e] G). *Good[ë] gouernaunce*, 1552 CD, is an error for *goddes g.* Goode, 44 AB (*om.* ‡ D), 6549 (god CD), and *goode*, 52 (D †), are mere accidents. *Goode Alceste*, 8141 (good BD) may be a "petrified vocative." Everywhere else *good* (var. B good(e)), except in plural and in definite forms, where grammar requires *goode* (cf. 335, 336, 627, 1247, 1254, 1556, 1667, 1763, 2743, etc., etc.).—goud, 1337 A (goode B, godę C, good D). (Cf. the *substantive*, § 14.)

grete (A.S. gréat, O. grǣt). I find no good case of *grete* except, perhaps, *yn purpos gret*, 7939 f (grete BD) (: contrefete *inf.*).

[1] *Secre* is no doubt right (secre John's, secree E Cp., secret Harl. 2392).
[2] Supply [ye] in AB. Cp. and John's have ʒe, ye ; Cp. has *falsë*.
[3] For cases of *sing. fals* (var. -e CD) before vowels, cf. 3140, 3646, 5043, 5656, 7061.
[4] Apparently Cp. and John's agree with A. Harl. 2392 reads *feuerere*.

§ 49.]   *of Chaucer's Troilus.*   117

gret, (i.) * 66, 94 [1] (D ?), 296 (D ?), * 528 [2], 1024, 1249, 1252 [3], 2522, 2595 (C †), 2788 (-ę D), 3361, 3709 (om. † C), * 4055, * 4058, * 4289, * 4357, 4718, 5518, * 6173, * 6501, * 6801, 8107, * 8156. [Var. B greetę; D greet.] — (ii.)   * 28 [4] (grete ease ‡ D), 65, 587 (C *om.* †), 1290 (gret [e]stat C, -e † D), 1810, 1966, 2250 (D †), 2377 (D ?), 2476, * 3377 (C †, D *om.*), 3475, * 4476, 5212 (D ?), 5559 (-e D), 7344 (C †), 7842 ([a] gret C), * 7992 (gret effect(*is*) C). [Var. D greet.]—gret hònour, 2654 (-e h. BD).

Note 1.—Such -e's as there are in A are none of them sounded. They are the following,—a ful gretę care, 1016 (a wol gret C, [a] ful grete D); in grete dishese, 2072 (gret C); a grete deuyneresse, 7885 (gret C); a bor as grete as, 7832 (gret CD).

Note 2.—In 515 B (*grete*), supply [a] and read *gretę* (gret AC, grete D); cf. also 1252. In 1903 BD *a grete rowte* might be read (And other of hire wommen ‖ a greté rowte), but *gret* is the reading of AC.

harde (A.S. heard, L. heard, herd, O. harrd), no moré harde grace, 713 (hard[e] D).—hard, (i.) 836 (-ę B, -e C), 2321 (-ę B, D †), 2326 (-ę B), 2356 (-e B †, hard here D), 2990, 3776, 6119 (-ę D); (ii.) 4199 (-e E). (Cf. 4757, 5802, 6035.)

heighe (A.S. héah, M. héh, L. hæh, hæhʒe, O. heh). Two cases of -e, —But that wot heighè god, 3869 (-[e] B, hy[e] D), wot ‡ I by god C); Thorugh purueyaunce and disposicion Of heyghe Ioue, 7906-7 (-[e] B, heye C, high[e] D). To which add,—in heuene hye, 4587 f ABC (heye E) (: gye *inf.* : companye).—highe, 3279 (heighę B, hey C, hyę D), heyghe, 4636 (heigh B, hey C, hyé D).

heigh, heygh,, (i.) 1717 (hey C, hyę D), 3128 (hey C; D †), 3739 (hi C, hie ‡ D), 4165 (hey C, high ‡ is E), 5853 (hey C, high D), 6799 (hey C, hię D), 7330 (hey C, high D), 7342 (hy C, hię D), 7872 ‡ D (high). (ii.) 4113 (hi C, hiʒ D), 5220 (hey C, high D).

longe (A.S. lang, long, O. lang), gon sithen longe while, 718 (seth gone long while (?) D); nought go (gon BC, gonę D) ful long[e] while, 1592 (-e B); longe tyme agon, 1807 BD (-[e] A (?), -[e] C); [5] longé tyme agon, 7688 (-[e] D (?)). Cf. the A.S. accusative phrases *lange þráge (hwíle, tíd.)*—In *Or that it be ful longe*, 832 f (long D) (: honge *inf.*), and *Ten dayes nys so longë not tabyde*, 6716 (-ę(?) C), *longe* is perhaps adv. longé lette, 7214 BCGCp. John's (more A, lenger D). [longe here (*hic*), 3661 C^c.] longe (*adv.* ?), 4698 (long D).

---

[1] Old-style figures indicate that B and D have -ę; an asterisk indicates that B alone has -e.   [2] Supply [a] in A.
[3] "For gret power and moral vertu, here." In B we might read: "For grete power and," etc.
[4] Old-style figures indicate that B and D have -e (elided); an asterisk indicates that B alone has -e (elided).   [5] Supply [*And*] in A, and read *long*[e].

118　　　*Observations on the Language*　　　[§ 49.

long, (i.) 143 (longe ? B), 2384 (-ę B), 3337 (-ę B), 5555 (-ę B, longe † D),[1] 5944 (mak[ë] long(e) sermon B, -ę D).

olde (A.S. eald, ald, L. ald, alde, olde, O. ald), of oldë tyme, 6833 BD (old[e] A, oftyn † C[e]).—oldę, 1481 (old CD); olde (*in address*), 4992. (Cf. *old*, (ii.) 6031, 7647.)

> Note.—All the other cases of *olde* (not *oldë*) that I have noted are either definite or plural. Definite cases (singular) are the following,—3189,[2] 3537 (wolde † C, old[e] D), 4766[3] (old[e] ? D), 4789, 4803 f (BC *defect.*, the old D) (: holde *inf.*), 6123 (D†), 7489, 7499 ; The newë lose out chaceth (cacheth † A, schakyth ‡ C) ofte the olde, 5077 f (: holde *p.p.* : colde *inf.*) ; myn oldë hat, 3162. (*Oldë* in all these except as indicated.) For the plural indefinite, see the following verses,—130 f, 160 f, 2933 f, 3139 f, 4041 f, 4728 f, 5086, 5634 f, 6921 f, 7009 f, 7015, 7571 f, 7822, 7841, 7844 (C†), 7874 f, 7925, 8212, 8217. (In all of these the reading of all the MSS. is *oldë* except as follows : -*e* (elided), in 5086, 7015 A (old B) ; -[e], in B in 7841, 7844 (C†), 7925, 8212 ; -[e], in D in 3139 ; old, 4728 f D ; oolde, 4041 f D ; oldde, 7822 B. [old[e]] ‡, 969 D.]—Plural definite,— -ë, 6742 (-[e] B), 6743 ‡ C, 8116 ; -*e*, 760 (old D), 6118 ‡ D (?).

proude (A.S. prút, L. prut), proudë bayard, 218 (-[e] D) ; proud (*before vowels*), 210 (-*e* B), 214 (pryde ‡ B).

salte (A.S. sealt), In heuęne and helle in erthe and saltë se, 2850 (-[e] BD).

wode (A.S. wód), Which that men clepeth wodë ialousie, 7576 (the wodë A).—wood, wod, (i.) 499 (-ę B, D†), 3635 (-ę B), cf. 2639 ; wod, (ii.) 3240 (-*e* B, *om.* † A), 4892 (-*e* B, *om.* † D), 5579 (-*e* B), cf. 5010, 6201.

> Note 1.—Some adjectives show an -*e* which is grammatically unjustifiable and never sounded. In B this is very common ; in A, however, it is pretty rare. Thus,—sikę, 575 (sik B, sek C) ; sykę, 7957 (sik B, in † seek C, sike D) ; but,—syk, (i.) 2601 (sikę BD) ; (ii.) 2608 (-*e* D), 2614 (sek C, seke D), 6776 (-*e* D, sek C).[4] See also *faire, goode, grete, highe, olde.*
> Note 2.—*It welę be to hirę lewe*, 5267 f C, is an error for *lewe* inf. (ABD) (: greue *inf.*) ; cf. 2778, 3487, 5273 f, 6581. Of monosyllabic adjectives, which in Anglo-Saxon end in a consonant and which take no -*e* in the *Troilus* in the uninflected forms, many examples are given in §§ 53, 55, 67, 69. Cf. also *bold* (2930, 4695, 7158), *broun* (109 f), *fayn* (6556, 6788, 6851 f, 7376 f), *hoors* (5809), *hor* (7647 f), *lyk* (2125 f, 5910, etc.), *towgh, towh* (2110 f, 2929 f, 6464 f), *vnwar* (549) (cf. note 3), *wan* (1636 f, 4897 f, 7584 f), *warm* (2732 f), *worth* (2163, 4382, 5160), *wyd* (5289). In some of these words there are variants in -*e* (not sounded) : thus, *hoor(e)* (7647 f D), *wann(e)* (1636 f D), etc.
> Note 3.—For dissyllables in the indefinite use, singular, cf. heuęnyssh, 8176, cf. 104 ; holsom, 4588 ; open, 1125 ; siker, syker, (i.) (ii.) 673, 920, 2455, cf. 4079 ; sonnyssh, 5398 ; sothfast, 5532 ; stedęfast, 5651 (stedfast BD) ; vnwàr, 304 ; a wonder thyng, 621, cf. 1120 D ; yonder sonne, 2322 ; on ydel, 948 f, 6457 f, 6635 ; yuel, 8000 ; ywàr, 1483 (i- B, war C, warę D) ; as Argus eyed, 6121 f ; rosy hewed, 2283 ; horned, 7013 ; lewed, 3240 ; blisful, blysful, (i.) 1765, 1917, 2176, 6323 (*voc.* ?), cf. 5778 ;

---

[1] C out of order.
[2] Old-style figures indicate that BD have *old[e]*.
[3] In B we must drop (*vp-*) and read *on* with A.
[4] *Sikë y me feyne*, 2613 D, is an error for *syklyche*, etc.

§§ 49, 50.] *of Chaucer's Troilus.* 119

dredful, 2130, 2343, d. herte 2186, 7694, B has *dredeful* in 2186, 2343, 7694; leful, 3862 (lefful C); skylful, (i.) 1477, 3780, (ii.) 3129; vnskilful, (ii.) 790; woful, (i.) 13, 1518, 2945, 5406, 5500, 6106, 6684, (ii.) 7683.
Sorwful is usually dissyllabic; *sorwẽful* (dissyllabic) is the regular pronunciation and spelling in AB, *sorwẽful* is favored by C, and D prefers *sorqwfull* (cf. 14, 1149, 1548, 5036, 6604, 6779); but the word is sometimes trisyllabic: thus,— Cryseyde ful of *sorw[ẽ]ful* (sorwẽful C, sorwẽfull D, sorwful John's) pite, 5393, where, however, Cp. has *sorwful* and *piete* (cf. also 7591 D, 7996 D); see §§ 57. c, 84. Cf. ernestful, 2812.

Note 4.—For adjectives in -*y* (A.S. -*ig*), indefinite, singular, (i.) before consonants, cf. almyghty (5355), angry (562), blody (5289, 7865 C), bysy (1359, 3884, 6307), cloudy (1853), dedly (5533), drery (13), hardy (2159, 7165), hasty (6230), heuy (3981), lusty, -i (157, 165, 951, 1837, 2184, 6147, 6756), myghty (1673), mysty (3902), redy (2081, 3545, 4627, 5870, 5873, 6378, 6420), sondry (440, 957, 5174), sory (14, 1179, 1549, 2141, 3886, 6503, 6990, 7445, 7461), thrifty (275), trusty (4665 ‡ D), vnmyghty (1943), vnweri (410, 1924), vnworthi (4126, 4991), wery (1296), worthy, -i (226, 979, 1265, 2784, 4011, 4701, 6696, 7226). For examples before vowels (with and without slurring of -*y*), see the Chapter on Metre. For the plural, see § 70; for the definite use, see § 57. d.

Note 5.—Adjectives in -*les* are the following (sing. and indef. unless otherwise noted): (i.) (ii.) boteles, 782 f (bootelees B) (see *graceles*); botmeles byhestes, *pl.*, 7794 (bottemeles C, botumles D); drynk[e]lees, 1806 (drenkynlees B, drynkeles C, drink[e]les D); endeles, 2168 (eufeyned † C, infynyte ‡ D *in a rather later hand*); gilt[e]les, 1413 (gilteles BC) (*perh. adv.*); the gilt[l]es in distresse, 2457 (gilteless B, gilteles C, giltles D) (*sg.* or *pl.* ?); graceles, 781 f (: causeles *adv.*: boteles); heleles, 7956 (heceles † A); hertcles, 7957 (I herde † telle C); knotteles, 7132 B (-[e]- D, knot[e]les AB); lyghtles, 3392 (-lees B); makeles, 172 f (: natheles: prees n.); resteles, 4426; roteles, 5432 (rootheles B, ertheles ‡ C); routhelees, 1431 f (-les B, reutheles C, rowtheles D); specheles, 5032, 5829; ster[e]les (= without helm; Ital. word here is *governo*), 416 (stiërlees (?) B, stereles C, ster[e]les D); vertules, 1429 f (vertuelees B) (: routhelees).

§ 50. The following adjectives of Germanic origin also show an -*e* in the *Troilus*:

badde (A.S. bæddel (?)), souned in-to badde, 6338 f (: ye hadde *ind.*); cf. sownen ynto gode, 1029 f.

lowe (O.N. lágr, L. laih, O. lah), But hold hym as his thral lowe yn distresse, 439 (low BD)[1]. Cf. the definite form,—my lowe confessioun, 1613; lowe, *pl.* or *adv.*, 2869 (lawe B, low D).

meke (O.N. mjúkr, O. meoc, P. Pl.c meke), 8210 f (: seke *inf.*).

schere (O.N. skærr, cf. A.S. scír), an arwë schere, 6210 f C (clere AB, cler D) (: here *adv.*).

wykke, wikke (cf. M.E. wicche, A.S. wicc(e)a 'wizard,' wicce 'witch'), -*e*, 403 (C *om.* †, wykkyd D); now is wykke iturned vn-to worse, 3916 (wyk D, wikked torned B, like † Cc); fro wikke I go to worse, 5502 (wo ‡ A, wikked D).

Note 1.—Cf. the following cases of the plural in the indefinite use,—wykke, 939 f (wyk D) (: thikke *indef. adj. sg.*), 1543 f (weke C, wyk D) (: thikke *adj. pl. or adv.*).

[1] Supply [*his*] in D.

Note 2.—*Wykked* also occurs. Thus,—7973 (wikked BD, wekedę C); cf. 1889, 3650. Cf. also the plural (39, 7118), the vocative (3679, where C has *welkede*), the definite use (§ 57. *b*).

Note 3—For *rakel* (cf Swed. dial. rakkel *sbst.*, O. N. reikall *adj.*) see the following places,—with r. hond, 1060 (-yl D); echę r. dede, 3271 (rackle B, rakil CD); thow r nyght, 4279 (rakle B, rakele C); *pred.* (before a consonant), 4472 (-yl C). In 4484 is *rakle* an inf. ?

§ 51. Romance adjectives preserve their final -e in the *Troilus* (Child, § 19; ten Brink, § 239). (A few Latin adjectives are included in the following list.)

I. Miscellaneous :

benigne, benÿgne (O. Fr. benigne), 8232 f (: digne *pl.*); -e he was, 4644 (beningę B, -nyng D). (For pl., cf. 431 f, 2868 f.)

contraire (O. Fr. contraire), 212 f A (contrarie BD, -rye C) (: on the staire : debonaire). (Cf. necessaire.) See also § 31, to which add references to 418, 637. Contrarie, *adj.*, 5690 f (: tarie *inf.*); cf. 5665.

dèbonaire (O. Fr. debonere, -aire), -e, 181 (-ar B, -er CD); cf. o goodly debonaire, 2846 f (-eyre D) (: clere *pl.*).

digne (O. Fr. digne), 429 f (: benygne *pl.* : resigne *ind.* 1 *sg.*); digne, cf. 961, 3856. (For pl., cf. 2865 f, 8231 f.)

eterne (O. Fr. eterne), 2853 f (: descerne *inf.* : werne *inf.*), 3217 f (: gouerne *inf.* : yerne *adv.*).

huge (O. Fr. ahuge), 3498 (D †), 6049, 6428. [Var. heuge C.]

iuste (O. Fr. juste), 1612, 1812 ; iust[e], 4069, 7619 (-e BCD).

large (O. Fr. large), 7167 f (: Arge *n. pr.*).

mansuète (Lat. mansuetus, cf. Ital. mansueto), 6557 f (*l. om.* † C) (: swete : mete *inf.*).

necessaire (O. Fr. necessaire), 5683 f (: fayre *adv.*) (necessarie AB, -rye D, C cut out). (Cf. contrarie.)

nice, nyce, nyse (O. Fr. nice), 1808 f (: vyse (A †) : cherishe *inf.*, -ice BCD), 1942 f (: vice), 2585, 5198, 5260 f (: vice). (For *pl.* cf. 3166 f, 4235 f.)

pale (O. Fr. pale, palle, pasle), 5402 f (: smale *adj. pl.* : bale *n.*), 6899 (C ?).

pryme, —at prymë face (=Lat. prima facie), 3761.

straunge (O. Fr. estrange), 6483 f (: chaunge *inf.*), 7223 (D †), 7995 f (strong † C) (: chaunge *n.*) ; his manère estraunge, 1077 f (straunge D) (: chaunge *inf.*).

trine (Lat. trinus, cf. Fr. trine), trine ‡ vnite, 8229 D.

II. For Adjectives in *-ble*, of all constructions, singular and plural, compare the following words in the places cited (C is fond of the spelling—*bele*, but sometimes has *-el*, *-il*).

[§§ 51, 52.] *of Chaucer's Troilus.* 121

able, 1292, 1821, 1988.
chàritàble, 7186.
còuenàble, 2222 f.
dìscordàble, 4595 f.
double, 1, 54, 7261.
èxcusàble, 3873.
feble, 7585.
hònouràble, 6798 f.
horrìble, 6613.
humble, 124, 433, 1913, 2154, 2214, 2938, 2983, 4197, 4329, 4790, 6161, 7683.

impossìble, 4153; cf. 783.
ìnuysìble, 8229.
muàble, 3664 f.
noble, 1404, 1416, 1732, 1822, 3739, 6747, 7342, 7686, 7920, 8115.
rèmuàble, 6344.
rèsonàble, 2220 f, 2991.
stable, 4593 f.
vnstàble, 3662 f.
visìble, 8229.

Note 1.—For the treatment of these words before vowels (elision or non-elision depending upon accent), see 1821, 2938, 3739, 4790, 6747, 7186, 7342, 7920, 8229. For *symple* cf. 181, 7183.

Note 2.—For *tęder* (O.F. tendre), see *tender of*, 3746 (tendre BD, -djr C); cf. *sobre was*, 7183 (-ere C). For *transitorie* (: memorie) see 3669 f.

Note 3.—French -é is of course preserved. Thus,—*loke that atempre be thy brydel*, 946 (atempree B, atempere † wel C, that thou † attempre be thy b. D); *sècre, secré*, cf. 744 f, 3128, 3154 f, 3601 (cf. also *sècret, secrèt* (?), (ii.) 2749, 2984, 3320); *prèue*, 3763 (priue B, pryve D, prime † C), cf. *prèuy*, 3629 (pryue BD, priue C).

§ 52. But some Romance adjectives take an -e in the *Troilus* that have none in French. In a few of the following instances one might be inclined to suspect the influence of a French feminine ending (cf. § 63). Some of the forms are vocative, but such are always indicated.

aduèrse (O. Fr. advers, avers), fortune aduerse, voc., 5854 f (: werse : diuerse *pl.*).

asùre (O. Fr. azur), a brochę gold of asure, 4212 f (g. and asure BCD) (: auenture : scripture).

clere (O. Fr. cler), 6210 f (schere C, cler D) (: here *adv.*); -ę, 3368 (cler C, -e D ?); cler, 5653 (-ę BD). [For def. form *clere*, cf. 7018 f; for pl. *clere*, cf. 2843 f, 2971 f, 4195 f, 6097 f, 6372 f, 6583 f, 6929 f, 7173 f, 7178 f, 7362 f, 7701 f.]

comùne (O. Fr. comun), fortune ys commune, 843 f (: fortune); she... traytour comune, 4667 f (: fortune : entune *inf.*); comune astrologer, 4257 (C †); by comune ‡ assente (?), 5008 D (on AC, oon B). [Cf. *pl.*, 5054 f.]

diuerse (O. Fr. divers), in diuèrsë wyse, 61 (dyuèrsę ‡ D). (Cf. Freudènberger, *Ueber das Fehlen des Auftakts*, p. 39.)

dyuyne (O. Fr. divin), of dyuynë purueyaunce, 5623 A (de- BD).
fyne (O. Fr. fin), of fyn[ë] force, 6784 (-ë BD). [fyne, 5139 f C (: myn) *should be* fyn *n.*]
mene (O. Fr. meiien), Criseyde mene was, 7169 (-[e] B)[1]. [Cf. the def. form,—this menë while, 2892; in this menę while, 3618 AB (in this wyse † C, in this while D).]
pure (O. Fr. pur), for pure ashamed, 1741 (-ë schamyd C)[2]. [Adverb?]
queynte (O. Fr. coint), swetë harmę so q., exclam., 411 f. (-t D) (: pleynte *n.* : feynte *pres. ind.* 1 *sg.*).
secounde (O. Fr. second), 7199 f (*pred. masc. sg.*) (secunde B) (: founde *p. p.*); cf. Ector the secunde, 1243 f (-ounde B, -ound D) (: wounde *n.* : abounde *inf.*).
souereyne (O. Fr. soverain), o lady souëreyne, 4978 f (-ayne B, -aigne D) (: peyne *n.*).

> Note 1.—Here may be added,—*the* blood *Thebàne*, 6964 f (Theban C) (: bane *n.*). The parallel form *Tròian Troiàn* (regularly *troyan* in C) has no -e, whether *adj.* or *sbst.* (cf. 1910, 4715, 4734, 4994 f (: man), 6489, 7240, 7272, 7275, 7283), except perhaps in the plural (cf. 145).
>
> Note 2.—*Recrèauntę* has an adventitious -e due to the scribe : *Or be recreaunte of* (-ę *for* B, *recreaunt of* D) *his owene tene*, 814. So *pleyne*, 5552 ABD (*pleyn* C).
>
> Note 3.—For examples of the singular of Romance adjectives in the indefinite use, see the following (accent recessive except as indicated) :—
> èternèl (5724 f), funeral (6665 f), fynàl (4807 f), general (163, 893 f, 919 f, 4644 f, 4804 f, 7185 f), infernàl (6205 f), moral (1252, 6334), mortal (2860, 3218), inmòrtal (103), natal (2992), egàl (2979), royàl (432, 435 f, 4642 f, 6329 f, 8193); angwysshous (3658), bounteuous (883 f), cheuàl[e]roùs (7165), còrageùs (7163 f), coueytous (4215)[3], desiroùs (1051, 2186), deynous (290), disdeỳnous (2302 D), doutoùs (5654), enuỳous (1942), ènuyoùs (4542), grenous (6154, 7594, 7967, cf. 5566), heỳnoùs (2702), ialous, ielous (3741, 3993), pitous, petous (111, 113, 422, 3760, 5345, 6161, 6918), dispitoùs (6562 f), tràytous (4542 A ; traytour BCD); absent (6824, 7000 BCD), absènt (3330 f, 7000 A), diligent (2986 f, 3327 f), innocent (2647, 2808), prèsent (4810, 7110), presènt (2887 f, 4142) ; caytìf (rather *sbst.* than *adj.*, 3224 B ; castif A, captỳf CD), èntentỳf (1923 f), testỳf (7165), cf. gỳltyf (3861, 3891) ; àngelỳk (102), cèrteyn (2633, 3374, 4601, etc.), yn certeỳn, cèr'eyn (697, 5570, 5607 C, 5667 f), vncèrteyn (5651), clos (2619), confus (5018), mat (5004), cùrteys (81), defèt (6981, 7582), discrèt (3319, 3785), esy (1083, 1705), èxpert (67), felon (6562), fortunat (1365), infortùnat (5406 D; -ed AB, ònfortùne C), fùtur (7111), gèntil (3746, 6336, 7294), ioly (2184, 7537), malapert (2929), pàrfit (4221, 7282), pepelyssh (6339), preìgnant (5841), secret (2749, 3320), secrèt (2984), sòdeyn (1752), soùr (4036 ‡ A), sùbget, -git (231, 8153), subtìl (1342), vnàpt (971), in veyn (4254, 4976, 7736). Some of these occasionally show variants in -e (not sounded). For adjectives in -*ious*, -*uous*, -*ial*, -*icnt*, -*uel*, see Chapter on Metre. For adjectives in -*ay*, cf. *gay* (2007 f), vèrray (6267, very D).

§ 53. In the definite use (that is, when preceded by a possessive or demonstrative pronoun or by the definite

---

[1] In C supply [*hirę*].   [2] D om. *for* (purë ashamyd).   [3] Dissyllable?

article) monosyllabic adjectives take an inflectional -e (Child, § 32; ten Brink, §§ 232, 241).

I. Ordinals:

our first[e] lettre, 171 (-e B, our chef[e] l. ‡ ? D); the firste syght[e], 1754 (the ferst[e] C, the ferst † D); the firste tyme, 2841 (-[e] D). (Cf. also 280, 2298, 4615, 6603, 7303.) the alderfirst[e], 2939 (the aldir ferste C; D †); with the firste ‖ it cam, 4725 (the ferst hit D). But,—the firste ‖ that, 7430 (see § 54).

the thridde ferthe fyfthe sixte day, 7568 (C † D †); Mayes day the thridde, 1141 f (-d D) (: bytydde *ind.* 3 *sg*); the thridde heuene, 2844 (-[de] D). (Cf. also 4660, 5353.)

this ilke ferthe book, 4688 (this ‡ ferthe b. D). (Cf. also 6839, 6856).

the seuenthe spere, 8172; here seuenthe hows, 1766 (seuente C, vij. D).[1]

that ilke nynthe nyght, 7466 (tenthe † C). (Cf. also 7044.)

the tenthe day, 6787 (the x[the] d. D). (Cf. also 6257, 6260, 6787, 7005, 7048, 7205.)

with his tenthe some yfere, 2334 (his t. sonne † B, his tensum † C, his x· somme D).

II. Monosyllabic superlatives:

for the beste, 581[2] f (-t C), 2409 f, 3890 f, 4171 f, 4831 f, 5539 f, 5950 f (-t C), 6090 f, 7969 f, 8113 f; the beste, 2533 f (-t C), 3295 f ([the] beste C), 3514 f (-t C), 3689 f, 3769 f, 5319 f, 5782 f (-t C), 6265 f (-t C), 7892 f (-t C); the best is 830 AD (-e BC); the faireste and the beste, 4122 f; my beste, 597 f (-t BC); thi beste, 1021 f (-t C, for the best D); the best[e] post, 993 (-e BC); the beste knyght, 1074 (-[e] BD); my best[e] frend, 1497 (-e C); thi beste gere, 2097 (-[e] D);[3] the best[e] harpour, 2115 (-e C); his beste wyse, 4436 (-[e] D); the beste weye, 5954 (-[e] D); o frend of frendes the alderbeste, 4439 f (no article in CD, which read *aldyr best, altherbest*). (Cf. also 474, 947, 1467, 3797, 5470, 5947, 5987, 6188, 7670.) But,—the best, 1825 f ACD (-e B) (: the thryftiest : the worthiest).

> Rhyme-words.—I ne lest (leste) *pres. subj.* (581), leste, lyste *pres subj.* 3 *sg.* (1021, 2533, 3514, 3689, 3890, 4171), leste *pret.* 3 *sg. ind. or subj.* (3295, 4831), reste *inf.* (597, 2409, 4122, 5950, 8113), *pres. ind.* 1 *sg.* (5319), *noun* (3769, 3890, 4439, 5782, 6265), vnreste (5539, 7969), wreste *inf.* (6090), moleste *inf.* (5539), in geste (3295), breste *pres. subj.* 3 *sg.* (597), Alceste (7892)

[1] Or,—Sat in here seuenthe hows of heuene tho.
[2] Old-style figures indicate that D reads *best*.
[3] Insert [*ryght*] in A.

at the laste, 916 f (att[e] laste B),[1] 1040 f (at ‡ last D), 1230 f (attë laste B), 1484 f, 1776 f (-t C), 3938 f (-t C), 5185 f (-t C), 8002 f (-t C), 8182 f; at the last[e], 8093 (-e BD); at the last[e], 2023 f (-e BC); at the laste, 5885 (-ë ‡ as C, -t † D); at the laste her-of, 3407 (-t B) (cf. also 1584, 1599, 1909, 3457, 3961, 4417, 5097, 6796, 7509); to the laste, 1340 f; April[2] the laste, 3202 f (-t C); my laste, 537 f (D †), 1955 f (-t C); his laste, 3640 f; the last[e] shour, 4709 (-ë B). But,—at the lastę the, 2009 (-të dede ‡ D); at the lastę this, 5034; at the last this, 5914 (-ę BCD).

  Rhyme words.—faste *adv.* (537, 916, 1040, 1230, 1776, 1955, 2023, 3938, 5185, 8002, 8182), laste *inf.* (537, 1040, 1955), caste *inf.* (1340, 1776, 3202), *pret. ind.* 3 *sg.* (1230, 3938, 5185, 8182), paste *pret. ind.* 3 *sg.* (1484), Horàste (3640).

at the leste, 1447 f, 2293 (-[e] BD), 2415 f (-t C), 3156 f, 4002 f, 6439 f (at leste ‡ D), 6888 f, 7313 f (attë leste B), 8041 f; at the leste how, 4678; oon the leste, 4152 f (oon ‡ of the leste E); the leeste ioye, 4162; the leste poynt, 4386 (-[e] D).

  Rhyme words.—heste, behest, byheste (1447, 2415, 3156, 4002, 8041), feste (1447, 4002, 4152, 6439, 6888, 8041), requeste *n.* (7313), at the meste (7313). [Var. B leeste, leest[e]; D leest.]

at the meste, 7310 f (attë meeste B) (: requeste *noun* : at the leste); the moste wondir, 2228 C (-[e] D, the grettest wonder AB); for the moste part, 3281 C (-[e] D, more AB); here most[e] fere, 4183 (-e CE); my most[e] nede, 6194 (-e CD); compare,—now is most[e] nede, 3259.

the nexte word, 2942 (-[e] B; D †); this nexst[e] wyke, 2358 (the nexte C); the nexte wise, 697 BC (-[e] D).[3]

the worste, 1452 (-[e] D); the worste, 341 (-ę so ‡ C, -t so ‡ D); the worste poynt, 342 (the worst y ‡ D); the worste trecherye, 3120 (-[e] D); the worste kynde, 4468 (-[e] D). (Cf. 1389, 1622, 6459, 7090.) [Var. ABCD werste.]

  III. Miscellaneous:

the bente mone, 3466 (-[e] B).

here blake wede, 177 (-[e] BD); cf. 2405 f. (For indef. *blak*, cf. 309, 642, 1619.)

the blynde lust, 8187; thy blynde and wynged sone, 4650 (blynd † D). (For indef. *blynd*, cf. 628, 1106, 3370 f).

here brighte face, 4670 (-[e] D); the bryght[e] mone, 7011 (-e C); Criseyde the brighte, 6879 f (-t CD) (: a-light (-e B) *pret. ind.* 3 *pl.* :

---

[1] Old-style figures denote that D has *last*.
[2] Three syllables (April AD, Aperil B, Aprille C).
[3] A reads: For this nys not yn certeyn the next wyse. Omit yn (with BCD Cp. John's) and read *the next[e] wyse*.

§ 53.] *of Chaucer's Troilus.* 125

nyghte *inf.*). (Cf. also 5325, 7071, 7379, 7602.) here fadies faire
bryghte tente, 7385 (faire bright[e] D).

here colde mouth, 5823 (-[e] B); my cold[e] care, 612 (-e C, the ‡
cold[e] D). (Cf. 2052 ‡ C, 5173.)

the dede slep, 2009.

his fixe and depe impressioun, 298 (B †, fyx C).

thi derke wede, 4273. (Cf. 5016.)

And nexst the derk[e] nyght the glade morwe, 944 (derke . . . glad[e]
B, derke . . . gladde C, -[e] . . . -[e] D).

the foule netle, 941 (C †, foul[e] D); thy foule enuye, 4937. (For
indef. *ful*, cf. 1981 and see § 55.)

his fulle myght, 7046 (-[le] BD) (cf. 610, 1052, 1419, 2637, 3278,
6438, 7902); at the fulle, 209 f (atte fulle B) (cf. 3055, 3359, 3376);
here ful[le] herte, 7083 A *should read* here woful h. (*so* BCD).

that glade nyght, 3071 (cf. 944, 4488).

this olde-greye, 4789 f (gray D) (: his eyen tw[e]ye).

his hote fyr, 445 (-[e] D). (Cf. 490, 6870. For indef. *hot, hoot*, cf.
1977 f, 2361, 2618, 5925 f, 7465.)

his lighte gost, 8171 (-[e] B).

my righte lode sterre, 7755 (-[e] D); my right[e] l. s , 6595 (-e C);
thi righte place, 4970 (-[e] BD); his right[e] lady, 2150[1] (-e C),
4505 (-e C); my right[e] lady, 6930 (-e C), 7016 (bryȝte C, my right
lady ‡ D); her right[e] cours, 2055 D (kynde ABC); the right[e]
lyf, 1936 (-e C). (For indef. *right, vpright*, cf. 1418 f, 3823 f,
3840 f.)

hire streght[e] bak, 4089 (streyte C, streiȝt[e] D, he[r] streyght[e] A).

the strong[e] cite, 7849 (-e BCD).

the swyfte fame, 5321 (C †).

My goode brother Troylus the syke, 2657 (D †) (: like *inf.* : syke *inf.*).

the white and eke the rede, 4226 f (: drede *n.* : rede *inf.*).

Antigone the white, 1972 f (: syke *inf.* : endite *inf.*); cf. 2147 f.

his wod[e] peyne, 2440 (-e BC); the wode ialousye, 7576 (wode BCD
G Cp. John's, *without the article*).

the fayre baye stede, 7401 f (-[e] BD); his bay[e] stede, 1709 (bayȝe
C); but,—his stede bay, 1066 f (: day : ay).

this blewe rynge, 3727 (-[e] D, blowe C).

    IV. Some examples are here given of the definite form of words
which occasionally show an -e in forms not obviously definite
(cf. § 49):

[1] Insert [*here*] in A.

this false world, 1505 (-[e] BD); thi fals[e] gost, 7884 (-e CD).

the good[e] wyse worthi fressh and fre, 1402 (goode BC); my goode brother, 2657 (my good trew brothir † D).

here goode softly wyse, 2752 (hire goodly soft[e] w. BD, hire goodeli softe w. C); his gode gouernaunce, 3269 (wise CD); his good[e] gouernaunce, 3323 (-e'C); my good[e] loue, 3851 A° (my good[e] myn B, myn goode myn C, good hert myn D); his goode chere, 6547 (-[e] D).

youre grete trouthe, 3834 (good[e] D).

his heigh[e] port, 1077 (hieghe B, hy[e] D)[1]; the heigh[e] worthynesse, 4451 (hye C, hiʒë D).

V. owene, owen, owne (A.S. ágen), is found only in the definite use. I. Singular. (i.) Before consonants; always dissyllabic, however spelled. Thus,—myn owenë lust, 407 (owne BD); thin owenë cheyne, 509 (own[e] BD, owen C); his owenë curtasye, 2571 (owen B, owne D); myn owenë lady, 7032 (swene † B,[2] ougne D) (cf. also 51, 442, 814, 1371 C (owne D), 1835, 1869, 1956, 2586, 2989, 4025, 4327, 4329 C, 6111, 6112, 6412, 6426, 6581, 6703, 6830, 6884, 6928, 7643, 7678, 7707, 7764, 7784, 8081); here owne place, 3060 (owen BD, owenë C) (cf. 2950, 3757 (owene BC, own[e] D), 3943); myn owen lady, 6525 (owene C, ougne D) (cf. 772, 5067, 5751); myn owenë herte, 5973 (swete B, ougne D) (cf. 3477, 5376 C); his owne herte, 4662 (owen B, own[e] D); thyn owen help, 795 (ow[e]n B, owene C, owne D); myn owen herte, 6214 AB (owene C, ougnë D) (cf. 1530 (own? B, ouenë C, own[ë] D), 6302 (own[e] B, owenë C, ougnë D)). (ii.) Before vowels, youre owene (*predicate*), 6517 (owen B, owyn C, ougne D.) II. Plural, his owenë nedes, 3266 (owen B, own[e] D, owene ‡ nede C); here owene men, 3438 (own[e] B, owne D).

Note.—For *myn owene throte*, 1410 A, read *my throte*. The form *owe* (6111 C) is no doubt due merely to the omission by the scribe of the sign of abbreviation.

§ 54. Occasionally, however, -e is dropped in the definite form of monosyllabic adjectives.

his good wil, 2294 (-e BC).

this good plit, 3981 (-e B, thus good p. A).

my good word, 7444 (godde C); youre good word, 7985 (C †).

---

[1] Read [e]*straunge* in D.
[2] This form occurs several times in B; as, 4025, 4327, 6412, 6581, 7032. Cf. *sweue*, 2586 B.

In these cases the phrases were perhaps felt as compounds; cf. O.N. *góð-vili, góð-virki*, etc., and notice the accent. But not so in,—
this heigh matere, 3358 (he B, heye C, hye D).
yowre heyghe seruyce, 4130 (heigh B, heye C, D †).
here heyghe compleynte, 5467 (heighe B, hire hyë pleynt C; D †).
thy wrong conceyte, 692 (-e B, wrang D, C †).
my lowe·confessioun, 1613.
Al be I not the firste that dide amys, 7430 (the ferste C, the furste D).
the laste, the last, see p. 124.
the pleyn felicite, 8181 (-e B); this mene while, 3618 AB (p. 122).
 Cf. the substantive use in:
Criseydë whiche that is thi lef, 5273 f (lief B, lyf C, the lefe D) (: a-gref: myschef). (For *lef, lief*, indef. sing., cf. 3706 f, 4461 f.)

> Note 1.—Cases before a vowel, such as *hire old vsage*, 150 (olde C, the ‡ old D), and *here playn entente*, 2645 (pleyne BC, pleyn D), of course prove nothing. *The next wyse*, 697 A, is an error.
>
> Note 2.—In
>
> > For which these wise clerkes that ben dede
> > Han euere yet prouerbed to vs yonge
> > That *firstë vertu* is to kepe tonge, 3134-6[1]
>
> (-[e] BC, The first vertu is to kepe wel the tonge D), the definite form is used by a sort of *constructio ad sensum*, though the demonstrative word (*the*) is omitted. Cf. Parforme it out for now is *most[ë] nede*, 3259, and perhaps also And thanne *at erst[ë]* shal we ben so fayn, 5983 (*at erste* B, *att erste* D †, *atte erst[e]* G), but here note *atte* in G.

§ 55. In vocative phrases monosyllabic adjectives appear in the definite form when they precede the noun (as in A.S. *léofa Béowulf*) (Child, § 34; ten Brink, § 235).

o blake nyght, 4271 (-[e] D).
o blynd[e] world o blynd entencion, 211 (-ë . . . -d B, -ë . . . -e C).
o bryght[e] Làthona, 7018 (-ë C).
thow foule daunger, 4163 BE (fole C; A †).[2]
Graunt mercy good[e] myn ywys quod she, 6322 (goodë B, go[o]d[e] D, Graunt mercy Iwis goode myn quod sche C).
goodë nece, 2288 (-[e] D), 3473 (-[e] D); good[e] nece, 1468 (-e C);
gode necë dere, 3817 (?) (-[ë] B, -ë C, good (?) D).[3]
gode brother, 3106 (-[e] D).

---

[1] From the *Roman de la Rose* : Sire, la vertu premeraine . . . C'est de sa langue refrener, 13117-21, II, 48, ed. Michel.
[2] For *foul, ful*, in the attributive and predicate uses (*indef.*), cf. 213, 1981, 5656, 6402, 6746 (foule A).
[3] Now doth hym sitte (sitten John's) now (*om*. BCGCp. John's) gode nece dere A.

goodë swetë, loue me, 6935 (-[e] D).
Now good[e] em for goddës loue I prey, 1394 (-e BG, my good eem ‡ D John's Hl. 2392, myn em ‡ C, And good[e] em Cp.);[1] o good em, 1584 (-e BC); good hert myn ‡, 3851 D.
leue brother, 3172, 5120 (derë ‡ D), 5203, 6670, 6840 (-[e] D).
leue nece, 1336 (louë † B), 5588.
leue Pàndare, 5114 (C ?).
o quyke deth, 411 (-[e] BCD).
Cf. the exclamatory line,—
o trust o feyth o depe asëüraùnce, 7622 (depë àssuraùnce ‡ C, depë àssuraùns ‡ D).
In 458 *good* is used in the voc. : Good (-e B, God CDG, Goode ? Hl. 2392) goodly (godely B, god Hl. 2392) to whom serue I (I serue CG) and (*om.* BD Cp.) laboure (-r DG).
But in definite or vocative phrases in which the adjective follows the noun no -e is added. Thus,—
myn owęnë lady bryght, 4327 f (: knyght) (cf. 7285 f).
o lufsom lady bryght, 6826 f (-e B) (: nyght), etc., etc. (Cf. ten Brink, § 235.)

§ 56. For adjectives of more than one syllable which do not stand at the end of the verse[2], the following rules as to -e in the definite and vocative constructions may be collected from the usage of the *Troilus:*

Of adjectives of more than one syllable those alone take -e which have a primary or secondary accent on the ultima, and are followed by a word accented on the first syllable.

The special cases of which the *Troilus* furnishes examples may be stated as follows:

I. Dissyllabic paroxytone adjectives take no -e when the following word is accented on the first syllable. The verse will not bear such an arrangement of accents as x́ ' xx '.

Example: *the wýkked spýrit*. (See others in § 57.)

II. For the same reason dissyllabic oxytone adjectives take no -e when the word that follows is accented on the second syllable.

Example: *his sodeýn comýnge,* 380. (See § 58.)

---

[1] C has but nine syllables ; AB Cp. become 9-syllable lines if *good* (*goode*) be read.
[2] The *Troilus* affords no certain means of judging how such words were treated at the end of a verse except in the case of some plurals (see § 71).

III. Trisyllabic proparoxytone adjectives (´ x ʽ) take -e unless the word that follows is accented on the second syllable.

Example: *the wòfullèstĕ wỳght*. (See others in § 59.)

IV. But trisyllabic proparoxytone adjectives take no -e when the following word is accented on the second syllable. The verse will not bear such an arrangement of accents as ´ x ´ xx ´.

Example: *his èxcellènt prowèsse* (see § 60).

V. For the same reason trisyllabic paroxytones take no -e when the following word is accented on the first syllable.

Example: *th' erràtyk stèrrès* (see § 61).

Examples under I.—V. follow (§§ 57—61).

Note.—Adjectives of more than three syllables are not common in the *Troilus*. The accentuation of *philosophical* is interesting in "To the, and the, philosophical Strode," 8220 (D †).

§ 57. I. Dissyllabic paroxytone adjectives take no -e in the definite and vocative uses when the following word is accented on the first syllable. (Cf. Child § 35; ten Brink, § 246.)

(a) Superlatives:

the grettest wonder, 2228 ([the] g. B, mostë C, most[e] D).

myn alderleuest lord, 3081 (-e C¹); myn alderleuest lady, 6939 ([myn] aldyr louelyest ‡ C).

The following of course prove nothing :—

the hàrdest is, 1814 (-e B; D †).

the faireste ànd, 4122 (-t BD), cf. 1832.

the grettest of, 4854 (-e C).

the kyndest and, 7892 C (*indef.* ABD).

Cf. in the plural,—

the worthiest and grettest in degre, 244.

the fresshest and, 4564 (-e B; C †; D †).

(b) the best[ë] sounded ioly harpe, 2116 (the bestë sowned B, the beste ‡ souned(e) C, the best ‡ sownyd D).

thilke couered qualite, 2873 (couerd B, thilk[e] couerid q. D).

this furrëd cloke, 3580 (-ed(e) C, furrid ‡ D (?)).

the heped(e) wo, 4898 (-ed B, -id D).

Note.—Compare *on of the beste enteched creature*, 7195 (on the best (?) B, on of the beste enteched(e) C, on(e) of the best entached D) (: dure *inf.*). On the idiom, see Einenkel, *Streifzüge durch die mittelengl. Syntax*, p. 87, and Kellner, Caxton's *Blanchardyn and Eglantine*, Introduction, p. xvii (E.E.T.S.). Cf. also *the newe abaysshed nyghtyngale*, 4075 (abaysed B, abasschit C, abaschid D †).

¹ Or, *leueste*.

my nakede herte sentement, 2885 (-d BD, hertis D).
this fals and wikked dede, 93 (wekede C, cursyd † D).
that wykkede dede, 3133 (-d BD).
that wikkede wyuere, 3852 (-d B, the wikkid serpent † wythir D).
the wykked spyrit, 7575 (wekede C).
thy wynged, 4650 (D †).
this wrecched, 5283 (-e C), 8180 (cf. 8214).

(c) that blisful, 6768; the blisful, the blysful, 1319 (C †), 1919 † (ʒe, blisful D), 4510, 6943.

this dredful, 1511 (C † om. this; dredeful B); hire dredful ioye, 1861 (D †).

thi greful, 4948 (gerful B, gery C, greffull D).

my sorwful, 4952 (reuful ‡ C, sorowfull D), 4963 (woful C, sorowfull D); this sorwful, 596 B (sorweful C, sorowful D), 4895 (sorweful AC,[1] sorowfull D), 5030 (sorweful C; sorowfull D), 5456 (woful ‡ C, sorwefull D), 5822 (sorweful C, sorwefull D), 5914 (woful C, woofull D), 6359 (woofull D); his sorwful herte, 6893 B (sorweful ACD); here s. h., 6543 (sorwe- CD).—the sorwful (before vowels), 10 (sorowful B, sory(e) D), 1537 (-we- C, sorowful D, the soruful (*dissyl.*) hernest B).

my woful, 5505 (sorweful C), 7733; here woful, 5814 (his † w. B); the woful, 5447 (sorweful C), 5801 (tho † w. B); this woful, 703 (thi w. BCD), 2446, 5022 (sorweful C), 5027, 5034, 6560, 7077; his woful herte, 6997; here w. h., 5884 ABD; the lasse wofulle of hem, 5794 (woful BC, woofull D). [Var. D woofull.]

the chyldyssh, 4010 [2] (childishe B, childis C, childische D).

thyn ire and folessh wilfulnesse, 793 (foolysh B, foly † C, folisshe D).

here snowyssh throte, 4092 (snouwhite ‡ C, snowe whit D [3]).

(d) thi blody, 3566 (-i C; D †).

the fery flood, 4442 (the firy feende † D).

youre frendly, 1333 (frende † B, frendely C, frend † D) (*l.* fremde),[4] 1417 (freendely B, frendeli C, lovely † D).

his goodly, 2353 (-ely B, goodli C); here goodly, 173 (-ely B, -eli C), 446 (-ely B), 2752 BD (-eli B, goode † A).

his happy, 1706 (-i C; D †) [5] (cf. 2467).

thyn heuy, 651.

the holy, 3384, 7860 ([the] C).

---

[1] Supply [*ek*] in C.   [2] Read *ielous* in AD for *ialousye* (*ielousye*).
[3] Omit (*On*) in D.   [4] Insert [*to me*] in A.   [5] Insert [*his*] in B.

§ 57.] *of Chaucer's Troilus.* 131

ourę lusty folk, 560 (-i B)[1].
his manly, 2955 (-i C).
his rosy, 4597 (-i C; E†), 6641 (-i B; D†)[2].
the sely, 4033 (-i C); this sely, 6892 (cely B), 7456.
that smoky, 3470 (this smoke reyn C, smokis † D).
the mestè stormy, 1863.
the sturdy ok, 2465 (stordy B, sturdı C, sturdy *pl* † D).
herę tery face, 5483.
the wel wılly planète, 4099 (the welę wylly p. D).
this worthi, 7924 (the worthy B); this ilke worthi, 8129. (Cf. 1243, 1402, 1416 CD, 2413.)
   Note.—For *merye* see above, § 46.

(e) yourę bittre,[3] 3021 (-tyr C);[4] the bittyr, 5372 C (hir bitter D); that bittre[3] hope, 7276 (-tir C, the bitter D).
the gilt[l]es[5] in, 2457 (giltęlees B, gıltęles C, giltles D).
this litel, 8178.
thin yuel fare, 2086 (euele C, evil D).[6]
the siker, 3763 (seker B, sekir C, sikir D).
the sothfast, 6388 ([the] -ę B); that sothfast, 8223 (the s. D); myn ow n hertès sothfast suffisaunce, 6302 (-ę B, sothęfast D).
the yonder hous, 2273 (-ę C[7], -ur D), 6938 (-yr C).

(f) Romance and Latin adjectives:
that noble gentıl knyght, 1416 (nobęle and worthi CD, noble worthi D).
this gentil man, 3805 (ʒonę g. m. C).
that wysę gentil herte, 3789 (that g. wisé h. C, wys[e] g. D).[8]
this myddel chaumbre, 3508 (-il CD).
the fàtal, 6364 (fathel B).
herę crùèl, 839 (*om.* † C); this crùwel, 6107 (cruël BD, crewel C); myn aspre and cruwel peyne, 5509 (cruel B, asper and crewel C, aspre ‡ crueH D), the cruel herte, 250 (crewel CD).
his rèal pàlais, 4376 (rial C; D†).
the cèrtayn, 5674.
this sòdeyn Dıomède, 7387 (cf. his sodeỳn comỳnge, 3801).
thılkë sòueyren (*dıssyl.*) pùrueyaùnce, 5732 (sòuęreyn D).
yourę ioly wo, 2190 (-i C, om. † D).
his pitous face, 5023 (pı(e)tous † fate D).

---

[1] Dele (*in*) in D.   [2] D may be emended by reading *carte* (as in ABC) for *char*.
[3] Dissyllable.   [4] Supply [*ın*] in A. The word is in this line used substantıvely.
[5] Sbst. *insontem* or *ınsontes.*   [6] In C omit (*al*).   [7] Lıne too short in D.
[8] Supply [*good*] ın A.

youre verray humble trewe, 2983 (humbele C); his verray slouthe,. 1371 (owene C, owne D).
the parfit blysse, 1976.

§ 58. II. Dissyllabic oxytone adjectives take no -e in the definite use when the following word is accented on the second syllable.

here natẏf beauté, 102.
his sodeẏn comẏnge, 3801.
his syklẏche manère, 2628 (siklẏch B, seklẏche C, siklẏ D).

Note.—Cf. *Com(e) hire to preye yn his propre persone*, 2572 (*propere* B, *his (owene) propere* p. C), and *I com my-self in my propre persone*, 4745 (*in* [*my*] p.p. D).

§ 59. III. Trisyllabic proparoxytone adjectives (′ x `) take -e in the definite and vocative uses, unless the word that follows is accented on the second syllable.

a) Superlatives:
the frèndlyèste wyght, 1072 (-[e] BD).
the frendlyest[e] man, 1289 (-e BC).
the fèrfullèste wyght, 1535 (ferefullest[e] B,[1] sorwefuleste † C,[2] frelyest † D).
the goòdlyèstë mayde, 1965 (good(e)lyest[e] B, god(e)lieste C, goodliest[e] D).
the wòrthièste knyght, 3623 (-[e] BD).
the wòrthièste, 1846 f (-t D) (: lyst, -e B[3] : at reste).
the wòfullèste wyght, 5178 (-[e] BD); the wofulleste, 4965 f (-t CD) (: vnneste *imv. sg.* : breste *inf.*).
the gèntilèste trewely, 7438 (-[é] D). [*gentileste*, 3100 B, should be *gentilnesse*.]
on the gèntilèst[e], 7419 f (-e BCD) (: on(e) the worthyest[e], 7420 f (-e BCD)).
the thryftiest[e], 1822 f (-e BC) ⎱ : the best[e] (-e B). (In these lines
the worthiest[e], 1824 f (-e B) ⎰ we may safely read -*e*, with B.)
I am one (oon B, on C) the (of the C) fairest (-e BC) out of (withoutyn D) drede
And *goodlyest*[e] (goodelyeste B) who-so (ho so CD) taketh hede, 1831-2. Cf. the drèdfullèstè thinges, 6611 (dredefullestè B, dredfullest[é] D).[4]

[1] Or, *ferēfullest*.　　[2] Or, *sorwēfuleste*.
[3] *lyste* should doubtless be read (*pres. subj.* 3 *sg.*).　　[4] C reads *thynge* for *thynges*.

[§§ 59, 60, 61, 62.] *of Chaucer's Troilus.* 133

Elision is seen in :
   the konnyngest of yow, 331.
   the gentileste and ek, 1073 (genlyest † B, gentillest D).
   the thriftieste and oon, 1074 (-t B, trustiest ‡ D).
Cf. the plural,—
   the worthièst and grèttest in degre, 244.
   the fresshest and, 4564 (-e B, frossest [and] C; D †).
     Note.—*Alderfirst*[e] and *alderbeste* are of course treated like monosyllables (see vv. 2939, 4439 f).

(*b*) Other adjectives, Romance as well as Saxon :
   youre fresshë wommanlychë face, 6607 (womanly[che] D). Cf. the plural, tho wommanyssh[ë] thynges, 5356 (wommau[y]sshë B, womanlichë C, the womanyssh[ë] D); and the vocative, o wommanlychë wif, 2948 (-[ë] BD), fresshë wommanlichë wyf, 4138 (-[ë] E, wemen lich[ë] C).
   this fòrknowỳng[ë] wyse, 78 (-ë BC, in this ‡ wyse D).
   Bygan for ioyë the amorousë daunce, 6093 (thamarousë B, the amerous[ë] CD).
   O cruel god o dispitous[ë] Marte, 1520 (dispitusë C, O thou c. g. o dispitousë marte B, *thou* being above the line).
   Cf. also, the Troiànë gestes, 145 A (the troyan BC *makes a bad 9-syl. verse, read* -[ë] ; troianys D).

§ 60. IV. But trisyllabic proparoxytone adjectives take no -e when the following word is accented on the second syllable. The verse will not bear such an arrangement of accents as ′ x ′ xx ′.
   the tèmpestoùs matère, 1090 (this tempestuos m. D).
   his èxcellènt prowèsse, 438, 1745. (But,—your excellèntë doùghter, *Sq. T.* 145.)

§ 61. V. For the same reason trisyllabic paroxytone adjectives take no -e when the following word is accented on the first syllable. Thus,—
   th erràtyk stèrres, 8175 (the erratyk B).
   his vnhàppy dède, 6003 (-i B); cf. myne vnresty sorwès, 7718 (C †).

§ 62. The following may serve as examples of the vocative of adjectives of more than one syllable.
   O moral Gower, this bok(e) I directe
   To the, and the, philosophical Strode, 8219-20 (D †).

o thow wykked serpent, 3679 (welkedę C, wikkid D).
o crueel day, 4292 (cruwel B, cruel C, cruel † ladi D).
despitous day, 4300 (dis- BC, dispitousę D).
inmortal god, 3027 (immortal D, o inmortal god *with slur* C).
enuyous day, 4296 (C †).
Thou mysbeleuęd and enuyous folye, 3680 (mysbeleuyd enuyous CD).
O olde vnholsom (on- C) and mysbyleued (-yd C, myslyued B, mysleuyd D) man, 4992.
o paleys desolat, 6903 f (-e D).
o paleys empty and disconsolat, 6905 f (-e D).
o thow woful Troylus, 519 (-H D).
o blysful light, 2843 (cf. 1007, 2145, 3547, 4159, 6945, 6962).
o brotel wele, 3662 (bretil C, Bbrotul ‡ 9-*syl.* D).
o verray cause, 2848.
redy to, 2847.
almyghty Ioue, 5741 (a. god C) (cf. 8105).
Thow myghty god and dredful for to greue, 6953 (dredęful B, miȝty . . . dredfull D) (cf. 2842, 2908, 5748, 7070).
lufsom lady, 7274 (louęsom CD) (cf. 6828).

But,—

o wommanlyche wyf, 2948 (-[e] BD).
fresshe wommanliche wyf, 4138 (-[e] E, wemen † lich[e] C).
O cruel god o dispitous[e] Marte, 1520 (dispituse C; O thou c. g. o dispitouse marte B, *thou* being above the line).

Note.—The presence or absence of -e, it will be observed, depends, at least in part, on the arrangement of accents in the line.

§ 63.
The *Troilus* shows few traces of the French inflection of adjectives.

Seynt Idyot, 903, and *the seynt* [i.e. *Criseyde*] *is oute*, 6916, throw no light on the vexed question of the forms *seynt, seynte* (which are discussed by Child, § 37, and ten Brink, § 242). In *o bele nece*, 1373 (beale B, CD *om.* o), and *a blaunche feuere*, 909 f (-[e] D) (: keuere *inf.*), we surely have to do with the intentional use of a French feminine adjective. Against *o lady souereyne*, 4978 (-ayne B, -aigne D) (: peyne *n.*) may be cited *my souereyn lady queene*, C. T. 6630 T. *Of dyuyne purueyaunce*, 5623 (de- BD) is comparable with *the seruyse divyne*, C. T. 122 (see ten Brink, § 242, Freudenberger, *Ueber das Fehlen des Auftakts*, p. 39). Compare also the list of French adjectives that have an inorganic -e (§ 52).

§§ 63, 64.] *of Chaucer's Troilus.* 135

In 6731 AB we have *infernals illusions* (enfernal C, infernaH D) (cf. Child, § 43; ten Brink § 243; Skeat, *Piers. Pl.*, ed. 1886, II, 130). In 2859 *amoreux* should be singular.

§ 64. Adjectives in the Comparative Degree usually end in the *Troilus* in -*er* (var. -*ere*). Thus,—

(*a*) fairer, 454 (-est † A), 6843; no fayrer creature, 7171; pl., fairerẹ, 5064 (-er BD). (In all these C has *fayrerẹ*.)

frendhour, 885 (frenlyer B, frendẹlyerẹ C, frendlier D).

gladder, 884 (D †, -ere C), 3199 (-ere BC).

grētter, 241 (-erẹ C); grettere help, 2531 (-er D); grettere hardinesse, 566 (-er BD).

hardere, 5567 (-er D).[1]

hotter, 1005 (-erẹ C, hatter D); h. is, 449 (hatter B, hattere C, hattẹr he is D). (Cf. pl., -erẹ, 1623 (-er B), 4999 (-er D).)

leuerẹ, 1027 (-er? D), 1437 (B? D?), 3433 (-er D), 3949 (C †, D †), 4332 (-er D), 5227,[2] 5229 (-yr D); -ere han, 5232 (-erẹ ȝit † C, -er ‡ than D); lèuẹre a, 3416 (-ẹr a BD).

liker, 3870 (-erẹ C, like † or D).

proudder, 1223 (-erẹ C).

rather, my r. speche, 4179 (-erẹ C); my ratherẹ speche, 8162 (-er BD).

outer, that outter hous, 3506 (other ‡ A, this vttir C, this ‡ litil D).

swyfter cours, 2470 (-erẹ C).

wiser be, 986 (-er of B, -ere C); wysere, 2087 (-er BD, -erẹ than C).[3]

worthier of, 251 (-ere C), *plural.*

So in the Romance adjective—

straungerẹ, 5050 (-er BD, strengerẹ ‡ C).

(*b*) lenger (A.S. lengra), 3541 (langer B, morē CD), 4703 (lenge[r] A), 7025 (-erẹ C, longer B), 7214 D (morē A, longë BC)[4]; lengerẹ, 1377 (-er D, longer B), 2050 (-er BD); lengere, 7022 (-er D, longer B). (So *lengest*, 474 (*adv.* ‡ D).)

(*c*) bettre (*dissyl*) (A.S. bet(e)ra, bettra), 1262 (-er D), 1445 (-erẹ B, -yr C, -er D), 3772 (-erẹ B, -irẹ C, -ir † D), 5964 (-er B, -ir D), 7308 (-er BD), 7432 (-er B, -ir † D); my b. arm, 2735 (-ere C, -ir D) (In all these, unless otherwise indicated, C has -*erẹ*.)

bet, (i.) 257 (betịr is ‡ D), 1211 (bettyr ‡ C, worth † A), 1213, 1315, 1514, 2539 (B †, D *adv.*), 2736 (betịr ‡ to D), 3963 (bet(ir) mynde D, bet *adv.* A), 4065 (bettịr ‡ than D), 7634 (best † C, bettir ‡

---

[1] Supply [ȝet] in C, [*it*] in D.   [2] CD insert *ben* (*be*), necessitating a harsh slur.
[3] Insert [*wel*] in A.   [4] Read *withouten* for *woth* in C.

wer įt D). (ii.) 5253 (betęre (it) is C, -įr is D), 5593 (-ęre is C, bettįr is D), 6404 (beste † D).

lasse, lesse (A.S. lǽssa), 703 f, 796 f, 1009 f (lesse(d) C), 2803, 2947, 3988[1], 5140 (allas † CD), 5465 f, 6981 f; for the lessë harm, 4000; lasse, 5240. (Cf. *plural*, 6206 f.) lassę nede, 2617 C (A † B †, the lessë nede D), *a doubtful line*.[2] Cf. otherę lassę folk (?), 4716. In *lesse he koude*, 2163, *lesse* has an adverbial force.

<small>Rhyme words.—Nouns in *-nesse* (drerynesse, etc.) (703, 796, 5465, 6981), destresse *n.* (1009, 5465), gesse *inf.* (6981).</small>

more (A.S. mára), I. as *adj. indef. sing.* in connection with nouns and pronouns,—nomorë hardë grace, 713 (n. m. hard[e] g. D); more vèrtu, 1264;[3] more feste, 1446 (festis † C); nomore feste, 6887; no more sorwe, 1491 (C †); routhe more, 1649 f (: sore *adv.* : lore *n.*)[4]; withoute more speche, 1582, 2506, 4352, 6751, 7494, 8079; more peyne, 2316; morë help, 2540 D (*perh. adv.*); the[5] morë thank, 2551[6]; morë pres, 2728; thi wo wax alwey more, 3084 f (: sore *adv.* : lore *n.*); the[7] more fere, 3414; withouten more lette, 3541 CD, 7214 A; his sorwe is muche more, 5561 (moore D) (: sore *adv.*); strof ... ay which of hem was more, 7182 f (mor D) (: euerę more *adv.*); more wo, 7415; Thorugh more (mor[e] B) wode and col the more fyr, 2417[8].—*more folk*, 4032, and *morë thyng*, 5205 (C † D †), are doubtless plural. II. more, moore, *substantive use*, 6452, 7772, 7974 (-[e] D); withouten more, 3815 f (: sore *adv.*)[9], 3998, 4795 f (: sorwes sore), 5038 f (: rore *inf.* : sikes sore), 6160 f (: yore *adv.*); withouten ony moore, 7560 f (moor D) (: sykes sore); cf. now is therę litel morë for to done, 3389 (A erroneously inserts *but*); no more[10] (*sbst.*), 1044, 3032 (*-e* as B), 3192 f (: sikes sore), 3515, 6689 f (: yore : lore *noun*), 7161, 8094 f (moor D) (: eueręmore *adv.* : of yore), 8106 (na mor[e] B).

<small>Note.—For *more* (of both kinds, *adj.* and *sbst.*,—and one or two in which the adverb-line is perhaps passed), cf. 796, 3518, 5183, 5187, 5933, 6047, 6321, 6363, 6492. Cf. what sholde I more seye, 1406, 2219; what sholde I more telle, 3435; what myght I more do or seye, 3892; what hym lyste he seyde vn-to it more, 5785 f (: sore *adv.*); what wole ye more, 7274; the harm that myghte ek fallen more, 1539 f (: sore *adv.*); not o word spak she more, 3899 f (D †) (: sore *adv.*).</small>

---

[1] Read [o]*this* in D.
[2] And hast the (*so* DG Cp. John's, *om.* ABC) lasse (lesse D) nede to (*om.* BD, the to C) countrefete.
[3] Supply [*he*] in B.
[4] As neuęre of thyng ne haddę I routhę more ([ne] D, no r. m. B, not r. m. C).
[5] The A.S. *þý*-construction. [6] Dele (*me*) in AD (or slur).
[7] The A.S. *þý*-construction. [8] Supply [*the*] in B. D reads,—*The morë wode*.
[9] Insert [*him*] in C. [10] Sometimes written *nomore* (B *namore*).

§§ 64, 65.] *of Chaucer's Troilus.* 137

more, I. *adj. use,* more nede is, 3699 (-e now † B, it nedith morë (i.e. *potius*) sodeynly C, D?); Ech(e) set by other more for other semeth, 643; more reward, 2218; out of more respit, 6500 (withoutë ‡ more respite D); cf. the more harm is, 7299 (C † D †). II. no more (*sbst.*) in *there is no more to done* and similar phrases, 574, 2511 (-e of CD), 3532, 7672; I kan no more but, 3232, 4035, 4115, 4156[1], 7731 (moor D); yet was there more to done, 7455; yet sey I more therto, 5734 (-e herto BD); nor axen more that, 1232; yf I more dorstë prey (?), 2521 (morë C, more y D)[2]; was worth more than, 4382 (worthy CD)[3]; withoutë more to, 2751 (-e is † B, *l.* to).

mo, moo (*plural*) (A.S. má, mǽ, *adv.*), 613 f[4], 614, 2490 f, 2566 f, 2651 f (*sg.* ‡ C), 3076 f, 3212 (more C), 4356 f, 4881 f, 5162, 5490 (moore D), 5787 f, 6303 f, 6592 f, 7127 f, 7626 f, 8044 f[5]. (Cf. 6521 f.).

Rhyme words.—wo, two, tho, so, fo, go, also.
Note:—Several of the passages cited contain the formula,—*withoutën wordës mo*. This occurs also in the form, *withoutën wordës morë* (cf. 5326 f, 6419 f, 8035 f.).

werse (A.S. wiersa, wyrsa), 4542 f (wors D); I go to worse, 5502 f (wors C); i-turned vnto worse, 3916 f (-s CD); in worse plyt, 1797 (-[e] D); with worse hap, 4088 (vois † B); ye may do me no werse, 5856 f. But,—wers though, 1950; wors that, 5144 (-e D); wors than, 7056 (-e D); wers of, 1947; *pl.* wers whi ‡, 1820 C (wors [why] ‡ D).

Rhyme words.—acurse (acorse) *inf.* (3916), 1 *sg. ind.* (5502, wors : fors C), curse (corse) 3 *pl. ind.* (4542), aduerse (5856), diuerse (5856). [Var. BC werse; D wurse, wurs.] (Cf. 2880 f.)

§ 65. The Comparative and Superlative of adjectives are sometimes formed by means of *more* and *most* (Child, § 38, *d*). Thus—

more bounteuous, 883 f.
more gracious, 885 f.
the more worthi part, 2413.
the more swet[e], 4061 f (more swete BC).
more fayn, 6851 f.
more parfit loue, 7282.
more kynde, 7283 f.

[1] Supply [*these*] in A.   [2] But supply [ʒow] in C and read *more.*
[3] worth(y) more than CD (if *worthy* be kept, we must slur *more than* (mor'n).
[4] The cases cited are adjectival unless the line-number is in old-style figures : in that case, the use is substantive.   [5] In A read *othes* for *other.*

most meke, 8210 f.
most is to hym dere, 4947 f.
the meste stormy life, 1863 (cf. § 87).
the most[e] fre, 1073 (cf. § 87).

§ 66. The Superlative of adjectives ends in -*est*. Thus,—
best (cf. 828, 2570, 2649, 2738, 4746, 4863, 5341, 6381, 6904, 7717 f, 8210); fairest, 5817 (fayrë ‡ C); leuest (cf. 1274); lothest am (cf 1322); shortest (7137 BD); trewest, 4665 (trusty ‡ D), etc. B, C, and D sometimes show a scribe's -e, which, however, is of course never sounded (for 6664 BD is to be emended).

For superlatives in the definite use or in the plural see §§ 53, 57, 59, 70.

Note.—In one case we may perhaps suspect that a single -*est* serves for two adjectives,—

And thus she lith with hewes pale and grene
That whilom *fressh and fairest* was to sene,

5816-17 (frosche and fayre ‡ werẹ C).

§ 67. The Plural of monosyllabic adjectives ends in -e.

In the following list no definite or vocative forms have been included without notice. An asterisk indicates that the adjective follows its noun (as, *eyen bryghte*); old-style figures indicate that the adjective stands in the predicate (as, *eyen are bryghte*)[1]. No cases are included (without notice) in which the adjective refers to a plural *ye* singular in sense. For *bare, fresshe*, etc., see note at the end of the section.

(*a*) blake (A.S. blæc. Sg. blak, cf. 170, 175), my clothes euerychone Shul blake ben, 5441.

bryghte (A.S. beorht, E.W.S. -breht, L.W.S. -bryht. Sg. bright, bryght, 166 f, 2054 f, 5402, 6525 f, 8075, etc.), a fewe bryghtë terys, 3893 (-[e] BD); bryght[e],* 4972 f (-e D) (: sight (sighte) *n.* : lyght (lighte) *inf.*) (*in* C : dispyt †). Before vowels,—bright, * 7006 (-*e* C, of thi bright[e] bemẹs(?) D), * 7909 (-*e* C, out ‡ A). [Var. C briȝte.] And sygnyfer his candeles shewed bryghte, 7383 (bryȝt C, candell . . . light D) (: alighte *pret. ind. 3 sg.* : yf she myghte).

bygge (*etym. dub.*), bygge bowes, 4702 (big[gë] D).

colde (A.S. cald, ceald. Sg cold, 5839 (-(e) BD); cold(e), 1783 f

---

[1] But these marks are not used with the singular forms given.

(cold CD), cf. 7465 f), *264 f (cold D), *4044 f, *4102 f, *6354 f, *7705 f[1], *8110 f (all these in the phrase *cares colde*); *-e* hem, *4611 (tolde † E).

> Rhyme words.—I tolde *ind.* (264), holde *inf.* (264, 8110), *p.p.* (4102), *subj. 2 sg.* (7705), byholde *inf.* (6354, 7705, 8110), folde *inf.* (4044, 6354), bokes olde (4044). [Var. D coolde.]

dede (A.S. déad. Sg., ded, cf. 723, 1494 f, 1527 f, 1739 f, 1930 f, 2135, 2441, 2784 f, 2921 f, 3923 f, 4414 f, 5162 f, 5819 f, 7609, 7866, etc.; dede, cf. 5041, 6922), *1624 f (*sg. in A, but read* asshe[n]; as lede ‡ D), 3134 f, 3194 BD (-[e] AC), 3734 (a dede † man A), *4781 f, 5754 f, 5894 f (D †), 6178 f; floures ... that winter dede made, 1137; shulle ... liggen dede, 5288 f (deed D).

> Rhyme words—rede *adj. pl.* (1624), rede *legunt* (3134), dede *n.* (3134, 5894), nede *n.* (5288), drede *n.* (5754, 6178), sprede *inf.* (4781), lede *inf.* (6178)

depe (A.S. déop. Sg. dep, 1236 C (-e ABD)), my ladyes depe sikes, 7038 (C †).

donne (A.S. dun(n)), 1993 f (dunne C) (: sonne *solem* : y-ronne *p.p.*).

dymme (A.S. dım(m)), *-e*, 1993 AB.

fayre (A.S. fæger. For singular, see § 49), floures fayre, 8204 f (fair D) (: a fayre *n.*)

felle (A.S. fel. Sg. fel a dede, cf. 6413), fel[l]e, *4706 f (felle BD)- (: quelle *ind. 3 pl.* : telle *inf.*).

glade (A.S. glæd. Sg. glad, cf. 592, 2623, 3489, 3493, 4633, 5067, † 5349, 5387, 5471, etc.), *1135 f, *1233 f, *1583 f, 2436 f (glad C; D †), *2857 f, *3453 f.

> Rhyme words—made *ind. 3 sg.* (1135, 1583, 3453), *ind. 2 pl* (2857), wade *inf.* (1233), Wade *nom. pr.* (3453), hadde *ind 3 sg.* (2436).

goode (A.S. gód. For singular, see § 49), good[e], *8222 f (garde † A) (: Strode *nom. pr.* : on rode); *-e*, *1808 (*om.*† D). But,— of good condıcıons, 1251 AD (-e BC)[2]; in good † chaunces, 2432 D.

grete (A.S. gréat. For singular, see § 49), *4722 f, *5630 (B †, grete clerkes D), *6499 f, *7601 f, *8122 f; grete àttendaùnces, 339 (gret C); gret ‡ effectis, 7992 C (*sg.* ABD).

> Rhyme words.—strete (4722), hete *n.* (7601, 8122), trete *inf.* (4722, 6499), bete *inf.* (8122).

leue (A.S. léof. Sg. lef, leef, lief (var. B leu(e); D leef, lef(e)), cf. 3302, 3706 f, 3711, 3712, 4461 f), 4744 f (: acheue *inf.* : leue *credo*).

lyghte (A.S. leoht, liht, shortened from léoht. Sg. lyght, cf. 5072 f, 5146 f, 6232, 6437 f, 6715 f, 7047 f, 7481 f), *2323 f (-t CD)

---

[1] Supply [*my*] ın A.   [2] Omit (*to*) ın D.

(: to the flyghte, -t BD), * 2471 f (-t CD) (: wighte *weight*). [Var. C ly3t; D light.]

madde (A.S. ge-mǽdd, *p.p.* Sg. mad, cf. 5055 f), * 6569 f (made B, he † made C) (: hadde *habuit*).—be ye mad, 1198 f (made B, madde C) (: a-drad *p.p. sg.*, adradd(e) C).

prowde (A.S. prút. For singular, see § 49), alle prowde (= omnes superbae), 1487 f (al[le] prowd D) (: lowde *adv.*).

quyke (A.S. cwic, W.S. cwucu, cucu, see Sievers, § 303. Sg. quyk, 2921), -e, 1137.

rede (A.S. réad. Sg. red, cf. 867, 1730, 1737 f, 2924 f, 3798 f, 4412 f, 7288 f), * 158 f, * 1136 f, * 1623 f, * 2936 f (*sg.* D †).

Rhyme words.—mede *pratum* (158, 1136), drede *n.* (2936), dede *adj. pl.* (1623), rede *ind.* 1 *sg.* (158), sprede *inf.* (1136).

salte (A.S. scalt. Sg. only in *saltë se*, 2850 (-[e] BD), see § 49), 543, 5592 (-[e] BD), 7278 (-[e] B); -e, * 7737; -e here, * 5834 (-t B). Cf. hise salte terys, 2171 C (-[e] BD, salty A).

sharpe (A.S. scearp. Sg. sharp, cf. (i.) 1876, 3268, 4373; -(e), 5560 (-p BC); (ii.) cf. 786, 4467; -(e), 7632 (*hardly adv.*)), * 470 ‡ A (*definite* BCD), 3906 (-[e] D ?); it maketh sharpe kervyng toles, 632 (-[e] D)[1]; -e, 7564.

shorte (A.S. scort, sceort. Sg. short, 7989 (-(e) D); in short, 2490 (-e B), 3076 (-e B)[2], 2041 (-[e] AD), 5298 (-[e] A), 6320 C (-[e] ABD), 7211.

sleye (Icel. slœgr), * 7261 f (slye C, slie D) (: lye *mentior* : yë); sley arn clerkes, 5634 (sleighe B, slye were D).

Note.—The rhymes show that *slye* (not *sleye*) is the correct form.

smale (A.S. smæl), * 2276 f (: tale), 4304, * 5399 f (: bale : pale); -e he[r],* 4089.

smerte; sorwes, peynes smerte, 794 f (-t D), 3792 f (-t D), 4910 f, 5088 f (-t D), 5803 f (peynë ‡ smerte D), 6163 f, 6561 f (-t C), 7087 f, 7412 f (-t C), 7689 f, 7783 f (-t C).

Rhyme words.—herte (*everywhere*), sterte *inf.* (3792), he sterte *pret. ind.* (6561).

Note.—Skeat seems to regard *smerte* in *sorwes (peynes) smerte* as a noun. At any rate he puts *Compl. Pite* 13, *B. Duch.* 593, *Compl. Mars* 10, *H.F.* 316, along with *the wounde smerte* (*H.F.* 374), under smerte *sbst.* in his Glossarial Index (*Minor Poems*, 1888, p. 440). But *his sorwes wer so smerte*, B. Duch. 507, and *Were my sorwes never so smerte*, Id. 1107 (cited *ibid.*), surely make against this. Besides, the substantive seems to be

---

[1] In D supply [yit].
[2] *With short[e] taryinge*, 7137 A Cp. (*schort[e]* C, *shortest* BDG John's), is the only case which seems to countenance *shorte* in the sing., but in this line the superlative is clearly right. For cases of the singular *short* before vowels, cf. 2578, 2743, 3298, 4638, 5552 (?), 5598.

§ 67.] *of Chaucer's Troilus.* 141

smert in the *Troilus* (cf. 5035, 5128, 5507; smert, 6780, may be a verb; C. T. 3811 T. is indecisive). Cf. also the entirely similar phrase *sorwes sore* (2427 f, 4794 f, 7718 f).

sore (A.S. sár. Sg. sor, 7002 (soor(e) B; D †); sor(e), 4263 (soor B)), *2427 f, *3191 f[1], *4794 f, *5037 f, *7038 f, *7559 f, *7718 f (C †); -e, *4613, *7397 BD (-e doun C, here sore sykes ‡ A).

Rhyme words.—more (*all cases*), lore *n.* (2427), rore *inf.* (5037) [Var. BD soore.]

sothe (A.S. sóð. Sg. soth, cf. 1254, 4199), 5333 (-[e] A).

stronge (A.S. strang, strong. Sg. strong and, cf. 7165), *57 f, *7051 f, *7227 f, *7564 f; -e, *4692 (strong D).[2]

Rhyme words.—longe *adv.* (*all cases*), *inf.* (7051), honge *inf.* (7564).

swyfte (A.S. swift), 4909 AD (-[e] B).

syke (A.S. séoc, Dur. Rushw. séc), 2903 f (*sbst.*), 3979[3], *4014 f, 4204 f[4], *7717 f (C †).

Rhyme words.—syke *inf.* (2903, 4014, 4204), pyke *inf.* (2903), lyke *inf.* (4204, 7717). [Var. BCD sike; D sijke.]

tame (A.S. tam), 3371 f (*sbst.*) (: lette-game : frame *inf.*)

wete (A.S. wǽt, wét), *7472 f (C †) (: hete *noun*), *8053 f (: lete *inf.*).

white, whyte (A.S. hwít. Sg. whit, cf. 642, 2011, and see § 49), 1993 (-[e] D), *3743 f (: for lyte : a myte), *4090 f (: lyte *adj.* pl. : delyte *inf.*), *4409 f (: lite *adv.*); -e, *158 (whit D), *1136 (*om.* ‡ D).

wronge (Icel. vrang-r. Sg. wrong, 4851, 7524 (-(e) B), *3646 f (wrong CD) (: longe *adv.*), *4233 f (: longe *pl.* : stronge *adv.*).

wrothe (A.S. wráð), 140 f (: bothe), 4784 f (: bothe), 6504 f (-th BD) (: bothe). (Cf. below, § 69.)

wyse (A.S. wís. Sg. wys, cf. 630, 1798, 5076 f, 5749, 7183, etc.), *954 f, 984 f, *3694 f, 3784 f, *4392 f, *4533 f, 7942 f. Cf. yf ye ben wyse, 4031 f (: aryse *pres. subj.* 3 *pl.*).

Rhyme words.—wyse *n.* (954, 984, 3694, 3784, 4392), seruice, seruyse (954, 984), suffice, suffise *inf.* (3694, 4533, 7942), aryse *inf.* (3784), deuyse *inf.* (4533), degyse *inf* (7942).

yone (A.S. geon), withinne ȝone ‡ wallis, 7096 C (the yonder AB, yonder D).

yonge (A.S. geong, etc. Sg. yong, (i.) 1721 (yung D), 7193; (ii.) 1837 (yung D)), 1204 (-[e] D); to vs yonge, 3135 f (-g B)

---

[1] Supply [*his*] in B.
[2] This line affords an excellent instance of the disregard shown for -e by D: "The grekys strong[e] about[e] troy[e] toun."
[3] Read *folk[es]* in B, *folkys* (for *follys*) in C.
[4] Supply [*that*] in C.

(: tonge); o yongë fresshë folkes, 8198 (-[e] D); yong and olde (*sbst.*), 130 (-e BC). [Var. B ȝong, ȝonge; C ȝonge.][1]

Further examples of the plural may be seen in :
>In May that moder is of monęthes *glade*[2]
>That *fresshë*[3] floures *blew* and *white* and *rede*
>Ben *quyke* a-gayn that wynter *dedë* made
>And ful of bawme is fletynge euery mede
>Whan Phebus doth his *bryghtë*[4] bemes sprede.
>Right yn the white bolę[5] so it bytydde
>As I shal synge on Mayes day the thridde, 1135-41.

(*b*) fele (A.S. feola, fela, Ps. N. feolu, -o ; really old neut. adj.), on of so fele, 4772 ; thow sleest so fele, 5174. [*fele*, 4706 f A, is *f. l.* for *felle*.]

fewe (A.S. féawe, -a, Ps. féa). I. Without *a*,—fewe lordes, 2672 ; fewe folk, 2732 (-[e] D); wommen fewe, 7051 (few B). II. With *a*,— a sely fewe poyntes, 338 (C † ?); a fewe wordes, 3743 (-[e] D) ; a fewe bryghte teres, 3893 (-[e] B); of wordes but a fewe, 6996 f (: shewe *inf.*); a fewe of olde storyes, 7822 (C †, sue † D) ; in a wordes fewe, 5942 f AB (in [a] w. f. CD) (: shewe *inf.*).

(*c*) So in the plural of monosyllabic superlatives :
meste and leste, 167 f (B † ; A ?; the moost and ek(e) the leest D) (: feste) ; most and leste, 4721 f (: requeste *n.*). (For " definite " plural phrases, *the meste and* [*ek*] *the leste, with the firste and with the beste*, cf. 6803, 7202.)

(*d*) Cardinal numerals (Child § 39. *c* ; ten Brink, § 247) :
tweyne, tweye (A.S. *masc.* twégen, Kent. Rushw. twǽgen, North. tuóege, tuége, etc.).

(1) tweyne, *1705 f (twene C), *2800 f, *2820 f (-n D), *3957 f, *4332 f, *5410 f (-n CD), *5804 f, *7634 f, *7711 f ; a nyght or tweyne, 3392 f (-n D, twey(e)ne C) ; we tweyne, 4049 f, 5138 f, 5450 f (-n D), 5920 f (twyne B), 7042 f ; vs tweyne, 5965 f (twyne B); tweyn (: peyne), *5412 f C. [4976 † f A, 5064 † f C.]
Rhyme words.—cheyne *n.* (1705), Eleyne (2800), peyne *n.* (2820, 4332, 5410, 5450, 5804, 5920, 5965, 7042, 7634), to seyne *inf.* (1705, 3392, 3957, 7711), reyne *inf.* (3392), streyne *inf.* (4049), compleyne *inf.* (5138, 5450, 7634, 7711), *subj.* 3 *sg.* (5920).

(2) tweye, *1255 f, 1267 f (swychë tweye), 1896 f (*absolute use*),

---
[1] ȝynge occurs in 184 C,—*hyse ȝyngë knyȝtis* (*yonge* AD, *ȝonge* B).
[2] monthes gladde B.   [3] fressch[e] B.   [4] bryght[e] B.   [5] bool B.

§ 67.] *of Chaucer's Troilus.* 143

*2917 †, 3665 f (*absolute*) (tweyen B), *4791 f (twye A, tway D), *4976 f B (tweyne † A, twye C †), 6075 f (a day or tweye, cf. 6045 f), *8091 f (twye B, tuey D) (cf. *4820 f, *4909 f); vs, ye, yow, bothe tweye, 2242 f (to † C), 2277 f (tweyne † C), 2739 f, 3982 f, 7670 f (tweyne B) (cf. 5771 f, 6165 f, 6991 f); a day or tweye, 6276 B (two A, too C, tweyne D). For the definite use (as, *the tweye, this ilke tweye*), cf. 494 f, 4035 f, 4156 f, 5032 f. —twey, with twey ‡ vesàgis, 7262 C (two AB, tuo D), cf. 3349 ‡ D (*definite*).

> Note.—D almost always has *twey* (but cf. 2383 f, 3074 f); C has *twey* in 6075 f, 7670 f.
> Rhyme words.[1]—deye *inf.* (1255, 4909, 6075, 6991), seye *inf.* (1255, 2739, 2917, 3665, 4820, 4909, 5771, 6045, 6165, 7670, 8091), *ind.* 1 *sg* (1267, 2277), pleye *inf.* (1896), *subj* 2 *sg.* (3665), preye *inf* (2739), *ind.* 1 *sg.* (2242, 6165), *ind.* 3 *pl.* (6045), leye *inf.* (2917, 7670), purueye 2 *pl. imv. or subj* (2242), a-weye (2277, 4976), chimeney(-eye) (3982), this olde greye (4791), what weye (4820), by the weye (6991)
> Note.—For two (var. C *to, too*; D *tuoo, to*), cf. 614 f, 645, 1671, 2777 f, 7736, 8226, etc ; *a-two*, 4317 f (on to C, a twoo D), 6543 f (oto C, in tuoo D), etc

fyue (A.S. fíf), *2117 f (: vpon lyue), *6760 f (: dryue *inf.* : blyue *adv.*), *7252 f (: on lyue); suche fyue, 1211 f (: thryue *inf.*); swych[e] fyue, 1213 (D †). [Var. BC fiue.]

sixe (A.S. sex, W.S. siex, syx), set the world on sixe and seuene (six B, sexe C, vj D), 5284.

seuene (A.S. seofon, siofon, -an, -en, Ps. seofen), the blysful goddes seuene[2], 4045 f (: to heuene); seuene (*dissyl.*) kynges, 7858 (vij BD); on sixe (*q.v.*) and seuene (seue C, seuen D), 5284 f (: to heuene).

nyne (A.S. nigon, R.[2] níone), ix. (= nyn) nyght, 5250 (nyne dayis ‡ ? C); ye sustren nyne, 4651 (ix that D); and othere of here wommen nyne·or ten, 3440 (nyne or (?) C, [3] a .ix. or .x. D [4]).

twelue (A.S. twelf), *1193 f, *2484 f (twelwe C), *6460 f, *7287 f (.vij. † C); swych[e] twelue, 5064 f (tweine † C). (All rhyme with *my-, thi-, hym-selue.*)

> Note.—But ten (cf. 60, 5982, 6602, 7569, 7713). Other numerals,—*thre* (cf. 2021, 3051 f, 3155 f, etc.), *twenty* (cf. 6069), *fyfty* (cf. 7856), *sixty* (cf. 441), *thousand* (cf 58, 457, 531, 546, 819, 1227, etc.), *thousandys* (8165, -es BD).
> Note.—In Anglo-Saxon, when the cardinal numerals from 4 to 19 are used absolutely, they form cases according to the i- declension (see Sievers, § 325 and note).

---

[1] No cases of the *definite use* included.
[2] Supply [*tho*] in A.
[3] But supply [*othere*] and read *nyne*.
[4] Supply [*of*] in D.

(e) Monosyllabic participles (see also § 68):
  with bygge bowes bente, 4702 f AB (bent D) (: mente 3 *pl.* : wente 3 *pl.*).
  with herte and eerys spradde, 6084 f (: he hadde).
  But cf. wommen lost thorugh, 3140 (C †).
(f) Romance adjectives:
  preste wynges, 5323 (-[e] BD). (For sing. cf. 3759, 4824.)
  tuskes stoute, 7817 f (: aboute : doute *n.*).
  knyghtes stoute, 7856 f (: route *n.* : aboute).
  floures blew and, 1136 AB.

> Note 1. For examples of the plural of adjectives that end regularly in -e in the singular, cf. *grene* (1906 f, 5816 f, 6095 f, 6374 f), *kene* (1143 f), *kynde* (7333 f), *newe* (2554 f, 3893 f, 6192 f), *trewe* (2695 f, 2959 f, 4613 f), *vntrewe* (1871 f). For examples of the plural of adjectives that come under § 49, cf. *bare* (7910), *fayre, fresshe* (1136, 3453, 8198), *goode, grete, hye, heyghe* (3460 f, 4910, 7093), *olde* (see note s. v.), *proude* (1487 f). For the plural of Romance adjectives that end in the singular in -e, cf. *pale* (3466 f), *straunge* (1109 f), *nyce* (1109), *ryche and pore* (6406 f), *square* (7164 f) (sg. not in the *Troilus*).
>
> Note 2. *Bonde* (A.S. bónda, *weak noun*) is used as an adjective (in the plural apparently) in "For as here lyst she pleyeth *with free and bonde*," 840 (bond D) (: withstonde *inf.*). For the singular, also adjectival, see "She wolde nought ne make hire-self *bonde* In loue," 2308 f (: vnderstonde *inf.* : in honde).

§ 68. Monosyllabic perfect participles *standing in the predicate* regularly take no -e in the plural. Thus—

(i.) Before consonants and at end of verse:
  they be gon, 2243 f (-e BD) (: anoon, or noon A).
  they were born, 4064 f (-e BCD) } (: by-forn).
  bothe two be lorn, 4065 f. (-e BD) }
  they were born, 5913 f (borne BD, bore C).
  we be lost, 3937 (cf. 3140).
  ye be brought, 3980 f (-e B, brouȝt CD) (: nought : thought *n.*).
  ben ... laft, 4180 f (last † C, lefte E) (: by-raft *p.p. pred. pl.*); cf. 4887 f, 4889 f.—ben wyst, 5739 (-e B), cf. 5681.
  they ben met, 4523 f (mette C^c) (: was it bet). So,—i-met, 1671 f (ymette D) (: net *n.* : set *p.p.*).
  this wordes seyd, 5573 (-e BD ; seydë ‡ *dixit* C).
  Til we be slayn (sleyne B) and doun oure walles torn, 6144 (torne D) (: lorn *p.p.* : sworn *p.p.*).
  thei be wont to, 7023 (wonte BD, wone C); cf. were woned to, 4553 (wonte B, wone C, wont D).

(ii.) Before vowels:
  thei ben met, 1237 (mette C ; D †); ben set, 4986.

[§§ 68, 69.] *of Chaucer's Troilus.* 145

ben fled, 5530 (fledde D).
Note.—So also when the subject is *ye* in a singular sense : cf. (i.) 4049, 5597 f (: assent *n.* : auysement) ; (ii.) 2191, 2267.

But in two or three cases the -e appears. Thus—

dred(r)es weren . . . fled[de], 463 f (fledde B) (: bredde *pret. ind.* 3 *sg.*, bred C †, bred D).

dores were faste y-shette, 3075 f (y-chette B, faste schette C, fast yshet D) (: lette *n.* : sette *pret. ind.* 3 *sg.*).

here speres were whette, 8123 f AB (whett D) (: mette 3 *pl.*).

And don thyn hod, thi nedes sped[de] be, 2039 (spedde BC ; D ?).

Cf. And fond two othere ladyes sette and she, 1166 A (sete B ; sate *pret.* 3 *pl.* D).

§ 69. Monosyllabic adjectives *standing in the predicate* do not always take -e in the plural (Child, § 41 ; ten Brink, § 234). Thus—

(*a*) hem that ben not worth two fecches. 3778 BCD (*sing.* A).
Cf. 3696, 4009, where *worth pl.* is followed by a vowel.[1]

wyse men ben war by folys, 635 (-e D, ware ‡ of B).[2]

dede were his iapes, 1076.

shal we ben so fayn, 5983 f (feyne B ; D †) (: ayen : seyn *inf.*).

tonges ben so prest, 1870 f (-e B) (: lest *n.*).

O verrey loues nice and blynde be ye, 202 (fooles nice and blynde B Cp. John's ; C † ; ἄλλως D ‡).

(*b*) So particularly when the adjective in the predicate refers to a subject *ye* (expressed or implied) used in a singular sense. Thus—

be ye mad, 1198 f (made B, madde C) (: adrad *p.p. sg.*, adradd(e) C).
Note.—In,—Be ȝe (*so* C G Cp. ; ye DE John's, *om.* AB) nought (not CD) war (ware BD) how fals (false Cp., that fals D) Polyphete, 2552, *ye is* necessary to the sense. We should read *war* and *false.* Cf. § 49. Cases before vowels (as, glad, 3019) of course prove nothing.

ye be wroth therfore, 1385 (-e D). Cf. p. 141.

Now beth nought wroth my blod my nece dere, 1679 (-e D) ; beth not wroth with me, 6508 ; so, before vowels, in 7972, 7977. [For sing. *wroth*, cf. (i.) 349, 842, 1012, 2158, 3127, 3572 f, 3886 f, 3924, 3952 f, 7827, 8138 ; (ii.) 581 (be ‡ ȝe wroth C), etc.]

(ye that) ben so loth to, 2996 (-e D). [For. sing. *loth*, cf. (i.) 3211, 3574 f, 4181 ; (ii.) 1893, 6384.]

beth al hol ‖ no, 3010 (-e D, hoole B).

ye ben to wys ‖ to, 3709 (-[e] ? C, wis B).

[1] For sing. *worth*, cf. 3675, 4382, 5428, 7245. [2] For sing *war*, see p. 146.

L

beth glad now, 5978 (-ę D ; C ?).

beth wel war, 4022 (-ę D) ; beth war of men, 8148 (-e D). [For sing. *war*, cf. (i.) 203, 1360, 2266, 4544 f ; (ii.) 2103, 3426, 4464, 7922 ; wa*re*, 6896 (war CD).]

and ye so feyr, 6533 (-ę BD).

So occasionally when the plural adjective is used attributively.

> Ten Brink's remark, " Im Plural des attributīv stehenden Adjectivs (gleichviel ob starker oder schwacher Flexion) tritt die Apocope [des flexivischen -*e*] kaum ein ; niemals, wenn der Adjectiv voransteht" (§ 236) is not borne out by the *Troilus* MSS. The following lines are significant :—
>
> And ben *of good condicions* ther to, 1251 A (goodę B, goodę condisciounys C, And to be of good c. therto D). We have no warrant to read *condicion*.
>
> Ne for no *wysę men* but for foles nice, 3166 (no wis man C, wysę man D). Here one is tempted to read *man*. (No note in the Cp. collation.) But *wyse men* is a quasi-compound, cf. 5749.
>
> Hath lordes oldę thorugh which withinne a throwe, 7824 (old C, high D).
>
> Note.—Cases before a vowel (as *ful*, 4223, 8176) of course prove nothing.

§ 70. For adjectives of more than one syllable which do not stand at the end of the verse, the rule as to -e in the plural is the same as that already stated as to -e in the definite and vocative constructions of such adjectives (§ 56).

Of such adjectives those alone take -e which have a primary or secondary accent on the ultima, and are followed by a word accented on the first syllable (cf. Child, § 40 ; ten Brink, § 233).[1]

Note.—For convenience, words in -*re* (-*er*), -*le*, have been included in the following list. A few sporadic cases of -*e* (as in *lewedę*) or -*e* (elided) will be observed

(*a*) the worthiest and grettest in degrè, 244.

the fresshest and, 4564 (-*e* B ; C † D †).

strengest folk, 243 (cf alderwisest han, 247).

---

[1] In the list that follows, no definite or vocative examples, or examples before a vowel, or *h*, are given without notice.

§ 70.] *of Chaucer's Troilus.* 147

(*b*) confòrted most, 249 (-id C, -yd D) (*predicate*).
thonked be ye, 1935 (*sg.* CD).
tresses vnbroyden hangen, 5479.
twynned be we, 5138, 7042.
here dorres sperid alle, 6894 (-ed BD, -ede C).
feyned loues, 8211.
payens corsed olde vyces, 8212.
(Cf. also 3931, 5670, 6186, 7482, 7702, 7907, 8143, etc.)

(*c*) ȝoure lewëde òbseruaùnces, 198 C (ȝour lewde obseruaunce ‡ D).
hire wykkede werkes, 997 (-ed B, -id D).
these wikkede tonges, 1870 (-yd D).
we wrecched wommen, 1867 (wreche[d] C; D †).
these wrecched worldes appetites, 8214 A (this B, the D).
(Cf. also 1905, 1906, 1907.)

(*d*) the blysful goddes, 4045 AB,[1] 7613.
maisterful or (*pred.*), 1841 (mastirful C, maystreful D).
sorwful[2] sykes, 4203 (soruful C, sorowful D), 7717 (sorweful CD).
sorweful[2] teres, 7737 (sorowfull D).
the sorwful, 6346 (sorwefull D).
wilful tacches, 3777.
o wofulle eyen, 4971 (woful B, cruel † C, wofull D).
hise woful wordes, 1658. (Cf. 5002, 5797.)
here woful wery gostes tweyne, 5804 f (wery woofull D).

(*e*) goosish peples speche, 3426 B (gos(y)lyche † A, C † *om.*, gosisshe D)[3].
here sonnyssh herys, 5478 (-e here B[4]).

(*f*) her sydes . . . fleysshly, 4090 (flessly C, fleschly C, fleishely D).
shaply ben, 6114 (shapely B, shappely D).
gyddé ‡ apis, 906 C (goddës apes ABD).
many wordes, 1233 (-ye BC, meny D).
In sondry londes sondry ben vsages, 1113 (sundry D).
sondry formes, 8076.
to yow angry Parcas, 6366 (angurry D).
vnthryfty weyes, 6192.
(For other cases, definite and indefinite, of the plural of adjs. in -y,
   cf. 233, 251, 742, 1112, 1203, 1233, 2171 A, 2324, 2436, 4046,
   4208, 4223, 4287, 6532, 7164, 7332, 8122, 8133, etc.)

---

[1] Supply [*tho*] in A   [2] Dissyllable throughout.
[3] A and D have *peple speche*, haplography for *peples speche*. The textus receptus has *goofish*, see Matzner s.v. *gofisch*. G has *goossish*. E has *gosissh*. Cp. has *goosissh poeples.*
[4] Read *here*[*s*] in B (: teres : eeres).

Note.—For *merye*, see above, § 46, p. 113.

(*g*) bittre[1] bondes, 3958 (bittere[1] C, bittir D); bittre teris, 5800 (bittere C, bittir D); bittre weren, 5798 (-tere C, bitter D); thi bittre peynes smerte, 5088 (-tere ? C, bitter D †).

with-innę tho yonder wallys, 7096 (with-inne ʒonë wallis C, with-ınnë yonder D).

(*h*) certeyn tymes, 4273; certeyn folk, 6396.

ye do hem còrteys be, 2868 (curteis B, curteys D).

esy sykes, 4205 (esię C).

tho that ben expèrt in, 2452.

o fatal sustren, 3575 (-(ę) D †).

gentil hertis, 2847.

ye humble[1] nettes, 4197 (vmbele[1] C).

parfit and, 7333 (-*e* B; C †; perfite D [2]).

the subtile stremes, 305 (subtyl C, sotil D).

folk vngìltyf suffren, 3860 (ongilti C, vngilty D †).

his throwes frènetỳk and madde, 6569 (feruentike † B, fren[e]tik D, frentyk † he made C).

The plural -e is shown in

the *Troiàne* gestes, 145 A (the troyan[e] BC, the troianys ‡ D),

and perhaps in

Fy on yourę myght and werkes so *diuerse*, 5857 f (: thow fortune aduerse : no werse) (cf. § 52, above; Child, § 42; ten Brink, § 241).

Cf. otherę besye (*dissyl.*) nedes, 355 (-y CD); cf. however, 7352 (A †).

Note.—In *amoreux hem made*, 2859, we have a French plural (*amerous* D). See also § 63.

§ 71.
The treatment of the plural of adjectives of more than one syllable at the end of the verse, is illustrated by the following examples. (Cf. also § 70, at the end.)

hem that falsęly ben apeỳred, 38 f, *rhyming with*

hem that ben des(es)peỳred, 36 f (despeyred B, dispeired D).

alderwisest han . . . ben plesed, 247 f (-id C, -yd D) *rhyming with*

thei . . . han ben . . . esed, 249 f (-yd D) (: apesed *p.p. sg.*).

the feste and playes pàlestràl, 6667 f (: funeral).

---

[1] Dissyllable throughout.
[2] In C read *parfit* (printed, *parfit*) and supply [*and*]; in D supply [*and*].

the thynges tèmporèl, 5723 f (temporall D) (: euery del : èternèl).
other thyng collateral, 262 f (thinges D, thyngis collatrial C).
Note.—*Thei be rungen*, 1890 f A, should read *Thei be runge*.

§ 72. Adjectives in A.S. *-lic* (*-lic*), O.N. *-ligr*, appear in the *Troilus* with the ending *-ly* or *-lich*.

Ten Brink (§ 270) seems inclined to recognize a tendency on Chaucer's part to use *-lich* instead of *-ly* when the following word begins with a vowel[1], but the *Troilus* MSS. do not given evidence in favour of such a tendency: one can only say that the ending *-ly* remains unchanged in the definite use, in the plural, and in the vocative, and that when the poet wishes for metrical or other reasons to add an inflectional *-e*, he employs the form in *-lich*.

In the following list *old-style figures* indicate that a vowel follows; *def.* = definite use (singular); *def. pl.* = definite use (plural); *pl.* = plural (indefinite use); *voc.* = vocative singular. Examples not distinguished by any of these signs are in the indefinite use, singular number, and are followed by a word beginning with a consonant. It will be observed that the *Troilus* affords no instance of an adjective in *-ly* or *-lich* (*-liche*) at the end of a verse.

For forms in *-lich*, *-liche*, see under *estatlyche*, *goodly*, *heuenliche*, *gosylyche*, *grysly*, *syklyche*, *wommanlyche*.

dedly, 5533 (dedely B), 5560 (dedely BC).

erthely, 5543 (erthly B, wordely C).

estàtlyche, 7186 (-liche B, statlyche (?) C, estàlich D).

fleysshly, 4090 (flessly B, fleschly C †, fleishely D) (*pl.*).

frendly, 538[2], 1234 (*pl.*), 1417 (lovely ‡ D) (*def.*), 5060. [Var. B freendly, frendely, freendely; C frendli, frendeli.]

goodly, 162 AB[3] (*def.*), 173 (*def.*), 277, 373, 405 (sauory B, sauery CD), 446 (*def.*), 458 (*voc.*), 1070, 1366 (goodlichë C), 2031 (perh. adv.)[4], 2113, 2210 (C ? D ?), 2353 (*def.*), 2752 (goode A) (*def.*), 2846 (*voc.*), 2970 (D †) (*voc.*), 3975 (*def. pl.*), 4315 (D †) (*voc.*), 4448, 5072 AB, 7081 (*def. pl.*), 7185. [Var. B godely, goodely; C goodeli, godli, goodli.]

gòsylychę peple speche, 3426 (goosish peples s. B, gosisshe peple s. D; C^e †). (See p. 147, footnote 3.)

grysly, 2785 (grysely B, grèsëllchë C)[5], 4817 (grisely B, gresely C).

helply, 6491 AB (helpyn *inf.* C, helpë *inf.* D).

[1] "Aus einem genauen Studium der Ueberlieferung . . . ergiebt sich u. a., dass Chaucer . . . vor anlautendem Vocal . . . vielfach *-lich* und *-liche* statt *-ly* gebraucht."

[2] In 538 C read *gladyth* for *gladede*.

[3] In AB the line is too long; CD Cp. Harl. 2392 om. *goodly*. G reads: And to the temple in her goodly best wyse

[4] In C read *haste* for *laste*.

[5] But in C supply [I] and read *grèsęlìchę*.

hèuęnlichę, 104 C (heuęnyꝛh B, heuęnyssh B, heuęnly D).
holy, 1203 (*pl.*).
homęli, 2644 C (*apparently adv. in* ABD, homly).
knyghtly, 1713 (-ę- BC).
lovęly, 1417 ‡ D (*def.*).
lykly, 4112 (I lykly was to sterue) (lyke ţo (?) D^c).
manly, 2348 (-lı C), 2955 (-li C) (*def.*).
oonly, 6330; saue only Ector, 1825 (oonly B, onlı C); oonly worthinesse, 6330 (oonęly B, onęly D).
shaply, 6114 (-ę- B, shappęly C) (*pl.*).
softly, 2752 (soft[e] BD, softe C) (*def.*)
sunnęlich was, 5398 C (sonnyssh ABD).
syklychè, 2613 (sikliche B, sekly C, sıke ‡ D (?)); his syklychę manère, 2628 (siklých B, seklýchę C, sıklý D).
well willy, 4099 ABC † (wel(e) wylly D) (*def.*).
wòmmanlýchë wyf, 2948 A (-lich[e] BD, -liche C) (*voc.*); womman-lichè wyf, 4138 (women lich[e] C, womanlich[e] D) (*voc.*); tho womanlichè thyngis, 5356 (wommanyssh[e] AD, womman[i]sshe B); yourę fresshë wommanlychè face, 6607 (-lıche BC, womanly[che] D); wòmmanlý, 287. (In 6940 *wommanly* is apparently an adv.)
worldly, 3655 (wordly B, wordęli C)[1], 3670 (wordly B, wordęli C), 4478 (wordly B, wordęlis ‡ C), 5497 (wordly BD, wordęly C).
worthęli, 1424 (worthi A, worthy BD).

With these may be compared:

sely, 338 (*om.* ‡ C) (a sely fewe poyntes), 871, 1768, 4033 (*def.*), 5165, 6152 (*pl.*), 6892 (*def.*), 7456 (*def.*). [Var. B cęly; C selı.]
vnsely, 35 (vnseely D).
weldy, 1721 (worthi ‡ C).

PRONOUNS.

§ 73. I. Personal Pronouns.

I (A.S. ic). Usually *I* or *y* in all four MSS. But the following cases of *ich* have been noticed : 678 ABC, 864 A (ıche here B), 2143 B, 2145 BD, 3474 B, 3549 B, 3715 B, 3770 B, 4319 B, 4660 AB, 4733 B, 4762 B, 4976 B, 4991 B, 5245 AB, 5287 AB, 5294 AB, 5411 B, 5419 B, 5467 B, 5585 B, 5727 A, 5999 A (ıchę B), 6053 AB, 6213 AB, 6312 B (ych A), 6403 AB, 6493 AB, 6589 AB, 6590 AB, 6781 B, 6928 B, 6933 B, 6942 B, 7062 B, 7110 B, 7234

---
[1] In B supply [*so*].

§ 73.] *of Chaucer's Troilus.* 151

AB, 7296 B, 7624 B, 7710 A, 7718 A, 7959 A (iche herte B), 7988 B, 8130 B. *ych* also occurs, 6312 A, 7745 A ; and, iche hym, 5594 B (cf. above 7959).

As *I* best kan to yow lord yeu*e ych* al, 1914 (I . . . Ich B, I . . . I † ȝow . . . I al C, y . . . y D †).

Clippe *ich* yow thus or elles *I* it mete, 4186 AB (ech*e* . . . [ellis] ich C, I . . . I D).

Why suffre *ich* it whi nyl *ich* do it redresse, 6403 (ich . . . ich B, I . . . I CD ; *om.* do BCD).

    Note.—*I* occurs in rhyme as follows : (1) with adverbs in -*ly*, 416, 430, 1103, 1269, 1629, 2087, 2511, 2619, 2760, 2910, 3594, 5351, 5545, 5679, 5926, 7486 ; (2) with *redy*, 983 ; (3) with *by, therby*, 1629, 5679.

thow (A.S. þú), 894, 909 (thou C), 933 (thou CD), 6633 (thu C, thou D), etc., etc.; thou, 898 (thow BD), etc. (In rhyme,—two cases,—thow, 2088 (thou C) (: now : how), 6695 (ȝow C, thou D) (: nowe, now BD).)

Thow in the reduced form -*ow* is very often attached to verbs. Thus :—
artow, 509 AB (art thou C, art(e) thou D) ; ertow, 5079 B (thow art A, are thou D) ; cf. 731, 5195, 5303, 5757. But,—art thow, 507 (artow B, art thou C, art(e) thou D), 3579 (art tow B), etc.
hastow, 554 (hast thou CD) ; cf. 617, 904, 962, 3145, 3681, 4297, 4301, 4453, 4945, 5039, 5057, 5148, 5158, 5301, 5751, 5755, 6868 + B, 6951, 6952.
sholdestow, shuldestow, 6714 (schuldist thow C, shuldest thou D) ; cf. 7651.
maystow, 623 (mayst thou CD) ; cf. 673, 2101, 3738, 4927, 7522, 8074. But,—mayst thow, 5208 (maistow B, mayst thou C, maist thou D) ; cf. 7493.
myghtestow, 4924 (mayst thu C, maist thou D).
dostow, 5177 (dost thou C, dost(e) thou D) ; cf. 7097.
ne hastow, 5512 (ne hast thou ? C, ne haue ye ? D).
ne haddestow, 4938 (ne haddyst thou C, ne haddist thou D).
wiltow, wyltow, 1011 (woltow B, wilt thow CD) ; cf. 4931.
woltow, 2446 (wiltow B, wilt thou C, wilt thow D) ; cf. 5513, 7520. But,—wolt thow, 2532 (wiltow B, wilt thou C).
nyltow, 792 (nylt thou C, nelt thou D), 8071 A (nyl to B, nil thou D) ; cf. 4269, 4912, 4965, 5151.
neltow, 5150 (nyltow B, nylt thou C, nylt(e) thou D).
nodestow, 4106 (noldestow B, noldist thou CD).
wostow, 588 (wost thou C, w. thow D) ; cf. 611, 775, 781, 843, 851, 855, 901, 956, 967, 3091.
wistow, 4486 (wistist thou C, wist thow D).
oughtestow, 6908 (auȝtist thow C, oughtest thou D).
canstow, kanstow, 757 (canst thou C, canst thow D †) ; cf. 5122 (canstu C), 5192.
darstow, 7642 (dastow A, durst(ist) thow C, darst(e) thou D).
dorstestow, 767 AB (durstyst thou C, trist thow D).
shaltow, 803 (schuldyst thou C, thou shalt D) ; cf. 5271 (shaltow(e)) B, 6391.
blamestow, 841 (-yst thou CD).
gabbestow, 5143 (-ist thou C, -est thou C).
intendestow, 6841 (entendist thow C, entendest thou D).
listow, 5056 (lyst thou C, liest thou D).
proferestow, 4303 (profrestuw B, proferist thow C ; D †).
sekestow, 4297 (-yst thou C, -est thou D).
sestow, 2888 AB (seest thou D).

seystow, 7524 (seistow B, seyst thou C, seest thou D); cf. 7654, 7886.
seydestow, seidestow, 912 (seydist thou CD); cf. 917, 918.
slombrestow, 730 (slomberyst thou C, slumbrist thow D).
thenkestow, 2458 (thynkestow B, thinkist thou C, thinkyst thou D); cf. 5511, 5750.

It will be seen that these forms are common in AB, very rare in C (canstu, 5122) and hardly found in D. AB have, however, full forms in *-est, -st thow* (*thou*), as well as the contracted forms.

Once the affixed -ow (= thow) is reduced to -e,—*Wher arte ?* (art D) (: *carte*), 7524.

Thart (= thow art), 4471 (thow art A, thu art C, thou art D).

he (A.S. hé), 21, 1164 f, and *passim*. he Ixiòn, 6575 (the ‡ I. D; C°†).

Note.—The colloquial contraction written *a* occurs (cf. *a* for *have*), but not in A: And on the Grekes ofte a wold a see, 7030 D (ost he woldē se A, oost he wold[e] se B, oftē wolde he se C). Perhaps the scribe intended *a* † *lough*, 3260 B, for *he lough* (and low AC, or lowe D). For elided or slurred *e* in *he*, see § 125. In 6440 C, *Antenòrē = Antenòr he ;* but cf. 5327 f.

she, 178 (scho B, sche C), 679 (sche C), 1166 f, 1689 f (sche C), 2832 f (sche C), 3995 (sho B, sche C † D), 4369 (sche CD), 5829 (sce C), 7479 f (sche C), 7667 (che B, sche C), and *passim ;* she Criseyde, 3968 B (cf. 1901 ?). For the elision or slurring of -e in *she*, see § 126.

it (A.S. hit), nom., acc., and with prepositions.

Usually *it* in all four MSS.; cf. 5686 f (: sit *sedet* ; yit), 5765 f (: yet : wit), 7124 f (: wit : yit), and *passim*.

But *hit* occasionally occurs (as, 297 D, 346 D, 1545 D, 2222 D, 3244 D); yt, 57 A.

Note.—Ten Brink's rule "dass Chaucer nach einem auslautenden Vocal, der nicht elidirt werden soll, stets *hit—nicht it—*schreibt" (§ 270) is not observed in the *Troilus* MSS.

me (A.S. mé) dat., acc., and with prepositions. (*a*) Dat. without prepositions, 142 (?), 403 f, 828, 1120, 1274; 3152 f, 3416, 4744, 5497 f. (*b*) Other oblique uses, cf. 1578 f, 4324 f, and *passim*. For *mē* with a preposition, see *by me*, 2076 f (: tyme : pryme). For elided or slurred -*e* in *me*, see § 126.

the (A.S. þé), dat., acc., and with prepositions. (*a*) Dat. without prepositions, 829, 2177, 4299 (thee D), 8094; 8100 f. (*b*) Other oblique uses, cf. 6771 f and *passim*. What eyleth the, 4993 f.

hym (A.S. him), dat., acc., and with prepositions. (*a*) Dat. without prepositions, 82, 188, 694, etc., etc. (*b*) Other oblique uses, *passim*. [Var. him.]

hire, here (A.S. hire), *dat. and acc.*, monosyllabic, not distinguished in spelling from the possessive (cf. (i.) bef. consonants ; 126, 131, 177, 286, 315, 361, 370, 388, 454, 481, 840, 976, 1050, 1360, 1687, 1778, 1999, 2010, 2069, 2205, 2239, 2450, 3311, 3398, 3523, 4094, 4824, etc. ; cf. (ii.) bef. vowels, 974, 1749; 3408, 3972, 4029,

[§ 73] *of Chaucer's Troilus.*

7223, etc.). Forms without -e occur even in A : thus,—her anoon *acc.*, 116 A ; to hyr spak, 3972 A ; as hir lyste, 3974 A ; sen her laughęn, 7144 A.—Notice the following cases in rhyme : here (*eam*), 2876 f (: to were = *weir*) ; of here, 3109 f (hire C) (: swere *inf.*); here (*eam*), 4484 f (hire BC) (: bere *inf.* : tere *inf.*), 5274 f (hire BC, her D) (: swere *inf.*).

It may be that when *hire* was emphatic it could be dissyllabic, even in the middle of a verse. Thus—

For-thi som grace I hope yn *here* fynde, 973 A (hyre C, hiré Cp , in her y D, in hyrę to B, in hir to G).

Biseching here syn that he was trewe, 7948 A (hire B, hirę that C, hir that D, hir[e] that sithe he Harl. 2392). [*Here* is not really emphatic. No variation in Cp. collation.]

In the following cases, however, a comparison of MSS. shows that the dissyllabic form is to be rejected : 977 C, 1056 A, 2159 C, 4827 A, 5365 C, 7212 C, 7226 C, 7454 AC, 7905 C.

Note.—In the light of the rhymes just cited, I cannot understand ten Brink's remark (§ 250, Anm. 3) . "Sicher, dass für den Sing. Fem. ihm [Chaucer] blos *hire hir* [not *here her*] geläufig war."

we (A.S. wé), 3707, 4856 f, 6176, and *passim*.

ye (A.S. gé), 26 f (ʒe B), 198 (ʒe CD), 202 f A (ʒe BC), 340 f (ʒe BCD), 5996 f (ʒe BC), 8055 f (ʒe BC, yee D) ; cf. 1364 f, 1373 f, 1667 f, 2860 f, 3441 f, *and passim*. For *yĕ* with a preposition, cf. *yow*.

they, thei (O.N. þeir), 60 (theyę B), 136 (thai B, the C), 763 ; cf. 134, 1167, 1260, 1302, 4224, etc., etc.

us (A.S. ús), dat., acc., and with prepositions, 1034, 1412, 1526, 1585, 6488, and *passim*. For examples of the dat. without prepositions, see 1181 f (: Pandarus : thus), 1868, 6010. (*Us* rhymes with *-us* in Pandarus, Troylus, Deiphebus, Tydeus, and with *thus :* cf. 620 f, 1181 f, 1207 f, 1286 f, 1517 f, 2273 f, 2404 f, 2563 f, 6842 f, 7400 f, 7414 f, 7841 f, 7925 f.)

yow, you (A.S. éow), dat., acc., and with prepositions, 331 f (ʒow BCD) (: prow *n.* : how), 1329 (ʒou B, ʒow C, *om.* † D), 4975 (ʒow B, you D), and *passim*. For examples of the dat. without prepositions, cf. 342, 431, 1421, 7728, etc., etc. [yowe, 4763 f (ʒowe B, ʒou D) (: now),] *yow* rhymes with *now, prow, how* (cf. 331 f, 2523 f, 2746 f, 3165 f, 3853 f, 4322 f, 4406 f, 4491 f, 4763 f (yowe A), 5540 f, 5988 f, 6492 f, 8103 f).

Yĕ in *fro ye*, 5 f (: Troye : ioye), is apparently a reduced *yow* (cf. *arte* for *artow*), whatever one may say of *ayeyn ye*, 334 AB (C †, ʒe D), where, on the whole, *ye* prob. = *yea*.

hem (A.S. him, heom), 908, 2791, 2805, 4227, 4521, etc., etc.

Note.—*Hem* is found in all MSS.; *him* or *hym* sometimes replaces it (as, 31 A, 303 BD, 518 B, 558 B, 911 B,[1] 1284 (?) CD, 2567 B, 4240 A); *them* is found only in D (see, e. g., 29, 31, 36, 50, 558, 4862, 5805); theym, 41 D.

§ 74. II. Possessive Pronouns.

my, myn (A.S. mín). I. Sing. (*a*) my *before. consonants*: my fo, 837 (myn C, my wo ‡ B); my brother, 2496 (myn C); my lord my brother, 2535 (myn . . . myn C) (cf. 2711); my dere brother, 2760 (myn C), etc., etc. ; mi spirit, 423 AB (myn C, the D). (*b*) myn *before vowels*: 16, 407 (D †), 432 (C †), 683, 772, 1134, 3081 (my D), 6112 (my D), 8081 (myne D), etc., etc. (*c*) myn *before* h: myn herte, 599, 606, 1652, 1664 (my D), 6593 (my D), etc.; myn hod, 2195 (myne D); myn hows, 3037 (my D); cf. 530, 1845, 1954, 3001, 3157, 6866; my dere hert allas myn hele and hewe, 461 (mi . . . myn B, myn . . . myn C); myn herte ayens my lust, 1560 (myn hest † . . . myn C, my hert . . . my D). (*d*) myn, *before consonants*: myn peyne, 1560 AC (my BD); on myn byhalue, 2543 AC (my BD); myn dere herte, 3685 AC (my BD); go litel myn tregedie, 8149. C, so far as I have observed, uses only *myn*, whether before vowels or consonants[2]; cf. 527, 612, 616, 2188, 2366, 2705, 2711, 2735, 3018, 3085, 3713, 3788, 3838, etc. (In some of these cases the n is written in C; in others it is represented by the familiar stroke.) Cf. myn swete herte, 5973 B (myn owne AD, myne C.) (*e*) *my* before vowels: my auctor, 394 (myn BCD); cf. the variants under *b*, above. (*f*) When the possessive follows its noun, *myn* is of course the only form used. Thus,—Com(e) nece myn my lady queene, 2799 ABD (nece myne myn C); cf. 1510, 2280 (myne B), 2320. And so when the possessive stands in the predicate (cf. 21, 3835, 5141 f (myne BD) (: for fyn)), and when the noun is omitted (cf. 3849, 6960). II. Plural: myn peynes, 2984 (my BD, myne C); my sorwes, 4014 (mynne C); my cares, 7705 B (D ?, myne C, [my] A); myne othere lordes, 2566 (myn D). —myne wordes, 4173 ABC (my E);[3] cf. 6680 ‡ C.—lordes myne, 4733 A (myn BD).—myn eyen, 7699 ABD (mynne C).

thi, thy, thyn, thin (A.S. þín) I. Singular. (*a*) thi *bef. cons'ts.*: thi brotheres wyf, 678 (thyn C, thy D); thi bed, 2602 (thin C); thy destene, 520 (thi B, thyn C), etc., etc. (*b*) thyn *bef. vowels*: thin

---

[1] "Som of *hem* took on *hym*."
[2] *myne* (5973 C) is merely a graphical variety.
[3] No variations noted in Mr. Austin's collation. 9-syl. in E.

owene cheyne, 509 (thyn CD); thyn auenture, 2604 (thin BD);
cf. 513, 795, etc.—thi synne and thyn offence, 556 (thi ... thin
B, thyn ... thyn C, thi ... thyn D). [thine, 5751 D.] (c)
thyn *bef.* h : thyn help, 672 (thi BD, that † C); thyn hert, 928 (thin
BD); thyn hod, 2039 (thin BD). (d) thyn *bef. cons'ts. :* thyn peyne,
589 (thi B thy D). C, so far as my notes indicate, uses *thyn* exclu-
sively,[1] whether before a vowel or a consonant (cf. 346, 524, 587, 653,
677, 801, 926, 935, 1018, 1916, 2481, 2588, 2597, 2696, 2723, 3237,
3580, 4829, 4946, 5079,[2] etc.). The other MSS. usually have *thi*
before a consonant (but cf. thin lif, 5079 D). (e) I have observed
no instance of *thy* before vowels. (f) When the possessive is in
the predicate, *thyn* is of course used, cf. 861, 1036, 3118 f (-e C)
(: engyn), 4354, 6303, 6950. So when it follows its noun : cf.
8232. Cf. to han for thyne, 3255 A (thyn BC, thin D). II. Plural :
thi prouerbes, 756 (thyne C, thy D); thi sorwes, 794 (thynne C);
thi bryght eyen, 4295 (thyne C).—thyne olde ensaumples, 760 (thin
BD); thyne eeres, 2107 (thyn B, thin D); thyne hestes, 3261
(thine B, thynne C, this ‡ D); thyne † heuenes, 3460 C; thin
hornes, 7015 (thyne B, thine D, thynne C); thyn eyen, 7522
(thynne C, thine D); thyn owene folk, 6951 (thynne C, thin D).—
thyne nedis, 2039 C (thi AD, thy B); thynne ‡ dremys, 7651 C.

his (A.S. his), so *passim* as possess. pron. with both masc. and neut.
nouns sing. and plu. Cf. especially *a friend of his*, 548, 3638 f
(: this); *a man of his*, 4883.

> Note 1.—No MS., except perhaps D, by far the worst of the four, is free
> from the spelling *hise* (-e of course never sounded) for the possessive with
> plural nouns. Examples are : hise auentures, 3 AB (cf. 471 AC, 2430 AC,
> 5535 A); hise foos, 994 A ; hise beste iapes, 2252 A (cf. 1658 AC, 1808
> A (hyse C), 2117 A (hese C), 2121 A, 2436 AC, 3339 AC, 7410 BC, 7452
> AC); hise hondes, 3026 AB ; hese worthi dedes, 8133 A ; hese eyȝen, 1948
> C; hese hondes, 2059 C, 8165 A ; hyse bony[s], 305 C.—C even uses *hise*
> for the singular : hise chere, 7591 C.[3]
>
> Note 2.—*Is* is occasionally found for *his*. Thus, 637 B, 4206 C, 6071 A,
> 6167 A. *Dethis = deth his* in 469 C (Lo here his lyf and from the
> *dethes* cure).

hire, here, possessive (= her) (A.S. hire).

In the attributive use before consonants A varies between *here*
and *hire :* for *here,* cf. 839 (C †), 5764, etc., etc. ; for *hire,* cf. 95,
107, 975, etc., etc. Varieties are, BC hyre ; BD hir ; C hyr ; D her.
(Cf. also, for further examples, 102, 108, 126, 173, 281, 282, 285,

---

[1] thynn fo, 4828 C.
[2] In some of these cases the n is written in C ; in others it is represented by the familiar stroke.
[3] Supply [so] in C.

427, 542, 846,[1] 1150, 1304, 1688, 1699, 1759, 1853, 1911, 2717, 3439, 6944, etc.) An examination of these cases, which are fair examples of the use of *here, hire* before consonants, will show that A has -ę in all of them (*herę* or *hirę*); that the usual form in B is *hirę*; in C *hirę* or *hyrę*; in D *her*.[2] Forms without the -ę are not common except in D, and are hardly found in A.

Good lines to illustrate this word are:—*Hirę* wommen soonë til *hirę* bed herę broughte, 1999 (hirę . . . hire ? . . . hirę B, hirę . . . hirę . . . hirę C, her . . . her . . . her D). *Hirę* gouernaunce *hirę* wit and *herę* manère, 3058 (hirę BC, her D). Al thoughtë she *herę* seruaunt and *hirę* knyghte, 3825 (hirę . . . hirę BC, her . . . her D).[3]

   Note.—Cases before vowels present no interest, for there elision would in any case reduce the word to one syllable. The spellings are in general the same as those already noted. (Cf. *e. g.* 305, 347,[4] 1335, 1619, 1737, 3060, 3408, 6426, 7228[5]. For cases before *h*, cf. 127, 655, 1742, etc.)

Absolute use:

A kynges herte semeth by *hires* a wrecche, 889 AB (hire C, her D).

And that I thus am *herës* dar I seye, 4450 (hirës B, ʒouris † C, her[ë]s D).

Shal han me holly *heres* til that I deye, 5106 (hiręs B, his † C, hirs D).

   Note 3.—It is doubtful if the possessive singular is ever *hirë* (disyllabic) in this poem. The following cases, which seem to require or admit that pronunciation, disappear as evidence on a comparison of MSS. : 1350 A, 1903 C, 1995 A, 1999 B, 5221 C, 7132 C, 7316 C, 7413 C †, 7510 C.

The following two passages admit of a dissyllabic *hirë*, but may also (if one likes the sound) be scanned as lines of nine syllables :

With a certayn of *here* owene men, 3438 (hire own B, hire owene C, her owne D).

I comende *hire* wysdom by myn hood, 7514 ABC (hir witte D).

oure (A.S. úre), gen., as singular possessive. In the attributive use the regular spelling of ABC is *oure*, D usually has *our* (cf. (i.) before consonants, 171, 558, 559, 1518, 1728, 2506, 5985, etc.; cf. (ii.) before vowels, 710, 1448, etc.). But *ourę* is also found in D (as, 5721); and neither A nor B is free from *our* (thus, our wreche, 7259 ABD (ourę C), cf. 965 B, 8157 B, 8186 B).

All these cases are monosyllabic. Indeed, there seem to be no

---

[1] This and 847 illustrate the indifference of A with regard to *hire* and *here* : That as *here* ioyes moten ouer gone So mote *hirę* sorwes passen euerychone (hirę . . . hirę B, hyrę . . . hirę C, her . . . her D).
[2] *Here* is rare in C (see 1853); *hire* is rare in D (see 6944).
[3] In B, read *though[tę s]he*; in D, *thoght[ë]*.   [4] *hyr* B.
[5] In most of these A has *here*.

cases of dissyllabic attributive *oure* (sing. or pl.) in the *Troylus* (see 5906, where *ourë* would give an intolerable verse, and 3598 C, where comparison of MSS. restores the monosyllable). Cf., however, the following predicate use: she shal bleuen oure, 5201 f (our D) (: owre = *hour*). In the plural possessive use the attributive form is the same as in the singular. Thus,—oure hierdes, 3461 (our D); oure walles, 6144 (our BD); oure ‡ cruel foone, 8229 D; cf. 1598, 2017, 4109, 4955, 5866, 8206.

your, youre (A.S. éower) (*a*) Attributive position:

Both forms are found in A before consonants. Thus: your, 429 (ʒour BD, ʒore C), 4955 (ʒour B, ʒoure C); youre (in A the usual form), yowre, 122, 1180, 1219, 1307, 1426, 1508, 2190, 2523, 2801 (oure † C), 3051, 4018, 4830 (-e B), 7099, 7236, etc., etc.. [Var. BCD ʒoure; BD ʒour; D your, yowr, ʒowr; B ioure, ʒowre; C ʒoure.] (For *youre*, cf. 337, 2526, etc.; for *youre* where h follows, cf. 334, 1378, etc.) *Youre* is monosyllabic in the attributive position, except perhaps in 2687, 3509; other exceptions (as, 198 AB, 1388 C, 5548 C, 7267 C, 7985 C) vanish on a comparison of MSS.

(*b*) In the predicate:

he is youre, 1672 f (ʒoure BC, ʒoures D[1]) (: oure *horam*); youres is Mi spirit which that aught[e] youre be, 422-3 (ʒour[e]s . . . ʒour[e]s B, ʒoure . . . ʒourë C, your[is] . . . youris D)[2]; he that is . . . youres fre, 2206 (ʒoures B, ʒouris C, youris D);[3] I haue ben yowrés also, 2944 (ʒoures B, ʒouris C, youres D);[4] cf. 4450 ‡ C; I was youre and, 6342 (ʒoure B, your D); I am youre ‡ all, 6303 D (thyn ABC); I am ʒoures ‡ bi, 4354 D (thyn AC, thin B).

hire, here, = their (A.S. hire), monosyllabic, not distinguished in spelling from here = her. Cf. (i.) *bef. cons'ts.*, 49, 63, 149, 151, 154, 705, 763, 907, 997, 1126, 1260, 1286, etc., etc. Cf. (ii.) *bef. vowels*, 51, 150, etc. The variant *heir* (5804 D, 7323 D; heire, 8218 D) deserves notice. *Their* is sometimes found in D (cf. 4861, 5369, 8123); *there* occurs in C 5803.

In,—Of *here* teris and the herte vnswelle, 5808 AC (hire B, *om.* † D), one has one's choice between *herë* and a 9-syl. line. 3304 A, however, should be corrected.

§ 75. III. Reflexive and Intensive Pronouns. The compounds of *self* (A.S. self, sylf, etc.) appear in the

---

[1] *rh.* houris D.   [2] In B supply [*that*] in 423; in C dele (*the*) in 423.
[3] In C supply [*al*].   [4] Supply [*al*] in D.

Troilus in the forms *-self, -selue, -seluen.* (Child,
§ 46; ten Brink, § 255. Cf. also § 79 below.)
my self, myn self, my selue, my seluen.

myself, (i.) 537 (my silf D, myn selue C), 669 (-ę B, myn self C),
2286 (myn seluen the † C), 5204 (myn seluë ‡ C; D †), 5286 (myn s.
C, my selfę D); cf. 3729, 4495, 4940. (ii.) 628 (myn saeluë ‡ sen C,
my seluë ‡ sen D), 927 (myn s. C), 7637 (myn seluyn C); cf. 2225,
3632, 4745; my self hate, 5501 (-ę D, myn self C).

myn self wil, 2094 (my s. BD); myn ‡ silf vnnethe, 7770 C.

my selue, 1191 f (myn s. C) (: twelue), 7286 f (meselfue B, myn
sellęue C, my silf D) (: twelue); my selue I, 5903 (my silf D, myn
seluyn wolde C).[1]

my seluen, (i.) 5439 (myn self[e] C, my silfę ‡ D), 6108 (myn
selue C, my self[e] D), 7635 (my self[e] D, myn self ‡ to C).

thi self, thy self, thyn self, thi selue, thi seluen, thyn seluen.

thi self, thy self, (i.) 963 (thyn s. C), 4466 (thyn s. C, thi silf
D),[2] 6750 (thyn s. C, thin s. D); cf. 717, 768, 2450 CD, 4098,
5079 A, 5266 BD, 5282, 6633. (ii.) Cf. 882, 2542, 5252; thi self
hire, 2450 (thi selft B, thyn self preye C, thy s. pray D). thyn self
fordon, 5753 (thi s. B, thyn s. C, thine s. D).[3]

thi selue, 3101 (-ën B, thyn -yn C, thy -yn D), 5062 f (thyn s. C,
thi silue D) (: swych[e] twelue).—thi self[e], (i.) 5253 (thi seluen B,
thynself ? C ‡, thinself[e] D); thi self[ë] helpen, 5190 (-en B, selue (?)
C; D †). (ii.) thi selue, thy selue, thi selfe, cf. 3141 (-yn ‡ C),
3212, 5513 (?), 8074.

thyn seluen, (i.) 622 (thi s. B, thyn seluë C, thi self[e] D), cf.
3098 ‡ C.—thi seluën, (ii.) 852 (thy self[e] D, C †), 5262 (thyn
seluyn C, thi self[e] D), 5512 (thyn self[e]? C, youre silf[e] ? D),
6700 (thyn seluyn C, thin seluen D), 7669 (thyn -yn C, thi
self ? D ‡).

hym self, hym-selue, hym-seluen.

hym-self, (i.) cf. 320, 896, 1460, 1864, 2163, 2249, 2558 BC,
3270, 3397, 5787, 5890, 6401, 6704, 6869, 6969, 6986, 7031, 7536,
7894. [Var. C hym selfę (320); CD hym silf.] (ii.) Cf. 457, 745,
815, 1544, 5746, 5824,[4] 6626, 6980, 7135 (seluyn C ?), 7148,

---

[1] Metre doubtful: My (Myn C) selue (self B, seluyn C, silf D, selfe G) I wolde
(wolde I C) haue (han B, a C) slayn (slawe C, slayne DG) quod she tho. (No
variations in Mr. Austin's collation.)
[2] Supply [*ne*] or read *silf[e]* in D.   [3] Supply [*so*] in C.
[4] Supply [*it*] in C. D, *himsilfe* (?).

7233. [Var. CD selfe ; C selue.] Before *he, his,* cf. 662, 5890 C, 6572, 8184 AB.

hym-selue, 2485 f (: twelue), 6461 f (hyme-s. BD) (: twelue).
hym self [y]beten, 741 (h. s. ybeten BD, h. s. i-bete C). hym-self[e], (i.) 2558 (h. self BC), 4907 (-en B, -e C, h. silf to (?) D), 6704 CD, 7396 (h. self ABD 9-*syl.*), 7940 (-en B, -e C). hym selue sle, 5581 (-en B, -[e] D, -[e] fle † C).

hym-seluen, (i.) 256 (-[e] CD), 302 (-[e] D), 604 (-e C, -[e] D †), 7586 (-yn C, -[e] D), himseluyn, 3397 C (-self ABD).

here-self, hire-self, here-seluen, *singular feminine.*

here-self, (i.) 7079 (hire-s. B, hir sowle D). (ii.) hire-self, here-self, 3619 (h. seluyn C, her self D),[1] 5299 (hir self D, hire self[e] wolde ‡ C), 5418 (h. selue C, hir selfe D); here self hym, 2716 (hire s. BC, her self al D).

hire-self[e] bonde, 2308 (-en B, here self[e] C, her selfe D); [2] here selue excusynge, 112 (hire seluen B, hyre selue C, herself[e] D).

here seluen, (i.) 3568 (hire s. B, hire seluyn C, her self D),[3] 5197 (hire seluen B, hire self[e] C, hir self[e] D), 5475 (hire-s. B, hir self[e] D).—hire seluen she, 1736 (h. self BC, her self D); here-seluen distorben, 5765 (hire-self C, h[i]re self C, hir self D),

oure seluen se, 2416 (-yn C, our seluyn D).

youre self, yow self, youre selue, youre seluen, yow seluen.

youre self, (i.) 2368 (ȝoure BC, ȝour D), 3751 (ȝ. BC, your D). (ii.) 118 (ȝourself B, ȝoure s. C, ȝour s. D),[4] 5896 (ȝ B, ȝ. sylf C, your silf quod D); your self, 3621 (ȝoure s. BC), cf. 5513 D; ȝoure selue ‡, 2951 C.

yow self, (i.) 1308 (ȝoure s. B, your s. D, ȝoure self[e] ‡ C), 2245 (ȝoure s. BC; D †), 3847 (ȝoure s. BC).[5] (ii.) 1323 (ȝoure s. C, ȝour self D, ȝoure seluen B).—yow seluen leste, 4172 (ȝoure s. B, ȝoure ‡ selvyn C, your self[e] D).

youre selue, (i.) 3510 (ȝ. seluen B, ȝ. seluyn C, your selvyn D); youre silf[e] (?), 5512 D.

youre seluen, (i.) 1216 (ȝ. B, ȝowre selve C, ȝour self[e] D), 7244 (ȝoure B, your self D †, *l. om.* † C), 7247 (ȝoure B, ȝoure seluyn C, your self[e] D), 7364 (ȝoure B, ȝoure sylf[e] C, your self D ‡); yowre seluen, 3967 (ȝoure BD, ȝ. -yn C).

[1] Supply [*a*] in A.
[2] If we read *make* (-*yn* C), we shall have *hire-self* in two syllables.
[3] In this v. ABC have *dane*, D *diane*, for *Daphne*. In D read *daphne her self[e] het.*
[4] Supply [*ye*] in B.　　　　　[5] yow self ‡ D (9-syl. ?).

hem self, hem seluen.

    hem self, (i.) 4683. (ii.) 915 (hym s. B),[1] 1543, 1875 ‡ D.
    hem seluen so, 4710 (h. self[e] D).

§ 76. IV. Demonstrative Pronouns.

    that (A.S. þæt), as demonstrative pronoun, *passim*. That = the, that oon(*e*), 5349 A (that oon B, that on C, the toone D).

    tho (A.S. þá), plural demonstrative (in substantive and adjective uses), cf. 924, 1078, 2452, 3272, 4016, 4223, 4285, 4813, 5087 f, 5293, 5356, 5797, 5835, 6025, 7033, 7096, 7569.

    thilke, *sing.*, 185 (the *i*lke C, that D ?),[2] 939 (-[e] D, thynke ‡ C), 2873 (-[e] D), 3305 (-[e] B, the *i*lke C, that D ?),[2] 4387 (-[e] BD, theilke C), 4501 (-[e] B, ilke C, that D ?),[2] 5732, 6196 (ilke C †), 6213 (that ilke CD), 6318 (theilke C), 7550 (theilke C), 8053 (-[e] B, that ilke C), 8202 ; thilke harme, 3560 (-[e] D).[3] [Var. B thylke, thylk[e].]

    thilke, *pl.*, 4114 (ilke CD), 5377 (theilke C), 5667, 5711 (-[e] B). [Var. B thylk[e]]. thilke effectes, 2857 (thi[l]ke B, thilk D).

    that ilke, *sing.*, 2347 (-[e] D), 5409 AB (that ylke D), 5435 (-[e] B, that ylke D), 5898 (-[e] B), 7466.

    this. Singular of course monosyllabic, and almost always written *this* (cf. 424 f (: is : i-wys), 484, 551, 1035, 1509, etc., etc.). *Thisse*, 1010 f A (this BCD) (: i-wysse : ysse *est*), is perhaps due to an attempt to indicate the unvoiced sound of final *s*.

    Plural variously written : *this* (7, 540, 5090, 5537, 5573, 6683, etc.), *these* (169, 561, 1188, 2350, 5952, 8086, 8116, etc.), *thise* (2110, 3460) ;[4] but always monosyllabic, as well before consonants as before vowels.

    For further examples of the plural, cf. 705, 742, 893, 903, 995, 1086, 1870, 1875, 2152, 2391, 2469, 3134, 4299, 4533, 5333, 5347, 5642, 6359, 6707, 6742, 6743, 7423, 7502, 7599, 7711, 7935, 8091, 8142, 8214.

    • Note 1.—2350 C is corrupt. In 2153 A, transpose *alle* and *these*. In 3193 A, insert [*as*]. In 4332 A, read *werë* and *these*.

    this ilke, *sing.*, 2791 (-[e] CD), 4688 AB, 6401 (this ylke D), 7232, 7876, 8115, 8129 ; cf. 1822 AB.

    this ilke, thise ilke, these ilke, *pl.*, 3349 (this ilk[e] BD), 4180 (-[e] B), 5915 (thes ilke D), 7674 ; cf. 4035, 4156, 4236, 5032, 5810.

---

[1] Supply [*thei*] in C.   [2] 9-syl. in D.   [3] Supply [*al*] in C.
[4] *This* and *these* are common in A ; *this* and *thise* in B ; D has often *thes* (561, etc.). Varieties are,—*thyse* (919 B, 2110 B), *theese* (1971 Cᶜ), *t[h]ese* (5090 D).

Note 2.—A remnant of the A.S. demonstrative þǽm, þám, þán, is seen in the phrase *for the nones* (561, 2466 f, 4847 f, 5090). The A.S. instrumental *þý* appears in *forthi* (cf. 445, 973, 1127, 4471, 4984, 5052, 5067, 5279), *forthi* (cf. 691, 1114, 1952, 5585).
Note 3.—For *at the* written *attë*, see § 53. II. Cf. *tother*, *attother*, § 79.

§ 77. V. Interrogative Pronouns.

who, *nom.* (A.S. hwá), 551 (ho C), 2338 (ho CD), 3593 (ho CD), 7626, etc.

whos, *gen.*, 2275 (whas B, hos C), etc.

whom, *dat.*, 6598 (ho *nom.* ‡ C; D †).

whom, *acc.*, 3428 (hom C, what ‡ that D), etc.; whom that I loue, 717 (hom that C).

what, I. *Sbst.*, nom., 828, 1214 f; acc., 320, 356, 3159 f. II. *Adj.*, nom., 401, 3512, etc.; acc., 552; of what man, 3992; what=why, 1347, 1377, cf. 1308. (Rhymes with *that* and *hat*.)

Note.—Remnants of the instrumental *hwý* are seen in *why* (cf. 1760 f, 3992 f) and in *for-whi*, *for-why*, 714, 1097, 2601 (also occurring as a variant of *forthi*).

which, see under Relatives.

§ 78. VI. Relative pronouns (and pronominal adjectives), and the interrogative (etc.) *which*.

that, *passim*. that = id quod, 7567. ho at = who that, 3861 C.

whos, *gen.*, 532, 700 (C †), 787 (whois C), 5025, 7680 (whoos D), etc.; the whos, 7339 (whos C †, the woos D), 7722 (whos (?) C).

whom, *dat.* and *acc.*, 189 (whan C), 533 f (-(e) D) (: from), 937, 2802; cf. 98, 1244, 1912, 6676, etc.; for whom that, 766 (C †).

who so, 147 (ho so C); cf. 77, 603, 857, 2880, 4104, etc.

what so,—in what wyse so yow lyste, 3889 (that ȝow C; D †).

what, as a "general relative,"—of what it be, 2418; euery gentil womman what she be, 8136; or of what wyght that stont, 3338.

which.

I. Interrogative (in both direct and indirect questions and in exclamations).

A. *Singular*. (1) *Adj.*, which hous, 2274 (wich C, whiche D); to enqueren which thyng cause of which thyng be, 5672 (which . . . whiche B); whiche ‡ opynyoun, 5635 D (whos AB). (2) *Sbst.* which of, 3040 (wich C). (3) = qualis, *interrog.*, which a labour, 199 BC (swych L A, such l. D); what thyng and which is he, 401 CD (-e B, what A); into wich helle, 5374 C (vnto which heH D; *st. not in* AB). (4) = *qualis, exclam.*, which a thonk, 803 (wych C; D †); which a dede, 5893 BD (swych A, wich a drede C).

B. *Plural*, which (= *quales* ?) doutances (*ind. quest.*), 200 (-ę B, with † D, which dotaunce[s] C).

II. Relative.

A. *Which* (without *the*).

(*a*) *Which* is used as a relative pronoun for all genders, with or without a following *that*. In the following examples the *which* is a simple relative (not attributive adj.); the presence of a following *that* is indicated by old-style figures in the verse-number.

(1) *Singular*, which, *bef. cons'ts.*, cf. 74, 78, 94, 106 (whiche B), 206, 527,[1] 1471, 7217. [Var. BC whiche; C wich, whych, wheche]—which, *bef. vowels*, cf. 261 (whych C), 7925 C; in which he, 366 (-e B, wich C); of which hym, 3345 (wich C, of the which D).—whiche, 54 (the whiche B), 1121 (wheche B, *om.* † D), 1415 (wich C; D †), 2231 (which [that] ? B; *l. om.* † C), 2492 (which BCD), 2677 (wiche B, wich C, which D), 2689 (which CD), 2843 (which BD), 3374 (which D, whiche = which she, *haplography*, C), 5273 (which BD, wich C), 7578 (of which ‡ he C, for whiche ‡ cause D).—whiche he, 1712 (wiche B, quych C, which D).

(2) *Plural*, of wich that, 4236 C (whom AB, wyche ‡ I E; in which that, 8199; which er, 3575; which I, 7569 (-e B, the whiche C);[2] whiche that 2858 (which B), 3427 (which as B, wich that C, which that D).

(*b*) *Which* as a relative adj. (not = *qualis*). (1) *Singular*, by which reson, 5710 (whiche D),[3] cf. 7578 D. (2) *Plural*, of whiche ‡ sykis, 4207 C (wych[e] ‡ D, swiche A, shwich[e] B *defect.*).

B. *The which.* Used either (*a*) as a purely relative pronoun, or (*b*) as a relative adjective (not = *qualis*).

(*a*) (1) *Singular*, the whiche, 3565 (the which BD; C †); *bef. cons'ts.*, the which, 603 ([the] whiche C), 7241 (-ę C). (2) *Plural*, the whiche he, 4884.

(*b*) (1) *Singular*, the whiche tale, 5328 (-[e] BC); the which[e] cote, 8016 (-e C, -e ?,D ‡); the whiche thyng, 4331 (the which

---

[1] C has *the wheche* for *to wheche.*
[2] Supply [*of*] in A.
[3] 9-syl., exc. in D; but we are hardly to read *which*[*e*]

[§ 78.] *of Chaucer's Troilus.* 163

B, the whech C).[1] (2) *Plural,* the whichë frendes, 6046 (-[e] BD; C †).

> Note 1.—In 5930 we are apparently to read: "Soth is the wo the which that we ben inne," but the MSS. vary. *Which* is sometimes miswritten by the scribe for *swich,* as 3299 D (cf. 2435 D).
>
> Note 2.—*Which . . . his* is equivalent to *whos* in "The kynges dere sone, The good[e] wyse worthi fressh and fre, *Which* alwey for to do wel is *his* wone," 1401-3. Cf. "*Which* with a thred of gold she woldë *it* bynde," 7175 C (but read *woldë byndë*). Cf., perhaps, "Er deth . . . Dryf out the gost *which* (so in ABD John's, whiche G, that CCp.) in myn herte *he* (so in ABDGCp. John's, om. C) beteth," 5572.
>
> Note 3.—*As* is used as a relative pronoun (= that) in 3244 C,—*this as thow dost* (this that AB, [this] that D), and in 3427 B,—*thynges which as neuerę were* (which(e) that A, wich that C, which that D).

swich, such (A.S. swilc, swelc). Examples are,—

I. Singular:

In A, swich, swych, such, (i.) 475, 550, 1794, 1970, 2153, 3338, 6627, 8001, etc.; (ii.) 296, 369, 521, 619, 762, 985, 1750, 1813, etc.—In B, swich, swhich, shwich, swihch, (i.) 127, 475, 550, 777, 1794, 1879, 1970, 3338, 3604, etc.; (ii.) 369, 521, 1351, 1750, 3320, 3382, 3604.—In C, swich, swych, swech, (i.) 412, 1794, 1879, 1970, 2153, 3338, 4070, etc.; (ii.) 296, 369, 521, 762, etc.—In D, such, (i.) 1794, 2153, 3338, etc.; (ii.) 2245, etc.

> Note.—Forms in silent -e occur in all four MSS. Thus,—in A, *swichę* (412)[2], *suchę* (1351); in B, *swichę* (291, 475, 562, 935, 1088, 2216, 2355, 3002, 3236, 7314, 7926), *swhichę* (412), *swuchę* (1663), *swiche* (619, 762, 955, 985, 1713, 2245, 3176), *swhiche* (296), *shwiche,* (2784); in D, *suchę* (550; cf. 2355, 4070). Cases in which we have an apparent -ë (before a consonant), as, *swichë,* 227 B, 4581 B (cf. 1393 C, 1970 D, 3306 C, 6627 D), all depend on bad readings; so also *swych[ë] auenture,* 5991 A (swich[ë] C, suchë D), in which we should read *swich* (*swych*) *an* (with B cp. John's Hl. 2392; *swiche an* G).

II. Plural[3]:

The plural ends in -e. Thus,—swiche fyue, 1211 (-[e] D, A †); swyche tweye, 1267 (such[e] D); suche tales, 1393 (-[e] B, -[e] D, -[e] tale[s] C); swiche sikes, 4207 (-[e] B, whiche C, wych[e] E). So we should read,—swych[e] fyue, 1213 (-e BC; D †); swych[e] sorwful sykes, 4203 (-e BE); swych[e] twelue, 5064 (-e D, -e tweine † C). Before vowels this -e is elided and often not written: cf. 1292, 2435, 3523, 3696, 3985, 4009, 4205, 6192, 6737. Cases of apocope occur: swich thornes, 2359 (sweche C, suche ? D);[4] if ye be swych youre, 1426 (swiche B, swich C,

---

[1] Either *the whiche thyng trewëly,* or *the whichë thyng trewęly.*
[2] Supply [*the*] in A.
[3] Variations in spelling not registered except as they concern final -e or MS. A.
[4] It is possible to read *swich[e]* if we read *sende* (mittat); BD have *send.*

such D); swych festes, 7792 (swich B, sweche C, suche D). For *suche thyngis*, 562 C, read *swech thyng*.

§ 79. VII. Other pronominal words.

same (O.N. samr, *definite* sami; cf. A.S. same, *adv.*), selue (A.S. sylf, self, *definite* -a), in the definite use,—the same prys, 1266; the same thing, 1269; cf. 2606, 4390 (the selue wyse C), 6087 (C †, the self[e] wit BD), 8018; the same hele, 7779; this same wyse, 5706 (the s. D); that selue wyse, 3197 (selwe C, self[e] D); this seluc swerd, 5902 (seluyn C, the same D). (Cf. myself, etc., § 75.)

som (A.S. sum), *adj. and subst.* I. Sing. (i.) 33, 555, 844; cf. 973, 1215, 1344, 2210, 2884, 3333, 4658, 7068, 7115, etc. Irrational e's are sometimes found, even in A: as, in some lond, 1123 ABD; somme swych fantasye, 3874 A (som B, sum C, some D †). [Var. BD some; C sum; D somme.] (ii.) 1197 (-e D), 2079 (sum C, some D †). II. Plural, some, (i.) 240 f (: ynome *p.p.* : ouercome *p.p.*), 2234 f (: by-come *pres. subj.* 3 *sg.*), 3449 f (: ycome *p.p.* : nome *p.p.*), 5630 f A (sone † B, som D) (: to come : ouercome *p.p.*), 5730 f (C †, som D) (: come *inf.* : ouer-come *p.p.*), 7246 f (som C, somme D) (: come *inf.*); somme, 5657 f A (some B, som D) (: to come); som men, 1132 (some B, some graue D), 1341 (sum C, some D), 2503 summe C, some D)[1], 7123 (somen CD, somme han A), 7167 (-e BD); some, 1866 ‡ D, 2669 ‡ D, 3333 ‡ D; some, 1132; som, *before vowels* (var. BCD some, D somme), 911, 1042, 2257, 2523, 4403; some han, 913; somme han, 7123 (som men B, somen CD).

And *some* (somme G) wole (wold BDG, wolde C Cp. Hl. 4912), mucche (muche B, fiete meche C, monche D, methe G, frete Hl. 4912) here (hire B, her D, he G, and Hl. 4912) mete (mone C, brede D, meten G, be hem self Hl. 4912) allone (alon CD, al on G, alone Hl. 4912). See ten Brink, § 327.

And *som* (some BCD) thow seydest hadde a blaunche feuere, 907, 909.

somwhat, sumwhat (A.S sumhwæt), *sbst.* (used also adverbially), cf. 672, 1646, 2078, 2394, 2410, 5187.

other (A.S. óðer). I. as *adj.* (*a*) *singular*, other (var. B oother; D othir),[2] both definite and indefinite, before both vowels and conso-

---
[1] Read *wold[e]* in D.
[2] *Othere* is sometimes found in the singular; see 352 C, 489 C, 4055 A, 4826 C, 7039 A. In 348 C, read *othir enchesoun* for *othir entencioun*.

[§.79.] *of Chaucer's Troilus.* 165

nants : cf. 348, 352, 444, 489, 577, 702, 707, 709, 1574, 1592, 1639, 1894, 2079, 2251, 2537 f, 2747, 3506 ‡ A, 3586, 3953, 4050, 4573, 4826, 6180, 6493, 7573, 8044 A, 8055;[1] non other, wyse, 5955 (not otherwyse C); o tyme ek and other, 2537 f (: brother); the tother side, 7050 A (that other BCD); at the other out it wente, 5096 (attother C, at other? D); noon nother, 7039 B. (*b*) In the plural of the attributive use (whether definite or indefinite), *othere* (dissyllabic) is the regular spelling of AC, *other* of B, and *othir* or *other* (var. *odir*) of D : cf. 179, 355, 463, 465, 1583 (oothere B), 1854 D, 2152, 2260, 2430, 2527, 2566, 3777, 4716, 5539, 5995, 8139 A. But *other* also occurs in A : cf. 26, 314 (other thing) (?), 1860.

II. As substantive : (*a*) singular, *other, another*, regularly : cf. 203, 643, 1449 (*neut.*), 2063, 2703 f, 3093 f, 3521, 3819, 4888, 5068 f, 5118 f, 5271 f, 5792, 5911, 7871 f. [Var. D othir.] *othĕrę* occurs : cf. 203 C, 3093 fB, 5253 A (prob. plural); an other in, 3618 (a nother B, another C, a nothir D), cf. 5351 A. (*b*) Plural. Forms as in I. *b* : cf. 1903, 3440, 5310, 6305, 6735 (oother B), 6738 (oother D); but I have not noted *other* in A.—these othere in (*pl.*), 893 A (other B; C?; other vertus ? D). For *othĕrë seyn*, 6735 C, read *othĕrę seyn* [*that*].]

Note.—For the genitive singular *otheres* (dissyllable), see 3792, 4532 (othir † D), 8127 (other † D); otheris, 3586 ‡ D. [Var. C otheris *dissyl.*] For the genitive plural *otheres* (dissyllable), see 8139 BD (othere *dissyl.* A).

ech (A.S. ǽlc), adjective and substantive; eche, 510, 2703 (ich B, èuerychę ‡ C), 3031 (ich B, ichę C); cf. 637, 643, 1127, 3263 A, 3266, 3850 D, 4182, 4890, 5069, 5911 A, 6204 ; ech for, 5074 (ichę C, echę D); echę rakel dede and eche vnbrydled chere, 3271 (ech . . . ech B, eche . . . eche C, echę . . . eke D). eche, 1432 (ech BD, vch C), 1479, 3819 (ech BC), 4532 (ich B), 4888, 5000 (ech B), 6149 (ech BD); cf. 2063, 2567, 3263 C (ich B), 3792, 4074, 5911, 7871, 8112; eche hym, 1071 (ech B, echę wight D †); eche a del, 3536 (ech B); ichę, 3275 C (eche D.; euęry wyght AB); ech, *bef. vowels*, 1078 (-*e* D), 4644 (-*e* BCD).—echone, 4880 f (echon C, euęrychon ‡ D) (: allone).

Note.—The *Troilus* MSS. give no evidence for a dat. *eche* (see ten Brink, §§ 255, 260 β).

euęry (A.S. ǽfre + A.S. ǽlc) counts as a dissyllable (cf. ten Brink, § 262). The usual spelling is *euery* (cf. 84, 101, 185, 268, 328,

---

[1] *Another* is variously written *an other, another, a nother, a-nother*, cf. 577, 709, 1894, 3953, 6493.

382, 397, 444, 844, 1097, 1273, 1280, 1478, 1613, 1675, 1686, 1800, 1889, 1975, 2033, 2074, 2262, 2472, 2663, 3023, 3068, 3196, 3275, 3339, 3369, 3445, 3469, 3670, 3850, 4527, 6012, 6341, 6998, 7121, 7478 (var. eueri, as 3074[1] C, 3322 C). But euerich (2251 B (euere-ich), 4338 B, 6533 AB), euerych (6180 ACD, 6533 D, 7683 B), eueryche (512 D, 2703 C ‡), and eueryche (6533 C) also occur. In the following lines we must read euerych, euery as a trisyllable, or regard the verses as consisting of nine syllables:

Euery thing that souned into badde, 6338.

Euerych (euery C) ioye or ese (ese (is) C) in his contrarye, 7742 (D †).

Note.—Certain apparent instances of trisyllabic euery (eueri) disappear on comparison of MSS. Such are 2676 A, 3074 C, 3334 C, 3362 A, 3671 A.

euerychon rhymes sometimes with words that have no final -e, sometimes with those that have. Thus,—euerichon, euerychon, 154 f (-oun B) (: Palladion), 5633 f ((: on : noon); euerichone, 176 f (-ychon B, echeon ‡ D) (: allone); euerychone, 847 f (-on C) (: ouer gon(e) inf.), 905 f (-on BCD) (: allone : grone inf.), 5611 f (-on CD) (: allone : mone n. moan) (cf. also 2683 f, 3254 f, 3507 f, 4880 ‡ f D, 5529 f, 5440 f, 8230 f).

any, ony (A.S. ænig), sg. and pl., cf. 20, 23, 848, 963, 1259, 8044, etc. [Var. C oni ; D eny.]

eyther (A.S. ǽgðer), adj. and sbst., (i.) 4792, 7869 (D †), 8127. (ii.) 5695. [Var. BD either; D eythir.]

Note —For eyther in ʒoure eyther loue, 4830 B, A has bothere, C bothers, D bothe, EG Cp brother†, John's bother, Harl. 2392 bothes

neyther (A.S. ne + A.S. ǽgðer), sbst., (i.) 5033 ; (ii.) 5792 (other † C). [Var. BD neither.]

bothe (O.N. báðir), adj. pl., 139 f, 4782 f, 5698 f, 6506 f (both BD, bethe C); bothe yow, 983 ; vs bothe two, 1034, hem bothe leste, 4521 (hem ‡ two ? D),[2] 6880 (-[e] B). (Cf also 687 (-[e] D),[3] 984, 1248 (bathë ? B), 1412, 1526 AC, 1572, 1585, 2277, 2373 (bathë B), 2825, 3262, 3784, 4007, 4065, 4160 BCD, 4312, 5254 ? D, 5794, 5894 (-[e] D),[4] 6176, 6512, 7497); bothe, 1414 (-é apaire ‡ D; bethe C), 2961 (both BD), 4528 (both BD), 4955 (both BD, bothe † ʒoure C), 5546 AD (both B), 5592 (both ‡ with D), 5595 (both B); bothe his, 2059 (both B); -e here (gen. sg.), 2914 (both B, -ë ‡ D).

[1] Read woyd[ed].   [2] brought[e] C, or supply [that].
[3] Old-style verse numbers indicate that B has both[e].
[4] Supply [we] in D.

[§ 79.] *of Chaucer's Troilus.* 167

Rhyme words.—wrothe *adj. pl. prcd.* (*all exc.* 5698), forsothe (5698).
Note 1.—There are no genuine cases of apocope (cf. 4955 † C, 5592 ‡ D).
In 1526 BD, for *bothę to deye* read *bothe deye* (with AC).
Note 2.—The genitive plural is seen in *ourę bothe labour(ę)*, 965 (*our bothe* D, *our bothis* C); *hirę bothe auys*, 3295. Cf., however, *yowrę bothere loue*, 4830 (*eyther* B, *botheis* C, *bothe* D, *bother* John's, *bothes* Hl. 2392, *brother* † EGCp.).

owene, owen, owne, see § 53, V., p. 126.

men = one. The use of *men* as an indefinite pronoun (= Ger. *man*) is seen in *men is nought alwey (y)plesed*, 3288 (man is C, men be D), and in *men was wont*, 5528 (men werę wonę C). In such cases as *men clępeth*, 6674 (callyn ‡ C, clepé ‡ an D), 7576 B (-ęth A, -yn C, -é D), *men seyth* (seyn BD) (see other examples in § 97), the verb may be regarded as plural (cf. *of whos folye men ryme*, 532 f, and see 241, 748, 7105 f). The form *me* does not occur in the *Troilus* (but see 5496 † C).

oon, on, o; noon, non, no (A.S. án, nán).[1] I. The full forms are found in all substantive constructions; so also in adjective constructions when the adjective follows its noun or stands by itself in the predicate. Thus,—

of yow oon, 350 f (on(e) BD, on C); to louę swych on, 369 (oon B); so goodly on, 373 (on(ę) B); quod first that oon(e), 5349 (oon B, on C, the toon(e) D); I louę oon(ę) best, 667 (on C, on(ę) D); cf. 203, 521, 619, 626, 955 (an B), 1668, 1923, 2259 f, 2666, 2770 f, 7271 f, 8227 f, etc., etc.

oon (*neut.*) thenketh the bere, 6115; oon (*neut.*) of the tweye, 494 (on BC; D †); auauntoure and a lyere al is on, 3151 f (oon(e) B, on(e) D, is al on C); euere yn oon, 816 (oon(ę) B, on C, on(ę) D); they felle at oon, 3407 f (atton(e) B, at on C, at on(e) D); on(e) of tho (*neut.*), 5087 (oon B, on C, oon(e) D).

whan ye ben on, 2825 f (oon B, on(e) D); cf. 4247 f, 5254 f.

oon the best, 474 (on(ę) D, on ‡ of the beste C); oon the beste knyght, 1074 (oon(ę) B, on D); on(ę) the fairest, 1831 (oon B, on(ę) D ‡ (?), on ‡ of the fayreste C).

clerkes grete many on, 5630 f (oon(e) B, grete cl. m. on(e) D).[2]

nas noon so faire, 101 (non BC, so fair was non(e) D); cf. 188, 1287, 1587, 1830, 1862, 2826 f, etc.); non(e) of tho, 924 (noon B, non C); thenk not on smert and thow shalt fele noon, 5128 f none B, non C).

pes ther may be noon, 6021 f (non BC, non(e) D); other bote is noon, 4050 f (non BC, noon(e) D); other wolę she non, 3153 f

---

[1] Cf. ten Brink, §§ 247, 264, 270.   [2] B † omits *clerkes*.

(noon B, non(e) D); swych a ryng I trowe that ye haue non, 3735 f (noon C, none D); nor other cure canstow noon, 757 (non(e) B, non C, *om.* † D); cf. 1451 f, 1702 f, 1809 f, etc.

cause non, 3993 f (noon(e) D); storye noon, 3341 (B † C †, non(e) D); lady noon, 6308 f (non C); bote noon, 7690 f (non BD; C †).

Pl., But whether that sche children hadde (hadde ‡ c. A) or noon, 132 f (non BC, non(e) D) (: goon *inf.*).

II. In the attributive position, *o*, *no* are the forms usually found before a consonant (but C is fond of *non*); *on*, *oon*, *non*, *noon*, before a vowel or *h*. Thus,—

o day, 1573 (a B, oo C); o thing, 3725 (on C); not o word, 3899 (a B, on C; D †), cf. 1023; o god, 6506 (on(e) D, on † good C); cf. 673, 1122, 1253, 2118, etc.

no deuocioun, 187 (non C); no man, 238; no shame, 374 (ne † CD); no maner weye, 495; cf. 437, 590, 600, 631, 640, 670, 685, 689, 714, 722, 733, 737, 1281, 4118, etc.

Pl., no dremes, 7644; no suche tales, 1393 (non swich tale † C); cf. 7089.

oon entente, 61 (on D); on assent, 5008 (oon B, comune ‡ D), etc.

noon other bote, 352 (non BCD); non yuel, 1666 (non BCD); non other wyse, 5955 (not ‡ C); cf. 1538, 3826, 6805, 7039, 7451, 7573, 8055, etc.

Pl., none other fownes, 465 (doon † A, non C, non othir ‡ fantasye D).[1]

noon helpe, 695 (non BCD); non hosbonde, 1839 (noon B, none (?) D); noon harm, 1886 (non CD), cf. 1661; noon hope, 3257 (non BC, no D); non heuy thought, 3981 (no B); noon hede, 4671 (non BD); noon honour, 6771 (non BCD); non(e) hate, 477 (non CD).

Note 1.—As indefinite article *a* is used before consonants, *an* before a vowel or *h*. an other, 540 (another C, a nother B, other *pl.* ‡ D), cf. *other*, above; an a, 171 (D *om.* ‡ an); an asse, 731; an errour, 1001, etc., etc.; an heuenysh, 104 (a ‡ perfit D); an heuene, 1722, 1911; an hors, 223; an hauk, 671; an hows, 1058; an hed, 1952 (han hed B); an herte, 2956; an hard request, 2990; an heigh matere, 3128 (D †); an halle, 3698; an helle, 7759; etc.

Note 2.—In 645 ABD, *Suth thus of two contraries is* a *lore* (on lore C), *a* apparently = the numeral rather than the article (see also the variants in the examples under *o*, above).

ought (A.S. áwiht, áht, ówuht, óht), (i.) cf. 578, 3309, 5947, 8100, etc.; (ii.) cf. 123, 1028, 3366, 7485, etc. [Var. B aught, ouȝght;

---

[1] In C, read *desyre* for *desyred*.

[§§ 79, 80.] *of Chaucer's Troilus.*

C ou3t, au3t; D aught, oght.] Woot *ought* my lord . . . this matere, 2711 (-(e) B, ou3t C, oght D); that I haue out myswent, 633 (aught B, ou3t C, oght D).

nought (A.S. náwiht, etc.), (i.) cf. 444 f, 1690 f, 5180, 5729 f, 6463 f, 7483, 7527 f, etc.; (ii.) cf. 4878, etc. [Var. BC nou3t; D noght.] For *nought, nowght*, as a strong neg. particle, cf. 576 f, 807 f, 4344 f; an interesting "transitional" case is 1660 f: But for to saue his lyf and elles *nought* (-3t C, not D) (: wrought *p.p.*).

§ 80. *Al*, singular.

I. In its strictly adjective use *al* (sg.) is commonest before the definite article (cf. 212, 1192, 1224, 1506, 1833, 1966, 2626, 2844, 3220, 3277, 7581) and other more or less definite words. Thus,— before *this* (cf. 504, 551, 1101, 1262, 1383, 1509, 1934, 2405, 2446, 2580, 2675, 2685, 2798, 2892, 3173, 3302, 3358, 6764)[1]; before *that* (cf. 1036, 3071, 4751); before *thilke* (cf. 2873, 3560); before *thi* (cf. 522, 589, 830, 2401, 2597, 3205); before *my* or *myn* (cf. 721, 873, 1954, 1956, 2083, 2770, 2977, 3020, 3085, 3235, 3843, 4140, 4146, 4749, 5602);[2] before *his* (cf. 265, 327, 665, 994, 1142, 1419, 1657, 2442, 2623, 2637, 3278, 3726, 6438, 6927, 7902); before *here* (poss. sg.) (cf. 2214, 2555, 2752, 2757); before *hire* (poss. pl.) (cf. 63); before *swych* (cf. 2824, 4241, 7125); before *youre* (cf. 4741).

Note.—In these uses the word is regularly written *al*; but *alle* (*alle*) is also found.[3] Thus,—alle this thyng, 2001 A (al BC, all the thinges D); alle this matere, 2514 AB (of ‡ this m. C; D (?)); alle the richesse, 3191 (al BC, al the ‡ rehetyng D (?));[4] alle this work, 3544 (al CD); alle that tale, 4245 (al BD; C†); alle oure labour, 948 (al C); alle his fulle my3t, 1419 C (alle his ful[le] C, al his fulle A, al his ful[le] D) (cf. 7046). Cf. also, for *alle* in these uses, B 212, 1192, 1506, 1509, 1934, 1954, 2083, 2405, 2824, 3220, 7125; for *alle his*, B 265, 994, 1142, 2623, 3726, 6927.

II. The half substantive use of the singular *al* (as in : *here is al, al is wel*, etc.) requires no special notice. The proper form is of course *al* (cf. 544, 952, 1045 f, 1406, 1757, 2000, 2297, 2583, 3101, 3148, 3370, 3482, 3494, 3687, 4459, 4641, 7378), but *alle* is sometimes found; the final -e, however, has no significance, and is never sounded (thus: alle, 2583 B, 3370 B; alle, 1406 B, 1757 B, 3482 B, 3687 B, 4459 B, 7378 B). For the substantive use of *al* (sg.) as object of a verb, where the proper form is of course *al*, cf.

---

[1] For cases where no noun follows the *this*, cf. 351, 386, 2544, 2591, 2716, 4638, 5062, 5734.
[2] Remark 1914 f.
[3] B 2626 is unmetrical, unless, with Furnivall, we supply [*to*].
[4] Supply [*his*] in B.

1302, 1914 f, 2409, 2680, 3102 BCD, 3766, 4027, 4166 f, 5636, 8180. Here too *alle* is found, both at the end of the verse (cf. 4166 f B) and elsewhere (for *allę*, cf. 1302 B, 3102 A, 3766 B; for *alle*, cf. 4207 B), but the -e is never sounded. For *al* (sg.) used substantively after prepositions (as, *yn al, for al, ouer al, with-al*, etc.), cf. 396, 437 f, 921 f, 1129 f, 2306, 2494, 2655, 2709, 3306, 3319 f, 7183 f, 7682 f. As before, the variants in -e are merely graphical (cf. 921 f B, 1129 f B, 2655 f B, 7183 f B, 7682 f B; for *allę*, cf. 396 B, 3306 C). Exception—with alle, 288 f (: falle *inf.*). This is the only case.

> Note. 1.—Observe: *he al hool*, 3855 ; *thy lady vertuous is al*, 891 f (alle B) (. in general : yn special) ; *whos I am al and*, etc , 4449 (*alle* B) ; *this* (= this is) *al and som*, 5855 (*alle* & *sommę* D), cf 5936.
> Note 2.—The spelling of AC is almost uniformly *al* (*att* occurs, however, in 386 A, for example). In D *att* is very common.

III. The form *allę* in the singular is found or required in the following verses:

In whom that *al[le] vertu* lyst abounde, 1244 (all[e] B, euęry D; C *is diff.* †).

As *alle trowth*e and *al[le] gentillesse*, 1245 (alle . . . alle B, al[le] . . . al[le] C, in all[e] trouth*e* and all[e] ıentilnesse D).

To euery wight that *alle prys* hath he, 1273 (al the prys C, al[le] pris D).

By *al[le] right* it may do me no shame, 1848.

In *al[lę] ioy*e and surętę out of drede, 1918 (alle . . . seurte B, al[le] . . . seurte CD).

Thurgh which is *al[le] sorwe* fro me ded, 1930 (Thorugh [which] is allé s. f. m. d. B, Thour wiche as † al sor f. m. d. C, Thurgh which is al[le] sorow fıo me dede D).

To flemen *alle manerę vic*e and synne, 1937 AB, (To fle[me]n alle mauer v. & s. C, To flemé al[lé] manerę v. a. s. D).

Of *alle ioy*e hadde opned herę the yatę, 3311 (al[le] B, alle . . . opęnyd C, al[le] ioy . . . opęnyd D).

With *alle ioy*e and *alle frendes farę*, 3447 ([and] B, al[le] i. & al[le] frendis f. C, al[le] . . . al[le] D).

And in despit hadde *alle wrecchednesse*, 4629 (al[le] C, despite had al[lè] D)

And *alle worldly blyss*e as thenketh me, 5497 (Ànd (and) alle B, And euęry wordęly ioy*e* C, all[e] wordly blisse D).

By *alle right* and in a wordcs fewe, 5942 (al[le] BC).[1]

[1] In CD supply [a].

As I that al[le] trouthe in yow entende, 6311 (all[e] D).
Thus Pandarus with al[le] peyne and wo, 6861 (alle D).
Enlumyned with the sonne of alle blysse, 6911 (enlùmynèd with sonne of a. b. B, enlùmynyd with the forme of a. b. C, enlùminèd with sonne of a. b. D).
And here I dwelle out-cast from alle ioye, 6978 (cast out C, out(e) cast(e) D).
And thus despeired out of alle cure, 7076 (oute BD; 7 lines om. † C).
But alle trouthe and alle gentilnesse, 7980 (al[le] . . . al[le] B, alle . . . al[le] C, alle trouth and al[le] D).
But subgit be to alle poesye, 8153 ABD (not in C).

It will be observed that in all these cases *alle* has a natural accent, and consequently needs an ictus, and that the noun that follows is accented on the first syllable. In these circumstances the form *al* is obviously impossible. In other words, the verse will not bear such a phrase as *al sorwe* when *al* is emphatic: the poet must use a form *alle*, or give up the phrase. Child (§ 30) has cited several cases of this *alle*. Ten Brink ignores tho idiom. Freudenberger, 'Ueber das Fehlen des Auftakts in Chaucers heroischem Verse, 1889 (Erlanger Beiträge, iv.), p. 35, remarks that Chaucer " vor Abstrakten im Singular häufig die schwache Form *alle* setzt, was auch die bessern Hss. meist haben," referring to ten places in the *Canterbury Tales* and to eight in the *Troilus* (1848, 1930, 3311, 3447, 4629, 5942, 7980, 8153). As to the grammar of the final -e, one hardly dares to hazard a guess.

If the noun that follows allows an accent on the second syllable, *allé* is of course unnecessary. Thus,—
As to my dome in àl Troyès cyte, 100 (allę B).
To àl honoùr and bounte to consente, 2529 (alle BC).

Note.—In *al nyght*, either *al* or *nyght* receives the accent, but not both. Hence,—àl nyght, 3705 (C (¹), allę B), 4308; al nỳght, 3710 (allę B), 3715 (alle B, al† wold D).

IV. *Al*, whether adjective or substantive, has in the plural (1) regularly the form *alle*, which is of course elided to *all'e* before (2) vowels, and (3) *h* in certain cases. When such elision takes place, we sometimes find (4) the -e left off, as in the case of all other words in elided -e.

(1) ye wysó proude . . . folkes alle, 233 f (folk[es] alle C, folkys alle D) (: thralle *inf.* : bifalle *inf.*).
alle ye, 340 (al[le] D).
of alle louers, 376.

Mystrusten alle or elles allé leue, 688 (al . . . al[le] C, aH . . . al
  tò leue D).
the Grekes alle, 1039 f (: falle *inf.*).
alle prowde (*omnes superbae*), 1487 (al[le] D).
here brighte thoughtes alle, 1854 f (aH D) (: falle *inf.*).
this othere termes alle, 2152 f (: calle *inf.*).
alle folk, 2695 (al[le] BD) ; cf. 2813.
hem alle thre, 2805 (C (?) ; al[le] D) (cf. 987, 3051).
on alle syke, 2903 (al[le] D).
thyne hestes alle kepe, 3261 (this hestis aH[e] D).
alle tho that lyuen, 3272 (al[le] BD).
of vs alle, 3600 f (of hem alle BC, of hem aH D) (: calle *inf.* : falle
  inf.).
as ye wommen demen alle, 3614 f (aH D) (: calle *inf.* : calle *reticulum*).
amonges alle, 3700 f (aH D) (: halle *n.* : falle *p.p.*) ; cf. 6614 f.
we shulle ben alle merye, 3794 (al[le] BD).
in alle nedes, 4614 (alle the B, al the D).
the goddes alle, 4930 f (aH D) (: calle *inf.* : falle *p p.*).
of sorwes alle, 5163 f (: byfalle *inf.* : calle *ind.* 1 *sg.*).
hom they wenten alle, 5392 f (aH D) (: out of the halle : falle *inf.*).
alle, 5670 f (aH D) (: falle *accidunt*) ; cf. 5712 f.
among vs alle fynde, 6488 (al[le] B).
houses alle, 6910 f (aH D) (: out falle *p.p.*).
this drede I most of alle, 7067 f (aH D) (: by-falle *accidat* : falle
  cadam) ; cf. 5762 f.
here corn and vynes alle, 7833 f (aH D) (: in stalle).
(Cf. also 561 f,[1] 903 f, 3527 f, 3530 ‡ B, 5090 f, 5130 f, 6143, 6533 f,
  6561, 6725, 6894 f, 6955, 7426 f, 7542 f, 7783.)
  (2) men myghte on vs alle y-se, 1439 (alle se C ; *om.* † D).[2]
the goddes alle, 3226 (al D).
his(e) wordes alle, 3339 ; cf. 4384.
I speke hem alle vnder correccioun, 4174.
myn othere thinges alle yfere, 5995 (al B, aH D)[3] ; cf. 8134.
to fayllen alle yfere, 6114.
(Cf. also 240, 463, 688, 2858, 3449, 3608, 4109 ‡ D, 4609, 5730,
  6141, 7246.)
  (3) alle here (*poss. sg.*) lymes, 282 (al D).

---

[1] In all the cases in rhyme cited is this parenthesis the rhyme-words are infinitives.
[2] Supply [*myghte*] in B.   [3] Supply [*ek*] in B.

alle here (*poss. sg.*) wommen, 3530 (al D, allé ‡ wommen B); alle
here sore sykes, 7397 (aH D); cf. 2513.
alle his goodly wordes, 7081 (7 *lines om.* † C, aH D).
alle hire (*poss. pl.*) goddes, 8213 (aH D).
    (4) ye lyue al yn lyst, 330 (loue al in rest C^c).[1]
al and some, 1448 [2], 2234 (alle C).
al hire folk, 1995 B (alle C, aH·D);[3] cf. 1704.
aH hise fyngres, 2117 (alle BC, al D).
hire folk weren al aweye, 2279 B (alle C, *om.* † D).[3]
thei slepten al ifere, 3588 (alle C).
Don olde affeccions al ouer go, 5086 (alle BC, aH D †).[1]
late hym haue al yfere, 2562 (alle B). [Singular?]
bretheren al yfere, 5868 (alle BCD).[4]
    V. But *alle* is the plural form before *the, this,* etc., when these
words count as a syllable (ten Brink's rule, § 255). Thus,—
alle ‡ the ladyis, 186 C (ay ABD).
alle youre obseruaunces, 337 (al D).
alle the men, 838 (al D).
alle these othere, 893 (alle this other B, al the other ? D ‡).
alle the othes, 1384 (al C, aH D; othes B, othis CD).
alle the weyes, 1907 (al D).
alle the folk, 1973 (al BD). [Plu. verb.]
aH the thinges ‡, 2001 D (*sg.* is right).
alle the dores, 3075 (aH D).
alle the temples, 3225 (al D).
alle these thynges, 3641 (al this wonder B, of this wonder CD);
cf. 2405 C.
alle youre wordes, 4409 (al B, alle these C).
alle the goddes, 4514 (al the goodnes † D).
alle the nedes, 4614 B (al the D, alle nedes AC).
alle youre frendes, 6218 (alle ‡ oure C).
alle this nyghtes two, 6683 (al B, alle these C, aH thes D).
alle these thynges, 8086 (al B, aH D).
    Note.—Alle these loueres (?), 2153 ‡ A, needs transposition (*these l. alle*).
al the peple, 1743 (alle B).
aH the thinges, 2001 D ‡ (alle this thyng A, al BC).
aH these thynges, 2350 (al this B, C †, al this thing[es] D).

[1] Can this *al* be adv.?
[2] Singular?
[3] A ‡ omits *alle*.
[4] Supply [*and*] in C.

al this folk, 2652 (alle thise folk C); al the world, 3119 (al BC, al
the peple D)[1]; cf. 1463, 3119, 3264, 3318, 4765.
al the prophesies, 7857 (alle D, -cy C).

Ten Brink (§ 255) leaves the impression that *alle* pl., is usually
apocopated before "syllable-building" article *the* (or pronoun), *but
not otherwise*. This is surely not accurate. We should expect such
apocope as well when *the* is reduced to *th'*, if the word following the
th' is accented on the second syllable. Thus we have,—

This yard was large and rayled aH the aleyes, 1905 (alle thaleyes
B, alle the aleys C, D *om.* al).[2]

Indeed it is hard to see how we can in any circumstances have the
order "*allë* × '" without apocope. Accordingly we find,—

Another day shal tòrne vs àlle to ibye, 6293 (aH D, com vs al D).
This is o word for al, this Troylus 4502 (al, that B). [Sing. ?]
Now hem he hurte and hem alle down he caste, 1284 (cf. *varr. ll.*),
is not a sure case. *Alle* may be merely the adverbial *al.* Similarly
the construction of *al* is not entirely unambiguous in,—

And of the furyes al she gan hym telle, 7861 (furies also ? C, furiès
she ‡ D). [Should we read *als* ?]

Me from disesis from alle peynys smert, 7783 C, should be emended
to *disese of allë peynys*, &c., as AD indicate.

On hys by-halue which that vs alle sowle sende, 2819 A, is also
clearly wrong. The reading of G: On his half which(e) that
soule vs alle sende, seems right, and is rather supported by
B † and C. Cp. and John's read: On (Of J) his halfe (half J)
which (*om.* J) that soule vs alle sende.

In 688 D, read *allë leue* for *al to leue*.

Note 1.—In 3765, *Consideréd allë thingës as they stòde* (*al[lë] thing[is]* D),
is of course to be read, not,—*Considered alle thingës*, etc. But cf.
Considered aH[ë] thyng it may not be, 2375 (*al[lë] thyng(e)*) B, *allë
thyng(e)* C, *al thing wel(e)* D). In 1920, *al* is doubtless a collective
singular.

Note 2.—In the following lines *thyng* is probably to be regarded as a
plural.
Ouer al[le] thyng he stood [for] to byholde, 310 (alle thing(e) . . . for to B,
alle thyng(e) [he][3] . . . for to C, al[le] thing (s)he stood [for] to D).
Nece al[le] thing hath tyme I dar avowe, 3697 (allë thyng(e) BC).

---

[1] In the case of collective nouns (like *world* = people), I have assumed that they take
plural constructions unless the text has some indication to the contrary (as, *e.g.*, al
the world *is* blind, 3370). This remark of course does not apply to *al this world* =
this universe, 3215, and such cases (cf. 3302). For doubtful instances, cf. 173, 804,
1573, 4086 (alle this world AB), 4446.

[2] A reads *garden*, repeated by error from the preceding line. *Yard* is surely
right (3erde B, 3erd CD). C omits *was*, which must be supplied.

[3] *thyngë* = *thyng he*.

In alle thyng(e) is myn entente clene, 4008 (al[le] B, alle thyng ... entent[e] C, al[le] thing al D).
That wost of alle thing(e) the sothfastnesse, 5742 (of al this thyng(e) B, of al this thyng C, of alle thing(e) D).
As to: Whan that he sey that al[le] thyng was wel, 3538 (alle thyng(e) B, woste alle thyng(e) C, wist[e] that al thing D), see p. 109.

§ 81. The genitive plural of *al* (cf. Child, § 44; ten Brink, § 255) remains in the *Troylus* in,—

alderbeste, 4439 f (alder beste B, aldyr best C, altherbest D).
alder best (*adv.*), 1001 (alder best(e) B, aldyr best C, althermost D).
alderfirst, 1062 [1] (altherferst D), 4736 (alderfirst(e) B, alther ferst D);
alderferst, 5494 (aldirfirst(e) B, aldirfirst D [2]); alderfirst[e], 2939 (aldir ferste C, altherferst[e] D [3]).
alder-lest, 604 (alderlest B, al there † lest C, altherlest D). [4]
alderleuest, 3081 (aldir leueste C, alther levest D), 6939 (aldyr loue-lyest ‡ C).
aldermost, 152 (althermoost D), 248 B (addermost A, aldyrmost C, althermoost D), 996 (aldyr most C, althermost D); [5] althermost, 4107 ‡ D°.
alderwisest, 247 (aldyrwysest C, altherwysest D).

ADVERBS AND OTHER PARTICLES.

§ 82. Anglo-Saxon adverbs in -e preserve their termination in the *Troilus* (Child § 69; ten Brink, § 246, Anm.).

Note.—Besides Anglo-Saxon adverbs, the following list includes a few later analogical formations. For *blyue, inne, oute, thanne, whanne*, see § 88.

blythe, 4836 f C, is an error for *blyue*.
bryghte (A. S. beorhte), 7383 f (-3t C, light ‡ D) (: alighte *pret.* 3 *sg.*: myghte *pret.* 3 *sg.*); bryght and shene, 4700 (-e B); shyneth bright, 1849 f (-e B, -3t C) (: put ... to flyght).
clene (A.S. cláene), -e, 4672, 7417, [6] 7561, 8058.
depe (A.S. déope), 1655 (-e C), 3434, 5251 f (: wepe *pres. subj. sg.*), 6621 f (: wepe *inf.*); -e, 272, 4341 (-e ‡ D).
dere (A.S. déore, W.S. díere, dýre), 8164 f (: pere *n.*: here *inf.*); -e, 810, 7329 (der D); -e haue, 4953. [Var. B deere.]

---

[1] A 9-syl. verse in ABD (C cut out).
[3] Supply [*the*] in D.
[5] For *arn* (*are*) C (D), read *erren*.
[2] Supply [*me*] in D.
[4] Supply [*him*] in D.
[6] Supply [*saide*] in B, [*is*] in C.

faire, fayre (A.S. fæg(e)re), 1413 f (: apeyre *subj*. 1 *pl*.), 4398, 5684 f (: necessarie [1]); -*e*, 1971, 6710 (*om*. † C).

faste (A.S. fæste), 534 f (-t B), 748 f, 917 f, 1038 f, 1229 f, 1282 f, 1361 (*om.* † A), 1742 f, 1773 f, 1957 f (-t C), 1983 f, 1985 f, 2022 f, 2239 f (-t C), 2249 f (-t C), 2360 (-[e] B), 2443 f, 2650, 2795 (-[e] B), 2999 f (-t C), 3936 f, 4029 (-[e] B, -[e] ‡ hent D), 4609 (-[e] BE), 4779, 4792 [2], 4884 (-[e] B), 4916 (-[e] B), 5182 f, 5336 f, 5576 (-[e] B), 5892 [3], 6901, 6959 (-[e] B), 7317 (-*e* ‡ haddę C), 8004 f (-t C), 8185 f; fast[e] for, 962 (-*e* C); -*e*, 3069 (-t BD), 4705 ‡ A (sharpe B, sharp C), 6736 (-t BC), 6817; fast (*before vowels*), 1174 (-*e* C) [4], 2789 (-*e* C), 7019 (-*e* CD); fast he, 190 (-*ė* ‡ he C) [5]; -*e* he, 360 ‡ D, 2180 AB, 7598 ; -*e* herę (*gen. sg.*), 7374 (-t B; *om.* † C); -*e* hadde, 7317 ‡ C ; -*e* homward, 2388 (-t BD).

    In all cases registered above in which *faste* occurs at the end of a line D has *fast*, except in 5182 and in 8185 (which is not found in D). Old style figures indicate that D has *fast*[e]. In 1361 D it is possible to scan *fast*.
    Rhyme words.—laste *inf.* (534, 1038, 1957, 5336, 8185), the laste, my laste (534, 917, 1038, 1229, 1773, 1957, 2022 (last[e] A), 3936, 5182, 8004), caste *pret. ind.* 3 *sg.* (1229, 1282, 2443, 3936, 5182), caste *inf.* (748, 1773, 2249, 2999, 5336, 8185), paste *pret. ind* 3 *pl.* (1742), thraste *pret. ind.* 3 *sg.* (2239), faste *pres. ind.* 1 *sg.* (2249), agaste *inf.* (1982).— faste *adv.* : faste *adv.* (1983-5).

foule, fowle, -*e*, 5684, 6239 (foul B) ; -*e* his, 6129 ; -ę fallę(?), 5124 (-*e* CD ; -*ė* B †).[6]

fresshe, 2985 D (frosch[e]? C, fresshly A, freshly B).

hard[e] (A.S. hearde), hard or, 1353 ; hard hym, 4373 (-*e* C).

heighe, heyhe, hye (A.S. héah, héage), heighe, 1486 f (hie C, hy D) ; hye, 3026 f (highe B, hyʒe C), 5861 f (heye B, high D, in ‡ hye C) ; heighe, 5658 (heigh B, high D), 6371 (?) (heigh B, hie † D), 6622 (heigh B, hye C, hie D) ; heyhe, 4985 (heighe B, hey C, high D).

    Note.—For *hygh and low*, 3260, and *hỹe or lowe*, 2369, see note to *lowe*.
    Rhyme words.—eye (*l.* ye) (1486), prye *inf.* (1486), glorifie *inf.* (3026), dye *inf.* (5861), melodie (3026), companye (5861) :

hoote (A.S. háte), drenken (*l.* dronken) hadde as *hoot* and strongę, 4232 (hote B); cf. I hadde it neuere half so *hote* as now, 4492 (hoote B, hoot D, ofte † C).

i-lyke (A.S. ge-líce), To seruen (-yn B, -*e* D) and ben (ben(e) D, ay ben C) ay (*om.* CD) *i-lyke* (*i-lik* C, *y-lyke* D) diligent, 2986 ; Was euęre *y-lyk*[e] (i-lik[e] C, yholde ‡ B) prest, 3327. (Cf. *lyk*, § 83.)

---

[1] So AB ; *-rye* D. We must read *necessaire*.
[2] Read ran[ne] in D.   [3] Supply [hire] in B, [her] in D.
[4] Supply [seyde] in D.   [5] But supply [ful] and read *faste*.
[6] But *hath* in A is the corrector's insertion.

late (A.S. late), 3310 f (: yate n.), 7104,[1] 7504 f (: yate n.); late, 1483 (lat B, -ë war C), 3218, 7106; latë ‡ is, 7433 (-e BC, -ë ‡ it (?) D).[2]

longe (A.S. longe, lange), 59 f (long D), 617 f, 1487, 1630 f (long D), 2212 (langë B), 2325 f (long D), 2330 (-[e] D, -e B), 2475 (-[e] ? D), 2680 (-[e] D), 3043 (long † shal D), 3647 f (long D), 4988 (-[e] D), 5133, 7054 f, 7225 f, 7495, 7565 f (long D); -e, 2008 [3], 2075, 3207 (-ë ‡ ich B)[4], 4159, 4270 (-ë ‡ as BC [5], -e [as] E), 5770 (alonë ‡ be C), 6350 (-e ‡ D), 6659 (lenger ‡ endure D), 6795; -e he, 723 (long D)[6]; -Chadde, 5832 (-e ‡ hire (sg.) C)[7]; longë ‡ of, 2807 A (-e his B, long his D, -e here (pl.) C); longë here (hic), 3661 C° (-[ë] D, alwey AB).

Rhyme words.—longe inf. (617, 1630, 7054), honge pres. subj. 2 pl. (2325), inf. (7565), wronge adj. pl. (3647), stronge adj. pl. (59, 7054, 7225, 7565).

Note.—In some of the following cases there may be confusion between the adverbial and the adjective construction:
For it were a long disgression.
Fro my matère and you to longe to dwelle, 143-4 (-ë dwelle C, for yow long to dwelle D).
Or that it be ful longe (long D), 832 f (: honge inf.).
Long streyght he hyre leyde, 5825 (-e B, a long ? C, longë streyt(e) D).
Ten dayes nys so longe not tabyde, 6716 (-e to ? ‡ C, -ë to D).
How longe it was bytwene, 7449 ABD ([how] longe C).
Thenk not longe to abyde, 7518.[8] (Certainly adj.=Don't regard it as tedious.)
To longe were it for to dwelle, 7847 (long it B, [al] to longe C, longe it D).

lowe (O.N. adj. lág-r), heng here hed ful lowe, 1774 f (lawe B) (: throwe n.); stoupen on hire stalk[e] lowe, 2053 f (: rowe n. : throwe inf.); lowe lowte, 3525 (-e ‡ to D; low ‡ risit (?) C); she stood ful lowe and stille alone, 178 (low BD); I . . . wol . . . folowe here spirit lowe or hye, 5861 (low B, forth ‡ C).

Note.—In "For hygh and low withouten ony drede I wole alwey thyne hestes alle kepe," 3260-1 (heigh † a lough B, hey and low C, hy or lowe D), and "And hye or lowe after (after that D) a wyght entendeth The ioyes that he hath youre myght it sendeth," 2869-70 (heigh or lawe B, hye or low D), the construction is probably adverbial rather than adjectival.

lowde loude (A.S. hlúde), 1485 f (-d D, froude † C), 2005 (-[e] D), 2162 f (-d D), 3520 f (-d D), 3585 (-[e] D, -e ‡ C), 7868 f; -e, 390 (-d D)[9]; -e ‡ he, 6568 C (deth ABD), 7607.

Rhyme words.—prowde adj. pl. (1485), the proude sg. (7868), koude ind. 3 sg. (2162, 3520).

---

[1] "But al to latë cometh the letuarye."   [2] AD easily emended so as to read late.
[3] Old-style figures indicate that D has long.   [4] But read, longe ich [it].
[5] In BC supply [when] and read longe.   [6] Supply [as] in AD.
[7] Supply [he] in B.   [8] Dele the first (to) in A.
[9] Supply [for] in C.

178 *Observations on the Language* [§ 82.

narwe (A.S. nearwe), narwe ymasked, 4576 (harde ‡ C, narwe ynia[s]ked A).

newe (A.S. néowe, W.S. ní(e)we, L. neowe), 222 (-[e] B, new y-shorn D), 440 f, 2985 f, 4541 f, 6628 f, 7013 f, 7020 (-[e] BD, -ę ‡ C)¹, 7696 f (new B), 7935 f (anewe ‡ C), 7946 f; newe and newe, 2958 f (new and newe BD); newe, 364 (new B), 1907 (new BD), 5119 (new D), 7373 (new D, newęly ‡ now C); -e his, 2766 (new B, now ‡ D); new hym, 4388 (-e BCD).

<small>Rhyme words.—hewe n. (440, 4541, 7935), trewe *adj sg. indef.* (7696, 7946), *sg. def.* (2985), *pl.* (2958, 7013), vntrewe *pred. sg.* (7935), rewe *inf.* (2958, 6628), knewe *ind. 3 pl.* (4541).</small>

rathe (A.S. hraðe), 2173 f (: bathe *inf.*), 4867 f (: skathe *n.* : bathe *inf.*), 7300 f (: skathe *n.*).

rowe,—loken rowe, 206 f (lokyd row D) (: browe *n.*).

sharpe (A.S. scearpe), 729 f (· harpe *n.*), 2119 f (: harpe *n.* : harpe *inf.*); -e, 4705 (sharp D, faste ‡ A). [Var. B charpe; C scharpe.]

shene (A.S. *adj.* sci(e)ne, scéne), 4700 f (: bytwene), 5901 f (: quene). [Var. B sheene; C schene.]

shorte; short[ë] for to syke, 2900 (schorte C). Cf. This (= this is) *short* and pleynę theffect of his message, 5552 (-e B, schort C, Thus shorte D).

smerte, 4905 f (: herte : sterte *inf.*).

smothe (A.S. smóðe), That han herę top ful heighe and smothe y-shore, 5658 (smoth D).

softe (A.S. sófte), 195 f (soft D), 279 (-[e] B, -e he C, soft he D),² 914 f (soft D), 2113 f, 3284 f (soft D), 3450 (-[e] BD), 3509 f, 4480 f, (-t B), 5202 f (soft B), 5884 ‡ C, 6710 f (soft B), 6982 f; -e, 1735 (softly ‡ synk D), 2914 (-t B, *om.* † D),³ 4377 (-t B), 6446 (-t B);⁴ soft vnpynne, 3540 (-e C); softe he, 3408 (-t BD). [soft † gan, 5024 B.]

<small>Rhyme words.—ofte (*all*); a lofte, on lofte, o lofte (914, 3509, 6710).</small>

sore (A.S. sáre), 667 f, 751 f, 827 (-ę ‡ to D), 1080 f, 1540 f, 1642, 1647 f, 2182 B (so[re] A; do ‡ C; *om.* † D), 2988, 3082 f, 3654 (-ę ‡ to D), 3748 (sor(w)e C), 3814 f, 3842,⁵ 3898 f, 4370, 5378 f, 5487 f (soor D), 5559 f (C?), 5783 f, 5848, 5879 (for † B),⁶ 6425, 6495, 7101 f, 7241 (D?); -e, 95 (therfor ‡ D), 1200; -e he, 3964 (é ‡ he B, -e I † D), 4313 (soor B); -e hath, 1618.—sorę, 1404 ‡ C.

<small>Rhyme words.—more *adj*, *adv.*, *sbst.* (*all except* 7101), soore *inf.* (667), lore *n.* (751, 1080, 1647, 3082, 7101), of yore (5378). [Var. BD soore.]</small>

---

¹ Perhaps adjective.
² *softe he* may be right.
³ *softe* [*vp*]*on* C.
⁴ Supply [*he*] in B.
⁵ In C read *sore* [*that*] *I*.
⁶ In C read *therwith*[*al*].

stille (A.S. stille),¹ 752 (stil[le] BD),² 2213 f (stiH D) (: bille *document*),
5183 f (: distille *inf.*); stille, 178 (stil D), 2000 (stil BD), 2579
(stil D), 3541 (stil D), 3790 (stile C, stiH D), 5016,³ 5183 f (: distille
inf.); stille ‡ gan, 1627 A (-e BC, stiH awey D).⁴ [Var. BC stylle.]
stronge (A.S. strange), 4232 f (: longe *pl.* : wronge *pl.*). [Cf. *hoote.*]
swythe (A.S. swíðe), 5413 f (: a thousand sithe : lythe *inf.*), 7747 f
(swith D) (: a thousand sithe : blythe *pred. adj. sg.*). [Var. B
swithe.]
swote (A.S. swóte), swoot[e] smellen, 158 (swote B, swete C, swete
smellyng flouris D).
thikke (A.S. þicce), 1541 f (thekke C, thik D) (: wykke *pred. adj. pl.*
(weke C, wyk D)); thikke, 6018.⁵ [Var. B thykke.]
vnnethe, vnethe (A.S. unéaðe), 3876 (-[e] B), 7583 (vnneth hym (?)
BD); -e, 354, 1089 (-e ‡ ȝet D),⁶ 5485 (-th B, vnnethis D), 6394
(vnnethes B), 6762 (-th B, -thë † vs D),⁷ 7770 (-th D); -e he, 4095
(-th B, -this D), 6398 (-th B, -th ‡ for D). [Var. C onethe.]—
onethe, 4920 ‡ C (wonder is the AB, wondrë is the D). (Cf.
vnnethes, § 91).

: ⁱ In 1089 the accent is on the first syllable ; in all the other cases, on the
second.

warme, though thou sittë warme, 4472 f (: harme *inf.*).
wete, ybathed was ful wete, 5477 f (: trete *inf.*).
wyde (A.S. wíde), 629 f (: gide *inf.*), 1700 f (: ryde *inf.*), 7458 f
(: chyde *inf.*); wydë where, 3246 (weyde C)⁸ ; wyde, 384, 1260
(meche ‡ knowe C, wyde know D). [Var. BD wide.]
yerne (A.S. georne), 2993 f, 3218 f (ȝe[r]ne B), 4774 f, 4863 f.

Rhyme words.—werne *inf.* (2993, 4774), yerne *inf.* (2993, 4863), gouerne
(gouuerne A) *inf.* (3218), descerne *inf.* (4863), eterne (3218).

To these may be added the Romance words *clere* and *ferme*.
clere, 1910 f, 6237 f, 6671 f (cler D), 6941 f.

Note.—In "*cler* stod on a ground of sykernesse," 3824 (clerę B ; clerë D,"
which om. *a*), *cler* is doubtless an adjective.
Rhyme words.—dere *adj.* (6237, 6671, 6941), here *inf.* (1910), here *ind. or
subj. 1 sg.* (6941). [Var. B cleere.]

ferme,—and thow this purpos holde *ferme*, 2610 f (: conferme *inf.*).

¹ Some of the cases cited may be adjectival. It is impossible always to distinguish
between *stille* adj. and *stille* adv. even in Anglo-Saxon (cf. Grein, s. v.).
² In C supply [*that*]. ³ Dele (*ony*) in A.
⁴ Transpose in A and read *stille* ; in B supply [*to*].
⁵ Supply [*ften*] in C. ⁶ A has *comynge*, D comyng, for *connyng*.
⁷ In D supply [*it*] and read *vnnethe*. Supply [*wel*] in A.
⁸ Supply [*so*] in D.

Note 1.—*Deuoute* appears to be an adverb in

    Hire old vsage wolde thei not letten,
    As for to honoure hire goddes ful *deuoute*,

150-151 (: *aboute* : *doute n.*); but it is possible that the construction is adjectival. In 5552 : This (= this is) short and *pleyne* theffect of my message (pleyn C, Thus . . . pleine D), the construction is perhaps adjectival.
Note 2.—*Scarcē* (with hiatus), 1128 D, should be *scarsly*.
Note 3.—For *maugre* (O. Fr. malgré, maugré), prep., cf. 4713.

§ 83. Exceptions to § 82.

ryght (A.S. rihte), cf. (i.) (ii.) 99 f, 171, 288, 307, 1022, 1200, 2090, 2636 f, 3070 (?) f, 4674, 7614 f; vnright, 7024 f.

    Aright (A.S. on riht) has of course no -e : cf. (i.) (ii.) 2085 f (-e B), 2346 f, 3070 ‡ f D, 3494 f, 5073 f, 6125 (-(e) B), 6919, 7480 f, 7943.

lyk (cf. A.S. gelíce), (i.) 5322 (-e BD); (ii.) 1080 (-e D), 1129, 2700 (-e B, as ‡ D). vnlyk that, 2741 (-e BD). (Cf. *ilyke*, § 82.)

    Note 1.—For *fayn* and *loth* in an adverbial sense, see § 85, note 1. For *adoun*, see § 88, note 1, p. 201.
    Note 2.—*Lest* (A.S. þý læs þe, L. leste) has lost its -e. Thus,—(i.) lest 319, 4013 (-e B), 4032, 4253 (list B, last C, leste E), 4815 (list B), 4828 (-e B), 5333 (-e D, 3if ‡ C) ; lyst ye, 2680 (list B, lest C, lest ‡ y D) ; (ii.) lest, 2133 (-e B) ; L he, 5091 (list B) ; lyst it, 321 (lest BCD).

§ 84. Adverbs in -*liche*, -*lich*, -*ly* (A.S. -*líce*, -*lice*, O. N. -*liga*).

Ten Brink (§ 270) thinks he has discovered a tendency on Chaucer's part to use -*lich* or -*lich*e before a vowel or h.[1] The following lists (I. and II.), which are meant to be exhaustive, exhibit the testimony of the *Troilus* MSS. on this question.

List I. contains all the adverbs which in any of the four MSS. show a form in -*lich* or -*liche*. When the same adverbs have also a form in -*ly*, references are added for that form.

List II. is intended to contain all adverbs in -*ly* not already included in I. Old-style figures indicate that the word that follows begins with a vowel or h. Variants in any way significant are registered, but trivial irregularities in spelling are not always noticed. It will be observed that occasionally some MS. has a form in -*lye* or -*lie* (see under *bisily*, *fermely*, *hardyly*, *lustily*, *preuely*, *shortly*, *sikerly*, *straungely*, *vnhappily*), but this spelling is unknown to A and is chiefly affected by D.

---

[1] "Dass er vor anlautendem Vocal oder *h* vielfach -*lich* and -*liche* statt -*ly* gebraucht."

The somewhat reckless insertion or omission of an interior *e* deserves attention (see especially *trewely* and *softely*). Some of these interior -*e* 's are due merely to analogy (cf. Child, § 71; ten Brink, § 262).

An examination of I. and II. shows that, so far as the *Troilus* MSS. are admissible as testimony, there is no tendency to use -*lich* or -*liche* before vowels and *h* to the exclusion of -*ly*, but that, on the other hand, -*lich* or -*liche* is not common before consonants. In A -*lich* (-*liche*) occurs 25 times before a vowel or *h*; in B, 39 times; in C, 16 times; in D, 8 times; whereas -*lich* (-*liche*) before a consonant is found only twice each in A and C, three times in B, and once in D. In all MSS. -*ly* is far commoner before a vowel or *h* than -*lich* (-*liche*). In the following cases (*a—c*) none of the four MSS. has -*lich* (-*liche*):—(a) before vowels, 771, 978, 1064, 1357, 1369, 1448, 2200, 2335, 2451, 2691, 2936, 2972, 2998, 3062, 3180, 3201, 3296, 3312, 3351, 3591, 3642, 3643, 3723, 4028, 4187, 4385, 4561, 4656, 4840, 4886, 5042, 5615, 5668, 5950, 6263, 6382, 6423, 6846, 6853, 6922, 6941, 6950, 7189, 7197, 7300, 7304, 7445, 7527, 7656 BCD, 7728, 7853, 8067, 8171, 8209, cf. 1578; (b) before *he, his, hym, hire* (poss. sg.), *heres* (sg.), *hastow, hawe, hadde*, 89, 209, 274, 306, 366, 1645, 2157, 2344, 2378, 2409, 2504, 3398, 3496, 3632, 3922, 4169, 4416, 4424, 4430, 4458, 4752, 5057, 5106, 5474, 5586, 5612, 5617, 5787, 5855, 6100, 6579, 6869, 6885, 7899, 7947 (-ly(e) D), 7998, 8007, 8169; (c) before *helpe*, 2315; before *how*, 7449. In all, then, we have nearly a hundred instances of -*ly* before a vowel or -*h*, not counting those places in which one or more MSS. have variants in -*lich* (-*liche*).

In most of the cases of -*lich* (-*liche*) before a vowel or *h*, the adverb is polysyllabic, and an ictus falls on the termination (as *cèrteinlìche*). One might be tempted to conjecture that under such circumstances -*lich* would be preferred to -*ly* as a means of avoiding an hiatus which the ictus would make particularly noticeable; but even here -*ly* is very common (see *bìsily, blỳsfully, cùrteysly*, etc.). In the present state of our knowledge, therefore, it is hardly safe to formulate a rule as to -*lich* or -*ly* before vowels and *h*, even in the cautious words of ten Brink (cf. also supra, § 72).

When the metre requires an additional unaccented syllable, the full form -*liche* is used, never -*lye* (see *sodeynlyche, tendreliche, wonderliche*). In rhyme -*ly* only is found.

I.

certeinliche, 6463 B (-ly ACD). certaynly, -eynly, (i.) cf. 713, 1257, 1571, 2763 f, 3401, 4616, 5295, 5459 ‡ D, 5622, 5681 f, 5714 f, 6681, 7197, 8079; (ii.) cf. 2451. cèrtaynly ‡ I (with slurred -y), 1531 A (cèrtein adv. B, sèrteyn C, cèrteyn D).

craftyliche, 2111 C (craftily AB, craftly D).

cruwellyche, 5966 A (crueliche B, crewelly C, cruelly D). cruwel[ly], (i.) 8119 (cruely B, cruelly D).

delyuerlyche, 2173 (-ly C, -lich D).

dignëliche, 2109 (dyneleche C, dignlych D †).[1]

ententiflych and, 332 (-liche B, -lich D, ententif(ul)ly C).

esilyche he, 317 (-liche B, -ly D). esily, (i.) 2073; (ii.) 2998.

eternaliche, 6202 B (-ly AD, -ally ‡ within C^c). eternally, (i.) 5137, 5449.

fer-forth-lich as, 2943 C (ferforthly D, feythfully AB).[2]

feruentlyche hym, 6046 A (-liche B, -ly CD).[3]

formeliche, 5159 B (-ly A, -aly C, formably ‡ D).

fullyche, 316 (-liche B, -ly CD); Therfore as (as a A) frend fullych yn me assure, 680 (-liche B, -ly y[n] D). fully, (i.) cf. 319, 2383, 2611, 2840, 3003, 3100, 3124, 3417, 3635, 3850, 4690, 4942, 4954, 7044, 7129, 7392, 8179; (ii.) cf. 391, 3180, 4656, 7720; fully his, cf. 4424. fully excuse (with slurred -y), 3652 (ful BC).

hastoliche, 5980 C (-ely AD, -ily B); hastileche the, 6787 C (-ely ABD). hastely, (i.) cf. 4284, 5577 f, 7656 ‡ A (-ily a BCD), 7675; (ii.) 4886, 7656 BCD.

nameliche, 743 BC (-ly AD); -elych of, 1297 A (-liche BC, -ly D); -elich, (i.) 5254 C (-ly B, nam[e]ly A, -ely D (?)); -elyche, 5996 (-liche BD, -ly C). namely, (i.) 165, 7466, 7927; nam[e]ly, (i.) 6220 (-ĕ- BCD).

onlyche, 5994 A (-lich B, only ‡ but (?) C, onely it D),[4] 7040 (-ly BC, onely D). only, oonly, (i.) 480, 1445, 3104 (onely B), 6330 (oonely B, onely D)[5]; (ii.) 3351 (C † D †); al oonly here (eam), 5758 ([al] only C, al onely D †).

outreliche his, 1795 B (vttirly A, vttirliche C, vttirlich D). outrely,

---

[1] C has: I wot thou nylt dyneleche ne mystileche endite. ABD have no mystileche.
[2] In A supply [I]; in D supply [had], or read have.
[3] In BD, read The which[e] at the beginning of the line. In C the verse consists of nine syllables, unless we read The wich[e] for ffor wich.
[4] CD need correction.   [5] Perhaps adjective.

§ 84.] *of Chaucer's Troilus.* 183

(i.) 8057 (-erly B, vttyrly C, vtterly D); cf. 382 f, 2089 f, 4328 f (outerely C); (ii.) outrely he, 5617 (vttirly D).[1]

pitouslyche, 6676 B (-ly ACD). pitously, pytously, (i.) cf. 2161, 2438, 2584, 5476, 5564, 5574 f (pitusely C), 5836, 6442 f (pitousely C), 6623 f, 7244, 7787; (ii.) cf. 5042, 5911, 6922; before *h*, cf. 6100, 6579, 6885, 7947 (pitouslye he D); dispitously hym, 8169 (ful ‡ pitously D).

pleynlich al, 2708 B (-ly AD †, -li C). pleynly, playnly, (i.) cf. 395, 2211, 4519; (ii.) cf. 1357, 1448; p. hire (*poss. sg.*), cf. 2378.

rowfullych his, 6353 A (rewfulliche B, pitously D).[2] rowfully she, 7092 (reu- C, rue- D, ioyful † B); rufully, 2907 f (reu- BC, rew- D).

scryvenlich ‡ or, 2111 D (scryuenyssh A, stryuenyssh B, coryously ne C).

secundelich ther, 2826 A (-ound[e]ly B, -undeli C, -ondly D).[3]

sobrelyche he, 1733 A (-liche B, sobirli C, soberly D), 6656 A (-lich B, sobirly D, soberëlichë ‡ grette C)[4]; sobrelich he, 6869 (sobrely D, soft[e]ly B, softely C); sobreliche he, 7536 B (-ly AD, soberely C)[5]; sobrelych on, 7292 A (-liche B, -ly D, sobirly C). sobrely, (i.) 3796 (-irli C), cf. 3000 f D, 6444 f; (ii.) 3201 (soberely C), 4840 (-irly D); sobrely he, 4430 (-irly C); s. hym, 4458 (-erely C). [sobrely for, 7372 D (*read* shortly).]

sodeynlychë red, 2924 A (so deynlyche B, sodeynli[che] C, sodenly[che] D), 3798 B (-lych[e] A, -li[che] C, sodenly[che] D); sodeynliche, 3934 C (-ly AB, sodenly D)[6], 6617 B (-lych A, -ly CD); -lyche his, 3198 A (-liche B, -li C, sodenly D); -leche his, 8022 C (-ly AD, -li B). sodeynly, (i.) cf. 231, 1758 f, 3636, 3699 (sodeynly A; D (?)), 3801, 4084, 5924 f, 6563, 6855 f; (ii.) cf. 3642, 4028, 6853; before *h*, cf. 209, 274, 306, 1645, 4416, 7899.

sorwfullyche he, 7996 B (sorwefully AC, sorwëful he D).—sorwfully, (i.) 114 (sorowful ‡ D), 596 A (sorwful *adj.* B, sorwëful C, sorowful D), 605 (sorweful (?) C, sorowfully (?) D †), 1513, 4012, 6421, cf. 1603 ‡ D; (ii.) 3643, 6423 (soberly ‡ D); s. he, 3922 (sorwfulli [he] sight D). [Var. B sorowfully, sorufully; C sorwefully, -li; D sorowfully, sorwefully.]

sternelych it, 3519 A (-lich BD, -liche C).

tendreliche wepte, 5015 A (-lych[ë] B, tenderely ‡ (?) C, tendirly ‡ (?) D)[7]; -lyche, 5031 (-lich B, èntirely C, tendirlichs D). tendrely,

---

[1] In B supply [*to*].   [2] Leaf cut out of C.
[3] In CD read *denyeth* for *denyeth* C, *deignith* D.
[4] In 6656 C supply [*tho*] and understand *sobereliche* as = *soberelich he*.
[5] In B supply [*ful*].   [6] Accent in D?
[7] A certainly has the right reading.

(i.) 111 (-erly BC, pytous ‡ and D), 7088 (-yrly C, -irly D), cf.
6445 f; (ii.) tendrely he, 5612 (-erly B, -erely C, -irly D).
trewęlychę the, 7414 B (-ely ACD); -elyche, 6077 (-eliche B, -ely
CD); -eliche, 1249 B (-ely C, -[e]ly A, tru[ë]ly D), 2246 C (-ely
AB, tru[ë]ly D); -[ë]liche, 6773 B (-elich (?) C, truëly (?) D,
-ewęly ‡ A); -[ë]lich as, 7350 B (-ely ACD); -elych it, 246 (-eliche C
-[ë]liche B, -[ë]ly D); -eliche he, 6476 BC (-ely AD); treweliche,
6743 (-ęlyche ‡ C (?), truęly D). [Var. D truëly.]—trewëly, (i.)
cf. 1326 f, 1713 f, 2909 f, 3001 f, 3020, 3677, 4331 f, 4778 f,[1]
5349 f, 5601 f, 5717 f, 5725, 6112, 6509, 6857 f, 7179, 7438 f,
7986, 8083; (ii.) cf. 5950, 6382, 6846, 7189, 7350, 7445, 8067;
t. how, cf. 7449. [Var. B trew[ë]ly (*common*); C treweli; D.
truëly, tru[ë]ly, trew[ë]ly, treüly, treuëly, truęly ‡ (6846), truly †
(7445).] trewly, (ii.) 1578 (trorwely † C, trew[ë]ly D); trewęly,
(i.) 6537 ‡ A (-ëly BC, truëly D); cf. also 8067 (trulyę yef D).
vnkyndelich and, 617 D (-ely A, -[e]ly B, onkendely C).
verraylyche, 4387 A (-liche B, -ly C, verily D); -lich hym, 6086 A
(verrily C, verily [him] D, ver[ray]liche ‡ it B).
womanlichę, 2753 C (-ly AB, -ly ‡ him D).[2] womanly with, 6940.
wondurliche, 729 B (wondyrliche C, wonderly A, -urly D); wonder-
lychë loude, 3520 A (-lichë B, -irlichë CD).

Note.—In 5466 C *child lichera deface* should be *chyldisshly deface*. In
6899, *with chaunged deedlych pale face* (*deellich* † B, *duit* & D, pale
dedlych *was* ‡ C), *deedlych* is apparently an adjective.

II.

bisily, bysily, bysyly, cf. 771, 2442, 3995 f, 5148, 5331, 5384, 5603 f,
6815, 6933 f ‡ C, 7046. [Var. C busily, busyly, besyly; D besily,
besily(ę).]
bitterly, cf. 4543.
blysfully, 6933 f (busily ‡ C), 8171 AB.
brennynly, 607 (brennyngly B, brenyngę (?) C, brennyng D †).
byhouëly, 1346 f (be- CD).
coryously (*trisyl.*), 2111 ‡ C, see *scryvenlich* in list I., above.
cowardly, 5858 (couardęly C).
curteysly, cf. 5252 ABD.
debonairly, 2344 (-erly CD), 2998 f (-erly CD).
dredfully, 2213.

[1] In 4778 *trewëly* is much more probable than *trewęly*.
[2] In C read *saluwe* for *seluyn*.

falsely, 38 (falsly B), 89 (falsely ‡ C, fàlsly ‡ broken D); falsly, 5855 (-ely CD).[1]
febely, 518 (fiebly B, febly CD).
feithfully, feythfully, cf. 1348 f, 2662, 4514, 4776 f AB, 7439 f (fey(i)thfully C, fei3tfully D).
fermely, 4330 f (formely † C), 4385 (formely † C), 6858 f (-lic D, frendely adj. ‡ (†) C).
fiersly, 4602 B (fersely C, freshly ‡ A, fersly D).
finally, fynally, fynaly, cf. 2409, 3398, 3848, 4877, 5547 f, 6089, 7377, 7398, 7790, 7818, 7998, 8007. finally, 682 (fynali B, fin(1)ally C, final adj. D).
frely, 3484 ‡ C, 4561 (-ly ‡ D).
frendly, 2972 A (freshely ‡ B, frenli ‡ sumtyme C), 3201 (frenly on C, frendly vn D), 3484 ‡ D. (In 6858 ‡ C *frendely* is perhaps an adjective.)
fresshly, freshly, cf. 2985 (frosch[ly] (†) C, fresshe D), 4602 A, 5119, 6753, 7373; freshely, 2972 ‡ B. [Var. C fresschely, froschely; D freisshly.]
generally, 86 (*line om.* † C).
gentilly, 1272 f.
gladly, cf. 1336, 3484 AB, 4187, 6936 ‡ B.
goodly (goudly, 3832 A), cf. 253, 2347, 2575,[2] 2691, 2805 f, 2936, 3496, 3832, 3877, 4627, 6936, 6941. [Var. B godely, goodely; C godly, goodely, goodli.]
gostly, 7393 (gostely D).
hardely, 1389 (-i C, -ily D), 2510 f (-i C, -ily D), 3055 f (-ily BCD), 6182 (-ily B, -eli [ne] C, -ily [ne] D), 7527 (-ili C †; D †), 7669 (-ily BC); hardyly, 2097 (-ily BCD),[3] 2802 f (-ily BD, -ili C), 7487 f (-ily BC, -ely(e) D).
heighly, 2818 (holy ‡ D, heyly [3ow] C).
hertely, 2362 f (-[e]- B, -ily D), 2762 f (-eli C, -ily D); hertely, 7304 (hertly B).
holly, hoolly, cf. 366, 2206, 2818 ‡ D, 2987, 3118, 4169, 5057, 5106, 5474, 6950, 8209. [Var. CD holy.]
homly, 2644 AD (in BC prob. adj.).
humbly, 2342 (humili C); humbely, 2804 f (humblely B, vmbely C, humb[e]ly D), 7717 (humili C).
inly, cf. 640 AB, 4448.

[1] In A read *haue* as = *haue ye*.
[2] Scansion ? In A read *good[ly]*.   [3] In A read *hardyly* [*right*] *yn*.

inwardly, 1349 f; ynwardly, 2817 ‡ D.
largely, 2792 (-li C).
lightly, lyghtly, cf. 1374, 1753, 2324, 2473, 2732, 3062, 3646, 5131. [Var. B lightęly; C ly3tęly (-li).]
lowly, 2207 (louli C), 6537 (lawę- B, louę- C, lou- D); lowęly he, 2157 BC (lowly D, louę- A).[1]
lustily, 6931 f (-li B, -ly(e) D).
manly, 5284 (namęli ‡ C), 6393.
mekely, 1101 f.
myghtily, 428 f, 6625 f (-[i]- D, -ely B).
nedfully, 5666, 5716 f (nedę- D); nedę-, 5736 (ned- B).
nedly, 5632 (nedę- B); nedę-, 5668 (ned- B, nedfully as ‡ D).
newęly, 7373 ‡ C (l. fresshly).
nicely, 7515 f.
openly, 5225 (opěnly it? D).
perpetuely (quadrisyl.); 4596 (-ualy B, -uël adj. ‡ C, -uell D †).
platly, cf. 3628, 3723, 5586.
preciously (trisyl.), 5252 ‡ C (see curteysly).
preuely, preuyly, pryuely, cf. 80 f, 380 f, 2200, 2261, 3592 f, 4427, 5316 f (previly(e) D), 5787, 6263, 7513 f.
richely, 1710 f (-[e]- B).
saufly, 5982 (sauęly CD); sauęly, 6850 ‡ C.
shortly, cf. 2567, 3018, 3312, 3390, 3543, 3959, 3998, 4278, 5003, 5312, 5333, 5615, 7372, 7395, 8189. [Var. B shorthly; C schortęly (-li); D shortly(ę).] shortęly, 3390 (-ily B, schortli C, shortly D); cf. 5544 C (shortly he D).
sikerly, sykerly, cf. 1605, 3000 f ‡ C, 3588, 4776 f CD,[2] 5314 f (sikirly(e) D), 7485 f. [Var. C sekirli; D sikirly.]
skarsly, cf. 1128 (scarcë ‡ in D).
skilfully, 5927 f.
sleyly, 1547 (sleughtęly B, sleli C, slely D), 2270 (sleigh- B, sly- C, sle- D)[3]; sleyghly, 6446 (sleighę- B, sly- C, s[l]e- D).[4]
softely, 78 f (C? D?), 1604 (-[e]- D, softly ‡ hym A), 1712 f, 2621 f (-[e]- (?) B), 2814 (-[e]- D, softly B †), 2817 (softly ‡ D)[5], 3000 f (-[e]- (?) B, sekyrly C, sobrely D), 3591 (-[e]- BD), 5017 (-[e]- B, softly ‡ D), 5577 f ‡ C, 6869 C (-[e]- B, sobrelich A, sobrely D); soft[e]ly, 2335 A (-e- BCD); softly, 1604 ‡ A; cf. 7516 f (where

[1] In AD supply [thus].   [2] In CD supply [it].
[3] In C dele (thus).   [4] Supply [he] in B.
[5] In B read [ful] soft[e]ly; in C, [ful] softeli.

§§ 84, 85.]   of Chaucer's Troilus.   187

 softely is no doubt the right reading). [Var. C softeli ; D softily.]
 sothly, cf. 4350, 5459, 5627, 6850, 7372 ‡ C. [Var. BD sothely.]
 straungely, cf. 7318 (-li(e) D); cf. 2508 f.
 thryftyly, 3053 f.
 vnfelyngly, 1104 f.
 vnhappily, -pyly, 666 (onhap[i]ly C, vnhappy[ly] D), 7300 (vnhap-
  p[i]ly(e) B, -happi[ly] C, -happely D).
 vulgarly, 6175 (-[l]y A, wolgaly C).
 warly, 3296.
 wikkedly, 1526 (wekedeli C).
 wofully, 1603 (sorow- ‡ D).
 worthily, 1271 f.
 wrongfully, 414 f (wronge- B), 2504 (wrongli † C), 7853.
 wylfully, cf. 1369.
 wysly, cf. 205, 949, 1064, 1459, 6710 (wisely (?) C), 7654 (wise- ‡ D).
  [Var. BD wyse-; BCD wise-.]
 wysly, cf. 2315, 3555 ‡ D, 3632, 3767, 4343, 4360, 4495, 4752, 5043,
  6026, 6106, 6519, 7728 (wisely as C‡). [Var. BC -e-; D wiss-, wisse-.]

  Rhyme words.—Adverbs in *-ly* rhyme usually with each other, but the
   following rhyme-words also occur : I (428, 1101, 1104, 1271, 1272, 1626,
   2089, 2508, 2510, etc.), by, therby (380, 382, 1626, 2362, 4776, 4778,
   5574, 5577), why (1758), grant mercy (1326).
  Note.—In 2111 AB, one *-ly* seems to be used for two adverbs (cf. Shak-
   spere's *fresh and merrily*) : "Ne scryuenyssh (stryuenyssh † B, coryously
   C, scryvenlich D) or (ne C) *craftily* (craftyliche C, craftly D) thow it
   (*om.* C) wryte."

§ 85. The following adverbs which have *-e* neither in A.S.
 nor in the *Troilus* deserve notice :
 amys (see Mätzner), cf. 491 f, 1398 f, 2133 f, 2593 f, 3015 f, 3112 f,
  3687 f, 3876 f, 3967 f, 4022 f, 4471 f, 5933 f, 7102 f, 7430 f, 7549 f,
  7641 f, 8047 f, 8090 f.

  Rhyme-words.—is, ywys, this.
  Note.—Cf. that yet is mys and, 5929 (that is amys D); that is mys, 6010 f
   (that is amisse D) (: is : this); al that was mys, 7789 f (amys ‡ CD).
 anon (A.S. on an), (i.) (ii.) cf. 75, 324, 349 f, 2096 f, 2636 f, 2840,
  3396, 3406 f, 3516 f, 3545 f, 3991 f, 4704, etc., etc. CD occasionally
  have *anon(e)*; B sometimes has *onon*. (Accent in 2636 ?)
 ful (A.S. ful. *adv.*), (i.) 151, 167, 3589, 5472, 6630, 6633 (fulle BD),
  7614, 7998; (ii.) 378, 626; ful humble, 124. [Var. D fuH.]

  Note.—Ten Brink, § 246 Anm., notices that "das steigernde *ful* (*ful wel*,
  ful hard u. s. w.)" has no -e. Of the above-cited cases all but two are
  instances of this "steigernde *ful*." These two, however, do not come
  under ten Brink's category : they are,—"Who koude telle aright or *ful*
  discryue," 6630, and "But fynally he *ful* ne trowen myghte," 7998.

hom (A.S. hám). See nouns, § 18.

nygh, neigh, neih, ney, *adv.* and *prep.* (A.S. néah, néh, *adv. and prep.*), (i.) (ii.) cf. 108, 180, 499, 543, 582, 2325, 3345, 5019, 5035, 5894, 6895. [Var. B neʒgh, neyghe ; C nyʒ, nyh, nyʒh ; D ny, nye, niʒ (4404 ‡ D).]

streyght, streyt, straught (A.S. streht, *p.p.*); streyght, (i.) 53 (streght B), 4802 (streught B†, streyt C), 5905 (streughte B, streyʒt C, streite D), 6655 (streght B, streyt C, streyte D); (ii.) 324 (streght B, styrte † C), 607 (streght B, streyt C), 6351 (streyte B, streite D); streygh[t], (ii.) 2258 (streght B, streyt C, streight † D); streyght he, 5825 (streught B, streyt C, streyte = streyt he D).—streyt, (ii.) 2546 (streght B, streight D, [as] streit C).—straught, (ii.) 3394 (streight BD, streyt C).

wys (really neut. adj. used as adv., cf. *y-wys*), god so wys be my saluacioun, 1466 (wis CD); god so wys me saue, 2063 (wis CD); as wys as I the serue, 3555 (wis C, wisly † D); as wys I neuere, etc., 6317 (wis BC, wisse D).

ynough, ynowgh, ynowh, ynow, inow (A.S. genóg, genóh), (i.) 2108 f, 2675 f, 2927 f, 3039 f, 4471, 4796, 5058, 5720, 6462 f, 6654, 7213, 7357, 7459, 7533 f; (ii.) 5346 (inow (of) C).

> Rhyme words.—towh, towgh, tough (2108, 2927, 6462), lowh, lough *pret. ind.* 3 *sg.* (2675, 3039, 7533). [Var. B inough, ynough(e); D ynow(e), inough, inowh.]

y-wys, i-wys (A.S. ge-wis, *adj. neut.*), (i.) cf. 425 f, 802 f, 1213 f, 1313 f, 1814 f ([y-]wys A), 5353 (iwiss(e) D), 8095 (i-wiss(e) D), etc., etc.; i-wysse, 1012 f (i-wis BC, ywys D) (: this(se) : ys(se)). Cf. *wys*.

Note.—In *euele, yuele, -ele* merely represents syllabic *-l*. Thus—*ful yuele fare*, 626 (enele C, evil D). This becomes consonantal before a vowel; as, *euele apayed*, 5304 (yuel B, euitt D), cf. 649 ; *yuele as*, 6601 (yuel B, iuele C, yuell D).

A few Romance words are used adverbially without termination :

certeyn, -ayn, -ain, (*a*) with accent on the ultima, (i.) cf. 492, 1475, 1476 ‡ B, 2654 f, 3631 f, 4118, 5720 f, 5780 (-(e) D), 7491 f; (ii.) cf. 5266. (*b*) With accent on the penult, (i.) cf. 674, 1809, 3996, 4782; (ii.) cf. 3938, 5864 (-(e) D). Cf. the use of *syker* in 2076.

complet, cf. 7191 (perh. rather adj.).

egàl, 5322.

plat, cf. 681, 1664.

seur, al so seur as day cometh, 5083 (sure D).

§ 85.] *of Chaucer's Troilus.* 189

Several adjective formations in *-les* (A.S. -léas) are used adverbially (cf. § 49, note 5). These are (i.) (ii.),—

causeles, 779 f (-lees B), 3853, 6139 ABD.

douteles, 1499 f (-[e]- D), 1579 C (-[e]- AD, trew[e]ly B), 2614 f, 4220 (-[e]- E),[1] 4630 (-[e]- D), 4764 f (-[e]- D)[2], 5092 (dought[e]les D), 5161 C, 5897 (douȝt[e]les D).

dredeles, 1027 B (-[e]- ACD), 3368 (-[e]- AD)[3], 3844 (-[e]- AD), 4738 B (-[e]- AD), 5940 (-[e]- A)[4]; -lees, 1041 B (dred[e]les AD), 1270 B (dred[e]les ACD).

endeles, 4685.

gilteles, 1413 BC (-[e]- AD) (perhaps adj.).

knot[te]les, 7132 (knotteles C, knott[e]les ‡ out D).[5]

nedeles, 2612 f.

Note 1.—*Fayn* and *loth*.—The adjective *fayn* (A.S. fæg(e)n) is used in connection with *wol* and *wolde* with the force of an adverb. Thus,— wolde I *fayn* remeue, 691 (fayne B); I wol right *fayn* with al my myght ben oon, 2770. Examples of this use may be seen in 3064 f (feyne B, feyn CD) (: ayen : seyn *p.p.*), 3497 f (: agayn ; rayn *n.*), 7358 f (-e BD) (: ayeyn); cf. 3769, 3854, 3945, 4359, 6432, 6550, 6914, 7595, 8104, in most of which the word that follows begins with a consonant. *Fayn* in this idiom has no proper *-e*, though B and D sometimes add one, which, however, is never sounded (so 2310 A).[6] (Cf. *fawe*, note 2 at end of § 46.) Similarly the adj. *loth* (A.S. láð) is used with an apparently adverbial force : God wot of thing ful ofte *loth* bygonne Cometh ende good, 2319-20 (lothe D†); For trewely ther kan no wight yow serue That half so *loth* yowre wratthe wolde deserue, 6509-10 (soth † C).

Note 2.—*Wonder* in connection with adjectives and adverbs (*wonder blyue, wonder wel*, etc.) is sometimes regarded as the first part of a compound ; but it was apparently felt as a separate word (cf. the adjectival use of *wonder* in such phrases as *this wonder maladye*, 419). For examples cf. *wonder blyue*, 7912 ; *w. cruwel*, 7831 ; *w. faste*, 5336 (marueilously slurred ‡ D); *w. ofte*, 139 † A ; *w. sore*, 751, 1540, 3964 ; *w. stronge*, 7564 ; *w. wel*, 288.

Note 3. For *scryuenyssh* or *craftily*, see note at end of § 84.

Note 4.—For *half* used adverbially (cf. A.S. healfe *instr.* with compar. ; healf- *in comp.* healf-dead, etc.), cf. (i.) 6510 (-e D), 7101, (ii.) 1152.

Note 5.—The following adverbs, etc., of various formation, are for convenience throwen together in a note :

ay (O.N. ei, cf. A.S. á, áwa, and see *o* below), (i.) cf. 186 (alle ‡ C), 2488 f, 3376 f, 6515 f, 7074 f, 7158 f, 7985 f ; for ay, cf. 4454 f, 4655 (aye D); tho forth ay, 1069 f ; (ii.) cf. 180, 5598 ; for ay and o, 2167 f C (and oo D).

eft (A.S. eft), (i.) 137 BC, 4322 (-(e) CD), 4374 (-(e) D), 4395 (-(e) B, ofte ‡ D), 4525 † D (erst ABC), etc. ; (ii.) 6391 (-(e) D), 6979 (-(e) D), etc.

est (A.S. éast). See *west*.

fer (A.S. feorr), (i.) 853, 2203 ; (ii.) 18 [7], 451, 565 (ferre [as] D), 888, 1301, 2305 (fayre ‡ C ; *om.* † D), 3275, 3325, 3502 [8] ; fer han, 4653 (B†);

[1] In E read *a[l]s[o]*.
[2] In D, read ȝe for *is* (yis ?) : otherwise *dout[e]les* is adj. ‡.   [3] 9-syl. verse.
[4] In C ‡ perhaps adj.   [5] In C read *thour[out]*.
[6] For 7595 D is to be emended by transposition. In 2310 C we are to insert [to], not to read *fayn[e]*.
    [7] Supply [I] in A.   [8] Read *lyggen* for *lyn* in C.

fer henne, 5908 (fere B); from a fer his, 313 (from affer C, from ferre her 9-*syl* D).¹ [D has usually *ferr*(e), *ferr*(e).]
forth (A S. forð), cf. 2345, 4809; tho forth ay, 1069 f; emforth, -(e), cf. 1328, 2082, 3841; fro this forth, cf 1094, 1529, 4976; ferforth (accented on either syllable) in the phrases,—so ferforth, as f. as, so f. that, thus f., how f., cf. 121, 2045, 2191, 4336, 5553, 5960. (In these examples no note as to whether a vowel or *h* or a consonant follows)
on . . . along (ylong) (A.S. on (æt) . . . gelang), *On* me is nought *ylong* thin yuel fare, 2086 (along CD, along(e) B)²; but it were *on* hym *along* ye, 3625 (-(e) B, on al † a long ye D).
tho (A.S. þá), cf. 1600 f, 1766 f, 2290 f, 2487 f, 2913 f, 3968, 5402, etc., etc.; er tho, 6811 (or this C, or thoo D).
✗ wel (A.S. wel), cf. (i.) (ii.) 12, 57, 68, 76, 131, 167, 288, 1177, 1677 f (wele ABD) (: del . stel); 2297 f, 3538 f, 3552 f, etc., etc. (Often written *wele* in BD and sometimes in A (cf. 246, 837, 1677 f), but of course the -e is never sounded.)
west (A S. west), est or west, 7795 f (est or weste B, est and west D) (: best *adv*. : lest *ind*. 3 *sg*.); est and west (*as sbst. acc.*), 2138 f (est and weste B) (: lyst *ind*. 3 *sg*.); by est or west, 7114 f (weste B, be(n) est or west C, by este or west D†) (. lest *ind*. 3 *sg*. : best *pred. adj. sg.*); by west and ek by este, 7556 f (by weste . . . bi este B, he † west . . . he † est C, by weste . . by est D) (: byheste *n*.).
youd. See note at end of § 86.

§ 86. Comparison of Adverbs (Child, § 70; ten Brink, p. 134). Comparative degree.

Of the "old" adverbial comparatives, A.S. *bet*, *wiers*, *iná*, *lǽs*, *néar* (*nýr*), *ǽr* survive in the Troilus (*a*); for *stð*, see § 88, p. 196. Other adverbial comparatives are adjective forms: (*b*) (I.) *bettre*, *more*, *lasse*, *derre*; (II.) A.S. comparatives in -*or* and their analogues.

(*a*) bet (A.S. bet), (i.) 275³ (b. hire ‡ C)⁴, 1363, 2524, 3963, 6832 (but † C), 7284, 7629 (beste † B), etc.; the bet, 481, 1177 f (bette BCD) (. let *p.p.*, lette BCD), 1589 (C †), 1921 f (bett B, bete C) (: beset *p p*), 2600, 3819 (the b. ‡ other (?) C); cf. 746, 3318, 3332, 4406, 5562, 6020, 7347, 7405; For yf it erst was wel tho was it *bet*, 4525 f (bette C) (: met *p.p.*). [Var. B bett; BD bett(e).]
bet, (ii.) 3264, 3965 (B † C †), 4333 (the bettir ‡ endure D); bet and bet shal, 3556 (. . . wil C).
wers (A.S. wiers, wyrs), wers bygon, 7691 (wors B, werse C, wurse D); wors(e), 2703 (wers(e) B, wers(e) Cᶜ, wors D).
In 5856 f, *no werse* (wurse D) (. aduerse *voc.* : diuerse *pl.*) is an adjective.
mo (A.S. má), euere mo, 1465 f (-more † D), 4268 f, 4603 f (euer more † moo E); cf. 418 f, 787 f, 6088 f, 7026 f, 7418 f, 7502 f. neuere mo, 2498 (neueuermore † C; D †); cf. 5645 f.

¹ Or supply [*a*] in D. ² Dele (*al*) in C.
³ Old-style figures indicate that D reads *better*, *betir*, *bettir*, *betre*, though the metre calls for *bet* (cf. 746 C). ⁴ Supply [*gan*] in A.

[§ 86.] *of Chaucer's Troilus.* 191

Rhyme words.—to and fro (418, 6088), two (418), also (5645), so (1465, 4603, 7502), wo (787, 1465, 4268, 7418), go *inf.* (4268, 4603, 6088, 7026, 7502), ago *p.p.* (7418), tho *adv.* (7026). [Var. BE moo.]

les (A.S. lǽs), preserved in *natheles* (A.S. ná þé lǽs), (i.) cf. 19, 170 f (: makeles : prees), 750, 916, 923, 1552, 3011, 3214, 3424, 3827, 3925, 4327, 5185, 5716, 6098, 6462, 6546, 6872, 7141, 7232, 7932, 8002; (ii.) cf. 5536, 5629; n. he, cf. 4814, 7547.

C usually has *neuere the les* (trisyllabic, as if *ne'ertheless*). Other variants are *nathelces*, 750 B, 916 B, 3011 A; *nathales*, 5536 B; *netheles*, 3925 D, 4327 D; *nathelesse*, 5716 D, 7232 D; *neuerles*, 6872 C; *nath[e]les*, 6098 A.

Note.—For *lest* (A.S. þý lǽs þe), see § 87, n. 3.

ner (A.S. néar, nýr), the ner the fyr, 449; the ner he was, 448.

Ner I come, 1647, may be either positive or comparative, and there is a similar uncertainty with regard to 2902 (nere D)[1], 4404 (niȝ ‡ D), and 6443 (neer B, ners he D). For the positive *ner*, *neer*, cf. 451, 582 C.

(*b*) II. bettre, betre (A.S. bet(t)re, *neut. comp.*), 2300 f (betere C); b. plese, 3728 (better BD, betere C); bettre his, 3729 (more BC, better D); the bettre, 2780 f (bettere BC); the b. pleyne, 2616 (bettere B, betere C, betir D); the bettre at, 6013 (bettire C, better D.) (All dissyl. except 3729, 6013.)

Rhyme-words.—lettre (2300, 2780), vnfettre *inf.* (2300).

more, (A.S. máre, *neut. comp.*), 647 f, 669 f, 753 f, 883 (C ?), 885 (-ę C), 931 (-ę C ‡ ⁻D ‡), 1082 f, 1820 AB, 2413 (D ?), 2424 f, 4061, 5380 f, 5488 f (mor D), 6007 f (D †), 6387 f, 6851, 7036 f, 7282 (C †), 7283, 7716 f, 7719 f, 8096 f (cf. 2540 C, 5610 D); -*e*, 2556, 3324 (D †), 4021, 4494 (-ë ‡ me C), 4919 (*om.* ‡ D), 6007 (mor B; D †), 7036, 7329 (-ë ‡ to C; D ?), 7744, 7751 CD (manęre ‡ A); more he, 448; more here (*sing.*), 2717 (C †); but,— nomore haue, 3013 (namorë han B, no more han C ‡).

morę than, 376[2], 532 (-e ‡ D), 537 (mor B; D (?)), 578 (-ę C (?); mor † D), 1425, 3162 (-ë B; C ? D ?), 3873, 4389, 5654; the morę that, 406 (-ë C ‡ D); morę ‡ thrust, 406 D; ne morę desirede, 567 (ner morę D); nomorę com, 1515; for euerę morę myn, 1915 (mo BC); euerę morę whan, 4243 (mo BC); nomorę come, 6130 (nomor B, no morë ‡ C); euerę morę lo, 4946 (cf. 2498 C)[3].

But,—morë than, 1226 (-ę C), 3289; morë that, 4493; morë thing, 539 (morę ȝe C, mor ye D).

Rhyme words.—lore *n.* (647, 753, 1082, 2424, 6387), sore *adv.* (669, 753, 1082, 5380, 5488), *adj. pl.* (2424, 7036, 7716), soore *inf.* (669), of yore (5380 8097), restore *inf.* (6007), more *adv.* (7716), no more *sbst.* (8096) [Var. BD moore.]

---

[1] Supply [*in*] in A.
[2] We can avoid *morę* in this verse, but only by reading *alle louèrs* instead of *alle lòuers*.
[3] *I kan no morę but*, 4654, seems to be substantive.

192   *Observations on the Language*   [§ 86.

lasse (A.S. lǽsse, *neut. comp.*), 284 (lesse B ; C †), 651 (lesse BD), 1986 (las[se] D, lesse hire B)[1]; lasse hadde, 886 ; the lasse, 2928 f (the les CD), 5278 f, 5794 (the lesse C), 5971 (the lesse D, lasse B, lesse [2] C) ; the lasse, 967.(the lesse, B, [the] lasse D).
  Rhyme-words.—masse *missam* (2928), passe *inf.* (2928, 5278).
derre (A.S. déorre, *neut. comp.*), boughten they . . . it derre, 136 f (dere BD) (: werre *n.*) ; to ben presed derre, 174 f (: sterre).
II. deppere (A.S. déoppor), 1570 (depter † B, depper D).
ferther (A.S. furðor), f. go, 3123 (-ere C, forther BD)[3] ; ferther-ouer, 5689 (further o. D, further now B) ; no ferthere out, 5969 (forther B, further D).
gladlyer (*dissyl.*), (ii.) 8140 (-lier B, gladder D).
hyer (A.S. héa(h)or), 2671 (heighere B, hey3ere C, hier D).
lengere, lenger, longere (A.S. leng) ; lengere, 1065 (langer B), 1683 (neuere C, neuere (?) D), 2478, 2699 (D †), 3010, 3183,[4] 3400 (-er B, -ere C, -er aftir D), 6370, 7273, 7562 (cf. 5370 C (-er D ?)[5] ; lengere, 2603, 2707 (*line om.* † C), 4870 [6], 8029 (langer B) ; lengere here (*hic*), 4970 ; longere, 2327 (lengere C). (In all the instances so far cited, unless there is a note to the contrary, B has *longer*, D *lenger*). lenger, (i.) 5610 (nothyng † C, more ‡ D), 5852 (langer B, more C †).
leuere vnwyst, 2594 (lever D).
rathere, rather (A.S. hraðor), (i.) cf. 835, 865, 3221, 3415, 4825, 5186, 5256, 5589, 5701, 6410 ; (ii.) rathere, 5650 (-er BD) ; -ere here (*hic*), 6111 (-er BD) ; -ere anoon, 5102 (-er sterue B, -ere s. C ; *om.* † D).
sonner, 1771 (sonere C).
  Note.—For *after* (adv. and prep.) cf. 30, 1581, 2434, 4888, 5597, etc. ; for *heder, hider, hyder,* cf. 5594, 6022, 6849 f, 6977 ; for *whider, wheder,* cf. 3233, 4944, 5309, 6791, 6849 f ; for *yonder,* yender, cf. 2231 f, 3505 f, 6928 (yende A), 6931, 7032, 7033 (for *yonder* as an adjective cf. *that yonder place,* 6943 ; *the yonder hill,* 6973 ; 3ondir ‡ *he,* 2369 C (yond A, 3onde B, 3end D[7]) ; yender ‡ *I,* 6975 D (yond A, 3onde BC) ; 3ondir *is,* 7525 C (3ond *is* B, yond nys A, yonde nys D)[8] ; for *outher, outher* (*other . . . or,* cf. 1501, 2433, 2436, 5193 ; for *other* (= or), cf. 3865 A (or BCD) ; for *neyther* (*neither*) . . . *ne* (nor), cf. 312, 1870, 3364, 5433, 5926 ; for *whether,* cf. 425, 1398, 2237, 5673 ; for *wher, where* (= whether), cf. 270, 2348, 2551 C, 2736, 2908, 3888, 5493, 5824, 6356.

---
[1] This line is best scanned "And ay gan loue hire lasse for to agaste." In B transpose *lesse* and *hire*.
[2] BC om. *tho*.
[3] Supply [*wol*] in A.
[4] Read *may* for *make* in A.
[5] This stanza is not in A B.
[6] D ? (supply [*in*] and read *blis*[*se*]).
[7] In A supply [*ye*].
[8] In 6928 B for 3onder saugh ich (yender saugh D, 3ondyr say C, yende saugh A) read yond saugh ich. 6936 B for 3onder so (-ir C, yonder D), read yond so (with A) ; in 7521 C for 3ondir sche, read yond she (-e D, 3onde B). For *yond,* cf. also 5685.

§ 87. The superlative adverbs *best* and *mest*, when preceded by the definite article, may take an -*ë* after the analogy of adjectives (cf. Child, § 70 ; ten Brink, p. 137, Anm.).

The following are all the cases in which *the* is used with these superlatives in the *Troilus*:

on the bëst[ë] sounded ioly harpe, 2116 (on the bestë sowned B, (vp)on the bestë souned(e) (?) C, (vp)on the best[ë] sownyd (?) D). the beste ynòrisshed, 7184 (best BD); the beste entèchëd, 7195 (best BD); [the] beste yprèysëd, 7836 (the beste C, the best D, the best [y]preysed B).

the mestë stormy life, 1863 (moost[ë] B, mostë C, most[ë] D).

the most[ë] fre, 1073 (moost[ë] BD).

When no *the* precedes, the forms are *best* and *most*. Cf. for *best* (i.) (ii.) 47, 332 f (: lyst n., leste B, rest C^c), 718, 1001 (alderbest), 1322, 1914, 2481 f (: yf the lyste, lest B, lyst CD), 2515, 2667, 2697, 2758, 3196, 3208, 3454, 3901, 4107, 4494, 4822, 4951, 6752, 6792, 6995, 7137, 7145, 7440, 7630, 7677, 7793 f (: west : lest *lubet*), 8064. For *most*, cf. (i.) (ii.) 152, 230, 242, 720 f, 1332, 1748, 2235, 2453 f (: wost *scis*), 2495 f (: wost), 3523, 4617, 4628, 4947, 5223, 5259 f (: ost : wost), 6283 f, 6955, 7067, 7426, 8120, 8143, 8210, etc.

> Note 1.—In none of these cases is *best* or *most* preceded by *the* or by a demonstrative or possessive pronoun. In all of them A has the form *best* or *most*. Variants in -e occur, but the -e is never sounded (for *most(e)*, cf. (i.) 1332 B, 2235 B, 5259 f D, 6283 f, etc.; for *best(e)* (i.) (ii.), see B in 1001, 2515, 2667, 3454, 4494, 7740, 7793 f).
>
> Note 2.—For *almòst álmost* (A.S. eal- æl-mǽst), cf. (i.) (ii.) 1855, 2906 f, 2995, 3138 f, 5368.
>
> Note 3.—*Best* and *mest* excepted, no superlative adverbs take an -e in the *Troilus*. Examples are (i.) (ii.) : *first, fyrst, ferst* (cf. 381, 659, 1875, 4076, 4834, 6318, 6930, 6944, etc., etc.), var. BD *first(e)*; *last* (cf. 7550 (-(e) B ; D (?))); *erst* (cf. 299, 842, 2425, 4389, 4512, 4518, 4525, 4830), var. BD *arst*; *next, nexst*, as adverb (cf. 2067, 3386, 4098, 4100), as preposition (cf. 399, 941 (9-syl.), 943, 944, 1729); *lest* (cf. 1925, 2236, 4110 [1]); *strengest feythed*, 1000 (*strenghest* B, *strengest fichid* C); see also *alderfirst, alderlest*, § 81.

§ 88. The following particles, of various formation, appear in the *Troilus* sometimes or always with an -*e* (cf. Child, § 72).

In this list are thrown together, for convenience : (i.) particles in A.S. -*an*, -*on*,—*aboute, abouen*, -*e*, *byforn, byfore, toforn, byhynden*, -*e*,

---

[1] Perhaps substantive in the accusative case.

bitwene, selde, sithen (etc.), *withinne, withouten, -e ;* cf. *aside, byside ;* (ii.) particles in A.S. *-a,—soone, yore ;* (iii.) *inne, oute, out, thanne, whanne ;* (iv.) *nowthe* (A.S. *nú þá*); (v.) *-mele* (A.S. *mǽlum*); (vi.) *atwynne, yfere, blyue, bothe ;* (vii.) *therfore, -for, wherfore, -for.* For *down, adown, gruf, asunder,* see notes at end of list. For *by weste,* see § 85, note 5.

aboute, abowte (A.S. ymbútan, onbútan), 149 f, 268 f¹, 1819 f ‡ C, 1904 f, 2478 f, 2556, 3523 f, 3950, 4692 (-[ë] D), 5063 f, 5342 f, 5364 (C †), 5377 f, 5937 f, 6231 f (C †), 6448 f, 6463, 6763 f, 7483 (abouȝte C ?), 7657 f, 7814 f, 7859 f, 8008 f; -e, 2553 (-t D, -ė for? C ‡), 4072, 6586; -e his, 3911, 4575 (D †), 6618, 7588, 7595; -e hym, 4562 (hym àboute alwey A, *which transpose*); -e her (*sing.*), 3642 (-yn C), 5479², 5531 (-e (?) ‡ B); aboutę thin, thi, 863 (-t C), 7019; -ę the, 4904; but,—abowtè this, 3380 (-ën B, -[e] D, -yn his C).

    Rhyme-words.—doute *n.* (149, 1819, 2478, 5063, 5937, 6231, 7657, 7814, 8008), route *n* (268, 1904, 5063, 5342, 5377, 6448, 6763, 7859), deuoute (149), lowte *inf.* (3523), with-oute (268, 3523), stoute *adj. pl.* (7814, 7859).

abouen, aboue (A.S. on-bufan); aboue, 230 f, 3720 f, 3869 f, 7367 f, 8193 f, 8207 f; abouë euęry, 6517 (-ėn B, -yn C, -e? D ‡); aboue, 3617 (vpon ‡ C), 8182; abouę ‡ thi, 3580 A³; -ę the goddes, 4930 (-ÿn goddis C); abouęn, (ii.) 6341, 6561 (-ë C, -yn D).

    Rhyme words.—loue *n.* (*all*), shoue *p.p.* (3869).

aside, asyde (as if A.S. on sídan), -e, 291 (on sydɇ D ; C †), 5886 (*om.* † C); -e his, 7290 (-e a BCD).

a-twynne (cf. O.N. tvinnr), 4508 f (a twyn D) (: bygynne *inf.*), 6276 f (a-twyn C) (: wynne *inf.* : with-inne). (Cf. *atwō*, etc., 6893 f.)

blyue (A.S. bí lífe), 595 f (bilyue B), 958 f (bylyue B), 1222 f, 1293 f, 2622 f, 2690 f, 3067 f, 4836 f (blythe † C),⁴ 5157 f (blyf C), 6017 f, 6526 f, 6759 f (biliue B), 7912 f; b[e]lyue, 2598 f (belyue C, blyue ? D).

    Rhyme-words.—thriue, thryue *inf.* (958, 1222, 1293, 2690), dryue *inf.* (2598, 2622, 3067, 5157, 6017, 6759, 7912), stryue *inf.* (4836, 6526, 7912), al my lyue⁵ (595), my lyue⁵ (1293), yn al his lyue (2622), his lyue⁵ (6526), on lyue (1222, 5157), of lyue (2690), hyue *n.* (6017), fyue (6759). [Var. D blive.]

bothe (bothen) . . . and (O.N. báðir *pron.,* cf. A.S. bá, bá-twá); bothe thow and I, 711 (bothen B); bothe fals and foul is, 6746 (-[e] B); so *bothe* . . . *and* in 168 (D †), 7131 (-[e] B), 8077 (-[e]

---

[1] Old-style figures indicate that D has *about.*   [2] Supply [al] in D.
[3] BC have *vpon,* D has *on* (l. *vpon*).   [4] In D read *a[l]s[o].*
[5] Expressing *time.*

B); bothe . . . and[1], cf. 97, 130, 167, 264, 464, 1396, 1397, 5340, 5705; bothe he . . . and, 1718 (D †); bothe heroner and faukon, 5075 (both B, bothe ‡ goshauk and C^c). But,—As seyden *bothę* the meest and ek the leeste, 6803 BD (bothe meste = both the meste C, A *om.* ek); cf. 167 AB (-e C), 1862 ‡ D, 2423 ‡ D.— bothen worship and seruyse, 82 AB (bothe C; D †).

byforn, biforn (A.S. befǫran), 221[2] f (aforn C), 376 f (byforne D), 1226 f. (byfor D), 2356 f (beforne C), 3144 f, 3917 f (aforene C, byforne D), 4062 f (biforne D), 5022 f (aforne C, beforne D), 5636 f, 5755 f (byfore : born A, beforn C), 5910 f (byfore C, beforne D), 6520 f (byforne D), 6644 f (beforne D), 7806 f (byfore C, beforne D); b. withouten, 5646 (-fornę B), 5663 (biforę B); b. oure, 5641; b. haue, 7463 (before BCD).

Rhyme-words.—corn (221), shorn *p.p.* (221), born, born(e) *p.p.* (376, 1226, 2356, 3144, 3917, 4062, 5755, 5910, 6520), lorn, y-lorn *p.p.* (376, 3917, 4062, 5910, 7806), sworn, i-sworn *p.p.* (5636[3], 6644), to-torn *p p.* (5022), thorn (2356). [Var. CD beforn.]

byfore, 5660 f, 5701 f, 6389 f (to-fore B); byfore, 2051 (beforn C, byfor ‡ he D), 3582 (byforne B, afore C, byfor D), 6120 (bifor B, to-forn C); be-fore certeinly (?), 5681 D (? byforn A, ? bifor B); byforę the, 1428 (byfor D); -ę that, 5739 (-ę the BD); -ę to, 5639 (befor B, beforn D). [Var. BC bifore; CD before.] (Cf. 5755 f A.) byfor noon, 7485 (biforę C, beforę D).

Rhyme-words —forloie *p.p.* (6389), yshore *p.p.* (5660), more *root* (6389), therfore (5660, 5701).

byhynden, byhynde (A.S. be-hindan); byhynde, 1604 f (-d D), 1724 f (-d D), 2192 f (-d D), 7174 f.—byhynden othere, 179 (-yn C, -[en] D).

Rhyme-words.—mynde (1604), fynde *inf.* (1724), *pl.* (2192), rynde *n.* (1724), bynde *inf.* (7174). [Var. (*at end of line*) C behynde, -hinde; D behinde, -hind, -hynd.]

byside, bysyde (A.S. be sídan), 1161 f (: gyde *pres. subj.* 2 *sg.*), 4623 f (: ryde *inf.*); -e hirę (*poss. sg.*), 1819 A, 3464, (*poss. pl.*) 1819 B; -e hym, 7045 (-e B[4], -ë was D[5]); there be sydyn schal, 3510 ‡ C. [Var. C besyde; D besíde.]

by-twene, bi-twene (A.S. betwéǫnan), 1908 f, 2791 f, 3096 (bytwyxèn B, betwixe C, bytwix[e] D), 3343 f, 4698 f, 6092 f (betwen D), 7449 f (botweyne B, bétwen D); by-twen[e] wyndes, 417 (betwexen B, betwexe C, bytwix[ë] D).

---

[1] Var. BD *both . . . and.*
[2] Old-style figures indicate that B has *byforne* or *byforne.*
[3] *swo* A, *sworne* B, *sworn* D   [4] But supply [*this*] and read -e (elided).
[5] But supply [*him*] and read -e (elided) (?).

Rhyme-words.—grene *adj. sg.* and *pl.* (1908, 2791, 6092), shene *adj. def. sg.* (1908), *adj. pred. sg.* (6092¹), shene *adv.* (4698), I wene *pres. ind.* (3343, 7449), queene (2791), contene *inf.* (3343). [Var. BC be-twene.]

inne² (A.S. inne), 387 f (in C, yn D), 821 f (yn D), 1091 f (yn D), 1936 f (in C, yn D), 1960 f (ther ‡ yn D), 3499 f (in C, yn D), 3753 f (in C, yn D), 5422 f, 5568 f (in C), 5921 f, 5930 f; inne, 7882 (in D).

Rhyme-words.—gynne *pres. ind. sg* (1936), bygynne *inf.* (387, 1960, 3499, 5921), bygynne *ind.* 3 *pl.* (1091), wynne *inf.* (387, 821), synne *n.* (821, 1936, 3753, 5422), twynne *inf.* (5422, 5568, 5930).

ther-inne (A.S. þǽr-inne), 3537 f (-in D), 4474 f (-ynne D), 5447 f (-in CD); ther-yn but, 1354 (-in BCD).

Rhyme-words.—bygynne *inf.* (3537), vnpynne *inf.* (3537), wynne *inf.* (4474), twynne *inf.* (5447).

mele (adverbial termination, A.S. -mǽlum, dat. pl. of mǽl, mél, *n., m.* (?)), stundemele (A.S. stundmǽlum), 7037 (stormyal † C).

nowthe (A.S. nú þá), 978 f (nouthe CD, nought † B): youthe : kouthe : posset.

Note.—*Now* is sometimes spelled *nowe*, even in A, but the -e is never pronounced (cf. 2357, 4674, 5691, 6693 f, 8101 f).

oute (A.S. úte, út, út of), But at the yate there she shoulde outë ryde, 6395; the seynt is oute, 6916 f (out D) (: route *n.*); thow art oute, 7882 f (: doute *n.*); oute of, 3857 (out C, out ‡ hym D), 4672 (out D); out of, 3894 (-e B).

out (*adv.*), *before consonants*, 1061, 4701, 4708³, 4872 (-ę D), 4874 (-ę (?) D), 4919 (-ę BD), 6912 (-ę D), 7733 (-ę D).

thurgh-out, thorugh-out; t. a, 3443 (throw-out C?); t. the, 4566 (thourout C); t. Troye, 5323 (thour-out C ‡).

selde (A.S. seld-, seldan), 1462 f (seld D) (: behelde *pret. subj.* 3 *sg.*); seldë sëynge, 5085 (*perh. adj.*); seelde, 1253 (selde B, seldë seyn C, seldom seyn D).

sithen, sethen, sith, syn (A.S. síð þám, síððan, etc.).

I. In causal sense:

A almost always has *syn*. Thus, (i.) 520, 1665, 2144, 2953, 3108, 4324, 4954, 5215, 6859, etc. etc.; (ii.) 721, 1133, 1380, 1856, 3429, 4006, 4767, 5081, 5107, 5164. Other forms found in A are: sith,⁴ (i.) 645, 696, 1345; (ii.) 598, 1380, 1524,

---

¹ A has *she[ne]*.
² Either pure adverb (as in *this Diomede is inne*), or prepositional (in such phrases as *lyf that I am inne*).
³ Read *brayn[es]* in D.
⁴ That no rule can be formulated as to *syn* or *sith* according as *th* does not or doe, begin the following word may be seen by comparing 645 and 696 with 520, 2144, 2953, 3108, 4324, 6859.

§ 88.]   *of Chaucer's Troilus.*   197.

1527, 3211; (*before* h) 1794, 3422; sithę, 719; sithęn that, 934; sithęn I, 720.

B, like A, commonly has *syn*. Other forms are: sith, (i.) 645, 696, 1665, 2144, 3256; sith, syth, (ii.) 598, 720, 1380, 1524, 1527, 3211; sith he, 1794, 3422; seth, (i.) 520; sen, (i.) 3993, 6859; seyn, (i.) 3980; (ii.) 4006; sithën thow, 934[1]; sithën thende, 1345.[2]

C has usually *sythę* or *sithę* before consonants (for sythe, sithe, before vowels, see 598, 1380, 1524, 1527, 4006). Other forms are: syn, (i.) 4319, 4954, 5057, 6859, etc.; (ii.) 5164; sith, (i.) 3422, 5171[3]; (ii.) 3429; seth, (i.) 520; sithë, (i.) 960 ‡, 2953 ‡, 3256 ‡, 5231 ‡, 6717 ‡ (cf. 1345); sythyn ‡ thyn, 891; sythyn that (or sythÿn that ?), 4971 ‡; sythyn al, 721.

D commonly reads *seth*. Thus,—(i.) 645, 696, 1665, 2144, etc., etc.; (ii.) 1524, 1527, 1856, etc.; *before* h, 1794, 3422.[4] Other forms are: syn, (i.) 4971, 4975, 5057; (ii.) 5087; synn your, 4977; sen, (i.) 4954, 4994[5]; sith, (i.) 520, 6909; sithę, 5146, 5171, 5215, 5254; sythe, 5174; sithe, 5107, 5164; sithé ‡ we, 6887; sithęn, (i.) 3980 ‡, 3993 ‡; (ii.) 4006; sithën ‡ that, 4319, 6859; -en I, 5231.

II. Temporal (= *cum*):

sith that, 2354 (-ę C, seth D), 4064 (syn they B, sithë they ? C, sethén thei ? D); sith I, 3627 (syn C, seth D).

III.

gon sithën longë while, 718 (-ë C°, seth ? D); sithën honge, 833 (sythén B, sethyn D, sythę ‡ me C); sethén do, 3086 (sythé C, seth[e] D, sithen B †).

IV. Preposition:

sith that day, 2497 (seth the D; C †); syn mydnyght, 3444[6] (sen B, sin C, tul D).

soone, sone (A.S. *sóna*), 234 (-[e] B, C †), 524 f, 553, 1160 f, 1296 f (D †), 2376 f (soene B), 2395 f, 3185 (D (?)), 3500 (-[ë to] B, -ë ‡ for to D), 3515 f, 4376 f, 4548, 4551 f, 4727 f, 4812 (-[e] B), 5432 (C(?); -[e] B), 5455, 5743 f, 5789 f, 5838 f, 5922, 5935 (D †), 6074 (C(?); -[e] B), 6432 f, 6641 f, 6754 f, 6958 f, 7008 f, 7210 f, 7265 f, 7454 f, 7574[7], 7578 (D ?), 7662 (-[e] B[8]; D †), 7671 f, 8082

---

[1] Read, *sith [that]/thow ?*
[2] Read, *sith the ende ?*
[3] Dele [*that*].
[4] Supply [*that*].
[5] Supply [*To*].
[6] Supply [*in*] in A.
[7] Supply [*for to*] in A.
[8] Or, *write* (*pres. subj.* 3 *sg.*) and *soon se*.

(cf. 1999, 5317 C ‡); soone, sone, 41, 1531 [1], 2693, 2951 [2] (D?), 3410 [3], 4309, 4358, 5938, 8204, etc., etc.; soon as, 2769 (-e CD); [4] soone he, 6657, 7595 ‡ C; -e hope, 3794 (soon B, -e y D); soonë on, 7727 (-e vpon CD); soonẹ, sonẹ, 2954 (soon B),[5] 4368 (-e C^c; D †), 8030 ‡ A (-ë BCD).[6]—eft soones, eft sones, 2553 (-ẹs ‡ D, -ys ‡ aboute? C), 2736 f (eftt sonys C) (: what to don is); eft-sone hym 4843 (-e hem C, -ẹs hem B, wel ‡ sone hym D.

Rhyme-words.—mone, moone *moon* (524, 1160, 2395, 6641), to done (1160, 1296, 2376, 3515, 4376, 4551, 4727, 5789, 6432, 6641, 6754 f, 7008, 7210, 7265, 7454, 7671), bone *boon* (4727, 6958), trone (5743, 5838).

thanne, thenne, than (A.S. þonne), *temporal and illative* [7]; thenne, 409 f BC (thanne A, than D †) (: brenne *subj.* 1 *sg.*), 1295 f (thanne C) (: henne *adv.*), 2638 f (than C, then D) (: renne *inf.*), 3471 f (than C, then D) (: henne *adv.*); thanne, 7790 f (than CD) (: whanne). *Before consonants:* (1) thennẹ, 865 (thannẹ B, than D; C †), 1052 A (than B, tho D); (2) then, 529 (than BD, thannẹ C), 803 (than BD, *om.* ‡ C); (3) thannẹ, 849 (D †), 2000 (than B, tho C; D †), 2247 (than BD) (cf. 2510, 3048, 3474,[8] 4922, 5218, 5496, 5741); (4) than, 221 (thannẹ B), 349 (ʒet ‡ D), 2167 (thannẹ C) (cf. 2461 ‡ D, 2710 ‡ D, 2832, 3347, 5249, 5686, 5693). In the following instances *thanne* (temporal or illative) seems to have two syllables before a word beginning with a consonant,—498 (-[ne] B, -nẹ ‡ D), 2966 (-[ne] B; D †), 7354 (-[ne] BD); than[ne], 7652 (-ne C); cf. 4585 ‡ C, 5138 † C, 6622 ‡ C. *Before vowels:* (1) thannẹ, 1489 (than D) (cf. 2973, 3158, 3255, 3346, 3485, 3718, 4845; (2) than, 874 (thanne BC) (cf. 1435, 1670, 2710, 3658, 3927). *Before* h : thanne he, 4313 ‡ D, 4459 (than B), 4585 (than D, thanne ‡ wolde he C); than hauẹ ye, 1413 (thanne C); than hastow, 4945 (thanne C); thanne hastow, 5301 (than CD).

than = *quam* (A.S. þonne, þon), (i.) 532 (D †), 537, 614, 1226, 2471, 2671, 3014, 3289, 3415, 3873 (thannẹ B), 4065 (thannẹ B), 4825, 5050 (then B, than ‡ is D), 5253, 5257 (C †); (ii.) 1425, 3988 (D †), 4497 (er † A); than he, 819, 3332 (thanne B, as C).

whanne, whan, when (A.S. hwonne); whanne, 2067 (when B, whan D), 3874 (when B, whan C, wher D †), 4001 (when B, whan C), 5355 (when B, whan CD) (cf. also, 71, 1002, 1237, 1672, 1689, 1849, 2095, 2255, 2386, 2577, 3445, 3925, 4001, 4257, 4665,

---

[1] Read *certayn* for *certaynly* in A.   [2] Old-style figures indicate that B has *soon*.
[3] Supply [*to*] in D.   [4] Supply [*I*] in B.
[5] Before *that*. If we read *soonẹ*, we have *neuere how*; if *soone*,—*neuẹre how*.
[6] Dele (*forth*) in A, and read *soonẽ*.
[7] In 2107 A, *than* = *whan* (*whan* CD, *when* B).   [8] Supply [*I*] in A.

4693, 4989, 5790, 5909).—whan (*bef. cons'ts*), 155, 1139 (when B), 2278 (when B), 3386 (when B, whi † C), 3513, 4071 (when B, whannę D), 4801 (cf. also 358, 545, 876, 914, 1369, 2107 (than A), 2185, 2209, 2569, 2669, 2805, 2825, 3036, 3044, 3294, 3418, 3450, 3985, 4043, 4076, 4237, 4243, 4423, 4521, 4624, 4915, 5207, 5482).—when (*bef. cons'ts*), 3195 (whan CD), 5249 (whan CD).

Before vowels both *whanne* (*whenne*) and *whan* (*when*) are found. Thus,—whanne, 85 (when B, whan C †), 4239 (whan B, when E) (cf. 4270, 4321, 4755); whan, 1483 (when B; C †), 1868 (when B) (cf. 2000, 2471, 2474, 3074, 3437, 3698, 4668, 4811); whenne, 404 (whanne C, whens ‡ D); when, 3083 (whan CD). Similarly before *he, here* (poss. sg.), *hem*: whanne 505 (when B, whan D) (cf. 1820, 2630, 5330); whan he, 323 (when B) (cf. 750, 1731, 2941, 3907, 4080, 4634).

Note 1.—*When* is the usual form in B, whether before a vowel or a consonant; but *whan* also occurs in B (as, 155, 3513, 4239, 4801).
Note 2.—No good case of *whannë* (*whennë*) or *whan*[*në*] occurs in the interior of the verse. Apparent cases are to be corrected, usually by the insertion of *that* (cf. 196 AD, 351 AB, 545 C, 1880 A (D ?), 2386 D, 3446 BD (C?), 3925 C, 4624 D (C?). *Whanne* (*whan* CD) occurs once in rhyme, in 7791 (: *thanne*).

therfore, therfor (A.S. þǽre + A.S. fore)[1]; wherfore, wherfor.[1]—therfore, 5661 f, 5699 f (there- B); wherfore, 2496 f (where- C, wherfor D). Before consonants,—therfore, 813 (-for B; C †; therfor ‡ hym (?) D), 855 (-for B)[2], cf. 5662, 7365, etc.; therfor, 17 (-ę B, *om.* † D), 574 (-ę C), 576 (-ę BC), etc.; wherfore, 430 (-for[ë] B, wherefore C, wherfor[ë] D).[3] Before vowels,—therfore, 472 (there- B, therfor D †), 680 (-for BD), 761 (-for D †), cf. 133, 1385, 1480, 3180, 5467, 5702, etc.; therfor, 488 (-e C), etc.; wherfore, 981 (wharfor B, therfore C, therefor D), 1100 (-for BD), 2423 (-for BD, wherefore C), cf. 3676; wher-forë ‡ er, 3123 (-fore BC, wherfor D)[4]; cf. wherfor he, 311 (war for C).

Rhyme-words.—to-fore (-forn A) (2496), byfore (5661, 5699), bore *p.p.* (2496), y-shore *p.p.* (5661).

to-forn,[5] to-fore (cf. by-forn, by-fore); to-forn, (i.) 1381 f (biforne B, before C, byforn D), 1042 (-nę B, -forë ‡ D), 1516 (-nę B), 2448 (-forę C, -for D), 3177, 3691, 4481 f (-ne BC); (ii.) 2077 (-ne B,

---
[1] These words are accented indifferently on the first or the second syllable.
[2] In C supply [*what*]; in B read *be*[*so*]*che*.
[3] BCD omit [*my*] (not necessary to the sense) before *lord*.
[4] But supply [*wol*] in A, and read *wher-fore*.
[5] Commonest in the phrase *God to-forn*.

-for D), 4168 (-ne B, -forn [I] E), 7326 (-ne BD).—to-fore, 2494 f BCD (to-forn † A), 5381 ‡ f C, 6418 ‡ f C.

<small>Rhyme-words.—y-born *p.p.* (1381), sworn(e) *p.p.* (1381), lorn *p.p.* (4481); wherfore (2494), bore *p.p.* (2494) [sore *adv.* (5381), more *adv.* (5381), more *adj. pl.* (6418)].</small>

whanne, whan. See after *thanne, than.*
wherfore, wherfor. See *therfore.*
with-inne¹ (A.S. wið-innan), 1061 f (-yn D), 2462 f (-yn D), 2815 f (her yn D †), 3818 f (-yn D), 4206 f, 4620 f (-in C, -yn D), 6277 f (-in C), 7332, 8023 f; -e, 1108 (-yn D), 1167 (-yn D), 5940 (-in B, that ‡ in C), 6075 (-in D), 7818, 7824 (-in D) (cf. 3443 D); -e here (*sg. poss.*), 1745 (-in BD), 1762² (-in D); -e his, 6837 (-in D)³; -e hym, 7135 (with[in] C).—with-innę the, 267 (-in D), 305 (-yn D), 7544 (-ë nyght BC); -ę tho, 7096 (-ë ȝonë C, -ë yonder D); -ę myn, 8060 (-in D).

<small>Rhyme-words.—bygynne *inf.* (1061, 2462, 2815 (?), 3818), wynne *inf.* (1061, 2462, 4620, 6277), blynne *inf.* (4206), twynne *inf.* (8023), a-twynne *adv.* (6277).
Note.—The form *in-with* is found in *in-with myn*, 4341 (riȝt‡ in D), and *in-with here* (poss. sg.), 7385 (with-innę CD); and this may perhaps be the right reading in some of the cases where the MSS. have *with-innę* or *with-inne.*</small>

with-outen, -owten, wit-outen,⁴ -owten⁵ (A.S. wið-útan), (i.) 1714,⁶ 1799, 1922, 2477, 3308, 3590, 3815, 4105, 5038 (-ë C), 5162 (-ë D), 5787 (-ën(e) D), 6020 (C †), 6303, 7681 (-ë CD), 8035 (-ë C), etc. [Var. CD -yn.] (ii.) 1757, 3077, 3260, 4655, 5066, 5646, 5663 (-ë D), 5733, 6255, 6258, 7127 (-ë ‡ wordis C), 7560, 8166. [Var. CD -yn.] with-outen awayte, 3421 (B †; -oute C; D †); -ęn answere, 5820 (-oute C); withoutęn his, 2365 (-yn C, -out D); -ën here (*sing.*), 5756 (-yn C); -ën ho, 2168 AB; -ën hond, 3030 (-yn CD).
with-oute, -owte, 270 f (-t D), 1321 (-en B), 1696 f (-t D), 2506 (-en B, -yn C), 3076 (-en B, -yn C), 3526 f (-t D), 3587 f, 4703 (-en B)⁷, 4795 (-en B, -yn C, without ‡ (?) D), 5257 (-en B), 5427 (-en B)⁸, 6033 (-en BD, -yn C)⁹, 6430 f, etc.; without[e], 1838 (-en B, -yn C, -out ‡ (?) D); -e, 4827 (-ęn B, -out thassent D)¹⁰, 7142 (-out B,

---

<small>¹ Preposition in 267, 305, 1108, 1167, 1745, 1762, 3443 D, 5940, 6075, 6837, 7096, 7135, 7332, 7818, 7824, 8060.
² *Hire* is dative in ABC (in all of which the line seems to consist of nine syllables), possessive in D. The line needs considering.
³ Supply [*and*] in C.   ⁴ 6020.   ⁵ 3590.
⁶ Old-style figures indicate that D has *without* (which, before consonants, makes the line short by one syllable in the cases in question).
⁷ *without eny* ‡ D.   ⁸ Dele (or slur) *I* in A.
⁹ Read *where*[*with*] in C.   ¹⁰ Supply [*ne*] in AD.</small>

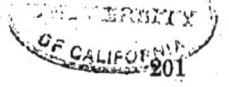

-ęn D)[1]; -e his, 5430 (-ęn B, -yn C†); withoutę the yates, 7541 (ouer † C); without ‡ bothe, 1862 D.

> Rhyme-words.—route *n.* (270, 1696, 6430), route *inf.* (3587), shoute *inf.* (1696), aboute (270, 3526), lowte *inf.* (3526), doute *n.* (6430).
> Note.—It will be seen from the foregoing examples that our MSS. use *with-outĕn* or *with-outĕ* indifferently before a consonant; the reading often varying in the same line. Compare also the following cases, in all of which a consonant follows: (1) (*A has* -ĕn) 361,[2] 2490, 2563, 2856, 3332, 3541, 3998, 4150, 4200, 4583, 5362, 5839, 6363, 6385, 6419, 6900, 7214, 8035[3]; (2) (*A has* -ĕ) 1668, 2651, 2725, 2751, 2974, 4352, 4881, 5326, 6160, 6654, 6751, 7494, 8079. It is to be observed that all the instances of *withoutĕ*, -ĕn, cited are prepositions, except the four in which *with-outĕ* (never -ĕn) occurs at the end of a verse. These last are adverbs.

yfere, ifere (*i. e.* i(n) + fere, dat., cf. A.S. gefér, on geférē), 1237 f, 1253 f, 1995 f, 2122 f, 2201 f, 2334 f, 2351 f, 2562 f, 3073 f, 3115 f, 3357 f, 3588 f, 3660 f, 4554 f, 4689 f, 5452 f, 5866 f, 5868 f, 5995 f, 6016 f, 6096 f, 6114 f, 6706 f, 7176 f, 7216 f, 8134 f.

> Rhyme-words.—chere *n.* (1237, 2351, 3073, 3588, 4554), deere, dere *adj.* (2562, 3115, 5868, 6016, 6114, 6706), here *inf.* (2201, 3588, 7216, 8134), here *hic* (1253, 3357, 3660, 4689, 5366, 5995), matere (1237, 2122, 2334, 3357), manere (4554), fere *companion* (5452), bere *feretrum* (5868), clere *adj. pl.* (6096, 7176), appere *inf.* (1995). [Var. B i-feere, i-fere, yfeere; CD in fere; D yn fere, in fer.]

yore (A.S. géara, L. ʒ(e)are), 6159 f, 6418 f (to-fore ‡ C), 6687 f; of yore, 5381 f (tofore ‡ C, of yoor D), 8097 f (of yoor D); yore ago, 6680 (yoor D).

> Rhyme words.—more *subst.* (6159), *adj. pl.* (6418), no more (6687, 8097), more, eueręmore *adv.* (5381, 8097), sore *adv.* (5381), lore *n.* (6687). [Var. BD yoore; C ʒore.]
> Note 1.—*Down, doun, adown, adoun* (A.S. of-dúne, dúne-stígian, adúne, adún-weard *Chron.* 1083) show no -e (except sometimes -(ę) in D): cf. (i.) (ii.) 110 f, 184 f, 299 f, 359, 1065 f, 1284, 1492 (adowyn B), 1744 f, 2202 f, 2938, 3815, 3921, 4434 f, 4625 f, 4896, 6795 f, 6924 f, 7174, 7222 f, 7368 f, 7386 f, 7675 f, 8013 f, etc., etc.
> Note 2.—*Gruf* in the phrase *fallen gruf* (O.N. falla á grúfu) occurs once: *fil gruf and* 5574, (grof CD).
> Note 3.—For *asunder* (cf. A.S. on-sundron) see 3502 f (a sundyr C, a sundre D), 4181 BE (a sondry A †, a sundir C), 4605 ABE † (asundęry C), 7346 f (a sundir C, a sondr D).
> Rhyme words.—thondre *n.* (-er B, -yr C, -re D), yonder (-re D), wonder *n.* (-ir C, wondr D).

§ 89. To the list in § 88 may be appended: I. *atwixen, -e, bytwyxen, -e, aweye, eke, often, -e, saue;* II. *here, there, where,* and their varieties,—particles in which the form of the termination has been influenced by various analogies (cf. Child, § 72, *b*).

---

[1] Supply [*nat*] in D.   [2] Dele (*ony*) in A and read *with-outĕn lette.*
[3] Cf. also 1820 CD, 1831 ‡ D, 6431 ‡ C.

atwixen, atwixe (cf. by-twyxen), atwixen noon, 6835 (attwexen B, betwixe CD); -e here (sg.), 5483. (See variants under *bytwyxen*.)

aweye (A.S. onweg, aweg), 1208 f (-y D), 2279 f (-y̆ D †), 4977 f, 5019 f, 5544 f (-y A, to dey C, to deye D), 6456 f (-y D), 6820 f (-y CD). [Var. BD awaye; C awoye.] awey̆, away̆, (i.) 572, 2600, 6263 f, 7431 f. [Var. C. awoy.] (Cf. 574 ‡ C, 1195 ‡ C, 1196 ‡ C.)

Rhyme-words.—pleye *inf.* (1208), deye *ind.* 1 *sg.* (1208), seye *inf.* (5019, 5544, 6456), seye *ind.* 1 *sg.* (2279), tweye (2279, 4977[1]), weye (6456), pleye *inf.* (6820), keye *n.* (6820).—day (6263), way (7431), weylawey (7431), may 3 *sg.* (6263).

bytwext. See *by-twyxen*.

by-twyxen, by-twixen, bi-twixen, be-twexen (A.S. betwix, betweox, betwuxt), 417 B (betwexe C, bytwix[e] D, bytwen[e] A), 585 (betwethë C),[2] 1896 (-e C), 3096 B (betwixe C, bytwene A), 3248 betwethe (?) C ‡), 4157 (betwixe C, bitweyne B, bytwix[e] E), 7249 (atwixen B, betwixe CD); -ën hope, 2392 (betwethë C),[3] 6993 (atwixë C, betwen[ë] D), 7570 (betwixë CD); -ën hem, 135 (betwixë C); bytwyxën hem, 7219 (betwethe C, betwixe D)[4]; bytwyxe vs, 5771 (betwixe C, bytwen D); bi-twyxën Orcades, 7334 (betwethë C, betwen[ë] D). [Var. B betwixen, bytwexen, betwyxen.] bytwext vs, 6165 (bytwyxe B, atwixe C, bytwixe D).

eke (A.S. éac, éc, cf. A.S. tó éacan), 2761 f (ëk C) (: bysеche *ind.* 1 *pl.*, bisike B, beseche B), 2918 f (ek C) (: beseche *inf.*, byseke BD, besek C), 4790 f (ek B) (: cheke *n.*: byseche *inf.*, -seke BD, beseke C), 6296 f (ek C) (: beseche *ind.* 1 *sg.*, beseke BD); ek, 3571 f (eke BCD) (: bysek *ind.* 1 *sg.*, biseke B, beseche C, byseke D); ekę, 475 (ek C, echę D), 1720 (ek BC), 4226 AE (ek BC), etc.; ek, (i.) 32 (om. † D), 1827 (ekę D), etc.

ofte (A.S. oft), 135 f (-t D), 196 f,[5] 212 (-en B, -[e] ? D), 625 (-en C, -yn D), 912 f (-t D), 940 f, 1145 (om. † D), 2114 f, 2319 (-en B, -e (?) C, om. † D), 2406, 2466, 3127, 3286 f, 3511 f (-yn † C), 4091 f, 4361 (-[e] B), 4479 f, 4485 (oft to B, al day CD), 4799,[6] 4876 (-[e] B, offte D), 5204 f (-t B), 5793 C, 5828 C, 5881 f, 6351 B, 6373 f, 6708 f, 6980 f (-t B), 7030 C (ofte a wold a = oftë wolde he D, ost A, oost B), 7945 (-t ‡ and B); oftë tyme,[7] 913 (-[e] D), 1850 (-y̆n C), 1877, 3971 (-yn C; B †), 5823 (-[e] B), 7939 (-[e] B), 7946 (-[e] B), 8121 (-[e] B); oft[e] tyme, 7172 (-e CD); ofte, cf.

---

[1] *twey(n)e* A.
[2] Old-style figures indicate that D reads *by-twix*[e].
[3] In D read *des[es]peraunce*.
[4] In D read *Troy*[e].
[5] Old-style figures indicate that B and D have *oft*[e].
[6] Supply [*hem*] in C.
[7] Variants of *tyme* not registered, see *tyme*, § 2, p. 3.

§ 89.] *of Chaucer's Troilus.* 203

344, 646, 740, 1782, 1876, 2419, 3168, 3903, 4561, 5164, 5166, 5400, 5828, 6037, 6351, 7052, 7078, 7589, 7685, 7931[1]; ofte he, 506 (-t B, offte D), 4579,[2] 6100 (-t B, -ë ‡ pitously C, -ę † ful D), 6969 (-t B); -e his, 445; 2343 (eft † C), 3976 (-t B), 4625 (-t B; D †); oftë hastow, 904 (-en B, -[ë] C); oftę, 346 (-t BD), 137 ‡ A (-t ‡ (?) D), 139 † A, 4395 ‡ D, 5828 D (cf. 3171 † D, 4561 ‡ D); oftę tymę, 5986 (oft B, oftyn ‡ there C, ofte ther D).

    Rhyme-words.—softe *adj. and adv.* (135, 196, 912, 940, 2114, 3286, 3511, 4091, 4479, 5204, 5881, 6708, 6980), on lofte, a-lofte, o lofte (135, 940, 3511, 5881, 6373, 6708).

often as, 3143 (-t D); -en herę-byforn, 3144; -en here (*eam*), 5387 (-[en] B, -ë D; C †); -en harme, 333 (-ë C, -[ë] D).—often for, 2331 (-e C, -[e] D); -en myght[e], 3351 (-[e] ‡ (?) D; C †); -en peyne, 4058 (-e CD, oft ‡ peynës (?) B); -en gan, 5024 (offte D, soft † B); -en was, 7465 (-[e] B, -e CD); -en seyde, 583 (-e C, -[e] D) (cf. 625); -en se, 4056 (-[e]. B); oftyn ‡ tyme, 6833 C; oftyn as, 3168 C. (Cf. 1876 ‡ C, 2419 ‡ C.) [Var. CD -yn.]

saue (O. Fr. sauf), -e, 395 (-ę ‡ that (?) D), 1241 (D ?), 1825, 3351 (C †, D †), 3632, 3729 (saf D), 4617[3], 4754, 7040, 8167, 8168; -e here (*pass. sg.*), 7176 (saf C); -e his, 1710 (saf C)[4], 6573; sauę Troylus, 2489. Cf. Myn honour sauf I wol, etc., 3001 (sauyn † C, savë ‡ I D).

here (=hic) (A.S. hér), 121 f, 292 f, 399 f, 1124 f, 1183 f (heere B), 1252 f (her D), 1337 f, 1577 f, 1680 f, 2058 f, 2189 f, 2714 f, 2729 f, 2836 f, 3355 f, 3483 f, 3489 f, 3661 f, 3678 f, 3790 f, 4053 f, 4149 f, 4690 f (heere B), 4970 f, 5102 f, 5205 f, 5558 f (heere B), 5582 f (heere B, her D), 5865 f (yfere † A, her D), 5870 ‡ C, 5976 f, 5993 f (her D), 6212 f (her D), 6297 f (her D), 6829 f BCD (there ‡ A), 7108 f (her D), 7361 f (her D), 7538 f. [1281 f D ‡ (see *there*), 4990 f D ‡ (see *there*).[5]]

    Rhyme-words.—chere *n.* (121, 292, 1124, 3483, 6297), manere (292, 1124, 3678, 5582), matere (1577, 2714, 3355, 4149, 7108, 7361), preyere (3483, 6297), here *inf.* (121, 399, 2189, 2714, 2836, 5205, 6829), yhere *inf.* (5976), lere *inf.* (2729, 5102), ye me lere *imv. or subj.* (1183), yfere *adv.* (1252, 3355, 3661, 4690, 5865, 5870 ‡ C, 5993), dere *adj. sg.* (1337, 1577, 1680, 2058, 2189, 3489 (drede † A), 3790, 4053, 4149, 4970, 5205, 5558, 5870 ‡ C, 5976, 6829), clere *adj. sg. and pl.* (6212, 7361), of fern[e] yere (7538).

[1] In most of these cases B reads *oft*; so sometimes D, and once, at least, C (7931).
[2] Old-style figures indicate that BD have *oft* (for *ofte*).
[3] In D read [y]dred.   [4] In D supply [*ful*].
[5] For the rhymes of these two lines see under *there*.

204 Observations on the Language [§ 89.

Before consonants *here* apocopates its -e, which, however, is regularly written except sometimes in D. For *here* (var. B heere; D her), cf. 868, 1054, 1096 (A †), 1115, 1188, 1282, 1409, 1462, 1515, 1728, 2076, 2208 (hire B), 2338, 2815 (D?), 3235, 3953, 4303 (hire C), 4844, 4902, 5139. Cf. also, here byforn, 2356 f,[1] 5910 f (there C, her D); here-to, 3362 B (herto CD, here ‡ myghte A); hertò, 5734 f BD (thertò A); here with al, 6441 CD (ther-with-al AB). For *here*, cf. 432, 1406, 1525, 1569, 2405, 2688, 2814, 2990, 3341, 3476; for *here* in compounds (*here after*, and the like), cf. 938, 3377, 3515, 4805; for *her* in such compounds (the second member beginning with a vowel), cf. 984, 1094 D, 1193, 3407; for here before *his*, *hym*, *haue*, cf. 469, 1544, 4415 A.

Instances of *herë* in the body of a verse are at any rate very rare. The strongest case is: "Intendestow that we shul *here* bleue," 6841 AB (but: here beleue C, her be-leue D)[2] where *here* is emphatic (or at any rate has the ictus). In the following apparent cases comparison of MSS. shows a better reading: 3362 A (*l.* here-to), 5594 A (*l.* hyder), 6826 C.

there (A.S. þǽr, þér), 1281 f (thare B, here D), 2095 f, 3366 f (thare B), 3411 f, 3428 f, 3469 f, 3593 f, 4162 f, 4990 f (here D), 5305 f (ther D), 5359 f (ther D), 6024 f (ther D), 6146 f (theere B), 6186 f (ther D), 6829 f ‡ (here BCD)[3], 7242 f (ther D), 7273 f (ther D), 7543 f (ther D), 7721 f (ther D).

Rhyme-words.—ere, eere *n.* (1281, 3593, 5305), gere *n.* (2095, 6186), were *ind.* 2 *sg.* (4162), *ind.* 3 *pl.* (3428, 3469, 7543), *subj.* 1 *sg.* (4990), *subj.* 3 *sg.* (2095, 3366, 3411, 5359, 6024, 7242, 7721), fere *n.* (3411, 3428, 3469, 3593, 4162, 6024, 7273), fere *inf.* (6146), ellys where (5359, 6186), tere *n.* 7242, 7543).

there, 3993 (ther BD); cf. 4049, 4198, 4227, 4368, 4570, 4658, 5111, 5760, 5761, 6022, 7033, 7455, etc.—ther, (i.) 4483 (-e C), 5606 (-e BC), 5614 (-e D); cf. 5505, 5630, 5649, 5685, 5843, 5859, 6021, 6156, 6308, 6316, 6509, 6532, 7085, 7609, etc.; ter mot, 5698 A (ther BD).

In compounds before consonants: thèrby, 447 (tharby B); therbỳ, 383 f, 5682 f; thèrfore, 472 (there-fore B, therfor D †); therfòre, 133 (therfor D); cf. for further examples, 17, 243, 247, 266, 274, 488, 574, 576, 627 f, 680, 761, 813, 855, 1161, 1251 f, 1385, 1434, 1480, 1576, 2094, 2137, 2935, 3180, 3378, 4232, 5467, 5662, 5702, 5734 f, 7365, etc., etc.

[1] See also § 88, under *byforn*.
[2] Cp. John's appear to agree with A, but Hl. 2392 has *beleuè*.
[3] For the rhymes see under *here*, which is the right reading.

there, 273 (ther BD); cf. 892, 1960, 2604 (thare B), 3247, 3406, 3415, 3510, 4902, 5048, etc.; ther, (ii.) 5243 AB (ther but D; C ‡) (cf. 7341).—there he, 1282 (thar B, that † C) (cf. 1418); there haue (*pres. ind.* 2 *pl.*), 3042 (ther B); ther helpeth, 5962 (-e CD). In compounds in which the second member begins with a vowel *ther* is usual: thus, ther-after, 5208; ther-inne, 5447 f (therin CD); cf. 333, 1354, 1454,[1] 1703, 2282, 4474 f; there-vp-on, 4805 C.

The strongest cases of dissyllabic *therë* are: That he cam *therë* ‖ and that he was born, 3915 (ther[ë] B, therë or CD)[2], and And *ther*[e] lat vs speken of oure wo, 5906 (therë C).[3] In 604 † C, 3420 A (*l.* therof), 5357 C (*l.* thennes), 6737 C (*l.* therof); comparison of MSS. affords a corrected reading.

> Note.—*ner* (= *ne ther* ?) occurs in 1262 A, but is perhaps merely a slip of the pen for *þer*.

where (A.S. hwǽr, hwér), 4239 f (whare B), 6582 f (wher D); euery where, 4724 f; ony where, 3534 f; ellys where, elles where, 5360 f (ellis wher D), 6183 f (ellis wher D), 7407 f (elles wher D).

> Rhyme-words.—feere *n.* (4239), ere *n.* (4724), gere *n.* (6183), tere *n.* (6582, 7407), were *ind.* 3 *pl.* (3534, 4239, 6582), *subj.* 3 *sg.* (5360), there (5360, 6183).

wher, (i.) 357 (-e [that] C), 1880 (-e C) (cf. 1291 A, 3874 ‡ D, 5795); no where, 4302 (no wher B, nower C, nowherë ‡ D); and in compounds of *wher* in which the second member begins with a consonant (as, *wher-so, wherby, wherfor*), cf. 311 (whefor A, war for C), 409 (where-to B), 430, 436, 981, 1100, 1387 f, 2423, 2496 f, 3123 (A ?), 3620, 3676, 5774 (whar-with B).

where, 3501 (whare C, wher D); wydë where, 3246 (wher CD); wher, (ii.) 1164 (-e B); where as, 1357 C (wher D, there A, ther B); wher as, 3358 BD (-e C, there A). In composition (*wher-on*, etc.): wher-on, 1776; where-of, 4489 (wherof BCD).—where he, 1285 (wher BD); wher he, 1461 (-e BC), 2236 (-e C); wher hym, 1291 BD (-e C, wher that A), 2034 (-e C); where hastow, 5158 (wher BD); wher hastow, 276 (-e BC); no wher hool, 954.

There are no cases of *wherë*. All apparent cases yield to comparison of MSS., as in 357 C (wherë ‡ hem), 1291 C (wherë hym), 1932 A, 4302 D.

> Note.—From a comparison of the rhyme-lists to *here, there,* and *where* (which are complete), it will be seen that these fall into two classes which do not cross: (*a*) rhymes to *here* and (*b*) rhymes to *there, where*. A

---

[1] Seems to be a 9-syl. verse.
[2] But the reading of Cp. is certainly right: *there* ‖ *and that that.*
[3] No note in Mr. Austin's collation.

striking instance of the difference in the sound of (*a*) and (*b*) is shown by 6581-5, where, the order of rhymes being *ababb*, the rhyme-words are: *dere, where, clere, were* (erant), *tere* (*n.*).

§ 90. *Ever* and *never* (A.S. *æfre, næfre*) are (as a rule) dissyllabic before consonants and monosyllabic before vowels and weak *h*.

The usual spelling, whether before vowels or consonants, is *euere, neuere* in ABC (and so often in D); but *euer* and *neuer* are not uncommon in BD, and *euer* is found in C 3605, *neuer* in A 2843, C 1362.

- - For the spelling *euer*, see B, 9, 418, 2299, 2494, 2681, 4243, 4268, 5772, 6785, 7892; for *neuer*, see B 294, 501, 534, 675, 910, 970, 3199. There are some petty variants: as, *nevir* (4942 D), *ewere* (7892 C), *evyr* (6025 D).

I. Before consonants both words are regularly dissyllabic: cf. for *euere*, 418, 584, 638, 1151, 1465, 1864, 1915, 1925, 1958, 2117, 2656, 3086, 3121, 3354, 3473, 3519, 3556, 3653, 4021, 4243, 4268, 4440, 4603, 4681, 4942, 4946, 4966, 5049, 5161, 5179, 5772, 5984, 6082, 6126, 6387, 6405, 6593, 6781, 7026, 7181, 7418, 7502, 7691, 7719, 7892, 8096.

For *neuere*, cf. 37, 294, 534, 539, 586, 639, 641, 675, 774, 910, 959, 1219, 1228, 1386, 1653, 1671, 1813, 2316, 2354, 2498, 2545, 2692, 2968, 3093, 3199, 3229, 3331, 3409, 3427, 3626, 3706, 3711, 3712, 3717, 4088, 4503, 4550, 4869, 4961, 5002, 5059, 5135, 5521, 5858, 5862, 6022, 6142, 6486, 6788, 7139, 7143, 7187, 7238, 7341, 7724, 8045. So before consonant *y* in the phrases *euere yet, neuere yet*: cf., for *euere yet*, 1325, 2080, 3135 AB, 7123; for *neuere yet*, cf. 657, 812, 1278, 1916, 3161, 3548, 3682, 3896, 4288, 4447, 7991.

II. Before a vowel both words are regularly reduced to one syllable by slurring: cf., for *euere*, 9, 318, 513, 541, 816, 1290, 1633, 2229, 2238, 2299, 2494, 2681, 4685, 5749, 6025, 6264, 6306, 6785, 6814, 7119, 7439, 7745, 8224. For *neuere*, cf. 501, 622, 1329, 1362, 1522, 1574, 1643, 2183, 3000, 3236, 3550, 3605 (neuere thoughte A), 4356, 4375, 5250, 6243, 6518, 6804, 7198.

III. Before *he* and *his* the same slur takes place as before a vowel: cf., for *euere*, 541 ‡ C, 2958, 5095, 6799 (C †), 7136, 7534; for *neuere*, cf. 1946, 4188.

But before other *h*'s, the dissyllabic pronunciation seems to be the rule: thus, euère haue (*subj.* 1 *sg.*), 1225 (euer B); neuère han (*inf.*), 3414 BC (neuère the AD); euere help, 1040 D ‡; neuère

[§ 90.] *of Chaucer's Troilus.* 207

how, 2954;[1] neuëre half, 4492; neuëre herte, 7746 AC (-ẽr D).
Cf., however, neuere haue (*inf.*), 6104 AB (neuëre haue C, -er? D ‡);
neuere han (*inf.*), 900 B (neuere a A; C †).

> Note 1. The only case of *ever* or *never* in rhyme is 7442-4,—*neuere*, 7742 f
> (-er D): *euere*, 7444 f (-er D).
> Note 2.—The following lines in which there are various readings (some
> MSS. following the word with a vowel, others with a consonant), may
> be compared, but are of little utility (presenting no instances which
> transgress the general rule, except for a manifest corruption or two): (1)
> for *euere*, cf. 236, 787, 1205, 5461, 6807, 7003, 7305; (2) for *neuere*, cf.
> 1755, 3605, 5101, 6317, 6528, 6811.

The rule, then, is clear enough. *Euere* and *neuere* are dissyllabic
before consonants; monosyllabic before vowels. This is the enun-
ciated (as to *euer*) by ten Brink, *Compleynte to Pite*, p. 176, n. to
v. 33, who indeed makes it so stringent that he changes *euer* to *ay*
in that verse. It seems doubtful, however, if the present state of
our knowledge allows us to emend in this way (and this is admitted
by ten Brink, *Ch's. Spr. u. Versk.*, § 263). The *Troilus* contains
some cases which seem to show that Chaucer allowed both *euere* and
neuere to count for a single syllable before consonants. I give the
sure, or tolerably sure, cases first:

> Quod Troylus for al that *euere ye* konne, 776.
> To ben hire helpe yn al that *euere they* myghten, 2709 (*om.* † D).
> As *euere she* was shal I fynde yn som route, 5065 (As she eüyr was D).
> She wolde come as soone as *euere she* myghte, 6874 (euer. D).
> Nas *neuere yet* thing seyn to ben presed derre, 174 (B †; -ẹr C, -ẽrẹ ‡
> seyn D).
> So hyd it wel I telle it *neuere to* mo, 613 (neuer D).
> Were hise nayles poynted *neuere so* sharpe, 2119.
> Now goode nece be it *neuere so* lyte, 2288 (-er B).
> For she was wys and louede hym *neuere the* lasse (not = natheles), 2928
> (neuer C; D †).
> To knowe of this ye were it *neuere so* lite, 7653 (D *om.* ye; neuer D).
> Cf. Be she *neuere so* faire or (ne so C) wel ishape (schape C), 3253 (no note
> in Austin).

Cases that are easily emended by comparison of MSS. are: (1) for
euere, 897 BC, 3316 BD, 4620 C, 7420 C; (2) for *neuere*, 739
BC (but perh. BC are right), 883 C, 1655 A, 2461 D, 7056 A,
7356 C, 7791 C; and some cases of *neuere the les* in C (as, 170 C,
750 C, 916 C) where *natheles* is the correct reading. Very doubtful
is 1144; and one does not like to dogmatize on 3253 or 4406.

Such of the above cases as are certain (for it will be observed that
emendation to *ay* is impossible in the four cases 776, 2709, 5065,
6874, and no emendation for *neuere* can be devised) seem sufficient
to show that ten Brink's rule is not rigid.

---

[1] That is, if we read *sonẹ* (*soon* B) *that*. If we read *sonĕ that*, we have *ncuẹre how*.

On the other hand in a few cases the dissyllabic forms are found before vowels. Thus,—

God helpę me so I neuere other mente, 1449.
Fro this forth shal I neuére eten bred, 1529.
And neuere other creature serue, 5110 (neuer D).
The obseruaunce euere yn youre absence, 5445 (C †, euer D).
Less secure are 897 AD, 4763 BD[1]; and certainly to be emended (as comparison of MSS. easily allows) are 3103 D, 3146 C, 6816 C.[2]
Similarly euëre hıs, 6799 C † and neuëre his, 4181 C‡, are to be corrected.

Note 3.—Such monstrosities as euerĕ and neuĕrĕ, sometimes perpetrated by this or that scribe, mean nothing, of course, and are easily corrected by comparison of MSS. (cf. e.g. the various readings in 2525, 2623, 3234).

§ 91. The following particles end in the *Troilus* sometimes or always in -*es*, -*s* (Child, § 73). This is sometimes an A.S. -*es*, sometimes a formation by analogy.

(i.) *ayens* (*ayeyns*, *ayen*, *agayn*, *afornyeyn*), *elles*, *nedes*, *to medes*, *towardes* (etc.), *vnnethes*; (ii.) *hennes* (*henne*, *hens*), *thennes*, *whennes*; (iii.) *ones* (*nones*), *twyes*, *thries* (*thrie*); (iv.) *alweyes* (*alweys*, *alwey*), *other weyes*, *amonges* (*among*), *togederes* (*to-gedre*); (v.) *algates* (*algate*), *ascaunces*, *certes*. In the following list the examples cited occur before a consonant (not *h*) unless there is a note to the contrary.

afornyeyn (A.S. foran, on-gægnes), afòrn yeyn vs, 2273 (a-for-ʒeynęs B, aforn [ ] C, aforyens D). (Cf. *byforn*.)

algates (cf. O.N. alla gǫtu, *adverbial acc.*), algàtes hem, 2866 (-is D); algàte, 2049 (-ę ‡ D), 2754 CD, 7434.

alweyęs, (cf. A.S. ealne weg, *adverbial acc.*), alweyęs arise, 2754 A (alwaȳes B, algate CD); alweȳs a, 6415 (alweyęs B, alwoȳ C, aH-yeȳ D). (Cf. weyes.)

àlwey, (i.) 782, 1403 (D †),[3] 1468 (-oȳ C, -eȳ D), 3084, 4477, 4942 CD (èuëre AB), 6505; àlwey here (*hic*), 3661 AB (cf. 1818 ‡ B); àlwey, (ii.) 1122, 1803. alwèy (i.), 1847, 2437 B (A ? C ?; àlwey C; D †), 5618 f; alweȳ hym, 2169 (àlwey D ‡). [Var. B álway; C alwoy; D alwei.] (Cf. alwaȳ, 6288 f C †; àlwoy ‡ his, 3328 C.)

amonges (A.S. ongemang, onmang), (i.) 7835 (omanges B, among[e] C); (ii.) 893 (amangë B, among[ë] C, almong D ‡), 2260 (-è B, -is C, -[is] D), 3700 (-is CD), 6614 (omanges B, amongis C, amongë D); among[ës] al, 4765 AD (-e B).

among, 1970 f (-e B) (: song *n*. (-ę BC)), 3110, 3702 (-ę B), 4658 f

---
[1] Where A seems to have two light syllables before the caesura : neuĕrĕ ‖ yif.
[2] So probably 7807 A. In 3327 read èuęre ylỳk[ę́].
[3] Supply [his] in C.

(: song n. (-e B)), 4727 (omangę B), 6148 (omangę B, amongę D), 7051 (-ę D, omangę B), 7944 (-ę D, omangę B); among (*before vowels*), 6488 (-e D, amang B, amongis C), 7911 (-e D,[1] amange B); among his, 5037 (amang B); among hem, 5359 (-e D, amange B, amongis C).

ascaùnces (etym. dub.), 205 (asscauunis C, askauns D), 292 (aschaunis C,[2] askauns D [3]).[4]

ayèns, ayeỳns, agaỳns, ayèn, (A.S. on-gægnes, on-gægn).

I. As preposition:

(*a*) *Before consonants*,—(1) ayèns, 603,[5] 1316 (aʒenis B, ayen D), 1561 (aʒeynist B, aʒen C), 2142 (aʒeyn B). [Var. B aʒeins; CD aʒens.] (2) ayeỳns, 3831 (aʒenis B, aʒenỳs (?) C ‡, ayens (?) D ‡). (3) ayèn, 2005 (aʒein B, aʒen CD), 5029 (aʒein B, aʒen C, ayenst D). Cf. here ayèns, 2465 (aʒenis B, aʒens C).

(*b*) *Before vowels*,—ayèn, 4837 (aʒeyn B, aʒen C); ayeỳns, 2499 (aʒeins B, aʒens C, ayens D); afòrn yeyn vs, 2273 (a-forʒeynęs B, aforn † C, a foryens D). Cf. ther ayènis, 1454 (aʒeyn B, aʒen C, ayens D).[6]

(*c*) *Before h*,—agayns his, 4362 (aʒeyns B, aʒen C, aʒens D); ayèns hire (*poss. sg.*), 5175 (aʒeyns B, aʒens C).

II. As adverb.

(i.) ayèn, 1476 (certeyn ‡ B), 1606,[7] 1694, 3061 f, 4425, 6972 (àyen ‡ D), 7277, 7964 [8] (cf. 5980 f, 6588 f, 6848 f, 7373 f, 7493 f, 7661 f); agaỳn, 3495 f (-e BC, ayen D), 5665 f (ageyne D); ayeyn, 7360 f (aʒeynne B, aʒeyn C, ayen D). (ii.) ayèn his, 280; agaỳn hym, 1533 B (ayen D; hym àgayn by A [9]). [Var. B aʒeyn, aʒein; C aʒeyn, ageyn, ageyne, aʒein, aʒen, aʒyn, aʒin; D aʒen.] ayènward, 3592 (aʒeynward B, aʒyn- C), 6243 (aʒin- C, aʒeynwardę B, *om.* † D).

Rhyme-words.—certaỳn (5665, 7493), seyn *ind.* 3 *pl.* (5665), seyn *inf.* (5980, 6848, 7373, 7661), seyn *p.p.* (3061), sleyn *p.p.* (6588), fayn (3061, 3495, 5980, 6848, 7358, 7373), rayn *n.* (3495).

certes (O. Fr. certes), (i.) 572, 773 (D †), 1618, 4108 f (: desertes *pl*), 4138, 5652, 5687; (ii.) 3651, 4320. [Var. BC certys; CD certis; C sertis, sertys.]

---

[1] Supply [*the*] in D.   [2] Supply [*what*] in C.
[3] If the reading of D were to be kept, both these lines would consist of nine syllables, and we should have to accent *àskauns*.
[4] In 292 *ascaunces* translates Boccaccio's *quasi dicesse*.
[5] Perhaps 9-syl. Supply [*the*] in C.   [6] 9-syl.
[7] Supply [*now*] in CD.   [8] Supply [*ne*] in ACD.
[9] Transpose, and read *agaỳn*.

elles, ellys, ellis (A.S. elles), (i.) (ii.) 345,[1] 688, 728, 948, 972, 1564, 1660, 2160, 2237,[2] 2775,[3] 3408, 3433, 3661, 3811 (D †), 3933,[4] 3996, 4183, 4186 (om. † C), 4204,[5] 4268,[6] 4353 (C ?), 4622 (om. ‡ D), 5085, 5718, 5729,[7] 5931, 7740 f (cf. 1501 C ‡, 5992, 5999, 6418, 6701, 7033, 7067, 7407, 7519, 7664, 7844, 8160). [Var. C ell (= ellis).]—elles-where, ellys-where, ellis-where, 5360 f, 6138 f, 7612, 7681. [Var. C ell (= ellis).]

    Rhyme-words.—wellys pl. (7740), helle ys (7740).
    Note.—I do not think a good case of *elles* (monosyllable) occurs (cf. 371, 3517 D, 4268 E, 4353 C).

hennes, henne (A.S. heonon, L.W.S. heonone); hennes, 4679 (-nis D), 7624 (henys ‡ C, hens ‡ D); hen[ne]s, 3009, 6766, 6970, 7016 (hens ‡ (?) D), 7254 (hennes D), 7258, 8080 (*leaf gone in* C)[8]; hen[ne]s hye, 6852 (hennes B, henys C)[9]; hens away, 572 (henne B, hene C); hens (*before consonants*), 574 ‡ D, 4267 A ‡ (hennës B, henys C, hen[ne]s E), 7220 ‡ D (*l.* he).—henne, 1294 f (: thenne), 3472 f (hende † B, hen CD) (: thenne), 5908 f (: brenne *inf.*).

medes, in *to medes* (A.S. tó médes, Siev. § 320), Myself *to medes* wole the lettre sowe, 2286 (Myn seluen † the medis C, My self † the medis D).

nedes, nede (A.S. néde, níede, nédes, níedes); nedes, 1524 (nede C), 3458 (nedes (?) A), 4004, 4362, 4551 (D †), 6015, 6681 (C ‡ D ‡), 7715,[10] 8025, cf. 5277 ‡ C. [Var. CD nedis.]—nede, 1756 f (: drede *n.*); nede, 4129 (nedis C), 6261 (C †; nedes ‡ D).

nones. See *ones*.

ones, onys (A.S. ǽne, *Pet. Chron.* ánes), 472 (D †), 549[11] (om. ‡ D),[12] 792, 2742, 4429, 4499 (D †), 6129, 6933, 6934, 7402; onys haue, 1566[13];—at ones, at onys, 90 f, 804 f, 2024 f, 2468 f, 2708 (D †),[14] 3192 (-es ‡ thei D), 4845 f, 5503 f, 6404 (D †), 6406; at ones er, 2961 (-ys or CD). [Var. BD oones; CD onis; B atonees.[15]]

    Rhyme-words.—bones *pl.* (90, 804), stones *pl.* (2024, 2468), the nones, nonys (2468, 4845), non is (5503).

for the nones, nonys, 561, 2466 f, 4847 f, 5090. [Var. B noones.]

other weyes. See *weyes*.

thennes (A.S. þanon), 3987 (thennë C, thennë D), 5396 (then[ne]s CD);

---

[1] D has *for good* ‡.   [2] Supply [*that*] in D, and read *liue* for *dye*.
[3] A is defective. Hiatus in D.   [4] Supply [*of*] in C.   [5] Supply [*that*] in C.
[6] *elles* (?) E.   [7] Supply [*it*] in B; l. [*co*]*me* in D.
[8] In these cases (3009-8080), except when otherwise noted, B reads *hennes*, C *henys*, D *hen[ne]s*.   [9] Supply [*if*] in D.   [10] Supply [*me*] in D.
[11] Old-style figures indicate that a vowel follows.   [12] Supply [*in*] in B.
[13] Supply [*haue*] in B.   [14] 9-syl.
[15] As to the pronunciation of *atones*, cf. the division *a-tonys* in C 2024.

§ 91.] *of Chaucer's Troilus.* 211

then[ne]s, 5357 (tennes B, theré ‡ B, thense *dissyl.* D), 6924 (tennes B), 7034 (thennes B, thenys C), 7143 (thennes B), 7248 (thennes B, thens ‡ D), 8177 (thennes B). [then[ne]s ‡ wolde he, 6839 C.]

thriës, thríe, thrye (A.S. þríwa); thries hadde, 6372 (cf. 2484 ‡ D); thrie, thryc, 1174 f (thry D), 1548 f (threye B), 2370 f.

Rhyme-words.—companye (1174), iupartie (1548), folye (2370), yn hye (1174), lye *mentior* (2370).

togedęres, togedre (A.S. æt-, tó-gædre), togedęres euere, 5984 (-ġidęres B, -gedir D, -gederę d[w]elle C); to-gedre[1] so, (to-giderę B, to-gederę C, to-gider D).[2]

to medes. See *medes.*

towàrdęs (A.S. tó-weardes), etc.; towardes, (i.) 523[3]; (ii.) t. hire, 2307; t. hym, 6080. [Var. BCD towardis; C -ys.] towàrd, (i.) 5017 (-ę BD), 6054 (-ę B, -ęs D; C †), 7004 (-ę B); to Troyewàrdes and, 59 (troy[e] wardis D); to meward shal, 6328 (-ę BD).—thèderwàrdęs ‡ gan, 2335 (thiderward B, thedirward C, thidirward D)[4]; cf. whedirwàrdés, 4944 D (wheder A, whedir(e) B, whedyr C); vpwàrdis ‡ at, 3047 D; her-àftirwàrdis ‡ for, 984 D (her afterward A, here efterwardę B, here aftyrward C), cf. 6193, 7291.[5]

Note.—Other words in *-ward*[6] are: ayènward, 3592, 5689, 6243; bàkward(e), 6215; *downward*, 1991, 2790, 6211; *èstward*, 4261 BE, 6640; *hòmward*,— 2388, 3463, 6845, 7545; *ınward*, 2810, 2817; *oùtward*, 2789; *ȕpward*, *ȕpwàrd*, 2913, 3047, 5821, 7471, 7723.

twyës (A.S. twíwa, *Chron.* 1120 twiges), 2484 (thriés ‡ D), 2940 (D ‡), 6460 (twiis C),[7] 6760 (twye B), 7252. [Var. BCD twies; B tweyes; C twiȝis, twyis.]

vnnèthes, vnèthes (A.S. unéaðe), 301 (-ë (?) C, -is D),[8] 1651 (-is D, onnethis C), 4911 (-è C, -is D). (Cf. vnnethe, § 82.)

-wardęs, -ward. See *to-wardes.*

weyes. He feleth other weyes dar I leye, 4500 (otherę wayes B, otherę woyis C, other-wise D). (Cf. alweyes, algates.)

whennes (A.S. hwanon), 408 (whenys C †, when[ne]s D); when[ne]s, 402 (whennes B, whennys C, when[ne]s D).[9]—whens ‡ euery, 404 D (whenne AB, whanne C).

[1] Disyllable.   [2] Supply [*me*] or [*I*] in D.
[3] Read a[*l*]s[o] in D.   [4] Read *soft*[*e*]*ly* in A; dele (*he*) in D.
[5] *Afterward* ‡ *ros*, 4261 A (*aftyrward* ‡ C, *estward* BE).
[6] Variants not noted, but no MS. has *-es*, *-is*, in the cases cited. In some MSS., however, -e is at times written, though never sounded. In this note no distinction is made as to whether vowel or consonant follows.
[7] Dele (*he*) in B. In C, dele (*be-*) and (*&*); then read *twiis*.
[8] Supply [*how*] in C. ("A later *to* stuck in." Furnivall.)
[9] In both 402 and 408 we may reduce *whennes* to one syllable by reading *cometh* instead of *comęth*.

VERBS.

§ 92. Present Indicative.—The First Person Singular of the Present Indicative ends regularly in -e (Child, § 48; ten Brink, § 184). Thus,—

I. In rhyme:

beseche, byseche, 855 f (be[se]che B) (: leche *n*.), 2505 f (: speche); cf. 1331 f, 3235 f, 3597 f, 4178 f, 5116 f, 6749 f, 7492 f, 7972 f; be[se]che, 5811 f (biseche B, beseche C, besheche D) (: speche); beseche, 6294 f (beseke BD) (: eke *adv*.); bysek[e], 3573 f (biseke B, beseche C, byseke D) (: ék *adv*. A, eke BCD).

defende, 2818 f (: amende *subj*. 3 *sg*. : sende *pret. ind*. 3 *sg*.).

defyne, 5052 f (: ruyne *n*. : deuyne *inf*.).

desire, 6954 f (: ire).

deuyse, 3277 f (: seruyse), 4921 f (: suffise *inf*.).

directe, 8219 f (: corecte *inf*.).

dye, 420 f (deye AC) (: maladye); cf. til I dye, 5061 f (deye C, dey D) (: éye); til that I dye, 6319 f (deye BC^c, dey D) (: ywrye *p p*. : eye); cf. also 4449 f, 5106 f.

gesse, 989 f (: goodnesse : wikkednesse), 1803 f (: dronkenesse : distresse).

grete (A.S. grétan), 4100 f (: the swete : planete).

herye, 3793 f (herie CD) (: merye *pred. pl*.).

hope, 932 f (: drope *n*.).

leue (*credo*), 993 f (: greue *inf*.), 4743 f (: acheue *inf*. : leue *adj. pl*.).

leye, 1046 f (ley D) (: seye *inf*.).

loue, 927 f (: loue *n*.), 1935 f (: loue *n*.).

lye (*mentior*), 2368 f (: thrye : folye); cf. 1385 f (: eye).

mene, 1666 f (: clene *pred. sg*.).

mete (A.S. métan), 4186 f (: swete *voc*.).

pace, 5467 f (pase C) (: deface *inf*.).

recomaunde, 7777 f (: comaunde *inf*.).

rede (*lego*), 159 f (: mede *pratum* : rede *adj. pl*.).

rede (*moneo*), 258 f (: lede *inf*.).

requere, 1443 f (-ire CD) (: chere *n*.).

resigne, 432 f (resyne C^c) (: digne : benygne).

sacrefise, 6786 f (: aryse *inf*.).

sayle, 7004 f (: bewayle *inf*. : fayle *subj*. 1. *sg*.).

serue, 15 f (: sterue *inf*.), 3555 f (: til I sterue).

√seye, 3124 f (dey *inf.* ‡ D) (: though I preye : wreye *subj.* 2 *sg.*), 4236 f (seyde † B) (: pleye *inf.*). (Cf. note, below.)
√stere, 1089 f (: clere *inf.* : matere).
suppose, 2339 f (: rose).
√swere, 3214 f (: spere).
swete,[1] 2550 f (: Polyphete : plete *inf.*).
telle, 2681 f (: dwelle *inf.*).
trowe, 2106 f (: glowe *inf.*).
warye, 7741 f (: contrarye).
wene, 3249 f (: Polixene), 3341 f (: bytwene : contene *inf.*), 5455 f (: sustene *inf.* : tene).
write, 4675 f (: endite *inf.*), 7989 f (wry3te C) (: endite *inf.* : lite *adj.*).

II. Before consonants :
bidde, 3717 AB (preye to (?) C, pray to D), 4312.
breke, 3157 BC (A ? D ?).
combre, 4941 (combere C ; D †) ; cf. suffre, 2947 (-er B, -ere C).
fele, 6679, 7632.
graunte, 785 (-[e] D), 1575 (-[e] B ? D ?).
iape, 1225.
kepe, 676.
loue, 2495, 5421, 6283.

mene, 4637, 7367.
quake, 3213.
recche, 5460, 8082 (-[e] B ; rekke D).
seche, 7303 (seke D).
sterue, 2615.
thanke, 1240 (-[e] D, -e it B).
thenke, 991 (thynke † to C, thenk *imv.* † D), 3249 (thynke BC, thenk it D).
vouchë sauf, 2268 (wouche ‡ D), 4752 (D †).

Before *th* :
bydde the, 1020 (-[de] D) ; coniure the, 3035 (D †) ; fynde that, 8121 ; mene this, 6168 (-e thus † C ; D ?) ; pose that, 3413 ABC° (suppose ? D ‡) ; preyë the, 6963 (-[e] D) ; reioyse thus, 7528 (reioyë C).

Before *y* (consonant) :
telle yow, 3620 ; trowe ye, 5538 (-e I C †).

III. This -e is regularly elided before a vowel. Thus,—
clepe, 8, 7126 ; hope, 47 (B ‡ (?) ‡), 2139, 2357,[2] 2610[3] ; late, 133 (latt B) ; fele 400[4] ; pleyne, 409 (C † D †), 534[5] ; consente, 414 ; compleyne, 415 ; hide, 581 (hid(d)e B) ; loue, 667, 1382 ; hope I (: redy), 983 ; drede, 1012 ; hate, 1018, 5501, 8095 ; answere, 1454[6] ; make, 1569, 7966[7] ; yeue, 1914 (C † D †) ; fare, 2593[8] ;

[1] Perhaps subjunctive.   [2] -e C ; D †.
[3] Read *hold*[e], later in line, in CD.   [4] Supply [*no*] in A (D †).
[5] *pleyn taught* † D ; *pleynë caught* B.   [6] 9-syl in D ‡.
[7] Supply [*ne*] in C.   [8] Supply [*her*] in D, or read *farë a mys*.

passe, 2680; mene, 2712; recche, 2954; warne, 3011; here, 3031; cause, 3113; rede, 3500[1]; excuse, 3878; clippe, 4186[2]; ende, 4660 (D †); suffre, 6403 (-fere C); write 7695; speke, 8225.[3]

I *know*e also and alday *here* and se, 1818 (know D).

Nece I *coniure* and heighly yow defende, 2818 (O nece I conioure & heyly defende C).

Yet eft I the *by-seche* and fully seye, 3124 (The pray y eft al-thogh thow shuldest dey D ‡).

For that I *tary*e ‖ *is* al for wykked speche, 7973 (-ie *is* CD).

IV. Elision before *h* :
by-come here (*poss. sg.*), 434.
speke hem, 4174 (cf. 4176 E).
loue hym, 5562 B (loueth † A).[4]

counte hem, 6726.
holde hym, 7734.
hope his, 8068.

V. Exceptions.

There are several genuine cases of -ẹ :

deyẹ ye, 6594 (dey D).

preyẹ the, 6693 (pray D); pray the, 6668 (-ẹ B, -ẹ ʒow C); pray to, 930 (-ẹ B), 1667 (-ẹ C); pray to god (?), 5101 A (preyẹ god BC, pray g. D); pray yow, prey yow, 1101 (-ẹ B), 2362 (-ẹ (?) B), 2491 (-ẹ B, -ë ‡ that C),[5] 6301 (-ë ‡ quod B),[6] 6494 (-ẹ B), 7984 (-ẹ B). Cf. also,—preyẹ to, 7726 C (prey[ë] god A, pray to D); pray to, 3717 D (preyẹ C, biddë god AB); pray with, 2145 A (-e I C, pray ich BD).[7]

seyẹ yow, 7361 (sey CD); seyẹ that, 5640 (sey D), 5692 (sey BD); -ẹ though, 5703 (sey D); sey nought, 1758 (sey for, 2738; sey not, 7365, 7366, 8142; sey no, 7771; sey this, 3165 (-ẹ nought B, sei not C, sey not D).

knowẹ not, 1267 (notẹ ‡ not D).

louẹ parde, 717; louẹ yow, 6296 (C ‡ ? D ‡ ?). Cf. also *lou*ẹ, 1332 ‡ B (-e ACD).[8]

menẹ that, 4133 (-ẹ ʒe † B, -ë ‡ wil C, thus he ‡ wyll E).

redẹ that, 495 (-e I CD).

settẹ the, 1452 (set BD).

Cf. also dwellẹ, 6978 ‡ C (-e ABD); hopẹ, 973 ‡ D (-e B; A ? C ?), 3794 ‡ D (-e ABC); leuẹ, 7418 † D; lyuẹ, 3647 ‡ D (-e ABC); makẹ, 3183 ‡ A (*l*. may); plight ‡ my, 6272 D (*p.p.* ABC); trowẹ,

---

[1] Read in B, *soon*[e *to*]. (D ?) [2] Insert [*ellis*] in C.
[3] Supply [*to*] in A ; [*I*] in B. [4] D too long. C has a different line.
[5] D ridiculously inserts *deiphebus*.
[6] *Preyẹ*, with -e fully sounded, may well enough stand for *prey ye = prey yow*.
[7] In B, read *god* for *and*. [8] Supply [*that*] in C.

3735 A (trow I B, trow y D, -e C). In 1491 *biddę* appears to be the right reading.

Note 1.—The final -e is often omitted at the end of a line in one or another MS. Thus,—assent, 2143 f C (-e ABD) *rh.* entent CD (-e AB); begyn 1934 f C (gynne AB, y bathë ‡ yn D) *rh.* in C (inne AB, yn D) *rh.* syn C (synne ABD); bryng, 2394 f D (-e ABC) *rh.* incomyng D (-e ABD); bysek, 3573 f A (-e BD, beseche C) *rh.* ek A (eke BCD); consent, 929 f CD (-e AB) *rh.* repente *ind.* 1 *sg.* ABC (-t D) *rh.* entent CD (-e AB); fast, 2251 f (-e AB) *rh.* fast *adv.* CD (-e AB) *rh.* cast *inf.* CD (-e AB); feynt, 410 f D (-e ABC) *rh.* pleynt D (-e ABC) *rh.* qweynt D (-e ABC); ges, 1372 f C (gesse ABD) *rh.* wrechednes CD (-sse AB); ges, 4569 f D (gesse ABC) *rh.* largesse ABCD *rh.* gladnes D (-sse ABC); repent, 926 f D (-e ABC) (see *consent*); repent, 1610 f CD (-e AB) *rh.* entent CD (-e AB); thenk, 2498 f D (-e A, thynke BC) *rh.* forthenk *inf.* D (-thynke ABC); trow, 2284 f D (-e ABC) *rh.* sow *inf.* D (-e ABC) *rh.* on know D (-e ABC); trost, 3208 f C (trist D, triste AB) *rh.* lest *subj. pres.* 3 *sg.* C (lyste AB, list D) *rh.* wost *pret. subj.* 2 *sg.* C (wyste AB, wyst D); trust, 1332 f CD (-e A, triste B) *rh.* lyst *pres. subj.* 3 *sg.* (-e AB, lust D) *rh.* kyst *ind.* 3 *sg.* (keste A, kiste B, kust D *later hand*).—So especially in verbs ending in *-eye, -aye.* Thus D has *prey, pray* in the following places in which the other MSS. have -e,—760 f *rh.* sey *dico* D (-e ABC) *rh.* deye *inf.* AC (dye BD), 1588 f *rh.* purvay *inf.* D (-e AC, pleye † B), 2218 f *rh.* say *inf.* D (-e ABC), 2244 f *rh.* twey D (-e AB, to † C) *rh.* purvey *imv. pl.* D (-e ABC), 2293 f *rh.* sey *inf.* D (-e ABC) *rh.* dey *inf.* D (-e ABC), 2755 f *rh.* plye † D (pleye *inf.* ABC) *rh.* lay *inf.* D (-e ABC), 2813 f *rh.* play *imv. pl.* D (-e ABC), 6531 f *rh.* obey *inf.* D (-e ABC), 8105 f *rh.* sey *inf.* D (-e AB), 8147 f *rh.* sey *ind.* 1 *sg.* D (-e AB), 8224 f *rh.* sey *dico* D (-e AB). So also,—sey, 1266 f D (-e ABC) *rh.* twey D (-e ABC), 1525 f *rh.* dey *inf.* D (-e ABC), 2280 f *rh.* twey D (-e AB, tweyne C) *rh.* awey D (-e ABC), 5431 f D (-e ABC) *rh.* deye *inf.* ACD (dye B); ley, 1046 f D (-e AB) *rh.* sey *inf.* D (-e AB); dey, 1209 f D (-e ABC) *rh.* pley *inf.* D (-e ABC) *rh.* awey D (-e ABC), 1512 f D *rh.* purvey *imv. or subj. sg.* D (-e ABC), 2954 f D (-e ABC) *rh.* sey *inf.* (-e ABC). In 1394 f, A has *prey*, D *pray*, while BC have *preye* (: seye *inf.* ABC, say D). Cf. prey, 5955 f CD (-e AB) *rh.* say *inf.* C (sey D, seye AB) *rh.* wey *acc.* CD (-e AB), 6935 f D (pray C, preye AB) *rh.* pley *inf.* D (play C, pleye AB) *rh.* sey *inf.* D (say C, seye AB); sey *dico*, 5585 f CD (-e AB) *rh.* dey *inf.* CD (-e A, dye B).—In the interior of the verse an -e necessary to the metre is sometimes omitted by the scribe: as,—*trow*[*e*], 1881 BD (-e AC); cf. 601 AD, 1020 D, 7726 A, etc.

Note 2.—The omission of elided -e is not uncommon. Cases of it occur in all the MSS. Cf. the following lines (old-style figures indicate that A omits the elided -e): I. before vowels : 240, 263, 406, 424, 759, 864, 1103, 1191, 1269, 1807, 1818, 1836, 1837, 2423, 2533, 2590, 2879, 2951, 3090, 3102, 3124, 3249 D, 3347, 3474, 3478, 3689, 3735, 4020, 4191, 5585, 5908, 7448, 7608, 7734. II. Before *h* : 3649.

Note 3.—Hiatus is very rare. "I *fyndë ek* in storyes ellys where," 7407, seems a pretty certain instance, though B has *fynde*, saving the metre by the insertion of *the* before *storyes.* Cf. also *louë oon*, 1923 AD (-e B, leus † C); *menë ‡ I*, 3463 A (-e B, -e it CD); *bathë ‡ yn*, 1934 D (bathe *inf.* AB, -ę ‡ *inf.* C); *takë ‡ it*, 7951 A (-e BD, tok ‡ C).

Note 4.—For the monosyllabic *se*, cf. (i.) 842 f, 1517, 1818 f, 2909, 5907, 5986, 6261, 6268, 7355, 7432, 7498, 7525, 7736 f, 8058; (ii.) se hym, 1418 ; se herę (*eam*), 7521. [Var. BCD see.]

§ 93. The Second Person Singular of the Present Indicative ends in -est (-ist, -yst), -st (-est) (Child, § 49; ten Brink, §§ 184, 186, 259). Thus,—

I. -est :
abydest, 7538 (-yst C).[1]
biddest, 5118 (-yst C, counsellest ‡ D).
coniestest, 5688 (-iect- B, comittist † D).
counseylest, 2613 (-ist C, -ist D ‡).
desirest, 7821 (-ist ‡ C).
deuysest, 5205 (demys † C, demist † D).
deynest, 4277 (-yst C).
dremest, 7645 (-yst C).
endurest, 785 (-yst C, -ist D).
errest, 4964 (-yst C).
farest, 5125 (-[e]st C).[2]
feynest, 6776 (-yst C).
hyëst, 4283 (hiȝost D).[3]

knowest, 4951 (-yn ‡ C, -ist D).
ledest, 1612 (-ist D †).
louest, 2481 (-is C, -ist D).
menest, 3179 (-ist C, -yst D).[4]
regnest, 8227.[5]
semest, 2601 (-yst C, -ist D).
sorwest, 5302 (-ist CD), 5763 (-ist C).[6]
stondest, 3089 (-ist CD).
suffrest, 3863 (-fered ‡ C, -frist D), 4309 (-frist D, sufferyst C, sooffrist(e) B).
thinkest, 2591 (-ist CD).
tornest, 196 (-yst CD).[7]
tristest, 720 (-yst C †, -ist D ?).
waylest, 556 (-yst C, -ist D).
wenest, 5688 (-ist D), 7885 (-yst ‡ C, -est ‡ D).

II. -st, -est :
(a) Monosyllables :
flest, 4277 (fleest BD).[8]
lyst (jaces), 2076 (list B, lycst D).
seist, seyst (dicis), 834, 932 (sest C) (?), 1033 (seyst(e) B), 5111 (seyest (?) D), 5784 (sest C), 7526 (seyest D), 7883 ; cf. 720 CD.
sleest, 5174 (slest BC) ; slest(e), 5117 A (slest BC, sleest D).

Note.—In 8154,—" And kys the steppes there as thow seest pace,"—it is perhaps better to read steppes and seëst.

(b) spekest, 2508 (-ist CD).
rennest, 6211 AB (-yst C ; D (?)).
entremetyst, 1019 ‡ C (?) (entremetist ‡ (?) D).
Cf. also the variants under I.

Note.—Forms in -is, -ys, un-Chaucerian and due to the scribes, are louis, 2481 C (-est AB, -ist D), and demys †, 5205 C (demist † D, deuysest AB).

[1] Supply [that] in CD (?).
[2] Supply [thow] in C.
[3] Supply [so] in C ; [for] in D ?
[4] Supply [wel] in A.
[5] Supply [&] in D.
[6] 9-syl. in C.
[7] Supply [ful] in AD (?).
[8] Supply [thou] in C ; dele (niȝt) in D.

§ 94. The Third Person Singular of the Present Indicative
ends in *-eth* (*-ith, -yth*), *-th* (*-eth, -ith, -yth*) (Child,
§ 50; ten Brink, §§ 184, 186). Examples are:

I. *-eth* (*-ith, -yth*):

He *spendeth iusteth maketh* festeynynges

He *yeueth* frely ofte and *chaungeth* wede, 4560-1 (all ending in *-yth* in C, in *-ith* in D[1]).

weneth, 216 (-yth C, -ith D).

gynneth, 218 (-yth CD).

priketh, 219 (-yth C, -ith D).

turneth, 324 f (-yth C, -ith D); soiòrneth (-yth C, -ith D): borneth -yth C, vnournith † D.[2]

serueth, 332 (-yth C, -ith D).

asketh, 339 (-yth C, -ith D).

thenketh, 403 (-yth C,[3] -ith D).

knoweth, 450 (-yth C, -ith D).

causeth, 551 (-ith D).

defendeth, 603 (-yth C, offendith † D): offendeth (-yth C, -ith D).

auayleth, 604 (-yth C): sailleth (-yth C, ffayleth † A): assaylleth (-yth C, -ith D); etc., etc.

The above cases are chosen from lines which all four MSS. give. Cf. also the following examples, also from such lines, in which AB have *-eth*, CD *-yth* or *-ith* or both: 625, 632, 667, 764 f, 766 f, 858, 1296, 1458 f, 1850, 1882 f, 2002, 2065, 2072, 2142, 2216, 2471, 2510, 2536, 3877, 4493, 4494, 4981 f, 7876, etc., etc.

It appears, then, that the usual ending in unsyncopated cases is *-eth* for A and B, *-yth* or *-ith* for C and D. But C sometimes has *-eth*: as, *seseth*, 1873; *axeth*, 2156; *desireth*, 2235; *causeth*, 2331; *crieth*, 4979, etc. That D sometimes has *-eth* is shown by the first list of examples; others are: *nedeth*, 2626; *endeth*, 5166; *beteth*, 5572; *floureth*, 6239; *dredeth* 7026, etc. The usual ending of D is *-ith*, as that of C is usually *-yth*.

Note 1.—Forms in *-it, et, -yt* are occasionally found. Thus,—*brestyt*, 258 C (read *brest*); *comyt*, 402 C (read *comth*); *jallit*, 142 C; *fallyt*, 212 C; *preuet*, 7311 B (perhaps meant for preterite); *louet*, 8001 B (possibly meant for preterite); *rennet*, 2839 B; *turnyt*, 1883 f C (: *spornyth*); *wexit*, 942 C. *Brennyt*, 5340 C, is probably meant for a preterite, and so perhaps *entendit*, 6832 C. It is barely worth while to note such spellings as,—*dauntcht*, 1484 B; *forzeteht*, 1460 f B; *geteht*, 1461 f B; *hang[e]ht*, 2071 B; *louyzt*, 8001 C; *pleyeht*, 840 B; *stynteht*, 3740 B; *thenketht*, 221 A; *doutheth*, 6251 B; *ettheth*, 1458 f B; *surmountheth*, 3880 B; *chasithe*, 5077 D; *occupie the* (for *occupiethe*), 7685 D.

Note 2.—A few examples of the third person singular in *-es, -s*, occur in B: *comes*, 5715 B (comth AD); *has*, 3457 B (hath BCD); *loues*, 1753 B (-ede AC, -yd D); *thankes*, 2306 B (thonked A, thankede hym C, thonkyd D). *Repeles*, *meddles*, *weres*, in A, 4956 f, 5001, 4744, are mere

---

[1] But *iustith* ‡ D.   [2] Cf. 4979-81-82.   [3] Supply [*wykke*] in C.

scribes' blunders for *repeted, meddled, weren*. In 5100 C, *trowis* should be *trewe is*. (Cf. Child, § 50; ten Brink, § 185.)

Rhyme words.—The ending *-eth*, 3 sg., rhymes usually with itself: cf., besides the places already cited, 1892-4-5, 2869-70, 4493-4, 4979-81-83, 5235-6, 5571-2, 6574-6, 7146-7. But see also *someth*, 643 f (-yth C, -ith D) (: the wyse it demeth AB, the wise demyn C, thes clerkis demith D), and *occupieth*, 5498 f (C †) (: men lieth).

II. The Present Indicative Third Person Singular in *-eth, -th (-e-* syncopated) is not uncommon. As we should expect, we find instances of it (*a*) in verbs ending in *a vowel*, or (*b*) in *m, r, v* (or *f*); but (*c*) it is not confined to such verbs.

(*a*) Verbs ending in a vowel:

lyth, lith, 1550,[1] 1800 (lyȝt C), 1826, 2658,[2] 2823 (lyȝth C),[3] 4890 (lith(e) D), 5005 (lieth D), 5078 (lyëth D),[4] 5120 (leyth C, lieth D), 5530 (lieth D ?),[5] 5816, 7648 (lieth D), 7650 (lieth † D),[6] 7780 (lieth D). (Cf. 1551 A, 7633 CD, 7782 C.)

pleyeth, 840 (-eht B, pleyth D).

pùrueieth, 5728 (-ueyth D, -ueyed ‡ A).

seth, seeth,[7] (*videt*), 4082 (sey ? C), 4410 (seeth (?) D),[8] 5625, 5636, 6595 (sey † C), 7546 (sey *pret.* C); seyth, 2339 (seth B, sey C, seyd † D); cf. 6820 C.

Whoso me *seth* he *seth* sorwe al at onys, 5503 (seeth . . . seeth B, seeth . . . seyth D).

seyth, seith (*dicit*), 1004 (syth B, sey ‡ C), 1181 (syth B), 1755, 1940 (sayith C), 2461, 3110 (soith B), 3153, 3344, 3638, 3876, 6265,[9] 7042, 7246 (sithe † C), 8014; *seith*, 1103 D, seems to be dissyllabic, but read *seydë* (cf. AB). In 2394: He song as who *seyth* (seith BD, seth C) sumwhat I brynge, are we to insert *he* before *who* or to read *seyèth* ? Mr. Austin's collation makes no note.

sleth, 7706 (sleeth D).

Note.—*fleth*, 5323 C, is a wrong reading. In D 4410 we are hardly to read *knoweth*.

(*b*) Verbs in *m, r, v* (*f*):

cometh, 402 (comth B, comyt C, -ith D),[10] 405,[11] 408 (-yth (?) C, -ith (?) D),[12] 1369, 1461 (comth B), 1728 (-yth B), 2320 (comth B),

---

[1] *li[e]th* (?) C; but supply [*now*] and read *lith*.   [2] Supply [*to*] in CD.
[3] Supply [*of*] in B.   [4] But read *now[ë]* and *lyeth* in D.
[5] But supply [*now*] in D, and read *lieth*.
[6] But supply [*him*] in D, and read *lieth*.
[7] *Seeth* is always monosyllabic in this list. A has usually *seth*, but *seeth* in 6595; D has usually *seeth*.
[8] Not a very certain line as to metre; apparently a nine-syllable verse.
[9] Supply [*that*] in A.
[10] If we read *whens* (so AD), we must read *comëth* (*-ith*); if *whennës* B (-ys C), *comth*.
[11] Old-style figures indicate that CD have *-yth* or *-ith*.   [12] Cf. 402.

§ 94.]   *of Chaucer's Troilus.*   219

   2338 (comth B, -yth (?) C, -ith D), 2420 (comth B), 2470, 2877 [1]
   (D †), 3721 (comth B), 5083 (-yth C), 5166, 6754 (come B, comth D),
   6789 (comth D, -yth C),[2] 7104 (-yth C, comth D), 7505 B (-yth B,
   comth D, com(e) ‡ A). (Cf. 4067 ‡ B, 5761 ‡ C, 7486 B);
   bicometh, 1880 BC (-eth A ‡, -ith D ‡), 1882; ouercometh, 6246
   (-yth (?) C †, -comth D †).
 comth, 5704 (-eth B), 5715 (comes B), 7034 (-eth B, -yth C),[3] 7516
   (-yth C), 7532 (-yth C).[4]   (Cf. 7486 D, 7506 ‡ D.)
   For al that *cometh comth* by necessite, 5620 (comth .... comth D).
 semeth, 889 (-yth C, -ith (?) D), 3030 (-yth C, -ith D); cf. 7969 D.
 meneth, 1472 A (-ith D, mene ‡ B, mene 2 *pl.* C^c). Cf. 1806 ‡ D,
   7513 C ‡ D ‡.
 bereth, 939, 940, 1272 (-ith (?) C, -ith D †), 1486 (berth B †), 6823
   (-yth C, kepith ‡ D).
 fareth, 956.
 swereth, 1739 (swerth B), 7793 (swerth B).
 byhoueth, 5666, 5716; cf. 5967 CD.
 dryfth, 7695 (dryuyth C, dryueth D).
 loueth, 4605 (-yth C, -eth E [5]), 7793 (-yth C),[6] 8109 (-ed ‡ D); cf.
   5562 † A.
 But,—
   cometh, 7486 (-yth C, -eth B, comth D); cf. 3904 ‡ D.
   semeth, 1201 (-yth C, -ith D), 5549 (-yth C),[7] 6664 (-yst † C,
     -yth D).[8]
   meneth, 1806 (leuyth ‡ C, menith D), 7798 (-yth C).
   fareth, 1080 (-ith D); cf. 652.
   dryueth, 7464 (drieeth C †, driueth D †). (Cf. 1085, 7903.)
   loueth, 1404 (-yth (?) C, -ith D), 1815 (-yth C, -ith D), 1862 (-yt C,
     -ith D), 2854 (-ith D).
 (c) Other verbs :
 liketh, 3227 B (-ith C, -eht ‡ A, lyke ‡ D); cf. 7729 C (D (?)).
 maketh, 1318 (-eht B, -yth C, -ith D)[9]; cf. 2468 C.
 nedeth, 1261 AB (-ith C † D †), 2475 AB (-ith ‡ C, -ith (?) D)[10]; cf.
   6699 ‡ C.
 speketh, 6599 (-en ‡ B, -ith C).
 thenketh (*videtur*), 1292 (-yth C, -ith D),[11] 1486 (B † ; -ith C), 2714

---
[1] Supply [*that*] in B.   [2] But supply [*that*] in C, and read *-yth*.
[3] In AD read *then[ne]s*.   [4] Supply [*that*] in D.
[5] Supply [*now*] in E.   [6] "That wonder was and *swereth* she *loueth* hym best."
[7] Supply [*me*] in C.   [8] Supply [*for*] in BD.
[9] Dele (*to*) in C.   [10] In D, read *long[e]*.   [11] Supply [*for*] in D.

eth ‡ B, -ith C, -ith ‡ D),¹ 5146 (-yth C, thinkest † D), 6942 (-ith C ; D (?)) ; me of-thynketh, 1043 (mathynketh B, me athinkith ‡ D).
But,—
  liketh, 1247 (-yth C, -ith D), 1527 (like † ȝow C, -ith D), 1615 (-ith CD),² 3196 AB, 4809 (-ith CD).
  maketh, 4669 (-ith D).
  nedeth, 1096 (-ith D),³ 1547 (-ith CD), 1582 (-ith CD), 3791 (-ith CD), 4305 (C † ; -eth D), 4485 (-yth C, -ith D), 4518 (-yth C, -ith D), 8211 (-eth D). (Cf. 740 A, 3699 CD.)
  thenketh (*videtur*), cf. 1392 ‡ D, 2714, 3222, 5497, 5772, 5926, 6483, 7235. Cf. thenketh (*putat*), 1118 (thynketh B, thenkyth D).

    Note.—In some cases of apparent -*eth* (-*yth*, -*ith*), a comparison of MSS. makes it certain or probable that the unsyncopated form is right. See 142 D, 195 C, 868 D, 1087 B, 1397 D, 1464 CD (*perhaps right*), 1568 C, 1876 C, 4674 B, 4901 D, 5967 CD ; and cf. also 1631 ‡ C (?), 3084 ‡ C, 3792 † B (?), 4479 ‡ CD, 5390 C †, 6598 C †. See other cases of syncopated -*yth* in the variants under § 95.

§ 95. The following examples of the third person singular in -*t* from verbs in *t, d, s*, occur in the *Troilus* (Child, § 51 ; ten Brink, § 186) :

ablt, 1084.
bet, 1498 (let B, redith C, ret D).
bitit, 1133 (betyt D) ; by-tyt, 6708 (bitit B, be-tydyth C, betidde ‡ D). (Cf. *tyt*, below.)
bytrent, 4073 (be- C ; bi- D (?)) ; cf. 5532 (?).
blent, 4667 (blent(e) B).
brest, 258 (brestyt C, brestith D), 4479 (brestyth C, brekith D).
drat, 3170 (dredith D).
forbet, 1802 (forbed(e) C, forbod(e) D †).
halt, 1122 (holt D), 3849 (holdyth C, holt D), 4216 BE (holt AC), 4478 (haldyth C ‡, holt D), 4589 (hast † C), 4606 (holt E), 6711 (holt C, halt(e) D) ; holt, 4562 D (held AC, hold B).
hent, 4667 (hent(e) B).
hurt, 6713 (hirt C).⁴ (*Preterite* ?)
last, 5250 (lestyth (?) C, last(e) D).
lat, 4862 (lat(e) them [not] D).
let, 1967 BC.⁵

[1] In B read *sith* for *soth*.   [2] In CD read *des[es]peraunce*.
[3] Insert [*other*] in A (D ?).   [4] Supply [a] in D.
[5] But AD have *led*, and a past tense seems almost necessary. "*led here lyf*."

lyst, lest, lust, cf. 518, 840, 852, 1308, 2136 f, 2233, 2479 f, 3243 f,
  3417, 3493, 3781 f, 5753, 7716 f, 7796 f, etc.; lyst(e), cf. 2479 f.
ouer-sprat, 1852 (ouersprad D).
put, 5683.
ret, 1498 D (see *bet*).
rist, 937 (ryseth C), 1897, 4894 (ryst(e) B, risith D), 5825 (rist(e) D);
  vp rist, 6105 (rist vp C).
ritt, 2369 (ride † B, rit C, ridith D); right, 6423 (rit(e) B, rauȝt ‡ C,
  ritt(e) D),—read *rit*.
sent, 2208 ABCD; but the metre is short by one syllable except in
  D, which reads *sent to*. Perhaps we should read *sent[e]*, pret.
sit, 12 (sitt D), 246 (sitt B, seyth † C, syt D), 976 (sitt B), 2020 (syt
  D), 3869 (is ‡ B, syt D), 5685, 5688 f (: it : yit), 5693, 5699, 5701,
  6596 (sitt(e) D), 7367 (sitt B, sitt(e) D), 7675 (settith D), 8207
  (sitt BD).
smert, 6780 (-(e) D). Perhaps noun.
stant, 602 (stonde † B, stondith C), 2273 (C (?); stont D), 2463
  (stond C, stont D),[1] 2477 (stont C, stond D †), 2698 (stont D),
  3338 (stont AD), 3627 (stont C), 3745 C (stont AD, stant(e) B),
  4404 (stont AC), 5212 (stont C), 5679, 6048 (stant(e) B),[2] 6596
  (stant(e) B, stont C), 8091 (stont B, stant(e) D); vndirstant ‡, 8005
  C (-stod A, -stood B, -stood(e) D).
tret, 1432.
tyt, 333 (tit B). (Cf. *bitit*, above.)
went, 1121 f (went(e) B) (: shent *p.p.*), 1897 (*om.* † B, wentë C).[3]
writ, 394 (writ(e) B, wryt CD).
wryth(e), 4073 (writh(e) B, written ‡ (?) D).
yelt, 385 (ȝelt B, ȝildyth C, yeldith D).

But forms in *-eth* are found. Thus,[4]—
beteth, 5572 f.
biteth, 4493 f (: delyteth).
dredeth, 7026.
eteth, 1458 ‡ : foryeteth : geteth. (Cf. *et*, Leg. G. W., 1389.)
knetteth, 4590 (endytyth ‡ C, kennyth ‡ D).
lasteth, 4664.

---

[1] Supply [*she*] in D. [2] Supply [*thus*] in D.
[3] May perhaps be preterite (*went*[e] *here*).
[4] Trifling variations in spelling are not registered.

lysteth, listeth, 671, 1785 (leste *pret.* C, lest D †), 4659 (lest[e] *pret.* (?) D).
nedeth, 1096, etc.
rideth, 1773, 6924 (redyn ‡ C)..
sendeth, 2870 f (: entendeth).
smerteth, 667 (cf. *smert*, Ch's. ABC, 152).
spredeth, 2065.
stenteth, 3740; stynteth, 4076.
stondeth, 2231 (l. om. C).

Cf. also hasteth, 949, 4549 (-ith ‡ D); threteth, 5571 f B (-yth C, treteth A, treth † D); thursteth, 7769 (trustyth † C); wasteth, 1478; and the Romance verb,—iusteth, 4560.

§ 96. The Plural of the Present Indicative ends regularly in *-en* or *-e;* but forms occur in *-eth-* (and rarely in *-es*) (cf. Child, § 52; ten Brink, § 186).

Before consonants, -en is commoner than -e; in rhyme, -e is commoner than -en. Before vowels or h, -en and -e (elided) are regular, -ẹn (apocopated) is rare. For *-eth, -es*, see § 97.

The following list is arranged as follows : I. -en before consonants. II. -en in rhyme. III. -en before vowels. IV. -en before h. V. Syncope : -ẹn, -n. VI. -e before consonants. VII. -e in rhyme. VIII. Elision : *-e* before vowels. IX. Elision : *-e* before h. X. Apocope : -ẹ. XI. Present plural of A.S. *fléon, séon, sléan, wréon*.

I. *-en* before consonants : (*a*) First Person :
seggen we, 4856 (siggen B, seyde ‡ C, sey we D).
seruen bothe, 6506 (-e D, were † C).
departen ye and I, 7436 (-yn 2 *pl.* C).

(*b*) Second Person :
preysen thus, 1180 (-in D, pryse C).
lyuen by, 1435 (-yn CD).[1]
slepen so, 1632 (-in C, -yn D).
faren wel, 2234 (-e C †, -yn D).
felen wel, 2368 (-e C, -yn D).
holden regne, 2871 (-yn D).
heren wel, 2994 (-yn CD).
liggen wel, 3511 (-yn C, -e D). (Conditional sentence.)
lysten for, 4652 (lest[e] to D).
comen be, 4989 (-[e] D, -yn to C).
louyn most, 5259 C (-eth AB, -eth 3 *sg.* D).[2]

[1] Dele (*that*) in A. [2] Query this line !

knowen wel, 6030 (-e C); cf. 2737 B †.
mystrusten me, 6268 (-yn C^e).
touchen nought, 7359 (-e C, -[e] D).[1]
yeuen me, 7778 (-yn C, -e D).[1]
requeren me, 7963 (-yn C, -e D).

(c) Third Person :

reden not, 241 (-yn C, -ith D; B †).
slepen softe, 914 (-e C, -(t)en B; D †).
writen clerkes, 954 (-e C, -yn D), 3694 (-yn CD), 4041 (-yn C); w. folk, 4680 (-yn D); w. `they, 6083 (-e CD);[2] w. that, 7179 (wotyn † C).
faren wel, 1248 (-e C, -yn D).
tellen that, 1270 (-e CD); t. xx., 6069 (-e C †, -[e] D), t. this, 6728 (-yn C, -e D).
fallen thikke, 1541 (-es A, -e C, -yn D); f. chaunces, 5760 (-yn C (?), -en D (?)).
louen wommen, 1819 B (-yn CD, -en ‡ a A); l. nouellerye, 1841 (-yn CD).
defamen loue, 1945 (-yn CD).
speken but, 1946 (-yn CD).
curen folk, 2665 (-e C, -ith D).
dreden shame, 2867 (-yn D).[3]
wondren so, 2874 (-in D).[4]
seruen the, 2882 (-yn D); s. best, 4107 (-yn CD^e).
techen bokes, 2933 (-in C, -yn D).
lyuen soth, 3272 (-yn CD).
dremen thynges, 3427 (-yn D, demyn C).
callen fals, 3656 (-yn D, tellen B, -yn C); c. loue, 4224 (-e C, clepen E).
comen nough[t], 3660 (-yn D (?), -[e] C).
bryngen folk, 4046 (-yn C, -eth B).
commenden so, 4534 (-yn CD).
drawen forth, 4546 (-yn CD, -[e]n B).[5]
desiren now, 4864 (-yn C).
vsen frendes, 5343 (-yn C).
bytiden by, 5719.
semen dede, 5754 (-yn C, -e D).

---

[1] Subjunctive ? [2] Supply [of] in C.
[3] In 4718 *dredden* (*dreden* B, *dreddyn* D) is of course preterite.
[4] Read *thing[es]* in A. [5] Apparently a 9-syl. verse.

purposen pes, 6012 (-yn C, -ed † D).
proceden thei, 6733 (-yn C, -en ? D).
wenen lese, 6744 (-e C° D).
knowen folk, 6778 (-en D (?), -yn C (?)); cf. 4951·C).
stonden for, 7482 (stode they C).
showen bothe, 8077 (-yn D).

II. -en in rhyme. Third Person:
dryen, 303 f (: eyen : dyen *inf.*).
treten, 742 f (-e C, -yn D) (: beten *p.p.*).
deseyuen, 1370 f (-e C; D †) (: receyuen *inf.* : weyuen *inf.* B (weylen † A)).
dremen, 1885 f (demen ‡ CD) (: semen 3 *pl.* : quemen 3 *pl.*).
semen, 1887 f (-yth † (?) C, -yn D).
quemen, 1888 f (-yn CD).
crien, 1950 f (cryȝen C) (: eyen *pl.* : dryen *inf.*).[1]
vsen, 3865 f (-yn CD) (: excusen *inf.*).
labouren, 4107 f (-on B, -yn CD°) (: honouren *inf.* : socouren *inf.*).
grauen, 4304 f A (-ë BCD) (: hauen *inf.* (-e BCD)).
growen, 4602 f (-yn C, grevyn † E) (: flowen *inf.*).

III. -en before vowels. (a) Second Person:
apeysen, 2864 (-yn D).[2]
bathen, 22.
compleynen, 4685 B (-ës A, -yn D).
demen, 3614 (-yn CD).
knowen, 240 (-ë C, -yn D).

(b) Third Person:
wepen, 7 (-yn D).
stonden, 418 (-yn CD).
techen, 698 (-yn D, cechyn † C).
tiren, 787 (-yn C, -in D).
erren, 996 (arn C †, arë D †).
wenen, 1356 (-yn CD), 1977 (-ë CD).
stoupen, 2053 (-ë C, -yn [on] D).
spreden, 2055 (-yn D, spryngin ‡ C).
longyn, 2431 D (-eth AB, -ith C).

shenden, 1675 (-yn C, -ë D).
slepen, 1630 (-in C, -yn D).
stonden, 428 (-yn CD).
suffren, 6195 (suffere *dissyl.* C, suffryn D).

hakkyn, 2466 D (-ë C°, -eth AB).
lyuen, 2858 (-in D).
lyggen, 3527 (-yn CD).
slepen, 3608 (-in C, slepe that ‡ D).
reden, 3905 (-yn C, -e in D).
drynken, 4058 (-yn C, -eth D).
holden, 4596 (-ith E †, hold † in C).
encressen, 5241 (-yn C).
haugen, 5479 (-ë [al] D).

[1] Subjunctive?
[2] Read *fers[e]* in D.

fallen, 5667.
comen, 5712.
deliten, 6095 (-e C).
passen, 6360.
lasten, 6764 (treüs lestith D).
speken, 6795 (spokè they C).

blamen, 7123 BD (-ë C, -ëd *p.p.* A).
commenden, 7124 (-yn C, comaundyn ‡ D).
tellen, 7841 (-yn C), 7925 (-yn C).

IV. *-en* before *h*.
(*a*) First Person : vsen here (*hic*), 4844 (-yn CD).
(*b*) Second Person :
maken hertes, 2865 (-yn D).
(*c*) Third Person :
redressen hem, 2054 (-yn D).
demen hot, 2618 (-ë CD).
knowyn hym, 3162 CD (*pret.* AB).
reuèsten hem, 3195 (-yn CD).
suffren here, 3860 (-re B, -fere C, -fryn D †).
seruen here, 3978 (-yn C, -eth D †).[1]
bryngen hors, 4707 (-[en] D).
deliten hem, 6097 (-es B, -e C, -ed D).
expounden hem, 7641 (-poungyn † C, -poune D).

V. *-en, -n.* (*a*) Second Person :
seyn ye, 1558 (sey D †); cf. 1275 C, 2367 D.
(*b*) Third Person :
seyn, (i.) 708, 5632, 5659, 5668 f (seyne B) (: agayn : in certayn), 6035 (seyn(e) B, say D), 6115 (say D, seith B, sen † C), 6246 (say D ; C †),[2] 6732 (seyn(t) A, seyn(e) D), 8002 (say D, seyn [that] C) ; cf. 1886 ‡ C. (ii.) 1833 (s. thour C), 5636, 7413 (sey D, sen † C) ;[3] seyn he, 7167 (sein(e) D ; C †).

Note.—*Seyen* (dissyllabic) appears not to occur in the *Troilus* (cf. *seyn* ‡, 6735 C, 8002 (!) C).

speken in, 6068 (-yn CD).
proceden of, 6723 (-yn C, -*e* B ; D †).
comen ayen, 7495 (-yn C).

Note.—Such cases as the last three are rare except as mere variants Cf., for the 2nd person : knowyn ek, 3757 C, 5993 C ; takyn it, 7969 C ; knowen how, 7688 D.[4] For the 3rd person, cf. lyuen vnder, 1259 B (-yn C, -eth A , *sg.* ‡ D) ; louen a, 1819 A ; auauntyn of, 3160 C ; fighten and, 4707 B ; takyn it, 6710 C : tellyn iwis, 6730 C ; dremyn and, 6740 C ; spekyn of, 7216 C ; speken for, 6599 B (*sg.* ACD). cf. §§ 136, *e*, 139.

[1] Supply [*ne*] in C.
[2] Supply [*that*] in D.
[3] Dele (*the proude*) in D.
[4] Read *long*[*e*] in D.

VI. -e before consonants. (a) Second Person :
make me, 1200 (-en B, -yn C); -e this, 3714.
mende ye, 1414 (wyn[ne] ‡ D (?)).
wene ye, 1975, 7267 (C?).
slepe ȝe, 2180 CD.
recche lest, 2236 (-yn D).
like ‡ ye, 2281 D.
wite ‡ what, 2737 D.
trowe ye, 3441 (-[e] D),[1] 4215 (-[e] B; D †), 6000 (-[e] B).
knowe ye, 4743 (-yn D).
thinke ‡ ye, 5511 D.
lyue ye, 5877.
speke not, 5988 (-[e] B, spake D).

(b) Third Person :
hunte faste, 748 (-ith D).[2]
wake whan, 914 (-en B; D †).
know[e] folk, 4860 ‡ D (weten A, witen B, wetyn C).
gynne sprynge, 7020 (-en B, -yn D, begynne ‡ C).
bytrayse yow, 8146.

VII. -e in rhyme. (a) First Person :
pleyne, 711 f (pleyn D) (: peyne n. : to seyne).
rede, 1185 f (: dede n. : rede inf.).
drinke, 1869 ‡ f C (inf. ABD).
byseche, 2759 f (bisike B, beseche C) (: eke, ek C).
deuyse, 6191 ‡ f C (2 pers. ABD).
hye, 6852 f (: vilonye). (Perh. subjunc.)

(b) Second Person :
eschuwe, 344 f (-ewe BCD) (: mysconstrue inf., -ewe BC, -ew D)
  2340 f (-ewe BCD) (: saluwe inf., -ewe D, salwe B, salue C).
endure, 682 f (: assure imv. pl.).
fare, 1194 f (: care n. : bare), 6601 f (: care n.).
mene, 1218 f (meue † CD) (: lene adj. pred. sg., eue † C, leve † D).
auyse, 1361 f (: wise n.).
requere, 1558 f (: chere : dere).
swete, 2028 f (smete † C) (: y-bete p.p. : hete n.).
leue creditis, 2226 f (: repreue n.).
constreyne, 2317 f (: peyne n.).
chese, 4851 f (: lese inf.).
deuyse, 6191 f (1 pl. ‡ C) (: wyse n.).

[1] Supply [now] in C. [2] The first part of 748 D is corrupt.

deface, 7278 f (: pace *inf.* : face).
speke, 7325 f (: wreke *inf.*).
   (*c*) Third Person :
endure, 34 f (: auenture *n.*).
write, 147 f (: Dite *nom. prop.*).
ryme, 532 f (: tyme).
plye, 732 f (pleye C, pley D) (: lytargie : melodye).
kepe, 763 f (-yn C) (: by-wepe *inf.* (-yn C)).
knowe, 1945 f (know D) (: bowe *noun* (bow D)).
resigne, 2867 f (: digne *adj. pred. pl.* : benigne *adj. pred. pl.*).
make, 4203 f (: take *inf.*).
lye *mentiuntur*, 4222 f (: folye), 4682 f (: vilonye),[1] 7844 f (: enuye *n.* : dye *inf.*).
ake, 4403 f (: wake *inf.*).
erre, 4616 f (: werre *n.*). (Subjunctive ?)
quelle, 4708 f (: felle (fele A) *adj. pl.* : telle *inf.*).
procede, 4809 f (*inf.* ‡ D) (: nede *n.*).
dwelle, 5347 f (: telle *inf.*).
bynde, 5525 f (: kynde *n.* : fynde *inf.*).
preue, 5631 f (: leue *inf.*).
falle, 5711 f (: alle *pl.*).
preye, 6046 f (prey CD) (. seye *inf.* : tweye).
rede, 6306 f (: drede *n.*).
mene, 6727 f (: bene *n.*). (Indirect question.)
carye, 7105 f (-ie D, *om* † C) (: letuarye).
declare, 7162 f (: square *adj. pl*).
cape, 7496 f (gape CD) (: iape *inf.*).
reyne, 7699 f (: pleyne *inf.*).
Cf. also the following cases of -e (3 *pl.*) in rhyme : 705, 788, 1092, 2153, 2452, 3131, 3143, 3432, 4063, 4229, 4271, 5508, 6046, 6382, 7153, 7640, 7826, 7896.
   VIII. *-e* elided before vowels. (*a*) Second Person :
lyue, 330 (loue ‡ C).
knowe, 340 (know BD, -yn C) ;[2] cf. 1107, 2873, 3757, 5993.
mene, 1311. [Indirect question.]
speke, 6217 (spek B, -é ‡ awoy C).
hate, 6508 (-ë ‡ be D).[3]
take, 7969 (-yn C).

---

[1] Perhaps subjunctive.   [2] Read *al*[*le*] in D.   [3] Subjunctive ?

(*b*) Third Person :
graue, 1132 (some graue D).
iangle of, 1885 (iangęle C, ianglyn (?) D).
deuỳne, 2830 (dèuyne ‡ C).
fele, 2853 B (feld † A, fele *inf.* † D).
yelpe, 3149 (ʒelp C, yelp D).
auaunte, 3160 (-e ‡ wommen B, -yn of C).
take, 4252 ‡ C (toke *pret.* ABE), 6710 (-yn it (?) ‡ C).
twynne, 4553 (twyn CD).
fyghte, 4707 (-ęn B, fight D).
trete, 6008
telle, 6730 (-yn C).
dreme, 6740 (-yn C).
speke 72,16 (-yn C).
clepe, 7262.
write, 7992.

IX. *-e* elided before *h*. Second Person :
yeue hym, 2861 (ʒaf ‡ *pret.* D).
suffre hym, 3705 (suffęre C),[1] 3723 (suffęre C).[2]

Note 1.—*knowe hem*, 3 pl., 4240 B (-yn C), should be preterite (*knewe* A, *knew* D).
Note 2.—Elided *-e* is occasionally omitted in writing.—Thus,—2nd pers., *know how*, 7688 (-*e* BC. -ęn D)[3]; 3rd pers., *com and*, 5761 (-en (?) D, -yth *sg* (?) C), *lat hem*, 1820 A (lat hym = hem B). Cf. also the variants under VIII., above.

X. Cases of apocope of -*e* are rare. (*a*) Second Person :
settę lite, 1517 (settè C, set[te] D).
trowę ye, 6231 (trow B, -è C ; D (?)).[4]
yeuę ye, 6598 (ʒeuyth † ʒow 3 *sg.* C, frome † your D).
sey right, 1275 (-ę B, seyn C, sey D †).
sey me, 2367 (say BC, seyn ful D).
Cf. also know wel, 3757 ‡ D, 5993 ‡ D.

(*b*) Third Person :
say may, 1707 (seyn(e) B, seyn C, sey D).
begynnę ‡ to, 7020 C.

Note 1.—In the case of *sey, say*, 2, 3 pl., the correct reading may be *seyn* (see V., above, and observe the variants there cited).
Note 2.—For the omission of -*e* at the end of the verse where the rhyme requires -*e*, see variants in the places cited under VII., above (*no cases in A*) ; cf. also *turment* ‡, 5003 f D. An -*e* necessary to the metre is occasionally omitted in the interior of the verse (*not in A*) : see variants under VI., above (in particular, *trow[e] ye*, 2 pl, 4215 B).

[1] Subjunctive? Supply [*that*] in C.
[2] Subjunctive?
[3] Read *long[e]* in D.
[4] Dele (*ek*) in A.

XI. The A.S. verbs *fléon, séon, sléan, wréon*, show in the *Troilus* the following monosyllabic contracted forms in the plural of the present indicative:

2nd person : sen that, 6007 (seen B, see D †, se ‡ ek (?) C); sen hym, 2995 (sen(e) D); se, see, cf. 1424 f (1 *pl.* ‡ D), 3508 f, 7247 f, 7765 f; se ye (?), 995 A.

sle me, 6267.

3rd person : seen, sen,— s. swete, 2618 (se D); s. alday, 3905 (sen(e) D); s. in, 5342 (see D, seyn C); s. here, 6707 (sen(e) D); s. hem, 6709 (sen(e) D).

wrien with, 1624 (wren B, wryen D). (Monosyllable.)

flen (= flyen, see ten Brink, § 158) from, 6018 (fleen B, flien, D; C †).

§ 97. **The Plural of the Present Indicative ends occasionally in -*eth* (-*ith*, -*yth*), -*th*.**

The following list is meant to be exhaustive for the four MSS. Old-style figures indicate that the subject is *men*. An asterisk indicates that the verb precedes its subject.

(*a*) Second Person :

knoweth what, 2737 A (-en B, wite D, knowith *imv. pl.* ‡ C).

causeth al, 4408 D (-es A, -ed B, can syre † Cᶜ).

loueth most, 5259 AB (-yn C, -eth *sg.* D).

grauntyth that, 7307 C (-e *inf.* AB, -e *subj.* 2 *pl.* D).

doth(e) me, 8063 B (do A, don C, don(e) D).

(*b*) Third Person :

redith not, 241 D (-en A, -yn C, -en [not] B).

hath ben, 242 BC (han A, have with D); hath this, *4299 B (han AC, haue D); hath go, 4547 D (han ABC); cf. 2467 D (?).

demeth, 644 f (-yn † C, -ith D) (: semeth *sg.*).¹

seyth wo, 694 (seyęth C)²; s. eche, 1127 (seyn BD); s. men, * 1809 (*om.* † D); s. impression[e]s, 2323 (sey C, seyn D); seith that, 6115 B (seyn A, sen C, say D).³

maketh of[t], 740 B (-yth C, -yn D; -eth *sg.* A).

huntith fast, 748 D (-e ABC).⁴

lyueth vnder, 1259 A (-en B, -yn C; -ith *sg.* D).

to suche as hym thenketh able, 1292 (thynketh B, thynkyth C, thinkith ‡ D).

---

¹ Subject : *the wyse*. Supply [*and*] in D.
² Subject : *thise wyse* A, *the wise* BCD. Perhaps singular.
³ Supply [*the*] in D.   ⁴ D has *ffor thy with* for *fro thyng which*.

bereth lyf, 1920 (-ith CD).[1]
gydeth yow, 2189 (-ith C; sg. D).[2]
doth these, * 2391 A (dos(e) B, don(e) D, don 3e 2 pl. C).
longeth yn, 2431 (-ith C, -yn D).[3]
furthereth most, 2453 (forthreth B, fer-rerith † C, furthrith D).[4]
hakketh ofte, 2466 AB (-ë C°, -yn D).
curith folk, 2665 D (-en AB, -e C).
adorneth al, 2844 (-ith D).
bryngeth folk, 4046 D (-en AB, -yn C).
drinketh ofte, 4058 D (-en AB, -yn C).
holdith a, 4596 E (-en AB, hold in C).[5]
lieth, 5496 f ABD (me hey † C) (: occupieth sg.).
goth plesaunce[s] (?), * 5761 C (gon plesaunces AB, gon(e) plesauns[es] (?) D).
clepeth an, 6674 (callyn ‡ [an] C, clepë ‡ an D); clepeth wode, 7576 B (-yn C, -e D, clepeth the A).
cometh swich, * 6737 AB (-yth C, -e D); cf. * 5761 C (?).
tretis lestith al, 6764 C (trewes lasten ABD).
weneth best, 7630 (-yn C, -e D).[6]
sleth my, 7706 ABC (sleeth D).
astreyneth me (?), 8146 D (commeueth sg. AB).

> Note 1.—In 1887 f C, semyth was doubtless meant for a singular by the scribe.
> Note 2.—In 217 C faylyt seems meant for a plural: faylyt thyngys.

The notes to the foregoing lists, together with the various diacritical marks, show that many of the examples are cases of the indefinite subject men, that others may be sing., and that still others may be accounted for in various ways (as perhaps by a confusion of constructions).

§ 98. The Northern Plural in -es occurs very rarely in the *Troilus* MSS.

Second Person:
causes al, 4408 A (-ed B, -eth D; C †).
compleynes euere, 4685 A (-en B, -yn D).

---

[1] Perhaps singular: "al that bereth lyf."
[2] "What maner wyndes gydeth yow (wynd D)."
[3] "And dide also hise other obseruaunces That to a louere longeth yn this cas."
[4] "It is oon of the thynges that furthereth most." In this succession of words there is often a confusion of numbers in modern speech.
[5] In E (Harl. 1239), read *bond* for *boute*, and *duryng* for *doyng*.
[6] Supply [to] in D.

Third Person :
bigiles, 7640 f B (-e ACD) (: while).
falles thikke, 1541 A (-en B, -e C, -yn D).
delites hem, 6097 B (-en A, -e C, -ed D).
dos(e) this, 2391 B (doth A, don(e) D, don ȝe 2 *pl.* C).

§ 99. The following Indicative Preterites (first and third person) of Anglo-Saxon verbs of the First Weak Conjugation occur in the *Troilus* (cf. Child, § 53; ten Brink, §§ 162, 165, 168-70).

(*a*) Stems originally short,—*lette, leyde, sette, shette*; (*b*) stems originally long,—*agylte, alighte, ayled, bente, bledde, blente* (A.S. *blende*), *blente* (A.S. *blencte*), *bredde, bytydde, demede, dyghte, dreynte, fedde, felte, ferde, grette, hente, herde, kepte, knette, kydde, kyste* (*keste, cussed*), *ladde* (*ledde*), *laste, lefte* (*lafte*), *lente, lyste* (*leste*), *mente, mette* (A.S. *métte*), *mette* (A.S. *mǽtte*), *myssed, nedede, radde, rente, reste, reynede, semed, sente, shente, spedde, spradde, stente* (*stynte*), *thraste, wende, wente* ; (*c*) irregular verbs,—*boughte, broughte, dwelled, raughte, roughte, soughte, taughte, thoughte* (A.S. *þóhte*), *thoughte* (A.S. *þúhte*), *tolde, wroughte.* For *hitte* (O.N. *hitta*), *thriste* (O.N. *þrýsta*), *trusted* (cf. O.N. *treysta*), see § 100.

Of these *ayled, demede, myssed, nedede, reynede, semed*,[1] are unsyncopated preterites formed on the analogy of the second weak conjugation (A.S. -*ode*) and replacing the proper Anglo-Saxon forms *egl(e)de, démde, miste, nédde* (but cf. *néadian,* -*ode*), *rínde, sémde.* For *cussed* (*kyssed*), a similar formation, see *kyste*. In these -*ed*, -*ede* preterites final -e is not sounded except in *nedede* (q.v.) and is often not even written.

Dwelled corresponds to A.S. *dwelede* (-*ode*), inf. *dwelian* (Siev., § 407, Anm. 1); *duelte* (A.S. *dwealde*, inf. *dwellan*) does not occur in the *Troilus.*

In *bente, blente* (A.S. *blende*, inf. *blenden*), *felte, lefte* (*lafte*), *lente, mente, rente, sente* (but also *sende*), *shente, wente,* A.S. -*de* is replaced by -*te* (cf. ten Brink, § 170 ε, ζ). *Brennen* (O.N. *brenna*, cf. A.S. *bærnan*) has both *brende* (: *amende* inf., etc.) and *brente* (: *sente* ind. 3 sg.) : see § 100.[2]

Several preterites of weak verbs belonging properly to the second conjugation show syncopated forms after the analogy of the first. These

---

[1] Ten Brink (§ 165) notices *demed, semed*
[2] Ten Brink (§ 170 ζ) appears to recognize only *brente.*

are, answerde (-swerede), caste (O.N.), made, pleyde, putte, rafte, shapte (O.N.), twyghte : see § 101.[1]
Syncopated perfects, after the analogy of the first weak conjugation, are shown by several verbs strong in Anglo-Saxon : breyde, dredde, fledde, lepte (var. lep), loste, sighte (sighed, siked), slepte (but also slep), smerte, [swelte,] wepte (but also wep) : see § 103. So also deyde (O.N. dœyja), pret. do). For highte, see § 103. For shapte, see § 101.
For other syncopated preterites from verbs of Germanic origin see glente, plighte, swapte, twyste (§ 100). For syncopated preterites from Romance verbs, see aspyde, caughte, cryde, hurte, paste, preyde (§ 104).
For rong (A.S. hringde), see § 103, note 2.
In the following lists (§§ 99-104) the cases cited are in the third person unless the contrary is indicated. In the infinitives given no attempt is made at exhaustiveness of reference, and elision is not indicated.

agylte (A.S. ágyltan, -gylte), 1st pers., -e hym, 3682 (-t CD).
alighte (A.S. álihtan, -lihte), 7380 f (-t D, -ly3te C) (: yf she myghte : bryghte adv.) ; she alighte, 6552 f (shalighte B, sche aly3t C †, she light D) (: myghte pret. 3 sg.).
ayled (A.S. egl(i)an, egl(e)de, see Cosijn, Altws. Gr., II, 163, § 120), ayled the, 4993 B (ailid D, eyleth A, aylyth C).
bente (A.S. bendan, bende), -e his, 725 C (bent D, lente AB).
bithoughte, see thoughte.
bledde (A.S. blédan, blédde), 2035 f (bled D) (: vnto bedde : he spedde ind.), 7563 f (: fledde pret. ind. 3 sg., is fledde ‡ A). [Inf. blede, cf. 4674 f, 7410 f.]
blente (A.S. blendan, blende), 7558 f (-t CD) (: wente ind. 3 sg. : wente n.). [Inf. blende, 2581 f, 5310 f (blynde BCD), 6889 f (blynde C) ; blynde, 3049 f (blende BCD).[2]]
blente (A.S. blencan, blencte), 4188 (blynte BC, blent[e] E).[3]
bought[e] (A.S. bycgan, bohte), bought, vs, 4007 AB (wrowte C, wrou3t D).[4] [Inf. beye, 8206 f.]
bredde (A.S. brédan, brédde), 465 f (bred CD) (: weren fled, weren fledde B). [Inf. brede, 4388 f.]
brende, see § 100.
broughte (A.S. bringan, bróhte), 3524 f (-t BCD), 5332 f (-t pl. ‡ D), 7143 f (-t D) ; -[e] there, 3428 (-e C, -t ‡ D)[5]; brought in, 3584 broute C, broght D) ; brought || whan, 4521 (-[e] C, -[e] (?) D). [Var. C brou3te ; CD brou3t ; D broght.] [Inf. brynge, -en, cf. 623, 3087, 3356, 5937, etc.]
   Rhyme words.—hym oughte ind. (3524), roughte ind. 3 sg. (5332), by-soughte ind. 3 sg. (5332), he thoughte ind. (7143).
bysette, see sette.

[1] Cf. ten Brink, §§ 173, 176.
[2] The rhymes show the correct form to be blende.
[3] Supply [ne] in C or read neuëre his. In E (Harl. 1239), read neuer.
[4] Supply [that] in C.   [5] Perhaps subjunctive.

§ 99.]   *of Chaucer's Troilus.*   233

bytydde (A.S. tídan, tídde), 1140 f (-tyd D) (: the thridde); bytidde, 8004 (bited B, betyd C †, betide D); be-tidde ‡ ful, 6708 D (bytyt *pres.* 3 *sg.* A, biuit C, betydyth D).¹ [Inf. bytyden, betyde, cf. 1708, 3486 f.]

demede (A.S. déman, démde), demede as, 4569 (-ed B, -yd CD). [Inf. deme, -e[n], cf. 799, 1457, etc.]

dreynte (A.S. drencan, drencte), 543 f (drenkte C) (: compleynte : pleynte). ⁀[Inf. drenche, -en, cf. 4603, 5172 f.]

dwelled (A.S. dwellan, dwealde; but also, later, dwelian, dwelede, -ode, Siev. § 407, Anm. 1), whil [that] she dwelled yn, 129 (-yd D, was dwellynge BCCp.); she duellid ay, 7074 ‡ D. [Inf. dwelle, -en, cf. 144 f, 2699 f, 3489, 6369.]

dyghte (A.S. dihtan, dihte, from Lat. dictare), 2033 f (-t BD, diȝt C) (: they myghte *ind.*).

fedde (A.S. fédan, fédde), -e hem, 2655 (fed[de] ‡ hem D), 6802 (fed BD). [Inf. fede, 5001 f.]

felte (A.S. félan, félde), 3187 f (-t D) (: swelte *inf.* : to-melte *inf.*), 3833 (-[e] D) (1st. pers.), 4118 (-[e] D), 4285 f (: melte *inf.*), 5027 f (-t C) (: melte *inf.*), 6354 ; -[e], 306 B (sholde A †, shold[e] D †), 5560 (-eth B, -ith CD); -e, 3192 (-t D); -e his, 2389 (-t BD); -e he, 3321 (-t D, wiste ‡ C); felt (*before vowels*), 1143, 2361 (ffelte the † thorn C, felt the iryn (?) D),² 7531 (-e CD) (1st pers.); felt his, 502 AB (-e D), 4513 (-e C, -t ‡ in D); felt this, 498 (-e Troilus D, fel to C ³); felt † that, 1146 A (fil B, fil ‡ hym D). felté ‡ here (*eam*), 4043 A (-e BC, -t D). [Inf. fele, -en, cf. 4539; 5128, 7671, etc.]

ferde (A.S. féran, férde), 739 f (-d D) ⁴, 1238 f (-d D) ⁴, 4371 f (-d D), 4633 f (feerde B); ferd (*before vowels*), 225 (-e C), 491 (-e BC),⁵ 2092 (-e C).⁶

    Rhyme words—answerede *ind.* 3 *sg.* (739, 4371), herde *ind.* 3 *sg.* (4633), yerde n. (739, 1238).

grette (A.S. grétan, grétte), 3797 f (-t D) (: sette *ind.* 3 *sg.*), 4430 f (: sette *ind.* 3 *sg.*), 6656 f (grete B, gret D) (: sette *inf.*). [Inf. grete, 4398 f]

hente (A.S. hentan, hente; cf. gehendan), 2009 f (-t CD), 2863 f (-t D), 4029 f (-t CD), 6453 f (hynte B, hent CD); -[e] faste, 1038 AD (-e B); hent here (*eam*), 2239 -e C, hynte B), cf. 4388 ‡ D.

---

¹ In B supply [*it*].   ² In D read [*be*]*gan*.
³ In B read *than*[*ne*].   ⁴ Indirect question.
⁵ Indirect discourse. Dele (*al*) in C.   ⁶ Indirect discourse. First Person.

Rhyme words.—entente *n.* (2009, 4029), sente *ind.* 2 *pl.* (2863), mente *ind.* 3 *pl.* (4029), wente *ind.* 3 *sg.* (6453).

herde (A.S. híeran, etc., hierde, hýrde, gé-hérde), 1731 (-[e] B, -ę the C, -d the D), 1984 f, 2185 f (-d D), 3641 f (-d D), 3907 f (-d D), 4458 f, 4634 f, 4838 f, 6541 f, 8086 f; -[e], 544 (-e C, -ę D), 1301 (-e C); -*e*, 106 (-d BD), 1536 (-d BD), 2675 (-d D, -ë ‡ alwoy C); herd (*before vowels*), 1602 (-e BC),[1] 1643 (-e BC; -D (?)), 4501 (-e BC, herd ‡ ferst (?) D); -*e* his, 2920 (-d D, -ę ‡ preye C^c); herd hym, 549 (-e B, -ë ‡ hym D, herdde C)[2] 1471 (-e C). [Inf. here, -en, cf. 30, 279 f, 398 (hire A), 2662, 3521, 3598, etc.; yhere, 5975 f (yheere B, [y]here C).]

Rhyme words.—yerde *n.* (3907), answèrede, -swèrde *ind.* 3 *sg.* (1984, 2185, 3641, 4458, 4838, 6541, 8086), ferde *ind.* or *subj.* 3 *sg.* (4634).

kepte (A.S. cépan, cépte), 5013 f (: wepte *ind.* 3 *sg.*); kept hire (*poss. sg.*), 130 AC (-e B). [Inf. kepe, -en, cf. 1553 f, 3136, 3261 f, 7411 B, etc.]

keste, see *kyste*.

knette (A.S. cnyttan, cnytte), yn knette, 3930 f (inknitt D) (: shette *ind.* 3 *sg.*).

kydde (A.S. cýðan, cýðde, cýdde), kyd anoon, 208 A (kydde B, ked C).

kyste, keste, cussed (A.S. cyssan, cyste); kyste, 812 f (-t CD), 3971 f (kyssed B, kist D), 4094 f (kist D), 4117 f (kiste CD), 4192 f (-t C), 5823 f (kiste D); keste, 1335 f (kiste B, kyst C, kust D)[3], 4361 f (kyste B, kyst C, kist D), 4417 f (kyste B, kyst C, kist D); kyste, 3067 (-t D, kist C), 3814 (kist C, kyssid D), 6440[4]; cussed tho, 2175 (kiste B, kyssid D, kyste the C). [Inf. kysse, cf. 3024 f, 6914 f.]

Rhyme words.—reste *n.* (3971, 4361), wyste *ind.* 3 *sg.* (812, 4094), *subj.* 1 *sg.* (4117), *ind.* 3 *pl.* (5823), nyste *ind.* 3 *sg.* (4192), lyste *pres. subj.* 3 *sg.* (liste B, lyst C, lust D) (1335), lyste *pret. ind.* 3 *sg.* (leste B, lest C, list D) (3971), truste *pres. ind.* 1 *sg.* (-t CD, triste B) (1335), thriste *pret. ind.* 3 *sg.* (threst C, thrist D) (4417).

ladde, ledde (A.S. lǽdan, lǽdde); ladde, 4556 (ledde B, led C, byd † D); ladde hem, 184 (-d CD, led B); ladde here (*eam*), 6455 (-d C, ledde BD); ladde here (*poss. sg.*), 7077 (ledde B); lad here (*eam*), 2901 (ledde BC, led D); ledde, 7581 f (: fledde *ind.* 3 *sg.*); led here (*poss. sg.*), 1967 (let BC); ledde, 8027 ‡ C (*l.* leyde). [Inf. lede, -yn, cf. 2534, 4559 f, etc.]

laste (A.S. lǽstan, lǽste), 315 f (-t D) (: caste *ind.* 3 *sg.*). [Inf. laste, -en, cf. 2606, 5339 f, 8187 f.]

[1] First Person. Supply [*that*] in D.
[2] Supply [*in*] in B.
[3] "Rather late hand."—Furnivall.
[4] *Antenore* (*Antenor he*) C.

§ 99.]   *of Chaucer's Troilus.*   235

lefte, lafte (A.S. lǽfan, lǽfde); lefte, 5813 B (lost[e] A, loste CD); lefte, 7947 (-t B, lafte D, lefte ‡ not C); lefte his, 1645 (-t D); lafte allas, 4754 A (lefte B, left D) (1st pers.); laft ǁ for, 3364 (left BD, lest † C). [Inf. leuen, cf. 5997.]

lente (A.S. lǽnan, lǽnde), -e his, 725 (bente C, bent D).

lette (A.S. lettan, lette), 2174 f (: sette : shette, *both pret. ind. 3 sg.*), 3315 f (let CD) (: bysette : mette *A.S. métte, both pret. ind. 3 sg.*). [Inf. lette, -en, cf. 150 f, 1817, 5191, 5963.]

leyde (A.S. lecgan, legde, léde), 2633 f (-d *p.p.* ‡ D),[1] 3897 f (-d D), 3970 f, 4797 f, 4842 f, 4886 f, 5825 f, 7236 f,[2] 7397 f, 7508 f, 7802 f; -e, 5813, 7140 (-e ‡ C), 8027 (ledde ‡ C); -e hym, 1600 (-d CD). [Inf. leye, cf. 2756 f, 2914 f, 3501 f, 4447 f, etc.]

    Rhyme words.—Criseyde (2633, 3897, 4797, 5825, 7236, 7397, 7508, 7802), seyde *ind. 3 sg.* (3897, 3970, 4842, 4886, 7236, 7397, 7508, 7802), prayde *ind. 3 sg.* (4797). [Var. B layde ; D leide, laide.]

lyste, liste, leste (A.S. lystan, lyste).   Pret 3 sg. Ind. and Subj. (no attempt is made to register the moods separately in this case.   (*a*) Forms at end of verse,—A *leste, lyste, liste;* B *leste, liste,* C *lest, lyst, leste, list;* D *lest, list, leste, lyst:* 189 f, 357 f, 1169 f, 1694 f, 1998 f, 3065 f, 3294 f, 3974 f, 4521 f, 4608 f, 4833 f, 6880 f, 7203 f (caste † D), 7469 f, 8099 f. (*b*) Before consonants,—lyste, 977 [3], 4155 (liste B, lust to D, they luste C), 8051 (list[e] B, leste C, liste (?) D), cf. 1785 C; lyst[e], 1423 (liste B, ȝe liste C, ȝe lyst[e] D), 3908 (list[e] B, liste C, lest[e] D); lyste, 3985 (list B (?), leste C, list D); leste, 4243 ‡ C; lyst not, 3345 (liste B, list C, lest D) is very likely present. (*c*) Before vowels,—liste, 1302 (luste C, lyst D); lyst, lest (B leste, liste; C lust, liste; D list), cf. 2034 (-*e* B), 4612 (-*e* B), 6414 (-*e* BC). (*d*) Before *h* (in *he, his, hym, here* dat., *hem*),—lyste, 2863 (list B, ȝe list D),[4] 5785 (liste BD); lyst, lest (B liste, lest; C list, lust, lyst; D lest, liste), cf. 2666 (-*e* B), 3365, 6548 (-*e* BD).[5]

    Rhyme words.—reste *n* (189, 1998, 3065, 3974, 4521, 6880, 7469, 8099), gest[e] *n.* (1169), in geste (3294), the beste (3294, 4833, 7203), wyste, nyste *ind. 3 sg.* (357, 4608), kyste *ind. 3 sg.* (3974), twiste *pres. or pret. subj. 3 sg.*[6] (4608), to-breste *inf.* (1694)

mente (A.S. mǽnan, mǽnde), 320 f (-t CD), 1449 f (-t D) (1st pers.), 1677 (-t D †) (1st pers.), 2306 f (-t CD), 2646 f (-t CD), 2968 f (-t CD), 4027 f (-t CD), 5095 f (-t CD), 6080 f (-t CD), 7231 f (-t

---

[1] Possibly subjunctive.   [2] First person   In D read *hand* for *haue*.
[3] Supply [*though*] in C.   D has *lest and*, but is quite unmetrical.
[4] In B supply [*whom*].   [5] In D supply [*here*].
[6] A has *it wyste* for *twyste*.

C † D); -e, 3274 (-t CD), 7210 (-t C)[1]; mente harm (?), 1523 (-t (?) B, -ë C, -t D) (1st person). [Inf. mene, cf. 3006, 3098 f CD.]

    Rhyme words.—descente (320), entente (1449, 2306, 2646, 2968, 4027, 6080 (entent ABCD), 7231), wente *ind.* 3 *sg.* (320, 5095, 6080), hente *pret. ind.* 3 *sg.* (4027).

mette (A.S. métan, métte), 3316 f (-t CD), 4393 f; mettę that, 1068 A (met with D, mette a B). [Inf. mete, -en, cf. 4512 f, 6347, 8066.]

    Rhyme words.—bysette *pret. ind.* 3 *sg.* (3316, 4393), or she lette (3316), shette *inf.* (4393).

mette (A.S. mǽtan, mǽtte), 362 f (-t D), 1175 f (1st pers.), 2010 f (-t D); -e he, 6612 ‡ C (mete *inf.* AB, dreme ‡ *inf.* D), 7601 (mett D); mett[e] ‡ that, 6614 D (*inf.* ABC). [Inf. mete, -en, cf. 4401 f, 6612, 6614.]

    Rhyme words.—lette *n.* (362), sette *pret. ind.* 3 *sg.* (362, 1175, 2010).

myssed (A.S. missan, miste), m. han, 3287 (mys(e)sid C, myssid havę D). [Inf. mysse, 4466 f.]

nedede (A.S. níedan, nýdan, nédan, -dde), nedëdë no, 7089 (neded[ë] BD, nedit (?) C).

radde (A.S. rǽdan, rǽdde (so always in W.S.), but also réd), -e, 2170 AB. [Inf. rede, -en, cf. 83 f, 668, 1188 f, 1214, 2261 f, 2407 f, etc.]

raughte (A.S. rǽcan, rǽhte), 1532 f (rauȝte C, raght D); ouer raughte, 7381 f (-t D, rauȝte C); rauȝt ful, 6423 C (right A, rit(e) B, ritt(e) D).[3]

    Rhyme words.—caughte *ind.* 3 *sg.* (1532), taughte *ind.* 3 *sg.* (7381).

rente (A.S. rendan, rende), 6362 f (-t D) (: wente *ind.* 3 *sg.*); -e, 2013 (-t BD), 3941, 5399.[4]

reste (A.S. restan, reste), -e here (*eam*), 7399 (ref B, reuyth C, rafte (?) D). [Inf. reste, 2411 f.]

reynede (A.S. rignan, rínan, rínde), reynede it, 4399 (-ed B, -yd C, -ed ‡ D). But also a strong pret. (A.S. rán), ron, 3482 (ron(e) D, reyne ‡ *inf.* C), 3519 f (rone D) (: anoon : gon. *inf.*). [Inf. reyne, 3393 f, 4961 f.]

roughte (A.S. rǽcan, reccan, róhte), 496 f (roght D),[5] 5329 f (-t D), 6813 f (-t D); rowhte, 5610 f (roughte B, roughthe Cᶜ, rought D); rought[e] not, 5093 (rouȝte C, route ‡ he (?) D).[6] [Inf. recche, cf. 797 f, 1423 f, 1519 f, 2558 f, 6109 f, 6250 f.]

---

[1] First Person.
[2] All the cases of *mente* cited (except 1449, 2306, 4027, 4699) are in indirect questions : some of them may well be subjunctive.
[3] The correct reading is *rit* = *rideth*.   [4] Supply [*her*] in D.
[5] Hardly subjunctive.   [6] Supply [*that*] in A.

Rhyme words.—thoughte *ind. and subj.* (?) 3 *sg.* (496, 6813), soughte *ind.* 3 *sg* (5610, 6813), by-soughte *ind.* 3 *sg.* (5329), broughte *ind.* 3 *sg.* (5329). [Var. C rou3te.]

semed (A.S. ge-séman, -sémde), s. she, 103 (-ede C, -yd D); s. that, 6086 (-yd CD)[1]; s. not, 7231 (-ede C †, -yd D); semed (*before vowels*), 496 (-yd D),[2] 2906 (-yd D); -ed he, 1721 (-ede C, -yd D); -ed here (*dat.*), 3307 (-ede C, -yd D). [Inf. seme, cf. 703, 747.]

sente, sende (A.S. sendan, sende); (*a*) sente, 1421 f (-t CD), 1916 f (-t CD †), 2421 f (-de C, -t D), 4801 f (-t CD), 5516 f (-t CD), 6650 f (-t CD), 7474 f (-t CD), 7813 f (-t D), 7840 f (-t CD); -*e*, 4427 (-t D); (*b*) sende, 2819 f (: amende *subj.* 3 *sg.* : defende *ind.* 1 *sg.*).[3] [Inf. sende[n], cf. 6047.]

> Rhyme words.—entente *n.* (1916, 5516, 7474), to rente (1916), assente *inf.* (1421), brente *ind.* 3 *sg.* (2421), wente *ind.* 3 *sg.* (6650, 7474), *ind.* 3 *pl.* (4801), stente *inf.* (7840), stente *pret. ind.* 3 *sg.* (7813).

sette (A.S. settan, sette), 359 f (-t D), 1176 f, 2012 f (-t D), 2172 f, 3078 f (-t D), 3542 f (-t D), 3795 f (-t D), 4431 f, 4896 f (sett BD), 7212 f (sett D); bysette, 3313 f (-set D, beset C), 4394 f (be- C); sette, 4673 (-t D); sett at, 444 (-*e* C, set D); sette hym, 2548 (sat C, sate D), -*e* here (*eam*), 1685 (-t B, sate there D †), 2303 (sat C, sat(e) D), 2313 (-t D); -*e* here (*poss. sg.*), 7083 (sett D);[4] set hym, 2149 (sette B, sat C, sete D). [Inf. sette[n], -en, cf. 3742, 5152, 5443.]

> Rhyme words.—lette *n.* (359, 3078, 3542, 7212), mette *A.S.* mǽtte *pret. ind.* 1 *and* 3 *sg* (359, 1176, 2012), mette *A.S* métte *pret. ind.* 3 *sg* (3313, 3542, 4394), er he lette, or she lette (2172, 3313), shette *pret. ind.* 3 *sg.* (2172, 4896), shette *inf.* (4896), y-shette *p p. pred. pl.* (3078), grette *pret. ind.* 3 *sg.* (3795, 4431), fette *pret. ind.* 3 *pl* (7212).

shente (A.S. scendan, scende), 7586 f (-t CD) (: wente *ind.* 3 *sg.* : potente *n.*).

shette (A.S. scyttan, scytte), 2175 f (-t D, schette *p.p.* C), 3568 f (-t D), 3591 f (-t D), 3928 f (swelt † D), 4894 f (shett D); -*e*, 2311 (-t D, schette C).[5] [Inf. shette, 4391 f, etc.]

> Rhyme words.—lette *n* (3591), sette *pret. ind.* 3 *sg.* (2175, 4894), fette *pret. ind.* 2 *sg.* (3568), yn knette *pret. ind.* 3 *sg.* (3928), er he lette (2175), thow ne lette (3568).

soughte (A.S. sécan, sóhte), 388 f (-t D), 5361 f (-t D, sout C), 5608 f (-t D, southe C), 6815 f (-t D), 7600 f (-t D), 8120 f (-t D); bi-, bysoughte, 3422 f (-t D, besoute C), 5331 f (be- C, besowte D);

---

[1] Supply [him] in D.
[2] "No semed it that she of hym roughte." I cannot scan this line.
[3] On (of John's) his by-halue (half BDG John's, halue C, halfe Cp.) which (-e G, with B, *om.* C John's) that (*om.* D) vs alle sowle (soule vs alle CGCp John's, same vs al B, vs soule hath D) sende.—The correct reading is doubtless :. On his halue which that soule vs alle sende.
[4] Supply [wo] in A.   [5] In D read *gan* for *to*.

238   *Observations on the Language*   [§ 99.

soughte, 7935 (-t B, thou3t ‡ D); bi-, bysoughte, 2439 (-t D, besoute C), 7816 (-t B, besou3te C, besou3t D). [Inf. seche, -en, seke, -en, be- (by-) seche (-seke),[1] cf. 704 f, 707, 763, 886 f, 2919 f, 3424 f, 4349 f, 4630 f, 4793 f, 5605, 6472 f, 7160 f, 7220 f, 7495 f, 7901 f, 8081 f, 8211 f.]

> Rhyme words.—thoughte *A.S. þóhte* (388, 5361, 6815), *A.S. þúhte* (7600), wroughte (7600), rooughte (5331, 5608, 6815), broughte (5331), oughte (3422), —*all ind. 3 sg.*; aboughte, *ind.* 3 *pl.* (8120). [Var. C sou3te, besou3te; D soght, besou3t, bysoght.]

spedde (A.S. ge-spédan, ge-spédde), 482 f (-d D), 2034 f (-d D), 2388 f (-d D), 4365 f (spede C); spede hym, 4882 (spedde BD); speddë he, 1771 (-[dë] D). [Inf. spede, 4737 f.]

> Rhyme words.—vnto bedde (2034), abedde (2388), bledde *ind.* (?) 3 *sg.* (2034), *subj.* 3 *sg.* (4365), cledde *ind.* 3 *sg.* (4365), dredde *ind.* 3 *pl.* (482).

spradde (A.S. sprædan, sprédde), ouer-spradde here (*poss. sg.*), 1854 (-d CD); ouer-sprad ‡ the sonne, 1852 D (ouer-sprat *pres.* 3 *sg.* ABC). [Inf. sprede, 1139 f.]

stente, stynte (A.S. for-styntan, ge-stentan, *-stynte, *-stente); stente, 273 f (-t D), 736 f (stynt D),[2] 1683 f (-t D), 7815 f, 7848 f; stent, 2716 ‡ f D (*l.* wente); stente, 1492 (stynte B, stint CD); stynte, 1554 (-[e] D, stinte C), 1961 f (-t D, stente BC), 4080 f (stint D, stente B); stynte, 2941 (-t D), 7291. [Inf. stynte, -en, cf. 2446, 4732, etc.]

> Rhyme words.—entente (736, 1961, 4080), wente *ind.* 3 *sg.* (273, 1683, 7848), sente *ind.* 3 *sg.* (7815).

taughte (A.S. tǽcan, tǽhte), 7379 f (-t D, tau3te C) (: ouer raughte *pret. ind.* 3 *sg.*). [Inf. teche, -en, cf. 2666 f, 4234, 6137 f.]

thoughte (A.S. þencan, þóhte), 386 f (-t BD), 497 f (-t BD), 1063 f (-t D), 2000 f (-t CD), 3307 f (-t BCD), 4640 f (-t D), 5385 f (fele ‡ C), 6816 f (-t D), 7141 f (-t D); -e somwhat, 1784 (-[e] BD, thoute C); -e she, 3825 (-[e] D, thought[e] [s]he B); -e thus, 1541 (-[e] BD), 1695 (-[e] BD, seyde ‡ C); -e this, 6868 (-[e] D; B †); -[e] now, 1364 (-e C, -[e] not[3] D thougth[e] not[1] B) (1st pers.); -[e] best, 2667 (-e BC)[4]; -[e] wel, 1786 (-[e] ferst D, -e C); -e, 361 (-t D, -e so C), 2381 (-t BD), 3483 (-t BD), 7535 (-t BD); thought (*before vowels*), 1472 (-e B, now ‡ C), 1749 (-e C, -t (?) D), 2839 (-[ë] ‡ a D, seydë ‡ o C), cf. 7935 ‡ D; bithought on, 545 (-t (hym) of D, thou3te C †); thoughte he, 276 (-t D), 380 (-t BD, seyde ‡ C), 1352 (-t BD), 2263 (-t D, thoute C), 3918 (-t B, -t ‡ it D), 7548

---

[1] *Seke, seche, by-seche, by-seke*, are all vouched for by the rhyme words, which include *speche, eke, meke*, etc.
[2] In C read *with* for *why*.   [3] Read *now*.   [4] Supply [*l*] in D.

§ 99.] *of Chaucer's Troilus.*   239

(-t ‡ amys D, seydë ‡ he C); -t he, 3539 (-e C), 5026 ‡ D.—
thoughtę ‖ that, 3310 (tought B, thoght ‡ althogh D); thouhtę ‖
ther, 5614 (-ghtę B, -ʒtę CD); thought ‖ whan, 3418 (-[e] B, -e C).
thoughtë his, 2035 (-[é] B, -e C, -t ‡ that (?) D).¹—thoughte ‖ how,
3282 (-t BD). (Cf. also the variants under *thoughte = þúhte*.)
[Inf. thynke (: drynke), thenke (:, synke, swynke), by-thynke,
by-thenke (: ınke), forthynke (: I thenke, *var.* thynke), thenken
(not in rhyme), athynken (not in rhyme), cf. 405 f, 975, 1859, 1868 f,
2340, 2499 f, 4536 f, 6154 f, 6636 f, 7241.]

    Rhyme words.—roughte *subj.* (?) 3 *sg.* (497), *ind.* 3 *sg.* (6816), wroughte *ind* 3 *sg.* (1063, 4640), *pl.* (3307, 5385), broughte *ind.* 3 *sg.* (7141), *pl.* (2000), soughte *ind.* 3 *sg.* (386, 6816), besoughte *ind.* 3 *pl.* (5385), oughte *ind.* 3 *pl.* (2000). [Var. BCD thouʒte; CD thouʒte; D thoght.]

thoughte (A.S. þyncan, þúhte), 3105 f (-t CD), 7223 f (-t BCD)³,
7597 f (he thought D); -e felen, 4539 (-[e] B, -t ‡ thei D; C †);
thowghte by, 3237 (thoughte B, -ʒt[e] C, thoght[e] D); thought[e]
tho, 3986 (-e C); -e, 6337 (-t BD), 7997 (-t BD), cf. 2683 ‡ D;
-e he, 2411 (-t B, -e *pers' l.* C, -t *pers' l.* D); -e hym, 3909 (-t
BD)⁴; -e his, 6893 (-t BD), 7563 (-t BD); -t he, 502 (-e ‡ his (?)
pers' l. C); -t hym, 294 (-e BC; D †), 5026 (-e BC, thought he *pers' l.*
D); -t here (*poss. sg.*), 2193 (-e B, -e *pers' l.* C; D †); thoughtę †
that, 306 (-e he B, -t † he D, -e for C). [Inf. thynke, 405 f.]

    Rhyme words —wroughte *ind.* 1 *sg.* (3105), *ind.* 3 *sg.* (7597), *ind.* 3 *pl* (7223), soughte *ind.* 3 *sg.* (7597), the oughte *pres. sense* (3105). [Var CD thouʒt; C thouʒte; D thoght.]

thraste (A.S. þræstan, þræste), 2240 f (-t C, cast ‡ D) (: faste *adv*). cf.
thriste, threste, § 100, p. 241 and note.

tolde (A.S. tellan, tealde), 261 f (-d BD) (1st pers.), 312 f, 2019 f
(-d D) (1st pers.), 2051 f (-d D), 2275 f (-d D), 5889 f, 6920 f
(-d B), 7012 f, 7569 f (1st pers.), 7616 f, 7875 f; -[e] tales, 3456
(-e C, -d ‡ the tale D); -[e] she, 7854 (-e D); -e, 613 B (C (?), -d
D, telle ‡ A); -d ek, 7848 (-e D, -e C †), 7855 (-e CD); -e here
(*dat*), 7815 (-d B); -d hym, 2580, 3650 (-e BC), 4081 (-e D, tok ‡
C); toldé ‖ who (*or* toldę who), 1656 (-[é] *or* -d BCD)⁵; who told ‡
yow, 3684 (-e hym B, -d him C, D (?). [Inf. telle, -en, cf. 142 f,
260, 794, 3155, etc.]

    Rhyme words —coldę *adj pl* (261), oldę *adj. pl.* (6920, 7012, 7569, 7875), holde *inf.* (261, 312, 2051, 7569), byholde *inf.* (312, 2275, 5889, 6920), holde *subj.* 1 *pl.* (2019), byholde *p p.* (7616), folde *inf* (5889).

---

¹ Supply [*But*] in C.   ² Perhaps -é (-[é]).
³ Perhaps subjunctive. "To asken here yf that here straunge thoughte Strictly, the verb is plural here.   ⁴ Supply [*a*] in A.
⁵ "Or he me *tolde* (told BCD) who *myght* (-e BC) ben his leche."

wende (A.S. wénan, wénde), 447 f, 1497 f (-d D)¹, 2254 (went[e] D), 3644 (-[e] D)¹, 4182 CE (-en *pl.* AB), 4382 f, 7056 f¹, 7974 f (-d D)¹, 8011 ; -e, 7627 (-d D)¹, 8048 (C †)¹; -d it, 3918 (-e BC, went D). [Inf. wene, -e, cf. 3333 A, 6775.]

    Rhyme words —brende *ind.* 3 *sg.* (447, 4382), defende *inf.* (1497), amende *inf.* (7056, 7974).

wente (A.S. wendan, wende), 272 f (C †), 317 f, 1147 f, 1681 f (went ‡ *p.p.* D), 1898 f (-t C), 2625 f (-t C), 2716 f (-t C), 2810 f (-t C), 3394 f, 3627 f (-t C)¹, 4423 f (-t C), 4749 f¹, 5012 f (-t D †), 5096 f (-t C), 5516 f (-t C), 5882 f (-t C), 6363 f, 6454 f (-t C), 6649 f (-t C), 6966 f (-t C), 7384 f (-t C), 7471 f (-t C), 7555 f (-t C), 7583 f, 7666 f (-t C), 7850 f (-t C). In all the above, except 2716, 6454, 7850, D has *went*; cf. also 3329 ‡ D. Before consonants,—wente, 2487 ‡ C (for *went he*), 2576 ‡ C, 2622 (-[e] C, -t ‡ to (?) D), 6988 (-[e] D), 8189 ; -[e], 163 (-e BC, went ‡ euery D). Before vowels, —ABC have regularly *wente*, D has regularly *went* : cf. 1285, 2301, 2576, 2726, 3068 ; but,—went, 1684 A, 2301 C. Before *h* (in *he, his, here*),— -e, 2487 (-t D, -ë tho C), 7937 (-t D); went, 267 (-e BC), 1055, 1897 (om. † B, -e for C)², 2264 (-e BC). [Inf. wende, cf. 2578 f, 3458 f, etc.]

    Rhyme words —descente (317), wente, went[e] *n* (1147, 1898, 3627, 6966, 7555), tente *n.* (7384), potente *n* (7583), entente, -[e] (2810, 3394, 4423, 5516, 5882, 7471, 7666), rente *n.* (4749), stente *pret. ind.* 3 *sg.* (272, 1681, 7850), mente *pret. ind.* (and *subj.* ?) 3 *sg.* (317, 5012, 5096), rente *pret. ind* 3 *sg.* (6363), hente *pret. ind.* 3 *sg* (6454), sente *pret. ind.* 3 *sg.* (6649, 7471), blente *caecavit* (7555), shente *pret. ind* 3 *sg.* (7583), glente *pret. ind.* 3 *pl.* (5882), assente *inf.* (2625, 2716).

wroughte (A.S. wyrcan, worhte), 1064 f (-t D), 3103 f (-t CD, I-wroughte ‡ B) (1st pers.), 4641 f (-t CD), 7356 f (-t D), 7599 f (-t D) ; wrowte, 4007 C (-t D, bought AB). [Inf. werke, -en, -yn, cf. 380, 2486, 4067, 4480 (werchyn C), 4836, 4899, 7356.]

    Rhyme words.—thoughte *A. S.* þóhte *ind.* 3 *sg.* (1064, 4641), thoughte *A. S.* þúhte *ind.* 3 *sg.* (3103, 7599), soughte *ind.* 3 *sg* (7599), oughte 3 *sg. pres. sense* (3103, 7356). [Var. B wroghte ; CD wrouȝt ; C wrouȝte ; D wroght.]

§ 100. A few Indicative Preterites (first and third persons) of Old Norse verbs of the First Weak Conjugation occur in the *Troilus*. With these may be associated several other verbs that form their preterites in *-te*, but are not found in Anglo-Saxon or Old Norse.

---

    ¹ First Person.
    ² But in 1897 AD *went* appears to be *pres.* 3 *sg.*

§ 100.]　　　　　*of Chaucer's Troilus.*　　　　　241

　　　(a) O.N. first conjugation,—*brende (brente), cledde (cladde), hitte, sterte* (?), *thriste* (cf. *threste, thraste*), *trusted* (from the noun, cf. O.N. *treysta*) ; (b) *glente, plighte, swapte, twyste.*
　　　The preterites in this list are all syncopated (-*de, -te*), except *trusted.*
　　　　Note.—For *caste, shapte*, see § 101. For *deyde*, see § 103.
asterte, see *sterte*.
brende, brente (O.N. brenna, brende ; cf. A.S. bærnan, and see ten Brink, § 141), 448 f, 490 f, 3267 f (-d D)¹, 4381 f (D †), 5366 f; -*e*, 4388 (hent ‡ D); brend hym, 440. (brinde B, brende C, brent (?) D).—brente, 2422 f (-de C, -t D). [Inf. brenne, cf. 5907 f, 6666.]
　　　　Rhyme words.—wende *pret. ind.* 3 *sg.* (448, 4381), 3 *pl.* (5366), *subj.* 3 *pl.* (490), amende *inf.* (3267), entende *inf.* (3267), spende *inf.* (5366).—sente *ind.* 3 *sg.* (-de C, -t D) (2422).
　　　　Note.—Ten Brink (§ 170 ζ) seems to recognize only *brente*, not *brende*, though he registers *brend* (p.p.) among the corrections, etc., at the end of his book (p. 225).
cledde, cladde (O.N. klæða, klædda; cf. A.S. cláðian, -ode), cledde, 4363 f (clede C) (: spedde *ind.* 3 *sg.* : bledde *subj.* 3 *sg.*); cladde, 6352 f (: hadde *ind.* 3 *pl.*). [Inf. clothen.= A.S. cláðian, cf. 7781.]
　　　　Note.—*Clothed* does not occur in the Troilus. Ten Brink (§ 173) notices *cladde*, but overlooks *cledde*, though he registers *cled*, p.p., B. Duch. 252.
glente (cf. Swed. glänta), 5885 f BD (*pl.* A, glent *pl.* C) (: entente *n.* : wente *ind.* 3 *sg.*).
hitte (O.N. hitta, hitta), hit hym, 209 A (hitte B); cf. 1284 C.
plighte (pret. of plicchen, quasi A.S. * plyccan), 2205 f (-t D, pliʒte C) (: myghte *ind.* 3 *sg.*). [Inf. plukke (A.S. pluccian), cf. 6065.]
sterte (cf. O.N. sterta, sterta), 2179 f, 4755 f (-t D) (1st pers.), 6073 f (sterede † Cᶜ), 6563 f (i-stert ‡ *p.p.* C), 7899 f ; -*e*, 1532 (-t D, stirte C); vp stirte, 4845 (vp sterte C, stert ‡ vp D)²; asterte, 2939 f (asferte † B, ouersterte C, astert D), 3912 f (-t D), 7855 f (-t C); me asterte, 1043 f (me stert D, may † sterte B). [Inf. sterte, 2719 f, 3791 f.]
　　　　Rhyme words.—herte *n.* (2179, 2939, 3912, 4755, 6073, 6563, 7855, 7899), sherte *n.* (4755), smerte *pres. subj.* 3 *sg.* (2179), *inf.* (1043), smerte *adj. pl.* (6563), conuerte *inf.* (6073).
swapte (cf. Eng. swoop, sweep), -*e* him, 4907 (swappid (?) D, schop C).³
thriste, thraste, threste (O.N. þrýsta, -ta); thriste, 4416 f (thryste B, threst C, thrist D) (: keste *ind.* 3 *sg.*, kyste B, kyst C, kist D); threste, 4916 f (thryst C) (: to reste *inf.*: breste *inf.*); thraste, 2240 f (-t C, cast ‡ D) (: faste *adv.*).

---

¹ Line out of order in ABC, but easily emended.
² "The noyse of peple vp stirte thanne at onys."
³ Read *him seluen* for *him self* in AD. Then read *swappid* in D.

　　　　　　　　　　　　　　　　　　　　　　R

242   *Observations on the Language*   [§§ 100, 101.

Note.—*Thriste*, 4416 f, and *thraste*, 2240 f, have the meaning of *thrust*; *threste* that of the A.S. þrǽstan. Forms from O.N. þrýsta and forms from A.S. þrǽstan appear to have become confounded.

trusted (from the noun; cf. O.N. treysta, treysta), -ed most, 7611 (trostedę C) (1st pers.). [Inf. tryste, triste, cf. 692 f, 3100 f, 3758 f, 4069 f, 8029 f; vntriste, cf. 3681 f; trust[e], cf. 1576; trusten, mystrusten, cf. 688, 690, 6132, etc.]

twyste (cf. A.S. -twist, *sbst.*, and M.L.G. twisten), -e 4916 (twiste BD).

§ 101. The following Indicative Preterites (first and third persons) of Anglo-Saxon verbs of the Second Weak Conjugation occur in the *Troilus* (cf. Child, § 53; ten Brink, §§ 172-3).

answèręde (-swerde, -swèred), asked, brydled, called, cursed, flekęred, folwede, gladede (-ed), herkęned, hied, huntede, liked, loked (-ęd), louedę (-ęd), made (cf. pl. makkeden), opęned, pleyde, putte, refte (rafte), shewed, thonked, twyghte, welcòmed. In the following alphabetical list are included also (a) from the Old Norse second declension,—caste, gayned, shapte, wanted, (b) four words of Germanic origin, not found in Anglo-Saxon, that form preterites after the analogy of the second declension,—bekked (see the word), houede, lakked, poked (?).

Syncopated preterites in *-de, -te*, after the analogy of the first conjugation, are answèręde (-swerde), caste (O.N.), made, pleyde, putte, refte (rafte), shapte (O.N.), twyghte. The other preterites of this declension end in *-ed, -edę, -ede* : no case of *-edë* occurs.

Several verbs of the first declension form unsyncopated preterites on the analogy of the second. For these, see ayled, demede, cussed (s.v. kyste), myssed, nededë (?), reynede, semed (§ 99). Cf. also trusted (from the noun, cf. O.N. treysta, pret. *-ta*) (§ 100).

Note 1.—For *cledde, cladde*, see § 100.
Note 2.—For the weak preterite *walkedę* from the strong verb *walken* (A.S. walcan), see § 103. For *quaked, quok* (A.S. cwacian, -ode), see § 103, note 2.

answèręde, answèrde, answèred, (A.S. andswarode); answèrędę, 737 f (-rde B, -ryd C, -rd D), 1982 f (-rde CD, -r[d]e B), 2187 f (-rde BC, -rd D), 3643 f (-rde BC, -rd D), 4369 f (-rde BC, -rd D), 4840 f (-rde BC, -rd D), 8088 f (-swarde B, -swerd D); answèrde, 4459 f, 6539 f (-d D); answèred, 1030 f (-rde BC, -rd D). *Before consonants*,—answèrędę, 5244 (-rde B, -rd[e] D), 6315 (-rde B, -rd[e] D, -rde ‡ C), 7523 (-rde B, -rd[e] D); -swèrde, 5876 (-[e] D, [he]

§ 101.]   *of Chaucer's Troilus.*   243

answerde ‡ herte C), cf. 5202 CD (*below*); -swèred, 4005 (-swarde B, -swerẹd him C, -swerịde him D), 4051 (-rde BC, -rịde D), 4334 (-rde B, -rid D, -rịde ‡ and C), 5302 (-rde C, -rde hym B, -rd him D), 6847 (-rde B, -rd[e] D, -rede C †). *Before vowels,*—answèrẹde, 4498 (-rde B, -rẹd C, -rd D), 5042 (-rde BCD), 5783 (-rde BC, -rd D), 5897 (-swarde B, -swerde C, -swerd D), 7638 (-rde BC, -rd D); answèrde, 2507 (-rẹd C, -rd D †), 2703 B (-r[d]e A, rr[d]e C^c, -rd D), 6686; answèrẹd, 2530 (-rde B, -rẹde C, -ıd D), 3767 (-rẹde BC, -rd D), 4019 (-rde B, -rẹde C, -rịde D), 6190 (-rde B, -rẹde C, -rd D), 6777 (-swarde B, -swerde C †, -swerd D), 7491 (-swarde B, -swerde CD), 7533 (-rd BD, -rde C); he answèrẹd and, 5097 (-rde B, he answerde C, he answerd D). *Before h,*—answèrẹde hym, 5202 (-rde B, -rde Troylus C, -rd[e] T. D); -swèrẹd hym, 2030 (-rde B, -rd[e] do CD), 3974 (-rde BC, -ride ‡ as D), 7230 (-rde B, -swèrede ‡ C, -ṇd D). answèred ‖ yf, 829 AB (-swerd[e] D, -swerde ȝyf C), 2136 (-swerde B, -swerıd ıf D, -swerde Pandạrus C). [Inf. answère, 2070.]

Rhyme words.—yerde *n.* (737), ferde *ınd. 3 sg.* (737, 4369), herde *pret. ınd. 3 sg.* (1982, 2187, 3643, 4459, 4840, 6539, 8088), *pret. subj. 3 sg.* (1030).

asked (A.S. áscian, áxian, -ode), (ı) 3593 (axen † B, seydë ho C, seid[e] ho D), 6471 (aixed B, axedẹ C, axed D); (ii.) asked him, 3411 (axed B, axẹd ‡ C, axid D), 5888 (axede C (?)); axẹd hym, 7587 BD (asketh A, axe C)[1] [Inf. aske, -en, axe, -en, cf. 1232, 1979, 3700, 5217, 5334, etc.]

bekked (cf. A.S. b{ecnan, bécnan, I., later béacnian, -ode, II.), b. on, 2345 (-ede C, -yd D).[2]

brydled (A.S. ge-brídlian, -ode), b. youre, 6340 A (bridẹled BD).

called (A S. ceallian, -ode, from O.N. kalla, kallaða), c. euẹre, 541 (clepid ‡ D, callyd in C). [Inf. calle, 902 f, etc.]

caste (O N. kasta, -aða), 314 f (-t D), 1227 f (-t D), 1284 f (-t BC † D), 1733 (-t adoun CD)[3], 2344 f (-t D), 2442 f (-t ‡ *inf.* D), 3939 f (-t CD), 5184 f (-t C), 8183 f AB[4]; cast ‡, 2240 f D (thraste AB, thrast C); -e, 75 (-t BD), 1492 (-t CD), 4696 (-t BD); cast (*before vowels*), 1159 (-e B), 7290 (-e BCD); -e he, 726 (-t BD); -e hıs, 1064 (-t *inf.* D †), 7292 ‡ D (threw AB, throwe *inf.* C); -e hym, 4672 (-t BD); -t here (*poss. sg.*), 7368 (-e B, kiste D)[5]; cast ‖ how,

[1] In D read *wher[of]*.   [2] Supply [*he*] in A.
[3] AB read *caste doun*.   [4] Supply [*was*] in B.
[5] Supply [*al*] in A, and read *ey[en]*.

4823 (-e B, -e he C, -t he D).[1] [Inf. caste, -en, cf. 1338 f, 1598, etc.]

> Rhyme words.—faste *adv.* (1227, 1284, 2240, 2442, 3939, 5184), at the laste (1227, 3939, 5184, 8183), laste *ind.* 3 *sg.* (314), paste *ind.* 3 *sg.* (2344).

clepid (A.S. cleopian, -ode). See *called.*

curssed (A.S. cursian, -ode), (i.) 6570 (-eth B, -ede C, -ed D), 6571 (-eth B, -ede C, -ed (?) D). [Inf. cursen, cf. 3738.]

flekered (A.S. flicerian, -ode), flekered ay, 5883 (fliked B, flekerede C, f[l]ykered D).

folwede (A.S. folgian, -ode), fol(e)wede, 7379 (folwed B, folwede C, folowed D). [Inf. folwe, -en, cf. 614, 3903, 5838, etc.]

gayned (O.N. gagna, -aða), 352 f (-yd D) (: feyned *ind.* 3 *sg.*: destrayned *ind.* 3 *pl*).

gladed, -e (A.S. gladian, -ode), -ede, 173 (-yd D, gladde[d] B); gladed her (*eam*), 116 (-ede C, -id D, gladded B); gladed hym, 7547 (-ede C, -eth D, gladded B). [Inf. glade, -en, cf. 734, 2064, 2630 f, 2659 f, etc.]

herkened (A.S. hércnian, -ode), herkened she, 2008 (herkned B, -enyd D). [Inf. herkenen, cf. 164 ; herken, cf. 1180.]

hied (A.S. hígian, -ode), h. not, 2999 (hyed B, hyed her D ; C †). [Inf. hye, cf. 3463 f.]

houede (cf. M.L.G. hoven), -e here (*eam*), 6396 (-ed BD). [Inf. houe, 4269 f.]

huntede (A.S. huntian, -ode), -ede hem, 1282 (-ed B, -yd D). [Inf. hunten, cf. 4622.]

lakked (cf. M. Dutch laken), l. routhe, 2365 (lak of *n.* CD) ; l. alwey, 7108 (-id C) ; -ede here (=her), 7187 (-ed BD). [Inf. lakke, -en, cf. 189, 5607, 6185.]

liked, lyked (A.S. lícian, -ode), (i.) liked wel, 2129 (-ede C, -yd D) ; (ii.) -ed, 2351 (-yd D, they likede ‡ in C), 6994 (-id C) ; -ed hire (*dat.*), 1996 (-yd D, -ede C). [Inf. like, lyke, lyken, cf. 431, 1130, 2655 f, 3455, 6496, etc.]

loked (A.S. lócian, -ode), -ede forth, 7507 C (-ed D (?), -eth AB) ; -ed, (ii) 1071 (-yd ‡ D (?)), 1359 (-yd CD), 7073 (-ede C), 7092 (-ede C ; B †) ; -ed he, 2833 (-ede C, -yd D) ; -ed in to, 2312 (-ede C, -yd D). [Inf. loke, -en, cf. 206, 629, 1350.]

louede (A.S. lufian, -ode), -ede Troylus, 1753 (-yd D, -es B) ; -ede neuer, 6520 (-ed BD) (1st pers.) ; -ede so, 7838 (-ed BD) ; -ed

---

[1] In AB it is possible to read *caste* (-[e] A), whether we allow the "extra syllable before the cæsura" or not.

§ 101.]   *of Chaucer's Troilus.*   245

so, 2489 (-yd C, -id D); louede || that, 1071 (-ed B, -id D (?)); -ed ‡ the, 8109 D (-eth AB); -ede hym, 2928 (-ed BC, -id D)[1]; -ede ek, 4991 (-ed BC, -yd D) (1st pers.). [Inf. loue, -en, cf. 798, 1944, 2854, 3639, etc.; vnlouen, cf. 8061.]

made (A.S. macian, -ode), 312[2], 1137 f, 1585 f (mode † B), 1963 (-e B), 2627 f, 2660 f, 3455 f, 6333, 6440 (-e D), 7415, 7792 (?); -[e], 5898 (-e BCD); -e, cf. 1148, 2160, 3220, 6341, 8203; made his, etc., cf. 479, 1145 (D †), 1153, 1637, 2007, 2253 (-ë ‡ her D), 3189, 4070 (-e ‡ D), 6862 (mad(yn) hym C), 6968, 7406; -e ‡ suche, 4070 D; -e this, 5324 (mad C); -e the, 7878; -ë ‡ and (?), 2170 CD. *Maked* seems not to occur, but cf. pl. *makkeden*, 4783 B. [Inf. make, -en, cf. 4177, 6825, etc.]

    Rhyme words.—glade *adj. pl.* (1137, 1585, 3455), glade *inf.* (2627, 2660), lade *inf.* (2627).

opened (A.S. openian, -ode), opened here herte, 4081 (opned B, openid C).

pleyde (A.S. plegian, -ode, North. also plægde), 1067 (pleyed D), 6872 ‡ f D (seyde ABC), 7537 f (pleyede C); pleyde he, 3456 (-ede C, pleyd D). [Inf. pleye, -en, cf. 671 f, 1206 f, 1902, 2599 f, 5122, etc.]

    Rhyme words.—seyde (6872 D, 7537), Cresseide (6872 D)

poked (cf. M.L.G. poken), p. euere, 2958 (-ede C, puked † B, procurid † D).

putte (A.S. potian, -ode), -e, 2264 (put D); put al, 4027 (putte BD). (Cf. 1985 D †.) [Inf. putten, putte, cf. 6170, 6174 (puten B).]

refte, rafte (A.S. réafian, -ode), refte hym, 484 AC (-t B); rafte hir (*eam*), 7399 D (reste A, ref[t] B, reuyth C). [Inf. reue, -en. cf. 188, 2744 f.]

shapt[e] (O.N. skapa, skapaða; skepja, skapði; cf. A.S. scieppan, sceppan, scóp, O.N. skapa, skóp), shapt here (*eam*), 2642 (-e B, schop C, schop(e) D (?)). For *shop*, cf. 207, 1146, 3393, 5617. [Inf. shape, cf. 3038.]

shewed (A.S. scéawian, -ode), (i.) 286 (-ede C, -yd D),[3] 7383 (-eth B, -ede C); (ii.) 487 (semede ‡ C). [Inf. shewe, -en, cf. 5943 f, 5953, 6052, 6994 f, 8057.]

thonked (A.S. þancian, -ode), (i.) 124 (thankked B, thankede C, thonkyd ‡ oft D), 3316 (-id D, thanked B, thankede C), 6546

---

[1] Supply [*and*] in D.
[2] "He neither chere (schyr C, cher G) ne (*om.* BCDG) made ne word (-e BG) tolde" No note in Austin. Are we to read "He neither chere made ne word ne (*or* he ?) tolde"?
[3] 9-syl., except in D, which has an ungrammatical *she* before the verb.

246   *Observations on the Language*   [§§ 101, 102.

(thankede C, thanked D); (ii.) -ed hym, 2306 (-yd D, thankes B, thankede C); -ed here (*dat.*), 2318 (-yd D, thanked B, thankede C), 2576 (-id D, thanked B, thankede C), 3972 (thankede C, thanked D). [Inf. thanke, -en, thonken, cf. 1933, 4045, 4436.]

twyghte (A.S. twiccian, - *ode), 5847 f (twy3t C, twight D) (: myghte 3 *sg.* : dyghte *inf.*).

wanted (O.N. vanta, -aða), ne wanted neuere, 6230 D ([ne] wantede C, ne wanteth A, ne wanthe (?) B).

welcòmed (A.S. wilcumian, -ode), w. hym, 7212 (-ede C, -[ed] B).

§ 102. The following Indicative Preterites (first and second persons) of Anglo-Saxon verbs of the Third Weak Conjugation occur in the *Troilus*,—*hadde, leuede, seyde* (cf. Child, § 53 ; ten Brink, § 162).

hadde (A.S. habban, hæfde), 92 (had[de] BD), 477 f (-d D), 2435 f (-d CD), 3517 (-d ‡ not D), 3712 A (B †; -e I C, -d y D),[1] 4231 ABC, 6567 f, 7008 (hade ‡ C, had[de] D), 7389 (-[de] D); cf. 2634 ‡ C, 4424 ‡ D; hadde, 1649 (-d B; D (?))[1], 3557 (-d D)[1], 4937, 7745[1], etc. ; had (*before vowels*), 6989 (hadde BCD)[2], 8017 (-de CD, hadde ‡ rent B); hade, 1718 C (hadde AB, had [a] D), 4635 ‡ C (had ‡ D, held AB); hadde (*before he, his, hym, here* (*poss. sg.*), here-vp-on), cf. 89, 188, 304, 663, 1992, 2783 (hade A), 3377, 4069, 5335, 7316, 7467; had hym, 2634 (-de ‡ prei3ed C), 6834 (-dé ‡ hym BD, -de ‡ sent C)[3]; hadde herd, 5007 (adde B); had herd, 750 (-de BC), 1002 (-de C), 5329 (-de BC); but,—hadde horn, 1727 (-de hed C; D †); cf. hade ‡ it, 5888 C; hadde av, 7074 (-[dé] B, -e C, *om.* D); -ë ‡ hym, 4069 A (?),[4] 6834 ‡ B; -ë ‡ his, 6927 C; hauede ‡ in (?), 5155 C.—hadde, 500 (hade C; D †), 1687 (-d BD), 2355 (-de BC, -[de] D),[5] 4835 (had BD); cf. 132 ‡ A, 2229 ‡ C, 7317 ‡ C; hade, 89 ‡ C, 1992 ‡ C; had (*before consonants*), 7102 (-de C)[6]; cf. 663 ‡ (?) D, 6927 ‡ D, 7229 ‡ D. [Inf. haue, hauen, han, cf. 13, 120 f, 122, 4305 f, etc., etc.]

    Rhyme words.—gladde *adj. pl.* (2435), madde *adj. pl.* (6567), madde *inf.* (477).

leuede (A.S. libban, lifgan, lifde, L.W.S. lifede, liofode), -ede yn, 5155 (-ed D, lyuede B, hauede ‡ C)[7]; lyued in, 5142 B (-ed D (?), leue

---

[1] First Person.   [2] Supply [seye] in D.   [3] 9-syl. in C.
[4] Read iust[e] cause and hadde hym.   [5] Or (?) ne hadde she AB.
[6] First person.
[7] First Person. 9-syl., if read as suggested: "I that leuede yn lust and in plesaunce."

§ 102.] *of Chaucer's Troilus.* 247

inf. A, lyuyn C). [Inf. lyue, -en, leue, -en, cf. 427, 520, 1635, 1663 f, 2066 f, 2212, 3626, 5142, 5430, 5852, 6660, 7444.]

seyde (A.S. secgan, sægde, séde), cf. 457 f, 722 f, 1005 f, 1184 f, 1964 f, 2159 f (seyede C), 2318 f, 2429 f[1], 2500 f, 3894 f, 3972 f, 4016 f[2], 4263 f, 4313 f, 4814 f, 4841 f, 4885 f, 5007 f, 5039 f, 5489 f, 5536 f, 5622 f, 5810 f, 5915 f, 6315 f, 6580 f, 6869 f, 6872 f, 6885 f, 7052 f, 7097 f, 7233 f, 7295 f (seide A), 7309 f, 7337 f, 7396 f, 7484 f, 7534 f, 7536 f, 7607 f, 7787 f, 7803 f, 8039 f, 8076 f, 8093 f; seyde, 752 (-[e] D),[3] 1361 (-[e] D, sayd[e] B),[4] 2037 (-[e] D), cf. 117, 330, 822, 870, 877, 1039, 1103, 1336, 1340, 1587, 1591, 1695 ‡ C, 1970, 2057 CD, 2060, 2176, 2181 ‡ C, 2215, 2228, 2248, 2250, 2267, 2284, 2338, 2362, 2378, 2395, 2404, 2444, 2509, 2686 (seide A), 2690, 2692, 2713, 2959, 3202, 3413, 3418, 3490[2], 3510[2], 4490, 5042, 5097 BCD, 6418[2], 6686; seyde (before *th*), cf. 1174, 1548, 1998, 2025, 2130, 2205 C, 3065, 3420, 3471, 4498, 5036, 7318; seyde, cf. 397, 507, 583, 873, 1052, 1294, 1412, 1494, 1912 AB, 2057 AB, 2162, 4641, 5097 A, 6421, 7146, 7549, 8087; -[e], 5188 (-e CD); -e he, 491 (-d BD)[5], cf. 380 C, 561, 1164, 1294 C, 1599, 2130 C, 4429, 7594; -e hym, 7790, cf. 195 C, 1230; -e here (*dat.*), 2241 (-ë B, -ë caste C, -[ë] cast D)[6], 3596 (-d D); seyd here (*dat.*), 2205 (-ë thus C, -[e] thus D), cf. 2713 D; -e how, 5419 (-d B, *om.* ‡ C), 5831. (In almost all the cases so far cited D omits final -e.)

seyde ‖ who, 1736 (-e ho C, -d ho D)[7]; seyde ‖ lord, 2028 (-d D, -ë C)[8]; seyde farwel, 4367 (seidë CD); -e ‡ furst, 5349 D (quod ABC); -e ‡ to fore, 6418 C (1st pers.); -e ‖ nought, 7146 B (-e AD; C †); -e ‡ to, 7315 C; seid ‡ than, 2710 D; seid ‡ wol, 2713 D; seid ‡ god, 2798 D. The construction of *seyd* in *seyd welawey*, 3146 (sayd C) is very curious.

seydë (*hiatus*),—seydë he, 421 (-[ë] D)[9], cf. 7548 ‡ C; seydë ‖ em, 2244 (-e hym B, -d hym D); seydë ‡ hire (*dat.*), 2241 B. [Inf. seye, seye, sey, seyn, cf. 492 f, 512, 574 f, 672 f, 3095, 3280, 7740, etc., etc.; see § 119, XIII.

Rhyme words.—Criseyde (457, 1005, 1964, 2318, 2500, 3894, 4016, 4263, 4313, 4814, 4841, 5007, 5039, 5489, 5536, 5622, 5810, 5915, 6315, 6580, 6868, 6872, 6885, 7052, 7097, 7233, 7295, 7809, 7396, 7484, 7607, 7787, 7803, 8040, 8076, 8093), mayde *n.* (1964), refreyde *inf.* (2429), breyde,

---

[1] Hardly subjunctive.   [2] First Person.   [3] Supply [*that*] in C.
[4] Supply [*faste*] in A.   [5] Dele (*al*) in C.
[6] But supply [*it*] in B, and read *seyde*.
[7] In A read *self* for *seluen*. Cf. *seydë ho*, 3593 C.   [8] In C read *swete* for *smete*.
[9] "And to the god of *loue* thus *seydë he*," or *loue* and *seyde he*.

abreyde *inf.* (5007, 6885), vpbreyde *inf.* (8076), deyde *ind.* 3 *sg.* (1184, 4814, 7387), -de, -ede *subj.* 1, 3 *sg.* (457, 4016), pleyde *ind. and subj.* (?) 3 *sg.* (1005, 7534, 7536), preyde *ind.* 3 *sg.* (2159), leyde *ind.* 1, 3 *sg.* (3894, 3972, 4841, 4885, 7233, 7396, 7803), seyde *ind.* 3 *sg.* (6868, 6872, 7534, 7536), breyde, abreyde *ind.* 3 *sg.* (722, 7607). [Var. CD seide ; D seid.]

§ 103. Several verbs that are strong in Anglo-Saxon show weak preterites in the *Troilus* (cf. Child, § 54, a; ten Brink, § 167).

(a) Syncopated preterites in -*de*, -*te*: *breyde, fledde, highte, lepte, loste, sighte (sighed siked), slepte, smerte, wepte* (to which add *dredde*, sometimes weak in A.S., and *deyde*, O.N.); (b) unsyncopated preterites in -*ed*: *lyed* (q. v.), *walked* (q. v.).

Note 1.—For *shapte*, see § 101. For *radde*, see § 99. *Swelt*, 3928 f D, is an error for *shette*.

Note 2.—*Quake* (inf. *quake*, cf. 2406 f, 3384 f, 4042 f, 6619 f), A.S. *cwacian*, -*ode*, shows a strong preterite *quok*, 6399 (-oo-B, quok(e) D), 7289 f (-(e) D, quook(e) B), *quook*(e), 2935 (quook B, quok C, quok(e) D)[1], cf. ten Brink, § 152 ; but the weak preterite *quaked* does not occur in the *Troilus*. *Rynge* (inf. *rynge*, cf. 4079 f), A.S. *hringan, hringde*, has pret. *rong*, cf. 2700[2], 4567.

abreyde, see *breyde*.

breyde (A.S. bregdan, brægd, bræd), 7606 f ; abreyde, 724 f (vpbrayd D) ; she abreyde, 5874 f (she brayde B, sche brayd C).[3] (For strong pret. *abrayd*, see B. Duch. 192, Ho. F. 110, and cf. ten Brink, § 140.) [Inf. breyde, cf. 4892 f, 5010 f; abreyde, cf. 3955 f, 6883 f.]

Rhyme words.—Criseyde (5874, 7606), seyde *ind.* 3 *sg.* (724, 7606).

deyde (O.N. deyja, dó, late deyða), 56 f (deyed B), 875 f (-d D, deyede BC), 1186 f (-ed B, -ede C, -d D), 4013 f (-ede B, deiede C, drede ‡ D), 4813 f (dyede B, deyede C, deide D), 5094 f (dyed B, deyede C, deyed D), 7339 f (deyede C, deyd D, seyde † B), 8197 f (deyed B). [Inf. deye, dye, cf. 573 f, 728 f, 758 f, 1027 f, 1257 f, 1524 f, 1526 f[4], 2160 f, etc., etc.; deyen, dyen, cf. 306 f, 1412 f, 8127, etc.]

Rhyme words.—Criseyde (56, 875, 4013, 4813, 8197), seyde *ind.* 1, 3 *sg.* (1186, 4013, 4813, 7339), *subj.* (?) 3 *sg.* (5094), deyde *subj.* (?) 3 *sg.* (5094).

dredde, dradde (A.S. on-drǽdan, on-drḗd, sometimes -drǽdde), dredde, 1959 (dredë ‡ I C, dred D),[5] 4489 (dred BD)[6]; -e hire (*acc.*), 2165 (dradde BC, drad D); dradde ay, 7933 (drede *inf.* BCD) : -e hire (*acc.*), 1540 (dredded B, dredde C, drede *inf.* (?) D). [Inf. drede, -en, cf. 84 f, 252, 6748.]

fledde (A.S. fléon, fléah), 7561 f BCD (fledde *p.p.* A) (: bledde *ind.*

[1] Supply [ek] in D.   [2] Supply [hem] in CD.
[3] *I breyde*, 7625 f, is apparently present.
[4] Noteworthy is the occurrence of *dye* in 1524 f (: *crye* ind. 1 sg. : *vilonye*) followed by *deye* (: *seye* ind. 1 sg.) in 1526 f.
[5] After *al* (= although).   [6] In an indirect question.

§ 103.] *of Chaucer's Troilus.* 249

or *subj*. 3 *sg*.), 7580 f (: ledde *ind*. 3 *sg*.); fledde he, 3192 (thei ‡ fled *pl*. D). (Is *fley* ‡, 5264 C, meant for a pret.?) [Inf. fle, flen, cf. 747 f, 1279 f, 1795 f, 4105, etc.]

highte, byhight[e] (A.S. hátan, heht, hét; cf. ten Brink, § 135); highte *promisit*, 7999 f (hyʒt C, hight D); byhight, byhyght *promisit*, 6873 f (be- D, bihighte B, behyʒte C), 7567 f (-highte B, behyʒt C, behight D).—highte *vocatus est*, 69 D (hyghte B, high[te] A), 2701 (-[e] D, hiʒte C †); so, with ellipsis of the relative,—thei hadde a relik *hight* (*heet* B, *hyʒt* C) Palladion, 153. Cf. hight Elẏsos, *vocatur*, 5452 AD (height B), and,—highte vòlturis, *vocantur*, 788 (-en B, -yn D, hyʒte C). *Hatte* (A.S. hátte, used both as pres. and as pret.) also occurs : The owle ek which that *hatte* Escaphilo, 6682 (hette B, hiʒte C, hete D); How that ye louen sholde on that *hatte* Horaste, 3639 (hat D (?)). For *heet*, vocatus est, see 153 B (above).

Rhyme words.—myghte, -[e] 3 *sg*. (6873, 7567, 7999), he sighte *ind*. (7999).

lepte (A.S. hléapan, hléop), -e, 2722 (lep C, lep(e) D). [Inf. lepe, 2040 f.]

loste (A.S. for-léosan, -léas), -[e] speche, 5813 (-e CD, lefte B); -e his, 441 (-t BD). [Inf. lese, -en, cf. 4850 f, 7161.]

lyed (A.S. léogan, léah), lyèd ‡ loude, 2162 D (ley ful AC, leigh ful B).[2] [Inf. lye, lyen, cf. 4775 f, 7887 f, 7890.]

sighte, sighed, siked (A.S. sícan, sác); sighte, syghte, 3922 f (-t CD), 5376 f D, 5879 f (-t D, seyʒt C), 7996 f (-t CD, sigchte B); sight[e] sore, 5783 (-e B, sighed D, seyde † C), sight and, 4313 (-e B, seyʒt C, siʒed D), 6421 (-e B, syhede C, sighed B).—sighed lest, 279 (sykyd CD); -ed sore, 3898 (-id D, sight[e] B, sikede C), 5559 (sighte B, -t[e] D; C †).— siked sore, 3814 (-yd C, syghid D);[3] syked sore, 5378 (syʒcde C, syhed D)[4]; syked for, 7078 (sighte B, sihed eke D). [Inf. syke, cf. 596 f, 751, 827 f, 1513 f, 1969 f,[5] 2658 f, 2900 f, 3654 f, 4012 f, 4202 f.]

slepte (A.S. slǽpan, slép, North. slépte, W.S. sometimes onslépte), slepte, 7602 (slep C); cf. *pl*. slepten al, 3588 (-yn C, slepyn[6] D). But,—slep, (i.) 7803 (slep(e) B (?), slepté (?) D, no ‡ word C); (ii) 2010 (-(e) BD). [Inf. slepe, -en, cf. 1998, 2183, 3262 f, 3499, 3509, 4378.]

smerte (A.S. smeortan, * smeart), 2015 f (-t D, sinerte † C) (: herte *n*.). [Inf. smerte, cf. 1042 f, 2373 f, 4024 f, 6110 f, 6280 f.]

---

[1] Indirect discourse.   [2] In D supply [*that*].   [3] After *al-though*.
[4] Indirect discourse, 9-syl. verse.   [5] Rhymes with *endite*, inf., and *the white*.
[6] Perhaps intended by the scribe for a present.

walkedę (A.S. walcan, wéolc), -ede ‡, 7585 C (-ęd D, -eth AB); -ede ‡, 1908 C (-eth AB, -ith D). But,—welk, (i.) 7598 (welk(e) B, walkędę C, walkęd D)[1]; (ii.) I welk allone, 1602 (-e B, walkyd D).[2] [Inf. walke, cf. 7029 f.]

 Note.—Ten Brink (§ 134) remarks that *walken* is "ausschliesslich schwach flectiert."

wepte (A.S. wépan, wéop), 5015 f (: kepte *ind.* 3 *sg.*); wepte sore, 1647 (-[e] D)[3]; -e, 5383 (-e for C †, -e for D); wepte ‖ bothe, 7088 (wepįd C); -ę she, 7409 (wep C).—But,—weep nought, 5800 (wep(e) B, wepyn † C, -įth ‡ D); wep ‖ ful, 7945 (weptę BCD); wep ‖ as, 2957 (-(e) D, wepte C). [Inf. wepe, -en, cf. 5591, 6445, 7598 f, etc.]

§ 104. A few Romance verbs show syncopated preterites in *-de*, *-te*, after the analogy of the First Weak Conjugation (cf. Child, § 53; ten Brink, § 180, 182).

aspỳde, 2337 f (-piede BC) (: ryde *inf.*); aspide, 6902 f (espied B, asspiede C, espide D) (: ryde *inf.*).—asplede wel, 2927 (-plęd B, -pỳed D). [Inf. espye, espie, aspye, aspie, aspien, espyen, cf. 1734 f, 2592 f, 3415 f, 3677 f, 3977, 4815 f, 5886 f, 6544 f, 7177 f, etc.]

caughte (O. Fr. cachier), 1533 f (kaughte B, cauhte C[c], caught D) (: he raughte *pret. ind.*); -e, 280 (cauȝte C, caght D); caught his, 7917 (-e B, -t D, cauȝte? C ‡).—kaught[ë] first, 6930 (caught[e] BD, cauȝte C). [Inf. kecche, 4217 f A.]

cride, 5875 f (cried D, cryede BC), 6568 f (cried BD, creyde C); cryde loude, 7868 (cried BD, cryęde C).—cride, 729 (criędę B, cryęde C, crięd D), 6579 (crięd BD, cryęde C), 7607 (crięde BC, crięd D); cride his, 8036 (crięd BD, cryęde C); crięd a, 5415 (cryęd BD, cryede ‡ C). [Inf. crie, crye, cryen, cf. 806, 1485, 3864 f, 5887 f, etc.]

 Rhyme words.—glide *inf.* (5875), Cupide (5875, 6568), Cipryde (6568).

hurte -e, 1284 (-t D, hitte C †).—hurt ‖ a, 6713 (hirt C, hurt ‖ [a] tymè D).

paste, 1483 f (at last † D), 2345 f (passede C : caste C, past D).—passed nought, 456 (-edę C, -yd D); -edę forth, 1639 (-ed BC, -id D). [Inf. passe, pace, passen, cf. 41 f, 371 f, 847, 1165 f, 2931 f, 3062 f, 4114 f, etc.; trespace, cf. 4017.]

 Rhyme words.—at the laste (1483), caste *pret. ind.* 3 *sg.* (2345).

---

[1] Indirect discourse.   [2] In D supply [*that*].   [3] Indirect discourse.

[§§ 104, 105.]   *of Chaucer's Troilus*   251

preyde, 2687 f (preyede C, prayd D)[1], 4799 f (preyede C), 6100 f (preyede C, preid D); preyede, prayede, 2157 f (preyde B, preyed C, prayd D), 4876 f (preyde B, praide D)[1]; preyede hem, 2786 (-ed B, preied C, prayed D).[2]—preydė here (*acc.*), 6480 (preÿėde ‖ sche C ‡, preide she (?) D).—praide ‡ god, 5400 D (bad ABC).[3] [Inf. preye, preyen, preyę, -ęn, prey, cf. 48, 2521 (?), 2841 f, 2920 f, 2926, 6678, etc.]

    Rhyme words.—Criseyde (2687, 4799, 4876, 6100), leyde *ind.* 3 *sg.* (4799), seyde *ind.* 3 *sg.* (2157), withseyde *pret. subj.* (?) 3 *sg.* (4876).

§ 105. Most verbs of Romance derivation make their preterites singular in *-ed, -edę, -ede*, without syncopation (cf. Child, § 53; ten Brink, § 179).

acceptid it, 6549 C (-eth AB, acceptë ‡ hit D).
acused, 2166 f (ascused C, accusid D) (: excused *p p.*).
altered his, 4620 (-yd ? C, -id D).
argumented he, 377 (-tede B, -tid C, -tyd D).[4]
assentyd, 1002 (-ed B) (: vntormentid *p.p.*).
avisid her, 2999 ‡ D.
causede, 7938 (-ed CD).
chaunged al, 2555 (-id D, chonged C).
compleyned ek, 2661 (-ede C, -id D).
comytted to, 6367 A (committed D, -eth B).
coueited ‡ so, 6001 D (*pres.* ABC).
couered she, 2412 (-id D). [Perh. subj.]
dampned al, 8186 AB.
declamed this, 2332 A (*pl.* BC, declarid *pl.* D).
departed hem, 4508 (-yd C, -id D).[5]
descendedę Tydeus 7843 (-ed BD, dessendedę C);[6] -ed ‡ doun, 7874 D (*pres.* ABC), cf. 7222 D †.
desiredę worthinesse, 567 (-ed BD); -ed she, 1229 (-id D); -yred but, 1417 B (*pres.* ACD).
deynedę sparen, 435 (-ed B, -yd D, -ęd to C).[7]
dressede hym, 2913 (-ed B, -id D).
entended bet, 6832 B (-it C †, -eth A, -eth D †).
falsedę Troylus, 7416 (-ed BD, -edé ‡ C).
feyned, 354 f (fayned B, -id C, feynid D) (: gayned *pret. ind.* 3 *sg.*:

[1] First Person.   [2] B has *hym* for *hem* (as often).   [3] Supply [*ful*] in C.
[4] Read (*by*)*gynnyng* in D.   [5] Supply [*the*] in C.
[6] 9-syl. in A only.   [7] In D read *in* for *if*.

destrayned *ind. 3 pl.*); -ed here (*acc.*), 494 (-ede C, -yd D †)¹; -ed hym, 7209 (fynẹde ‡ C).

formede, 2138 (-ed B, fourmyd D).²

graunted the, 3181 (-id D); -ed hym, 3422 (-yd D, -id it C)³; -ed on, 7312 (-yd C).⁴—grauntede ‖ anoon, 2636 (-ed B, C †; -id he D †).

ymagyned he, 6980.

impressid in, 4385 D.

iaped thus, 6872 (-et B, -ede C, -ed ‡ he D).

obeyed as, 3423 (-ede C).

percede and, 272 B (procede †A, perceyvid ‡ D, persẹydyn ‡ *pl.* C).

peyned hym, 2659 (-id D, p(l)eyned C); -ede hym, 6438 (-ed BD, -yde C).⁵

pleynyd and, 6594 C.

plitede she, 1782 (plyted B, pleytede C, plytid D).

purpòsed [pes], 6012 D (-en *pres. pl.* ABC).

purueyed ‡ thyng, 5728 A? (-ueieth B, -ueyth D).

receyued ‡ vnto, 6944 D. [Hardly to be scanned.]

rehersẹde ‡, 2767 C (*inf.* ABD).

remembred me, 7109 (-id C).

scorned hem, 303 (-ede C, -yd D).

sorted hym, 8190 AB.

souned into, 6338. [9-syl.]

streynẹde ‡ him, 3913 C.

tariéd ‡ so, 7225 D (*pres.* ABC).

tasted, 639 (-id C, -yd D).

torned here (*acc.*), 5517 (turnede C, turned D); -ed hym, 7509 (turnede C, -ed D); tornede on, 3286 (-ed B, turned C, -id D); tornẹd he, 6448 (turned BD,⁶ -ede hym † C).

vaylydé ‡ this, 6812 C.

venged ‡ hir (*acc.*), 7831 D (wrak AB, wrok C).

waytede on, 3376 (-ed B, -id CD).

§ 106. The Indicative Second Person Singular of Weak Preterites ends in *-est* (Child, § 53, c; ten Brink, § 194).

iàpedèst, 508 (-yst C, -ist D), 917 (-ist C, iaped[est] B, ympedist † D).

---

¹ In C read [*s*]*he*.
² A is a bad 9-syl. verse.
³ Supply [*that*] in D.
⁴ 9-syl.
⁵ Supply [*al*] in B.
⁶ Supply [*that*] in D.

§§ 106, 107.]   *of Chaucer's Troilus.*   253

seydest, 909 (-ist CD), 5143 (-ist C); seydestow, seidestow, 912 (-ist thou CD), 917 (-ist thou CD), 918 (-ist thou CD).¹
preyedest, 910 (-ist C, praydist D, preydest B).²
deydest, 3105 (-ist D, dydest B, deyedist C).
louedest, 3562 (-ist CD).
bysoughtest, 8097 (be- D).
dedest, 3205 (-ist CD, didest B); dedyst, 6960 C.
koudest, 622 (-yst C, -ist D).
woldest, 5103 (-yst C).³
myghtestow, 4924 AB.

But,—thow fette, 3565 f (fet D) (: thow . . . lette *imv. subj. sg.* : shette *pret. ind.* 3 *sg.*).

myght, 619 AB, seems meant by the scribe for *pret. ind.* 2 *sg.*, but C has *may3t*, D *mayst*.

The indicative preterite form in -*est* is often used in constructions properly subjunctive, as in late Anglo-Saxon (cf. Sievers, § 365, Anm 2; ten Brink, § 195). Thus,—

I nolde that thou . . . wendest, 1024 (-yst C, -ist D).
ne haddestow, 4938 (-yst thou C, -ist thou D).
wististow, 4486 C. AB (*wistow*) and D (*wist thow*) are unmetrical. Read, perhaps, *wisté thow*, and cf. wyste *pret. subj.* 2 *sg.*, 3211 f (wiste B, wost C †, wyst D) (: triste *pres. ind.* 1 *sg.* : lyste *pres. subj.* 3 *sg.*).
dorstestow, 767 (durstyst thou C, trist ‡ thow D).⁴
woldest, 4944 (-1st C, wilt ‡ C); cf. 4487, 5103.
nodestow, 4106 (noldestow B, noldist thou CD).
sholdest, 774 (schuldyst C, sholdist D); cf. 6714, 7651.
myghtest, 7890 (my3tist C, mightest D †).
Cf. oughtest, 8069; oughtestow, 6908 (au3tist thow C, oughtest thou D).

§ 107. Second Person Singular of the Indicative Preterite of Strong Verbs (cf. Child, § 54 b; ten Brink, § 193).

thow foundé me, 3204 (fond[e] B, fondist C).
thow me bere on, 5425 AB (bare D).
were, 4160 f (you were E) (: there : fere *timor*); -e, 510 (wer ‡ wont(e)

---

¹ Supply [*that*] in A.   ² Dele (*to*) in C.
³ Perh for subjunctive. Supply [*thus*] in C.
⁴ Supply [*hire*] in B; 9-syl. in D.

D), 3559[1], 5424 ABD; werę wonęd, 901 (were wont(ę) B, werë ‡ wonę C, werę wont D)[2]. But,—was thow, 4996 (art(ę) ‡ thou D).

§ 108. In the First and Third Persons Singular of the Indicative Preterite of Strong Verbs no MS. is free from occasional forms in -e, which, however, is of course never pronounced (cf. Child, § 54). Thus,—

stod(ę) she, 172 (stood(ę) B, stod C, stood D).

tok(e) hede, 820 (took B, tok C)[3]; -(e) hire (poss. sg.), 126 (tok C), 3053 (tok C), 3067 (tok C); -(e) his, 2387 (tok C), 2545 (tok C), 3436 (took(e) B, tok C); -(e) he, 379 (tok C), 6565 (took B, tok C); tok(e) and, 3024 (took B, tok C); -(e) it, 3811 (tok C).[4]—tok(ę), 1646 (tok C).

com(ę), 1640 (cam C), 2024, 2682 (com B)[5]; bycom(ę), 1072[6]; com(e), 1629, 1647,[7] 2647 (com B),[8] 3592, 7515 A; -(e) here (dat.), 1687 (cam to D); -(e) hire (acc.), 2572 (com B; com(e) C (?)).

wrot(ę), 2299 (wrot C); wrot(e), 7787 (wrot C).

wax(e), 2341 (wex BC, wax D).

quook(e), 2935 (quook B, quok C, quok(e) D)[9]; see § 103, note 2.

fill(ę), 4243 (fel B, lestę C, fillę ‡ pl. E).

shop(ę), 4914 (schop C).

Other examples are: (1) in B, -(e), before vowels or h,—1360, 1641, 1724, 1774, 2275, 3593, 3821, 3921, 4419, 6392, 6609, 6890, 7441, etc., etc.; -(ę), 826, 1640, 1690, 1787, 2645, 2789, 3207, 3437, 3836, 4725, 6838, 7093, 7534, 7565, 7579, 7803, etc.; (2) in C, -(e), as before, 549, 1677, 2547, 3070, 4563, 6925, etc.; -(ę), 141, 2645, 2902, 3612, 7208, 7506, etc.; (3) in D, -(e) and -(ę), passim. The phenomenon is commonest in D, and B comes next. For examples of this -(e) in rhyme, cf. 2265 BD, 2410 B, 2413 B, 2689 B, 2691 B, 3519 D, 3803 B, 4677 BD, 6652 B, 7289 BD.

For weak preterites from strong verbs, see § 103. For quok and rong from verbs weak in Anglo-Saxon, see § 103, note 2.

---

[1] Protasis. Read were [in] in A.
[2] But supply [uhi] in B, and read werę.
[3] 9-syl. in AB   Read hed[e] in CD.
[4] Perhaps subjunctive.
[5] Supply [for] in D.
[6] Read frendlyest[e] in BD.
[7] Read wept[e] in D.
[8] Read Criseid[ë] ‖ innocent in D, or supply [al].
[9] Supply [ek] in D.

§ 109. The Plural of the Preterite Indicative of both Strong and Weak Verbs ends in *-en, -e,* for all persons (Child, § 55; ten Brink, § 194).

In the following list the *persons* are not distinguished. The examples given are arranged as follows (cf. § 96): I. -en before consonants; II. -en in rhyme; III. -en before vowels; IV. -en before *h*; V. syncope: -ęn, -n; VI. -e before consonants; VII. -e in rhyme; VIII. -e elided before vowels; IX. -e elided before *h*; X. apocope of -e.

The examples comprise the following preterites: (*a*) A.S. First Weak Conjugation (cf. § 99),—*alighte* (VII.), *bente* (VI., X.), *boughte* (I., VII.), *broughte* (VI., VII., VIII., IX.), *felte* (I., III.), *fette* (VII.), *herde* (III.), *kyste* (VII.), *lafte* (VIII.), *ledde* (II.), *mente* (VII.), *mette* (A.S. métton) (VII.), *redde (radde)* (IV., VIII., X.), *-rente* (VII.), *sente* (VII.), *sette* (I., VII., IX.), *shette* (II.), *soughte (bysoughte)* (VII., IX. n.), *spedde* (IV. VIII., IX. and n.), *stente* (III. VII.), *thoughte* (A.S. pohton) (VII.), *thoughte* (A.S. puhton) (VI., VII.), *tolde* (VII., VIII.), *wende* (II., IV., VI., VIII.), *wente* (III., VII., VIII., IX. n.), *wroughte* (III. VI., VII., VIII.); cf. *yede* (II.); (*b*) *glente* (cf. § 109) (VII.); (*c*) Second Weak Conjugation, A.S. and other verbs of Germanic origin (cf. § 101), *caste* (I.), *folwede* (V.), *lyked* (VIII., IX. n.), *made* (I., III., VI., VII., IX.), *pleyde* (VII. VIII.), *rafte* (VIII.), *shewed* (VIII., IX.), *stremede* (III.); (*d*) A.S. Third Weak Conjugation (cf. § 102),—*hadde* (I., III., VI., VII., VIII., IX.), *seyde* (I., III., IV., VI., VII., VIII. X.); (*e*) Weak preterites from Strong Verbs (cf. § 103), *dredde* (I., VII.), *fledde* (II.), *highte (byhighte)* (II., IV., VI., IX.), *slepte* (III.), *wepte* (I.); (*f*) Romance verbs with syncopated preterites (cf. § 104),—*caughte* (IX.), *cryede* (VIII., IX.), *paste* (VII.), *preyde* (VII.), *quytte* (IX.); (*g*) Romance verbs with unsyncopated preterites (cf. § 105),—*apoynteden* (I.), *assegeden* (I.), *assembled* (VIII.), *bisegede* (VIII.), *caused* (VIII.), *comenseden* (III.), *commendeden* (III.), *declamed* (X.), *destrayned* (X.), *entrechaungeden* (IV.), *ioyneden* (III.), *turnede* (VIII.); (*h*) Strong Verbs,—*braste* (VIII.), *come* (V., VIII., IX.), *drowe* (VIII.), *ete* (VII.), *felle (fille)* (I., II., III., VII., VIII., X.), *founde* (I., VIII.), *gonne (gan) (bygonne)* (I., III., IV., VI., VIII., IX. and n., X.), *hange* (III), *hielde* (III.), *knewe* (VII., VIII., IX.), *laye* (III., VIII.), *lete* (I.), *quod* (X.), *ride* (II.), *ronne* (I.), *aryse* (IX. n.), *sete* (III. VIII.), *seygh (say, sey)* (IX., X.), *spake (spoke, speke)* (II., III., VI., VIII., IX., X.), *sponne* (VII.), *stode* (I., VII., X.), *sye* (II.), *toke* (VIII., IX.), *were* (I. III., VI., VII., VIII., IX., X.), *wesshe* (I.), *yaf* (IX.).

I. -en before consonants.:
   assègëden neigh, 60 (-ȝe- C, assegid wel D †); bysègëden the, 7859 (be- B, besegedè C, besegèd[è] D);
   casten to, 88 AB (-yn C); -en what, 2570 (-yn CD).
   boughten they, 136 (-ȝte C, boght[e] D); cf. 8164.
   founden no, 137 (-yn ‡ the (?) D).
   weren to, 283 (wherè C, weryn D); cf. 463, 3531, 4744 (A †), 7892, 7942.¹

---

¹ Subjunctive?

hadden prys, 1109 (-yn D).
gonnen, 1184 (gunne C, gun[ne] D); gunnen, 1235 (gon- B, gonë C, gun[ne] D); cf. 2668, 2704, 3452, 4541, 4720, 6891.
wesshen they, 2269 (wesche C, wysshyn D).
fillen forth, 2276 (-yn D, fellyn C); cf. 1583.
apoynteden ful, 3296 (-yn D; C †).
felten sith, 4064 (-yn C).
wenden ben, 4182 AB.
setten tyme, 4554 (-e C, -yn D).
dredden to, 4718 (-yn D, dreden B).
makkèden the, 4783 B (made A †, madyn alle CD); **maden dye,** 8165.
ronnen doun, 4792 (-e C, ran[nen] D).
leten falle, 5797 (-yn CD).
seyden, 6803 (C ?), 6854 (-e C, -e D (?)), 7712 (-e CD).
stoden for, 7477 (-ę C, stood[e] B).
wepten for, 8185 AB; cf. 4909 C.

II. -en in rhyme :
fellen, 3 f (: tellen *inf.*).
shetten, 148 f (C †; *line om.* † D) (: letten *inf.*). [After *though.*]
wenden, 217 f (-yn C; D †) (: descenden *inf.*).
riden, 473 f (-yn D) (: diden 3 *pl. ind.* : abyden *p.p.*).
spaken, 565 f (-yn C, -e D) (: maken *inf.* : awaken *inf.*).
yeden, 2021 f (ʒeden B, ʒedyn D, ridyn C) (: ryden *p.p.* : abyden *p.p.*).
hyghten, 2708 f (-yn D, hiʒtyn C) (: myghten 3 *pl.*).
mysledden, 4710 f (-yn D, -leden B) (: fledden, -yn D, 3 *pl.,* 4711).
syen, 7179 f (seyen C) (: espyen *inf.* : (e)yen).

III. -en before vowels :
Cf. wroughten, 63; fellen, 134; bihelden, 177; herden, 1168; stenten, 1188; seten, 2277; comèueden, 2859; spaken, 3056, 6879, cf. 6795; commendeden, 3059; slepten, 3588; weren, 4632, 5798, cf. 2279 ‡ A; madyn, 4783 CD; stremeden, 4909; wenten, 5392; hangen, 5479; hadden, 5912; gonnen, 6578; ioyneden, 7176; seyden, 7479. (Variants not registered.)

In some of these cases hiatus occurs in one or another MS (not A) · as, wente alle, 5392 B; speke in, 3056 D; ffelte in, 4158 C; cf. leye at, 3587 C (lay[en] A, layen B, lyen D). See also IX. note.

IV. -en before *h* (in *hym, here* acc., *hem, here* pl.) :—
Cf. redden, 2791; èntrechaùngëdèn, 4210; wenden, 5345, 5363, 5386; gonnen, 5384; bihighten, 6859; spedden, 6864. (Vari-

§ 109.]   — of Chaucer's Troilus.   257

ants not registered.) Hiatus,—speddë hem, 6864 D (cf. also IX., note). Thus *seyden* here and howne, 4872 (-e BC, saidë D).

V. -ęn (syncope):
  folęwëdęn yn, 1904 (folwëdęn B, folwëde C, folǫwdyn D).
  comęn vpward, 3047 (-yn C, come D).
  (Cf. 3470 ‡ C, and the references under VIII., IX.)

VI. -e before consonants:
  were wrothe, 140 (-ę B, -yn D); were neuere, 1671 (-[e] D); were they, 1997 (-en B, -in C †); were faste, 3075; were bothe, 5894 (-en B, were we C; D †); were sene, 6637 (waren B, wer ysen D).
  broute me, 424 ‡ C.
  highte volturis, 788 (-en B, -yn D, -зte C) (in pres. sense).
  gonne fro, 1279 (gunne C, ded[e] ‡ D); cf. 4238, 5371 C (D?), 5790.¹—bygonne we, 1597 (B † C †; bygun ‡ we D).
  made loue, 1762 (-ę D); m. many, 1900 (-yn CD); m. ‡ swich, 3468 C (-yn D).
  bente neuere, 1946 (-en B, -yn C, -t ‡ D).
  spoke no, 2204 A.
  wroughte me, 4196 (-[e] B, -en E, -зtyn C).
  hadde worthynesse, 4631 (-yn CD); hadde ye, 8055 (-yn C); cf. hadde neuere 3712 ‡ B.
  wende that, 5378 (-en B).²
  seyde softe, 6982 (-yn C).³
  thoughte (=seemed) tho, 7023 (-[e] B, -зte C, зt[e] *sg.* D †).

VII. -e in rhyme:
  stente, 60 f (stynt D) (: went *ind.* 3 *pl.*, -e B : entente), 5002 f (-t C) (: wente *ind.* 3 *pl.* : to-rente *pret. ind.* 3 *pl.*).
  tolde, 131 f (: holde *inf.* : olde *pl.*), 7328 f (: holde *p.p.*).
  felle, 145 f (: telle *inf.* : dwelle *inf.*).
  dredde, 483 f (-d D) (: spedde *ind.* 3 *sg.*).
  paste, 1743 f (-t C, past † D) (: faste *inf.*).
  broughte, 1999 f (-зt C, broght D) (: oughte 3 *pl.* : thoughte þǫ́hte *ind.* 3 *sg.*).
  ete, 2269 f (*inf.* ‡ D) (: strete *n.*).
  made, 2859 f (: glade *adj. pl.*).
  sente, 2862 f (-t D) (: hente *pret. ind.* 3 *sg.*).
  wroughte, 3305 f (-t B, -зt C, wroght D), 3604 f (-зt C, wroghtyn D), 5388 f (-зt C, wrought D), 7224 f (-зt CD).

[1] *gan* C (l. *gunne*), *ganne* D.   [2] 9-syl.   [3] Subjunctive?

S

Rhyme words.—thoughte *þóhte ind.* 3 *sg* (5388), 3 *sg. indir. quest.* (3305), *þóhton ind* 3 *pl.* (3604), *þúhton* 3 *pl. indir. quest.* (7224), bysoughte *ind.* 3 *pl.* (5388).

were, 3427 f, 3467 f, 3535 f (ware B), 3931 f, 4237 f, 6584 f (wer D), 7541 f (wer D).

Rhyme words —fere, feere *fear n.* (3427, 3467, 3931, 4237), there (3427, 3467, 7541), where (3535, 4237, 6584), tere *n.* (3931, 7541), eyen clere (6584).

sette, 3450 f (set D) (: fette *inf.*).

sponne, 3576 f (spunne C) (: bygonne *p.p*).

thoughte (A.S. þóhton), 3605 f (-ʒt C, thoghtyn D) (: wroughte 3 *pl. ind.*).

stode, 3765 f (stood D) (: for gode).

wende, 4528 f (-d D) (: complende *inf.* A, comprehende BC, comprehend D), 5367 f (: spende *inf.* : brende *pret. ind.* 3 *sg.*).

knewe, 4538 f (knowe † B) (: hewe *n.* : newe *adv.*), 6083 f (knowe † B) (: trewe *pred. adj. sg.*), 6486 f (: newe *adj.* : trewe *adj.*).

mente, 4699 f (-t D) (: wente *ind.* 3 *pl.* : bente *p.p. pl.*), 4834 f (-t D), (: wente *subj.* 3 *sg.* : entente), 8056 f (-t C †, D) (: entente).

wente, 4701 f (-t D), 4802 f (-t CD), 5000 f (-t C), 6797 f (-t D); went[e], 58 f (-e B), 2751 f (-e B ; C †).

Rhyme words.—entente, -[e] *n.* (58, 2751), sente *ind.* 3 *sg.* (4802), mente *ind* 3 *pl.* (4701), stente *pret. ind.* 3 *pl.* (58,5000), to-rente *ind pret.* 3 *pl.* (5000), assente *inf.* (6797), bente *p p. pl.* (4701).

mette (A.S. métton), 4704 f (met D) (: lette *n.*), 8121 f (: whette *p.p. pred. pl.*).

preyde, 4858 f (preyede C) (: Criseyde).

stente, 5002 f (stent C) (cf. next word).

to-rente, 5003 f (-t C, turment ‡ D) (: wente *ind.* 3 *pl.* : stente *pret. ind.* 3 *pl.*).

bysoughte, 5387 f AB (besouʒte D) (: thoughte *þóhte ind.* 3 *sg.* : wroughte *ind.* 3 *pl.*).

lyste, 5793 f (: twyste *inf.* : nyste *ind.* 3 *sg.*).

glente, 5835 f (-t C, glente *sg.* BD) (: entente : wente *ind.* 3 *sg.*).

hadde, 6336 f (: into badde), 6350 f (: cladde *ind.* 3 *sg.*).

fette, 7215 f (fett D) (: sette *pret. ind.* 3 *sg.* : lette *n.*).

thoughte (=seemed), 7223 f (-t B, -ʒt CD) (: wroughte *ind.* 3 *pl.*). [Ind. question.]

pleyde, 7475 f (pleyede C) (: Criseyde).

seyde, 7628 f (*sg.* ‡ C) (: breyde *pres. ind.* 1 *sg.* : Criseyde).

aboughte, 8119 f (aboute D) (: soughte *ind.* 3 *sg.*).

§ 109.] *of Chaucer's Troilus.* 259

Final -e is to be supplied in *alight*[e]¹, 6876 f (-e B, aly3t ? C, light D) (: nyghte *inf.* : brighte *def. adj.*).

VIII. -e elided before vowels.

Cf. bisegede, 149; hadde, 153, 909, 1302, 4528, 5381; seyde, 176, 5348; fille, felle, 470, 3407, 3894, 5413; wente, 473; toke, 911, 4252; were, 916, 3073, 3265, 4247, 5909, 6875; tolde, 1165; pleyede, 1235; cryede, 1697; founde, 2023; sete, 2336; turnede, 2432; gonne, 2684, 5364; knewe, 2750; spake, 3305, 6096, cf. 4208; laye, 3591; rafte, 4911; wroughte, 5789; radde, 7100; come, 7237; lafte, 7689. (Variants not registered.)

In all these instances A has -e (elided). In several, D omits -e; as,—had, 153, 909, 4528; fil, 470; told, 1165; cried, 1697; gun, 2684; wer, 5909; etc. So sometimes B : as,—beseged, 149; had, 153; went, 473; took, 911; cried, 1697; torned, 2432; fel, 3407; com, 7237; left, 7689; cf. caused, 4408;—and C: as,—tok, 911; lay, 3591. -yn (syncopated) is found in C 153, 916, 1302, 1697, 2750, 3073, 3894, and in D 2023, 2432; -ÿn in C 5909, D 176; -e in D 3265.—*Drowe* pret. ind. 3 pl., 3516 D (drew C), should be *p.p.* (as in AB).—For the omission of elided -e in A, see,—shewed, 159 (-ede C, -yd D); sped, 1111 (spedde B, did ‡ D); brast, 1411 (bruste B, brostyn C, brest D); lyked, 2351 (-ëdë‡ in C, -yd‡ *sg.* D); assembled, 2652 (-bledin D, -blid D, assemlede B); gon, 2793 (gonnë‡ it B, gan on C, gun on D); wrought, 4555 (-3te C, wroght D); tok, 5793 (tooke B, hent C, toke D); went, 7690 (-é BC), cf. 1995; cf. ye caused al, 4408 B.

IX. -e elided before *h* (in *he, his, hym, here* acc., *here* pl., *here* adv., *hem*).

Cf. made, 472, 6097; come, 1704; cryede, 1728; sette, 2269, 5348; were, 2436, 3523, 7564; hadde, 3706; knewe, 4240; gonne, bygonne, 4919, 7590, 7830; toke, 6863; spedde, 6881. (Variants not registered.)

In all these instances A has -e. Cf. were, 6829 B (wer D, werë‡ here C, were‡ there A). D omits -e in 1728, 3706, 4240, 5348, 6097, 7564, 7590; B, in 4919, 5348, 6863; C, in 1728, 7590, 7830. C has -yn in 472, 3706, 4240, 6881 †, 7564. For the omission of elided -e in A, see— spak hem, 1110 (-e B); brought hym, 2023 (-e B, -3te C, broghtyn ‡ at D); gan hym, 2629; byhight hem, 3161 (biheighte B, behy3t C, behight D); shewed his, 4206 (-id is C, sweyd † E); yaf hym, 4795 (3af C; B † D†), cf. 2861 D; quyt hym, 4867 (-tt D, quite B); seygh here (*acc.*), 5382 (seigh B, saw C, say her [so] D); tok here (*poss. sg.*), 5392 (took B; toke C, D (?)); caught here (*pl.*), 6965 (-3t C†).²

Note.—A few cases of hiatus occur in one or another MS., but these are easily corrected. Thus,—wentë arm, 2201 (-en B, -yn C, *om.* † D); arysë euerychon, 2683 (-en B, -yn C, risyn D); gonnë‡ it, 2793 B; likëdë‡ in, 2351 C; sought[ë] hym, 2022 (-3të C, soughten B, soghtyn D); speddë hem, 2032 (spede B, sped[ë] from D); werë‡ here (*hic*), 6829 C. See also III., IV., above.

X. Apocope. A few genuine cases occur:

¹ Perhaps present tense.   ² Supply [*the*] in D.

were born, 4064 (-e BC), 5913 (wer D); were woned, 4553 (be D); war caught(e), 2267 B.[1]
say (*vidistis*) the, 656 (say CD); sey ye, 1362 (sey[e] ‡ ʒe D).
gan to, 3957.
quod they, 4856 ABC (D ?).
declamed this, 2332 B (-ede C, declarid D, declamed ‡ *sg.* A).
destrayned, 355 f (-yd D) (: gayned : feyned, *both pret. ind. 3 sg.*).
[Indir. discourse]
Cf. bygun ‡ we, 1597 D; gunne ‡ to, 1994 C (gan ‡ to D); gun ‡ they, 3452 D; gunne † the, 5791 C (gan the peynes ‡ A); gan ‡ to, 6891 D; had ‡ that, 1302 D; hadde ‡ ye, 3711 A; bent ‡ neuere his, 1946 D; redde ‡ me, 7100 C; seide ‡ that, 7479 D; stode ‡ they, 7482 C; were ‡ wrothe, 140 B, were ‡ clerkes, 5634 D, were ‡ there, 6829 A; were ‡ wont(e), 7023 D.

§ 110. **The Singular of the Present Subjunctive of both strong and weak verbs ends in -e in all persons** (Child, § 56; ten Brink, §§ 184, 188).

I. First Person.
  (*a*) Before consonants :
    er that I parte, 5 (or [that] I p. D).
    lest thow deme I trust[e] not, 601 (tryste B, truste C).
    thow I desir[e], 650 (-e BD, desese † C).
    as euere I thriue, 1205 (as euere thryue I BC).[2]
    if that I breke, 2980.
    er that I departe, 6297.[3]
  (*b*) In rhyme :
    whil I leue, 931 f (lyue BD) (: foryeue *subj.* 2 *sg.*, *inf.* D).
    er that I sterue, 1007 f (er than C) (: deserue *inf.*).
    now is tyme (is it tyme CD) I wende, 1305 f (: to an ende).
    yf I . . . endite, 1352 f (B †) (: lyte, litel † A).
    wene I lye, 1385 f (ly D) (: eye).
    counseylest me . . . that . . . I me feyne, 2613 f (: peyne *n.* : pleyne *inf.*).
    though I . . . preye, 3127 f (prey D) (: seye *ind.* 1 *sg.* : wreye *subj.* 2 *sg.*).
    til I sterue, 3556 f (sterwe C) (: serue *ind.* 1 *sg.*).

---

[1] In ACD supply [*that*] and read *were*.
[2] Supply [*this*] in AD.
[3] Supply [*that*] in C.

§ 110.]   *of Chaucer's Troilus.*   261

though I . . . compleyne, 3847 f (pleyn † D) (: to seyn[e] AD, to seyne BC : peyne *n.*).

but I retorne, 4325 f (-tourne B, -turne CD) (: soiourne *inf.*).

yf I . . . twynne, 5420 f (: inne : synne *n.*).

til I . . . vnshethe, 5438 f (C †) (: to dethe).

yf so be that I . . . passe, 7059 f (pace BD, pase C) (· grace *n.*).

yf . . . I falle, 7068 f (fatt D) (· byfalle *subj.* 3 *sg.* : of alle).

(*c*) Elision :

though I praunce, 221 (how ‡ y p. D).

though I speke, 1104 (yf I ‡ spak D).

yf I lye, 3216.

so thriue I, 3552.[1]

though that I tarye a yer, 4037.

or I soo werche, 5013 D (do ABC).[2]

al sey I nought, 3098 A (-*e* B).

yf that I me put in, 7064 (putte C).

II. Second Person.

(*a*) Before consonants :

but thow it fynde, 831 (fynde ‡ it C, but if thow fynd it D).

se that thow . . . requere, 895.

and thow . . . holde, 2610 (-[e] CD).

if thow remembre the, 3203 D (if it r. the B, if it rememberid ‡ be C, if it remembreth the A).

that . . . thow deme, 3236.

though thou sitte, 4472 (sit[te] D).

that thow retorne, 6215 (C †).

that thow . . . sende, 6958 (C ?).

(*b*) In rhyme :

that thou dwelle, 789 f (: helle *n.* : telle *ind.* 3 *pl.*).

(I) . . . pray . . . thow foryeue, 930 f (-ʒiue B, -ʒeue C ; *inf.* D) (: leue *subj.* 1 *sg.*).

that thou me recomaunde, 1049 f (: comaunde *inf.*).

that thow . . . wreye, 3126 f (wrey D) (: seye *ind.* 1 *sg.* : preye *subj.* 1 *sg.*).

whider so thow wende, 3233 f (wynde C) (: ende *n.*).

how thow pleye, 3663 f (pley CD) (: tweye : seye *inf.*).

that . . . thow wynde, 4282 f (wende B) (: kynde *n.* : bynde *subj.* 3 *sg.*).

or thou olde †, 5079 f C.

---

[1] In C read *this* for *wis*.   [2] Supply [*thus*] in C.

what so thow seye, 5104 f (sey D) (: deye *subj.* 1 *sg.*).
That prey I the thow take (tak B) and it conserue, 6673 f (: serue *ind.* 1 *sg.* : sterue *ind.* 1 *sg.*).
I the beseche . . . that thow foryeue, 6750 f (-yiue B, -ʒif C) (: dreue *p p.* : leue *vicere*).
that thow . . . write, 7656 f (: lete : endite *inf.*).

(*c*) Elision :
if thou wene, 575.
lest thow deme, 601 (C †).
if thow . . . deye, 800 (dy D).
yf thow late hym, 1408 (lat B, late C, lete D, *all three plural*).
yf thow write, 2113.
that thow knowe, 3249 (know D).
that thow . . . . cause, 4466 (causë ‡ it D).
yf thow deye, 5285 (dey D).
my conseyl is . . . thow . . . . go and make, 5777 (mak BC).
if that thow trowe, 6694 (C †).
if thow . . . . ligge, 6774 (leve C, lye thus D).[1]
whe[the]r yet thou thenke, 7098 A.
if thow werk yn, 952 (wyrke B, were † C, work on D).

III. Third Person.
(*a*) Before consonants :
touche ‡ loue, 744 C (*l.* toucheth).
god forbede, 1198 ; cf. 2775, 3603.
cesse cause ay cesseth maladye, 1568 B (-eth . . . -eth A, sese . . . seseth the C, cesyd *p.p.* . . . cecith D) ; cf. cesse wynde it wold aryse, 2473 (sese C^c, cesid (?) D).
though a man forbede, 1801 (D †).
god sende, 2359 (-[e] BD), 8065 ; god . . . so sende, 8151 ; cf. 3163 (-e hele), 3185, 6871.
though she bende, 2463 (-[e] D).[2]
wher it be bet she byde, 2736 (sche abide C, to ‡ bydé *inf.* (?) D).
if that she vouche saf, 2776 (-eth B, -ith D, thou ‡ vouche C).
I pose a womman graunte me, 3152 (-ede C, -ith D).
if it remembre the, 3203 B (cf. II., above) ; er deth delyuere me, 7763 (-uereth D ; C^c (?)) ; mysmetre for, 8159 A (-metere B, misse-metre D).
god . . . brynge, 3808 (bryng ‡ at D).
god . . . so quenche, 4298 (D †).

[1] In later hand in C. Supply [*or*] in D.   [2] Supply [*she*] in D.

§ 110.] *of Chaucer's Troilus.* 263

   so . . . that it cause, 4347 (is † cause CD).
   god vs graunte, 4368 (C (?); graunt D †).
   yif that it lyke yow, 4763 (if it like B, if it likith D); cf. 1527 ‡ C, 4144 ‡ A.
   God leue that, 4987 (len[e] D, leue ‡ ay C).
   if Criseyde . . . now loue the, 5274 (-eth BD, -yth C).
   but yf . . . remorde yow, 6153 (-moue C †).
   god . . . as wysly glade so, 6519.
   though he wepe and make, 6779.
   er Calkas sende, 6871.
   bytyde what bityde, 7113 f (: syde).
   although she come, 7504.
   though . . . commeue, 7749 (re- C, remorde D).
   that noon myswryte the, 8158 (miss(e)-write D) [1].

(b) In rhyme :
   god me blysse, 436 f (blys C, blesse D) (: prowesse :. distresse *n.*);
   god vs blesse, 7575 (blisse BD, blys C) (: heuynesse).
   thowh . . . breste, 599 f (-t C, or (that) ‡ . . . to-brest D) (: my beste · reste *n.*).
   yf the lyke, 829 f (: syke *inf.*); cf. 3653 f.
   but if . . . shende, 965 f (-d D) (: ende *n.*).
   so god you saue, 1199 f (: ye raue : caue *n.*).
   lest . . . slake, 1376 f (: take *inf.* : make *inf.*).
   if . . . assente, 1420 f (-t (?) D, -e *inf.* AC) (: sente *ind.* 3 *sg.*).
   er [that] . . . deuoure, 1480 f (er that BC) (: houre).
   so she . . . saue, 1823 f (: haue *inf.*); cf. 2944 f, 4220 f, 4343 f.
   so god me spede, 1829 f (: drede *n.* : hede *n.*).
   who-so it rewe, 1874 f (rew D) (: vntrewe *pl.* : an newe).
   god so wys me saue, 2063 f (: haue *ind.* 1 *sg.* · yaue *subj.* 3 *sg.*).[2]
   til that . . . departe, 2075 f (: Marte).
   although it . . . smerte, 2182 f (-t D †, -e ‡ *inf.* C) (: sterte *ind.* 3 *sg.* : herte).[3]
   recche . . . wher he bycome, 2236 f (: some *pl.*).
   whether that he lyue or elles sterue, 2237 f (leue . . . sterue C, dye † . . sterue D) (· serue *inf.* : deserue *inf.*).
   whan that so he bygynne, 2569 f (whan so that he bygyn D, whan so euere ‡ he gynne (?) C) (: wynne *inf.*).
   god hym amende, 2816 f (: defende *ind.* 1 *sg.* : sende *subj.* 3 *sg.*).

---

[1] Dele (*to*) in BD, or read *myswrite*.
[2] In C, read *eche* for *sche*.   [3] In A read *so*[*re*].

god hym brynge, 2891 f (bring D) (: heriynge).
yf this . . . displese, 2949 f (-plees B) (: ese *n.* : apese *inf.*).
how sore that me smerte, 2988 f (-t CD) (: herte *n.*); cf. 3748 f, 3842 f, 6495 f, 7587 f.
god forbede, 3387 f (: nede *n.*), 4819 f (: drede *n.*), 6218 f (: nede *n.* : hede *n.*).
til the sonne shyne, 3610 f (: deuyne *inf.* : myne *inf.*).
er that . . . breke, 3750 f (to-breke ‡ D) (: wreke : speke *infs.*).
til . . . sende, 3773 f (: ende *n.*); cf. 6865 f.
Ioue . . hym race, 3857 f (arace BC) (: place *n.*).
(god) . . . auaunce, 4228 f (avance E) (: myschaunce *n.*).
god . . . bynde, 4281 f (: kynde *n.* : wynde *subj. pres.* 2 *sg.*).
til that fayle, 4935 f (: bywayle *inf.*).
though the body sterue, 4984 f (: serue *inf.*).
rather than my felawe deye, 5186 f (dey D) (: scye *inf.*).
that . . . wepe, 5253 f (: depe *adv.*).
the deuel spedé hym (spede hym BD, haue hym C)[1] that recche, 5292 f (: wrecche *n.*).
god . . . gyde, 5355 f (guide D) (: side *n.*).
til deth me mete, 5444 f (: swete *adj.* : in quiète).
that he . . . fynde, 5578 f (i-fynde C) (: out of his mynde).
yf . . . compleyne, 5917 f (: peyne *n.* : tweyne).[2]
yf so be that . . . take, 6224 f (: make *inf.*).
yf that . . . me assayle, 6257 f (messaile B, me asayle C; D †) (: fayle *n.*).
though . . . smerte, 6425 f (-t C) (: herte *n.*); cf. 6495 f, 7587 f.
that . . . he dryue, 7028 f (: on lyue).
yf that it byfalle, 7065 f (so falle C) (: of alle : falle *subj.* 1 *sg.*).
bytyde what bityde, 7113 f (: syde *n.*).
yf . . . masterte, 7706 f (me asterte C, me astert D) (: herte *n.*).
god encresse, 7722 f (-cresc CD) (: cesse *subj.* 3 *sg*).
so that it neuere cesse, 7724 f (sease D, sere † C).
god . . . auaunce, 7798 f (-ns D) (: myschaunce *n.*); cf. 4228 f.
though hym greue, 8001 f (: leue *inf. lœfan*).
er that he dye, 8150 f (: thow nenuye).
liste, lyste, lyst (1843), leste A (liste, lyste, leste B; liste, lyste, leste, lest, lyst, lest C; liste, leste, list, lyst, lest, lust D), 679 f (as thou lyste C), 693 f (yf thow lyste AC), 1022 f (as thou lest C), 1334 f, 1843 f, 2030 f (ȝe lest C), 2195 f, 2268 f (ȝe

---
[1] In D read *Adieu* for *And dey*.   [2] Supply [ȝif] in C.

list D), 2534 f, 3101 f, 3210 f (thou lest C), 3430 f (ye lyst D), 3513 f (ye lyst D), 3688 f (ye lest D), 3759 f (ye lyst D), 3807 f, 3889 f (ye lest D), 4172 f, 6209 f (thow leste AC, ye leste D), 7629 f (sche luste C), 8074 f (thow lyst A), 8140 f.

Rhyme words.—wyste *pret. subj.* 1, 2 *sg.* (679, 3210), er ye wiste (2268), tryste, triste *inf.* (693, 3101, 3759, 7629, 8074), truste, triste *pres. ind.* 1 *sg* (1334, 3210, 3430), geste *n.* (2195), Alceste (8140), beste *def. adj. sg.* (1022, 2534, 3513, 3688, 3889, 4172), the worthieste, (1843), *at, to, for reste* (1843, 2030, 3807, 3889), keste *pret. ind.* 3 *sg* (1334), brest[e] (-e B) *pret. subj.* 3 *sg.* (2195).

(c) Elision.

For examples of elision before a vowel, cf. 31, 44, 597, 1034, 1114, 1472 B, 1673, 1941, 2104, 2237, 2297, 2721, 2798, 3217, 3637, 3768, 3782, 4066, 4360, 4735 (remembre I), 6223, 6779, 6787, 7321 (deliuere it), 7500, 7724, 7797, 8113. For examples of elision before pronouns beginning with *h*, cf. 45, 558, 695, 1248, 2898, 3387, 4227, 5124, 6703, 7490; happe how happé may, 7159 (happen how happyn may D).

Note 1.—In cases of elision *-e* is sometimes omitted in writing. Thus,—(a) before vowels,—sey, 1004 ‡ C (seyth A, syth B, seith D); com, 2519 (*-e* C, *-e* D (?)); prey, 3388 (*-e* BC, prayeth ‡ *imv.* D); set, 3674 (sette B, set (not) D); lat, 4088 (B†, let C); worth, 5409 (wurth D, wurthe ‡ C); dryf, 5572 (-ue BD); glad, 6317 (*-e* CD); tak, 7452 (*-e* CD) ;—(b) before *hym*,—war, 1953 (*-e* D); lat, 2692 (let C, lete D), bryng, 2693 (*-e* B) There are no good cases of hiatus *who-so axè* ‡ *hym*, 7587 C (-eth A, -ed B, -ed him wher[of] D), and *the deuel spede hym*, 5292 A (haue C, spede B; D†) should be corrected ; *so god me sende hele*, 3163, is regular.

Note 2 —Before a vowel or *h* it is not always possible to determine whether *lyst* (ind.) or *lyste* (subj.) should be read : cf e g., 119, 398, 857, 1379, 2860, 4018, 4589, 8133, where A has *lyst*, *list*, with 3528, 4134, 5291, 6062, 6685, 8133, where A has *lyste*.

IV. Contracted forms (all persons).

Monosyllabic (contracted) forms are seen in *se*, *see*, and *sle*. Thus,— 1st Pers., se ich neue[r] Ioues face, 5999, cf. 3652 f, 7748; 2nd Pers., I wol now that thow se, 990 f, cf. 6769; 3rd Pers., god yow see, 1170 f (se CD); though he se a man, 1457 (9-syl. in A); yf this man sle hère hym self, 1544 (sla B, heɪe sle hym D). Cf. § 111, III, note 2.

§ 111. Exceptions to § 110.

I. First Person.

But if that I consente that it so be, 413 (conseute that it be BC, if [that] I consent that hit so be D).

II. Second Person.

the best is that thow tellẹ me, 830 (telle ÇD)

whether thow thy[n]kẹ ʒet vpou, 7098 B (thynke ʒit [vp]on C, thinkịst yet vppon D, whe[the]r yet thou thenke vpon A).

III. Third Person.

helpe me (in *God helpe me so, as helpe me god*, and similar phrases), 1449 (-p BC), 1675 (-p D), 2089 (-p D), 2211 (-p D) 2298 (-p CD), 2315 (-p BCᶜD), 2367 (-p BD), 2397 (-p BCD), 4408 (C †), 5275 (-p B), 6194 (-p BC), 6256 (-p B)[1], 6726 (-p BC), 6849 (-p B), 7340 (-p B), 7362.[2]

help me (in *God help me so*, etc.), 1218 (-ę B, help ‡ y D), 1267 (-ę me C ‡), 3706 (-ę C), 4463 (-ę CD), 6516 (-ę BCD), 6755 (-ę D).[3]

help god, 3900 (-ę B, *om.* † D).

God yeldę the, 1048 (ȝeld D).

sendę yow, 1489 (-d D; C (?)).

yf the lykę than, 2101 (lestę B, lystę C, *if thou list* D); cf. 3227 ‡ D.

Ioues . . . yeuę me sorwe, 2694 (gif C); Ioues yeuę the sorwe, 7888; god yeuę youre, 4407 (ȝif C, ȝeuę ȝow ‡ D); I biddę god so yeuę yow, 4312 ([so] C)[4]; preye I god so yeuę yow, 7437 (ȝeuę ȝou C, *to* ‡ *yeuę you inf.* D)[5], 7774 (ȝeuę ȝow C); cf. 33 ‡ D.

yf it comę to, 4067 (-ęth B).[6]

loue . . . bynd this acord, 4592 (*line om.* E).

ne trust no wyght, 5053 (-ę B; C †).

wo worth that day, 5425 AB (-ę D); cf. 1429-32 (*four cases*); cf. 5409 ‡ C.

Venus lat me, 6323 (let CD).

yf she writę thow, 7662 (writë D, ȝif ‡ that sche writę C).[7]

Note 1.—*Red* seems to be imperative in " Hese worthi dedes who-so list hem here *Red* Dares," 8133-4 (redę D).—In several passages it is impossible to determine with certainty whether *lestę* (*lystę*), subjunctive, or *lest* (*lyst*), indicative, is to be read : cf. for example, 686, 1407, 1820, 2245, 2865, 2978, 3215, 3888, 4104, 5245, 6020, 6295, 7360, 7751, 7780 ; see § 95, p. 221.

Note 2.—In *If harm*(e) *agree me*, 409 (agre CD), *agree* has of course but two syllables.

§ 112. The Plural of the present Subjunctive of both strong and weak verbs ends in *-en*, *-e* for all persons (Child, § 56, *c*; ten Brink, §§ 184, 188). Thus,—

I. First Person:

though we comen in, 6184 (-yn C) (pret. ?).

---

[1] D ridiculously reads *Ioue heuen quene*.　　[2] In A insert [*here*].
[3] Supply [*the*] in C.　　[4] *so* later hand in D.
[5] In B supply [*I*]; in C, [*riȝt*].　　[6] B has *of* † for *if*.　　[7] Read *soo*[*ne*] in D.

§ 112.] *of Chaucer's Troilus.* 267

whil we dwellen there, 6186 (-e CD, dwelten A).
though that we . . . apeyre, 1414 f (if that B; C (?)) (: faire *adv.*).
we our tales holde, 2017 f (-d D) (: tolde *ind.* 1 *sg.*).
turne we, 2794 (torne B); torne we, 3061 (turne CD)[1], 4425 (turne CD).
lest we . . . reue, 2807 (byreue BD, be- C) (: leue *n.*).
it is tyme that we wende, 3050 f (: ende *n.* : blynde, blende *cœcare*).
yf we . . . hye, 6852 f (: vilonye).
er that we . . . wende, 7254 f (wynde C) (: shende *inf.* . ende *n.*); cf. 2961 ‡ f D.
but that we shape vs, 5935 (D †).

II. Second Person:
though . . . by-hete, 539 f (be- CD) (· swete *voc.*). . . .
but . . . telle what, 1216 (-e vs BC; D (?)).
though that ye sterue, 1572.[2]
so ye endite, 2247 f (: write *inf*).
that ye . . . honge, 2327 f (-g D) (: longe *adv.*).
he wole . . . that ye brynge, 2728 f (bring CD) (: rekenynge : taryinge).
er that ye wende, 2961 f (winde C, wende ‡ 1 *pl.* D) (: ende *n.*); yf that ye wende, 6157 f (: rende *inf.* : shende *inf.*).
digne me, 2981 (deigne (?) B, digne (?) C, deigne D †).
whil that ye me serue, 3016 f (: deserue 2 *pl. subj.* or *ind.*). [Ind. ?]
so that . . . greue, 3846 f (· at preue).
what so ye me comaunde, 5956 f (: demaunde *n.*).
yf that ye drecche, 6108 f (: wrecche *n.* : recche *inf.*).
er that . . . cause, 6110 (-yn D; *n.* ‡ C).
er ye . . . fynde, 6313 f (: vnkynde *pred. adj.*).[3]
tyme is that ye ryse, 6349 (C †) (: suffice *inf.*).
yf ye vouche sauf, 7285 (*line om.* C).
lest [that] ye . . . breke, 7395 f (*om.* † B; C †; lest that, etc., D) (: speke *inf.*).
that . . . ye not holde, 7702 f (-d B, vnfolde C*ᶜ* †) (: byholde *inf.* : colde *adj. pl.*).
graunte it that ye . . . rewe, 7727 f (: trewe *pred. adj. sg.*).
that . . . ye . . . recomforte, 7758 f (-con- C) (: comporte *inf.* : desporte *inf.*).
that ye ne take, 7988 f (B †) (: make *inf.*).

---

[1] Supply [*to*] in B.
[2] Supply [*that*] in CD.   [3] C has *3yf* † for *er*.

yf . . . seche, 8218 f (: speche *n*).

For instances of -*e*, elided before a vowel, cf. 1385, 1405, 1472 C°, 1476, 3771, 3942, 4760, 4987, 5460, 6103, 6608. For -*e*, elided before *hym*, see *make hym*, 1445 (mak B); *lat hym*, 1408 B (-*e* C, lete D, late ‡ *sg.* A); *suffre hym* (-fẹre C), 3723 (cf. 3705). But -*e* is of course preserved in,—loke that ye *thonke humbely*, 2804 (-en, B, -[e] D, thanke C).

III. Third person:

though wrecches on it crien, 1950 f (cryȝen C) (: eyen *n. pl.* : dryen *inf.*).

though wommen dreden with, 3164 B (-in C, -e AD).[1]

how-so it be that . . . delite, 1341 f (: a lyte : endite *inf.*).

though . . . to-rende, 1875 f (vnrende ‡ D) (: ende *n.*).

lest more folk aryse, 4032 f (: wyse *pred. adj. pl.*).

who wot . . . what they signifie, 6734 f (: glotonye).

er that thei fynde, 7496 (ffynden D).

but men lye, 7891 f (: iupartie : dye *inf.*).

although they holde hem, 4235 AC (hold B).

that they ne fynde in, 4861 (-yn C).

IV. Contracted forms:

fle we, 2649 (flee B, fle [we] D).

whan ye . . . se, 7765 f (seȝ D).

V. Apocope of -*e* :

And coyë (*inf.*) (koy D) hem they (that they D) *sey* noon harm of me, 1886 (seyẹ B, seyn † *ind.* 3 *pl.* C).

Cf. letọ ‡ we *her*, 2017 D (*imv.* ABC); letẹ ‡ we, 3060 D (*imv.* ABC); ne stond ‡ we, 3405 f D (*imv.* ABC).

§ 113. The Preterite Subjunctive Singular of Strong Verbs ends in -*e* for all persons. The Preterite Subjunctive Singular of Weak Verbs shows in the first and third persons the endings -*de*, -*te*, -*edẹ*, -*ed* (cf. Child, § 56; ten Brink, § 195). For the indicative form -*est* in subjunctive constructions in the second person singular of weak preterites, see § 106, above.

I. Strong Verbs.

(*a*) First Person:

---

[1] A erroneously reads *womman* for *wommen*.

§ 113.] *of Chaucer's Troilus.* 269

yf that I so withstode, 5214 f (: for the townes goode).
were, 4053, 4991 f (wer D) (: there); -e, 526, 529, etc.; -e here
(*poss. pl.*), 51 (-ę ‡ their D); nere I, 1494 (ner D).
(*b*) Second Person :
er thow me slowe, 5168 (slewe B, slouȝ D, slow ‡ 3 *sg.* C).
wolde neuerę god but thow were, 936, cf. 521.
(*c*) Third Person :
were, 226 f, 723 f (where C), 765 f, 2098 f, 3302 f, 3367 f, 3409 f
(there ‡ D), 3413 f (there ‡ D), 3949 f, 3984 f, 4181 f, 5357 f
(wer D), 6022 f (-ee- B, wer D), 7240 f (wer D), 7720 f (wer
D), 7944 f (-ee- B), 7965 f ; were (*before consonants*), 528 (-e
BCD), 1027 (ware B, werę (?) D), 1749 ‡ D (were C, was
a A, as † a B), 2715 (D †), 3379 (-ę CD), 3416 (B?), 4011 ‡
A (-e BCD), 4332, 4359 (-ę ‡ D), cf 7847 BCD ; -e, 608 (C †),
836 (-ę C), 860 (wer D)[1], 3359 (wer B)[2], 4353 (-ę ‡ C (?)),
6236 (-ę ‡ C), etc.; -e he, 2705 (-e it C)[3] : -e hym, 3433 (wer
D, -e ‡ he C); -e here (*poss. sg.*), 1777 (-e D)[4]; -e here (*hic*),
143 C (-e a D; A ? B ?); -e honour, 1790[5]; were ‡ and,
5070 A (-e BCD).—nere, 4184 f (were BC ; D †), 6011 (ner
D †); -e, 2128 (were A), 2495, 2559 (ne were C, ner D), 6285
ner D) ; -e he, 2929 (ner B) ; -e his, 6437 (ner D).

Rhyme words.—a-fere (226), fere, feere *n. fear* (723, 765, 3302, 3413, 3984
4181, 6022, 7965), ere, eere (723, 765, 3302, 3409, 3949), gere *n* (2098),
tere *n* (7240, 7944), nere *subj.* 3 *sg.* (4181), there (2098, 3367, 3413,
5357, 6022, 7240, 7720), where (5357), stere *inf.* (226, dere ‡ A).

me were leuere dye Than she . . . vnderstode, 1028 f (· sownen
ynto gode) ; though that she stode, 1032 (stod C).[6]
it sat[e] me, 1202 (-e BD);[7] although . . . sat among, 5359
(-e BD).
who so that me yaue, 2062 f (: haue *ind.* 1 *sg.* : saue *subj.* 3 *sg.*).
spake, 2204 B (*ind. pl.* A, his wordis ‡ CD).
al-though he lay[e] softe, 3284 (?) ; as thow he leye, 6575 ‡
C[c] ; as though . . . lay on, 772 (-e C) ; lay in (*apodosis*), 6222
(leye C, were ‡ D).
al come it, 3310 (-e late D †).
lest . . . fille, 320 (fel C, fil D).[8]
yf she toke it, 3811 (that . . . toke B, that . . . tok C, ellis ‡
she toke D).

[1] 9-syl. verse in ABC (unless one reads *werē it*) ; *wer it* in D=*wer't*.
[2] In D read *were at* [*the*] *ful*.   [3] In D read [*an*]*hangid*.
[4] But read *were her em*(*e*) *n*[*e w*]*old*[*e*] in D.   [5] In C supply [*with*].
[6] Supply [*that*] in C.   [7] Supply [*a*] in AB.   [8] Supply [*self*] in D.

yf that loue . . . late his, 4604 (lete B, let C; D †).

er that . . . spak out, 3385 (-e B, speke ‡ *pres.* C, spakè ‡ out D).

or . . . slow I, 5168 ‡ C (2 *sg.* ABC).

(d) Exceptions:

First Person: nerę but (*apodosis*), 6313 (werę C, ner D).

Third Person: werę sent, 105 (war B, was D); werę wyst, 321, 615, 6222 (wer D); were there, 1223 A (is BCD), 3411 (wer B, was C); werę leuere, leuest, 1274, 1437, 5227 (C (?), wer D)[1]; werę to, 1440, 3479 (-e ‡ C); werę ‡ worthi, 2784 C (was ABD); were brought, 3149 (D †); werę my, me, 3217, 4943 (wer D); werę right, 3840 (C?); werę lost, 4606 (-e BCE); werę wel, 5099 (wer D); werę rathere, 5650 (wer D); werę fals, 5656; werę routhe, 6244; werę ‡ folye, 6626 C (was ABD).—nerę no, 5649 (ner B, wer D).

II. Weak Verbs.

(a) First Conjugation (cf. § 99):

as his herte bledde, 4366 f (blede C) (: cledde *vestivit* : spedde *ind. 3 sg.*).

whom he brought[e] there, 3428 (-e C, broght D).

bysought on, 1st pers., 769 (besouthe C).

al dredde I, 1959 (drede BC, dred D).[2]

as . . . dwelled here (*hic*), 3rd pers., 121 (-ede C, -yd[ę] al ‡ D); duelled ‡ ther, 3rd pers., 7242 D (-eth AB, -yn † C).

til that he herde, 2036 (-[e] D).[3]

though that she . . . herde, 1032 f (-d D) (: answered *ind. 3 sg.*, -swerde BC, -swerd D).[4]

lyste, see § 99.

yf that he mente, 1750 (-t ‡ but D, myʒte ‡ C), cf. 5011 f (?).

vs nedede for, 6006 (-ed BD, -ith ‡ not C).

I rought[e] not, 1032 (-e BC),[5] 2513 (-ʒte C, roght[e] D); nought rought[e] ‖ I, 4944 (-e C, -t D). Cf. § 145, III.

yf I . . . sente, 2532 f (-t CD) (: consente *inf.* : entente *n.*).

that . . . shente, 3rd pers., 1442 f (-t CD) (: assente *inf.*); yf here whiel stynte, 848 (-t D, styntyn † C).

were it thyng that me thoughte vnsittynge, 1392 (-t B; -ë ‡ C, thinkith ‡ D).

if I it tolde, 1314 (-d D); cf. 767 BCD; who-so talės tolde,

---

[1] Dele (*be*) in D.   [2] In C supply [*to*].
[3] In D supply [*that*].   [4] In C supply [*thot*].   [5] In C supply [*that*].

3644 f BC (-d D, tolle † A) (: colde *inf.* : holde *inf.*); she told
here-self, 2716 (-e C, told ‡ hym D).

wolde I that he twyste, 4611 f (-t C) (: lyste *pret. subj. 3 sg.*
: wyste *pret. subj. 3 sg.*).[1]

yf that ych ... wende, 6312 f (· defende *subj. 3 sg.* : entende
ind. 1 sg.); yf I wend[e], 5581 f (-e BCD) (: despende *inf.* :
pretende *inf.*); though ... wende, 3rd pers., 227 (-[e]
ind. ‡ D).

er she wente, 2716 f (-t C, stent ‡ D) (: assente *inf.*); that ...
ne wente, 2739 (wend[e] D ‡); cf. 4832 f (-t D).

(*b*) Second Conjugation (cf. § 101):

al lakkede here, 522 (-ed B, -id D).

al ... made it, 3rd pers., 2929.

although ... pleyde, 3rd pers., 1006 f (-d D, -ede C) (: Criseyde :
seyde *ind. 3 sg.*).

put out, 3rd pers., 3810 (putte BC).

(*c*) Third Conjugation (cf. § 102):

hadde, 1st and 3rd pers., 3770 (-[de] D, had for B; C †), 4998
BC (-[de] D, -de A), 7296 (-[de] D), 7900 (hadd ymade B,
had ymade D)[2]; cf. 6590 ‡ D, 8047 ‡ C; hadde, 1628 (had
D), 2594 (had D), cf. 3117, 5145, 5245, 6419, 6590, 6646 A,
7296, 8047, 8128 A; had I, 7101 (-de B, -de ‡ I C); hadde
his, 3496 (had ‡ myght D), 7548 (had D); had herd, 7086
(-de B, hade C (?)); hadde had, 227 (-[dë] had (?) BD, -de
had C).—yf I ne hadde spoken, 5895 (nadde i-spoken B, ne
had[de] spoken D); I ne hadde trowed, 7099 (nadde ytrowed
B, that I ne hadde trowid C, I me hadde trowed D); I ne
hadde y-brought, 4758 (ne hadde brought B, ne had ‡ her
broght D); ne hadde I, 4052 (nad I CD), 4161 (nade I BE,
naddi C).[3]

though I lyuede, 6242 (-ed BD, leuede C).

what wyght that it with-seyde, 4877 f (: Criseyde : preyede
ind. or subj. 3 sg.); lest I seyde, 2133 (seyd D); yf he seyde,
3420 (-[e] D)[4]

(*d*) Strong verbs with weak preterites (cf. § 103):

er that I deyede, 460 f (dyede B, deyd D) (: seyde *ind. 3 sg* :
Criseyde); lest he ... deyde, 5091 f (dyed B, died D, deyede

---

[1] A has *it wyste* † for *twyste*.
[2] Doubtful case Impossible to decide between *hadde mad* and *hadde ymad*.
Similar cases are 6646, 8128; cf. also 4758, 5895, 7099
[3] In C supply [*my*].   [4] In A read *there*[*of*].

C) (: seyde *subj.* 3 *sg.* : deyde (dyed B, deyẹde C, deyed D) *ind.* 3 *sg.*); whanne he deyde, 5330 f (deyed BD, deyede C) (: Criseyde).

how sore that hym smerte, 5848 f (-t C) (: herte).

it semed as he weptẹ, 2906 (-t CD, veptẹ B).

(*e*) Romance verbs with syncopated preterites (cf. § 104):

al cost it, 6801 (·e CD).

(*f*) Other Romance verbs:

cessedẹ she (*apodosis*), 849 (cessed B, sesed C, sesid D †); cesid ‡ the, *3rd pers.*, 2473 D.

lest any wight devynid ‡ or, 3300 D (*inf.* ABC).

I pose a woman grauntedẹ me, 3152 C (graunte AB, -ith D).

as though I labourẹd me, 5671 AB (-borẹd D).

but yf ... passed oure, *3rd pers.*, 4109 A (-id C, passe ‡ D).

(*g*) Exceptions:

and (= if) it haddẹ ben, 125 (had D).

though he ... haddẹ poured, 299 (hade C, had D); haddẹ nedẹ, 886 (had D).[1]

who-so haddẹ with hym ben, 1276 (had D).[2]

(yf that I) ... had loued, 1501 (haddẹ BC).

(wolde ... Ioue) ... That I the haddẹ where, 4998 (haddë BC, -[de] D); and (= if) ich haddẹ swych, 5727 (had D).

lest ... seyde, *3rd pers.*, 4829 ‡ B. Cf. nededẹ (*a*, above).

For *lystẹ*, see § 99.

§ 114. The Plural of the Preterite Subjunctive of both strong and weak verbs ends, like that of the present, in, *-en*, *-e* for all persons (cf. Child, § 56, *c*; ten Brink, § 195).

that ye dredden this, 1452 (-yn D; dreden B, drede C).

though we comen in, 6184 (-yn C) (pres. ?).

while we dwelten there, 6186 (dwellen B, dwelle C, duelle D).

lest ... men wende, 489 f (: brende *pret. ind.* 3 *sg.*).

though al the town behelde, 1463 f (-d D) (· selde *adv.*).

though alle herẹ foos it herde, 2513 f (-d D) (: with yerde).

(god forbede) ... that ye ... wroughte, 3604 f (-t C, -tyn D) (: thoughte *ind.* 3 *pl.*).

to aske ... yf that they blythe were, 4524 f (: enquere *inf.* : fere

---

[1] Perhaps indicative.
[2] In C *haddė* or 9- syl.; but read *this day* for *yesterday* and *addẹ* is preserved.

n.); lest this tales . . . were, 5333 f (: fere n.); assayinge how here speres were whette, 8123 (-en B, -[e] D); Were hise nayles poynted neuere so sharpe, 2119.[1]
though ʒe . . . . dreynte, 5592 f B (-t D, drenche † A, drenk † C) (: pleynte n. AB, pleynt CD).
he dorste not ye dwelte lengere, 7273 (-[e] B, duelle no C, dwelle ‡ there inf. C).
(if thei) . . . seyde hire (poss. pl.), 1126 (seying ‡ D).
if [that] thei ferd in, 1124 (-e B, fer ‡ with D).[2]
if . . . ye it toke, 1314 (told † B).
were hanged, 1 pl., 1438; were (before vowels), 2 pl., 4011 (-e bete C), 6309 (wer D).
hadde, 3 pl., 4230,[3] 4232, 5638 (had D).[4]
wyst he that ye ferde, 5580. [Indic. ?]
though al this town criede, 5247 (cryed BCD).
that we tok oure leue, 6843 (-e BCD).
who that ther come, 7478.

Exceptions:
al seyde men soth, 3143 (seyd B, seid as D, seidyn as C).

Note.—In *lest it folk aspied*, 6050 f (espied D, aspie † A, aspiede † sg. C), we should read *aspyde* (: bytyde pres. subj. 3 sg. : syde n.). In 1438 (see above), *were honged* may be regarded as a case either of apocope or of elision. In 4065 D *were* should be *be* (so AB, ben Cc); in 4358 ‡ C, *after ʒe were go* should be *after that ʒe go*.

§ 115. The Imperative second person Singular of Weak Verbs in the *Troilus* usually follows the Anglo-Saxon inflections: that is, it shows -e (A.S. -a) in the Second and Third Conjugations, and in the First Conjugation either ends in -e (A.S. -e) or has no ending, according as the stem-syllable was originally short or long (cf. Child, § 58; ten Brink, § 189).

In the following lists the examples given occur *before consonants* in the places cited, unless the contrary is indicated. An accompanying *thou*, *so*, or *as* is noted. As to the possibility that the construction with a preceding *thou* is subjunctive, see below, V, note, and § 117, II.

---

[1] Either *Werĕ his* or 9-syl.
[2] Supply [*that*] in A, as indicated. BD have *that*. C is cut out here.
[3] Read a[*l*]s[*o*] in C.   [4] Read swo[*rn*] in A.

T

I. First Conjugation,—(a) verbs with stem originally short:

leye (A.S. lego), 2079 f (lay C, ley D) (: seye *inf.*), 2602 f (ley D) (: pleye *inf.* : to seye)

telle (A.S. tele), tel[le] which, 3254 (tel me CD)[1]; telle, 595. But,— telle, 681 (tel† D), 693 (tel BC, *om.* † D), 862 (tel C, tellë ‡ me D), 864 (tel C, teH D), 2479 (tel B, tellë ‡ D), 3210 (tel C, tellë ‡ if D); cf. 765, 1010, 2514, 5146, 6693[2]; tel me, 721, 5055 (telle C, teH[e] ‡ D), 5301 (-H D); tel thi, 696; tel thou, 2696 CD (teH † yow A, tel † how B).

lette (A.S. lete), thow me nought ne lette, 3567 (that ‡ thou ne lette *subj.* D) (: fette *pret. ind.* 2 *sg.* : shette *pret. ind.* 3 *sg*).

selle (A.S. sele), -e, 4304 (so ‡ selle C).

> Note.—For the imperatives of *bidden*, *lyen*, see V. *Heue* (A. S. hefe) occurs only with elided *-e* (7522).

II. First Conjugation,—(b) verbs with stem originally long:

bryng (A.S. bring), 5744 (-(e) BD).

hyd (A.S. hýd), h. not, 595 (-(e) BD); so hyd it, 613 (-(e) BCD). But,—Be diligent and trewe and ay wel *hide*, 950 f (: tyde *n.* : abyde *inf.*).

kep (A.S. cép), 3174 (-(e) BD); k. hire (*eam*), 3107 (-(e) BC, so ‡ help D); so kep alwey, 3108 C (saue ABD).[3]

kys (A.S. cys), 8154 (-(se) BD).

kyth (A.S. cýð), 5200 (-(e) CD, right ‡ B); kygh now, 5281 (right † B, kith D, kith (k)now(e) C).

lef, leef (A. S. lǽf); leef, 7881 (lef C, lef(e) BD); lef al, 5514 (leef B, leu(e) C, leueth *pl.* D †).[4] But,—lev(e), 5194 (lef C), 2585 ‡ D (lat AB, let C); leu(e), 2093.

lef (A.S. lýf, léf), 6741 (leu(e) BCD). But,—bileu(e), 2587 (beleuë ‡ and C); so leu(e) it, 7322 (len(e) ‡ B).

red (A.S. rǽd), 8134 (-(e) D).[5]

send (A.S. send), send(e) me, 1614 (-d B, send[e] me D).[6] But,— thow me grace sende, 3547 (synde C) (: ende *n.* : wende *inf.*).

thynk, thenk (A.S. þenc); thynk, 937 (-(e) BC, thenk D); thenk, (i.) 1436 (thynk(e) B, thynkyth ‡ C), 3130 (thynk B, think C),[7] 5128

---

[1] Tel (Telle G) which (-e G) thou wylt of euerychone AB (the Cp. collation has no note on this line); Tel me, etc. CD. If we read *tel[lë]* in ABG and *tel* in CD, all five MSS. have 9-syl. verses. *Tel* is unmetrical in AB; *tel[lë]* in CD would make a full verse. [2] In 6693, *telle* might be taken for an infinitive.
[3] No *so* in AB. [4] In A read *we[r]k*
[5] Might be construed as subjunctive. If imperative, the verb may be either singular or plural.
[6] But insert [*swich*] in D and read *send(e)*. [7] Supply [*what*] in D.

(-(ę) D, thynk(ę) BC), cf. 2595, 3568, 4128, 5279, 5759, 7518 (thynkįth ‡ C); thenk, (ii.) 890 (thynk B, thyng C), 1053, cf. 5079, 5262, 5270; thenk here (*hic*), 2465 (thynk(e) C).

werk (A.S. wyrc), (i.) 2078 (work D).[1]

trow (A.S. tréow), trow(ę), 6209 (-ę *pl.* B, -ęth *pl.* D).[2]

> Note.—For *dred(e)*, imperative of *dreden* (weak in Chaucer), see 3550 (dred C), 6719 (dred C).

III. Second Conjugation:

bridle (A.S. ge-brídla), bridle alwey, 4477 (brydęle C, bridęl D).

calle (A.S. cealla), -e, 3244 (cal CD);[3] -e hym, 3243 (cal CD, cal ‡ hem B).

glade (A.S. glada), 870 (-dde BC).

herkene, herke (A.S. heorcna, hercna); herkęne (*or* herkenę) for, 5691 (-ęnyth ‡ *pl.* D); herkene it, 658 (-en B, herkęnyt it *pl.* C, herkęnith it *pl.* D); herkęne of, 5515 (-yn ‡ with D, werkęne † C). herke, 602 (-[e] D, herkęne *or* -enę C), 624 (-[e] D, -ęne *or* -enę C), 1023 (-[e] BD).

loke (A.S. lóca), 946 (-oo- B, lokę D †); -e, 862, 2405 (se ‡ thes D).

loue (A.S. lufa), -e, 807; -e hire (*eam*), 679, 5278; louę ‖ for, 1481; -ę me, 6935.

make (A.S. maca), 2102 (-ę thow B, thow makę D); so make vs, 8231 (mak B, or take ‡ D); makę the, 3545 (mak C); -ę no, 5112 (mak C); -ę redy thou, 5870 AD (mak B).[4]

pulle (A. S. pulla), -e, 958 (pul D, felle ‡ it C).

> Note.—For the imperative of *rewen* (a weak verb in Chaucer), see § 117, II.

IV. Third Conjugation:

fecche (A.S. feta, see Siev., § 416, *n.* 9), 6685 f (feche CD) (: wrecche *n.*).

folęwe (A.S. folga), -ęwe me, 3581 (-ǫwe B, -ow D, folwe C); folwe alwey, 4969 (-ǫw B, -ǫwe D)

V. Exceptions:

To I. See under *telle*, above, and compare,—

byd (A.S. bide), byd for, 3184; but,—bidde hym, 5571 (bid BC).

ly (A.S. lige), ly stille, 2038 (li BC); but,—lyę right, 2604 (ly C, be † D).

set (A.S. sete), set the, 5284 (sett D); set a cas (=put case, suppose), 1814 (sotte C, set y ind D †).[5]

---

[1] In C read *for-thy* for *for thyn*; in D supply [*shal*].
[2] In AC change þow (þou) to yow and trowe becomes pl.
[3] Supply [*that*] in D.   [4] In D read *my ber[e]* for *me her* † *ber*.
[5] In A read *y[wys]*.

To II. See under *hyd, send, trow(e)*, above, and compare,—
quenche (A.S. á-cwenc), thou ... quenche, 5173 f (-ch D) (: drenche *inf.*).
so spede it, 2147 (-ë ‡ it C, -e D †).
wende (A. S. wend), thow wende, 5308 (: blende *cœcare* : sende *inf.*).

To III. See under *loue, make*, above, and compare,—
put (from A.S. potian?) not, 783; put thyn, 5781 (C †).

To IV. haue (A.S. hafa), 831, 1608[1], 3183, 3262, 5282 (D?);
-e al, 3173 (-ë ‡ al D); -e here (*hic*), 1054 (D?), 1409 ‡ A, 2405, 3953 (?), 7521.

seye (A.S. saga), 925 (sey BCD); sey, 928 (-e B), 2496, 2603 (-e B), 2605 (-[ë] ‡ C). [Var. C say, sei.]

Note.—With regard to the exceptions above noticed, it should be observed that forms like *déme, hýre, telle, cwell* occur in Late West Saxon, and forms like *ner, sel*, etc., in Northumbrian (Sievers, § 410, *n*. 3). In phrases like *thou sende, thou wende*, one is tempted to regard the verb as subjunctive (cf. § 117, II). *Fellë it*, 958 C, is an error for *pulle it*.

VI. Verbs of Germanic origin, but not found in Anglo-Saxon:
beblotte, 2112.[2]
iompre ek, 2122 (iumpere C).
trust (O.N. treysta, *imv.* treyst), ne trust no, 5053 (-(e) B)[3]; thow trust to, 6773 (-ë me CD).[4]
vnneste, 4967 f (-t D, wonest † C) (: the wofulleste : breste *inf.*).

§ 116. The Imperative second person Singular of Verbs of Latin or Romance derivation ends in the *Troilus* in -*e* (cf. ten Brink, § 189).

In the following lists an accompanying *thou, so,* or *as* is noted (cf. § 118, p. 280).

I. Before consonants or in rhyme:
scorne, 576 (-e me CD).
repreue, 669 (reproue ‡ thow D).
assure, 680 f (-eure B; assure ‡ *ind*. 1 *sg.* D) (: endure *ind.* 2 *pl.*).
delite, 704 (A?).
suffre, 755 (-fere C, lete † D), cf. 947.
thow hym gyde, 1162 f (: by syde).
thow ... purueye, 1511 f (-vey D) (: deye *ind*. 1 *sg.*).
eschuwe, 2103 f (-ue B; that thou eschewe *subj.* CD) (: saluwe *inf.*).

---

[1] In A read [vp]on, thus avoiding hiatus. [2] Supply [ek] in C, [thy] in D.
[3] Perhaps 3 *sg. subj.* [4] No *thou* in BCD.

But,—eschewę thou, 634 (eshewę B, -chew D, excusę † C).
compleyne, 2584 f (· peyne n.).
thow me enspire, 3554 f (thou me en- D, thou me this ny3t enspire C) (: desire inf. : in the fyre).
delyuęre, 5177 (-er D ; C ?).
deuyne, 5251.
receyue, 5872.
thow dispone, 6663 f (: to done).
offre, 6669 (-fęre C).
thou nenuye, 8152 f (thou ‡ enuye D) (: dye subj. 3 sg. : poesye).

II. Before vowels :
persèuęre in, 951.
plaunte, 957.
accepte, 1614 (D ?).
reherse, 2114.
saue, 3108 (so save D,_so kep ‡ C).
departe, 3246 (-e ‡ it D).[1]
parforme, 3259 (-forne BC, -fourme D).[2]
prey, 3560 (prey [al] C).
gide, 6685 (guide D, gyde ‡ pl. C).
defende, 8230.

III. Before h :
pray hym, 2543 (prey C, preye B).
dįstreyne herę (poss. sg.), 6959.
delỳuęre herę (acc.), 8106 (-ęr BD).

IV. Apocope :
prey ‖ now, 2584 (-ę B, pray D, preye C) ; cf. II., III.

§ 117. The Imperative second person Singular of Strong Verbs has in the *Troilus*, as in Anglo-Saxon, no -e (Child, § 18, b ; ten Brink, § 189).

An accompanying *thou, so*, or *as* is noted (cf. § 118, p. 280).

I. Regular :
abyd, (i.) 2070 (-(e) D ; quod ‡ C), 2075 (-(e) D, abit C), 2604 † C.
(ii.) 2070 AB (-(ę) C, -(e) D)   (Cf. byd(e), under II, below.)
beet, (i.) 925 (bet(e) CD).
com, (i.) 5164 (-(e) CD). But,—com(e), 7501.
dryf, (ii.) 6722 (-u(e) BD).

---

[1] But supply [so] in D, and read *departe*.   [2] Read *most[e] nede* in ABCD.

farwel,[1] 1053 (-(e) D); farewel, 1033, 2609 (far C), 3703 (far C), 4367 (*pl.* ?) (far BCD), 6916 (far C), cf. 6390, 7539; far(e) now wel, 5320 (far C); far(*e*), 878, 2084 (do ‡ A).

gnaw, (i.) 509 (-(e) B, gnow(e) D).

help, (i.) 10 (-(e) D), 2093 (-(e) B), 5252 (-(e) BD); so help ‡ her, 3107 D (kep A, kepe BC); thow help(e) me, 6 (thow help B); helpe me god, 2211 (*perh. subj.* 3 *sg.*) (help D, helpe god *subj.* C).

Note.—The imperative *help* has in some cases become almost a mere interjection (see 533, 1007, 3566, 3573, 5812); but lines like 1047, 3570, 3573, allow us to see the original construction (cf. helpe, *sbst.*; p. 17, note). In 3900 we perhaps have a *subj.* 3 *sg*.

hold, (i.) 2105 (D †), 4311 (-(e) D, -e ʒow(?) C), 5782 (-(e) D); so hold, 5117 (-(e) BD, held C). (ii.) 2124; hold here (*acc.*), 5194 (-(e) D). But,— hold(e), 2619 (-d CD), 4474 (-d BC).

lat, (i.) 616 (-(e) D), 701, 760, 2038 (-(e) D, -(e) A), 2585 (leve ‡ D), 5199 (lett D), 5759 AB (let D)[2]; cf. 856, 1021, 2137, 2141, 2486, 2515, 2607, 5061, 5112, 5283, 5313, 7644. [Var. CD let; D let(e).] (ii.) 702 (let(e) D; C †); cf. 4968, 6752, 6756, 6844, 6845, 7492; lat here (*acc.*), 5193 (let(e) D)[3] (cf. 5249 C, 5500, 6722). But,— lat(e), 3255 (lat B, let CD), 3582 (lat BC, let(e) D); cf. 2038 A, 3262; lat(*e*) hym, 2562 (?) (lat B, let C, let(*e*) D).

Note.—How completely the adhortative first person plural and the periphrasis with *lat* had become synonymous may be seen from such passages as the following:

But *fle we* now prolixite best is .
For loue of God and *lat vs* faste *go*. . .
And *late vs* of here saluynges pace, 2649-50, 2653, (lat . . . let C, let(e) . . . let D)..
So *go we* seen the paleys of Criseyde
For syn we yet may haue nomore feste
So *lat vs seen* here paleys at the leste, 6886-88 (As go B, As goo D, Go C; Yett let(e) ys goo se D). Compare also,—
Now *late here slepe* and *we* oure tales holde, 2107 (lat BC; Now lete we her slepe & forth our talis hold D).
Now *late hem rede* and *turne we* a-noon, 2794 (lat B, let(e) D).
Now *late here wende* vn to here owne place
And *torne we* to Troylus a-yen, 3060-1 (lat B, let C, Now let(e) we her wend to, etc. D); cf. 1772-3.

In all these cases, as well as those in which Chaucer addresses his audience, we should probably regard the *lat* as imperative plural (see 1079, 4515).

ren, (i.) 7019 (ren(ne) BD).

ryd, (i.) 2098 (-(e) BD); rid(e), 2105 (ryd C, ride D †).

---

[1] The variations noted concern merely *far*; the second part of this quasi-compound is written *wel*, *well*, or *wele* (never dissyllabic). The accent is on *far* in 1033, 3703, 4367 CD, 6916; 6390 BD, 7539; on *wel* in 1053, 2609, 4367 AB, 6390 A.

[2] Supply [*thi*] in A.   [3] Supply [*of*] in B.

§ 117.] *of Chaucer's Troilus.*

rys, (i.) 6756 (-(e) D), 6770 (r. ‡ vp C, ris(ę) D). (ii.) 5199 (-(e) BD); cf. 5255, 5307, 6751 A. But,— rys(ę), 6751 B (rys C, aris(ę) ‡ D).

se, (i.) 894, 1697 ABC (*perh. pl.*), 2405 ‡ D, 7659.

spek, (i.) 2542 (-(e) D), 2584 (-(e) BCD), 3954 (-(e) CD) (*perh. pl.*).

stond, (i.) 962 (-(e) B).

tak, (i.) 344 (-(e) BD, *om.* ‡ C). (ii.) tak it, 4463 (-(ę) B, -(e) D, tak now C); tak herte, 5279 (-(e) BD; C †). But,— tak(ę), 5514 (tak C, -eth D †), cf. 6668; tak(e), 8231 ‡ D; tak(e) hede, 5769 (tak C ?).

wassh, (i.) 5308 (wessh B, wasch C, waissh(e) D).

wep, (ii.) 7881 (-(e) B, -(ę) CD).

worth, (ii.) 2096 ((-e) C, worth thow B, worth(e) thou D).

yef, (i.) 6671 (ʒef B, ʒif C, yif D); y. thow, 2148 (ʒif BC, ʒev(e) D).[1] But,—yeu(ę), 1035 (ʒif BC, yef D); so yeu(e), 6677 (ʒeu(e) BC).

II. Exceptions.

In a few cases forms in -e (sounded) occur. These cases are,—

thow breste, 6208 f (to-breste *pres. subj.* 3 *sg.* BCG Cp. John's, which is no doubt the correct reading) (: leste *subj. pres.* 2 *sg.* AC, 3 *sg.* B, 2 *pl.* D).

thow ... rewe, 7070 f (: trewe *pred. adj. sg.*).

thow write, 2111 f (: endite *inf.* : a lyte).

In these instances it will be observed that *thow* precedes the verb, and we are perhaps justified in regarding the forms as jussive subjunctives (cf. § 115, V, note). *Thow helpę me*, 6 (thow help B) cannot well be used as an argument against this view, for apocope is frequent in the subjunctive mood (see § 111). The imperatives *rewe*, 5743 (rew C), 5838 (rew BD), and *writ*(e) *here* (dat.), 7671 (writ(e) (to) hire C), are indecisive, since they stand before a vowel or *h*. It should be remembered, however, that *rewen* is a weak verb in Chaucer. There are many other cases in which -e is written in the imperative singular of strong verbs, even in MS. A, but in none of these instances is the -e pronounced : see above (I.) under *com, far, help, hold, lat, ryd, rys, tak, yef,* and add,—

awak(e), 729; awak(e) he, 751 (awak B, -ë ‡ he D).

ber(ę), 6212 (ber B).

byd(ę), 2604 (-d B, abyd ‡ C, tabide † *inf.* D); byd(e), 3582 (bid B, byd C).

ches(e), 2040 (sches C).[2]

writ(e) here (*dat.*); 7671 (-(e) (to) hire C).

---

[1] In C read *wit* for *wilt*.   [2] Supply [*And*] in A.

wyt(e), 2085.

Note.—For the imperatives of *bidden, lyen*, see § 115, V. For the imperative of *heuen*, see § 115, I, note. For the imperative of *dreden*, see § 115, II, note. *Flen* (cf. §§ 96, 103) has *fle* (4968).

§ 118. The Imperative second person Plural of verbs, strong or weak, native or naturalized, ends in the *Troilus* in -*eth*, -*eth*, -*th*; but forms in -*e* and forms without any termination are very common. (cf. Child, § 59; ten Brink, § 189).[1]

Commands in the second person plural are expressed in Anglo-Saxon in three ways: (1) by the regular imperative plural in -*að*, (2) by the regular subjunctive plural in -*en*, and (3) by a form in -*e*. This last form is used only when the subject *gé* immediately follows the verb and is especially common in prohibitions, but in no construction or situation is it employed to the exclusion of the forms in -*að* and -*en*. It was doubtless originally a subjunctive, but in West Saxon it became indistinguishable from the imperative and indeed it is sometimes co-ordinated with -*að* in the same sentence (as,— *nime gé . . . ond settað*, Cura Past., 345, 15; *ne fare gé né ne fyliað*, Luc. 17, 23)[2]. See Sievers, § 360, Anm.; Cosijn, *Altws Gr.*, II, §§ 75, 77; Mätzner, *Engl. Gr.*, II, i, p. 138, ed. 1864; Hennicke, *Der Conjunctiv im Altenglischen*, Göttingen, 1878, pp. 11, 12; Hotz, *On the Use of the Subjunctive Mood in Anglo-Saxon and its further History in Old English*, Zürich, 1882, pp. 13-15; Fleischhauer, *Ueber den Gebrauch des Conjunctivs in Alfred's altengl. Uebersetzung von Gregor's Cura Past.*, Erlangen, 1885, pp. 4, 5, 87; Wohlfahrt, *Die Syntax des Verbums in Ælfric's Uebersetzung des Heptateuch und des Buches Hiob*, München, 1885, pp. 2, 3; Prollius, *Ueber den syntact. Gebrauch des Conj. in den Cynewulfschen Dichtungen Elene, Juliana u. Crist*, Marburg, 1888, p. 5; P. T. Kuhn, *Die Syntax des Verbums in Ælfrics Heiligenleben*, Leipzig-Reudnitz, 1889, p. 10.

In the *Troilus* the form in -*eth* and the form in -*e* are both common, and they are often joined in the same sentence. The form in -*e* is usually felt as an imperative; but when *ye* precedes (as in *ye me lere*, 1182) the construction may have retained some of its original subjunctive force (cf. in the singular, *thou quenche*, etc.; see §§ 115, V, and note, 116, 117, II). Forms in -*e* (apocopated) or without ending also occur, and some of these may be due to an extension of the singular form to the plural or to the petrifaction of a singular in an idiomatic use. Cf. especially *lat* in the periphrasis *lat us* with inf. (*latteth* is altogether unknown to Chaucer).

In the examples that follow (I.—IV.)-an accompanying *so* or *ye* is noted.

I. -eth (var. CD -ith, -yth)[3]:

preyeth, 29 (-[e]th), 32.
biddeth, 40 (-ith ‡ D), 43.
ye . . . dwelleth, 119 (-yt B; D †).

refuseth, 255 (-eth ‡ C, grucchith D), 2296 (refuse ‡ it C).
douteth, 683 (-eht B).
disblameth, 1102 (des- B).

---

[1] *Rewes*, 6163 A, is a scribe's error.
[2] So also the imperative and the subjunctive in -*n* may be co-ordinated in the same sentence. Thus,— *ne ondrǽdað éow né gé ne onforhtion*, Ælfric, Deuter. 31, 6.
[3] Before consonants unless the contrary is noted. Old-style figures indicate that a vowel follows.

[§ 118.]   *of Chaucer's Troilus.*   281

sitteth, 1298 (sitheth B).
quaketh, 1387.[1]
herkeneth, 1400[2] (cf. 52, 2195,
    5958, 6034 (bef. *how*), 8148).
loketh, 2220.
letteth, 2221 (-e[t]h B).
thanketh hym, 2293 (thonk[ith]
    D).
abydeth, 2800.
so techeth, 2883, 4135.
draweth, 3019 (-et B).
careth, 3512.
wyrcheth, 3785 (werk- B, werch-
    ith C, wurkith D).
liggeth, 3790 (lith C).
kneleth, 3807.

swowneth, 4032.
iuggeth ye, 4154.
helpeth, 4688.
so . . . shappeth, 5587; so s.
    how, 5596 (-eth ? D).
suffreth, 5866 (-feryth C).
taketh, 5955 (B ?), cf. 3790.
so reweth, 6163 BD (-ith C,
    rewes A)
thenketh, 6238 (thynk- B, thynk-
    yth C, thinketh D).
maketh, 6248.
leueth, 6278.
vp casteth, 8201 (D ?).
loueth hym, 8205.[3]

   Compare also 232, 259 D (bef. *him*), 538, 687, 1388, 2511, 2737
C, 3790 (bef. *hym*), 4050, 4990, 6182, 6221 (bef. *hede*), 6252, 6525,
6668 C (bef. *hede*), 7250, 7266 (bef. *heed*), 7281, 7749, 7762, 8200
(bef. *hom*), 8203, and the examples cited under II.—IV.

   Note.—Observe the variations of ending in B 119, B 683, and cf.,—takyt,
   232 C; herkenyt, 658 C; trusteht, 2330 B; herknet, 8148 B; herkenet,
   2195 B; douteht, 683 B.

II. Syncopated forms[4]:

refuseth, 255 C (-eth not AB, grucchith not D).
aryseth, 1306 (-e D, -eth lat B).
castith, 1307 D (cast ABC).
biddeth, 1659 C (byd AB, bid D).
takyth hede, 1666 C (tak A, take BD), cf. 1376 D; -eth, 2801 C
    (take AD, tak B); -yth, 3051 C (tak AB, -e D).
tellith, 2190 C (tel AB, tel D †).
bryngyth, 2217 C (bryng A, -e B, bring D).
spekith, 2372 D (spek AB, speke C).
sleth, 2821 C (sle ABD).
comith, 3511 D (-e ABC).
haueth, 3595 (-yth C, haue BD); -yth, 2218 C (haue ABD); havith
    here (*hic*), 3727 D (-e ABC).
seth, 3805 (se B, sey C, y-sey D).

---

[1] Supply [*not*] in B.
[2] In A cut out (*yow*).   [3] Supply [*that*] in B, [*the*] in D.
[4] Old-style figures indicate that a vowel follows

seith, 4018 C (do AB, doth D).
so shapeth you, 5596 D (-eth how AB, -yth to C).
duelleth, 6111 D (dwelle ABC).
troweth, 6209 D.
thynkıth, 6249 C (thenk A, thynke B, thinke D); cf. 1436 C, 5979 C, 7518 C.
dryueth, 6277 C (dryf A, dryfe B, dryue D).
fareth now wel, 6349 AD (B?), 7784 C (fare AD), 7994 (farth B, farith C); -eth wel, 7775 AD (farwel C). But cf. 5869.
comaundıth, 6495 C (-eth me ABD).
meruelleth, 6525 D (wondreth AB, -derith C).
  Note —It will be observed that syncopated forms are not common in A.
III. Forms in -e :
ye me lere, 1182 (leere B, lere *inf.* D).
loke ye, 2733 (-eth B, -ith C, -ith [ye] D), 2737 (-ith CD, lakketh † B); loke that, 2804 (-ith D); loke thanne, 3158, 3718[1]; looké || alwey, 2194 B (loke D, loke that C, lok [that] A).
avise yow, 2815 (-eth BC, -ith D).
so help[e] to, 3577 (-eth B, now helpyth C, now helpith D).
stynte ‡ al, 3948 B (stynt *p.p.* ACD).
thenk[e] thowgh, 4128 (thynk that B, -eth thouȝ D ; C †).
smyte of, 4415.
take not, 6498 (-eth B, -yth C)[2]; cf. 3704.
hèrkene it, 658 (-en B, herkeuyt C, herkenith D).
telle it, 1181 (tel BD).
cache, 1376 (tache C, takıth D).
late, 2029 (lat BC, lete D); cf. 4148 (?), 5905.
refuse, 2239 (refuse ȝe it = ȝe't D); cf., however, 2296.
aquyte hym, 2285 (aquit it C).
ye . . . inhelde, 2886 (in hielde B, iuheld D).
rewe, 4766 (-ıth D, rew? B).
so yeue hym, 4772 (ȝif B, grauntith ‡ me D); foryeue, 5948 (-ȝeue BC, -yeveth me D), 7707 (-ȝeue BC, -yef D).
receyue, 4983.
so loue here (*acc.*), 5278.
 IV. Forms in -e or without ending :
  (*a*) Before consonants :
help me, 535 (-e D).
yif me, 1378 (ȝif BC, yeve D); yeue me, 6515 (ȝeue C, ȝif C, yef D).

---

[1] Supply [*that*] in BD. [2] In 6498 A *take* might easily be construed as infinitive.

§ 118.]   *of Chaucer's Troilus.*   283

vnderstonde for, 1443 (-ė ‡ B, -d CD)[1]; stond not, 3405 (stant B, stond we *subj.* 1 *pl.* D).[2]

tel me, 1586, 1589 (B †); telle me, 1395 (tel BC), 2363 (tel CD).[3]

lat youre, 1469 (C †, lete ? D); lat this, 1482 (lete D); so lat me, 1522 (lete D); lat be, 2229 (let C, lete D), 3405 (let CD)[4]; lat preue, 3890 (let CD); lat now, 3981 (lete D); lat sle, 4143 (let C); cf. 117, 1194, 1204, 1399, 1635, 3040, 3598, 3602, 4855, 5586 ‡ C.

awake ‖ ye slepen, 1630.

byd me, 1659 (biddeth C, bid ʒe D).

loke that, 2194 C (lok [that] A, looke ‖ alwey B, loke al wey D).

ne bryng me, 2217 (-e B, -yth C).

yif me, 2289 (ʒif BC, ʒef D).

stynte that, 2327 (stynt D).

thenk which, 2822 (thynke B, think C, thenk † one D); so thynk that, 4128 B (thenk[e] thowgh A, -eth thouʒ D; C †).

foryet this, 5458 (-ʒet BC, -yete D).

so lef this, 5558 (leuyth C, leue D), 5586 (leue D, lat be C).

farewel, 5869 (far BC; D †)[5]; fare now wel, 7784 AD (-eth C). But cf. 6349, 7775, 7994.

dwelle rathere, 6111 (duelleth D).

trowe me, 6209 B (-eth D; -e *sg.* AC).

hold forward, 6860 (-e BD), cf. 6447.

make good, 7276.

wre you, 1465 (were † B, wri C, couere ‡ D).

y-se who, 2338 (I-see B, lo ‡ C); se ye, 995 (se now BC).[6]

o fle not, 2339.

sle nought, 2821 (sleth C).

(*b*) Before vowels or h :

rys, 1196 (-e BD),[7] 2029 (-e D); arys, 5577 (-e D).

tel, 1207 (-telle B, -H D; C †).

tel, 2190 (-ith C; D †), 2280.

trist, 1391 (trustith ‡ me D).

com, 1395 (-e D), 2823 (-e CD, com [of] B), 2827 (-e C, -è ‡ of D).

thenk, 1478 (thynk B, think C); thynk, 7749 C (-eth AD); so thenk, 6160 (thynke BC, thinke D). Cf. 1459, 2824.

---

[1] In B we should supply [*yow*] and read -*e*.   [2] In A supply [*ne*].
[3] Infinitive ?   [4] In A supply [*ne*].
[5] Dele (*now*) in A ; insert [*my*] in B.
[6] Probably the correction *ye* to *now* should be made and *se* regarded as singular.
[7] Supply [*and*] in D.

284 · *Observations on the Language* [§ 118.

tak hede, 1666 (-e BD, -yth C); tak it, 1337 (-e CD).
ber, 2226 (-e CD).
cast, 2241 (-e C, -e [it] B); cf. 1700.
se how, 3804 [1], 6594 ABD.
sey, 3948 (sei C, seie D).
lat, 4346 (let C); cf. 5906, 5963, 5964, 6263, 6858, 6860; lat hem, 4164 (let D).

Further examples of the imperative plural in -e or without an ending may be seen in,—

> But *lat* be this and *telle* me how ye fare.
> *Do* wey youre barbe and *shewe* youre face bare
> *Do* wey youre book *rys* vp and *late* vs daunce
> And *lat* vs don to may som obseruaunce; 1194-7 (tel . . . swow †. . . .
>   ryse . . . lat . . . lat B; tel . . . schew . . . lat . . . lat C, let . . . shew . . . risë vp . . . let . . . lete D).

> *Lat* be [to me][2] youre frendly.[3] manere speche
> And *sey* to me, etc., 1333-4 (lat . . . say B, let . . . sey CD).

> . . . em I preye
> Swych answere as yow lyst yow self *purueye*, 2244-5 (D †).

> *Lat* be youre nice shame and youre folye
> And *spek* with hym in esyng of his herte
> *Lat* nicete not do yow bothe smerte, 2371-3 (let . . . speke . . . let C, lete . . . spekith . . . lete D).

> For loue of god *make* of this thyng an ende
> Or *sle* vs bothe, 2960-1 (mak . . . slo C ; D †).

> *Lok*e al be wel and *do* now as yow lyste, 3430 (look . . . [and] do B, loke . . . y do *ind.* D).

> *Lat* Troye an Troian fro youre herte pace
> *Dryf* out that bittre hope and *make* good chere
> And *clepe* ayen the beaute of youre face, 7275-7 (late . . . dryue . . . make . . . clepe B ; let . . . dryue . . . make . . . clepe D).

The freedom with which imperatives in -*eth* are co-ordinated with these truncated forms is shown by the following passages,—

> *remembre* yow . . . and *thenketh*, 24-26 A (-breth . . . thenketh B, remembre . . . thynke D †).

> . . . *aryseth* and *lat* vs daunce
> And *cast* youre wydwes habit to myschaunce, 1306-7 (ariseth lat . . . cast B, arise and lete . . . castith D).

> *Sey* on *lat* me not yn this fere dwelle
> So wol I don now *herkeneth* I shal yow (*om.* BCD) telle, 1399-1400 (let . . . herkenyth C, let . . . herkenith D).

> *Auiseth* you on it whan ye han space
> And of som goodly answere yow *purchace*, 2209-10 (avise ʒow . . . purchace C, avisith . . . purchace D) ; cf. 2815.

---

[1] Supply [*can*] in B.   [2] *to me* om. in A, but found in BCD.
[3] frende B, frendely C, frend[e] D. Read *fremde*.

§ 118.]   *of Chaucer's Troilus.*   285

Nay nece quod Pandare *sey* not so
Yet at the leste *thanketh* hym I preye
Of his good wil and *doth* hym not to deye
Now for the loue of me my nece dere
Refuseth not at this tyme my preyere, 2292-6 (thonketh B, thankith ...
  refuse ‡ it C, thonk[e] ... refusith D).

Now *stynte* that ye ......

But *hasteth* yow to don hym ioye haue
For *trusteth* wel to longe don hardnesse, etc., 2327-9-30 (trusteth B, hastyth
  ... trosteth C, stynt ... hastith ... trustith D).

Rys take with yow yowre nece Antigone

The lasse pres the bet *come* forth with me
And *loke* that ye thonke humbely
Hem alle thre and whan ye may goodly
Youre tyme y-se *taketh* of hem youre leue, 2801-3-4-5-6 (ris tak ... com ...
  loke ... taketh B, rys taketh ... come ... loke ... takyth C, rys
  take ... com ... lokith ... takith D).

Stynteth right here and softely yow *pleye*, 2814 (stynteth ... *om.* † B,
  styntith ... ȝe pleye C, styntith ... soft[e]ly ȝow play D) (: I preye *ind.*).

Com of therfore and *bryngeth* hym to hele, 2835 (brynge C, come ... bring
  ȝe hym D).

Now *beth* al hol no lengere ye ne *pleyne*, 3010 (peyne C, no lenger that ȝe pleyn
  D) (: feyne *inf.*, feyn D).

And *eseth* there youre hertes right y-nough
And *lat* se which, etc., 3039-40 (ese † ... lat C, esith ... let D).

Tak nece myn youre leue at alle thre
And *late* hem speke and *cometh* forth with me, 3051-2 (lat B, takyth ...
  comyth C, take ... let ... comith D).

And yf ye lyggen wel to nyght *come* ofte
And *careth* not what weder is on lofte, 3511-12 (carith C, comith ... carith
  D).

Ne *wondreth* not ne *haueth* of it no fere

Lat no wight rysen, 3595-8 (-dereth ... haue ... lat B, -deryth ...
  hauyth ... let hem C, -drith ... have ... let no (?) D).

Haue here and *bereth* hym this blewe rynge

And *sey* my, etc., 3727-30 (haue ... bere ... sey C, havith ... berith
  ... sey [my] D).

For *trusteth* wel ... So (To † A) *speke* youre self, 3748-51 (spek B, trostyth
  ... speke C, trustith ... speke D).

... *se* how this lord kan knele
Now for youre trouthe *seth* this gentil man

And seyde *kneleth* now, 3804-5-7 (se ... se ... kneleth B, how wel ...
  sey ȝone ... knelith C, how wel ... y sey (=y-se ?) ... knelith D).

And euere more on this nyght yow *recorde*
And *beth* wel war. ..

Foryeue it me, etc., 4021-2-5 (ffor-ȝif C, ȝe ‡ recorde D) (: mysericorde *n.*).

286   *Observations on the Language   [§§ 118, 119.

Beth glad forthi and *lyue* in sykernesse, 4355 (leuyth C, be . . .- lyuęth D).

And *shappeth* yow his sorwe for to a-bregge
And nought encresse leue nece swete
Buth rather to hym [cause] of flat than egge
And with som wysdom *ye* his sorwes *bete*, 5587-90 (shapeth . . beth. . . .
beete B, schapyth . . . be . . . bete C, shapeth . . . beth ,·. . bete D).

So *shappeth* how distourbe this goynge

And *lat* sen now, etc., 5596-9 (shapeth B, schapyth to . . . let C, shapęth
you . . . lett D).

. . . *beth* glad now yf ye konne.
[1] And *thynk* right thus, 5978-9 (thynk B; thynkįth C, thenkë D).[2]
So *rewes* on myn aspre peynes smerte
And *doth* somwhat. . .
And *lat* vs stele away by-twext vs tweye
And *thenk* that folye is, etc., 6163-6 (reweth . . . thynkę B, rewith . . .
thyng C, reweth .·. . lete . . . thinkę D).

And forthi *sle* with reson al this hete

Thus *maketh* vertue of necessite
By pacient and *thenk* that lord is he, 6245-8-9 (by paciens . . . thynkę
B, this makyth . . . beth pacient . . . thynkįth C, be pacient . . .
thinkę D).

And *thenketh* wel. ·. .

Dryf out the fantasies yow with-inne
And *trusteth* me and *leueth* ek yourę sorwe
Or *her* my trouthe I wol not lyuę til morwe, 6273-7-8-9 (thynketh . . .
dryfe . . . herę C, thynkyth . . . dryuęth . . . trostyth . . . leuyth . . .
herę D, me thinketh ‡ *ind*. . . . dryue D).

Now *hold* yowrę day and *doth* me not to deye, 6447 (do B, help ‡ this day and
do C, holdęth . . . letë ‡ D).

Now *writeth* swete and *lat* me thus not pleyne, 7762 (-yth . . . let C,
-eth . . . letę D).

§ 119. The Infinitive ends in the *Troilus* in -*en*, -*ęn*, -*e*, -*ę*
(cf. Child, § 60; ten Brink, § 190). In *to seyne, to sene, to done*, the -*ne* of the A.S. gerund or dative-infinitive is preserved.

Variants in -*yn, -in* are found; -*yn* is particularly common in C.

The spelling -*ene* in *for to trostene*, 690 C, *to chaungen* . . .
and . . . ȝeuenę, 4721-2 B, is rather a scribe's eccentricity than a reminiscence of the gerundial ending.

Note.—The prefix *y-* (very common with the *p. p.*, see §§ 121-2 *passim*) is occasionally found with the infinitive: *y-se*, see § 119, XII.; *y-the*, 1755 f (the ACD); *i-the*, 5101 f B (the A, he ‡ C, thee D) (cf. § 119, XI.); *y-here*, 5975 f (yheere B, [y]here C, here D). But in 1439, 5500 (*y-se*), the -e of the preceding word may have been carried over, and in 1755, 5101, we may choose between *neuer the* and *neuer y-the*.

[1] Here begins a new stanza, but the construction continues.   [2] D omits *And*.

[§ 119.] *of Chaucer's Troilus.*

The examples are arranged as follows,—I. -en before consonants; II. -en in rhyme; III. -en before vowels; IV. -en before *h*; V. syncope, -en; VI. -e before consonants; VII. -e in rhyme; VIII. -e (elided) before vowels; IX. -e (elided) before *h*; X. apocope of -e; XI. hiatus; XII. contracted forms,—*fle, sle, the, wre*; XIII. gerundial infinitives,—*to seyne, to sene, to done* (with the other infinitive forms of these three verbs).

I. -en before consonants (of all kinds, except *h*):

seken bote, 763 (sychen C, seche D).
suffren loues, 971 (soueren B, soffere (?) C, suffre D).
helpen sely, 1768 (-e C, -[e] D).
wexen dymme, 1993 (-e dunne CD).
gladen lo, 2064 (-yn D; C †).
lyuen for, 2212 (leuyn C, lyvyn D).
helen the, 2400 (-e CD).
auaylen now, 2515 (-e C; D †).
dishesen for, 2735 (-esen D, -esin C, -sese D).
axen red, 2783 (-in D).
wrathen yow, 3016 (-e C ‡ ?, -yn D, wreth[e] B).
cursen slouthe, 3738 (-yn CD, corsen B).
maken chere (clere † A), 4506 (-e C, -yn D).
Cf. also 139, 252, 380, 435, 838, 1529, 1598, 2480, 2640, 4248, 4539, 4622, 5288, 5607, 5694, 6445, 6870, 7161, 7916, etc., etc.

Note.—The spelling -*yn* is rare in A: see *she may ledyn Paris*, 2534 (-en B, -e C).[1]

II. -en in rhyme:

tellen, 1 (: fellen *pret. ind. 3 pl.*).
wayten, 190 (-e D) · beyten *inf.*, 192 (-yn C, -e D, baten B).
descenden, 216 (-yn CD) (: wenden *pret. ind. 3 pl.*).
quyken, 295 (queken C, qwykyn D) : stiken *inf.*, 297 (-yn D, quekyn C); quyken, 5293 (-yn CD) : pryken *inf.*, 5295 (-yn C).
dyen, 306 (deyen BC) (: dryen *patiuntur*: eyen *n. pl.*); dyen, 1412 (-ey- BC): lye *inf.*, 1409 (lyen CD) (: eyen); deyen, 1621 (dyen BD): bywryen *inf.*, 1622 ([be]- B) (: eyen); dyen, 3027 (dey3en C) (: eyen). (See *eyen*, n. pl., § 4, p. 8.)
maken, 562 (-e CD) : awaken *inf.*, 564 (-yn C, wake D) (: spaken *ind. 3 pl.*, -yn C, -e D); maken, 3734 (-yn CD) (: shaken *p.p.*, -e C, -yn D).
weylen, † 1369 (weyuen B, weyue CD) : receyuen *inf.*, 1367 (-e CD) (: deseyuen *ind. 3 pl.*, -e C; D †).

---

[1] In D supply [For].

lyuen, 1663 f (-yn D, leuyn C) (: dreuen, -yn C, dryuen B, -yn D : schryuen, -yn D, screuyn B, schreuyn C, *both p.p.*); lyuen, 2066 (-in D, leuyn C) (: (y)dreuen *p.p.*, dryuen B, dreuyn C, -in D).

cryen, 1731 : aspien *inf.*, 1734 (-yen BCD) (: eyen *n. pl.*). Cf. 3977, etc., below.

dryen *pati*, 1951 (: eyen *n. pl.* : crien 3 *pl.*).

wàryen, 2704 (-ye C, -ien D) : vàryen *inf.*, 2706 (-ie C, tarien † D) : tàryen *inf.*, 2707 (-ien D, *l. om.* C).

comen, 3097 (-yn CD) (: becomen *p.p.*, -yn CD).

excusen, 3867 (-yn C, -e D) (: vsen *ind.* 3 *pl.*, -yn CD).

espyen, 3977 (aspien BD) (: eyen *n. pl.*, iʒen D) ; espyen, 7177 (asspyen C) (: syen *viderunt*, seyen C : eyen *n. pl.*, yen BD). Cf. 1731, above, 4296, below.

escapen, 4084 (as- D, eschape C) (: shapen *p.p.*, -e C).

honouren, 4104 (-yn C, *to h*onouryn D) : socouren *inf.*, 4106 (-on B, -yn CD) (: labouren *ind.* 3 *pl.*, -on B, -yn CD^c).

spyen, 4296 (tò ‡ espÿen C, tò ‡ aspìen D) (: ywryen *p.p.* : eyen *n. pl.*, eyʒyn C, yen D). Cf. 3977, above.

flowen, 4600 (-yn CE, flewen B) (: growen *ind.* 3 *pl.*, -yn C, grevyn † D).

byholden, 5023 (-yn D) : colde *inf.*, 5024 (-en B, -yn CD) (: folden *p.p.*, -yn CD).

comforten, 5384 (-yn C, -e D) : disporten *inf.*, 5386 (-yn C, -e D).

wryten, 8128 f (-e BD) : endite *inf.*, 8130.

> Note.—The commoner infinitive ending in rhyme is *-e* (see VII., below). The ending *-en* is often used to give variety to stanzas which also contain the infinitive in *-e* at the end of one or more verses. Thus the rhymes in 5293 ff. are,—*quyken* inf., assente 1 *sg.*, *pryken* inf., *tormente* inf., entente, sholde, wolde (cf. also 1 ff., 190 ff., 295 ff., 561 ff., 1408 ff., 1730 ff., 3095 ff., 4082 ff., 4600 ff., 5293 ff.).

III. -en before vowels :

drawen, 1347 (-ë? C, -[ë] D).

lyuen, 1635 (-ë D, leuin C).

taryen (*dissyl.*), 2104 (-ye C).

quenchen, 3900 (-in C, -yn D †).

fynden, 5053 (-yn C, -ë D).

asken, 5334 (axen BC, askë ‡ hem D).

distorben, 5765 (-in C, -yn D).

bryngen, 5937 (-yn C, -[ë] ‡ D).

causen, 5971 (-yn C, -ë D).

congeÿen, 6842 (cùngë ‡ và C, cunueien ‡ D).

bifallen, 7325 (-ë D, -yn that C).
Cf. also 194, 620, 836, 1029, 1595, 2242, 2476, 2724, 5191, 5768, 7444, etc., etc.
  Note.—The ending -yn is rare in A: see *werkyn in*, 4899 (-en B, wirke D)..
  IV. -en before h:
fynden here (*hic*), 399 (-ë BC, -yn D)
byholden here (*eam*), 1350 (-yn D, -holdyn C).
dissimulen he, 3276 (-yn CD).
esen hem, 4632 (-yn D).
distorben hym, 6065 (-ë CD).
beren hym, 6066 (-yn C, -[e] D).
rennen hom, 6848 (-e CD).
Cf. also 370, 388, 1238, 2377, 2926, 4609, 5100, 6052, 6551, 7677, 8069, etc.
  V. Syncope,— -ẹn.
    Note.—In most of the cases cited under A, and in some of those under B and C, the caesura falls immediately after the infinitive.
  A. Before vowels:
spekẹn, 387 (-e BD, spek C).
seruẹn, 817 (-e BD, -yn C †) cf. 2986.
herẹn, 1013 (-e BD, -yn C).
castẹn, 1744 (-e B, -yn C, cast D).
louẹn, 1843 (-yn C, -e BD).¹
axẹn, 1981 (-e ? D, -ith C, -en fendes B).
tellẹn, 2578 (-e BC, tel D).
rysẹn, 3598 (-e B, -yn ? C, arise ? D).
lokẹn, 3822 (-e CD, -e vp[on] B).
to amendẹn, 6501 (-e D, tamende B, to amendyn C).
syngen, 7000 (-e BC, syng D).²
stelẹn, 7115 (-e B, -ẹ D; C †).³
laughẹn, 7144 (-e B, laugh D, lauʒhẹ ne ? C).
holdẹn, 7554 (-e BD, -é al C).
trowẹn, 7626 (-e BC, truste ‡ D).
  B. Before h:
plesẹn hym, 1562 (-e CD).
helẹn hym, 4794 (-e BC, help ‡ D); cf. 7412.
clawẹn hym, 5390 (-e CD, clowen B).
preyẹn here (*eam*), 6678 (prey CD) ⁴

¹ Supply [*if*] in D.   ² Dele (*to*) in A.   In C read *gan* for *may*.
³ C reads *ostel* for *ost stele*.   ⁴ Dele (*to*) in A.

U

To rauysshęn here syn thow hast not ben there, 5305 (-asche C, -issh D); cf. the same phrase in 5299, and see 7258 BC.

lyuen haue (1 *sg.*), 7305 (lyue BD; C †).

> Note.—In many cases in which the proper reading is no doubt elided -*e* (preserved, for the most part, in A) one or more of the other MSS. show the syncopated ending -*en* or -*yn*. Examples are: I. Before vowels, 189 C, 192 C, 370 C, 714 C, 922 C, 966 B, 1742 C, 1744 C, 1797 C, 1828 C, 1871 C, 1979 C, 2002 CD, 2041 C, 2538 C, 2679 C, 2720 C, 2721 C, 2732 C, 2779 C, 2794 C, 2918 C, 2933 C, 3008 C, 3176 C, 3206 C, 3607 C, 3615 C, 3636 C, 3700 BC, 3910 C, 4258 C, 4506 D, 4785 C, 5065 B, 5100 B, 5142 C, 5380 B, 5925 C, 5938 C, 6017 C, 6055 C, 6118 C, 6125 C, 6227 C, 6501 C, 6558 C, 6720 C, 6972 C, 7258 B(?), 7348 C, 7468 C, 7493 C, 7516 C, 7658 C, 7664 C, 7829 C, 8028 C, 8044 D. II. Before h (in *his, hym, hem, hire* (poss. sg., acc.), *here* (hic), 1515 C, 2121 C, 2379 C, 2743 C, 3328 C, 3386 C, 3476 C; see also 1460 C, 4494 C, 4551 C, 4613 C, 5261 BC, 5880 C, 6653 C, 7047 C, 7412 B; *comyn hasteliche*, 5980 C.

C. Before consonants:

hopen the, 865 AB (-ę D, -ë rathere C).

louęn sholde, 3639 (-en ‖ oon? B, -yn ‖ on C, shold love ‖ on D).

trowen that, 7661 A (B †, -ë sche C, -ę that D).

Cf. also 1453 AC, 1563 C, 2606 C, 2950 C, 3817 D, 5520 C, 6174 B, 6858 B, 7700 C.

VI. -ë before consonants (of all kinds except *h*):

mùlteplïë that, 486.

hide fro, 587 (-en B, -yn C).

loke wyde, 629 (-en B).

seme lesse, 703.

loue such, 798.

fare wel, 1177 (-en B).

synge clere, 1910 (-en B, -in C, -yn D).

thanke but, 1933 (-en B, -[e] D).

slepe neuere, 2183.[1]

iape faste, 2249 (C ?).

desire fresshly, 2985 (-en B, -yn CD).[2]

make resistence, 3832 (-en B, -in C).

deye mot, 4083 (-en B, dien D).

fele noon, 5128.

handle for, 5434 (-dle(e) B, -delyn C, -diłł D).

come by, 5628 (-en BD).

fynde bote, 5921.

oblige me, 6076.

stele pryuely, 6263 (-yn C).

cleyme kyngdom, 7850 (-en B, -yn C).

[1] Supply [*not*] in D.   [2] Dele (*to*) in C.

Cf. also 734, 747, 1339, 1773, 2204, 3356, 4337, 4378, 5574, 6369, 8131, etc., etc.

VII. -e in rhyme:

endite, 6 (: write *ind.* 1 *sg.*).
pleyne, 11 (: peyne *n.* : to seyne).
sterue, 17 (: serue *ind.* 1 *sg.*).
auayle, 20 (: trauayle *n.*).
falle, 290 (: with-alle).
wyte (= blame), 825 (: lyte) ; cf. 1470 f, 7698 f.
neuene, 876 (nemene C) (: yn heuene).
keuere, 910 (: feuere).
comaunde, 1050 (: recomaunde *subj.* 2 *sg.*).
wade, 1235 (: wordes glade).
salùwe, 2101 (salue BC, -ewe D) (: eschuwe *imv. sg.*, -ue B, -ewe CD).
here, 2199 (: yfere *adv.*).
vnfettre, 2301 (onfetere C) (: lettre : bettre *adv.*).
bygynne, 2459 (be- CD) (: wynne *inf.* : with-inne).
denye, 2574 (-y CD) (: curtasye : companye).
declare, 2765 (: Pandare).
forbede, 3309 (: hede *heed n.* : nede *n.*).
pace, 3312 (pase C, passe D) (: grace).
wende, 3458 (wynde C) (: ende *n.*).
delyuere, 3854 (-er D, del[y]uere B) (: wyuere *n.* : slyuere *n.*).
adawe, 3962 ([a]- B, to dawe C) (: drawe *inf.*).
fonde, 3997 (: on honde).
fysshe, 4004 (: rysche *n.*).
syke, 4014 (sike C, sijke D) (: syke *adj. pl.*).
houe, 4269 (: Ioue).
melte, 4287 (mette † B) (: felte *ind.* 3 *sg.*).
selle, 4303 (: helle : dwelle *inf.*).
rewe, 4612 (: trewe *adj. pl.*).
trete, 4720 (: grete *adj. pl.* : strete).
werne, 4773 (: yerne *adv.*).
lythe, 5416 (: swythe *adv.* : a thousand sithe).
to abregge, 5587 (tabrigge B) (: egge *n*) ; cf. 3137 f.
leue (*credere*), 5629 (: preue *ind.* 3 *pl.*).
sorwe, 5971 (: morwe).
glose, 6072 (: suppose *ind.* 1 *sg.*).
fere, 6145 (: there).
gnawe, 6399 (: sawe *n.*).

glaze, 6832 (-se CD) (: maze n.).
borwe, 7089 (: sorwe n. : morwe).
wreke, 7323 (: speke ind. pres. 2 pl.).
loue, 7365 (: aboue).
seche, 7495 (: byseche ind. 1 sg. : speche n.).
honge, 7562 (: stronge adj. pl. : longe adv.).
vnbòdye, 7913 (on- C, vnbodie D) (: paròdye n.).
ryue, 7923 (: of lyue).
restore, 8036 (: more).
haste, 8187 (: faste adv. : caste inf.). Etc., etc., etc.

Note.—For forms without -e in rhyme, see below, X., note 2.

VIII. -e (elided) before vowels (variants not registered).

Cf. 49 (lyue), 123 (enquere), 194 (smyle), 224 (endure), 347 (deme), 392 (loue), 616 (sterue), 699 (walwe and wepe), 806 (wepe and crie), 1203 (bydde and rede), 1204 (daunce), 1256 (mene), 1456 (deme), 1868 (wepe and sitte), 2256 (dyne), 2284 (humme), 2406 (glade), 2840 (dye), 4091 (stroke), 4541 (dispise), 4956 (suffre), 4962 (ende), 5426 (lyue), 5844 (dresse), 7154 (wowe), 7577 (crepe), 7820 (smyle), etc., etc.

Note.—The elided -e of the infinitive is sometimes omitted in writing. Thus, in A see 204 (cast), 560 (bryng), 818 (thenk), 1493 (brest), 1857 (put), 2215 (chaung), 2554 (bryng), 2734 (bryng), 4899 (brest), 6588 (com), 6794 (pley), 6818 (glad), 6948 (mak). See also 33 B, 192 BC, 275 D, 370 D, 387 C, 460 B, 476 D, 522 B, 714 D, 833 D, 1040 BD, 1057 D, 1079 D, 1184 B, 1203 D, 1347 D, 1427 B, 1540 B, 1732 D, 1744 D, 1772 D, 1797 BD, 1812 B, 1817 B, 1979 D, 2040 D, 2156 D, 2289 BD, etc., etc.

IX. -e (elided) before h :

bygonne he, 6610 (by-gynne B, be-gynne C, begynnë ‡ for D); mete he, 6612 (dreme D ; mette he pret. ind. ‡ C).
lete his, 192 (let C); kepe his, 627 ; loue his, 817 (C †); saue his, 1660. Cf. 1468 (stynte), 2121 (here), 2167 (telle), 3328 (ese), 3957 (wete), 5726 (cause), 6624 (here), 7047 (make).
dresse hym, 1156 (-yn D); make h., 1407 (mak B; imv.? D); lyke h., 1760 ; graunte h., 1789 (-t B); drawe h., 2271 (-w D); bidde h., 3309 (bid BCD) ; telle h., 4488, 7221. Cf. 1460 (gouèrne), 2379 (loue), 2380 (guèrdone), 3428 (auyse), 3743 (feffe), 3759 (fecche), 3913 (streyne), 4396 (make), 6065 (plukke), etc.
reherce here (gen. sg.), 2741. Cf. 289 (lyke), 1150 (make), 2743 (take).
loue here (acc. sg.), 4494 (-yn C). Cf. 2300 (auyse), 7460 (excuse), 7462 (excuse), 7489 (make), 8096 (hate).
lese here (gen. pl.), 6744 ; vp frete here, 7833. Cf. 151 (honoùre), 907 (mucche).

come here (*adv.*), 1462, 5582 (com BD, -ÿn C); dwelle here, 3476 (-yn C, dwełł D).

lyue haue (1 *sg.*), 7305 BD (lyuęn A). But,—comë hath, 6717 (-en B, -ë? C, -e ayen ‡ D).

constreùe how, 2875 A (-strùe BD); caste how, 6752 (-t BC, [us] caste D); trowe how, 7265 (-w B). But,—rehercè how, 4239 (-en B, -yn C, -on E).

take hede, 7120 (tak B). But,—takė hede, 8069 D (-en AB).

com hom, 4871 (-e in C). But,—bryngė hom, 4800 B (-[e] hem A, -yn hem C, -[e] home D).

come hastely, 5980 (-[ë] B, -yn C).

Note.—For hiatus before *h*, see XI., below

X. Apocope of -e (before consonants).

There are several genuine instances of apocope. Old-style figures indicate that a cæsura follows the infinitive ending, so that the -e may be pronounced if one cares to admit the "extra syllable before a pause."

louę for, 16 (*prob. noun*); l. he, 46 (*prob. noun*) (D *is different*); l. swych, 369; l. yow, 537 (D †); l. til, 686; l. the, 2043. But,—louë, 798, 2854.

hope the, 865 D (hopen AB, hopė ratherę C).[1]

lat Criseÿdë, 5119 (letę C, let D).

tellę yow, 2198 AB (tellë CD).[2]

spekę for, 2511 ABG (of this CD). (No note in Mr. Austin's collation.)

berę the, 2583.

comę soupen, 3402 (cum C)[3]; -ę but, 5661; c. therfore, 5662; c. sholde, 5726; c. for, 6023 (com C); c. that, 7021; c. ye, 7791; com spekę, 5316 (-ę CD). Cf. 5717 (?).

makę desseueraunce, 4266 (C †); makę the, 7515 CD (-en peplę ABG) (no note in Mr. Austin's collation).

lyuę to, 4759; l. til, 6279 (leuę to C; D †).

puttę that, 6174 (-ęn B, put D).

wenę that, 5730, 6775 AB (seyn C, sey D).

holdę forth, 6858 A (-ęn B, -e ourę CD).[4]

---

[1] No note in Mr. Austin's collation. G reads: Thanne wolde I hopen rather for to spede.

[2] For which (whiche G) I am come (I come BGCp., come I C, come y D) to (*om.* B Cp) tellę yow newe (new B, *om.* CDG) tidynges. No variants are noted for John's MS

[3] In C it is possible to read *cum[e] suppe*; in D, *comë soupe*; but the line would then be intolerably harsh.

[4] CD and John's give a 9-syl. line. Lat vs holdę ourę purpos fermėly (frendely † C). AB read *forth* after *holde*. Cp. also has *forth*, but reads *holdęn*. G has: Lette vs holde for the purpos fermely.

294   *Observations on the Language*   [§ 119.

trowe that, 7661 D (-ęn A, -ë sche C; B †).
preyę for, 48 (pray D); prey yow, 2521 (-ę ? B, -e C, pray as D, prey as G).[1]
seyę, see XII., below.

    Note 1.—For *wetę, dorrę*, see § 123; for *hauę*, see § 124.

In many cases the apocope disappears on comparison of MSS. Thus,—

worschepę preuyly, 380 C (*l.* werken).
tellę the, 580 A (l. tellę it).
tellę ʒow, 7134 C, 7308 C (cf. 7309 C).
bring me, 623 D.
cogh bygan, 1339 C.
dyę there, 1418 C.
love no, 1563 D.
plinę no, 1581 C.
bynd with, 1813 D.
bathę begyn, 1934 C.
endurę to, 1949 D.
trust to, 2041 D.
spekę sumwhat, 2106 D.
spekę therof, 2688 C.
drechę to, 2349 C.
tellę ʒow, 2626 D.

wend to, 3060 D (?).
kepę wele, 3136 D.
yevę no, 3607 D.
makę chere, 4396 D.
tornę to, 4781 B (?) (turnę tyl C ?).
helpę to, 5190 C (?).
mervailę wheder, 5309 D.
failę certeyne, 5607 D.
tell you, 5925 D.
schortę myn, 6459 C (shortę your † D).
writę ʒit, 6635 C°.
wrytę to, 7754 C.
stelę by, 7115 D.
letę no, 7273 C.
cloth shal, 7781 D.
shewę me, 8057 D.

    Note 2.—In 3817 the readings of ABCEGCp. John's are: Now doth (do G) hym sitte (syttyn D, sitten John's) now (*om.* BCCp. John's) gode (good BD) nece dere. The weight of MS. authority seems to be in favour of omitting the second *now* and reading *sittē*.—In 1226 B, we may perhaps read *wondren more* for *wonder more* (wonderyn C, wondryn D, iapę ‡ A); cf. 1453 D, 5309 C (wondere; wondren AB, mervaile D).—In 6118 the question is really between *at-renne but not at-rede* and *at-renne and not at-rede*; cf. *C. T.* 2451 T.

    Note 3.—Occasionally -e in the infinitive is not written at the end of the line, but the rhyme always[2] indicates that it should be restored. Instances are rare in A and B, but in C and D they abound. For A, see 462 (rew), 4260 (throw), 4975 (lyght); for B, see 313 (hold), 392 (repent), 1338 (cast), 2956 (rew), 4017 (trespas), 4402 (wak), 6994 (shew), 8021 (bihold); for C, see 73, 193, 389, 492, 750, 908, 1420, 1441, 1524, 1775, 1958, 1986, 2078, 2252, 2529, 2556, 2558, 2574, 2624, 2639, 2715, 2757-8, 2795, 2841-2, 2919, 2997, 3100, 3200, 3384, 3500, 3681, 3758, 3924, 4069, 4339, 4418, 4447, 4500, 4530, 4919, 5029, 5154, 5459-60, 5519, 5543-4, 5769, 5833, 5850, 5858-9, 5952, 6043, 6076, 6188, 6243, 6274, 6280, 6446-7, 6720, 6752-3, 6822, 6867, 6878, 6914, 6932, 6934, 6997, 7029, 7349, 7574, 7590, 7593, 7595, 7667, 7771, 7839, 7931, 7983. In 4973 f, C needs correction. For D, see 256, 665, 2599, 2639, 3043, 3699, 4276, 4536, 5272, 8133, and *passim*.

[1] No note in Mr. Austin's collation.   [2] *I. e.* when not another inf.

[§ 119.] *of Chaucer's Troilus.*

XI. Hiatus:

deyë in, 674 (dyen B, deyen CD).
demë other, 799 (-en B, -yn CD).[1]
folwë if, 1134 (-en B, -yn C).
stoppë euery, 1889 (-en B).
fyndë in, 4140 (-en B); fyndë at, 6866 (-en B); fynd[ë] || out, 7453 (-en B, -ë CD).
endurë al, 4333 (-en B, -yn C).[2]
bryngë vs, 5354 (-yn C); bryngë it, 7657 (-en B, -yn C).
compleynë in, 7086 (B†).
writë yf, 8140 (-ë yif D).
Cf. also 360, 979, 1184, 1350, 2120, 2793, 2898, 2923, 3079, 3154, 3304, 3742, 3946, 4166, 4238, 4504, 5314, 5420, 6047, 7049, 7122,[3] 7178[4], 7503, 7629.

> Note.—In all the cases cited above A has -*ë* (with hiatus), but in all of them the hiatus may be removed by reading -*en*, except in 360, 1184, 5314, 5420; in these four lines a word has dropped out of A, the restoration of which reduces the -*e* to -*e* (elided).[5] None of the four MSS. is free from hiatus in the infinitive form, but it is rarest in B.[6] Other examples (not in A) may be seen in the variants under III. (above); cf. also 796 D, 1843 D, 2886 D, 3317 D, 3822 B, 4524 D, 4835 C, 6233 D, 7538 CD, 7554 C, etc.

hidë his, 381 (-en B, -yn C, -e his? D).[7]
endurë he, 2730 (-en BC, -e he D).
suffrë hym, 2996 B (-en A, sufferyn C, suffryn D).[8]
likë here (*dat.*), 3455 (-en B, -yn C; D†).
dwellë here (*hic*), 3483 (-yn D); cf. dwellen here, 3489 (-yn D, -ë C).
bryng[ë] hem, 4800 (-yn C, -ë hom B, -[ë] home D).
Cf. also 292 C, 481 C, 504 C, 542 D, 1885 C, 4038 D, 5149 D, 5334 D, 6052 D, 6065 C, 6136 D, 6534 D, 6987 C, 7121 C, 7201 D, 7480 D, 7816 D.
tellë how, 2091 (-en B, -*e* her D); cf. 7869 D.
rehercë how, 4239 (-en B, -yn C, -on E). But,—constreüe how, 2875 A (-strüe BD); caste how, 6752 (-t BC, [us] caste D); trowe how, 7265 (-w B).
comë hath, 6717 (-en B, -e? C, -e ayen ‡ D).
takë hede, 8069 D (-en AB). But,—take hede, 7120 (tak B).
tellë half, 3186 (-en B, -yn C, -e? D).

---

[1] In C read *other* for *ouȝt*.   [2] Dele (*the*) in D.
[3] Supply [*Ne*] in A (?).   [4] Furnivall prints *speke*[*n*] in A.
[5] In 5420, it is possible to explain the hiatus in A on the ground of the cæsura (*lyue* || *yf*), but BCDECp. John's have *if* (*ȝif*, *yif*) *that*, which makes the verse regular.
[6] In the majority of the lines just cited Cp. has the form in -*en*.
[7] 9-syl., except in D.   [8] Dele (*to*) before *serue* in C.

brynge hom, 4800 B (-[e] hem A, -yn hem C, -[e] home D) ; com hom, 4871 (-e in C).

XII. *Fle, sle, the, wre*:

fle, (i.) 747 f (flee B, sle † D) (: secre : be *sit*), 1795 f (flee B) (: he), 3386 f (: be *inf*. : tre), 3670 f (: he : be *inf*.), 4105 (flen C, flie *monosyl*. D), 5422 ‡ D (sleen A, slen B, sle C). (ii.) 4648 (*before caesura*).—flen, 1279 f (fleen B, flen(e) D) (: ben *p p*. : ben *sbst. pl*.).

sle, (i.) 747 † f D (fle AC, flee B), 4143 (sla B), 7834 (slee D), 8049 (slee D). (ii.) 6108 (sla B, sle ʒif C, sle yif D), 7635 ‡ C.—slen, sleen, (i.) 1750 (slan(e) B, sle CD), 5422 (slen B, sle C, fle ‡ D), 5929 (sle D), 6409 (sle CD). (ii.) 2443 (sle D), 3850 (sle D) ; slen hym, 815 (sleen B, sle D), 823 (sle D)[1]; slen how, 5848 (slan(e) B, sle D).

the, 341 f (: be *sit* : ye), 1755 f (ythe B) (: be *inf*. : parde), 5101 f (ithe B, be ‡ C, thee D) (: to be : me), 7523 f (: me : se *inf*.).

wre ; Hymself to wre at hem he(r) gan to smyle, 329 (wrie *monosyl*. B, wrythe ‡ C; were ‡ D) ; byhoueth . . . vnwre his wounde, 858 (onwrye *monosyl*. C, vnwry D).

XIII. *Seyn, to seyne ; sen, to sene ; don, to done.*

The Anglo-Saxon Gerundial (or Dative) Infinitive is preserved in the *Troilus* in *to seyne, to sene*, and *to done*. The only sure case of final -e pronounced in the interior of the verse is in 7487 (*to done*, see below).

to seyne, 12 f, 591 f,[2] 712 f,[3] 1605 f, 1706 f, 2071 f, 2211 f, 2441 f, 2644 f, 3272 f, 3390 f, 3835 f, 3959 f, 3998 f, 4372 f (seine D), 5165 f (seyn C), 7398 f (seyn C), 7712 f. All these are cases of *soth for to seyne* and similar phrases. In 7531 f, *soth to seyne* (: I durste leyne = wager) is the reading of C, *soth(e) to seyne* (: durste I leyne) that of D ; G has *soth(e) to saye* (: durste I lay) ; AB read *dar I seye* (: dorste I leye, laye) ; Mr. Austin's collation has no note on these two lines. In 3845 f, *what al this is to seyn* (seyne BC), *to seyne* is the correct reading, as is shown by the rhymes, *compleyne* (ind. 1 sg.) and *peyne* (noun).

> Rhyme words.—peyne *n.* (12, 591, 712, 1605, 2071, 2211, 2441, 3835, 3959, 4372, 5165, 7398), cheyne *n.* (1706), Eleyne (2644), tweyne (1706, 3390, 3959, 7712), pleyne *inf.* (12, 1605, 2441), 1 *pl. ind* (712), feyne *inf.* (2644, 3998), restreyne *inf.* (3272), reyne *inf.* (3390), destreyne *inf.* (4372), compleyne *inf.* (7712).

But *seyn, seye, seyę*, and *sey*, are found in the gerundial construction with *to*, as well as *seyne*.

---

[1] In C read *hym*[*self*].
[2] Supply [*soth*] in D.
[3] Old-style figures indicate that D has *scyn*.

§ 119.] *of Chaucer's Troilus.* 297

seyn,[1] (i.) soth to seyn, 1769 (say C, sey[e] D ‡) ; platly for to seyn, 3628 f (seyne C) (: reyn *n.* : certeyn *adv.*); vsen . . . to seyn, 3866[2] ; that (this) is to seyn, 4020 (say C, seie D), 6037 (seyne C), 7261 (seyne C); now is this abusion to seyn, 5722 f (seyne B) (: certeyn *adv.*) ; the sothe for to seyn, 7375 f (seyne BD) (: ayen AD, aȝein B, aȝen C : fayn *pred. adj. sg* AC, fayne BD) ; what al this is to seyn, 3845 f (seyne BC), *should be* seyne, *as the rhymes* (compleyne *pres.* 1 *sg.*, peyne *n.*) *show*. (ii.) this is to seyn, 3280 ; soth to seyn he, 4635.

seye, (i.) ther is no more to seye, 574 f[2] ; soth (for) to seye, 2601 f, 3197 f ; sothly for to seye, 5459 f (sey C, certemly to sey D) ; shortly al the sothe for to seye, 5615 f (seyne † B) ; shortly for to seye, 7372 f (seyne·† B, seyen C) ; what is this to seye, 2916 f (saye C) ; shame it is to seye, 3091 f ; I it forbar to seye, 3207 f ; were impossible . . . to seye, 4153 f (say E); which chargeth nought to seye, 4418 f (sey C, seie D) ; no litel thyng of for to seye, 4530 f (sey C) ; he nyst[e] what to seye, 5018 f ; seyd(e) that was to seye, 5833 f (sey C) ; haue I for to seye, 7771 f (sey C) ; I began yow for to seye, 8163 f

Rhyme words.—in the weye (3091), aweye (5018), dreye *adj. pl.* (3107), dreye *adj. pl.* (hardly *adv.*) (5833), tweye (2916, 4153), deye *inf.* (574, 5459, 5615, 7771, 8163), pleye *inf.* (2601, 3091, 3197, 4153), leye *inf.* (2916), *imv. sg.* (2601), bywreye *inf* (3207), obeye *inf.* (4530), preye *inf.* (5833, 7372).

seye, that is to seye ‖ for, 3095 (seyne C, sey D) ; that is to seye ‖ that, 3126 (seyn B, seine C, sey ? D).

sey, to sey a soth, 2222 (seyne B, seyn C †).

seyn, seyen, seye, seye, sey, are also used in infinitive constructions without *to*. Thus,—

seyn,[3] (i.) 514,[4] 1839 (sey C), 2539 (sey B),[5] 2825 (seyne B), 3707 (sey ? D), 3809, 4464 (seyne B, seie D), 4829 (seyde ‡ B), 5520 (seyne B, sendyn ‡ C)[6], 5699 (seyne B), 5862, 5982 f (seyne BD) (: ayen AD, aȝein B, ageyn C : we ben so fayn AC, feyne BD), 6050 (C †), 6141, 6775 C, 6850 f (: ayen AD, aȝein B, aȝen C : fayn *adj. sg.* AC, feyn B, fayne D), 7239 (sen C), 7642, 7659 f (seeyn C) (: ayen, aȝein, aȝen, ageyn). (ii.) 396 (sayn A, say C), 398 (sayn C), 512, 804 (say C), 1011, 2532 (seyne D), 5515 (seyne B),

---

[1] In 1769, 3280, 4020, 4635, 6037, 7261, *seyn* comes before the cæsura.
[2] Old-style figures indicate that D has *sey* or *say*.
[3] In all cases cited except 512, 1839(?), 2539, 4829(?), 5520, 6626(?) *seyn* comes before the cæsura (when not in rhyme).
[4] Old-style figures indicate that D has *sey* or *say*.
[5] Dele (*That he*) in B.   [6] Supply [*herte*] in A.

298 *Observations on the Language* [§ 119.

6071 (C †), 6414 (say C), 7428 [1], 8095; seyn he, 3923 (seie D), 7157...

seyën sholde, 6989 A (seynë B, sey[ë]n C, *om*. † D).

seye, (i.) 492 f (sey C), 672 f, 924 f, 1044 f, 1258 f, 1396 f, 1406 f, 1546 f, 2078 f (say C, y sey *dico* † D), 2219 f, 2291 f, 2741 f, 2842 f (say C), 2922 f, 2953 f, 2963 f (seye *pres. subj.* 1 *sg.* BC, sey *pres. subj.* 1 *sg.* D), 3398 f, 3503 f, 3666 f (seyen B)[2], 3892 f (seyne B), 4033 f (seie D), 4450 f (saye B, say C, seye D), 4501 f (say C), 4818 f, 4911 f, 5033 f (seye D), 5187 f, 5431 f, 5543 f (sey C), 5769 f (say C), 5872 f (sey C), 5952 f (say C), 6043 f (say C), 6164 f, 6446 f (sey C), 6458 f, 6934 f (say C), 7349 f (say C), 7531 f (to seyne CD),[3] 7669 f (sey C), 8092 f, 8106 f, 8208 f. (ii.) seye,[4] 2084 (seyne B, seyn C),[5] 6233 (seyn C). ·[In all these instances D has *sey*, unless the contrary is noted.]

Rhyme words.—weye *n.* (492, 4818, 5952, 6458), aweye (6458), awey (aweye) (5543 : to dey C), tweye (492, 1258, 2741, 3666, 4033, 4818, 4911, 5033, 5769, 6043, 6164, 7669, 8092), pleye *inf.* (672, 1546, 3398, 6934, 7349), *subj.* 2 *sg.* (3666), deye *inf.* (924, 1258, 1406, 2291, 2963, 3892, 4911, 5431, 5872, 6446), *subj.* 1 *sg.* (2953, 4550), *subj.* 3 *sg.* (5187), leye *ind.* 1 *sg.* (1044), *imv. sg.* (2078), *inf.* (3503, 4450, 4501, 7531, 7669, 8208), preye *ind.* 1 *sg.* (1396, 2219, 2291, 5952, 6164, 6934, 8106), *inf.* (2741, 2842, 2922, 2968), *pres. ind.* 3 *pl.* (6043), beye *inf.* (8208).

seye,[6] 451 (sey C), 1337 (say B, seyn C), 3120 (seyn BC), 4108 (seyn BC, seie D), 4139 (seyn CE), 4777 (seyn C), 5493 (sey ? D). [D has *sey*, unless the contrary is noted].

sey, (i.) sey yis (*l.* this *with* C ?), 4222 (seyn BC)[7]; sey yow, 7740. (ii.) 1316 (seye B, seyn C); sey hym, 195 (seye B, seyde ‡ C).

seyne in the form *seine* occurs in 6626 without *to*,—sholde ... seine it was folye (sey CD),— cf. also variants under some of the forms above registered,— but it will be observed that the full gerundial form is found only in rhyme.

to sene,—fairest (-er) was to sene, 454 f (: Polixene); fairest was to sene, 5817 f (: grene *adj. pl.*); it ioye was to sene, 4070 f (to seene B) (: tene *n.*).

But *to sen* and *to se* also occur : *to se*, indeed, is by far the commonest form.

to sen, to seen, (i.) so lyk a man of armes ... He was to sen, 1717

---

[1] Dele (*me*) in D.   [2] In B, rhymes with *pleye* and *tweyen*.
[3] In CD the rhyme is *leyne inf.* (=wager) ; in AB the rhyme is *leye* (*laye*), which is clearly right.
[4] In 2084, 6233, *seyë* may be read (with hiatus) if one admits the "extra syllable before the cæsura."   [5] In B supply [*I*].
[6] In 3120(?), 4139, 4777, it is possible to read *seyë* if one admits the "extra syllable before the cæsura."   [7] Supply [*that*] in BD.

§ 119.]   *of Chaucer's Troilus.*   299

(senę ∥·D); first to 'sen (*purpose*), 3384 (se CD); it thoughte hym no strokes To here or sen Criseyde . . . wepe, 3910 (se his D); youre desport Was al to seen Criseydes eyen, 4972 (sen BC, se D); it hardere is To sen that sorwe, 5568 (to sen him C, to se the sorwe D); It was his sorwe vpon hem for to sen, 6821 f (sene D) (: ben *sunt bene* D). (ii.) she was right swych to sen, 5524 (seen B, se CD); to seen here (*gen. sg*), *purpose*, 446 (sene B, sen C, se D); to sen here (*acc.*), *purpose*, 7941 (see D); cf. 5568 C.

to se, (i.) hath gided the to se my, 569 (sen B); ye ben faire to se, 1669 f; It was an heuene vpon hym for to se, 1722 f; he hath to se me swych delit, 1794; it ioye was to se, 1902 f; sobrely and frendly for to se, 3201 f; This was no litel sorwe for to se, 3935 f; ycomen hym to se, 5028 f (see D); it a deth was for to se, 5518 f (see D); Which that I drede neuere mo to se, 5521 f (see D); I nolde leuen for to se, 5997 f (see D); coueyteth . . . to se me, 6001; the pure spirit wepeth To se yow wepen, 6283 (see D); comen Troylus to se, 6645 f (see BD); to longen here to se, 6960 f (see B); thei stoden for to se, 7477 f; ther com this bor to se, 7835 f (see D). (ii.) to se ‡ his, 3910 D.

sen, seen, *inf.*, without *to*, (i.) 293 (seth † D), 1386 (se CD), 6886 (sene B, see D)[1]; cf. 5599, 6133, 6147, 6258, 6299, 7112, 7238, 7446, 7573. (ii.) 2242 (seyne B, se CD), 4961 (D †), 7264 (syn B, se D); cf. 6512, 6691, 6972, 7371, 7476; sen here (*acc.*), 6391 (se BD), 7144 (sene D, se lauʒhe ? C); seen here (*gen. sg.*), 6888 (sen C, se D); sen how, 5599 BC.

se, see, *inf.*, without *to*, (i.) 1659 BD (son C, do A), 1673 (sen C; B †), 1700 (sen C, sene D), 4124 (sen BC), 8074 (sen B, see D); cf. 245 f, 1365 f, 1530 f, 1879 f, 2067 f, 2177 f, 2398 f, 2416 f, 2515 f, 2972 f, 3442 f, 4056 f, 4187 f, 4321 f, 4446 f, 4853 f, 5350 f, 5947 f, 6700 f, 7030 f, 7522 f, 7662 f, 7751 f, 8003 f, 8139 f. (ii.) 644 (sen C; D †), se here (*acc.*), 6979 (seen B, sen C).

y-se, *inf.*, without *to*, (i.) alle y-se, 1439 f (alle se C; D †); tyme y-se, 2806 (is[e] D, tyme se BC); wrecche y-se, 5500 f (wreche se C, wrecchë see D); wel y-se, 5710 f, 7110 f ([y]se C, [y]see D). [Var. B y-see; D i-see.]

to done,—that thow hast to done, 1019 f; I haue to done, 1298 f; hadde nought to done, 3517 f; his erand was to done, 1157 f; were it nought to done, 1788 f, theron was to heuen and to done, 2374 f; what was best to done, 2570 f, now is there (but) litel more for to

[1] Supply [*As*] in C.

done, 3389 f; how yow was best to done, 4746 f, what thenkestow to done, 5750 f (doon B); it was ek to done, 6433 f; as the semeth best is for to done, 6664 f; it is nought to done, 6741 f; the beste is thus to done, 6755 f (doon B); it is for to done, 7266 f; yet was there more to done, 7455 f; there is no more to done, 7672 f (doon B); as he was woned to done, 4378 f (doon B) (*similarly* 4553 f (don D), 4729 f, 5788 f (doon B)); it wonted is to done, 6640 f; as was his wone to done, 7010 f. [Var. BD doone.] feyned hym with Calkas han to doon[e], 7209 f (done CD) (: soone *adv.*). She hath ynow (-e G) to done hardyly, 7487 ACG (to don[e] B, to do[ne] D).[1] to bidde hym ought to done, 3309 (don BC, do ne D); to haue ynowh to done, 6407 (don C, doone D); what to done he nyste, 356 (don B, do D).

to done,—what to done || best were, 1781 (to do D, what to donë best ‡ and C); what to done || for ioye vnnethe he wyste, 4095 (don B, do D).

Rhyme words.—mone, moone, *n.* (1019, 1157, 3389, 6640, 6741), bone *n.* (1019), sone, soone *adv.* (1157, 1298, 2374, 3517, 4378, 4553, 4729, 5788, 6433, 6640, 6755, 7010, 7209, 7266, 7455, 7672), persone (1788, 2570, 4746), trone *n.* (5750), thow dispone *imv.-subj* (6664).

to don,—(i.) a thyng to don yow pleye, 1206 (do D); a body and a myght To don that thyng, 1719 (do D); is he . . . aboute me to drecche And don me wrong, 2557 (do D); I may ben he . . . to don yow my seruyse, 2975 (do D); prey [I] yow To don myn herte . . . an ese, 3475 (do D); bad a boone . . . to don that reuerence, 4731 B (do D, to don hym ‡ that reuerence A); the enspire This womman thus to shilde and don vs lese Daun Antenor, 4850 (doun C, done D); be suffred me to erre . . . ne don so gret vnright, 5212 (do (me) D); what frendes ich haue . . . to don the wrathe pace Of Priamus and don hym stonde in grace, 6054-5 (doo . . . make D); make hym . . . to conuerte And don my red, 6074-5 (doo D). (ii.) what for to doon, 887 (don BC, done D); what to don is, 2737 (doon B, done CD); comytted to don execucion, 6367 (done D); comaundeth me . . . To don al, 6496 (doo D); she wolde fayn(e) to don his herte an ese (*syntax ambiguous*), 2310 (do D; C †); hasteth yow to don hym ioyé haue, 2329 (do D); gon to don his sacrifice, 3381 (done D); al prest to don hire byde, 4824 (do D); to don his sorwe to falle He rought[e] not what vnthryf[t] [that] he seyde, 5092 (to make his CD); glad to don hym that seruice, 5471 (doo D); to the . . . goddes . . . He preyde . . .

[1] No note in the Cp. collation.

[§§ 119, 120.] *of Chaucer's Troilus.* 301

To don hym, 5613 (doon B, doone D); That he noldę don his peynę and al his myght To don it for to don here herte an ese, 6478-9 (done . . . to done it for to doo D).

to do,—what is me best to do, 828 f (: wo : so); a kynges sone yn armes wel to do, 1250 f (: two : therto); for to do wel is his wone, 1403 (don BC, [for] to do D); yourę beste is to do so, 1467 (don C); to wys is he to do so gret a nyse, 1810 (don BC); vouche saf for to do so, 2776 (don C, [for] to do D); ryse To knele and do yow honour, 2912 (don C); to wys to do so gret folye, 3709 (don BC); gracę for to do so, 3770 (hadde to don so C †); what thenkestow to do, 5511 f (doo BD) (: for-do *inf.*, -doo D, 5513 : to *prep.*).

don, *inf.* without *to*, (i.) 19 (donę B, do D), 852 (do D), 1496 f (done D) (: anoon : agon *p. p.*); do yow don by force, 6137 (don . . . don C, doo . . . doonę D); cf. 120, 600, 1197, 1400, 1553, 1560, 1842, 2330, 2951, 4320, 4973, 5957, 6327, 6413, 6762, 7200, 7203, 7631, etc. (ii.) 2591 (do CD); cf. 1474, 3725 (done D), 4952, 4957, 5245, 5456, 5602, 5604, 6150, 6295, 6475, 6604, 8071, 8097, etc.; doon, 824 (don C, done D); for forms before *he, his, hym, here, hem, how* (*don* is usual in ABC; D has *doon, doone, done, do, doo*), cf. 563, 2066, 2459, 3008, 3400, 4550, 5365, 6478, 7284, 7503, 7828; don hardnesse, 2330 (but it is perhaps better to take *don* as *p. p.*, as the reading of B, *ydon*, indicates). In 2734 AB, *don harm* should be *don him harm*, as in C (do hym harme D). In 7349 A, *done* should be *don* (don B, don can C, doo can D).

do, *inf.*, without *to*, (i.) 795 (don BC), 1848 (don C), 6345 f (: for-do *inf.*, -doo D, 6343 f); cf. 692, 1232, 1659, 2042, 2373, 2699, 3022, 3690, 3708, 3769, 3969, 4320, 4912, 5121, 5439, 6588, etc.; for-do, 238 (-don B, vndo D), 5513 f (-doo D) (: to do : to *prep.*). (ii.) 2503 (don BC, done D), 2557 (don B), 3892 (don BC, done D), 5419 (doon B, doo D, don ‡ what C); vndo, 3583 (vndon B, ondo C, vndo ‡ the D).

§ 120. The Present Participle ends in the *Troilus* in -ynge, -yng. (Cf. Child, § 64; ten Brink, § 191.)

The form *-ynge* is regular in rhyme (see, however, II., last example), but the *-e* is never sounded in the interior of the verse (except for syntactic reasons, see II., note 2). D almost always has *-yng*, both in and out of rhyme, but I have not taken the superfluous trouble to register this lack of *-e* in that MS. Minute variations in spelling are also sometimes disregarded in the following lists.

The participle in -*ende* occurs only twice,—*ryndende*, 2334 C (corrupt), 2338 f C^c (where it spoils the rhyme).

> Note.—I have registered "gerunds" with nouns in -*ynge* (§ 10) in preference to confusing them with participles.

I. The following list includes such present participles as rhyme with an infinitive in the *Troilus*. All the rhyme-words are recorded in each case.

lyuynge, 1320 f (leuenge C) (: rynge *inf.* : wytynge *n.*).
vnsittynge, 1392 f (: brynge).
sterynge, 4078 f (: synge : rynge).
durynge, 4596 f (-g C (?), doyng † D) (: concordynge *ptc.*, -yng CD : brynge).
makynge, 5517 f (: brynge).
portraynge, 7079 f (-treynge B, portering † D) (: recordynge *ptc.*, according † D : sprynge).
arguynge, 7135 f (: taryinge *n.* : brynge).

II. Here follow all other cases of the present participle (or participial adjective) in rhyme. An asterisk indicates that the rhyme-word is a noun (or "gerund") in -*ynge* (see § 10).

wepynge, 111 f (: excusynge *ptc.*).
pleynge, 267 f (pleyinge BC, pleying D) (: lokynge *ptc.*).
answerynge,* 282 f.
konnynge,* 302 f (kun- C, cunnyng D).
comynge,* 378 f, *1644 f, *5649 f (D †), *5676 f.
sittynge, 2099 f (: lokynge *ptc.*).
ymagynynge, 6817 f (-g C, -gening D) (: festenynge *n.*, thing ‡ D).
excusynge,* 7937 f.
But,—comynge, 5737 f (-yng D) : thing *n.* : byfallyng *n.*

III. Present participles before consonants. (D has almost always -yng.)

touchyng, 265 (-ę BC); towchyng, 2108 (-ę BC; D †), 3274 (-ę BC).
pleynge, 280 (pley(n)- C).
lykynge, 309 (lokynge † C).
ymagynynge, 372 (-ing (?) D, -enynge (?) C).
bewalllyng, 547 ‡ D.
kèruyng, 632 (-ę B).[1]
rydyng, 2334 (-ę B †, ryndende † C).
fàllyng,—the happy fallyng strok, 2467 (-ę BC; D †).
hèlpyng, 2635 (-ę BC).

---

[1] Supply [*yet*] in D.

[§§ 120, 121.] *of Chaucer's Troilus.* 303

làngwysshỳng, 3083 (-syngẹ B, -syng C).
herỳngẹ, 3188.[1]
thònkyngẹ 4394 (D †).
wèpyngẹ, 5237 (-ing *sbst.* † D).
dispùtyngẹ, 5746.
schaùngyngẹ ‡, 6918 C (changed *p. p.* ABD).

> Note 1.—In 309 the accent is perhaps on the first syllable; in 2108, perhaps on the second.
> Note 2.—In *this fòrknowyng[ẹ] wyse*, 79 A (-e BC), the sounding of *-e* is due to the definite construction (see § 59). This is the only case in the *Troilus* in which *-e* is sounded in the present participle in the interior of the verse (cf. 7804 ‡ C, 7951 ‡ A, 8098 (read *hauyngẹ* [*vn*]*to*; G, Cp., and Harl. 2392 have *vnto*). Cf. IV, V, notes, below.

IV. Before vowels.

For *-ỳnge*, cf. 1705,[2] 4691, 4747, 4755, 5404, 5502, 5951, 7075, 7804, 7975.

For *-ỳng*, cf. 65, 908,[3] 1055, 4542, 4750, 5099, 5116.

For *-ynge*, with the accent on the preceding syllable (as, flètyngẹ), cf. 1138, 1640, 2789, 3534, 3982, 4210, 4624, 4967, 5491, 5913, 6387, 6430,[4] 6758, 7188,[4] 7502, 7571, 7697, 8033, 8135, 8173, 8175 (hèrkẹnyngẹ).

For *-ỳng*, with the accent on the preceding syllable (as, byhòldyng), cf. 9, 101, 186, 547, 631, 2024, 3348, 4395, 4693, 7386, 7604, 7719, 8020.

> Note.—In 7333, *and* (after *konnyng*) restores the metre: ACDG omit *and*, BCp John's have it. 7804 C is to be corrected by the insertion of *ay*.

V. Before h (in *his, hym, here* (acc., poss. sg., poss. pl.), *how, hound*).

For *-ỳnge*, cf. 2900,[5] 4381, 5819, 6066, 6836, 7048.

For *-ỳng*, cf. 3359, 4789, 4905, 5025, 5764.

For *-ynge*, with the accent on preceding syllable, cf. 318, 1157, 1738, 2893, 5374 C, 5377, 8123.

For *-yng*, with the accent on preceding syllable, cf. 384, 3004, 3606.

> Note.—In 5951 C, *makyngẹ here* (hic) should be corrected.

§ 121. The Perfect Participle of Weak Verbs ends in the *Troilus* in *-ed, -ẹd, -d, -t.* (Cf. Child, § 62; ten Brink, §§ 163, 166-9, 176, 180-3.)

Instead of *-ed*, C and D often have *-id* or *-yd*, and so occasionally B, For *-id, -yd* in A, see, for example, 182, 308, 1004, 6894. B has

---
[1] In A read *theffect* for *the feyth.*
[2] Old-style figures indicate that the accent may stand on the preceding syllable.
[3] In A, supply [*make*] before *hem.*   [4] 9-syl. verse.
[5] Old-style figures indicate that the accent may stand on the preceding syllable.

woundud in 1618 f. C sometimes shows *-it* : as, *gydit*, 569 (cf. 558, 987, 1438, 1707, 2705, 4075, 6707 f, 6709 f, 7548); cf. *woundet*, 1618 f C. For *-ede*, *-de*, *-te*, see notes 1, 2, below.

Perfect participles rhyme usually with each other or with words that have no *-e*. Very rarely a perfect participle is found rhyming with the preterite of a verb: the only examples in the *Troilus* are,—

excused *p. p.*, 2164 f, *rh.* acused *pret. ind.* 3 *sg.*

vntormentid, 1004 f, *rh.* assentyd *pret. ind.* 3 *sg.* (or possibly *p. p.* ?).

y-shette *p. p.*, 3075 f, *rh.* lette *n.*, *rh.* sette *ind.* 3 *sg.*

bente *p. p.*, 4702 f, *rh.* mente 3 *pl.*, *rh.* wente 3 *pl.*

spradde *p. p.*, 6084 f, *rh.* he hadde.

whette *p. p.*, 8123 f, *rh.* mette 3 *pl.*

In the last four cases the participles are in the plural (see §§ 67. e, 68).

In 1123 B, 2175 C, 7561 A, the reading should be corrected (see notes 1, 2 below).

Note 1.—C, which is especially fond of the ending *-ede* in the preterite, not infrequently extends this termination erroneously to the participle: cf., for examples,—*-ed*(*e*) in C 1509, 1907, 2119, 3467, 3931, 4111, 5407, 5878, 5900, 5945, 6528, 8062; *-id*(*e*), 4237 C; *-ed*(*e*), C 299, 1907, 6894; *-ed*(*e*), C 648 f, 3285 f; *-id*(*e*), 316 f C. Cf. also *rowed*(*e*), 962 f B; *disesed*(*e*), 3285 f B. Even A is not free from this spurious *-e*: thus,—*pronunced*(*e*), 4875 A; *formed*(*e*), 7180 A; *falsed*(*e*), 7419 A; cf. 1906 A, 7458 A. In all cases this *-e* is of course purely a scribe's caprice and never pronounced. Similarly *-de* is occasionally written for *-ed* (as, *arayde*, 1285 B, l. *arayed*; cf. 646 B, 3383 B, 4062 B, 4289 D, 7612 f B), or for *-d* (as, *adradde*, 1200 f, l. *adrad*; *ferde*, 1209 B, l. *ferd*, etc.). In a few cases, however, the plural of a monosyllabic participle in *-d* ends in *-dde* (see §§ 67, e, 68). *Fledde*, 7561 f A (: *bledde ind.* 3 *sg.*) should be preterite indicative.

Note 2.—The ending *-te* instead of *-t* is found again and again in one MS. or another, as a comparison of MSS. in the places cited below (I.-VIII.) will show (see, *e. g.*, 1237, 1670, 6051, 6909). Even A is not free from this spurious *-e*: thus,—*hath sent*(*e*) *after*, 6643 AB (*-t* CD). In all cases, however, the *-e* is clearly a scribe's fashion or whim, except in a few instances where it is used to denote the plural of a monosyllabic participle (see the cases under §§ 67. e, 68, above). Bad readings are,—*shente* p. p. (: *wente* pret. 3 sg.), 1123 B (should be *shent* : *went* pres. 3 sg.), and *schette* p. p. (: *sette* pret. 3 sg. : *lette* pret. 3 sg.), 2175 C (should be *pret.* 3 *sg.*).

Examples.

In the following lists (I.-X.) variants are seldom registered; and, except in a few instances, no record is made of the initial letter of the word that follows the participle.

I. Anglo-Saxon verbs of the First Conjugation (cf. § 99).

afered, 967 f, 3324 f (aferd D); -[e]d, 1691 (-[e]d(e) B, -ed ? C, aferd D); aferid, 1209 ‡ C (ferd A, ferd(e) B ; D †).

agast, 715, 1396, 3579 (agarst A), 3938, 6306, 7256. (Inf. agaste, 1986 f.)

agilt, 4299 f, 4923 f; agylt, 8047.
beleued,—cf. mysbeleued, *adj.*, 3680 AB.
bente, *pl.*, 4702 f AB (-t D) (: mente 3 *pl.* : wente 3 *pl.*).
blent, 2828.
bought, 4953 f, 7328 (bout(e) D); ybought, 810 f, 4161 f (bought D).
brought, 424, 915, 1303, 3088, 3149, 3611, 3980 f, 4465, 4954 f, 7924; brough[t], 7279 (-t BCD); ybrough[t], 6466 f (-t B, brought D; C †); ybrought, 4441, 6374.
yburyed (*trisyl.*), 2396.
dight, 4615 f.
dreynt, 7866.
dwelt, 7074 (dwellyd C, duellid ‡ *ind.* D).
eched, 4171.
felt, 25, 27, 2851, 2884, 4125; feled, 5646 AB (-id D).
ferd (*fared*), 5756, 7721.
ferd, see *afered, forfered*.
for-fered. This may be the right reading in 6073 (*so* Cp.; for fered A, for ferde ∥ out B, for fer C †, for drede ∥ out D). [§ 135, III. 1, n 1.]
fulfild, 1717; fulfilled, 5853 (-filld B, -fyld C).
heled, 1082, 4054, 5098.
hent, 509.
herd, 197, 750, 754, 969, 1002, 1186, 2051, 2537, 2632, 2953, 3340, 3395, 5007 (hard(e) B), 5329, 6113, 6809, 6931, 6992, 7086, 7343, 7974.
heried,[1] 4098; heryed (*dissyl.*), 4599 (y-herid(e) D), 4655; yhered, 2058 (yheried BD, i-heried C); iheried, 2849; yheryed, 4646.
hid, 618, 5158, 5972 (hidd(e) B, hed C, hidde † in D).
yknet, 4576 f.
kyst,—vnkyst, 809.
lad, 872, 6757; led, 1638.
laft, 4180 f (left(e) E, last † C), 4943 f (left C, laffte D), 6123 f (left C, laft(e) D); ylaft, 4889 f (ileffte D, ilaste † C).
lered, 3248 f (lernyd † C); ylered, 969 f.
let, 1179 f, 3559, 7665 (lettid C).
leyd, 2048, 2630, 3529 f, 5845 (berid † D).
met, 1237, 4523 f; imet, 1671 f.
myssed, 3379.
plyght, 3624 f, 6272; plight, 5107 ‡ f D.
queynt, 4975, 6092, 6906.

[1] *Heryed* is dissyllabic in all the examples except the first.

x

red, 8160; yred, 5461.

yrent, 8017.

reyned,—byreyned, 5834 f (be-reigned D).

sent, 105, 2399, 2783, 3329 f, 6051, 7785; ysent, 6834.

set, 643, 1670 f, 2878, 3182, 3328, 4213, 4330 (i-set B, schet C), 4788, 4986, 5837, 6040, 6103; yset, 4573 f, 4846, 5336. beset, 521, 879, 1919 f (y-sette D); byset, 4255; biset, 898. But,—sette, *pl.*, 1166 A (sete B, sate *pret.* 3 *pl.* D).

shent, 1123 f (y- D), 4301 A, 4741 ‡ D.

shet, 2000 ‡ D (hust ABC), 6897 (shitt D); schett(e), 2175 f C; schitt, 3936 D (hust ABC); byshet, 3444 (beshit D). But,—y-shette, *pred. pl.*, 3075 f (y-chette B, schette C, y-shet D) (: lette *n.* : sette *pret. ind.* 3 *sg.*).

ysought, 4159 f (isout C). vnsought, 809 f.

sped[de], *pl.*, 2039 (spedde BC; D?).

spilt, 4925 f.

spradde, *pl.*, 6084 f (: he hadde).

stynt, 3948.

taried (*dissyl.*), 2824, 7499, 7712.

thought, 5204, 5216. bithought, 1310.

told, 197 ‡ A, 1381, 1760, 1780 f, 2370, 3350, 3638, 3846, 4039, 4592, 6159, 6687, 7806; told(e), 913 f AB (-d CD), 1220 A (-d BCD), cf. 7463. ytold, 4803.

tyd, 900, 1309, 1549.

wend, 5046 (went C), 8045.

went, 1681 ‡ f D, 5597 f, 6909, 7100 A, 8171-f A (-e B); ywent, 6807 f (wente B, went CD); myswent, 633 f.

whette, *pl.*, 8123 f AB (whett D) (: mette 3 *pl.*).

wrought, 578 f (y-wrogth B), 1662 f, 1757 f, 4132, 4345 f, 5758, 7530 f.

II. Old Norse verbs of the First Declension (cf. § 100).

brent, 7873 (brend C); ybrend, 4739 (brent D †, brent(e) B), 6672 (brent CD).

fletted, 7907 f (kyttid † C [1], flitted D).

hit, 867 (hurt ‡ C).

reysed, 7834 f.

hright, 6683 (schriht C).

trusted, 1499 (tristed B, trustid C, trustyd D); mystrusted, cf. 1516.

[1] *flittid* in the next line in C.

III. Anglo-Saxon and Old Norse verbs of the Second Conjugation (cf. § 101).

answerẹd, 4807 (-swerd(e) B, -swerịd C, -swerd D);[1] answèrëd, 3383 (-id CD, -swerde † B).

ybathed, 5477.

ybedded, 6709 f.

blyssyd, 308 (blissed B, blessed C, blessid D).

vnbrydled, 3271 (-dẹled B, -dẹlid CD).

called, 394, 548, 874, 1093, 2502, 3775, 7814.

cast, 2474 f, 2938, 8059; outcast, 6978; forn-cast, 3363.

cleped, 66, 5424; -id, 548 ‡ D; ycleped, 5166.

clothed, 156.

cursed, 4996; acursed, 4913, 4294.

fetẹred, 4768 AB (fetrid D).

fysshed, 1413 (fichid C).

gladed, 987.

hamẹled, 2049 (-ịd C, lessɪd ‡ D).

[h]alwed, 3110 (halọwed B, halwid C, halọwid D).

hanged, 1438; an-honged, 2705.

lernyd †, 3248 f C (l. leryd).

loked, 4002.

lost, see V., below.

louẹd, 500, 1501; ilouẹd, 594 (-ịd D, louéd ‡ C); belouẹd, 131 (-ịd C, -yd D).

ilyssed, 1082.

maked, (i.) 1193 (-yd C, made D). (ii.) ymạked †, 4576 (ymasked BCp., -id CD); in 2567, And shortly madè eche of hem his fo (makes B, mad C), we should clearly read maked (with Cp. and John's).

mad, maad, (i.) 251, 553, 904, 3100, 3681, 7926; mad(ẹ), 3145 (mad C), 3377 (mad his C †, mad(e) his D). mad, (ii.) 2956 (mand B), 5139, 5540 (mad the C); mad(e), 7900 (y-mad(e) BD, mad C);[2] mad(e) haluendel, 6698. In most of the cases cited B and D read mad(e).

opned, 3311 (opẹnyd CD).

played, 2325 (pleyẹd C, pleyd D).

put, 1698, 1851, 2191, 3363.

raft, 7621 (reft(e) D); reft, 7623 (raft C, raft(e) D). byraft, 4182 f

---

[1] In D, read ben for hem. [2] In B ymadë leche = ymad a leche.

(-reft(e) D), 4887 f, 4890, 4945 f (bereft C, berafft(e) D), 6122 f (beraft(e) D).

shadwed, 1906 (-wed(e) [wel] A).

shamed, 8090 ; ashamed, 2132.

shewed, 4690, 7810 ; -ẹd, 7812 (-ịd D, -īd C); yshewed, 7614.

sorwed, 5545.

spared, 6567.

sperid, 6894 (-ed BD, -ed(e) C).

thonked, 1935, 4451 ; -ẹd, 517 (-ĕd B, -yd C, -ịd D); ythonked, 4664.

trowed, 5045, 8041.

twyght, 5234 f.

warned, 4511.

wedded, 6707 f, 7338.

wondred, 1277 (-id D, -derd C).

wont, wonẹd, wonted. (*a*) wont, (i.) 183, 2605 (C(?)), 4975 (*om.* † B; C(?)), 5443 (wonẹd C), 5788, 6909, 7023, 7025 ; men was wont, 5528 (werẹ wonẹ C). (ii.) 510 (-yd C), 6982, 8073 ; wont here (*poss. sg.*), 5416 (-yt ‡ was C).—(*b*) wonẹd, (i.) 901 (wonẹ (?) C), 1485, 4378, 4553, 4697, 4729. (ii.) 3397 (-t BCD).—(*c*) as it wontĕd is to done, 6640 (wonte ? B, wone ? C, wonte ? D). For *woned* = dwelt, see 276 f (-yd CD) (: astoned *p.p.*).—In most of the cases above cited (*a—b*) C has *wone* (monosyllabic), B *wont(e)*, and D *wont(e)* or *wont*.

wounded, 1618 f, 1711.

IV. Anglo-Saxon verbs of the Third Conjugation (cf. § 102).

had, 1503, 1504, 2943, 5057 f, 5153, 6493, 7119, 7691.

lyued, 5755 ; ilyued, 7296.

seyd, 611, 740, 905, 935, 969, 1129, 1131, 1467, 1475, 1509, 1687, 1955, 2768, 3173, 3531 f, 3778, 3788, 4054, 4459, 4656, 5573, 6078, 7102, 7639, 8132 ; seyd(e), 5833.

V. Verbs originally strong (cf. § 103).

adrad, 1200 f (adradde C) (: be ye mad) ; ydrad, 4617.

fled, 87, 3933, 5530 ; yfled, 5323. In 463 *fled[de]*, pl., rhymes with *bredde*, pret. ; *fledde*, 7561 A, should be preterite.

hight, 1577, 5107 f (be- C, plight D), 6289 f ; yhight, 6904 f ; byhight, -hyght, 6717 f (hight D), 7467 f.

lost (cf. A.S. gelosod), (i.) 462 (D †),[1] 809, 3140 (C †), 3937, 4108 (lorẹ C), 4268, 4606, 4949, 5068 (-t(e) D), 5230 (-t(e) D), 6129 (-t(e) D), 6783, 8008 (-t(e) D); ylost, 5945 (-t(e) BD); fòrlost,

---

[1] Supply [*wol*] in C.

§ 121.]   *of Chaucer's Troilus.*   309

5418 (soore ‡ lorn(e) D). (ii.) lost, 2824, 5040 (-t(e) B),[1] 6244, 7069; forlòst, 3122 (-t(e) B, fordon(e) ‡ D)[2]; lost haue, 7001 (-t(e) D), 7766 (-t(e) D); lost held, 4635 (lorn hade C, lorn had D).
  lorn, (i.) 373 f (-n(e) B, borne † D); cf. 3918 f, 3943 f, 4065 f, 4483 f, 6141 f, 7808 f; ylorn, 5912 f (ılorne D, bore † D). (ii.) 5621 (-n(e) B), cf. 6275; lorn hade, 4635 C (lorn had D, lost held AB). He wend it *lost* he thoughte he nas but *lorn*, 3918 (lost . . . lorn(e) BD, lost . . . forlorn(e) C). He seyde (seid D) he nas but lor[e]n (lorne G) waylawey, 5619 ABD Cp. (not in C; He seide I am but lorn so weylaway John's).
  lore, 4108 C (lost ABD); forlore, 6386 f (fore † B).
    Rhyme words.—born *p.p* (373, 3918, 3943, 4065, 5912), sworn *p.p* (6141), torn *p.p.* (6141), byforn (373, 3918, 4065, 5912, 7808), toforn (4483), thorn (3943), more *n. A.S. more,-u* (6386), byfore (6386).
rewed, 5803.
rowed, 962 f.
siked, 7101.
  VI. Verbs of Germanic origin not found in Anglo-Saxon.
awhaped, 316 f.
bystowed, 960 f.
bywared, 636 f.
gert, 7408 C (hurt A, hirt(e) B, hurt(e) D); though girt, 5282 (thurgh gird(e) D).
grounded, 6334.
hust, 2000 (shet D), 3936 (schitt D).
smytted, 7908 f.
stokked, 3222.
twynned, 5138, 5450, 7042.
vntŷd, 1837 (-teyd B, onteyed C).
  VII. Romance and Latin verbs with participle in -t (cf. § 104).
abayst, 2936 (abassed C, abasshid D), 3964 (baist(e) B, abaschid D).
  Cf. abaysshed, 4075 (abaysed B, abasschit C; D †).
caught, 214 (caut C), 557, 2027, 2267, 2357, 7066; kaught, 4049, 4768; ycaught, 1668 (caght D, lauȝt C),[3] cf. 534.
hurt, 1080, 7408 (gert C).
quyt, 334, 529, 1327 f, 3861, 4068.

combèst, 3559 (-bust B, cumbrid ‡ CD).
enhàbyt, 5105 (-it B, enabit(id) C, an habıt(e) D).[4]

[1] Supply [*how*] in D.   [2] Read [*y*]*wonne* in A.
[3] Supply [*y*-] in CD.   [4] Read *her*[*ie*] in A.

èxecùt, 3464.
vncircumscript, 8228 (-t(e) D).

VIII. Romance and Latin verbs with participle in -ed (cf. § 105).

recouẹred, 37 ; couẹred, 2873 A (-id D, couerd B).
apeyred, 38 f.
plesed, 247 f.
by-iaped, 531 ; cf. 318 f.
astonyed (trisyl.), astoned, 1512, 1688, 3931, 8091.
disposed, 1767.
considẹred, 2375, 3765, 3827, 5933 (-sidred D), 7711.
delyuẹred, 3065.

delibẹred, 4873 B (-uẹryd C, -uẹrid D ; A †).
medẹlid, 5001 C (medled B, medlid D ; A †) ; cf. ymedled, 3657.
suffred, 5211 (-fẹrid C).
eschewed, 5740.
assembled, 5920 (-bẹlyd C).
ypreysed, 7836 f.
depeynted, 7962 f.

Cf. also 85 f, 87 f, 249, 274 f, 1274, 1447, 1690, 1710, 1765 f, 1872, 1924 f, 1925 f, 2164 f, 2166 f, 2262, 2272, 2467, 2477, 2588, 2811, 3170 f, 3171 f, 3247 f, 3263 f, 3265 f, 3287 f, 3288 f, 3366, 3622, 3875, 4026 f, 4028 f, 4376, 4653, 4700, 4730, 4892, 4929, 4937, 4955 f, 4956 f, 5215, 5221 f, 5222 f, 5301 f, 5303 f, 5304 f, 5455, 5470, 5487, 5637, 5670, 5715, 5766, 5832 f, 5924, 5959, 6186, 6310, 6514, 6540, 7076, 7123, 7191, 7270, 7347, 7482, 7610 f, 7612 f, 7698, 7702, 7741, 7877, 7905 f, 7960 f, 8046, 8073, 8084 f, 8085 f, 8143, 8179, etc., etc.

Note.—*Passen*, pret. *paste, passed* (§ 102), has p.p. *passed, ypassed* ; see 24, 2180, 4241, 4249, 4470, 6838, 7044, 7109.

IX. Roman participles in -ẹd (syncopated).

turnẹd, 4242 C (tornẹd B, tournèd AE).
criẹd, 5249 (cryẹd B, cryẹd C).
purueỹẹd, 5668 (-uyẹd D) ; pùrueyẹd (or purueyẹd ?), cf. 5717.
But,—pureỹ[é]d, 5718 (-ed B) ; purueỹéd, 5670, 5714 (-[e]d D).
enlùmynẹd, 6911 (-yd C, -ed BD).
Cf. also 992 C, 997 C, 2082 C, 2634 C, 6952 D, 7673 C, etc.

X. Adjectives in -ed.

Of adjectives formed from nouns by means of the participial termination -*ed*, the following will serve as examples :—

feythed, 1000 (fichid ‡ C).
sucred, 1469.
helmed, 1678.
rayled, 1905.

benchéd, 1907.
sonded, 1907.
fethẹred, 2011.
Cf. also §§ 57. b, 71.

Note 1.—It is of course impossible to draw a hard and fast line between such adjectives and genuine participles : *ytressed*, 7173 ; *ypleyntcd*, 7960 f.

Note 2.—The prefix *y-, i-* (A.S. *ge-*) is common in the perfect participles of both native and borrowed verbs: see the lists above (I.—X.) and cf. *yclosed*, 2053; *yplesed*, 3288; *idarted*, 4902; *yformed*, 4977; *ypleyned*, 6350; *yserued, iserued*, 6800, 8084 f; etc., etc. In cases like *wyse ylored*, 969 f (wyse lered BCp., old[e] lerid D; C†), where the word preceding the participle ends in -e, it is not always easy to determine whether the scribe has carried over the -e to the participle, or whether the *y-* is Chaucer's own (cf. 1260, 5945, 6637 (adj. *sene*), 7109, etc.).

§ 122. The Perfect Participle of Strong Verbs ends in the *Troilus* in *-en, -ęn, -n; -e, -ę* (cf. Child, § 61; ten Brink, § 196).

Instead of *-en* C usually has *-yn*: so often D, and occasionally B. *-in* is also now and then found. Variants of this kind are commonly disregarded in lists I.-IV., below. Examples are,—*ybetyn*, 741 f D; *holdyn*, 1326 D, 4516 CD, 8043 C; *brostyn*, 2061 CD; *comyn*, 2528 CD, 2904 D, 3599 CD, 4397 BC; *foldyn*, 5021 f CD; *brokyn*, 5809 BCD, 7567 C; cf. 86 f CD, 205 f CD, 1151 D, 1661 f D, 1680 CD, 2020 f CD, 2068 f C, 2177 CD, 2938 CD, 3095 f CD, 3292 CD, 3298 C, 3533 CD, 3576 CD, 3732 f D, 4060 C, 4739 D, 4777 D, 5375 C, 5606 C, 5918 C, 6032 C, 6077 CD, 7234 C, etc. For *-in*, see *dryvin*, 2068 D; *holpin*, 2404 C, 2526 C; 4112 C. *Writon* occurs once, 7666 B.

Note.—Instead of *-n, -n(e)* occurs now and then (see especially V., below), but this is very rarely the case in A.

The examples are arranged as follows,—I. -en before consonants; II. -en in rhyme; III. -en before vowels; IV. -en before *h*; V. syncope, -ęn or -n; VI. -e before consonants; VII. -e in rhyme; VIII. -e (elided) before vowels; IX. -e (elided) before *h*; X. apocope of -e; XI. hiatus; XII. the perfect participles of *sleen*; XIII. the perfect participles of *seen* (including the adjectives *sene, ysene*).

I. -en before consonants:
holden trewely, 1326 (holde C)[1]; h. was, 4516; h. me, 8043.
foryeuen be, 1680 (-ʒouyn C)[2].
brosten ben, 2061[3].
holpen what, 2526 (-[e] D)[4]; h. there, 4112 (-ęn † hem D); h. for, 5918 (helpyn C, helped D).
comen was, 2528[5], 4397; c. to, 2904 (-e C); c. benędicįte, 3599; c. Troylus, 6645 (-e CD); icomen was, 4510 (comyn D †).
yolden chere, 2938 (i-ʒolden B).
boden go, 3533 (bedyn C).

[1] In B supply [no].   [2] In AB read *wel* for *wols* (*wol*) I.
[3] In D supply [am].   [4] D is 9-syl.   [5] In C read *which* for *with*.

312   *Observations on the Language*   [§ 122.

shapen was, 3576; forshapen was, 1151.
founden by, 4777 (-e B, -e C); f. salue, 5606; f. were, 7965 (-e D, fonde C).[1]
fallen was, 5375 D (-yn C) (stanza not in AB).
broken (*adj.*) voys, 5809; b. that, 7567.
wreten wel, 6077 (writen B, writyn C); ywriten nor, 7422 (wretyn ‡ C, ywretyn D).
faren syn, 6829 (-e C, farne *l.* -en B).
woxen lesse, 6981 (waxen B, waxe CD)[2]; w. was, 7190 (waxen C, waxe D); w. wellys, 7737 (waxen C, wexen D); ywoxen was, 6638 (ywaxen D, wexen ‡ *inf.* C), 7071 (iwaxen C, waxen D).
wopen for, 7087 (wepid C, wepte † D); bywopen thus, 5578 (-wepen B, -wepyn CD).[3]
knowen were, 7944 (-e C).
ytaken for, 8128 (taken B, had[de] taken D).

II. -en in rhyme:
spoken, 86 f (C †), 205 f.
wroken, 88 f, 207 f (ywrokyn D).
broken, 89 f (-e C), 208 f (ybrokyn D).
ybeten, 741 f (beten A, ibete C).
dreuen, 1661 f (dryuen B, dryvyn D); dryuen, 2068 f B (dreuyn C, dryvin D, (y)dreuen A).
schryuen, 1664 f (screuyn B).
ryden, 2018 f (redyn C).
abyden, 2020 f.
becomen, 3095 f.
shaken, 3732 f (-e C).
shapen, 4082 f (y- BD, [i]schape C).
ywryen, 4293 f.
folden, 5021 f.
ycomen, 6875 f (come C).
nomen, 6877 f (-e C).

Rhyme words.—Other participles in *-en*, and I. Infinitives: lyuen (1661, 1664, 2068), comen (3095), maken (3732), escapen (4082), byholden (5021), colde[n] (5021), spyen (4293); II. treten *ind.* 3 *pl.* (741), yeden *ind.* 3 *pl.* (2018, 2020); III. eyen *n. pl.* (4293). Observe the rhyme *yeden* : *ryden* : *abyden*.

III. -ën before vowels:
clomben, 215 (clumbyn D).

[1] Supply [*that*] in AC, [*why*] in D; otherwise the line is a disagreeable 9-syl. verse.
[2] In BCD perhaps infinitive.   [3] In D read *ne* for *you*.

thurgh shoten, 325.¹
yolden, 801 (ʒuldyn C); ² cf. 5455 ‡ C.
founden, 1325 (-e C, -[ën] D), 1374 (-[é] C, -[en] D), 2596 (fonden C, found[e] ‡ me ? D), 4060 (fonden B), 6032.
shapen, 2177, 4272.
comen, cf. 2255, 7286.
holpen, 2404 (-[en] D).
wreten, 3292 (writen C, writyn D) ³; cf. 4198.
spoken, 3298 (-e D).
taken, 4712 (D †), 7234.
Cf. also 3683, 3853 (cropen), 4734, 5074, 5280, 5616, 6431, 7268, 7377, etc.

IV. -en before *h* :
taken hede, 501.⁴
dronken hadde, 4232 (drenken A).
holden haue, 4762 (-d ‡ my D).
ycomen hym, 5028 (comyn C, icommyn D).
yeuen here (l. *hire* A.S. hýr, with B), 5168 (yoven D).
yknowen here (*acc.*), 5381 (knowyn C, knowen D).
vnbroyden hangen, 5479.⁵
a swollen herte, 6564 (sorweful ‡ C).
comen heder, 6847 (C †).
songen hadde, 7008 (sungen had[de] D, songe ‡ also C).
wonnen han, 7353 (-en ‡ the D).
wreten here (*dat.*), 7666 (-on B, -e to C, -yn ‡ to D).
woxen helle, 7739 (waxen C, waxe D).
shapen hadde, 7914 (-e C, -en ? D).

V. Syncope :
shorn, 222 f (-ne B, yshorn D) (: corn *n.* : byforn).
born, (i.) 375 f (*in* vp born) (-ne BD), 897 f (-ne B), 1228 f (bor D), 1653 f (-ne BC); cf. 2354 f, 3146 f, 3915 f, 3945 f, 4064 f, 4438, 4994, 4996, 5913 f, 7053, 7063 (-yn C), 8062; born(e), 6518 f ABD (born C). (ii.) cf. 4265, 4960, 5407, 7074 (-yn C), 7320; born haue, 7639 (-n(e) D).—yborn, 1383 f (-ne B, ibore C); yborn al, 382 (-n(e) B, iborn C, [y]born D).
 Rhyme words.—lorn, ylorn *p.p.* (375, 3915, 3945, 4064, 5913), sworn, isworn, sworn(e) *p.p.* (897, 1383, 1653), byforn (375, 1228, 2354, 3146, 3915, 4064, 5913, 6518), toforn (1383), thorn *n.* (2354, 3945).
sworn, (i.) 899 f (-ne B), 3154, 6143 f (-ne B, isworn C, iswoine D);

---
¹ In D supply [*thurgh*]. ² In C read *that for* for *therfor*.
³ In B read *while* for *whiche*. ⁴ In D supply [*neuer*]. ⁵ In D supply [*al*]

sworn(e), 1384 f AB (swore C, sworn D); swo[rn], 5638 f (sworne B, sworn D); isworn, 1655 f (sworne B, isworne C, sworn D), 6646 f (sworne BD, sworyn C).

> Rhyme words.—born, yborn *p.p.* (899, 1384, 1655), lorn *p.p.* (6143), torn *p p* (6143), by-, toforn (1384, 5638, 6646).

torn, 6144 f (-ne D) (: lorn *p p.* : sworn *p.p.*); to-torn, 5020 f (-ne CD) (: byforn).

fallẹn yn, 555 (falls BC).
growẹn vnder, 1488 (grow B, wox ‡ D).
foundẹn àlwey, 3837 (found D).
yoldẹn ywys, 4053 (ȝolde BC, ȝoldẹn D).
yeuẹn vs, 5633 (yeue D).
spokẹn as, 5895 (i- B, speke C).
comẹn and, 6867 (-yn C); cf. 6560 C (?).
vnknowẹn of, 7942 (-knowe C); cf. 6910 † D.

> Note 1.—C is fond of *-yn* when ABC have *-e* (elided): see VIII., below.
> Note 2.—For *lorn, ylorn,* see § 121, V.; for *slayn,* see XII., below; for *seyn,* see XIII., below.

VI. -e before consonants (not *h*):
come was, 155 (-en B, -yn CD).
to-hewe was, 1723 (-en B, -yn CD).
knowe be, 1877 A (yknowen B).
smet[e] be, 2230 (-e C, smyten B, smytyn D).[1]
holde fully, 2383 (-en B, -[e] D).
vnbore dar, 3111 A (-e BD).
ywrete ben, 4535 (wryten B, wretyn C, writyn D).
bete doun, 4739 (betten B, drawyn ‡ D).
vnderstonde god, 8161 (-ę B, -en D †).

VII. -e in rhyme:
ybete, 2025 f ([i]bette B, i-betyn C), 2314 f (-tte B), 4011 f (-bette B, bete C).
blowe, 4829 f (i- BC, yblow D); yblowe, 384 f (-w D).
bonde, 255 f (-d D), 2308 f; bounde, 859 f (-d D); vp bounde, 3359 f (-d D).
bore, 2497 f. (Cf. also VI., above).
i-, ycome, 3446 f (come BCD), 6434 f; ouercome, 243 f (ouęr- C), 5731 f (-com D, ouęrecome B). For *welcome,* see § 2.
idrawe, 3695 f (ydrowe B); out drawe, 5888 f (drawe ‡ CD); withdrawe, 5548 f (-drare † C).

---

[1] A has *be smet* for *smet[e]* be.

dreue, 6752 f (dryue B, dryf *inf.* ‡ D).
bygete, 970 f (be- C).
be-, bygonne, 1133 f, 1864 f, 2045 f, 2319 f, 2669 f, 3577 f; bygon[n]e, 3121 f (-nne B). [Var. CD -gunne; C -gune; D -gun.]
falle, 3701 f (yfalł D), 4933 f (-H D), 6615 f, 6912 f (-H D).
yfare, 3419 f, 5831 f (fare C).
folde, 5909 f (-yn CD), 6351 f, 7603 f.
founde, 3360 f (-d D), 5290 f, 6327 f, 7197 f (y- B); y-founde, 5256 f (stound ‡ *n.* D).
graue, 2945 f, 4341 f.
ygrounde, 4705 f (-d D).
holde, 4101 f (y- D ‡), 5079 f (-en B; C †), 6937 f, 7329 f (D †); byholde, 7615 f (be- CD).
knowe, 638 f (-w D), 5145 f (y- B, i- CD); vnknowe, 4830 f (-w D).
nome, 3448 f, 6553 f (y- B, i- D); ynome, 242 f (nome C).
ronge, 7425 f (runge D); runge(n), 1890 f (ronge B, (i)runge C, yrung D).
ronne, 2549 f; yronne, 1992 f, 2926 f ([y]- C°, yrun D).
ishape, 3253 f (schape C).
yshore, 5658 f (yshoor D).
shoue, 3868 f (sowe † D).
songe, 8160 f (sunge D); y-, isonge, 5461 f, 7422 f (ysong B).
sowe, 385 f (-w D, sawe B).
ystonde, 7975 f (istounde C); withstonde, 253 f (-d D), 5960 f (-stande D); vnderstonde, 5958 f (-stande *inf.* ‡ D), 6067 f, 7977 f.
itake, 4040 f.
ythrowe, 4668 f (-w D), 5144 f; ouerthrowe, 5047 f (-w B), 7823 f.
wonne, 777 f (won D), 2047 f, 2583 f, 2828 f (won D); ywonne, 2321 f, 3122 f ([y]- A, ywunne D), 5977 f (Antenore wonne = Antenor i-wonne C).
wrie, 3462 f (i- C, ywrye D); ywrye, 6316 f (-wrey D).
y-yeue, 4453 f (iȝeue BC, [i]ȝeue D).

Rhyme words.—Other perfect participles in *-en,* and the following,—I. *nouns*: to the grounde, to grounde (859, 4705), wounde (859, 5256, 5290), hete (970, 2025), sonne (1864, 1992, 2319, 2321, 2669), tunge(n), tonge (1890, 5461, 7422, 7425, 8160), in, on honde (2308, 6067, 7975, 7977), strete (2314), iape (3253), frape (3253), hawe (3695), loue (3868), halle (3701), mowe (4668), throwe (5047, 7823), sto[u]nde (5290), eye (6316), cf. welcome (6434, 6553); II. *adjectives*: bare *indef. sg.* (5831), secounde *indef. sg.* (7197), the grete (2314), the olde (5079), donne *pl.* (1992), hye *pl.* (3462), colde *pl.* (4101, 6351), some *pl.* (242, 243, 3446, 3448, 5731), alle *pl.* (3701, 4933, 6615, 6912); III. *adverbs*: fawe (5548), to-fore, to-forn (2497), byfore (5658), wherfore (2497), therfore (5658), aboue (3868); IV. *infinitives*: 970, 2308, 2926, 3419, 3462, 4011, 4040, 4933, 5079,

5731, 5909, 6067, 6327, 6351, 6752, 6937, 7603, 7823; V. *other verbforms: pres ind.* 1 *sg.*,—trowe (638), haue (2945), leue *vivo* (4453); 1 *pl.* konne (1864); 2 *pl.* konne (777), swete (2025), 3 *pl.* konne (2669); *pres. subj.* 1 *sg* konne (1133), dye (6316); 2 *sg.* konne (2549, 2583), foryeue (6752); 3 *sg.* saue (2945, 4341); 2 *pl.* yf ye konne (2828, 5977); *pret. ind.* 3 *sg.* tolde (7615); 2 *pl* tolde (7329), sponne (3577).

VIII. -e (elided) before vowels (variants not registered).

Cf. 474 (founde), 530 (iblowe), 616 (vnknowe), 809 (vnknowe), 1163 (come), 1260 (yknowe), 1367 (shape), 2917 (come), 3092 (bigonne; -ę A), 3111 BD (vnbore), 3630 (come), 3634 (come), 3844 (founde), 3948 (foryeue), 4293 (stole), 4642 (come), 4719 (yeue), 5207 (yeue), 6321 (founde), 6373 (molte), 6952 (ywroke), 7254 (take)[1], 7394 (come).

> Note.—In some of these cases syncopated forms occur in B, C, or D: as,— ȝeuęn, 5207 B; forȝeuęn, 3948 B; comęn, 2917 B (-yn C); comyn, 3630 C, 3634 C; founden, 6321 D; moltęn, 6373 D; etc. Sometimes, too, the ending is omitted altogether: thus,—com, 1163 B, 3630 B, 7394 B; found, 3844 D; vnknow, 616 BD, 809 BD; etc. (cf. grow, 1488 B; wox, 1488 D). Even A occasionally omits the ending before a vowel: thus,—wrong, 5833 ACD (-e B); hold, 7066 AB (-e C, -ęn D).[2]

IX. -e (elided) before *h*:

wonne hym, 28 (D †).

founde his, 3378 (-d D, fonde B, fond C).

come he, 3396.

take here (*dat.*), 3986.

y-yeue hym, 4218 (i-ȝeue BC, yeue D ‡).

X. Apocope of -e (before consonants):

Genuine cases are rare. Such are perhaps,—

fond no, 2263 (-ę B).

comę this, 6560 (-yn C, -ęn D).

Apparent cases occur now and then, but usually disappear on comparison of MSS. Examples are,—

comę to, 2198 A.

spokę with, 2565 D.

bygonnę to, 3092 A.

hold my, 4762 D.

wretę to, 7666 C.

yborę was, 8013 A.

vnderstondę god, 8161 B.

XI. Hiatus.

Hiatus very rarely occurs, and is of course always easily corrected by adding -n. Examples are,—

boundë in, 663 A (-en B, -yn CD).[3]

spokë in, 3298 D (-en AB, -yn C).

iboundë in, 4891 A (-yn CD, ybounden B).

brokë alday, 5280 C (-en ABD).

---

[1] In A read hen[ne]s. [2] In A supply [I]. [3] Supply [hym] in C.

songë also, 7008 C (-en hadde AB, sungen had[de] D).

XII. Perfect-participle of *sleen*.

The perfect participle of *sleen* has various forms. The usual form before vowels and consonants is *slayn* (var. D sleyn, slayn(e); BD slayn(e); B sleyn(e); C slain): cf. 608, 1420, 4301 BCD, 4940, 5860, 6144, 6417, 7299, 7864, 7867 C, 7868, 8170, 8183. For *slay* (p. p.) *youre self*, 5896 A, read *slayn* (so BC, slayn(e) anon D). In rhyme we find,—*slayn*, 5855 f (slayne D) (: desdayn *n*.), and *sleyn*, 6590 f (-ne B, slayn CD) (: ayen AD, aȝein B, aȝen C); but also *slawe*, 3563 f (-w D) (: shawe *n*.), 5546 f (: withdrawe *p.p.*), 5890 f (: drawe *p.p.*). In 5903 either *slay[e]n* (cf. ten Brink, § 196 : " wohl niemals *slayen* ") or *slawe* must be read in the interior of the verse, —My (Myn C) selue (self B, seluyn C, silf D, selfe G) I wolde (wolde I C) haue (han B, a C) *slayn* (*slawe* C, *slayne* DG) quod she tho (too D). Mr. Austin's collation of Cp. and the John's MS. has no note on this line.

XIII. Perfect-participle of *seen*.

seyn, (i.) 174 (seyen C)[1], 3063 f (: ayen : fayn), 7962 (sen C, seyn [with] B). (ii.) 3902 (sen C)[2], 5624[3].—yseyn with, 6811 (sen C, sene D); beseyn that, 2347 (by- BD).

seighen byfore, 5639 A (seyn BD); seyghen byfore, 5660 A (seyn(e) B, seyn D).

yseye, 1253 (yseyn B, seyn CD).

sen at, 6804 C (wyst A, wist(e) BD).

sene, 3713 f (seene B) (: I wene *ind*.), 6637 f (-ee- B, ysen D) (: shene *adj. postpos*.), 7259 f (-ee- B) (: queene), 8078 f (-ee- B) (: tene *n*); sene his, 8117 (seen B, sen D †); sene, 3731 (-ee- B, seyn D), 6394 (sen D).

yseene, 700 f ([y]sene C, ysene D) (: queene); isene, 6269 f (i-seene B, [i]sene D) (: tene *n*. : shene *adj. def*.).

Note.—The forms in *-ne* represent the A.S adjectives *geséne* (*gesýne*) : cf. ten Brink, § 148.

§ 123. Præterito-present verbs.

(i.) *wot, not, oughte*; (ii.) *kan, dar, thar*; (iii.) *shal*; (iv.) *may*; (v.) *mot*.

I. *wot*.

Pres. Ind. 1 Sing. wot, woot, (i.) 670 (-(e) BD)[4], 2087 (-(e) BD)[5], 2109 (-(e) D †; C †), etc.; (ii.) 1829 (-(e) BD), 2525 (-(e) D)[6],

[1] In B read ȝit for þat. [2] In A supply [a]. [3] In D dele (*for*).
[4] Supply [*for*] in D. [5] Supply [*wel*] in A. Cf. 1621. [6] Supply [*wel*] in D

2785 (not(e) D, wot [I] C; B †), 5044 (what D, wote *pl.* C), etc.; wot(e), 1960 ABD (wot C)[1].

Pres. Ind. 2 Sing. wost, (i.) (ii.) 633 (wyst C)[2], 717 (-(ẹ) B), 721 f (-e B, wyst C), 882 (wyst C), 2451 f (-e B)[3], 2493 f (wist C), 2514 (wolt ‡ C; D (?)), 2908 f, 3088 f, 3098, 3141 f, 3181, 4930 (wotịst D), 5262 f (-e D, wooste B), 5742 (-(e) D), 6281 f (wooste B, wist C, woste D), 6705 (-(ẹ) D, wist C), etc. [Var. BD woost; B (633) whost.]—wostow, 588, 775, 781, 851 (wastow B, wyst thou C, wost thow D), 901, 3091. [Var. CD wost thou; D wost thow.]

Rhyme words.—most *adv.* (721, 2451, 2493, 5262, 6281), almost (2908, 3141), bost *n.* (3088, 3141), ost *n.* (5262, 6281).

Pres. Ind. 3 Sing. wot, woot, (i.) (ii.) 1975 f (wote C) (: hoot *pred. adj. sg.*); cf. 826 (A †), 2080, 2711, etc. B shows less liking for *wot(e)* and more for *woot* than in the 1 pers.; C has *wot*(e) in 807.— for-wòt, 5733 A (fòr-woot B, fòrẹwitt D).

Pres. Ind. 1 Pl. we wote alle, 5044 C ‡ (*should be singular*).

Pres. Ind. 2 Pl. wetë wel, 1323 AC (-en B, wite D); witë ‡ what, 2737 D.—wotẹ ye, 3686 (-oo- B, wot C †); wot ye, 3501 (-oo- B, what C, wytẹ D), 3739 (-ẹ D, whoot B), 5916 (-oo- B, wote CD); wot your, 3621 (-ẹ D, wetẹ C), wot that, 1665 (-oo- B, wetyn C, wytẹ D), 5974[4]; wot the, 2731 (-ẹ D, wetẹ C), 5576 (woote B); wot, 2281 f (wootë B, he wrote ‡ D) (: not *nescio*), 5923 f (woote B, wote D) (: hot *pred. adj. sg.*).

Pres. Ind. 3 Pl. weten folk, 4860 (witen B, wetyn C, know[e] D); wotyn ‡ that, 7179 C (writen ABD); wot no, 1978 (-ẹ B; D ‡).

Pret. Ind. 1 Sing. wyste, 3682 f (wist CD) (: vntriste)[5]; wyst I, 1644 (-e B, wiste C, wist D)[6], 2968 (wiste B, woste C), 3210 (wiste B, wost C, wist D).[7]

Pret. Ind. 2 Sing. wistist thou, 4486 C (but see under *subj.* 2 *sg.*).

Pret. Ind. 3 Sing. wiste, wyste, 811 f (-t D; C †), 3112 (-[e] ‡ D)[8], 4071 f (-t C), 4095 f, 8028 f (wistt D); -[e] what, 7231 (-e B, *om.* † C); -[e] wel, 8087 (-e D); -e, 565 (-t he D, woste he C)[9], 4634 (-t D); -t he, 76 (west B, woste C), 301 (-e B, woste he C)[10], 3367

---

[1] BD regularly add -e, which is never sounded, however, though false readings sometimes force one either to pronounce it or to emend the verse by a comparison of MSS. (thus, 670 D).

[2] *Wyst* might be called *pret. subj.* in this line.   [3] Protasis.

[4] Supply [*that*] in C; [*a*] in D.

[5] "Whi hastow mad Troylus to me vntriste That neuere yet agylte hym that I wyste."

[6] Supply [*as*] in D.   [7] Read *telle* [*me*] in D.

[8] Supply [*that*] in A.   [9] Supply [*as*] in D.

[10] But supply [*how*] in C, and read *woste he*.

§ 123.]   *of Chaucer's Troilus.*   319

(-e B, -t D);¹ -e he, 3321 ‡ C; wostë ‡ alle, 3538 C (wist[e] ‡ that D); wist ‡ non, 2646 D.

Rhyme words.—kyste *pret. ind.* 3 *sg.* (811, 4095), tryste, triste *inf.* (4071, 8028), twyste *n.* (4071).

Pret. Ind. 2 Pl.   wysten of, 1586 (westen B, wistyn C, wist[en] D) *(indirect question).*

Pret. Ind. 3 Pl.   wyste, 5824 f (wiste BCD) (: kyste *pret. ind.* 3 *sg.*); wyst[e] neuere, 6383 (wiste B); wyst what, 2646 (wiste B, woste al C, wist ‡ non *sg.* D).

Pret. Subj. 1 Sing.   wiste, wyste, 678 f (wist D), 4119 f (woste C), 4350 (-[e] D, wostë C); -[e], 765 (-e BC), 6285 (-e BD, nyste C); -é how, 3944 (-[e] D); wist I, 8104 (-e B, wist † hou D); wist[e] outrely, 4328 (-e B, woste C, wist D).

Rhyme words.—liste *pres. subj.* 3 *sg.* (678), kyste *pret. ind.* 3 *sg.* (4119).

Pret. Subj. 2 Sing.   Sith I so loth was that thi selfe it wyste, 3211 f (wiste B, wost C †, wyst D) (: triste *pres. ind.* 1 *sg.* : lyste *pres. subj.* 3 *sg.*).

Note.—In 4486 C *wistist thou* is used in a subjunctive construction (= if thou didst know). Cp. and John's have *wystistow*; *wistow* ABG, *wist thow* D, which make a disagreeable 9-syl. line and are not grammatical, should be emended (see § 107).

Pret. Subj. 3 Sing.   wiste, wyste, 3307 (-[e] D, weste[e] B, woste C), 4610 f (-t C)² (: liste *pret. subj.* 3 *sg.* : twyste *same* ³), 7269 (woste C); -e, 6005 (-t D); wist he, 5580 (-e BCD); wyste of, 1830 (woste C, wist D).⁴

Pret. Subj. 2 Pl.   wyste, 2267 f (wiste BC, wyst D) (: lyste *pres. subj.* 3 *sg.*); -e, 1224 (wiste C, wist BD); wiste how, 6280 (wist D).

Inf.   wyte, wite, 1397 (wetyn C, wytyn ‡ D), 3991 (wete C); wete, 6468 (wit as B, wete as D).

Perf. Part.   wist, wyst, (i.) 513 (-(e) B), 615 (- (e) B), 3116 (wost C), 3246 f (-e B) (: lyst *pres. ind.* 3 *sg.* : tryst *n.*), etc., etc.   For *vnwist, vnwyst, wnwist,* (i.) (ii.) cf. 2594, 3445, 3612, etc.

II. *not.*

Pres. Ind. 1 Sing.   not, (i.) (ii.) 410 (wot(e) ‡ D), 1626, 2282 f (note D) (: wot *pres. ind.* 2 *pl.*), 3851, 4320, 5463 (nott D), 6500 (knowe † D), 7530 (knowe ‡ D); cf. 426, 1120, 2291, 2451, 2551, 2963, 4495, 4698, 4842, 6589.   [Var. B noot; D not(e).]

¹ Supply [wel] in D.   ² 3 *pl.* in E ‡.   ³ *it wyste* † A.
⁴ Al (As D) wolde (wold CD) I that noon (*so* ABG, no man CD) wyste (woste C, wist DG) of this thought (-e B). No note in Mr. Austin's collation.

320   *Observations on the Language*   [§ 123.

Pres. Ind. 2 Sing.   nost, (i.) 5304 (wost C, knowest D)¹, 5763 (wost C ‡², knowest D).

Pres. Ind. 3 Sing.   not, 800 (noot B, not(e) D).³

Pret. Ind. 3 Sing.   nyste, 356 f (-t CD), 4193 f (-t C), 5011, 5341,⁴ 5794 f ((I) nyste D); nyst[e], 6381 (-e B), 7566 (-e B, nist ‡ what D ; C †); nyste how, 7145 (-t B †).⁵

    Rhyme words.—lyste *pret. subj. 3 sg.* (356), kyste *ind. 3 sg.* (4193), *ind. 3 pl.* (5794), twyste *inf.* (5794).

Pret. Subj. 1 Sing.   nyste, 6285 C (wist[e] A, wiste BD).

Pret. Subj. 3 Sing.   nyst[e], 7791 (-e ‡ C, nist[e] D); nyste, 494 (*om.* † D).⁶

    Note.—The forms *nyst thou* in 4269 C and *nyst(e) thou* in 4965 D are blunders for *nylt thou*.

III. *oughte.*

Pret. Ind. 1 Sing.   ought[e] konne, 647 (ouȝte C, me oghte to ? D)⁷; ought[e] be, 7710 (auȝte C); I ne ought[e] not⁸, 1805 (ne aught[e] B, ne auȝte C, I oght[e] not D); oughte I, 7002 (auȝte C, ought D); ought half, 5927 (auȝte C).⁹

Pret. Ind. 2 Sing.   oughtest, 8069 ; oughtestow, 6908 (auȝtist thow C, oughtest thou D); oghtist, 649 D. (But see § 107.)

Pret. Ind. 3 Sing.   oughte, 649 (*om.* † C, oghtist D), 3106 f (-t D; ȝe ouȝt *pl.* C),¹⁰ 3325 (-[e] B, auȝte ‡ to C, oght ‡ be D), 3423 f (-t D), 3522 f (-t CD), 5805 (-[e] D, hem owen † to B, auȝte ‡ to C), 7357 f (-t D, nouȝt *adv.* ‡ C), 7919 (-[e] B, auȝte C †, aught[e] D), 8006 (-[e] D, auȝte ‡ to C)¹¹; cf. 5971. [Var. B aughte ; C ouȝte, ouȝt ; D oght.]—ought[e], 710 (auȝte ‡ C, oght[e] D), 744 (ougthte B, auȝte ‡ C, oght ‡ to D); aught[e], 423 (auȝght[e] B, auȝte C, oght ‡ euere D).—oughte, 2683 (thouȝte ‡ C, oght ‡ thei D), 3832 (-t BD), 5058 (-t BD), 5233 (-t D; aught 3 *pl.* B).¹² [Var. B aughte, aught ; C auȝte, ouȝte ; D oght.]—oughts he, 2322 (-t B, auȝte C, oght ‡ ȝe 2 *pl.* D).—ought (*bef. vowel*), 1691 (aught B, auȝte C, oght D).¹³—oughte, 3871 ‡ A (-[e] B, auȝte ‡ C, oght[e] D) ; ought ‡ the, 5971 (aught[e] lasse B, auȝte lasse C, ought ‡ the D).—out,¹⁴ 7459 (ought BD, auȝte C).

---

¹ Dele the second (*nat*) in D.   ² 9-syl. in C.
³ "If thow thus *deye* and she *not* whi it is." The distinction in sense between the subjunctive *deye* and the indicative *not* in this verse is marked.
⁴ Supply [*So*] in A.   ⁵ Supply [*for*] in C. B needs [*herte*] for the metre.
⁶ Read [*s*]*he* in C.   ⁷ Read *conne* for *come* in C.
⁸ So, rather than *I ne ought not*.   ⁹ Supply [*to*] in D.
¹⁰ Supply [*do*] in D.   ¹¹ Impersonal. Supply [*that*] in D.
¹² In C dele (*Hadde*).   ¹³ C is too long.   ¹⁴ "It out i-now suffise."

[§ 123.] *of Chaucer's Troilus.* 321

Note.—In 1691, 2683, 5805, 8006, *oughte* is past in sense; in the rest of the cases above cited it is present in sense. In 649, 2683, 3106, 3423, 3522, 5805, 8006, the construction is impersonal with the dative (*the, hym, here, hem oughte*); cf. 647 D (*me oght to?*).
Rhyme words.—wroughte *ind.* 1 *sg.* (3106, 7357), me thoughte *ind.* (3106), bisoughte *ind.* 3 *sg.* (3428), broughte *ind.* 3 *sg.* (3522).

Pret. Ind. 2 pl.   oght ‡ ȝe, 2322 D; ȝe ‡ ouȝt, 3106 f C.   (See under *pret. ind.* 3 *sg.*).   (In sense of present tense.)

Pret. Ind. 3 Pl.   oughte, 1997 f A (aughte B) (: broughte *ind.* 3 *pl.* : thoughte *ind.* 3 *sg.*), 4275 (aughten B, auȝten C, ouȝten D)[1]; oughte, 4637 (-t B, ouȝt C, oght D); aught of, 5233 B‡; oght ‡ thei, 2683 D.

Note.—In 1997 and 2683 *oughte* is past in sense; in the rest of the cases above cited it is present in sense.

Pret. Subj. 3 Sing.   oughte, 7708 (auȝte C, ought D).

IV. kan.

Pres. Ind. 1 Sing.   kan, (i.) (ii.) 11, 459, 492, 718, 1044, 2243, 2530, 2590, 7731; cf. 1635 f, 7304 f, 8132 f.   [Var. CD can; B kann(e); D cann(e).]

Pres. Ind. 2 Sing.   kanst, (i.) (ii.) 511 (can C), 2607,[2] 2697, 3141, 5154 (ka[n]st B), 7644; cf. 1045 D, 5759 C.   [Var. CD canst; D canst(e).]—canstow, 757 (kanstow B, c. thou CD)[3]; kanstow, 5122 (canstu C, canst(e) thou D).—thow kan wel endite, 7655 (kanst B, canst C, canst(e) D).[4]

Pres. Ind. 3 Sing.   kan, can, (i.) (ii.) 147, 203, 234 f, 259 (may ‡ D), 3002 (gan † B, ȝe can C), 5774, 6120, 6134, 7136 f, 7573; cf. 1291 f, 1459 f, 6357 f.   [Var. D cann(e).]— kan(e), 4666 A (kan B, can D).

Pres. Ind. 1 Pl.   konne, 1867 f (cunne C, kun D †) (: bygonne *p.p.* : sonne); kon haue, 6481 (kan B, can CD).

Pres. Ind. 2 Pl.   konne, 776 f (cunne C, conne D) (: wonne *p.p.*), 2551 f (cunne C, conne D)[5] (: ronne *p.p.*), 2827 f (kanne B, cunne C, kun D) (: wonne *p.p.*); konne, 985 (kun D, cunne ‡ conseyl C), 1374[6] (kanne B, cunne C, kun D); can ‡ now, 3002 C; can ‡ don, 5856 C; kan ye, 4405 (can C, kunne ? D); kan recorde, 6180 (can C †, canne D).

Pres. Ind. 3 Pl.   konne, 1260 f (cunne C) (: sonne), 1971 (donnen † B, cunne C, kun[ne] D), 1974 (kunne C, kun[ne] D), 2672 f (cunne C, kun D) (: bygonne *p.p.* : sonne); konne, 838 (cunne C, kun D),

---

[1] Supply [*pleyne*] in B, [*the*] in C.   [2] Supply [*wel*] in C.
[3] Supply [*non*] in D.   [4] Supply [*this*] in C.
[5] Indirect question.   [6] Conditional; perhaps subjunctive.

Y

1001 (kun D, cunnyn an C); cunne how, 1921 C (*pret. subj.* ? ABD); konne telle, 1980 (kan B, can CD); kan leye, 559 (cunne C, can D); kan not, 1357 (can CD), 2875 (may ‡ D); kan sen, 7476 (can D, c. ouȝt *sg.* C)[1]; kan a, 6712 (can CD).

Pret. Ind. 1, 3 Sing. koude, kowde, coude, 629 (-[e] D), 798 BC (-[e] D, wolde A), 2163 f (-d D) (: loude *adv.*), 2263 (-[e] D), 2758 (couthe D, koude she BCp.), 3276 f (· cloude), 3454 (couthe D), 3521 f (-d D) (: loude *adv.*), 3800 (B † D †), 3802 (couthe D), 4110 (couthe C), 4564 (myght[e] D), 5237 (C ‡ (?)), 6452 (couthe B), 6651, 7139; koude, kowde, 193 (coute C, couth D), 367 (kouth B, coude C, couth wel D),[2] 660 (coude B, curere † C^c, couth D), 3054 (coude C, couthe D), 3480 (*om.* † B; coude CD),[3] 3536 (coude C, cowd ‡ wel D), 7110 (coude CD),[4] 7991 (couthe ‡ wel C; D †); koude he, 1144 (cowd D; A †),[5] 3317 (coude C, couthe D), 4638 (coude C, couthe D), 8092 (coude D, koude ‡ not B); koude his, 665 B (coude C^c, cowd D, koude (al) his A); koude here (*gen. sg.*), 5337 (myghte B, myȝte C, myght D); koude he, 4207 (coude he C, cowde he D; B †).

Pret. Ind. 2 Sing. koudest neuere, 622 (coudest B, coudyst C, coudist D).

Pret. Ind. 2, 3 Pl. koude, 7480 (coude CD); -ë ye, 4200 (coude C; cowde ? D); kowde how, 1921 (koude B, couthe D, cunne C) (subj. ?).

Pres. Subj. 1 Sing. if I konne, 1134 f (kun D) (: begonne *p.p.*).

Pres. Subj. 2 Sing. if that thow konne, 2582 f (cunne C, kunne D) (: wonne *p.p.*).

Pres. Subj. 2 Pl. I not whether ye . . . konne, 2551 f (cunne C, conne D) (: ronne *p.p.*); yf ye konne, 5978 f (cunne C) (: ywonne *p.p.*).[6]

Pres. Subj. 3 Pl. if they kan sen, 7476 (can D, can ‡ ouȝt *sg.* C).[6]

Pret. Subj. 1 Sing. koude, kowde, 3342 (couthe D, thow I coude † C), 4344 (coude C †, couthe D); koude, kowde, 1206 (coude C, cowd ? D), 2667 (cow(e)de A, coude C, cowd [I] D), 3138 (coude C, couthe D).

Pret. Subj. 3 Sing. who koude telle, 6630 (coude D, wil C ‡).

Pret. Subj. 2 Pl. koude, 7335 (couthe C, coude D); koude han, 8046 (coude haue D, wolde ‡ a C).

[1] Perhaps subjunctive. Supply [*of*] in A.   [2] Read *wel couth* in D.
[3] Read *mich*[e] in D.   [4] Read *ys*[e] in CD.
[5] In this line *koude he* is concessive (= *though he could*).
[6] Perhaps indicative. In 7476 A supply [*of*].

Pret. Subj. 3 Pl. koude, 7700 (couthe ‡ pleyne C, coude ‡ p. D); kowde how, 1921 (koude B, couthe D, cunne *ind.* ‡ C) (ind. ?).

   Note.—Of the above cited subjunctives, the following are in apodosis, and therefore perhaps doubtful : 1206, 1921, 2667, 3138, 3342, 4344, 6630, 7335, 8046. The rest are in protasis, except as indicated in the citation.

Inf. konne, 2925 f (cunne C, kun D) (: y-ronne *p.p.*), 3219 f (cunne C, kun D) (: sonne), 7767 (cunne C, kanne D); konne, 647 (come † C; know[e] ‡ D (?)).

Perf. Part. kouth in, 4723 A (B † D †); vnkouth, (i.) 1236 (-(e) AD), 4639 (-(e) BD, vnkow A).

V. *dar*

Pres. Ind. 1 Sing. dar, (i.) (ii.) 396, 451, 1258, 1622,[1] 2834, 2946, 3180 (dare? CD),[2] 3503, 4108, 5272, 5434, 7659, 7990 (D †), etc. [Var. CD dar(e).]

Pres. Ind. 2 Sing. darst not, 768 (C?); dar not, 6776 (darst BC, darst(e) D)[3]; dastow, 7642 (darstow B, durstjst ‡ thow C, darst(e) thou D).

Pres. Ind. 3 Sing. dar, 5863 (-(e) CD),[4] 6130 (-(e) CD),[5] 6566 (durst(e) D).

Pres. Ind. 2 Pl. dar ye, 2832 (-(e) C, dore ‡ D (?)).

Pret. Ind. 1 Sing. dorste, 1859 (durste C, durst D).

Pret. Ind. 2 Sing. dorstestow, 767 (durstyst thou C, trist ‡ thow D).[6] (Perhaps subjunctive, see § 106.)

Pret. Ind. 3 Sing. dorste, 1287 (durste C, durst[e] D), 7273 (-[e] B, durste ‡ ȝow C, durste D); dorst[e] yow, 27 (-e B, durst[e] D);[7] dorste, 3294 (-t B, durste C, durst D) (cf. 5334, 7073); dorste hire (*acc.*), 7091 (-t B, durste C, durst ‡ compleine D)[8]; dorst he, 503 (durste C, durst D); dorst hir (*acc.*), 98 B (durste C, durste mone D, dorst (make) hire A).

Pret. Ind. 3 Pl. So as they *dorste* (dorsten G, dorst B, durste C, durst D) how (hough G, so as C, how ferre D) they wolden (wolde C Cp., wold D) procede, 3297.

Pret. Subj. 1 Sing. dorste, 7667 (-[e] B); dorste, 3219 (-t BD), 7532 (-e leyne † C)[9]; dorst I, 924 (-[e] seye BD, -e seye C), 3212 (-e C), 6720 (-e CD), 6915 (-e CD); dorst haue, 899 (durst a C †); dorste,

---

[1] Supply [*bc-*] in B. [2] CD should be emended by means of AB.
[3] Read (*a*)*rise* in D. [4] Supply [*fere*] in B. [5] C is defective.
[6] Supply [*hire*] in B. 9-syl. line in D. [7] Possibly subjunctive.
[8] Read *pleyne* for *compleyne* in C. [9] Supply [*that*] in D.

2521 (-t B, -e C, -[e] D)¹. [CD have -u- in all these cases, AB -o-.]
Pret. Subj. 2 Sing. See Pret. Ind. 2 Sing.
Pret. Subj. 3 Sing. desiryng . . . to haue here herte dere In swych a plyt she *dorst*[e] make hym chere, 4396 (durste C, that sche durst ‡ him make D).

> Note.—Of these instances of the subjunctive preterite (1, 3. person), the following, being in protasis, may be regarded as certain : 2521, 3219, 6915, 7708. The following are in apodosis (as, *I dorste leye* i. e. wager) : 899, 924, 6720, 7532, 7667 ; cf. *how dorst I*, 3212.

Pret. Subj. 2 Pl. And yf so be that pes her-after take . . . Why lord the sorwe and wo ye wolden make That ye ne *dorste* come ayen for shame, 6227 (dorst[e] B, durstyn C, durste D) (=because you would not, or did not, dare).

Infin. to dorre don, 7203 (durre (to) do B, to dore den Cᶜ †, to doo † D).

VI. *thar*.

Pres. Ind. 3 Sing. he. thar nought, 2746 (hym thar BCp. John's, him thar G, him dar C, hym ogh‡[e] D).

Pret. Subj. 3 Sing. *thorste*, 3414, in which the correct reading seems to be : *Yow thorste* neuere han the more fere. The variants are curious : Yow dorste (*so* A, Thow thruste B, He thourrste C, Yow durst D, ȝou thurst G, ȝow thruste Cp., Ye thorste John's, Yow thurste Harl. 2392) haue neuere (*so* AD John's, neuere han BCG Cp.).

VII. *shal*.

Pres. Ind. 1 Sing. shal, (i.) 398 (sal B), 922 f (shalle B)², 1047 f, 1912 f, 2094 CD (wil A, wol B), 3633 (ow ‡ D)³, 4168 f, 4806 f, 7210, 7680 f, etc. [Var. C schal ; D shaH.]

> Rhyme words.—general (922, 4806), special (1047), fynal (4806), al (922, 1047, 1912, 4168, 7680).

Pres. Ind. 2 Sing. shalt, (i.) (ii.) 349 (schal thow B, that ‡ C), 808, 2041 (shal trow[e] B, schal trostyn C), 2598 (schat C)⁴, 3546 (xat C)⁵, 5206 (schat C)⁶, 5266 (schat C, shalt(e) D), 5315 (shaH this D), 6767 (shalt(e) D), 7657 (schat C, shalt(e) D), 7662 (shal B, schat C, shalt(e) D)⁷, 7671 (shal B, schat C), 7825 (-(e) D), etc. [Var. C schalt.]—shaltow, 803 (schuldyst ‡ thou C, thou shalt ‡ have D), 5271 (shaltow(e) B ; *pret.* C ‡ ; D †), 6391 (shaH thou D).

---

¹ Scansion doubtful. ² "Now may I iape of the if that I shal."
³ "And by that feith I shal'(=owe) Pryam of Troye." ⁴ 9-syl. in D.
⁵ Supply [*for*] in A, [*in*] in D. ⁶ Supply [*this*] in A. ⁷ Read *soo*[*ne*] in D.

§ 123.]   *of Chaucer's Troilus.*   325

Pres. Ind. 3 Sing. shal, (i.) 236, 651, 1131 f (schalle B †) (: al : wal), 2358, 3640 (shalt † A, wól D), 5255, etc. [Var. BC schal; D shall, shaH, shat.]

Pres. Ind. 1 Pl. shal, shul, (i.) 2106, 3502 (shullen not B)[1], 5068, 5452, 5983 (schal ‡ ȝe *C*), 6178, 6761 (cf. 804 ‡ D, 5456 D, 6185 ‡ C); (ii.) shul here (*adv.*), 6841 [2]. —shulle, 3794 (shul BD, schuln C), 5984 (shal B, shaH D, schal ‡ eueremore C); we schul[le]n twynne, 5932 C (*pret.* ABD). [Var. C schal, schul; D shaH, shat.]

Pres. Ind. 2 Pl. shal, shul, (i.) 1177, 6151, 7217, etc., etc.; (ii.) shal ek, 6133; shul ek, 6147; shul han, 122. [Var. BC schal; C schul; D shaH.]—shullen dar, 3503 (schul[le]n C, sholdyn neither D).—Ye shul (schal C, shal GCp. John's) nomore haue (han BC Cp. John's) soueraynte (-eynte BDG, -eignete Cp. John's, -anitee E, seurete of me C), 3013.

Pres. Ind. 3 Pl. shal, shul, (i.) 5449, 7256, 7257, etc. etc. (ii.) shal it, 1365; shal han, 122. [Var. BC schal; C schul; D shaH.]

Pret.[3] 1 Sing. sholde, 923 (-[e] D)[4], 1025 f (D †) (: nolde 1 *sg.*), 1257 (-[e] D), 1438 (-[e] BD), 3219 (-[e] D), 3239 (-[e] BD), 3335 f (-d D) (: wolde 3 *sg.*), 5118, 5298 f (-d B) (: wolde 3 *sg.*), 6241 (-[e] B); shold[e] don, 1474 (-e C; A †). [Var. B scholde; C schulde; D shulde.]—sholde to, 2291 (-d B, -[é] hym D, schuldë him C); cf. 5271 D †, 6850 ‡ C.—sholde, 17 (-e sterve ‡ D), 1410, 2349, 3435, 6023, etc., etc. [Var. B shold, schold; C schulde; D shold, should, shulde.]—shuld I, 8095 (shold B, shulde D).—sholde han, 5213 (shulde haue D, schulde also C); sholdé haue, 5228 (-[e] B, schuldé C; shuldë D).

Pret. 2 Sing. sholdest, 774 (schuldyst C, sholdist D); sholdestow, 6714 (schuldist thow C, shuldest thou D); shuldestow, 7651 (shold-estow B, schuldist thow C, shuldest thou D). Cf. 803 ‡ C, 3124 ‡ D, 5271 ‡ C.

Note.—Of these 774, 6714, 7651, may perhaps be regarded as subjunctives see § 107).

Pret. 3 Sing. sholde, shulde, 76 f (-d D), 521 f, 728, 2120 (B †), 3374 f (-d D), 3603, 4511 f, 4878 f, 5852 f, 6185 (we ‡ shul[le] C),[5] 6474 f, 6610 (-e ‡ D), 6621 (-e ? C), 6825 (solde B), 7269 f, 7364 (D ?), 8127 f, etc., etc. [Var. BD shold[e]; C scholde, schulde.]—sholde,

---

[1] In C read *ly[gge]n*.   [2] "Intendestow that we shul here bleue" (var. be-leue).
[3] In the case of *sholde, -en, wolde, -en*, and *nolde, -en* no attempt is made to distinguish between the indicative and the subjunctive.
[4] In C supply [*that*].
[5] "Vs sholde neyther lakke gold(e) ne gere" (*impersonal*).

shold, 1498, 3826 (D?), 7913. [Var. C schulde; D shulde.] Before *he, his, hym, here* (acc.), *han* (inf.), *haue* (inf.),—sholde, shulde, shold, shuld, 228, 813, (-[e] ‡ he D), 1638, 2841, 3399, 3856, 3924, 6417, 7636 ABD. [Var. B schold, scholde; CD schulde.].—sholde holde, 4726 (-[e] BD).—sholde destroyed, 68 (shulde ‡ be D); sholde cause, 5726 (shulde D); cf. sholde, shold, schulde, shulde, 306 † A, 2381 CD, 7427 CD, 7767 ‡ C.

Rhyme words.—Only *wolde* and *nolde*.

Pret. 1 Pl. sholden, (i.) 5932 (schul[le]n C, shulde D); shuld[en] al, 8188 A (sholden B); schulde, 5288 ‡ C.

Pret. 2 Pl. I. sholden, (i.) 4737 (-[e] B, -yn D)¹, 6027 (-e CD), 6219 (-e BD, -yn C); sholdyn, 3503 ‡ D. II. sholde, 2993 (-en B, -[e] D), 3626 f (-d D) (: nolde *pl.*), 6171 (-on B, -en D, -yn C †), 7243 (-en B)².—shulde, 6488 (shold B, schulde C, shulden D).—scholde, 3719 ‡ C; shulde ‡ ye, 4973 Cᶜ.—louen sholde òn, 3639 (shòlden louen oòn B, schulde louyn on C, shòld love òn D). [Var. to I., C schulde, schuldyn; D shulde. Var. to II., C scholde; D shulde, shulden.]

Pret. 3 Pl. sholden, (i.) 73 (-e C, -[e] D), 3386 (-[e] B, xulde C, shold ‡ fle D),³ 3799 (-e B, -d anon *sg.* ‡ D; *line* om. † C), 4798 (-e C, -[e] D); cf. schuldyn, 6171 C †. [Var. C schulde.]—sholde, 2923 (-[e] B, -en D, schulden C), 6989 f (schold B, schulde C, shulde D †) (: wolde *ind. 3 sg.*); shulde, 1496 (schulde C, sholden B, shold[e] D); shulde, 4681 (sholde B, shold ‡ cause D); sholde han (*inf.*), 872 (schulde C, shold D),⁴ 3273 (shold D, schulde a C); sholde his, 4815 (-d D, schulde C) —sholde hire (*gen. pl.*), 4848 (-en B, -yn D, schulde C).

Pres. Subj. 1 Pl. shulle, 5288 (shul B, shall D, schulde ‡ C).⁵

Pres. Subj. 2 Pl. shul putte, 3719 (scholde ‡ C, shal † he *ind.* D).

Note.—5288 is after *though* (hypothetical future case); 3719 is in protasis.

VIII. *may.*

Pres. Ind. 1 Sing. may, (i.) (ii.) 922⁶, 1008, (mowe B, mow D), 1563 f (3 *sg.* CD), 2183⁷, 7435 f, 7772 f, 7984 f, 8059 f.

Pres. Ind. 2 Sing. (i.) (ii.) In A,—mayst, 600, 806, 1045, 2070, 2450, etc., etc.; maist, 5699. In B,—mayst, 600, 806, 1045, 5244; maist, 2070, 2450, and usually. In C,—mayst, 2450, 3027,

---
¹ Supply [*that*] in D. ² 9-syl. ³ Dele (*the*) in C.
⁴ Insert [*led*] in C; [*in*¹ in D. ⁵ 9-syl. in C; but supply [*a*].
⁶ Supply [*I*] in B. ⁷ Supply [*not*] in D.

[§ 123.] *of Chaucer's Troilus.*

etc.; mayȝt, 619, 806, 2070, etc.; mayȝ thyn, 6633; mayt, 600, 7795. In D,—mayst, 619, 806, 1045¹, etc., etc.; maist, 5208, 5244, etc.; maist(e), 5295; may, 600.

maystow, 623 (mayst thou CD),² 673 (mayt thou C, mayst thow D), 2101 (mayst thou CD), 3738 (mayst thou C, may thow D), 4927 (mayst thou C, maist thou D), 7522 (mayst thu C, maist(e) thou D), 8074 (maist(e) thou D); cf. 5208 B, 7493 B. [Var. B maistow.]

Pres. Ind. 3 Sing. may, (i.) 147,³ 253, 3831 f, 3901 f, 4428 f, 5826 f, 6512 f, 7354 f, etc.

Pres. Ind. 1 Pl. may, (i.) 987, 1663, 6176, 6179 ‡ C, 6191, 6752 C,⁴ 6753,⁴ 6792 (That we may). (ii.) 2416, 6179 ABC; may haue, 6887 (D ?).—mowe, 6168 (mow B, now † C, may D (?)).

Pres. Ind. 2 Pl. may (i.) 54 (shall D), 1490⁵, 3688,⁶ 4124 ‡ D, 4843 ‡ D, 4956, 5519, 5555 (C † D †)⁷, 5856 (can C), 5990 (D †)⁸, 6013, 6299⁹, 6320, 7360, 7698, 7744. (ii.) 30, 4843 ABC, 7987; may his, 3752; may here (*acc.*), 3528 (C †); may here (*gen. sg.*), 8139 (B †); may here (*inf.*), 5747 BC (A ? D ?), 7000 (A †), 7315 (mow B, schul C), 7679 (schul C), 7952.—mowen ellys, 5992 (-ë B, moun *dissyl.* C, mow[ë] D).

Pres. Ind. 3 Pl. may, (i.) 120, 644¹⁰, 756 (moun *monosyl.* C), 2242 (may it ? C)¹¹, 2732, 4124 (may ‡ ȝe 2 *pl.* D), 4307 (C †, mowen D †), 4853, 4932,¹²·5710¹³, 6118, 6706, 7495 (mough D). (ii.) 839 (C ?), 4056, 8116 (*om.* B † (?)), 8213.—mowe not, 5740 ABD (*the passage is not in* C). [In several of the instances cited the subject is *men.*]

Pres. Subj. 1 Sing. may, (i.) 863, 1530, 2486 f, 3561,¹⁴ 6324, 6785 f, 6979, 7551 f, 8080 f.¹⁵

Pres. Subj. 3 Sing. may, (i.) 1017 BCD (wole A),¹⁶ 1616, 1949, 2875, 5941 (schal C), 6262 f, 7159 f. (ii.) 3819 (may ‡ the C).¹⁷—mowe neuere, 959 A (may BCD).

Pret. Ind. and Subj. 1 Sing. myghte, 4120 (-[e] B, myȝte C, miȝte D); mygh[te], 1797 (myght[e] BD, myȝte C); myghte, 3230 (myȝte C, might D); myght¹⁸ (*bef. vowels*), 19 ‡ D, 1651, 3473, 3892, 7460; myght hym, 3744 (myȝte C); -e here (*acc.*), 6972 (-t B,

---

[1] Supply [*But*] in D. [2] Read de[ue]l in C.
[3] 9-syl. in CD. [4] Indirect question.
[5] 9-syl. Perhaps subjunctive. [6] Supply [*that*] in D. [7] Dele (*as*) in A.
[8] 9-syl. [9] Subjunctive ? Supply [ye] in A. [10] Supply [*and*] in D.
[11] Purpose-clause. [12] C reads : what may me now the calle. Supply [*now*] in D.
[13] 9-syl. But read *mowen* or *which[e]* ? D has *whiche*. [14] Read (*re*)*turne* in D.
[15] Several of these are hardly to be distinguished from indicatives.
[16] Supply [*that*] in D.
[17] Some of these are hardly to be distinguished from indicatives.
[18] Var. C *myȝte* (in all), D *might*.

328　　　　　*Observations on the Language*　　　　[§ 123.

myȝt C, might D).[1]—myght best, 2515 (myȝte ‡ 3 *sg.* C, might[e] (?) ‡ D).—myght[ë] ∥ I, 5121 (-ë B, myȝte C, myght D); -[ë] I, 7652 (myȝtë C, myȝt[ë] D, myght[ë I] B).[2]

Pret. 2 Sing. myghtest, 7890 (myȝtist C, mightest D †); myghtestow, 4924 AB.

> Note.—7890 is perhaps subjunctive (see § 107).—In 619, readings vary: Parauntor thow myght (*so* ABG, mayȝt C, mayst D) after swych on longe. (No note in Mr. Austin's collation.)

Pret. Ind. and Subj. 3 Sing. myghte, 373 (myȝt[e] B), 1075 AB, 2204 f, 2379 f (-t C), 2655[3], 2838 (-t ‡ the D), 3186, 3925 f (-t B, myȝt C, miȝt D),[4] 4697 f (-t B), 4822 (-[e] B),[5] 4823 (-[e] B), 5647 (-[e] B), 5849 f (myȝt C), 5880 f (myȝt C), 6551 f (myȝt C), 6874 f, 6995 f (myȝt C), 7155 (-[e] B), 7157 (-[e] B), 7192 f (-t B, myȝt C), 7382 f, 7998 f. [Var. D *might*[*e*] or *myght*[*e*] in most of the verses above-cited; C myȝte.]—myght[e], 1029 (-e C), 1536 (-e C), 2064 (-e BC)[6], 2499 (-e C, mygth[e] B), 2525 (-e C)[7], 3282, 3734 (myhte? A)[8], 4351 (-e BC, miȝt ‡ not D), 4445 (-e CD), 5792 (-e C, -ë ‡ other B), 6535 (-e C), 7171 (-e C), 7566 f (-e B), 7583 B (miȝt[e] D, see below), 8100; cf. 1656, 4564 D. [Var. BD might[e]; C myȝte, myȝt[e]; D miȝte.]—myghte, 2660 (mygth B; D(?)), 2941, 3362,[9] 5485, 6923 (myȝt C); cf. 1539, 5033. [Var. B myght (*in all except* 2660); C myȝte; D myght, might (*in all*).]—myght (*bef. vowels*), 638 (-e C), 2135 (myȝtë ‡ no C, might ‡ no D), 3442, 4002 (-e C), 7788 (-e C); cf. 2922, 4033. [Var. C myȝte, myȝt; D miȝt.] —myghte his, 2411 (-t BD); myghte him, 562 (-t BD); myght he, 370 (-e C), 3923 (-e C); -t haue (*inf.*), 1277 (-e han B, miȝtë ‡ han C, might[ë] haue D), 1796 (-t han C), 7102 (-t han B, -e a C); might he, 1519 (myght B, miȝt C); cf. 823, 2956, 3728, 3955, 4911, 6645, 7583. [Var. BC myȝt; C myȝte; D might, miȝt.]—myght holden, 5260 (may C); myght neuere, 5644 AB (might D; *not in* C); myght to, 8151 AB (miȝt D); myȝt non, 7317 C (might D, may A, may it B); cf. 1539 ‡ D, 2135 ‡ D, 3264 ‡ D, 4351 ‡ D, 5033 ‡ D; myȝte, 1739 ‡ C, 5370 ‡ C (myght D?).—myghtë here (*inf.*), 3586 (-[ë] BD, myȝtë C); myghtë ‡ other, 5792 B; myghtë ‡ here (*acc.*), 1056 A (myȝte B, might D).

---

[1] Supply [*to*] in A.
[2] How myght (myȝte C, myȝt D) I (*om.* B) than (thanne C) do (don BC Cp. John's, doo D) quod Troylus.
[3] Supply [*wel*] in D.　　　　[4] Supply [*that*] in C.
[5] CD are too short, even if -*ë* be read.
[6] Supply [*me*] in C.　　　　[7] Supply [*wel*] in D.
[8] For *myhte a dedë man* in A, read *myhtë dedë men*.　　　[9] Read *here*[*to*] in A.

§ 123.]   *of Chaucer's Troilus.*   329

Rhyme words.—with sighte (2379), from sighte (6995), in highte (7192), bryghte *adj. pl. or adv.* (7382), plighte *pret. ind. 3 sg.* (2204), sighte, syghte, *pret. ind. 3 sg.* (3925, 5880, 7998), twyghte *pret. ind. 3 sg.* (5849), alighte *pret. ind. 3 sg.* (6551, 7382), highte *pret. ind. 3 sg.* (7998), byhygt[e] *pret. ind. 3 sg.* (byhighte B, behyȝt[e] C, behighte[e] D) (7566), byhight[e] *pret. subj. 3 sg.* (bihighte B, behyȝte C, behight[e] D) (6374), lyghte *inf.* (3925, 6995), fighte *inf.* (4697), dyghte *inf.* (5849).

Pret. 1 Pl.   myghte, 1596 (-en B, -yn D, myȝtyn C †); myghten, (i.) 6850 (-e B, myȝtyn C, might[e] D).

Pret. 2 Pl.   myghte, 6172 (-en B, myȝtyn C, myght[e] D).

Pret. 3 Pl.   myghten, (i.) 1815 (myȝte C, myght[e] D), 2524 (-[e] B, myȝtyn in C, might[en] in D), 2709 f (myȝtin C, mightyn D).— myghte, 614 (-[e] BD, myȝtyn C), 1726 (-[e] BD), 1751 (-[e] D) [1], 2031 f (myȝt C, myght D), 2734 (-en B, -[e] D, myȝte ‡ C) [2], 3609 (myȝtyn C, myght ‡ this D), [3] 6612 (-[e] B). [4] [Var. C myȝte ; D mighte, -[e].)—myght[e], 3351 (-e B, myȝte C †;.D ?), 3605 (-e B, myȝte C, might[e] D).—myghte, 1439 (om. † B, -t D †), 2702 (-t D), [5] 7324 (-t BD). [Var. C myȝte ; D miȝt, might.]—myght (*bef. vowels*), 286 (myȝtyn in C) [6], 3264 (-e B, might ‡ not D), 3318 (-e C), 6948 (-e C ; D †). [Var. C myȝt, -e ; D miȝt.]—myghte hym, 279 (-t BD) ; -e hire (*poss. sg.*), 5337 (-t D, koude A) ; myght hym, [7] 3415 (-e C). [Var. C myȝte.]

Note.—Of these examples of the *pret. 3 pl., men* is the subject in 279, 286, 1439, 1726, 1815, 2702, 3415, 3609, 6948 ; *al the world* is the subject in 3264, 3318, 5337.

Rhyme words.—hyghten *pret. ind. 3 pl.* (2709), dyghte *pret. ind. 3 sg.* (2031).

Infin.   mowen,—To mowen (so ABG Cp. John's, moun C, wyn D) swych a knyght don (so BC Cp., om. A, doon G, to D John's) lyue (leuyn C) or dye (deiȝe C), 2679.—to mowe ‡ dwelle, 7213 C (maken AB, make D).

IX. *mot.*

Pres. Ind. 1 Sing.   (i.) (ii.) mot, moot, 224 (-(e) BD, is ‡ ffor C [c]), 573 (-(e) BCD), 1621 (-(e) B, must D, me muste C), 4037 f (-e BCD) (: in his fote ; foot B, foote D : sot *sbst.* (=*soot*), soot B, sote CD), 4129 (-(e) BD), 5408, 6284 (-(e) C) ; cf. 2889, 3429 C, 4676, 6681, 6784, 7692.

Pres. Ind. 2 Sing.   most, (i.) (ii.) 520 (must(e) C, must D), 5129

---
[1] Or singular : Now myghte som enuyous iangle thus.
[2] Supply [*hym*] in AB. ACD may be singular.   [3] Supply [*for*] in B.
[4] Dele (*as*) in A. C is out of order.
[5] "So heynous that men myghte on it spete" (*heynous* or *myghte on*).
[6] "Shewed wel that men myght yn here gesse" (9-syl., but D supplies *She* †).
[7] A has *hem* †.

330 *Observations on the Language* [§ 123.

(moost B, must(e) C, muste D †), 5310 (mayst ‡ C, must(e) D), 7822 (must D, *om.* † C).

Pres. Ind. 3 Sing. mot, (i.) 2456 (moot B, mot(e) D); cf. 1524, 1701, 3406, 3636, etc., etc.—mot(ę), 6247 A (moot B, mot(ę) (?) C; D †). (Cf. *pret.* 3 *sg.*)

Pres. Ind. 2 Pl. mote, 2754 C (moste A, most B, must D).

Pres. Ind. 3 Pl. moten ouer, 846 (-yn CD)[1]; mote hire (*poss. sg.*), 847 (-yn C); motę spenden, 6038 (moot B, mot C †, must D).[2]

Pres. Subj. 1 Sing. mote I, 1220, 7270 (mot B); mot I, 341 (-e BD)[3], 1210 (-e BCD), 2230 (-e BCD)[4], 4048 (-e C), 7347 (-e CD), 7523 (moot B, mote C; D ?). (All these in wishes : as, *so mote I gon, as mot I the*.) I bidde god I neuere mot haue ioye, 3717 A (-e BG, I preye to god neueremore haue I ioye C, I pray to god y neuer more have ioy D; no note in Mr. Austin's collation).

Pres. Subj. 3 Sing. to good[e][5] mot it turne, 1175 (-e BCD); so mot he neuere the, 1755 (-e BC); sory mot he ben, 2141 (-e BCD); longe mot youre lyf in ioye endure, 4988 (-ę BD, motë ‡ ȝe 2 *pl.* C).

Pres. Subj. 2 Pl. mot ye lyue, 1487 (-ę BCD); motë ‡ ȝe, 4988 C (3 *sg.* ABD).

Pret. Ind. 1 Sing. most (*bef. vowels*), 3429 (mot C, must D), 4676 B (must D, mot A)[6]; moste here (*poss. sg.*), 5232 (-t B, must D; C †); y must ‡ nedis, 1621 D; I must[e] nedis, 6681 D † (mot AB, mot C †). (In all these cases with the force of the present tense and with the meaning of modern *must.*)

Pret. Ind. 3 Sing. moste, 74 (-[e] BD); 3401 (-[e] BD), 3465 (-[e] B; D ?)[7], 4000 (-[e] BD), 4878 (-[e] BD), 5373 C (-[e] D), 8025 (-[e] B). [Var. C muste; D must[e], muste.][8]—most[e], 4551 B (muste C, must[e] D).[9]—moste, 2385 (-t BD), 3999 (-t B), 4004 (-t BD, mot ‡ C), 6368 (-t B), 6433 (-t D).[10] [Var. C muste; D must, -e].—most at, 3382 (-e B, muste C, moost D).—moste his, 6441 (-t BD); -e hem, 4551. [Var. C muste; D must.]

Note 1.—In all these cases of the *pret. ind.* 3 *sg.* the verb has its proper preterite function. The modern sense (in which *must* is equivalent to a present tense) is seen in *moste*, 216 A (schall B, mot B, must D). C shows four instances of this latter use : *muste* ‡ *ben*, 6261 C (muste D, mot AB), *muste* ‡ *for*, 6422 C (mot AB, mot(e) D) ; *me* ‡ *muste nedis*, 1621 C, 7715 C. D several times substitutes *must* (in a present sense) for *mot* (etc.) of

---

[1] Read *ioye[s]* in C.   [2] In 6038 the subject is *men*.
[3] Supply [*that*] in C.   [4] In A read *to deth[e]* and *smet[e]*.   [5] goode BC.
[6] Supply [*I*] in B.   [7] Dele (*At*) in AB (?). In D read *must[e] ō(y)leue*.
[8] In 4000 D has *most[e]*; the usual vowel in this word, however, is *u* for CD, *o* for AB.
[9] In D supply [*day*].   [10] Read (*re*)*torne he* in D.

the other MSS., cf. 1701, 2586, 3406, 3670 : in these four cases a consonant follows, but in none of them (except perhaps in 2586, which is otherwise unsatisfactory) are we to read *mustë*]. Cf. also 4266 ‡ E.

Note 2.—*Must* is used impersonally in *me muste nedis deyen* (pres. sense), 1621 C (I mot A, I moot(e) B, y must D)[1]; *hym most obeye* (pret. sense), 3999 B (he moste A, he muste CD); *mustë ‡ hem bleue*, 7543 C (they moste b[l]euen A, they most[e] bleuen B, thei muste b(e)leue D), which is probably subjunctive. In none of these lines is the impersonal construction apparently the genuine reading. (See Child, § 67, and cf. *Englische Studien*, XIV, 391.)

Pret. Ind. 2 Pl. moste, 2754 (-t B, mot(e) C, must D); 3758 (-t B, muste C, must D). (Both in present sense.)[2]

Pret. Ind. 3 Pl. men moste, 4056 (-[e] B, mustyn C, must[e] D); men mostë axe, 1979 (miste ? C, must[e] D)[3]; men mose, 6016 (most B, moste nedis C †, musten † entercomen D); men . . . must spenden, 6038 D (mote A, moot B, mot C). (All in present sense.)

Pret. Subj. 1 Sing. most I, 1884 (I muste be C, y must[e] be ? D); I moste come, 6023 (-[e] B, muste C, must[e] D). (In both cases = *I should have to*.)[4]

Pret. Subj. 3 Sing. moste, 74 (-[e] BD), 3401 (-[e] BD). [Var. C muste ; D must[e].]—most[e], 5226 (moost[e] B, mot † C, must[e] D).—moste, 3758 (-t B, muste C, must D); -e he, 2160 (moost B, muste C, must D); -e han, 3733 (-t B, muste C, must D). (In all these cases = *would have to*.) Cf. *mustë ‡ hem*, impersonal, 7543 C.

Pret. Subj. 3 Pl. mosten folk, 2592 (mustyn CD); they most[e] b[l]euen, 7543 (muste b(e)leue D, mustë ‡ hem *impers. sg.* C). (In these = *would have to*.)

§ 124. Other irregular verbs.

This list includes *be, wol, nyl, do, go,* and *haue*.

I. *to be*.

Pres. Ind. 1 Sing. am, (i.) (ii.) 10, 223, 6160 (nam BD; may ‡ C), 6782 (nam B), 7069 (nam BD).—nam, 7609 (am C, nam(e) D).

Pres. Ind. 2 Sing. art, (i.) (ii.) 277, 555 (ert(e) D), 648, 1045 (D † ?), 5163 (-(e) D), etc. [Var. B ert (*usually*).]—artow, 509 (art thou C, art(e) thou D), 731 (art thou C, art(e) thow D); art thow, 507 (artow B, art thou C, art(e) thou D), 3579 (art tow B; C (?)).

---

[1] Supply [*that*] in B.   [2] 3758 may be construed as subjunctive.
[3] If *moste* be read, the verse becomes 9-syl.
[4] But in 1884 perhaps rather in a present (future) sense "How bysy if I loue ek most I be."

Note.—In "Al wrong by god what seystow man wher arte," 7524 f (arte ABCG, arte D; no note in Mr. Austin's collation) (· carte *n.*), *arte* is plainly a colloquial form of *artow* · perhaps it represents the ordinary pronunciation of that contraction. Cf. *fro ye* (: Troye), 5, in which *ye* may be regarded as a similarly weakened form of *yow*.

Pres. Ind. 3 Sing. is, 3622 f (: this), and passim; helle ys, 7739 f (is C) (: wellys *pl.* : ellys); his, 1943 C, 7150 B; ysse, 1013 f A (is BCD) (: thisse : iwysse).[1]—nys, 203 AC (is B)[2], 574 C (is ABD), 684 (ne is C, nis D), 697 (nis B, is D),[3] 2824 f (is CD) (: is), 4570 (ne is C, ther is ‡ (=thei's) D), 7085, etc.; nyis *monosyl.*, 7451 C (is ABD).

Pres. Ind. 1 Pl. (i.) be, 3937 (ben C, beeth D), 7346 (ben B, ben(e) D; C†); be we, 5920, 6847 (C†), 7042 (cf. 5138); ben now, 5986 (ben(e) B, be D); been so, 6511 (ben BC, be D); ben ‡ we, 4049 C. (ii.) ben, 5930 (be D)[4]; be, 5921 (ben BC).

Pres. Ind. 2 Pl. (i.) be, 1320 (ben BC), 3881, 3980 (ben BCD), 7721 (ben CD)[5]; be ye, 202 ABC, 2191, 2552[6], 3599, 4049 (ben C); ben, 1201 (be D), 1669 (be D), 3709 (ben(e) D), 4407, etc.; beth bothe, 984 (ben BC, be D). (ii.) ben, 1433 (be BD), 2825 (ben(e) D), etc.; be ywonne, 2321 (ben BC, be ȝe D)[7]; ben he, 1332 (be D); ben his, 3718 (D†)[8]; ben here (*adv.*), 2836 (ben(e) D).

Pres. Ind. 3 Pl. (i.) Before consonants *ben* and *be* are both found in A, but *ben* (the regular form in BC) is the commoner. D usually has *be* or *ben(e)*, but *ben* occurs in D (*e.g.*, 3134). Cf. 1137, 3134, 3696, 4887, etc. Cf. been, 4205 E; byn, 4595 E. In rhyme,— be, 48 f, 2039 f, 2858 f, 2879 f, 5709 f, 5718 f 7033 f (bee B), 8143 f; ben, 6819 f (bene D) (: to sen). Other forms are,—they *beth* with, 6020 C†, and *arn* (*are*) : arn thei, 999 A (are BC, they are the D); arn clerkes, 5634 A (ern B, were D)[9]; arn woxen, 7737 A (aryn C, are D)[10]; arn, 996 C (are D), *is an error for* erren ABG; no note in Mr. Austin's collation). (ii.) Before vowels *ben* is the usual form, except in D, which commonly (though not always) has *ben(e)*: thus,—1000 (be D), 1973 (ben(e) D), 4180 (been E), etc. Before *h*,—ben his, 2560 (ben(e) D); ben here (*gen. sg.*), 6582 (D†); ben here (*adv.*), 2815 (be D)[11]; ben hertes, 2959 (ben(e) D).

---

[1] This monstrous form serves at least to emphasize the fact that the *s* is unvoiced.
[2] Dele (*that*) in C.   [3] Dele (*yn*) in A.
[4] Supply [*that*] in D.   [5] Dele or slur (*that*) in D.   [6] Supply [*ye*] in AB.
[7] Read [*y*]*wonne* in D.   [8] Supply [*that*] in B.   [9] Not in C.
[10] Leaf cut out of B.   [11] Read *her*[*with*]*yn* in D.

[§ 124.] *of Chaucer's Troilus.* 333

Rhyme words.—charite (48), aduersite (2858), benignite (2879), necessite (5718), subtilitee (8143), me (2039, 5709, 8143), the (2039, 2879), ye (2858), fre (7033), se, y-se *inf.* (5709, 7033).—to sen (sene D) (6819).

Pres. Subj. 1 Sing. be, (i.) (ii.) 832, 859, 2945, 3240 f, 4128 f, 6213 f, etc.

Pres. Subj. 2 Sing. be, (i.) (ii.) 3663, 4473, etc.

Pres. Subj. 3 Sing. be, (i.) 23 f, 308, 349, 1036, 2418 f, 5994 f, etc.

Pres. Subj. 1 Pl. (i.) be, 5450 (ben *ind.* C †)[1], 6144. (ii.) ben, 6276.

Pres. Subj. 2 Pl. (i.) be, 1365 (ben C; B †), 1385 (ben C), 1422 f (: se *ind.* 2 *pl.*), 1426 (ben C), 1935 (*sg.* CD)[2], 2491 f (: me), 5597 (ben CD); And be ye wys as ye ben faire, 1669 (be ... be D); ye heryed ben for, 4655 AB (be D). (ii.) be, 3012 (ben C), 6102 (ben C, be *sit* ‡ D); whanne ye ben his, 1672 (be D).

Pres. Subj. 3 Pl. (i.) ben, 1488 (be BD, hem ‡ C); be, 2243 (ben C), 3158[3], 4769 f ‡ B (*sg.* A; D (?)). (ii.) be his, 4599 (*sg.* B †).

Pret. Ind. 1 Sing. was, (i.) 2497[4], 4733 f (y-wis † D) (: Calkas); cf. 4733 f, 4756 f, 7338 f.—nas, (i.) 2498 BCD (na[s] A).[5]

Pret. Ind. 2 Sing. were, 4160 f (you were E) (: there : fere *timor*); were, 510 (wer ‡ wont D), 3559[6], 5424 ABD; were woned, 901 (were B, were wone C (?))[7].—was thow, 4996 (art(e) ‡ thou D).

Pret. Ind. 3 Sing. was, (i.) 2, 64 f (: Calkas), 4397 f, 5895 f, etc. In 4438, D has the ridiculous form *wesse* (: blesse *inf.*).—nas, (i.) 101 (was BCD), 208 (was D), 1281 (was B), 1769[8]; cf. 281, 6477, 6809, 6831, 6985, 7142, 7177, 8006, 8029. (ii.) nas houre, 6826 (nas oure C, *om.* † D).

Pret. Ind. 1, 2, 3 Pl. were. See § 109.

Pret. Subj. Sing. were. See § 113.

Pret. Subj. Pl. were. See § 114.

Imv. 2 Sing. be, 950, 951 (fe † C), 4472, etc. Once in rhyme,—thow ne be, 6962 f.

Imv. 2 Pl. beth, 431, 1679[9], 2755 (both B, be C), 3010, 3019 (betht B), 4355, 6508[10], 6522, 7977 (be C), 8148 (be B), etc.; buth, 3938 (beth B, be C, beeth D), 5589 (beth BD, be C)[11]. [Cf. 6249.]

Infinitive. A shows: ben, before vowels, 2642, 3323, 3794, and usually; ben, before h, 1823, 2973, and usually; ben, before consonants, 1921, 5446, etc.; be, before vowels, 938, 981, 1536, 4322,

---

[1] Dele (*with*) in D. [2] "thonked be ye."
[3] In C read *be nou3t* for *ben ou3t*; in D read *be* [n]oght.
[4] In C read *for sith* for *forsothe*. [5] Supply [*more*] in D.
[6] Protasis. Read *were* [*in*] in A. [7] But supply [*whi*] in B, and read *were*.
[8] Supply [*al*] in D. [9] Old-style figures indicate that D has *be* (pl.).
[10] Supply [*as*] in D. [11] Supply [*cause*] in A; [*of*] in C.

5197; *be*, before *h*, 468, 1438, 2383, 2526, 7023; *be*, before consonants, 255, 760, etc., etc.

B shows: *ben*, before vowels, 938, 981, and usually; *ben*, before *h*, 1438, and usually; *ben*, before consonants, 758, 1921, 4739, etc.; *be*, before vowels, 350, 609, 1536, 5759; *be*, before *h*, 7023, 7066; *be*, before consonants, 4414, 6178, etc., etc.

C shows: *ben*, before vowels, 938, 2642, and usually; *ben*, before *h*, 468, and usually; *ben*, before consonants, 373, 7491, etc.; *be*, before vowels, 1536, 5461, etc.; *be*, before *h*, 7023, 7066; *be*, before consonants, 74, 7644, etc.

D shows: *ben*, before vowels, 649, 5740, etc. (*ben*, before *h*, seems not to occur); *ben*, before consonants, 3507, 5621, etc.; *ben(e)*, before vowels, 2986, 3142, 3794, etc.; *be*, before vowels, 938, and very commonly; *be*, before *h*, 1438, and always; *be*, before consonants, 255, 1921, and commonly.

At the end of the verse all four MSS. have regularly *be* (see 37 f, 849 f, 1482 f, etc., etc.); *ben*, inf., does not occur in rhyme in the *Troilus*.

Perfect Part. A shows: *ben*, before vowels, 585, 2488, etc., etc.; *ben*, before *h*, 125, 2356, 7680; *ben*, before consonants, 247, 249, 1609, 2081, etc.; *be*, before vowels, 4469, 6505; *be*, before consonants, 242, 638, 1878, 5900, 6590.

B shows: *ben*, before vowels, 585, etc., etc.; *ben*, before *h*, 125, 2356, 7680; *ben*, before consonants, 242, 247, etc.

C shows: *ben*, before vowels, 585, etc., etc.; *ben*, before *h*, 2356; *ben*, before consonants, 247, 249, etc., etc.; *be*, before *h*, 125; *be*, before consonants, 638, 1878.

D shows: *ben*, before vowels, 2488, 7296, 7680, 8008; *ben*, before consonants, 5305, 5756; *ben(e)*, before vowels, 585, 6913; *ben(e)*, before *h*, 2356; *ben(e)*, before consonants, 249; *be*, before vowels, 4469, and usually; *bee*, before vowel, 6129; *be*, before *h*, 125; *be*, before consonants, 247, 638, etc., etc.

At the end of the verse: ben, 1276 f (bene D) (: ben *bees* : flen *ind.* 3 *pl.*); be, 1877 f (se *inf.* CD) (: se *inf.*), 5352 f (bee D) (: se *inf.* : she), 5899 f (: she : me); y-be, 5770 f (i-be BD, be C ‡) (: she : preuete).

Note.—Infinitive and perfect participle coalesce in: I haue and shal *Ben* humble (be D), 1913; cf. 7680.

II. Will.[1]

Pres. Ind. 1 Sing. A has usually *wol* or *wole* (*wole*). Thus,—wol, (i.) 990, 1294, 1560, 1955, 2512, 3001, 6255, 6846; (ii.) 53, 1330, 1358, 1400, 1564.—wole, 981, 1033, 2077, 2665, 2719, 2770, 2851, 2933, 3226; wole, 427, 599, 1222, 1363, 2247, 2894.—wol han (*inf.*), 3581; wole haue (*inf.*), 2733.—A also has *wil* : thus,—(1.) 266, 2094, 5121; (ii.) 2144.

B almost always has *wol*. Thus,—(i.) 266, 981, 990, 1033, 1294, 1531, 1955, etc., etc.; (ii.) 53, 427, 1330, 2247, 2894, etc.; before *h*, 2733, 3581. Other forms in B are : wole, 1053; wil, (i.) 589[2], 3226; wil, (ii.) 1222, 2144; will, (ii.) 599; wel, (i.) 1560.

C has usually *wele* (*wele*). Thus,—wele, 758, 981, 990, 1033, 1531, etc.; wele, 549, 1222, 1330, 1363, etc.; wele han, 3581. But *wil* also occurs : thus,—(i.) 2719, 2933, 3001; (ii.) 1400, 1564; wil han, 2733.

D has : wole, 1231, 1560, 2077, 2512, etc.; wole, 1222 (?)[3], 1363, 2144; wol, (i.) 1955[4], 2665, 3001 (?); wol, (ii.) 1400, 1564, 2247; wol haue, 3581; wul, (ii.) 2894; wil, (i.) 266, 990, 1033, 1409, etc.; wil, (ii.) 427, 1358; wyl, (i.) 1294; will, (i.) 7445†; will, (ii.) 1330.—In 2733 D, *wole have* (inf.) should be *wole have* (supply [*ye*]). In 3137 D, *wole abregge* should be *wilne as now tabregge*.

Note.—589 appears to be a 9-syl. verse : "I wole (wil BD, wele C) parten with the al thyn pyne." Mr. Austin makes no note. G agrees with A.

Pres. Ind. 2 Sing. wilt, wylt, (i.) (ii.) 3254,[5] 3551 (wolt B), 4301 f (whi † B) (: agilt *p.p.*), 4926 f (-(e) D) (: agilt *p.p.* : spilt *p.p*); cf. 719 † C, 2109 † D, 2148 † C, 3045 ‡ C, 4944 ‡ C.—wolt, (i.) (ii.) 2040 (wilt(e) B)[6], 2514 † C, 3178, 7669 (woldest ? D), 7881. [Var. CD wilt, wylt]—wyltow, wiltow, 1011 (woltow B, wilt thow CD), 4931 (wilt thou C; D †); woltow, 2446 (wiltow B, wilt thou (thow) CD), 7520 (wilt thow C, will thou D);[7] wolt thow, 2532 (wiltow B, wilt thou C).

Pres. Ind. 3 Sing. Not different from 1 *Sing.* (cf. 1456, 1481, 2042,

---

[1] For scribe's confusion between *willan* and *wilnian*, see 2963 A, 3137 D, 5277 C.
[2] 9-syl. verse.
[3] Line too long.
[4] Supply [*scyd*].
[5] AB are short by two syllables; CD are 9-syl. : Tel (Telle G) (CD insert *me*) which (-e G) thow wylt (wilt BCDG) of euerychone. No note in Mr. Austin's collation.
[6] Supply [*And*] in A.
[7] Supply [*now*] in CD

6290, etc., etc.). The following forms may be noted,—wyl be, 1545 A; wyl no, 1015 C; wyll how, 4133 ‡ E; wyllę, 537 C; welë ‡ nedis, 5277 C[1]; wolë ‡ ben, 6265 A; welę ‡ wondere, 6857 C (*l.* wolde); wele ‡ away, 6290 C.

Pres. Ind. 1 Pl. wolę go, 2256 (wol BD, welę C); wol the, 4305 (nilę D, welë ‡ no C); wole hym, 2541 (wol B, welyn C); wil haue, 2717 † C; wele ‡ no, 4305 C (wol the AB, nilę the D).

Pres. Ind. 2 Pl. A has usually *wol* or *wolę* (*wole*). Thus—wol, (i.) 1297, 3774, 3816, 3969, 4010, 4654, 5865; (ii.) 1578; wol han (*inf.*), 5579.—wolę, 2686, 2825, 2866, 3708, 3725, 4133, 7274, 7345; wole, 6034, 6188 (*subj.* ?).—*Willę* occurs once (2963).[2] In 1473, *wole* should be *wolde*, and in 2713 *wole* should be *wolę* (supply [*me*]). In 3946, read *pulle*[*n*] and *wolę*.

B has usually *wol*: thus,—(i.) 1297, 2825, 2866, etc.; (ii.) 1578, 6034; wol haue (*inf.*), 2831 (*subj.* ?), 5579.—But,—wolę, 2713; welę, 3725; wel, (i.) 3774; wil, (i.) 1396 (*subj.* ?), 4010.—In 3946, read *pulle*[*n*] and *willę ye*.

C has *wil* or *welę* (*wele*). Thus,—wil (i.), 2686, 3708, 3816, 3946, 4010, 4133, 5865; welę, 1297, 2713, 2825, 3774, 7274, 7345; wele, 1578[3], 6034; cf. 6188 (*subj.* ?); wele haue (*inf.*), 5579.

D has: wil, (i.) 1297, 2686, 2825, 2866, 3725, 5865; wol, (i.) 2713, 3774, 3816, 4654; wol, (ii.) 1578; wolę, 4010, 4760 ‡ (*subj.* ?); wiH, (i.) 7242, 7345; wiH, (ii.) 6034 (cf. 2715 †) (*subj.* ?), 6188 (?) (ye wiH = ye'll); wiH have (*inf.*), 5579.—wolyn ‡ dweH, 3493; wole ʒe, 3946.[4]

Pres. Ind. 3 Pl. wolę, 3033, 4222 (wyl E)[5], 4785. [Var. BD wol; C welę.]—wol, (i.) 3776 AB, 5249 AB (wul D), 7423 (C ‡), 7428. [Var. C welę; D wil, wiH.]—wol hem, 7256 (wil C, wiH D)[6]; wol hate, 7426 (wele C, wiH D).—wolen til, 3610 (wollen B, welyn C, willyn D).—wolë mucche, 907 A (*but read* wolde *with* CG Cp.; wold[e] BD).

Pres. Subj.[7] 1 Sing. lest I wol ‡ of, 716 B (wold A, wolde C; wold ‡ the D).

Pres. Subj. 3 Sing. wolę (*in protasis*), 715 (wil BC; D †); wol haue (*in protasis*), 5968 (wele C, wiH D); wol don (with *if*[8] = *whether*),

---

[1] The correct reading is *wilncth fro*. [2] The correct reading is *wilnë that*.
[3] Dele (&) [4] But read *pulle*[*n*] and *wolę*.
[5] Supply [*that*] in E. [6] Subjunctive (?).
[7] Subjunctive constructions cannot always be distinguished with certainty from indicative.
[8] A has *of* for *if*.

[§ 124.] *of Chaucer's Troilus.* 337

852 (welẹ C, wil D); lest that the cherl wolẹ falle, 1017 A (may BCD).¹ Cf. welë ‡ nedis, 5277 C. *Er I wol forther go*, 3123 B (welẹ C, wolẹ D, *om.* † A) is perhaps indicative.

Pres. Subj. 2 Pl. wolẹ (*ind. quest.*), 1396 (wil BC, wol D); -ẹ (with *but yf*), 4760 ‡ D; wolẹ (with *but = unless*), 462 (wol B; *om.* C † D †); -e (with *if that* in *ind. quest.*), 6034 (wol B, welẹ C, wiłł D); -e (*in protasis*), 6188 (wol B, welẹ C, wiłł D †); wol, (i.) 1659 (welẹ D) (*in protasis with* but), 7704 (welẹ C, wiłł D) (with *that*, objective clause of purpose); willẹ (*ind. quest.*), 2963 (wilne B, wiln C †, wolde D †); wol ‡ have (with *though*), 2831 (*pret.* BCD).

Pret. 1 Sing. wolde, 2919, 3490 (wold ‡ go D), 3854, etc. [Var. BD wold[e].]—wolde, 865, 3769², 7462 (wilde ? C, wolde ? D). [Var. BD wold.]—wold I, 2232 (-e C, walde B), 3342 (-e B, -ë † not C).—wolde here (*dat.*), 2091 (-[e] telle D); -e hym, 2966 (D †), 3715 (-d B; D †); -e haue (*inf.*), 5168 (-e a CD), 8041 (-d B, -e a C); wold han (*inf.*), 1499 (-e a C, -d haue D).—wolde, 2512 ‡ C, 2770 ‡ C, 8140 ‡ D (?).

Note.—In 5903 the correct reading is perhaps *wolde han slawe* (see § 122, XII.); Mr. Austin's collation has no note; ABCDG read,—My (Myn C) selue (self B, seluyn C, silf D, selfe G) I wolde (wolde I C) haue (han B, a C) slayn (slawe C, slayne DG) quod she tho (too D).—In 3864 A *woldẽ on* should be *wolde vpon* (*so* BC, wold vpon D).

Pret. 2 Sing. woldest, 4487 (-ist C, -ist ‡ thou D), 5103 (-yst C).³

Note.—In 4944 we should perhaps read: Nought roughte I whider that thou woldest me stere. Mr. Austin's collation has no note; ABCDG have : Nought (Nouȝte G) rought (rouȝte CG) I wheder (-yr C, whidere B, whedirwardes D, whider G) thow (that thou C) woldest (-ist C, wilt D) me (*om.* D) stere. *Woldest* may be regarded as a subjunctive (see § 106).

Pret. 3 Sing. wolde, 77 (-[e] BD), 2957 f (-d BD), 3064 (-[e] D)⁴, 3333 f (-d *pl.* D), 3458 (-[e] D, wald[e] B), 4509 f, 4828 (-[e] D), 4833, 4885, 6475 f, 6653 (-[e] B), 6874 (-[e] B), 6987 f, 7267 f, 7595 (-ë ‡ he D), 8126 f (-d B), etc.; wold[e], 7578 (-e C; D ?); wolde, 1776 (-d BD), 3287 (-d D, wald B)⁵, 3301 (-d BD), 3344 (-d D, walde B), 4276, 7241 (-ẹ D, woolde B); wolde he, 6901; -e hem, 3303 (-d BD); wold of, 716 (-e C, wol ‡ B, wold ‡ the D); wold he, 4621 B (-e C, -e ‡ ryde A; -d he D (?)); wold hire (*acc.*), 1355 (-e BC), 2678 (nulde C, nold D) (for other cases of *wolde* or *wold* before h in *hym, haue, han,* cf. 501, 2164, 3497, 5045, 7999, etc.).—wolde come, 7949 ACD (wol B); wold ‡ do, 6550 A (wol B, wiłł D, *line om.* † C); cf. 527 ‡ C, 1294 ‡ C, 2459 ‡ C, 2745 ‡

¹ Supply [*that*] in D. ² Supply [*And*] in D. ³ Supply [*thus*] in C.
⁴ Dele (*deiphebus*) in B. ⁵ In C read *mys(e)sid.*

z

C, 5890 ‡ C, 7241 ‡ D, 7789 ‡ D.—woldë ‡ on, 3539 A (-e vpon BC, -d vpon D); -ë I (?), 1830 A (-d BD, -de C); -ë ‡ he, 6839 C¹; -ë ‡ holde, 7999 C.

    Rhyme words.—byholde *inf.* (2957), sholde, shulde *sing.* (3333, 4509, 6475, 7267, 8126), sholde *pl.* (6987).
    Note 1.—In 6510 we may read *wrathë* and *woldę* or *woldë* and *wrathę* : That half (-e D) so loth (-e G, soth C) yowre (ʒoure BC, your DG) wrath-the (wreth BD, wrethe C, wreith G) wolde (-d B) deserue. Mr. Austin's collation has no note.—In 3830 *woldë* (-d BD) *the excellence* admits either *woldë* or -ę.
    Note 2.—The following cases, in which *woldę* appears in wishes (*as wolde god*, and the like), may be put together as indubitably subjunctive,— wolde, 459 (-[e] D), 519 f (: sholde 3 *sg.*) 936 (-[e] D), 4119, 4229, 4607 (B†), 4997, 6487², 6590, 6971 (B has *wold*[e] in all but 519); -e, 526 (-d B).

Pret. 1 Pl.   wolde, 3373 f (-d D) (: sholde 3 *sg.*); wold[e], 6854 (-e b(o)leue CD).³

Pret. 2 Pl.   wolden, (i.) 6226 (-e C, -ę ‡ D), 7754 (-e C); (ii.) 343 (-ë C, -[ë] D); wolden han (*inf.*), 2831 (-yn C, wol B, wold D), 5896 (wold B, -e a CD); woldyn ‡ assent, 2715 C; woldyn ‡ in, 7713 C (nolde AD).—wolde, 2328 (-[e] D, walde B), 2972 (-yn C, -[e] D), 6281, 6536 (-[e] B); -e, 2715 (-yn C, will D)⁴, 6497 (-yn me C, -ë ‡ as D), 8046 ‡ C; -e han (*inf.*), 4348 (-d B, -ë ‡ han C, -ę ‡ me D); woldę ‡ be, 3888 C.

Pret. 3 Pl.   wolden, (i.) 919 (-e C, -[e] D), 1453? (-[e] B, -[e] D?)⁵, 2503 (-[e] D), 3297? (-ę C, -d D)⁶, 6233 (- ęn it? D); (ii.) 2517. [Var. C -in, -yn; D -yn.] wolden han (*inf.*), 915 (-e B, -e a C, *om.* ‡ D)⁷.; wooldyn † ouʒt, 1997 C.—wolde, 150 (-[e] B, nolde C, nold ‡ they D), 3119 (-ë on C, would vpon D), 4819 (-[e] D), 4832 (-[e] D, -e [that] B), 4837 (-[e] BD)⁸, 4879 f (: sholde 3 *sg.*)⁹, 7700 (-en BD, -yn C), 7828 ‡ C; wold[e], 907 BD (C†); wolde, 2520 (-d B, -yn D, -d *sg.* C), 3867 (-d BD, -yn C†); -e hym, 2630 (-d D); -e han (*inf.*), 4839 (-d D).; -e here (*gen. pl.*), 7323; wold afferme, 2673 BD (-yn C, -e *sg.* A).¹⁰—wold ‡ deme, 1546 A (-e BC, -d of D); wold[e], 3333 f D (wolde *sg.* ABC).

---

¹ But read *then*[ne]s and *wolde he*.   ² Supply [*if*] in AC.
³ Supply [*that*] in CD.   ⁴ If we read *it werë good*.
⁵ Men wolden (-yn C, -e Cp., wold BD, wole G)wondren (wonderyn C, wondur D)) to (*om.* B Cp. John's, that G) se (sen BC Cp., seen G) hym come (-yn CG) or (and CD) gon (gone D, goon G).
⁶ So as they dorste (-en G, dorst B, durste C, durst D) how (hough G, so as C, how ferre D) they wolden (wolde CCp., wold D) procede.
⁷ Supply [*they*] in C.
⁸ The subject is *al the world*.
⁹ The subject is *substaunce* (i.e. majority) *of the parlement*.
¹⁰ In C read *of* for *oftin*.

III. *nyl*.

Pres. Ind. 1 Sing. nyl, (i.) 758 (welẹ C)[1], 1231 (wolẹ D), 1562, 2246 (wolẹ A), 3009 (wolẹ D), 6846 BC (wol A, wil D). [Var. C nil; D nel.] nyl, (ii.) 2897 (wolẹ D), 3284 (nel D), 6406, etc.—nel not, 1409 (nyl B, nil C, wil D); nel haue, 1100 (nyl B, nel ‡ neither D).

Pres. Ind. 2 Sing. nylt, (i.) (ii.) 2085 (nelt D), 2109 (C †; wilt † D), 2140 (nelt D)[2], 5190 (nyl thy B, nelt D †).—nyltow, 792 (nylt thou C, nelt thow D), 4912 (nyl-tow B, nylt thou C, nylt(e) thou D), 8071 (nyl to B, nil thou C); cf. 4269, 4965, 5151; neltow, 5150 (nyltow B, nylt thou C, ńylt(e) thou D.)

Pres. Ind. 3 Sing. nyl, nil, (i.) 2474 (welẹ C, nel D), 6538 (nilt D), 6719 (sche nẹ wil C, nilt D); cf. 777, 1015, 5275, 6478 ‡ C; (ii.) nyl he, 6704 (nylt D).[3]—nel ‡ be, 1545 D.

Pres. Ind. 1 Pl. we nilẹ thee, 4305 (wol AB, we welé ‡ no C).

Pres. Ind. 2 Pl. nyl me, 6594 AB (nilt D); nyl not, 7265 (nil D).

Pres. Ind. 3 Pl. nyl, (i.) 37 (*perh. sg.*) (nylt D); nil it, 3776 C (wol not AB, nel hit D).

Pret. 1 Sing. nolde, 1023 f (I nẹ wolde C[c], nold D) (: sholde 1 *sg.*), 5997[4]; nold[e], 5248 (nylde C, noldẹ ‡ D); nolde, 5899 (-d B, I nẹ wolde C); nold I, 1118 (-ẹ ‡ nat B), 1393 (-d BD, woldẹ C), 1566 (-e C)[5]; I nold ‡ not (?), 3742 (nold[e] setten B, -e settë C, -[e] set D).

Note.—In 2558 the correct reading seems to be *ne wolde I* (so B Cp.): A has *nold I*, which is unmetrical; D has *wold y*, but improperly omits *ne*; C reads *wolde I*, but has'ʒit for *ne*.

Pret. 2 Sing. nodestow, 4106 (noldestow B, noldist thou CD). (For subjunctive, see § 106.)

Pret. 3 Sing. nolde, 77 f (-d D) (: sholde 3 *sg.*), 2134 (-e B, -d hit D), 2308 (-[e] D, wolde A), 3409 (wolde C, wold[e] D ‡), 4787 (-[e] B, nuldè C; D?), 5299 f (: sholde 1 *sg.*), 7314 (-[e] B); nulde, 2574 C (nold[e] D, wolde A, wold[e] B), cf. 1777 D; as nold[e] god, 5228 (-e CD); noldẹ han, 5803 (nulde an C), 7087 (nold B, woldẹ † a C; D?); -e herẹ[6] (*gen. sg.*), 7572 (-d B); -e his, 7593 (-d B); nulde hire (*acc.*), 2678 C (nold D, ne wold AB).—noldẹ don, 6478 (nyl C, wil † D); nold, (i.) 2643 A (-e BC, wold D).[7]

Pret. 2 Pl. nolde, 3625 f (-d D) (: sholde 2 *pl.*); nolde, 7713

---

[1] Supply [*not*] in D.   [2] Supply [*that*] in D.
[3] Supply [*thus*] in D; dele the first (*thus*) in B.
[4] Supply [*Whom*] in C; [*for*] in D.   [5] Supply [*han*] in B. Read *sey*[*ë*] in C.
[6] A has *he* †.   [7] Supply [*to*] in D.

(woldyn C)[1], 8042 (-d B, nolden ? D) ; -e han, 8043 (-d B); nold han, 1503 (nylde an C).

Pret. 3 Pl.   nolde, 150 C (wolde A, wold[e] B, nold ‡ they D), 5851 f (: sholde 3 sg.)[2], 7828 (-[e] B, -en D, wolde C).

IV. do.

Pres. Ind. 1 Sing.   do, 719 (C †).

Pres. Ind. 2 Sing.   dost, (i.) (ii.) 2595, 3238 (-(e) B, doost D), 3244, 4278 (D?), 6960 (doost B, dedyst C, hast D) ; dostow, 7097 B (dost thou C, dost(e) thou D, dost[ow] A).

Pres. Ind. 3 Sing.   doth, (i.) (ii.) 626, 671, 1270 f (-o D ; B †), 2369 f (-e D), etc. B and D sometimes add an irrational -e, which of course is never pronounced (see 1031, 3876, 5542); so also in 7757 A.

Pres. Ind. Pl.   (1) Before consonants,—don, 1237 (doon B, om. † D), 2471 (do D), 3647 (don(e) D) ; cf. 2669, 3724, 6707, 7978 ; doon, 705 (don C, done D †), do, 426 (don C †), 3143 ‡ D, 3967 (B †), 5575 (doo D), 8063 (doth(e) B, don C, don(e) D); doth, 2391 A (dos(e) B, don- C, don(e) D), 2469 (don BC[c], don(e) D).[3] (2) In rhyme,—do, 1111 f (: tho : so)   (3) Before vowels,—don, 134 (-(e) D); cf. 345, 1526, 5086, 7217, 8085. (4) Before *he, hem, here* (adv.),—don, 1124 (doon B, do D), 5845 (-(e) D, don folk C), 7935 , do, 2868.

Pret. Ind. 1, 3 Sing.   dide, 3653 (dede C, did? D †); dude ‡ dye, 7845 C ; did[e] ‡ byseche(?), 3424 D ; dide || for, 4233 (dede C) (cf. 699 ‡ D, 1064 ‡ D, 7292 ‡ C); dide, dede, 2316 (did C, dyd D), 2430, 2788 (ded D),. 3766 (did D) (cf. 3121[4], 4497, 8099, 8100) ; Than he dede erst thurgh hope and *dide* his myght, 2425 (dide . . . om. ‡ B, dede . . . dede C, om. † . . . dede D †). For elision before *his, hym, hem,* cf. 2014, 2654, 3354, 3813.

Pret. Ind. 2 Sing.   dedest, 3205 (-ist CD, didest B) ; dedyst, 6960 ‡ C.

Pret. Ind. Pl.   deden, (i.) 82 (-yn C, dede him D †); diden, 471 f (deden C, dedyn D) (: riden *ind. pret.* 3 *pl.* : abyden *p.p.*); deden hardely, 3055 (-yn D †, diden B, dudyn C); dede al, 4247 (diden BE, dedyn C); ded[e] ‡ flene, 1279 D.

Pres. Subj. 1 Sing.   do, (i.) (ii.) 590, 4142, 5103 (werche D), 5224. [Var. D doo.]

---

[1] In A read *dayes ten* for *ten dayes*.   [2] Double subject.
[3] In 7321 *al that doth it care* appears to be singular in A (alle that doth B, alle that don C, all that doth D, alle that doth(e) G)   (No note in Mr. Austin's collation.)
[4] Perhaps subjunctive

Pres. Subj. 2 Sing. do, (i.) 636, 2401 (9-syl. in CD), 5131, 5276. [Var. D doo.]

Pres. Subj. 3 Sing. do, (i.) (ii.) 980, 2903, 6201 (put ‡ D), 6305.

Pres. Subj. Pl. do we, 2030; do no, 4022 (don C); do me, 7773; doon vs, 1412 (don BC, do D); don amys, 3015 (do D).

Pret. Subj. Sing. dede his, 369 (dydde B); dide hym, 3764 (dede C, did † D).

Imv. 2 Sing. do, (i.) 833, 1022, 2886, 5176 (doo D), etc.; ne do thou, 586.—*do on*, 2039 C (don AB; D †), 3580 (don B, do this C).[1]

Imv.[2] 2 Pl. doth, (i.) 1407 (do CD), 1663 (doth(e) D), etc.; doth hym, 2294; doth herof, 3781 (C †).—do, (i.) 2268 (doth D), 3430 (y ‡ do *ind.* D), 3891, 4018 (doth D, seith ‡ C); do ye, 2915.

Inf. do, don, to done, etc. See § 119, XIII

Perf. Part. (1) Before consonants,—don, 63 A (doun B), 2366 (do D), 3044, 3228 (ido B, ydo D), 5148 A (doon B, doon(e) D), 6419 (don(e) B, do C, doon(e) D); cf. 2544, 2577, 3256, 3917, 4460, 4552, 4923, 4939, 6470, 7429, 7721; harm idon is don who-so, etc., 1874 (ydon . . . don D); do, 3086 (D (?), don ‡ euere C; B †), 4024 (don BC, don(e) D), 4402 (don C)[3]. (2) In rhyme,—do, 1095 f (: Cleo *n. pr.*), 1389 f (: wherto), 1878 f (done D) (: go *p.p.* : so); fordo, 74 f (: Appollo : to go). (3) Before vowels,—don, 1129 (-(e) BD), 1446 (do D), 3703; cf. 1010, 2083, 2530, 3340, 3997, 7102, 8047, 8090; fordon, 525 (-doon B, don(e) D †), 8050 (-(e) D); vndon, 4577 (-(e) D, ondon C).

V. *go.*

Pres. Ind. 1 Sing. go, (i.) 5502 (goo D), 5869 f (goo D) (: wo *n*), 5938 f (goo D) (: two : so).[4]

Pres. Ind. 3 Sing. goth, gooth, (i.) (ii.) 514, 1084, 1418, 3242, 5355, etc.; 3950 f (: wroth *pred. adj. sg.* : oth). B and D sometimes have an irrational -e, which is of course never pronounced.—forgoth here (*gen. sg.*), 6426 (-(e) B).

Pres. Ind. 2, 3 Plur. gon, (i.) 5761 (-(e) D, goth *sg.* C), 6740 C (goth *sg.* ABD); (ii.) 6159 (-(e) D).[4] go, (i.) 7494 (gon C, -n(e) D).

Pres. Subj. 1, 2, 3 Sing. go, (i.) (ii) 1363 f (so : no), 2774 f (: so : two), 3123 ‡ A, 3125, 3155, 5777, 6407 f (: also : two), 7490, [Var. D g. o]—for-go, (i.) 4953.

Pres. Subj. 1, 2. Pl. go, 1570 f (. two : foo), 3771 f (: wo : so), cf.

---
[1] In D slur *do on* and read [*vp*]*on.*   [2] All the cases cited refer to a single person.
[3] Supply [*me*] in B, [*so*] in D.   [4] Perhaps subjunctive.

1299 f, 4358 f; go we, 1700 (gow we B), 2199, 2248, 2690, 2809, 3514, 6187 (goo D), 6765 (goo D), 6886 (goo D); gon, (i.) 7361 (goon D).

Pret. Ind. 1, 3 Sing. wente, (see § 99).—yede, 3 *sg.*, 7206 f (ȝode B, ȝede C) (: Diomede); ȝede, 3 *sg.*, 3548 ‡ C; foryede he, 3 *sg.*, 2415 (-ȝede BC).

Pret. Ind. Pl. wenten, wente, yeden. See § 109.

Pret. Subj. 1, 3 Sing. wente. See § 113.

Imv. 2 Sing. go, (i.) 574, 1481, 2609 (so ‡ C), 5285 (goo D), 8149 (go . . . goo D); go hens, 572.

Imv. 2 Pl. goth, (ii.) 3513 ‡ D; go, (i.) 5601 (goth(e) D).[1]

Inf. gon, (1) Before consonants,—gon, forgon, 53 (-(e) B, go D), 357[2] (C?; go D), 1996 (go BD), 4623 (go CD), 5141 (-goo D), 5624; cf. 1204, 4857, 5417, 5946, 6284, 6432, 6649.—go, forgo, 2256, 3533 (gon C, gon(e) D), 4226 (-ȝon B, -goo E), 5246 (gon C, goo D), 7116 (gon BC, goo D); cf. 1458, 2029, 3582, 5136, 5261, 5989, 7895. (2) In rhyme,—gon, 117 f (gone BD), 1453 f (goon B, gone D), 1627 f (-e BD), 2094 f (-e BCD), 2137 f (-e CD), 2258 f, 2311 f (-e B; D †); cf. 2769 f, 2796 f, 3036 f, 3404 f, 3518 f, 3543 f, 4048 f, 5017 f, 5255 f (goone D), 6023 f, 7270 f; goon, 133 f (gone BD, gon C), 2014 f (gon BC, gone D); gone, 846 f (gon C) (: euerychone), 2686 f (gon C) (: euerychon : anoon).

> Rhyme-words.—bon *os* (2014), ston *n.* (2311, 5017), oon, on *num adj.* (2258, 2769, 3036, 3404, 5255, 7270), noon, non *num. adj.* (133, 1453, 2137, 4048, 6023), anoon, anon *adv.* (117, 1453, 1627, 2014, 2094, 2137, 2258, 2686, 2769, 2796, 3036, 3404, 3518, 3543, 4048, 5017, 5255, 7270), euerychon (2686), euerychone (846), begon *p.p.* (117), ron *pret.* 3 *sg.* rained (3518).
> Note.—The rhymes show that in *gone* the -e is merely parasitic. The only ambiguous rhyme is *euerychon, -e.*

go, 75 f[2] (: Appollo : fordo *p.p.*), 628 f (: so : therfro); cf. 838 f, 1033 f, 2650 f, 3291 f, 3421 f, 3490 f, 4267 f, 4316 f, 4422 f, 4519 f, 4604 f, 4798 f, 4825 f (gon † A), 4884 f, 4966 f, 5086 f (D †), 5119 f, 5150 f, 5786 f, 5905 f, 6087 f, 6171 f, 6217 f, 6589 f, 6890 f, 7025 f, 7347 f, 7501 f, 7624 f.—(3) Before vowels,—gon, goon, 517, 863, 3425, 3486, 5408, 6017, 7058; cf. 2598, 6850, 7151, 7173. [Var. BD gon(e); D goo, go.] (4) go henne, 1294 (gon BC), 3472 (gon C, gette B).

> Note.—In 4181 A has the reading *go-ne* (printed with hyphen): So loth to hem a sondry (asonder B, a sundir C, a sonder E) go-ne (gon it BCCp., gone it E); *leaf wanting in* D; *stanza wanting in* G. Of course *gon it* is right.

[1] Addressed to a single person (perhaps singular)
[2] Old-style figures indicate that *to* precedes the infinitive.

Perf. Part. (1) Before consonants,—gon, goon, agon, forgon, 718 (gone ‡ D (?)), 2107 (go D), 3381 (gon(e) D), 4284, 4527 (ago B, gon(e) D), 4547 (go D), 6598 (gon(e) D †); wo bygon, 2959 (bi- B, be- C); go, 1592 (gon BC, gon(e) D). (2) In rhyme,—gon, 2243 f (-e BD), 3736 f (-e D), 4336 f (-e D), 5309 f (goone D); agon, 1495 f (-e BD), 1807 f (-e D), 4244 f (ygonne † E), 5442 f (gon (?) B, igone C, gone (?) D), 5842 f (-e BD, igon C), 5979 f (-e D), 7688 f (-e D); bigon, bygon, begon,—with *wo, wel. wers, sorwfully*,—114 f (-e BD), 1379 f (-e BD), 1682 f (-e D), 5126 f (-goon D), 5484 f (-e D), 6310 f (-goon D), 7691 f (-goon BD); ago, 5752 f (agoo D, *line om.* † C), 6680 f (ago(n) C, agoo D), 7417 f (agoo D); [a]go (?), 1880 f (ago B, go C, gone D); go, cf. 4358 f C. (3) Before vowels, —gon, 8008 (ben BCD); wo-by-gon, 4372 (-gan B, woo-be-gon C, woo-bigon(e) D) (cf. 6397).—For *went*, see § 121. I.

Rhyme words.—ston *n.* (3736, 5126), won *n.* (5842), oon *num. adj.* (4244), noon, non *num. adj.* (1379, 1807, 3736, 5126, 5342, 6310, 7688, 7691), euerychon(e) (5442), anoon (114, 1495, 4244, 4336, 5309, 5484, 5979, cf. 2243), gon *inf.* (114), don *inf* (1495);—do *pp.* (1880), so (1880, 5752), fo (5752), two (6680), Escaphilo *nom. pr.* (6680), wo (7417), mo (7417)

VI. *haue*.

Pres. Ind. 1 Sing. *haue* is the regular form before consonants: cf. 611, 628, 670, 988, 1133, 1298, 1327, 1467, 1760, 1780, 1955, 2370, 2565, 3173, 3251, 3340, 3350, 3531, 3902 BCD, 4024, 4039, 4349, 4460, 4592, 4691, 4953, 5770, 6032, 6159, 6183, 6272, 6327, 6687, 6783, 7234, 7343, 7419, 7463, 7752, 8197. —haue, 2060 f (: yaue *pret. subj.* 3 *sg.* : saue *pres. subj.* 3 *sg.*), 2942 f (: saue *pres. subj.* 3 *sg.* : graue *p.p.*), 4319 f (: saue *inf.*). —haue herd, 2537, haue hight, 6289,—and so of course before a vowel or weak *h.*—For *haue* before consonants, (not *h*) see 197 ‡ C, 1179 ‡ A, 1381 ‡ D, 2596 ‡ D, 3902 ‡ A, 7752 ‡ C. Cf. also, —hauë ‡ honour, 5232 C; have ‡ in, 6042 D, 6946 ‡ A (B?)

Pres. Ind. 2 Sing. hast, (i.) (ii.) 557, 696, 845, etc.—hastow, 276 (hast thou CD), 4297 (hast thou CD), etc., ne *hastow*, 5512 (ne hast thou? C, ne have ye? D).

Pres. Ind. 3 Sing. hath, (i.) (ii.) 1255, 1952 (hauyth C), 3457 (has B), etc., etc.—nath, (i.) 1862 AB (ne *hath* C), 7562 (ne *hath* C, ne ‡ hath D).

Pres. Ind. 1 Pl. han, (i.) 4853 (have D), 5545 (have D), 5654 (hañ D), 5904 (haue CD), 6757 (haue D), 7519 (haue CD);[1] (ii.) 3779

---
[1] Supply [*for*] in AD (or, in D, read *haue*).

(have D, ȝe ‡ han B); han herd, 1186 (have D).—hauę, 5642 (han D).¹—hauë ‡ nat, 7519 D.

Pres. Ind. 2 Pl. (1) Before consonants *han* is the regular form in ABC, *hauę* in D²: cf. 25, 27, 28, 1446, 1668, 2209, 2325, 2878, 3395, 4102, 4154, 4401, 4954, 5860, 6505, 7353, 7712, 7721, 8059. But *hauę* is found in all four MSS.: thus,—3735 AB, 4768 AB, 5860 B, 7353 C; and when *ye* follows (*hauę ye*) *hauę* is the regular form in all four: cf. 1373, 1413, 3042, 5855 (han ȝe C),³ 5977, 6829, 7619, 8040.⁴ (2) Before vowels,—han, 2964 (have D, han ‡ routhe Cᶜ), 3779 ‡ C, 4742 (haue D). (3) Before *h*, han herd, 2051 (have D), 2632, 2953 (have D), 5469 (have D, ȝe han ‡ D), 5538 (C (?); haue D); han hight, 1577 (have D); haue herd, 6992 (han B; C †).

Pres. Ind. 3 Pl. (1) Before consonants *han* is the regular form in ABC, *hauę* in D: cf. 241, 247, 553, 706, 802, 913, 999, 2478, 3034, 4293, 4299, 4547, 5249, 6877, 7119, 7123 A. But *hauę* occurs in 6877 C, *han* in D 241, 247, 2669; and *hath* is found in 242 ‡ BC, 2467 (?) ‡ D, 4299 ‡ B, 4547 ‡ D. Cf. also,—hauë ‡ suffred, 6778 D (*read* haue [y]suffred). (2) Before vowels,—han, 199 (have D), 1129 (have D), 1973 (have D), 3135, 3194 (han(e) D), 6143 (hauyn C, haue D), 6632 (haue D), 7614 (haue D), 7975 (haue D); cf. 6778. (3) han here (*gen. pl.*), 5658 ABD.

Pret. Ind. 1, 3 Sing. hadde. See § 102.
Pret. Ind. 2 Sing. haddest. See § 106.
Pret. Ind. Pl. hadden, hadde. See § 109.
Pres. Subj. 1 Sing. hauę, 33 AB, 1095, 1740, 3717 ‡ D; haue, cf. 1225, 1609 (*or indic.*), 3632, 3717 ‡ C, 4752; haué myght(e), 8067 ‡ BD (*read* trew[e]ly and hauę).
Pres. Subj. 3 Sing. haue, 955, 1834, 2723, 2771, 7750 ‡ C (hath AD), 7994; haue ‡ spase, 7305 C; haue, cf. 220, 6465; haue he, 21,⁵ 1932 (-e ‡ he A)⁶; haue his, 805; haue ‡ in, 6465 D; haue ‡ hym, 5292 C.
Pres. Subj. 2 Pl. hauę ye, 1667, 2772.⁷
Pret. Subj. 1, 3 Sing. hadde. See § 113.
Pret. Subj. 2 Sing. See § 106.
Pret. Subj. Pl. hadde See § 114.

¹ Supply [*as*] in D.   ² D has *han* in 4653.   ³ *hauę* [*ye*] A.
⁴ *hauę* [ȝe] BC   ⁵ Supply [*my*] in D, or read *hauę* ‡ *he*.
⁶ Supply [*so*] and read *haue he* in A.
⁷ Transpose *clyne* and *the quene* in C.

§ 124] *of Chaucer's Troilus* 345

Imv. Sing. Haue now good nyght, 3183, 3262; haue here my trouthe, 3953.

Imv. Pl. Ne wondreth not ne haueth of it no fere, 3595 (haue BD, hauyth C); haue, 2218 (-yth C), 3908, 4015; haue here (*adv.*), 1409, 3727 (havith D), 6028.

Inf. (1) Before consonants both *han* and *haue* are common in A, B, and C; but *have* is the regular form in D. For *han*, see 467 AB, 638 B, 769 ABC, 872 AB, 900 BC, 915 AB, etc., etc.; for *haue*, see 467 C, 501 AB, 638 A, 899 AB, etc., etc. Cf. 1100, 1277, 1354, 1499, 1566, 1580, 1638, 1796, 2522, 2523, 2717, 2733, 2956, 3255, 3273, 3287, 3581, 4002, 4057, 4683, 4764, 4770, 4774, 4839, 5045, 5046, 5106, 5168, 5232, 5522, 5582, 5653, 5803, 5890, 5896, 5899, 5900, 5968, 6019, 6138, 6247, 6383, 6417, 6431, 6481, 6645, 6887, 7102, 7209, 7268, 7344, 8041, 8046. For *an=han*, see 5803 C. In—To (*om.* C) slepe and after tales *haue* (han BG Cp., hauyn C, have D, han a E) reste, 3066, *han* is unmetrical; cf. Ye shul (schal C, shal GCp. John's) nomore *haue* (han BC Cp. John's) soueraynte (-eynte BDG, -eignete Cp. John's, -anitee E, seurete of me C), 3013; cf. also 2717 ‡ D, 3414 ‡ D, 3799 ‡ D, 5968 ‡ C, 6138 ‡ C. (2) In rhyme,—haue, 120 f, 1821 f, 2329 f, 2541 f, 4221 f, 5228 f, 6036 f, 7779 f; hauen. 4305 f (haue BCD) (: grauen *ind.* 3 *pl.*, -e BCD).

Rhyme words.—saue *inf.* (120, 2329, 5228, 6036, 7779), *subj.* 3 *sg.* (1821, 4221), graue *inf.* (2329, 6036), craue *inf.* (2541), graue *n* (7779).

(3) Before vowels *han* is the commonest form in ABC, *have* in D: cf. 13, 122, 349, 803, 1574, 2224, 2460, 2587, 2831, 2840, 3733, 4348, 5047, 5213, 5967, 7443, 7636. But *haue* is found in all four MSS.: thus,—50 AB, 122 C, 349 B, 709 AB, 2454 AB, 2562 A, 2831 B, 3485 AB, 3786 ABC, 5047 B, 5271 AB, 6407 ABC, 7443 C, 7636 B. In 2224 D *havyn of* is found (han ABC). (4) Before *h* (*hym, his, here* (*hire*), *had*), both *han* and *haue* are found in A, B, C, and D: cf. 1503, 2164, 2504, 3352, 3856, 4395, 5579, 7747; for cases before other *h*'s, cf. 857, 3497, 6104, 8043. C has *an* for *han* in two instances: an had, 1503 C; an hyȝed, 3947 C.

Note.—The clipped form *a* for the infinitive occurs several times in C (rucly in A and D) Thus,—in C 501, 638, 899, 915, 1499, 1638, 2956, 3273, 4002, 5045, 5046, 5168, 5890, 5896, 5899, 5900, 5903, 6417, 6645, 7087, 7102, 8041, 8046; in A 900; in D 5168, 5896. The form *ha* is rare,—see 5106 C, 5900 D, 6417 D. In all the citations in this note a consonant follows the infinitive.

METRICAL CHAPTER.

§ 125. Weak -*e* is elided before a vowel and often before *h* (see Child, §§ 74—76; ten Brink, § 269); but final -*e* in the definite article may be preserved (see § 128).[1]

Elision of weak -*e* takes place before *he, his, him, hire* (gen. dat. acc. sg., gen. pl.), *hem;* before *haue* (pres. ind. or subj., inf.), *hast, hath, han* (ind. pl., inf.), *hadde;* before *how* and *here* (adv.); before French "*h* mute" in *honour, horrible;* before irrational *h* in *Hoiaste.*

Examples of elision before *h* in pronouns are unnecessary (for possible exceptions to the rule, see § 126). Examples before *h* in the other words mentioned follow: variants are for the most part left unregistered; the occurrence of a caesura after the elided -*e* is indicated. —

dere (*adv.*) haue (*ind.* 1 *sg.*), 4953; blame haue (*ind.* or *subj.* 1 *sg.*), 1295; Diomede || haue (*ind.* 2 *pl.*), 8040.

wratthe || hast, 933; cause hast, 6913; ioye hastow, 6951.

mone hath, 4598; herte hath, 6501; loue hath, 879 AB; loue || hath, 960; nece (||?) hath, 8090; purueyaunce (||?) hath, 5639; sore hath, 1618; Troye hath, 6220; Criseyde || hath, 7610.

a lawe (||?) han (2 *pl.*), 2878.

loue hadde (3 *sg.*), 304, 663; ioye || hadde, 3311; cause || hadde, 4069; Criseyde || hadde, 5487; longe || hadde, 5832.

on lyue han be, 5899; ye koude han, 8046; moste (*sg.*) han, 3733; men sholde (||?) han, 872; sholde (3 *pl.*) han, 3273; I wold han, 1499; she wold (||?) han, 2164; he wolde han, 3497; ye me wolde han, 4348; they wolde han 4839; nolde (*sg.*) han, 5803, 7087; ye nolde han, 1503; ye nolde (||?) han, 8043; som tyme (||?) han, 5967 (see note 2, below); cf. also, wolden (2 *pl.*) han, 2831.

I dorst haue, 899; he myght haue, 1277; who myght haue, 7102; I wolde haue, 5168, cf. 8041; she wolde haue, 501; who wolde haue, 5045.

In all the following cases of elision before *how,* except 6005, 7145, *how* is preceded by the caesura: loue, 1752; nece, 4405; Troy, 6005; swete, 4120; at the leste, 4678; thoughte (*ind.* 3 *sg.*),

---

[1] With reference to the treatment of the final vowel in elision, the following readings are not without interest, though some of them can hardly be called evidence: *tellit* (= telle it), 580 C; *myghty* (= myghte I), 7444 A (my3ty C); *drie* (= drie I *patior*), 6659 C; *pose* (= pose a), 3152 B; *excuser* (= excuse her *inf.*), 7462 D, see 7460 D (cf *dethes* = deth his, 460 C); *leue* = leef he, 6247 C.

[§§ 125, 126.] *of Chaucer's Troilus.* 347

3282; cast (*pret. ind.* 3 *sg.*), 4823; kowde (3 *sg.*), 1921; he
nyste (*ind.*), 7145; if ye wiste (*subj.*), 6280; happe how happe
may, 7159.
allone here (*hic*), 806; hadde here-vpon, 3377.
Ne shal I neuere haue hele || *honour* ne ioye, 6104 (neuere haue ||
honour C, Shal I neuer haue hele h. ne ioye D). Cf. And that
ye d[e]igne me so *muche honoure* (inf.), 2981 (muchel B, mechil
C, And yow deigne me so honoure D †).
In *place horrible* makynge ay his moone, 6613.
How that ye louen sholde (sholden louen B Cp., schulde louyn C,
shold love D, shulde louen G, shulden loue John's) on that *hatte*
Horaste (horast G, on hat h. D, oon atte h. E), 3639. That
Horaste = Orestes (cf. § 139) is evident from Gower's *Confessio
Amantis,* bk. iii. (I, 352), where the forms *Horestes* and *Horest*
(elided) occur: Chaucer merely uses the name without intending
an allusion to the classical Orestes.

Note 1.—In some of the examples just given, the word affected by elision
is one that loses its -e rather readily before a consonant: so especially of
the "auxiliary verbs," and of the nouns *loue, necs.*—It should be observed
that in phrases in which an auxiliary verb precedes the infinitives *han* or
haue, we have often what is to all intents and purposes a single verb-form
of which the infinitive *han* (or *haue*) is the unaccented part (or scarcely
more than a suffix). In such cases the infinitive had of course no full
pronunciation, and in some instances we actually find it written *an* or *a*
(§ 124, VI., note at end). Elision before such a form as this has really
little in common with elision before a fully sounded *h,* of whatever origin.
Note 2.—Proparoxytone words ending in -e apocopate -e before consonants
(ten Brink, § 257): *swètnesse hàue* (638), *Pàndare* || *here* (adv.) (868),
Pandare herde (876), and the like, have therefore no significance as
examples of elision (cf. also *sòm tyme hàn,* 5967, where *som-tyme* is
practically a compound, and see § 2, p. 3).
Note 3.—For the treatment of words like *chaumbre, lettre, temple, vncle,*
before *h,* see § 136, *f, g.* Cf. *heuene* (dissyl.) *hye* 4587 (§ 14). For *euere,
neuere* before *h,* see the details in § 90.

§ 126. Hiatus, whether before a vowel or before *h* in the
words mentioned in § 125, is very rare.
In a few instances, the evidence for hiatus is either conclusive or,
at any rate, considerable. Thus,—
Al this *Pandarĕ* || *yn* his herte thoughte, 1063 (C cut out). *Pandare*
is the reading of ABDEGCp. John's Phillipps; Durham has
Pandar; Hl. 2392 has *Al this tho Pàndarè in herte thoht.* Shall
we read *Pandarus* (see § 139)?
Now *good[ĕ] em* for *goddes loue* I prey, 1394 (goode BG, Now my
good eem D John's Hl. 2392, Now myn em C, And good[ĕ] em

Cp.). C has but nine syllables, and, unless *goode* be read (cf. p. 128), the same is true of ABCp.

Al *wolde I* (wold I B, wold y D) *that* noon (no man CD) *wyste* (woste C, wist DG) *of* this thought, 1830. (No note in Mr. Austin's collation.) Read either *wolde I* or *wyste of*.

But hasteth yow to don hym *ioye haue*, 2329 (ioy[é] D; no note in Austin, except *doon* Cp).

Iwys so wolde I (wold I B) and I *wistë how*, 3944 (wist[e] D; no note in Austin). Rather *wistë how* than *woldë I*.

Were it so that I *wist[e] outrely*, 4328 (wiste B, ȝ[i]t were it so that I woste outerely C, ȝit were it so that I wist vttirly D, Were it so that I wiste entirely G; no note in Austin).

As nold[e] god but yf I *sholde haue*, 5228 (nold[e] . . . shold[ë] B, nolde . . . schulde C, nolde . . . shulde D, nolde . . . schuldé G; no note in Austin.)

And stod forth mewet (meuyth † D) *myldë* (-[e] D) *and* mansuete, 6557 (*line om.* C, And stode forthe full myldé and manswete G; no note in Mr. Austin's collation).

Trewe as stel in ech condicion, 7194 (Trew B; no note in Mr. Austin's collation). Either hiatus or 9-syl.

I *fynde ek* (eke G) in storyes (stories DG, storyes C, the stories B) ellys (ell C) where, 7407. The reading of B avoids hiatus; no note in Mr. Austin's collation.

The same hele I shal noon *hele haue*, 7779 (no note in Austin).

Of the examples just given the surest are the three before *haue* (inf.) (2329, 5228, 7779), that before *how* (3944), and that before *and* (6557). Reasonably sure is 4328 (before *outrely*), and so, perhaps, is 1830 (before *I*). 1394 may be a verse of nine syllables, but hiatus makes a much smoother line; 7194, however, will run very well as a nine-syllable verse.—Here perhaps should be considered *haddë had* in 227, though *had* (p.p.) is a part of the verb *have* not mentioned in § 125:

And wende no thing *hadde had* swych myght, 227 (no thing(e) had, had swiche myȝt B, hadde had swych amyȝt C, he (*no* and) wend no thing had had such myght D; Cp. agrees with A except that it has *swiche;* And wend no thyng hade had sueche myght G; no note as to John's). Possibly *swiche* in BCp. is for *swich a*[1]: Cp. is a good MS. is all respects, but B is not to be trusted as

---

[1] Cf. 4581 B.

to its -*e*'s. However, *hádde hád* is surely more euphonious than *hád had* ($\underline{}$ ×).

The following two lines may perhaps be more safely regarded as nine-syllable verses than as verses with hiatus, for *loue* almost always loses its -e in the *Troilus*, whether a vowel or a consonant follows (§ 8, p. 14). In both verses the reading is quite secure (no note in Austin).

Loue ayens the (*om.* C) which who-so defendeth, 603.

Loue hym made al prest to don hirę byde, 4824.

In 421, it is perhaps safer to read *loue thus* than to allow the hiatus *seyde he* (but cf. ten Brink, § 270. 2):

And to the god of loue ǁ thus *seyde he*, 421 (seyd he D).

In the following two lines the reading *comýnge* must be looked at with suspicion (see § 10). In the first it may be avoided by hiatus (*cause of*); in the second, it causes hiatus, which, however, may be avoided by inserting *ek* (with CD). Apart from these two lines, there are no instances of *-ynge* in the *Troilus*, whether before a vowel or a consonant, except *thus forknowyng[é] wyse* (§ 59, *b*).

The cause of his comynge (-yng D) ǁ thus answerede, 2187.

Of here comynge ǁ and of his also, 4517 AB (comynge and ek C, comyng and eke D; no note in Austin).

Other lines in which hiatus, though possible, is on the whole unlikely, are:

Quod Pandarus now is *tyme I* wende, 1305 (*so* ABG, now is it tyme C, Now quod Pandarus is it tyme y wende D; no var. in Cp. noted).

I am on(e) (oon B Cp, on G, on of C) the *fairest* (fayreste BC) ǁ *out* of drede (withoutyn drede D), 1831 (no note in Mr. Austin's collation except on *oon*). The choice lies between the *fairest[e]* ǁ *out* and a 9-syl. verse.

Hym to reuoken she *dide* (did B, dede C) *al* hire (hir D) peyne, 3960. Mr. Austin's collation shows no variants. *Reuoke* and *dide al* certainly give a more agreeable line than *reuoken* and *dide al;* but it is unsafe to assume hiatus. *Hire* is improbable. G has *Hym to reuoke she dide her bysy peyne*, the last word in a later hand.

Nought (Nouȝte G) *rought* (rouȝte CG) *I* wheder (whidere B, whider G, whedyr that C, whedirwardes D) thow woldest (wilt D) me (*om.* D) stere, 4944 (no note in Mr. Austin's collation). The choice lies between *roughte I* and *woldest* (cf. § 136, b).

She *told ek* (tolde ek CD) how Tydeus (Cithideus † C) er she

stente, 7848 (no note in Austin). The choice lies between *tolde
ek* and *Tydēus* : cf. Tydeus sone that doun descended is, 7877,
and see § 141.

In a considerable number of verses the reading of one or another
MS., necessitating hiatus, is easily corrected by comparison of MSS.,
so that the hiatus disappears. Examples are :

Now *Pandare* (so ABDCp., Pandar G, Pandarus E John's) || *I* kan
(kanne B) no more (mor G) seye, 1044 (cut out of C). Here
Pàndarè, with its impossible accentuation, should without doubt
be rejected in favour of *Pandarus* (§ 139). Cf. Pàndarè || and,
5747 (Pandarus C, Pàndare || in BCp. John's).

And how he *myght*[e] *here* (acc.) beseche of grace, 1056 (BCp.
John's have *best* after *he*).

I *loue* (leue C) *oon* (om. G) which (which that BE Cp., wich that C,
wheche that G) is most (moost is B Cp., most is G) ententyf,
1923. Read *which that.*

But Troilus *thoughte his* herte bledde, 2035 (thought[e] his B,
Troylis that thouȝte his h. b. C, Troylus that thought that his
herht bled D, But Troylus thought his herte bledde G; no note
in Mr. Austin's collation). Clearly we should read *But Troilus
that* thoughte *his herte bledde. That* is almost necessary for the
construction.

And gan to smyle and seyde (seyde hym BDG) || Em I preye, 2244
(no note in Mr. Austin's collation).

Ye shul (schal G, shal Cp. John's) *nomore* (namore Cp., no moore
John's) || *haue* (han BCp. John's) souereynte, 3013, (souereignete
Cp. John's, seurete of me C). Read *han* (or *haue*) *sòuereȳnetè*
(cf. § 137).

And what *myschaunce* || *in* this world yet is, 3132 (myschauns[e] C,
meschaunce in this world ȝet ther is B, what mischef yet in this
world ther is D; Cp. John's insert *ther* before *is*).

If that ich *grace had* (so BG, ich a grace hadde Cp., I hadde grace
A, y had grace D, I hadde C *omitting* grace) for (om. CD) to do
so, 3770. The choice lies between *gracĕ haddĕ* and *haddĕ gracĕ*.

Of swiche (swhich B, whiche C, wych D) sikes *koude he* (om. B)
nought blynne (bilynne B), 4207. (No note in Mr. Austin's
collation.) Cf. § 138, 1.

That pride *enuyè i*re and auaryce, 4647 ACDE Phill. 8252 Harl.
2392 (That pride and ire enuye and anaryce BCp.; That pride
enuye and ire and auarice G John's Selden B 24; That ire enuy

[§ 126.] *of Chaucer's Troilus.* 351

and auerice Durham II 13). Hiatus is doubly suspicious on account of the unusual treatment of *-ye* (as *-y̆ĕ*) in the interior of the verse (see p. 84).

And though I *myght[ĕ]* || *I* wol not do so, 5121 (myghtë B, myȝte || I nuldë not C, myght || I woldë nat D, myȝte || I woldë not G). (No note in Austin's collation.)

A (And D) dieu (dey D) the deuel *spedę* (haue C) *hym* that (that it BD, at hit G) recche, 5292. The insertion of *it* restores the verse. (No note in Austin.)

Whanne I (om. B) the (thyn C) processe (procès C, procès D) *haue iŋ* memorie, 6946 (haue in myn C, I haue in my D; no note as to Cp. John's; whan wil ye this processe haue in memory Hl. 2392; When I the processe haue in memorie G).

The[r] (Ther BD, There CG, Wher John's) she (he † G) was born (borne BDG, boryn C) and (and there C, and ther D John's) she dwelt (dwellyd CG, duellid D) *hadde* (had BG, om. D) *ay*, 7074.

And that to *late is* now me to rewe, 7433 (to late is now for me to rewe B, to late it is now for to rewe C, And to late it is now for to rewe D). (No note in Mr. Austin's collation.)

And graunte it that ye *soone* || *on·* me rewe, 7727 (sone vpon CDG; Cp. John's also have *vpon*).

Other examples[1] are : (*a*) before vowels,—1099 D, 1277 C, 1305 AB, 1405 C, 1608 A, 1956 B, 1957 A, 2287 A *(hondë* acc.; see § 13), 2386 D, 2744 C, 2807 A, 3495 C, 3611 D, 4970 C°, 5070 A, 5258 C, 5401 C, 5436 C, 5885 C, 6073 D, 7110 CD, 7917 D ; (*b*) before *h*,—*herdë* (pret. sg.) *hym* (549 D), *tymē* || *hath* (1877 A), *speddë* (pret. pl.) *hem* (2032 AB), *hestë hath* (4587 A), *demaundē he* (7222 D), *scydē* (pret. sg.) *he* (7548 C), *willē hath* (7905 C).—In 6605 A, for *tëndressë how* (with impossible accentuation) read *tendernesse how*. In 5747 A, for *Com Pàndarè* || *and* (with impossible accentuation) read *Com Pàndare in* || *and*, with BCp. (Com(e) Pandare in and John's, Com pandarus and C, Com(e) Pàndarè and D). In 7652, read *than[në] don* rather than *myght[ĕ] I* : C has the *-e s* right.

Instances of consonant + *-re*, *le* not slurred before a vowel are perhaps not strictly cases of hiatus, for it is by no means certain that Chaucer's ordinary pronunciation was *lettre, temple* rather than *letter, tempel*, or *lettr, templ*.

But wel ye wot the *chaumbre* (-er B, -ir C) *is* but lite, 2731.

And of myn *ordre* (ordere C) *ay* (om. C) til (til that C) deth (they C) me mete, 5444.

I thenk (thynke C) ek how he *able is* (abele he is C, able he is D) to (for to BCCp.) haue, 1821. Read, however, with BCp.

Humble (-bele C, -blely † D) *in* (his D, in his BCECp.) speche and

---

[1] Cf. also note 3 at the end of § 92, V.

yn his lokynge (tellynge C) eke, 4790. Read, however, with B etc., *humble in his.*

A considerable number of instances of apparent hiatus are due to the reading *-e* instead of *-en* in forms in which both endings are known to Chaucer's language. Thus rather often in the infinitive (§ 119, XI.) and in strong perfect participles (§ 122, XI.), and occasionally in other verb-forms, as *dede* (pret. pl.) *al*, 4247 (read *diden* with BE Cp.; dedyn C) and *they sholde hire* (gen. sg.), 4848 (read *sholden* with BCp. John's; -yn D) : cf. the variants in § 96, III. (pres. ind. pl), § 109, IX., note (pret. ind. pl.). Similarly, for *here selue excusynge,* 112, read *here seluen* (hire seluen B, hyre seluè C, herself[e] D); for *aboue euery*, 6517 (§ 88), read *abouen* with B (-yn C, -e? D ‡), for *ofte haslow*, 904, read *often* with B (ofte C, oft[e]D).

> Note 1.—No doubt unelided *-e* before a vowel is to be changed to *-en* whenever such a change is possible, even if the cæsura might protect hiatus. Thus,— *But yf thow late* (ʒe lat B, ʒe late CG, ʒe lete D) *hym deye* (dy[e] D, deyen G; no note in Austin) ‖ *I wole sterue*, 1408 ; *God leue hym werke* (-en BCp. John's, -yn G, werk[e] D) *as he can deuyse*, 2898.—With regard to erroneously substituting *-e* for *-en* and thereby necessitating hiatus, B is the least culpable of the four MSS. and Cp. appears to be almost exemplary (cf. § 119, XI., note).

§ 127. Before *h* in words other than those mentioned in § 125, there seems to be no special inclination to elide *-e* : the *-e* is sometimes preserved (see list I.) and sometimes lost (see list II.).

In the examples that follow (lists I. and II.) variants are for the most part left unmarked; the occurrence of a cæsura after the elided or unelided *-e* is indicated.

I. -ë retained :

leuè (*sbst.*) hom(e), 126 A (read *leue* and *hom*).

Pandàre ‖ herkene, 658 (Pandàris C).

nomore harde grace, 713.

hadde ‖ horn, 1727 (or,—haddé horn ‖).

here seuenethe hows, 1766 (or,— here seuenethe hows).

the best[e] harpóur, 2115.

that ye thonkè (*subj.*) ‖ humbely, 2804.

so god me sende hele, 3163.

thilke harm, 3560.

myghte (3 sg.) here (*inf.*), 3586.

worse hap (*sbst.*), 4088 ; hertë ‖ happe (*subj.* 3 *sg.*), 7159.

sholdé (3 *sg.*) holde, 4726.

thi self[e] ‖ helpen, 5190 (read *seluen* with B).

termè holde, 7572.

fatè ‖ helpeth, 7915 A (read *fate* ‖ *hym helpeth* with AD ; C †).

Note.—No importance attaches to *vncle* (dissyl.) *herde,* 2185.

§§ 127, 128.] *of Chaucer's Troilus.* 353

II. -e lost:

had, hadd*e* (*ind.* 3 *sg.*, see § 102) herd, 750, 5007, 5329;[1] had (*subj.* 3 *sg.*, see § 113) herd, 7086.

abedd*e* ‖ half, 1152 (§ 14); ought (*sg.*) half, 5927 (§ 123, III).

wer*e* hanged, 1438.

fast*e* ‖ homward, 2388.

no fors hardyly, 2802 (§ 21).

soon*e* hope (*ind.* 1 *sg.*), 3794 (§ 88).

ioy*e* ‖ halt, 4478 (§ 21); lou*e* halt, 4606 (§ 8); myght (3 *sg.*) (‖ ?) holden, 5260 (§ 123, VIII); hope ‖ halt, 6711 (§ 2).

both*e* hèronèr, 5075 (§ 88).

the more harm is, 7299; cf. 1523 (‖ ?).

Note.—Some of the examples in list II. have no significance, since the word affected is one that loses its -e freely even before a consonant: so especially of the "auxiliary verbs" (including *were*), of the noun *loue*, of *more*, and of the phrase *no fors* (which, besides, is, in the instance in question, accented on the *no*).

§ 128. Elision of weak -e in monosyllables.

The cases that come under consideration are *the* (definite article) and *ně* (simple negative, 'non'). *The* before a vowel or weak *h* may suffer elision or preserve its -*e* at the will of the poet. *Ně* is regularly elided.[2] Whether elision in these cases amounts to full ecthlipsis may be doubted. Ten Brink decides for ecthlipsis (§ 269), but the metre is quite as well satisfied by reducing the -*e* to a consonant *i* (*y*). The spelling *nyis* for *nis* (*ne is*) in 7451 C seems to be significant in this regard. On the other side we have the evidence of *toon* and *tother*, and the testimony of Hart (1569): see Jespersen, *Studier over engelske Kasus*, Förste Række, Copenh., 1891, p. 154.

I. Elision of *the*.

the aduersite, 25 (D *om.* the).

theffect, 212 (the effecte B; D ?); the effect, 2651 (theffect B); cf. 2305, 3188, 4422, 4519, 4657, 4806, 6740.

the assege, 464 (thassege B, the sege D); thassege, 4724 (thessage B, the sege D (?)); cf. 1192, 1208, 6142, 7220.

at the ende, 1876 (at ende BD, an ende C); cf. thende, 1345 B.

the aleyes, 1905 (thaleyes B, thé a. D).[3]

the alderfirst[e], 2939 (the aldır ferste C; D ‡ *om.* the); cf. 4439.

the experience, 4125; cf. 3830.

the affeccioun, 4432 (thaffeccion B; C ‡ *om.* the).

---

[1] Supply [*which*] in A. [2] See exception at end of IV., below.
[3] Supply [*was*] in C.

A A

the ambassiatours, 4802 (thembassadours B, theem-bassatourys C);[1]
thembassadours, 4807 (the embassadourys C, thambassiatours D).
theschaunge, 4808 (the chaunge CD); cf. 4820, 4822, 5540 C.
at the other, 5096 (attother B, at other D).
the ymage, 5526 (C †); cf. 1458.
the ordre of causes, 5679.
thaqueyntaunce, 6485 (the acqueyntau[n]se C, the acqueintauns ? D).[2]
thencheson, 6995 (then(e)cheson B, the encheson C, the entencioun ‡ D); cf. 681 ‡ B.
the est see, 7472 (thë ‡ C, thë est see D).
thauentaylle, 7921 (thauantaile B, the auentayle CD).
thentent, 7993 (the ent. BD, the ‡ centence ? C).[3]
th erràtyk, 8175 A (the erratyk B).

Compare also 1696 C, 2361 D, 2663 D, 3378 CD, 4827 D(?), 7829 C, and the variants under *thilke* (p. 160).

Similarly before *h* :

thonour, 120 (the honour BCD).

Note 1.—For *it shal of*, 5768 C has *the hèd shal of*, clearly the "correction" of a scribe.

Note 2.—Before *h* in the following words *the* of course suffers no elision : harpe, 731 ; harm, 839, 1539, 3167 ; haste, 2031 ; hil[le], 943 ; hardest, 1814 ; heuenes, 1989 ; hood, 2266 ; happy, 2467 ; hond, 2689 ; holy, 3384 ; herte, 3913, 5808 ; halle, halles, 5394, 7093 ; hous, 5485 ; hote, 490. So also *the* (A.S. þý) in *the hottere*, cf. 1623.

Note 3.—Sometimes one or another MS. has a reading which seems to require or suggest *the* (definite article) before a consonant (not *h*) : thus,— 200 C, 2052 A (?), 2341 A (?), 3191 D (?), 3345 D, 3386 C, 3567 B, 3597 C, 4333 D, 4845 D, 6926 BD, 7392 B, 7993 C, 8232 D. The cases cited may all be corrected by comparison of MSS. But in 4906, ABCD agree in reading : *His hed* to the wal *his body to the grounde* (no note in Austin).

II. But *e* in *the* may remain unelided. Thus,—

By alle (al B, aH D) *the* (tho Cp.) othes that I haue to (*om.* BCD) yow sworn(e), 1384. Probably we should read : By alle the othes that I haue yow sworn. *Allë the othës* or *allë the othes* is hardly to be thought of.

The olde (The old D, Wolde † *for* þolde C) daunce and euery poynt therinne, 3537.

The cause ytold (tolde John's) of here comynge (-yng D) *the* (*om.* C) olde (old D, *om.* B), 4803. *Comÿngë the olde* is unlikely.

The newe (new BD) loue out (-e BD) cacheth (chaceth B, schakyth C, chasithe D) ofte (oft B) *the olde*, 5077 (no note in Austin).

---

[1] Supply [*thei*] in B.
[2] Thaqueyntaunce (The aqueyntau[n]se C, The acqueintauns D, The acqueyntaunce G) of these (this BC, thes D) Troians (Troyans B, Troylus C, Troiaunes D) to (for to C) chaunge. (No note in Mr. Austin's collation.)   [3] Supply [*the*] in B.

Here *oft the olde* is perhaps preferable to *oftë the olde.*

The obseruaunce (-ns D) euere yn youre absence, 5445 (C *inserts* I *before* in).

And whiten gan *the* (eche † C) *orisonte* (orisoune B, oryʒonte C, orisent D) shene, 6639.

III. Some lines may be read in two ways, one of which preserves the *-e* in *the*, the other of which elides it.

And sith (sithen B, sythe C, seth D, sitho Cp.) *the ende* (thende B Cp. John's) is of (*om.* BCDCp. John's) euery tales strengthe, 1345.

Lo herte (hert D) myn as wolde (wold BD) *the excellence*, 3830 (no note in Austin).

Bygan (Bygunne C, Began D) for ioye *the amorouse* (thamarouse B, the amerous CD, thamorouse Cp. John's) daunce (dauns D), 6093.

IV. In *në* the *Troilus* regularly elides *-e* before a vowel. There is but one exception : 649 (see end of list).

ne acheueth, 1893 (nacheueth B ; CD *om.* ne ; eschewith † D).

ne enforce I, 5678 (nen-force B).

naxe in guerdon, 6957 (ne axe CD).

For he that nough[t] nassayeth nought nacheueth, 7147 (nouʒt asayeth nouʒt ne cheuyth C, nouʒt assaieth nouʒt acheueth D).

He ne eet ne dronk for his malencolye, 7579 (ne et(e) BD, he nother † et C).

He ne eet ne dronk ne slep ne word [ne] seyde, 7803 (ne word(e) seyde BD, He net ne drank ne no word he ne seyde C).

But litel bok no makyng thow nenuye, 8152 (D *om.* ne).

So *nam, nys* (§ 124). Particularly interesting is *nyis* for *nis* (7541 C). For *nere, noot, niste, nyl, nylt, nolde, noldest,* see §§ 124, 125.

A single exception is :

Ek the *ne oughte* (aught B) not ben yuel apayed, 649 (And ek thou not to ben euele payede C, And eke thow oghtist not ben evil apayed D ; no variants in Austin, except *nat* Cp. for *not*). The reading seems to be well established. In : I *ne* (*om.* D) *ought* (aught B, auʒte C, oght D) not for that thyng hym despise, 1805, read ne ought[ë] not.

§ 129. Elision of close *-e.*

I. Of the elision of (close) *-e* in *me, we, he, she, ne* (neque), there are several examples. Ten Brink (§ 269) is inclined to regard such instances as full elision (*ecthlipsis*), but this seems doubtful, except perhaps when the vowel which follows is itself an *e*.

And yet me of-thynkẹth that this auaunt me asterte, 1043 A (mathynkẹth ... may † sterte B, me athinkith ... me stert D ‡).

me offendeth, 605 (me off. C ‡ ; D †).

me assaylleth, 607 (massaileth D † ; me ass. C ‡).

me allone, 1021 (malon B, me a. D ‡); so 2486.

mauyse, 1361 B (me auyse C, me a. D ‡ ; A †).

me enspire, 3554 AB (me enspire D, nyȝt ens. C).

me anon, 5172 BCD (A?).

me assayle, 6257 (messaile B, me a. C ‡ ; D †).

And go we anoon for as yn myn entente, 6187 (C †).

In to the gardeyn go we and ye shal here, 2199.

he answèrẹd, 5097 (B om. he; he answerde C, he answerd D).

she abod, 127 (D om. she; sche bod C); cf. 2736 ‡ C.

she abreyde, 5874 (she brayde B, sche brayd C).[1]

she alighte, 6552 (shalighte B, she light D; C †).

Ne yn hym desir doon (l. noon)[2] otherẹ fownes bredde, 465 (Nyn hym C).

Ne auaunter certeyn seyth men is he non, 1809 (Navauntour B; D ‡).

Nen-tendement considere ne tonge telle, 6358 (Ne †-mendement B).

Ne of ladyes ek so fayr a companye, 6810 (Nof B).

Ne encens vp on here auter sette a fyre, 7829 (Nencens B, The ensens ‡ C, Ne eucense D).

Ne (Ny B, Ne y D) neuere (G inserts man) saw (saugh BCp., ne say C) a more bountenous

Of here estat (-e B, astate D) ne (non C) a (om. BCDG John's; nagladder Cp.) gladder (-ere John's) ne (om. D, nor B) of speche

A frendliour (frendelyere C) na (ne a DE, ne non C, ne G) more gracious, 883-5.

Examples of hiatus are :

Whi hastow (D inserts thus) mad (-e B) Troylus (Tr. made Cp., tr. mad C, tr. me made D) to (om. D) me (om. D) vntriste (-truste B, -trust CD), 3681 (no var. noted for Jn's). But the reading in Cp. is perhaps to be preferred.

As for a frend ye may in me assure, 7987.

And after this (om. C) with sikyngẹ/he abreyde (vpbrayd D), 724.

---

[1] In D read of swogh for A swogh.
[2] none B, non CD. For desir C has desyred †; for hym BD John's have his; for fownes D has fantasye. Cp. reads : Nyn him desire noon other fewnes bredde.

§ 129.]   *of Chaucer's Troilus.*   357

I thenk ek how he/ *able is* (abele he is C, able he is D) to (for to BC) haue, 1821.

That sorwest thus and *he answered* (answerede C, answerde hym B, answerd him D) nay, 5302.

That yf that *he encrese* myghte or eche, 6473 (C † D †).

In furye as doth *he* (the D) *Ixion* in helle, 6575 (In furie as ᶜthow he leye in helleᶜ Cᶜ).

To which (-e D) no word (-e B) for sorwe (sorw B) (for sorwe no word D) she answerede (-swerde BC, -swerd D), 4369; cf. 5897.

Cf. also: mè alsò, 5978; gò we ủncle, 2809; hè ‖ allàs, 3919; he into, 3939 BC (he hym into A; D †); hè iwỹs, 4023 f; hè ‖ aboùte, 4904; he òfte, 6980 f; he ònys, 7402; shè ‖ allàs, 3945; shè alsò, 4419; that shè vntrèwe bè, 7660 f.

In 1097: For-whi to euery louere (louer BDGJn's.) I *me excuse* ABDG Cp. Jn's. (C *cut out*), e in *me* may or may not be elided.

Note 1.—There are no instances of elided *the* (pron. 2 pers.) or *ye* (pron. 2 pers.). For instances of hiatus with these words, see, for *the*, 3139 (*thè alègge*), 4100 A (*the Ìmenèus*), 4299 (*thè agilt*), 4454 (*thè ‖ oblìged*); for *ye*, 682 (*yè endùre*), 6598 (*ye aùdiènce*). Cf. also *the oùghte*, 3106 f; the *òftë*, 3127, and see note 2, below.

Note 2.—When the word that follows is a monosyllable, elision of *me* (etc.) is not to be expected, whichever of the two words has the ictus. See 528 (*mè ‖ it*), 1011 (*mè ‖ and*), 1102 (*mè ‖ yf*), 3768 (*mè is*), 4265 (*mè is*), 5176 (*mè at*), 5411 (*mè ‖ and*), 5671 (*mè in*), 6278 (*mè ‖ and*), 6607 (*mè ‖ o*); 2017 (*wè oure*), 2030 (*dò we às*); 90 (*hè ‖ and*), 226 (*hè a*), 299 (*he èrst*), 326 (*hè ‖ yn;* cf. 358, 377, 543, 720 ‡ A), 1165 (*hè yn*), 1210 (*hè ‖ as*), 1363 (*hè ‖ and*), 1663 (*hè and Ì;* cf 5545 f), 1743 (*hè and*), 2158 (*hè of*), 2166 (*he aỹ*), 2281 (*hè I*), 3855 (*hè al hoòt*), 5185 (*he ‖ it*), 4633 (*hè ‖ yf;* cf. 1441), 4634 (*hè it;* cf 2636), 6448 (*he àl*), 6646 (*he òn*), 6999 (*he òf*), 7103 f (*he is*), 7802 (*he ỹn*), 8198 (*hè or shè*); 467 (*shè on*), 660 (*shè ‖ and;* cf. 2274, 2341, 5879, 6552), 937 (*shè ‖ of;* cf 1028, 1268), 1691 (*she oùght*), 1808 (*she is*), 3829 (*she ‖ òf*), 5072 (*shè is*), 5573 (*she òn*); 1811 (*ne àls*), 5926 AD (*yè ne Ì*); for *the* (2 pers.) see 585, 648, 766, 922, 2485, 2619, 5149, 7667; for *ye* see 1314, 2885, 3042, 4215, 4331, 4359, 7237, 7352, 7436.

Note 3.—In 98 A · Of ony fiend to whom *she dorst* make hire mone, we should omit *make* (with BCDEGCp.).

II. *Ne I* is several times reduced to a single syllable (sometimes written *Ny*). Thus,—

Ne I nyl forbere yf that ye don amys, 3015 (Ny nyl B Cp. John's, Ne y wil D ‡).

Ne I wele not serteyn breke ȝoure defence, 4141 CE (Ne I wole certeyn A, Ny wol certein B).[1] Cp. reads *Ny*, but otherwise appears to agree with A.

---

[1] B is unmetrical : supply [*not*].

Ne I nyl not rakle as for to greuen here, 4484 (Ne I wil C, Ny nyl BCp., Ne rakyl nel y be for to grevyn here D).

Ny say not nay but in conclusioun, 7366 B (Ne I sey C, Ne sey AD). (No note in Mr. Austin's collation.)

Ne I sey not this al only for these men, 8142 (Ny sey B Cp. John's). See also 883, just quoted.

III. Ten Brink (§ 269) remarks that the elision of close -*e* occurs "nur vor vocalischem Anlaut, nicht vor *h*;" but there seems to be no good reason why weak *h* should have interfered with the operation of this elision, and in one verse of the *Troilus* one is tempted to follow B in reading *maddë* for *me hadde*: Allas I *madde* ytrowed on ȝoure lore, 7099 B. The other MSS., however, except D, read differently: I *ne haddë* trowed AG; that I *ne hadde* trowid C; *me haddë* trowed D; no note in Mr. Austin's collation. Both *me hadde* and *ne hadde* make sense. If the former reading be adopted, the line means, "Would I that I had trusted myself to your counsel!" If the latter, "Alas! to think that I should not have trusted your counsel!" But *ne hadde* is ambiguous: it could mean, "Would that I had not trusted!" which is contrary to the obvious purport of the passage. Perhaps this explains the reading *me hadde*, as a scribe's purblind attempt to correct what he did not understand. —In 2017, D has: Now lete *we her* slepe and forth our talis hold, but ABCG omit *we* (no note in Mr. Austin's collation) before *her* and insert it before *oure*, having no *forth*.—Similarly in 3939 A reads: For this or that *he hym* into beddë caste, where the correct reading is undoubtedly *he into bed hym caste* (so BCp.; he into bedde him cast C; For this or for that he into the bedde him cast D); and in 2413 D reads Thus to the more worthi part(e) he hym held, where ABC have no *hym*.

Note 1.—For hiatus before *h* see, *e. g.*, 4135 (*mè* ‖ *how*), 5207 (*mè* ‖ *hast*), 5222 (*mè* ‖ *his*), 5563 (*mè* ‖ *hath*), 6947 (*me hàst*), 7328 (*mè hath*); 3779 (*we hàn*), 6757 (*wè han*); 83 (*hè hath*; cf. 3667, 3917, 4402, 7464), 301 (*he how*), 318 (*hè hadde*; cf. 750, 6986), 491 (*he hàdde*; cf. 1718, 2435 f, 6086 f, 7808), 695 (*he hàth*; cf. 1794, 2870), 2051 (*hè hym*; cf. 3542), 3907 (*hè here* poss. sg.), 4029 (*he here* acc.), 4459 (*he hym*), 7455 (*he here* acc.; cf. 2157, 7143); 124 (*shè hym*), 1823 (*shè here* poss. sg.), 3424 (*she hỳm*; cf. 7567), 4835 (*she* ‖ *hadde*), 7467 (*she hadde*); 3851 (*ne how*). Cf. also *the hadde* (4998), *ye han* (25, 28, 1446, 1577, etc.), *yè his* (5590), etc. Elision is of course out of the question in such cases as *me hàtē* (1798), *me hèlpeth* (4688), *me holly* (5106), *he hèld* (1288), *he hèrde* (2036), *he hènte* (2863 f), *he hèng* (3921), *the hèrye* (3793 f), *the hàrme* (4478), *ye hèlpe* (1405), *ye here* inf. (3774 f, 7217 f), *ye hàte* (6508).

Note 2.—In 7910, the reading of C: *ffrom day to day til they be in were of ioye*, makes sense, but is certainly to be rejected in favour of *ben bare of* ABD.—In 1972 read *ye wys* A instead of *ȝe i wis* CD (B has *ȝe ys*). In 4979 C *ye ilkë* is to be corrected.

IV. A remarkable case of the elision of close -*e*, and one which seems to indicate that the phenomenon in question is not full ecthlipsis, is 2199 :
   Into the gardyn go *we* || *and* ye shal here. So ABCDG; no note as to Cp. John's.
V. Instances of the elision (*synclisis*) of close -*e* in other words than the monosyllables just discussed are very rare (cf. § 33).
   As he that feltë *pyte on* euery syde, 5486 (pitie Cp., pitë haddë B, pitë feltë D). Here the cæsura comes after *pyte*. Perhaps we should scan *feltë pytë*, but that seems not so likely. C lacks the stanza. Cf. also 2662 ‡ C, 7462 ‡ D.
   On euery nymphe and *döitë inferndl*, 6205 (deytë BD, deth † C). Possibly *deitë*, with synæresis.

> Note.—The -*e* in *Dane* (= Daphne) seems to have been weak (cf. the rhyme *Diane* : *Dane*, K.T. 1205-6) : hence we have ordinary elision in *O Phebus thenk whan Dane here seluen shette*, 3568 (diane her self shet D).[1] No doubt the -*e* in *Tarbe* is of the same kind : *Flexippe she* Tharbe *and Antigone*, 1901 (fflexippe & Schetarbe & Antigone C, Flexipe & she tarke and Anteigne D); *Antigone hire sister* Tarbe also, 2648 (Tharbe B, Tarb C, Marbe D). So *Alète* (= Allecto) in *Megera* Alète *and ek Thesiphone*, 4686 (Megera aliete thow thesiphone D). On the other hand, we have final close -*e* slurred in *Flexipe* in the (doubtless erroneous) reading of D in 1901 (just quoted). As to these -*e*'s cf. ten Brink, § 94.

§ 130. Elision (or slurring) of final *o* and final *a*.

I. Final *o* in the preposition *to* is treated like final -*e* in the definite article. It is safer to regard the elision in this case, too, as not complete ecthlipsis. The elision is commonest with the infinitive.

to auaunce, 518 (tauaunce B, to a. D).
tassayen, 921 B. (to assay[e]n A; to asayen C, for cesyng † D); tassaye, 7146 (tasaie B, to asaye C †, to assaie D).
to arede, 1217 (thede † B; C † D †).
to endite, 1342 (to en. CD), 1785 (tendite B; C ? D ?).
to entende, 1938 (tentende B; D †).
to appere, 1994 (tapere B, to apere CD).
to auyse, 2300 (tauyse B, to ‡ vyse D).
tonfolde, 2787 B (to vnfolde AD, to onfolde C).
to abrygge, 3104 (tabregge B, to abregge CD); tabregge, 3137 f (to a. C, abregge D †); cf. also 5088, 5587.
to encrese, 4177 (tencrese BC, ten(en)crece E); cf. 5588 C.
to aproche, 4538 (taproche B, ta-proche C).

---

[1] The reading of D shows that Chaucer's caution in distinguishing *Diana* and *Daphne* in the passage cited from *The Knight's Tale* is evidence that he "knew his public."

to abyde, 4652 (tabide B, to ‡ abyde D); tabyde, 6396 (to a, ↑ D);
cf. also 6716, 6859 C (?), 7133, 7518, 7546.
to acheue, 4741 (tacheue B, shal ‡ cheue D).[1]
to enqueren, 5672; cf. 4526 C.
to arede, 6232 (tarede B, torede C).
to amendęn, 6501 (tamende B, to amendyn C, to amende D).
tenbrace, 6587 (to embrase C, to enbrace D). (9-syl. verse.)
tabreyde, 6883 (to a. CD, to breyde B).[2]
tacoye, 7145 (ta-coye C, to accoy D).[3]
to vnlouen, 8061 (to vnloue CD).
Cf. also 1781 D (teschewe), 1986 (?) B, 2682 C, 6796 B, 7816 C.

But instances of this slur also occur when the word that follows *to* is not an infinitive:

Vn to ony louere and his cause auayle, 20 (D †).

For to euęry wight som goodly auenture, 1366 (to euęrychę C, for euęry D); And his comyng vnwyst is to euęry wyght, 3754 (teuęry B, vnwist to euęry C).

And into a closet for to auyse herę bettre, 2300 (tauyse B, in a closet for to vyse D ‡).

Out wente anoon to Elyne and Deiphebus, 2726.

That passed was and thus he drof to an ende, 6838 (tanende B).

Examples of hiatus with *to* are:

to àrten hirę, 388 (for to àrtyn C; B †).[4]
tò èntrepàrten wò, 592 (intyrpartyn C).
to èche, 887 f.
to v̀se, 1096 f.
to èuęry lòuęre, 1097; to èuęry wight, 1273.
tò argùe, 1779 f (BCD *om.* to).
tò agàste, 1986 f, is doubtful.
to v̀sen, 2123 (to v̀se D).
to èrre, 5211 f.

Note 1.—For examples with monosyllables, see 14 (tò a), 1057 (thèr to ‖ ànd), 2529 (to àl (alle BC) honoùr), 3328 (to èse inf.), 3360 (tò ut), 3462 tò vs), 4814 (tò ut), 4818 (vntò ut; cf. 5187), 5779 (vntò vs).

In a few instances *to* suffers elision before *h*:

As for to honoure hirę goddes ful deuoute, 151 AB (CD *seem wrong*).

To honouren hem that hadde worthynesse, 4631.

---

[1] Read [to] shende in B. [2] Read (be)gan in D.
[3] Supply [herte] in B, [for] in C. [4] Dele one (hirę) in A.

To honouren yow as wel as folk of Troye, 6482 (*To* honourë CD).[1] Cf. also 4104 D.

I thenk ek how he ablë is for *to haue*, 1821 B Cp. (I thynke ek how abele he is for *to* haue C, I thenk ek how he able is to haue A, I thenk eke how able he is to have D, I thyng eke howe able he is to haue G, Ek wot I wel he worthy is to haue John's, Yit wot I weel he worthi is to haue Harl. 2392). Perhaps *able is*.

Cf. also,—*to* his (?), 2546 C; *to* hir, 7666 CD;[2] *to* hire, 7671 C; vnto her, 3762 D; into harm, 7739 C.

But *to* is the usual form before *h*. Thus,—to han, cf. 13, 769, 2224, etc.; to haue, cf. 50, 709, etc.; to here (*dat.*), cf. 443, 2094, etc.; to here (*poss. sg.*), cf. 5226, etc.; to hym, cf. 858, 998, etc.; to his, cf. 2179, 2219; vnto his, cf. 2627; etc. For cases before strong *h*, cf. e.g., to holde (128 f, 161 f, etc.), to herkenen (164), to helpen (836), into helle (872 f), into halle (2255 f), to hyde, (6393 f), to haten (7442), etc.

Note.—Sometimes a similar slur seems to take place in *to, into, vnto*, before a consonant; but most of the cases noticed are aberrations of the scribe, easily cured by a comparison of MSS. Thus,—*to seche*, 704 A; *to lede*, 6379 A; cf. also 1318 C, 1327 C, 2196 D, 2519 D, 2956 A, 3699 D, 3939 D, 4356 D, 6178 D, 6355 B, 6678 A, 7000 A, 7218 B, 7350 A, 7406 C, 7518 A, 7740 C, 8158 B.

Men wolden (wold BD) wondren (-deryn C, wondur D) *to se* (B Cp. John's *om* to; to sen C; to se D) hym come or gon, 1453.

To late here go thus *vnto the* Grekes ost, 5261 AB (into C; C *om.* thus; thus to D). No note in Austin.

II. Elision of final *-o* is rare except in *to*:

He cursed Ioue *Appollo and* ek Cupide, 6570 (C *om.* ek).

Of Ioue *appollo of* mars of swych rascaylle, 8216.

Note.—The following cases disappear on comparison of MSS. *go awoy*, 574 C (go wey AB, go hens D); *do awoy*, 1195 C (do wey ABD), cf. 1196 C; *do on*, 2039 C (don ABD), 3580 A (don B); *tho and*, 834 C (ABD *om.* and); cf. in 1559, AD have *No ywys*, but we may read *No wys* (with B[3] C Cp. John's)[4] In 3027, C reads: *O immortal god quod he that mayst not deyʒen*; ABD have no *O*); cf. 7424 D, where for *O yrolled* we should read *O rolled*.

III. The *Troilus* affords one good instance of elision (slurring) of final -*a*:

Megera. Alete. and ek Thesyphone, 4686 (Megera aliete thow thesiphone D).

---

[1] In B supply the second [*as*].   [2] In C, however, perhaps *wrete* (p.p.) *to hire*.
[3] In B supply [*he*].
[4] Cf. 2196, where A has *now ycome*, but *now come* (BC) is the correct reading. Cf. also 7070 D.

§ 131. Slurring of final *y*.

Final -*y* is sometimes united with the initial vowel of the following word (*synclisis*).

Obviously, in the case of adjectives accented on the penult, this slur can take place only when the word that follows either has no ictus or is accented on the second syllable. Thus we have : "How bÿsy ẏf I loue ek most I be," 1884; and so in the case of most adjectives in -*y* there is no slur before an initial vowel : as,—*gredy*, 4600; *hasty*, 6229 (hastif B, hastyth † C); *redy*, 3372, 7327, 7733; *sondry*, 1112; *sory*, 2436, 8089; *sturdy*, 2465; *wery*, 5369, 6636 (slur in D); *vnwery*, 1924; *worthi*, 1243, 1424. See also *lady* (§ 5), *ruby* (p. 94), *euery* (§ 79), *ony* (§ 79), adjectives in -*ly* (§ 72), adverbs in -*ly* (§ 84).

The commonest instance of the slur is in the phrase *many a, many án* : as,—This knoweth *many a* wys and worthi wyght, 1265 (meny a D). So also 163, 165, 166, 540, 810, 934, 1148, 1236, 1726, 1900, 3145, 3147, 3657, 3953, 3989, 4072, 4301, 4555, 4701, 5289, 5755, 6147, 6505, 6527, 6585, 6696, 6968, 7301, 7409, 7424, 7557, 7640, 7945, 8124. Variants have not been registered, for in none of the cases cited is there any doubt as to the true reading, so far as this phrase is concerned. The *Troilus* knows only the slurred *many a;* no unslurred example occurs which a comparison of MSS. does not correct (thus, *e. g.*, 4695).

Other instances are :

And I with *body and* soule synke in (into CD) helle, 6216.

Charitable estatlyche *lusty and* fre, 7186 (D Cp. John's *om.* and;
   Scharite abele statlyche lyȝt lusti & fre C; G agrees with A,
   except for the spelling *estateliche*).

I shal therof as *fully excuse* me, 3652 (ful BC; *but* Cp. John's *seem to haue* fully).

> Note 1.—Here and there one or another MS has a slurred -*y*, which comparison of MSS. causes to disappear. Thus,—*lády vntò*, 1164 A (§ 5); *hardy(e) as*, 7193 D; *sauery and*, 942 C; *worthy and*, 2163 C (cf. 1951 C, 4382 CD, 5160 B); *wery on*, 6636 D, *certaynly I*, 1531 A (cf. 3938 C); *gladly as*, 592 D; *hardıly and* (?), 2097 C; *nedfully as*, 5668 D; *wisely as*, 7728 C. In 5427 A : *How sholde I a fyssh withoute water dure*, omit *I*
>
> Note 2.—In 4873 C *ffor wich delyueryd* (l. delibered) *was by a parlement*, omit *a* (with ABD Cp. John's).

A similar slur of final -*ey* is found in 3287 A : *But yn swych cas men is nought* alwey yplesed; but the correct reading is *alwey plesed* (so BCp.; alwey plesid D; man is not † wel plesed C). In 2986, however, the preponderance of MS. authority is in favour of *ay i-lyke* :

§ 131.] *of Chaucer's Troilus.* 363

To seruen (-yn CG, serve D) and ben (bene D) *ay* (*so* ABG; *om.* DE;
C *has* ay ben *for* ben ay) *I-lyke* (ylike B, I-lik C, y-lyke D, I-lyke G)
diligent (Cp. John's appear to agree with A).

An effect precisely similar to the slur of final *-y* takes place when a
word in *-ye* (unaccented) suffers elision before a word the first syllable
of which has no ictus. The instances of this phenomenon are in the
Troilus confined to words in *-rye* like *contràrye*,[1] and to the word
remedye (the forms of which may be seen in full at p. 86, cf. ten
Brink, § 87, Anm.).

    By sort and by *augùrye ek* trewëly, 4778 (trew[e]ly B, By sort and
augury eke truly D).

    In *consistòrie among* the Grekes soone, 4727.

    By eche (*l.* his) *contràrie is* euery thing declared, 637 (-rye *is* BC).

    Retorneth in his part *contràrie agayn*, 5665 (-rye agayn B). But
the form *contràire* also occurs: see § 51, p. 120.

    Be *necessarie al* seme it not therby, 5682 (necessarye *al*(le) D).
But *necessaire* occurs: see § 51, p. 120.

    And som(e) so ful of *furye is* and despit, 3879 (furie *is* BCD).

    Anoy smert (-ę D) drede (dred[e] C) *fury and* ek (ekę D) sikęnesse
(seknesse C), 5507 (furye *and* BD, furie *and* C).

    For which the grete (gret[e] D) *furye of* his penaunce, 6091 (furie
of C).

    In *furye as* doth he Ixion in helle, 6575 (-rie *as* B, -ry *as* D; In
furie as thow he leye in helle C).

    And God *Mercùrye of* me now woful wreche, 6684 (-rie *of* B, -rye
on C; D *om.* now).

    Into *mysèrie yn* which I wol bywayle, 4934 (Into myn deth ‡ C).

    And certeinly in *story it* is yfounde, 7197 B (stori as it is founde
C, story as it is founde D, storye it is yfounde Cp., storye it is
founde A).

    Though that I *tarye a* yer som tyme I mot, 4037 (tar*ie a* BCD).

    For that I *tarye is* al for wykked speche, 7973 (tar*ie is* CD).

When the word that follows has the ictus, there is of course no
synclisis. See examples in § 30 under *còpye, fòlye, pàrtie*, and in § 31
under *augùrye, fùrye*. In 4915 *furye and*, BC have the slur, but AD
have none. Of *merye, mery* (§ 46, p. 113) the *Troilus* affords no
example before a vowel.

---

[1] In 6240 C, read *filthe it* for *folye it*.

§ 132. Weak *e* in two successive syllables (*syncope* or *apocope*).

Ten Brink's rule: "Enthalten zwei aufeinander folgende Silben je ein schwaches *e*, so verliert eines von diesen nothwendig seinen Silbenwerth, sei es durch Syncope oder Apocope durchaus, sei es annähernd, jedoch für das Bedürfniss der Betonung und des Verses vollkommen ausreichend durch Verschleifung" (§ 256), has been abundantly illustrated in the preceding chapter.

In the case of *-ede* in the preterite singular (§§ 99-105) the *Troilus* shows not a single exception to the rule, except perhaps in 7089: Here (Hire BC, Hir DG) *nèdedè* (neded BDG, nedit C) no (noun B John's, none CG Cp.) teris for to borwe (see 146, I, *b*). In 129 A, *dwèlled[è] yn* should be *wàs dwellỳng yn*. In the case of *-eden* in the preterite plural (§ 109), there are several exceptions (cf. ten Brink, §§ 194, 256), *màkkedèn* (apparently the correct reading in 4783, see § 109, I.), *strèmedèn* (§ 109, III.), *iòynèlèn* (§ 109, III.), *assègedèn*, *bysègedèn* (§ 109, I.), *comèndedèn*, *comèuedèn* (§ 109, III.), *èntrechaùngedèn* (§ 109, IV.).

For the application of this rule in the inflection of nouns see the genitives *fadęres*, *fadres* (§ 36), *heuęnes* (§ 36, n. 1), *somęres*, *widęwes*, *wydwes* (§ 35, I.), the plurals *arwes* (§ 38, IV.), *candęles*, *heuęnes* (§ 38, V.), and *maydens* (§ 39, III.); and the numerals *seuęne* (§ 67, *d*);[1] cf. *owęne* (§ 53, V.), plural *othęre*[2], *otheres* gen. sg. pl. (§ 79).

So in verb forms: as,—*flekęred* (A.S. flicerian) *pret. sg.* (§ 101),— *fetered* (A.S. ge-feterian) *p.p.* (§ 121, III.), *hamęled* (A.S. hamelian) *p.p.* (§ 121, III.), *opned* (A.S. openian) *p p.* (§ 121, III.), cf. the adjective *fethęred* (§ 121, X.).

The weak *-e-* (either not found or usually syncopated in A.S.) which, according to ten Brink (§ 61, III.), is inserted "zwischen *v* und Dauerlaut," and sometimes after *th*, is, of course, syncopated or slurred like the *e*'s just discussed: *sweuęnes* pl. (§§ 38, V.; 44), *euęre*, *neuęre* (§ 90), *brothęres* gen. (§ 36), *brethęren* (§ 41), and *fethęres* pl. (§ 38, V.). The morphological value of this *-e-*, however, is rendered dubious by the occurrence of such spellings as *fyngęres* pl. (§ 38, V.: *fyngres* A), *monęthes* (as well as *monthes* : § 38, I.) pl, taken in connection with the tendency of some Middle English scribes to use *ene* (*ele*, *ere*) indiscriminately for *ne* and *en* (or *ŋ* ?), etc.: see *heuene*, with variants, § 14, p. 42, cf. p. 38, and the C spellings *chaumbere*, *lettere*, *letteris*,

---

[1] Cf. the ordinal *scuęnęthe*, *scuęnthe* (§ 53, I.). [2] Cf. ten Brink, § 272.

coupelys, etc., (§§ 29, 38, V.), *-bele* for *-ble* in Romance adjectives (§ 51, II.), *susterin, schilderyn* (§ 41), *angery* for *angry* (562), *sundery* for *sundry* (440, 742, 957, 5174). Cf. also the next paragraph.

In native verb-forms, too, an *-e-* is sometimes written where it has no etymological status : as,—*herkenen* inf. (164, cf. 1180), *fortheren* inf. (8070, *ferthren* B), *herkened* pret. sg. (§ 101), *herkeneth* 3 sg. (1116), *herkeneth* imv. pl. (§ 118, I.); but cf. *wondren* (A.S..wundrian) *inf.* (1453, 5309, 6857), *handle* (A.S. handlian) *inf.* (5434), *wondred* p.p. (§ 121, III.), *vnbrydled* (A.S. brídlian) *p.p.* (3271, vnbrideled B), *bytokneth* 3 sg. (7876), *wondreth* imv. pl. (6525).[1] A similarly intrusive *-e-* shows itself in some Romance and Latin verbs : as,—the infinitives *coueren* (2597), *discoueren* (675), *recoueren* (4248), *delyueren* (3958), and *deliberen* (4831), *couered* pret. (§ 105), the participles *considered, couered, recouered, delibered, delyuered*, (§ 121, VIII.); but cf. the infinitives *remembren* (4470) and *suffren* (971, 2996, 5865), the imv. pl. *suffreth* (5866), the pret. *remembred* (§ 105), the participles *assembled, medled* (§ 121, VIII.), and the adj. *sucred* (§ 121, X.), though in these instances, too, C usually interpolates the irrational *-e-*.

§ 133. Apocope or syncope of weak *e* after an unaccented syllable which is capable of bearing an accent.

The metrical fact conveniently expressed by ten Brink (§ 257) in the rule: "Nach unbetonter, jedoch tonfähiger Silbe muss ein schwaches *e* verstummen," has been abundantly illustrated in the grammatical chapter.

For apocope see *housbonde, som tyme, oft tyme, welcome* (or *welcome?*) (§ 2), *louere, lyere, makere, morter, redere* (§ 7), *frendship, lordship* (§ 7), *answere* (§ 8), *syknesse* (§ 9), *felawe, wyndowe* (§ 15), *fortune, pursuyte* (§ 21), *seruise* (§ 26), *manere, maner, preyere* (§ 28), *goter* (§ 28, note at end) *Eleyne* (2532), *Pandare* (§ 139); cf. also *angwyssh, aungel*,[2] *concord, curtyn, raket, relyk, skarmyssh, trauers, yssue* (§ 22).[3] This principle may, of course, also prevent the addition of an inorganic *-e* : see *-ynge, -yng* in substantives (§ 10, III.) and participles (§ 120, III.), and cf. *forward* (A.S. foreweard, § 11), and the spelling *excesse* (§ 32).

For syncope see the plurals *seruauntz* (§ 39, I.), *resones, Troians* (§ 39, III.), *louers, maneres, porterys, preyers* (§ 39, IV.), the subjunctive

---

[1] C, however, shows *wonderyn, wondere, onbrydelid, handelyn, betokenyth, wonderith.*
[2] Cf. ten Brink, § 221.   [3] *Refuyt* (§ 22) can appeal to O. Fr. *refuit*.

làboured (§ 113), and the participles ànsuered (§ 121, III.), enlùmyned, pùrueyed (¹) (§ 121, IX.).

Doubtful lines ¹ are the following :

Ymagynynge that trauaylle nor grame, 372 ABG (-ing . . . travaill & game † D, neyther trauayle nor † gaine C).

Ne remuable (renuable B, resonable D, removeable G) fortune deface (to deface D), 6344 (cut out C).

Than wold (-e D) I of luse (his BD) battaylles endite, 8130 (leaf cut out C).

§ 134. Apocope of weak -e after a syllable having a secondary accent (ten Brink, § 258).

Apocope of weak -e after a syllable which has a secondary accent is on the whole not common. Examples are : haselwode || there, 7537 (but, haselwode || thoughte, 6868, see § 6), prescience, 5683 (§ 24). For preservation of the -e, see secrenesse, selynesse, wortthynesse (§ 9), sauegard[e] (§ 21), chàritàble, còuenàble, discordàble, èxcusàble, hònouràble, rèmuàble, resonàble (§ 51, II.) Cf. also, in the " definite " inflection, wòmmanlỳche, fòrknowỳnge, àmoroùse, dìspitoùse (§ 59, b), and superlatives like goòdlyèste (§ 59, a),—but, of course, the tèmpestoùs matère, his èxcellènt prowesse (§ 60).

In several Romance words in which the -e is not apocopated in the interior of the verse it makes little difference whether the syllable that precedes is regarded as bearing the main or the secondary accent : infortùne, òrisònte (§ 21), gèntilèsse (§ 25), còueytìse (§ 26), crèatùre (§ 27), impossìble (§§ 21, 51, II.), inuysible (§ 51, II.). For the treatment of final -es after the secondarily accented syllable, see §§ 37—39.

> Note.—Ten Brink's remark that weak -e "in Wortauslant" "nach nebentoniger Silbe" "zahlt im Vers wohl in der Mehrzahl der Falle nicht als Silbe mit ; wie es scheint sogar nach Muta cum Liquida, wo Verschleifung eintreten kann" (§ 258), does not hold true of the Troilus unless elided -e be included in the reckoning.

§ 135. Apocope of weak -e immediately after the syllable bearing the main accent.

I. Ten Brink (§ 260) holds that -e never counts as a syllable (except in rhyme) in certain words and forms which he enumerates (§ 260, (α—η). His list, however, requires modification.

(a) The accusative herè must be read as a dissyllable in 7948 : Biseching here (hirè B) syn that he was true, That she wolde come, etc.,

---

¹ Cp. John's throw no light on the scansion. In 372 Cp. has grace †; in 6344 Cp. John's agree with A letter for letter; in 8130 Mr. Austin notes no variation from A.

§ 135.] *of Chaucer's Troilus.* 367

unless we accept *hire that* C (hir that D); the repetition of *that* is ungrammatical, however, and there seems to be no good reason for rejecting the reading of the best MSS. (Mr. Austin's collation makes no note.) In 973, Forthi some grace I hope yn *here* fynde (hyrĕ C, hirĕ Cp., in her y D, in hyrę to B, in hir to G), the dissyllabic form has pretty good MS. authority; besides, the word is emphatic in sense besides having an ictus.—The singular possessive *hire, here*, is probably never dissyllabic in the *Troilus*, though one or two lines are doubtful (see § 74). The plural possessive, however, seems to be fairly entitled to two syllables in : Of *here* teris and the her*te* vnswelle, 5808 (hire B, *om.* † D; no note in Austin; G, which is beneath contempt in this stanza, reads : Of hir teres and the herte gan vnswelle). As a verse of nine syllables the line would certainly be no credit to its author (cf. § 146).—In 423 : Mi spirit which that aught[e] *youre* be (ȝoure C, ȝoures G Cp., youres John's Hl. 2392, ȝour[e]s B), *yourès* is doubtless right.—In 4173 : For *myne* wordes here and euery part (*so* ABC, my E; no note in Austin), we have our choice between *mynĕ* and an unpleasant nine-syllable verse. *Allę* before *myne* would be an easy insertion.

(β) *Somĕ* (pl.) is found once, if And *somĕ* wolde muche here mete alone, is, as it seems to be, the correct reading of 907 (see the variants, § 78).—The *Troilus* gives no support to the hypothesis of a "dative *eeche*" (see § 78).

(ε) Final -*e* never counts as a syllable, according to ten Brink, "in den Formen *were* und *made* nicht nur im Sg., sondern auch im Pl. bei apocopirtem -*n*." But the *Troilus* affords several examples of *were* in the subjunctive singular (see 1027, 2715, 3379, 3416, 4359 : § 113), and several of *werĕ* in the indicative and subjunctive plural (see 140, 1671, 1997, 3075, 5894, 6637, 8123 : §§ 109, VII., 114). For dissyllabic *made* ten Brink would substitute always *maked* in the singular, *maden* in the plural. The substitution of *maden* for *made* depends upon the general principle that in the plural -*en* rather than -*e* shall stand before consonants,—a principle which, however probable, can hardly be regarded as well established; the substitution of *maked* for dissyllabic *made* in the *Troilus* would necessitate considerable tampering with good MSS. (see § 101).

(ζ) That *sone* may retain its -*e* as a syllable is certain (§ 6, p. 10); for *wone*, however, see § 2. The *Troilus* affords no certain example of -*e* pronounced in Romance words in -*le* in the interior of the verse (§§ 30, 126).

(η) In 5681 *beforë* or *beforen* seems necessary : Of thinges wyst (wiste BG Cp. Durh.) *byforn* (*bifor* B, *before* DG, *byfor* Cp., *biforn* John's, om. Durh.) certeynly (full certeinlye Durh.).[1] *Therë* appears to be necessary in : And *ther* (*there* GG) lat (lete D, lett G) vs speken (-e D) of oure wo, 5906 (no note in Austin). In 3915, however,—That he cam *there* (*ther* BG) and (or CD) that (that that Cp.) he was born,—the reading of Cp. *that that* is clearly right. In 6841 we should doubtless read *here beleue* rather than *herè bleue* (see p. 204).

II. Other special instances of apocope deserve notice.

(1) The form *loue*, whatever its construction, shows a marked tendency to apocopate *-e*. Thus,—the noun (§ 8), the pres. ind. 1.sg. (§ 92, V.), the imv. sg. (§ 115, III.), the inf. (§ 119, X.).

(2) Ten Brink's remark (§ 261) that *-e* is " stets silbenbildend im Plural des attributiven Adjectivs, wenn dieses vor seinem Substantiv steht" (cf. his § 236) is contradicted by one line in the *Troilus* (1251, § 69). In this passage *good condicôns* occurs (notice the accent, and see § 54). Cf. also, *wỳse men* 3166 (*man* CD), which perhaps may be regarded as a sort of compound (the singular is written *wysman* in 5749 AC, *ways man* in C, *wise man* in D). *Lordes oldę* occurs in 7824. Cf. also 4, below.

(3) When a monosyllabic adjective in the definite construction immediately precedes a substantive accented on the second syllable, the inflectional *-e* of the adjective is necessarily lost (see § 54). Thus,— *this heigh matère* (3358), *yowre heyghę seruỳce* (4130), *here heyghę compleỳnte* (5467), *thy wrong conceỳte* (692), *my lowę confessioùn* (1613), *the pleyn felicitè* (8181). A plural *-e* must also disappear under similar circumstances : *of good condicions*, 1251 (§ 69).

(4) In a very few phrases the constant association of an adjective with a noun seems to have resulted in the formation of a sort of compound, freed from the necessity of the "definite" inflection of the first part (see § 54). Such are *good wil* (his good wil, 2294), *good word* in the sense of *commendation* (my, youre good word, 7444, 7985). Less certainly of this sort is *this good plit*, 3981. *Meanwhile* might be thought to belong here, but *this mënë while* occurs (2892) as well as *in this menę while* (see § 52). Cf. also 2, above.

(5) Monosyllabic adjectives standing in the predicate do not always take *-e* in the plural (§ 69). Monosyllabic participles standing in the predicate seldom take *-e* in the plural (§ 68).

(6) For the use of *alle*, *allę* as the plural of *al*, see § 80.

---

[1] The passage is not in CE.

(7) The comparative *more*, adj. (§ 64), subst. (§ 64), or adv. (§ 86), often loses -*e*.

(8) In the case of certain adverbs in -*e*, the possibility of a confusion with some adjectival construction makes suspicious what might otherwise be regarded as good examples of apocope; see *longe, low*, and cf. the Romance words *cler, pleyn* (§ 82).

> Note.—*Lyk* (cf. A S. *gelíce*) may be due to adjective influence (§ 83). *ilyke* also occurs (§ 82). For *ryght*, see § 83; for *lest*, see § 83, n. 2, for *down, adown*, see § 88, n. 1; for *grif*, see § 88, n. 2. all these words have lost their -*e* for good and all.

(9) Verb forms in -*eye* lose -*e* more or less freely. Thus,—inf. *seye* (§ 119, XIII.), *preye* (§ 119, X.); pres. ind. 1 sg., *deye, seye, preye* (§ 92, V.); pres. ind. pl. *sey* (§ 96, X.); subj. pl. *sey* (§ 112, V.); pret. ind. pl. *say the*, 656, *sey ye*, 1362 (§ 109, X.). Note also that in the imv. sg. of A.S. *licgan* (A.S. *lige*) we have *ly* and *lye* (§ 115, V.), and in the imv. sg. of the Romance verb *preyen, prey* (§ 116, IV.).

(10) In *as helpe me Gòd* and other idiomatic invocatory or optative phrases containing a subjunctive, the arrangement of the accents, fixed by sense and usage, brings together the subjunctive -*e* and another unstressed syllable after the accented root-syllable of the verb. Since the accentuation of phrases of this kind cannot be interfered with, the -*e* of the subjunctive disappears in Chaucer's verse. Thus,—*help me God, as help (helpe) me God (Iuno, Pàllas, hère Pallàs), as wysly helpe me God, God help (helpe) me so, helpe me so the mone, And helpe me god so at my most[e] nede, God yeue your herte care, Ioues yeue the (me) sorwe, I bidde god so yeue yow bothe sorwe, Yet preye I God so yeue yow right good day. So wo worth that day*, etc. The aggregate of instances of apocope that come under this head is not far from thirty (see § 111, III.).

(11) In a considerable number of instances the curtailed form of the Imperative Plural loses its -*e* entirely (§ 118, IV.). Some of the cases may be due to an extension of the singular form to the plural or to the petrifaction of the singular in an idiomatic use (cf. especially *lat* in the periphrasis *lat us* with the infinitive).

(12) The form *haue* (§ 124, VI.) has always apocope before a consonant. Thus,—pres. ind. 1 sg., pres. ind. pl. (also *han*), pres. subj. sg., pres. subj. pl., imv. sg. and pl., inf. (*hauen* occurs once in rhyme, 4305, *rh. grauen* ind. 3 pl.). In the pret. ind. and subj. sg., both *hadde* and *hadde* occur (§§ 102, 113).

(13) In the imperative singular of *tellen, telle* or *tel* is the usual form (see many examples in § 115, I.): there is no certain instance of *telle*.

(14) The praeterito-praesentia and the verb *wil* show considerable confusion, the singular form having sometimes intruded into the plural or even ousted the historically correct form. In the preterite, however, the *Troilus* shows no very striking proportion of forms with apocope of -e. See the paradigms, §§ 123, 124.

III. When the special cases discussed in I. and II. are provided for, a considerable number of examples of apocope are left. For obvious reasons the following words are not here considered: the nouns *wille, wil* (§ 2), *sight, sighte* (§ 9), *flyght, flyghte* (§ 14), *wey, weye* (§ 14), *tryst, tryste, trust* (§ 15); the nouns already treated in §§ 7, 11, 22; nouns in *-ynge, -yng* (§ 10); the adjectives already treated in §49; *cler, clere* (§.52); the adverbs *oute, out, sith, thanne, than, whanne, whan* (§ 88), *aweye, awey* (§ 89), and adjectives and adverbs in *-lich, -liche, -liche, -ly* (§§ 72, 84); participles in *ynge, -yng* (§ 120). There remain the following instances:[1]

(1) In nouns:[2] (a) Germanic,—*hope* ‡ (§ 2), *wel-come* * (§ 2), *wone* * (§ 2), *erthe* ‡ (§ 3; cf. *ertheles*, § 49, n. 5), *hegge* ‡ (§ 6, only case of the word in the poem), *dore* ‡ (§ 8), *kynde* (§ 9), *nede* (§ 9), *strete* * (§ 9), *trouthe* (§ 9), *tid* * (§ 9), *while* (§ 9), *hewe* (§ 14), *teer* * (§ 14), *yate* (§ 14), *bole* ‡ (§ 15), *hede* (heed) (§ 15); (b) Romance,—*grace* (?) (§ 21), *nece* (§ 21; no case in rhyme), *fayre* * (§ 21), *science* * (§ 24), cf. *prescience* * (§ 24). (c) Proper names,—*Criseyde* (1774, 4969), *Diomede* * (6455), *Eleyne* (2788), *Pandare* (§ 139) *Poliphete* * (2704).

Note 1.—In several of the nouns just cited the disappearance of -*e* may be regarded as merely a return to a form etymologically more correct. For *col, losse*, etc., see § 18 and cf. p. 38, note 1. The form and etymology of *ferde* (?) are too uncertain to rely on *ferd* as a genuine case of apocope (see § 15, § 121, p. 305).

Note 2.—There is no instance of the apocope in *tyme* except in the phrases *somtyme* and *ofte tyme*, which, as compounds, come under the head of § 133. There is no certain instance of *herte* (§ 3); the two lines 889 and 4529 admit of a satisfactory scansion with *hertë* (see p. 6). In one verse, 3197, *wyse* (§ 3) is required if the reading of AB be followed; CD have -*ë*; there is no note in Mr. Austin's collation.

Note 3.—The case of the noun *helpe* is curious. This word occurs several times in the *Troilus*, but never in rhyme and never with -*ë* in the interior of the verse (it is always *helpe, help*, or *helpe*, § 9). In the *Canterbury*

---

[1] For instances of apocope that depend on false readings easily corrected by a comparison of MSS., see, for example, *herte, lyne, myte, sonne, tonge* (§ 3), *eye* (§ 4), *spere* (§ 6), *hete* (§ 8), *leue, -nesse, reste, rote, sorwe, soule, trouthe, tyds* (§ 9), *game* (§ 12), *fere* (§ 14), *hede* (§ 15), *ioye*, (§ 21), *gyse* (§ 26), *cure* (§ 27), *stille* (§ 46), *lasse* (p. 136), *twoye* (p. 143), *sone, stille, vnnethe* (§ 82), *raughte, besoughte, tolde* (§ 99), *praide* (§ 104).

[2] An asterisk indicates that the word in question is found in the *Troilus* in rhyme with some word in -*e*, but that it is not found with -*ë* in the interior of the verse; a double-dagger indicates that the word occurs neither in rhyme nor with -*ë* in the interior of the verse; a word left unmarked is found both in rhyme with a word in -*e*, and with -*ë* in the interior of the verse.

§ 135.] *of Chaucer's Troilus.* 371

Tales (see Child, § 16) it occurs but once in rhyme (260), and in that case its rhyme-word *vhelpe* (A.S. *hwielp*, m.) has no right to final *-e*; in the interior of the verse *helpẹ* is never found (in 9202 T. read *helpe vnto*). So far as the forms of the rest of Chaucer's poetry have been recorded, the word occurs nowhere in rhyme and only once with *-ẽ* in the interior of the verse. This highly exceptional instance is *Leg. G. W.*, 1616: *Withouten deeth but I his helpẹ be*, where one is tempted to think of *helpe*, weak substantive, formed on the analogy of *huntẹ* (A. S. *hunta*).

(2) In adjectives a few examples of apocope besides those already discussed occur in the endings of adjectives. *At the lastẹ* || *the*, 2009; *at the lastẹ* || *this*, 5034; *the firstẹ* || *that*, 7430; *louẹ the wers* || *though*, 1950; *hym is wors* || *that*, 5144; *now is wors* || *than*, 7056; *good goodly*, voc., 458 (p. 128); *swych thornes*, 2359; *swych festes*, 7792.

> Note.—In 5144, 7056, cited above, *wors* may be regarded as adverbial in construction.

(3) In adverbs and prepositions (§§ 88-89): *aboutẹ, abouẹ, bothẹ, theryn, withinnẹ, withoutẹ, oftẹ* (in *oftẹ-tymẹ*), *sauẹ*.

(4) In verbs.—Besides the cases already mentioned, apocope of *-e* occasionally takes place in the inflection of verbs. See pres. ind. sg. (§ 92), pres. subj. sg. (§ 110), pret. ind. sg. (see § 99, under *broughte*, *felte, lefte, lyste, mette, thoughtẹ, tolde;* § 102 under *seydẹ*, cf. subj. pl. *seydẹ*, § 113; § 103, under *highte*), imv. sg. (see *makẹ*, § 115, III.; *byd, set*, § 115, V.), inf. (§ 119, X., a considerable number of examples; see especially *comẹ*, which is fond of *-ẹ; wetẹ, dorrẹ*, § 123), p.p. (§ 122, X., rarẹ).

> Note 1.—Ten Brink's remark (§ 261) that the *-e* is silent rather less often in the present subjunctive than in the present indicative does not hold good of the *Troilus*. In the ind. pret. sg. *thoughtẹ* and *seydẹ* seem to show a tendency to apocope, but there are not instances enough to generalize from, even if any principle other than the abrasion of frequent use suggested itself.
>
> Note 2.—*Gan* (3957) and *quod* (4856) are merely examples of the singular form used in the plural (see § 109, X.).
>
> Note 3.—In the case of *weptẹ, wcptẹ*, pret. sg. (§ 103), one cannot be certain that *weptẹ* is not an error for the strong form *wep*, which also occurs.

IV. Apocope of *-e* is apparently not influenced by the quality of the consonant that begins the following word, for there is hardly a consonant before which *-e* is not sometimes apocopated. There are perhaps more examples before *th* than before any other letter, but this may doubtless be explained by the fact that a number of monosyllables, either ill adapted in general to bear an ictus or apt to lose their stress altogether when not actually emphatic, begin with *th*. Such are,—the definite article *the;* the pronouns *thow, the, thin, this, that, tho;* the particles *that, there* (relative), *than, though, thurgh:* see, e. g.,[1] 267,

---

[1] Several of these places are cited merely for comparison: viz.,—376 (*than* perhaps has an ictus), 3162 (*than* has an ictus); 1950, 5144, 7056, in which the word in *th*, coming immediately after the cæsura, may have an ictus (cf. also III., 2, above).

305, 376, 413, 495, 532, 863, 1048, 1425, 1452, 1799, 1950, 2009, 2788, 3162, 3310, 4133, 4592, 4904, 4930, 5034, 5144, 5758, 6395, 6455, 6803, 7019, 7056, 7096, 7537, 7541, 7544, 7662, 7824, 8178. Apocope before *who, which, where, whan* (see, e. g.,[1] 1656, 1736, 2272, 3418, 4243, 4521) can hardly be ascribed to any other cause (though *who* is sometimes spelled *ho*, § 77). So always perhaps in cases like *trouę ye* (6231), *yeuę ye* (6598), *sendę yow* (1489), for apocope before *y* is not common enough to allow us to ascribe it to the "semi-vocalic" character of that sound.

Since a good many cases of apocope fall before the cæsura, the recognition of the doctrine of the "extra syllable" in that situation may reduce materially the number of silent -e's in the *Troilus* (see § 144 for the evidence). But it is important to remember that, even if it can be established that Chaucer occasionally allowed the extra syllable before the cæsura, we are not therefore justified in assuming that we have an instance of this license when its sole utility would be the preservation of a final -e. There are too many examples of undoubted apocope *elsewhere in the verse* to make such an inference anything but a begging of the question.

The upshot of all this appears to be that apocope, except in the case of a few words like *louę*, etc., must be regarded as a license for the nonce and cannot be brought under any rules but those of metrical exigency (see Child, § 92).

§ 136. Syncope or slurring of -e in final syllables when the noun accent falls on the syllable immediately preceding (cf. ten Brink, § 259).

Undoubted instances of full syncope are perhaps rare, but, since it is seldom possible to distinguish between full syncope and slurring (ten Brink's "Verschleifung") with certainty, it seems best to discuss the phenomena under a single head. The sign of syncopation (-ę-) has been used for convenience, but without any intention of implying full syncope in all cases.

(a) *-es*: in the plural, *louęres* (§ 39, IV.); in the possessive pronoun *hęręs* (but also *heres, yourès*, § 74). For *-ęs, -s*, in adverbs, see § 91.

(b) *-est* in pres. ind. 2 sg.: *lyst* (jaces), *seist, seyst, spękęst*, and

---

[1] In 2272, 3418, 4243, 4521, however, the word in *wh*, coming immediately after the cæsura, may have an ictus.

§ 136.] *of Chaucer's Troilus.* 373

probably *rennest*,[1] are genuine (§ 93, II.); *flest* and *sleest* are not to the point; in 8154 the question is between *steppes* and *seëst* or *steppës* and *sēēst* (§ 93, II., note), but the former gives much the smoother verse.— *-est* in pret. 2 sg. is almost always fully sounded: in 4944 perhaps *woldest* is to be read (see the variants, § 124, II., note); in *louedest*, 3562 (-ist CD, § 106), read *louedest* (rather " verschleifung" than full syncope).

Note.—Possible cases of syncopation in the superlative ending *-est* are: *myn alderleuest lord*, 3081 (-e C), and *myn alderleuest lady* [myn] aldyr louelyest ‡ C), 6939: in both of which either *leuest* or *leuestë* satisfies the metre. Compare the extraordinarily common syncopation in this ending in the Elizabethan dramatists.

(c) *-eth* : for syncope in the ind. 3 sg., see § 94, II. (forms like *abit, halt, lyst*, in § 95) ; for syncope in the ind. 3 pl. in *-eth*, see § 97 ; for syncope in the imv. pl., see § 118, II. (cf., however, the curtailed imv. pl. in *-e, -ę*, § 118, III., IV.).

(d) For syncopated weak preterites in *-de, -te,* and unsyncopated weak preterites in *-edę, -ed*, see §§ 99—105. Pairs are *dwelte* (§ 114), and *dwelled* (§ 99), *kyste* and *cussed* (§ 99), *made* and *maked* (§ 101), *sighte* and *siked* (*sighed*) (§ 105). A. S. *andswarode* appears before consonants as *answęrede, answèrde, answèrēd*, before vowels and *h* as *answęręde, answèrde, answèręd, answèrēd* (§ 101), the last form before a syllable that has the ictus. In Romance verbs *aspyde* and *cride* (§ 104) are assured by rhyme; *cride, criẹd* occur before vowels, and *cryede* is found in the plural (see §§ 109, VIII., IX., 114); *paste* (§ 104) is assured by rhyme and *passed* by the subj. sing. *passed* before a vowel (§ 113); *preyde* is assured by rhyme, but we have *preyëde hem*, and this suggests the correction of *praydë here* (see § 104).—In verbs that make their preterite in *-ed (-ede)* exclusively, syncope (or slur) of this ending is rare : *louedę* || *that* occurs, however, in 1071 (§ 101), but *louëde, louëd* is the usual form; cf. also *louede ek* (4991), *louede hym* (2928), *loked into* (2312; but *lokëd he*, 2833), *leuede* || *yn* (5155, if the verse is 9-syl.), *lyuede* || *vnto* (subj., 6242); *liked wel* (2129) is perhaps not quite secure (§ 101).—For weak perfect participles, see in general, § 121. Worth notice are *afered* and *ferd* (§ 121, I)., *maked, maad* and *mad* (§ 121, III.); *abaysshed* (4075), *abayst* || *and* (2936) (§ 121, VII.); *purueyëd alle* (5670), *purueyëd* || *certaynly* (5714), *purueyed* || *but* (5668) (cf. § 121 IX.); *criẹd* || *than* (5249). *I-loued the* (594) occurs, and, before vowels or *h*

---

[1] In 6211, where John's reads *Troye ay rennëst* (smoother, perhaps, but lacking in authority).

are found—*beloued* ‖ (131), *mysbeleued* (3680), *shewed* (7812). In 6947 *werreyed* ‖ *on* is doubtless the correct reading (see under Synizesis). Note *pleyed tyraunt* (2325); *vntyd in* (§ 121, IV.). For *wont, woned* 'accustomed'; *woned* 'dwelt,' see § 121, III.

Note.—In the preterites *flekered, opened*, etc. (§ 101), we should read rather *-ered, -ened* than *-erḙd, -enḙd* (§ 132), and so in *couered*, etc.

(*e*) *-en*. Syncope is regular in the participles *born, shorn, sworn, torn* (§ 122, V.), *lorn* (§ 121, IV.), *slayn* (§ 122, XII.), *seyn* 'seen' (§ 122, XIII.); instances of *-en* before vowels, as *fallen, growen*, are of course suspicious, and may almost always be reduced to the elided form (*falle*, etc.) by comparison of MSS. (§ 122, V.). In the infinitive *seyn* (cf. the gerund *to seyne*) syncope is regular, but *seyen* also occurs (§ 119, XIII.); as to *hauen, han, haue, haue̦*, see § 124, VI.; for infinitives in *-en* before consonants (no sure instance) and before vowels or *h*, see § 119, V. In the pres. pl. of *seyn, seyn* is common (§ 96, V.), but *seggen* also occurs (§ 96, I.), cf. *liggen* (§ 96, I., III.); for *han*, see § 124, VI.; for *arn*, see § 124, I.; for the plurals of *shal* and *wil*, see §§ 123, VII., 124, II.; for plurals in *-en* before vowels, see §§ 96, V., 109, V. For the treatment of adverbs in *-en*, see §§ 88, 89.

These final *-en*'s are all inflectional, but other final *-en*'s may suffer syncope (or be slurred) under similar conditions, *i. e.* when they are immediately preceded by the accented syllable, and when the following word begins with a vowel (or weak *h*). Final *-ene*, under the same conditions, loses *-e* by elision and, thus becoming indistinguishable from final *-en* in sound, is treated like *-en* with regard to slurring. It is accordingly difficult to ascertain what the full forms of the Modern English *heaven, welkin, own* (proprius), etc., were in Chaucer's language, — whether *-en, -ne, -n*, or even *-ene* (see pp. 38, 42, 126). A similar uncertainty prevails with respect to *-er, -re, -el, -le, -em, -me* (see below).

The question between full syncope and slurring in the case of *-en* is often very nice. When *-n* is written (as in *born, sworn*), there is of course no doubt; but when *-en* (*-ene*) is written, no certain conclusion can be arrived at. Of the different ways in which it is phonetically and metrically possible to read *-en* before a vowel (or weak *h*), that seems preferable which, allowing the *-e-* to disappear, makes the *-n* vocalic and retains it at the end of its word as a very light "extra syllable." This method seems almost certain for lines in which the cæsura falls directly after the *-en*, particularly if the cæsura coincides

§ 136.] *of Chaucer's Troilus.* 375

with an insistent pause in the sense. Ten Brink (§ 272) takes the ground that -*en* should be emended to elided -*e* when the latter is possible: "Ueberall da, wo tonloses *n* apocopirt werden kann, wird man besser solche Apocope and in Verbindung damit Elision als Verschleifung annehmen, so beim Part. Perf. Pass. mancher Verba, und durchweg beim Inf. und dem Plur. Präs. oder Prät. des verbi finiti." This seems too sweeping. There is nothing against the -*en* slur *a priori*, and Chaucer certainly had no objection to it, for, if our texts be manipulated throughout in accordance with the rule suggested by ten Brink, there will still remain cases enough in which the -*en* slur, or something precisely the same in its effect on the ear, must be left undisturbed (see *heuene, heuen, or heune*, § 14), to say nothing of kindred phenomena with regard to *el, -le, -er, -re, -me, -em* (below). There seems to be no good reason, then, why Chaucer should always have preferred elided -*e* to slurred -*en* in forms in which, as in most infinitives, for example, a choice was open to him. True, the evidence of the best MSS. is that he *usually* preferred the elided -*e*; but there is no antecedent probability of a rigid rule; indeed, it does not seem unlikely that now and then his ear may have been better satisfied by the fuller form, especially, one might conjecture, before the cæsura. Nothing short of an autograph MS., however, can ever settle such questions as this.

(*f*) -*er*.—Final -*er* may be slurred when the following word begins with a vowel (or weak *h*). Whether this slur amounts to full syncope of -*e*- must be left undecided. For convenience, the mark of syncope (-*e*-) has been used, but with no intention of necessarily implying anything more than ten Brink's "Verschleifung" (§ 272). Examples of both slurred and unslurred -*er* have been given in the Grammatical Chapter: see *feuer* (p. 55), *brother* (p. 62), *tender* (p. 121), *other* (§ 79), *tymber, wonder* (§ 18, p. 61), *fader, moder, suster, doughter* (§ 18, pp. 62, 63), *coler, corner, daunger, dyner, leyser, quarter, soper, squyer* (§ 34, I., p. 90), *other, eyther, neyther* (§ 79), *ferther* (§ 86). Here belong the comparative adjectives *leuere* (§ 64, p. 135), *hardere, hotter, leuere, wysere, lengere* (*ibid.*), and the comparative adverbs *leuere, rathere, ferther, lengere, rathere* (§ 86); for the proper ending of these words in Chaucer is -*er* not -*ere*. As to the comparative adjective and adverb *bettre* (*better*), one may hesitate whether to put it here or in the next paragraph, but the classification is of no consequence for our present purpose (for forms and slurs, see §§ 64, 86, observing the variants under *bet*, pp. 135, 136). Cf. also the variants under *màner*, the reduced form of *manère* (§ 28, p. 82). *Euere* and *neuere* may be placed here or in the next paragraph : for a full discussion of their behaviour before vowels and consonants, see § 90. *Angre* perhaps belongs here (§ 19 : read *anger* ?) : it is not slurred in the *Troilus*. For *after, whider, yonder, other or, neither, whether*, see note at end of § 86. *Ouer* before consonants (except *h*) regularly counts as two syllables (cf. 2598, 2634, 7508 ; *ouer-thwart*, 3527) ; but before a vowel or *hys, hym*, a slur is common, as : *ouer vs*, 4269 ; *ouer his*, 2756 (on ‡ D) ; cf. 386, 3070, 4638, 5062, 5734 ; see also 2170, where cæsura intervenes : And radde it *ouer* ‖ *and gan the lettre folde* AB. But we have also *ouer al* (=uberall), 921 f (ouer alle B, oueral C ; D †) (: in general : I shal) (cf. 5689 ‡ B), and, on the other hand : There is in loue som cloud is *ouer that sonne*, 1866 (ouere B, -er ‡ the C, some cloudis in ‡ that sunne D), and *And that the mone hath lordship ouer the nyghtes*, 4598 (-ere B ; D †) (cf. 243 ‡ f C). In 1259, 1488, we are hardly to read *vnder* before consonant : instead, we may read *lyue* for *lyueth* in 1209 and *growe* for *growen* in 1488.

Note.—An interesting line is : *For al so syker as thow lyst here by me* (sekyr C), 2076. Here it would be impossible to tell whether one should read *syker às* or *syker as*, if it were not for the rhymes *tyme* and *pryne*.

Under the circumstances defined at the beginning of the last paragraph, -*re*, -*ere*, are reduced to -*re* (by elision), -*ere* (by elision and syncope), and are thus slurred with the following word, producing the same effect as the slurring of -*er* (last paragraph). As before, the precise nature of the slur (or syncope) cannot be determined. The uncertainty in scribes' spelling between -*re* and -*er* (-*ere*) renders impossible a rigid distinction between the words that belong here and those that belong in the preceding paragraph. Examples both of slurred and unslurred -*re* and -*ere* have been given in the Grammatical Chapter : see *answere* (§ 8) ; *chaumbre, -er, iaspre, lettre, ordre, poudre* (§ 29) ; *louere* (§ 7, p. 11) ; and, for unslurred forms before vowels, *chaumbre, ordre* (§ 29), *endere, fyndere,* [*harpour,*] *holdere, louere, lyere, makere* (§ 7). Compare the proper name *Cassandre* (=Cassandra) : *Cassandre Eleyne or ony of the frape*, 3252 (Cassaundir C) ; *Cassandre hym gan right thus hys drem expounde*, 7819 (Cassandre bygan B, Cassaundere hym gan ry3t thus expounde C)[1] ; *That called was cassandre ek* (om. BC) *al aboute*, 7814 (cassaundere C.).[2] Of slurred

---
[1] A is no doubt right. No note in Mr. Austin's collation.
[2] No note in Mr. Austin's collation.

[§§ 136, 137.] *of Chaucer's Troilus.* 377

verb forms the following will serve as instances; *why suffre ich it*, 6403 (suffere C); *if that ye suffre hym*, 3705 (ȝif [that] ȝe suffere hym C); *and ye suffre hym*, 3723 (suffere C); *How may ye suffre allas it be repeled* (repeles † A), 4956 (sufferyn that it be C); *I shal wel suffre vnto the tenthe day*, 6260 (suffere C); *suffure vs*, 5865 B; *And if that yow remembre I am Calkas*, 4735; *deliuere it* subj. 3 sg., 7321; *ne iompre ek* imv. sg., 2122 (iumpere C); *perseuere yn* imv. sg., 951; *delyuere here* (eam) imv. sg. or inf., 8106 (deliuer hire B); *And gan to motre I not what trewely*, 1626 (motere C); *recouere a blysse* inf., 3023; *recouere another* inf., 5068 (rekeuere a nother C); *mokre and* inf., 4217 (mokere C, moke A).

(*g*) Final *-el, -le* are treated in the same way as final *-er, -re* (see *f*, above). Thus,—*yuel apayed*, 649 AB (C †); *yuele* (adv.) *as*, 6601 A (-el B); cf. *yuel* sbst. (§ 18, p. 62), where the cases of slurs before consonants are, as indicated, easily corrected by comparison of MSS. For *lytel, muchel*, see § 48. For words in *-le*, see *netle* (§ 3) *temple* (§ 14), *ensample, moeble peple, title, vncle* (§ 21), *egle, table* (§ 21). Romance adjectives in *-le* (§ 51, n. 1, p. 121); *bridle* (imv. sg.) *alwey*, 4477 (-dele C, -del D); *iangle* (ind. 3 pl.) *of*, 1885 (-ele C, ianglyn of D); *rakle* (inf.) *as*, 4484 (-ele C; D †). Cf. *deuël haue* (p. 54), *epistol hem* (p. 55).

Note.—Apparent cases of slur or apocope like *-er, -re, -ere*, before consonants (not *h*) are almost always easily corrected by comparison of MSS. For examples, see the variants under *lettre* (§ 29), *bet* (§ 64, cf. 481 D), *yonder* (§ 86, note at end). Cf. *And I ther* (*om*. C) *after gan rome* (roman B) *to and fro*, 1601; *Nentendement considre ne tonge telle*, 6358 (see readings of ten MSS. in § 144). In the latter case, at least, we must allow the "syllable before the cæsura." For apparent slurs of *-el* before consonants, to be corrected by comparison of MSS., see variants under *yuel* (§ 18).

(*h*) *-em* (or *-me*). See *botme it*, § 14, p. 39.

§ 137. The treatment of interior weak *-e-* ("schwaches e zwischen dem Hauptton und dem Nebenton," ten Brink, § 262) varies, sometimes in the same word. Thus,—

(*a*) In compounds, whether Germanic or Romance : *lodësterre* (§ 2), *wodëbynde* (§ 3), *fellëfare* (§ 5), *lechëcraft* (§ 6), *stoundëmele* (§ 9), *mylnëstones* (§ 12), *lettëgame* (§ 15), *sauëgarde* (§ 21), but *forward* (§ 11), *stedefast* (§ 49, n. 3); (*b*) in nouns in *-nesse* (§ 9) : *kyndënesse, rudënesse*, but *fiebḻenesse* (read *feblesse*, see § 25, I.); (*c*) in adjectives and adverbs in *-les* (§§ 49, n. 5, 85) : *botëles, dredëles, drynkëles, endëles,* heléles, hertèles, knottèles, makeles, nedèles, resteles, roteles, routheles, specheles, sterēles, causeles, douteles, graceles, gilteles and giltles (cf. lyghtles, vertules); (d) in adjectives and adverbs in -ly, -lich, -liche (§§ 72, 84): byhouèly, hastèly, hertely and hertely, mekély, namely, softely and softly, sternelyche, treièly and trewely (trewly), vnkyndely, digneliche, fermely, formely, largely, nicely, richely, secundelich, straungely, but erthely, nedely, nedly (cf. helply, lowely, lowly, febely)[1]; (e) adjectives in -ful: blysful (p. 147), dredful (pp. 119, 130),[2] ferfulleste (p. 132), sorweful, sorwful (pp. 119, 130, 147), but once, perhaps, sorwèful (5393); (f) nouns and "gerunds" in -ynge, -yng (§ 10): festenynge, rekenynge, cheterynge, slomerynge, titeryng, wonderynge, but tokenynge, whysprynge (p. 31); (g) Romance nouns in -ment (§ 34): accusèment, auisement, element (cf. the plural, p. 104), entendement, iuggèment, parlément, sentement; (h) Romance nouns in -aunce (§ 23), -aunt (§ 34, IV.), -ence (§ 24): delyueraunce, desseueraunce, disauenaunce, ordenaunce, perseueraunce, sustenaunce, difference, reuerence, but remenaunt (cf. remembraunee) (cf. mountenau[n]s, 2792 C ‡; rememb[e]raunce, 7807 ‡ C); (i) Romance nouns in -ie (§ 30): baudery[e], frenèsye, poesye, poëtrie, prophesie (cf. the plural, p. 103), remèdye and remedye, trecherye, but nouellerye; (k) miscellaneous English words: euërich, euèry(?), euery, euerychon (§ 79), heuenyssh (§ 49, n. 3), cf. scryuenyssh (§ 84, n. at end), nathelès (§ 86), felawship (§ 7); (l) miscellaneous Romance and Latin words: collateral (p. 149), funeral, general (p. 122) but generally (§ 84, II.), cheual[e]rous (p. 122), frenetyk (p. 148), appetit (§ 34, VII.), conquerour (§ 34, II.), sorceresse (§ 25, II.; cf. deuyneresse), dùetè, nicelè, but suiete, seurte (§ 33), sòuereyne (p. 122) and souereyn (pp. 131, 134) (cf. sòuereynètè, § 126). On the forms April, Aperil, Aprille, see § 32, n. 3, p. 88.

> Note 1.—Interior -e- has given place to -in- in nyghtyngale (§ 3), A.S. nihtegale.
> Note 2.—Lorely, sunnelich, heuenlichę (§ 72) are false readings.
> Note.—Of interior e's due merely to the scribe (and of course not pronounced) many may be found among the variants registered in the Grammatical Chapter. Such are frendęschipe (§ 7), gladdęnesse, goodęnesse, sikęnesse, wittęnesse (§9).

§ 138. Syncope of other vowels than -e- and of consonants is rare (cf. ten Brink, § 263).

(1) The nicety of the question between lileue and bleue 'manēre' may be seen in the following lines. In all of them bleue may be read without doing violence to the measure, but in 6019 alone is bleue

---
[1] Hardely is for hardily.   [2] Cf. dredfully, nedfully (§ 84).

[§ 138.] *of Chaucer's Troilus.* 379

compulsory, in 6841 *here bileue* is certainly more probable than *here bleue* (see p. 204), and in 1820 *nomore . . . bileue* is at least quite as satisfactory as *namorë . . . bleue.*

> And whanne (when B) hem leste nomore ‖ lat hem *byleue,* 1820 A (bileue B ; CD have an entirely different line ; Austin notes *leue* from E, but registers no variants from Cp. John's).

> And euery wight han (haue CD) liberte (liberteis C) to *bleue,* 6019 (beleue CD ; no note in Austin).

> Intendestow that we shul here (her D) *bleue,* 6841 (beleue CD Harl. 2392 ; no note as to Cp. John's).

> Syn (sythe D) that (*om.* D) we (3e C) seyden (-e CD) that (*om.* C) we wold (wolde CD John's) *bleue,* 6854 (beleue CD Harl. 2392).

> Or al the nyght they most (moste Cp., mosten John's, muste D, muste hem *for* they most C) *b[l]euen* there, 7543 (bleuen B, bleue C, beleue D Harl. 2392).

Another doubtful case is 4207, in which we must choose between *bilynne* (A.S. *blinnan*) and hiatus :

> Of swiche (swhich B, whiche C, wych D) sikes koude he (*om.* B) nought *blynne* (so ACD, bilynne B ; no note in Austin).

(2) Of the A.S. *bi life* the usual form in the *Troilus* is *blyue,* which occurs frequently (§ 88) ; but in

> Thow shalt gon ouer (to) nyght and that *blyue,* 2598 (belyue C, bylyve E, as blyue D Hl. 2392 ; Cp. John's appear to agree with A),

belyue (*bylyue*) is doubtless correct.

(3) The noun *errand* (A.S. *ǣrende*) occurs but once in the *Troilus,* in v. 1157, where the MSS. vary as to its form : *erand was* A, *herand* B, *ernde* D (Cp. John's appear to agree with A ; the leaf is cut out of C) ; cf. § 7.

(4) The treatment of *rauysshen* by the *Troilus* MSS. is interesting. In 5299, 5305, 7258, we have our choice between *rauysshen* (with syncope or slur) and *rauysshe* (with elision).

> To (Go BC) *rauysshe* (rauyshe B, rauysch C, rauisshe D) here ne (*om.* C) kanstow (canst thou CD) not for shame, 5192 (stanza om. in Cp. ; no variation noted from John's).

> To *rauysshen* (rauasche C, rauissh D, rauysshe John's) hire but yf hereself it (*om.* C) wolde, 5299.

> To *rauysshen* (rauasche C, rauissh D) here syn (sithe that D) thow hast not ben there, 5305 (no note in Austin).

That *rauysshen* (rauisshe D, he rauassch shal C) he shal yow with his speche, 6136 (no note in Austin).

From hen[ne]s (hennes B, henys C) forth the *rauesshynge* of a (to rauysshen any B Cp. John's, to rauych ony C, to rauissh any D) queene, 7258.

Cf. the verbal noun *ràueshỳng* (p. 29), *ràuysshỳng* (p. 30).

(5) Other more or less certain instances of syncope (or slur) of vowels are seen in :

And *finally* (fynali B, finially C, fynally G, final D) cause of wo that ye (the C, thow D) endure, 682 (no note in Austin).

Ne scryuenyssh (strynenyssh B, coryously C, scryvenlich D, skryuenyscher G) or (ne C) *craftily* (craftyliche C, craftly D Cp., craftili G) thow it (om. CE) wryte, 2111.

Vp to (Vnto G) the (om. B) *holwghnesse* (holughnesse B, halownesse G) of the seuenthe (seueneth G) spere, 8172 (cut out of C; stanza not in D; no note in Austin).

Lord trowe (trow B) ye a *coueytous* (covetours D) or (om. CD) a (om. D) wrecche, 4215 (stanza not in G; no note in Austin).

Ye bothe for the *seson* ‖ and for the feste, 168 (BC *om. the second for*; D *reads* and eke for; no note in Austin). (Cf. 7275 C).

And yn here *bosom* ‖ the lettre doun he thraste, 2240 (And in her bosom doun the lettre cast D; no note in Austin).

O olde *vnholsom* ‖ and mysbyleued (myslyued B, mysbeleuyd C, mysleuyd D) man, 4992 (no note in Austin).

<small>Note.—In *Maugre Polydamas or Monesteo*, 4713, we should doubtless read *Mònestèd* (trisyllable) rather than *Polydamas* : the movement of 4715, which rhymes with 4713, seems to be conclusive : *Polyte or eke the Troian daun Rupheo* (cf. also 4716). For *Pàndarus*, *Pandgrùs*, when these forms occur, we should doubtless read *Pàndare*, *Pandàre*, with elision or apocope of *-e* (see § 139).</small>

(6) Syncope *th* of is certain in *wher* = *whether* : *wher*, 2348 (whe[r] A, wher(e) C), 2736 (wher(e) C), 2908 (whei(e) C), 3888 (wher(e) B, whether ‡ C, wher D †), 5493 A (ther † B, whe·der D †; stanza not in C), 5824 (whether (?) C ‡, wheither? D ‡), 6356 (wher(e) B); *wher(e)*, 270 (C †, whethir ‡ D) ;[1] *whether* (monosyl.), 2551 B (wher C, whether? AD); cf. 7663 ‡ D. In 7098 A *uher* should be *whether* (emended by Furnivall). In 2348, 2736, 5824, 6356, a vowel or weak *h* (*he*, *hym*) follows, so that *whether* would be possible (§ 136, *f*), but 270, 2908, 3888, 5493, in all which consonants follow, are decisive. So far as the *Troilus* is concerned, the syncopated form

---

[1] The scribe of C mistook *where* for the adverb of place.

[§§ 138, 139.] *of Chaucer's Troilus.*

wher seems to be confined to the unstressed part of the foot, but one cannot be certain of this, since it usually begins the verse (270, 2736, 2908, 3888, 5493, 5824, 6356).—For *other, or*, see note at the end of § 86.—Other words in *-ther* occasionally syncopate or slur *-e-* when the following word begins with a vowel or weak *h*, but there is no evidence that they lose *th* : see § 136, *f*. In 5309 C read *whedyr thou art gon* for *whedyr thou art thus gon;* in 372, the reading of C, *neyther*, which, if correct might suggest syncope of *th*, is pretty certain to be wrong.

(7) For the few instances in which *euere* or *neuere* before a consonant (not *h*) counts for but a single syllable, see § 90. We have no certain means of knowing whether there was syncope of *-v-* in these cases; if so, we should expect to find readings like *ere, nere* or *er, ner* (cf. *where, wher*, for clipped *whether*). A trisyllabic foot, however, seems more likely than ten Brink's *eur, neur*, in spite of *paraunter* for *parauenture* and *mysaunter* for *mysauenture* (see § 27).

(8) The exclamatory *benedicite* occurs three times in the *Troilus*, each time as a trisyllable : 780 f (: be *inf.*), 3599 f (: he), 3702. In 780 the spelling is *bèndisteè* in B, *bèndistè* in Cp. John's, *benediste* in C. This seems to settle the pronunciation of the trisyllabic clipped form as *bèndisteè* rather than *bencite* (Child, § 96 ; Skeat, *Prioresses Tale*, etc., p. 141 ; ten Brink, § 263) or *bendcite* (ten Brink, *ibid.*). The dissyllabic *benste* (*Towneley Myst.*, pp 85, 99, quoted by Mätzner, *Poesie*, p. 109) might come through *bendistee* as well as through *bencite*. (Cf. also Kolbing on *Ipomadon A* 4480 (p. 421), A. Kaufmann, *Trentalle Sancti Gregorii*, p. 55, *Erlanger Beitr.*, No. 3).

(9) In one instance, *comprehende*, inf., is perhaps shortened to *comprende* : As muche ioye (ioy D) as herte (hert D) may (myght D) *còmplende*, 4529 (comprehende BCG, comprehend D, comprende Cp. John's).

(10) *Dèsespeìr, despeỳr* (§ 34, VII.), *desèsperaùnce* (1615 f), *despeỳred* p.p. (36 f, 42, 779), occur in the *Troilus*. There is naturally some confusion in spelling : thus A reads *desespeyred* in 36, 42, and *desespered* in 779, though the metre shows that the shorter forms are right; and C reads *desperaunce* in 1615, where the metre requires *desesperaunce*; A *desper* in 1091, where the metre requires *desespeir*.

§ 139. Apocope of consonants (cf. ten Brink, § 264).

I. Apocope of *-n* in verb-forms has already been referred to in § 136, *e*. See the material in the Grammatical Chapter under Present

Indicative Plural (§ 96), Present Subjunctive Plural (§ 112), Preterite Indicative Plural (§ 109), Preterite Subjunctive Plural (§ 114), Infinitive (§ 119), Perfect Participle (§ 122).

II. On the so-called apocope of *-eth* in the Imperative Plural, see § 118.

III. Many proper names have lost a final *-s*, sometimes with further change of form (cf. ten Brink, § 264). The following list is thrown together for convenience, with no attempt at classification.[1]

Achìlle, 8169 f (-Ħ D) (: wille *n.*); Achìlle thorugh, 7922 (-es BCD). But,—Achìlles, 3216 ; Àchillès, 1501 f (: douteles).

Adoòn, 3563 (Adon BCD). [Adonis.]

Amète, 664 f (: bete *inf.* A.S. bétan).

Arge, 7168 f (: large); Arge, 7297. [Argos.] But,—Argus [the guardian of Io], *as Argus eyed*, 6121.

Dēiphèbe, 8015, 8017 (Deyphèbe C). But,—Dēiphèbus (before vowels, *h*, and consonants), 2487, 2493, 2507, 2510, 2528, 2571, 2581 (Delphebùs ‡ D), 2634, 2686, 2778, 2787, 3068 ; Dēiphebùs, Deyphebùs (before vowels, *h*, and consonants, and in rhyme) 2483, 2565 f, 2627, 2643, 2654, 2696 f, 2726 f, 2760, 3046 f (D ?), 3063.

Dìomède, Dỳomède, 6378 f (: blede *inf.*), cf. 6546 f, 7387 f, 7404 f, etc. ; *-e*, 6409, 6469, etc. ; *-e* he, 8120 ; *-e* here (*gen. sg.*), 7880 ; *-e* haue (*ind. 2 pl.*), 8040 (Diamede C); Dìomède ‖ that, 6455 (Dy- B).

Dite, 146 f (Dyte CD) (: write *pres. ind. 3 pl.*). [Dictys.]

Horàste, 3639 f (: his laste); *-e*, 3648 (-ast D, -este C). [Orestes, cf. § 125.]

Iùuenàl, 4859 (-Ħ D).

Lukàn and, 8155 (-can BD).

Mercùrye (*trisyllable*), 3571 (Mercure B, -ie C, -y D), 8190 A (-ie B); Mercùrye ‖ of, 6684 (*-ie* B, Mercùryè ‡ *trisyl.* D).

Mỳda, 4231. [Midas.]

Omèr ‖, 8155 ; Òmer or [2], 146 (Omere C, Homere D).

Ouỳde, 8155 (Ouìde D).

Pandàre, 610 f (: care *n*), 3445 f, 3947 f, etc. ; Pandàrè (before consonants), 2292 (-dàris C), 2360 (-dàrus C), 2500 (-dàrus C; D †), etc. ; Pandàré (before vowels), 1063 ; Pandàré ‖ herkęne,

---

[1] A consonant (not *h*) follows unless the contrary is noted. The list gives the forms of ABCD.
[2] A *of* †.

§ 139.]   *of Chaucer's Troilus.*   383

658 (-dàris C); Pandàre, 4397 (-dạrùs C, -d[à]re D), 5244 (-dàr answerd[e] D), cf. 829, 1002, 1152, 2136, etc., etc.; Pandàrẹ, 3471 (-dàrus C, -dàre D), 5468 (-dàre BD); Pàndare, 736 (-dạrys C †), 1038, cf. 1030, 2577, 2761, etc.; Pàndare ‖ here (*adv.*), 868 (-dạrys C); Pàndare ‖ herde, 876 (-darys C); Pàndarẹ, 582, (Pandàre ‡ D; C †), 2646 (-dạrus C), 2957 (-dạrus C), cf. 5015, 5303, 6644; Pàndarè ‖ I, 1044; Pàndarè ‖ and, 5747 (Pàndarùs C, Pàndare in ‖ BCp. John's). But,—Pàndarùs, 618 f (-is C), 1178 f, 1205 f, 1514 f (-is C), etc.; Pàndarùs (before consonants), 1142 (-dàrè D), 1170 (-dàris C, -dàre D), cf. 761, 2024, 2227, 2311, etc.; Pàndarùs (before vowels), 1191 (-è C), 2022 (-è D), etc.; Pàndarùs (before *h*), cf. 6917, 6920, etc.; Pàndạrus (before consonants), 1575 (-dạris C, -dạre D), cf. 2178, 8072; Pándạrus hym, 2337 (-dare D), cf. 2059 (*he*), 3050 (*it*)[1]; Pàndạrùs ‖ alweỳ, 2437 (-dàre B, -darùs ‖ was C, -dàrẹ ‖ was D); Pàndạrùs ‖ and, 932 (-darỳs C, -dàre D); Pandạrùs ‖ that, 3604 (Pàndarùs BC, Pàndarè D).

Pòlyphète, Pòliphète, 2552 f (Polyfete D) (: swete 1 *sg.* : plete *inf.*), 2701 f (: spete *inf.*); Pòliphètẹ ‖ they, 2704 (-phèté ‖ gun[ne] they ‡ D).

Pòlymỳte, 7301 (-myʒt C, Polymites D).[2] But,—Polỳmytès, 7851 f (Poli- B, Polymites C, Polemites D) (: Thebès : Ethỳoclès).

Polỳte, 4715 (Polìte B, Pòlyte D).

Prỳam may, 5583 (Prìam BC; D †); Prỳàm (before consonants), 4804 (Prìàm B, Prìàm(us) D; C †)[3]; Prỳàm (before vowels), 3633 (Prìàm B, Prìàme C), cf. 5868, 6647, 7589;[3] Prỳàm his, 4801 (Prìàm BC, Prìàm(us) ‡ herẹ (*gen. pl.*) D).[4] But,—Prỳamùs was, 4719 (Prìamùs BD); Prìamùs ‖ and, 6055.

Quyrỳne, 4687 f (Qwyrine D) (: pyne *n.* : fyne *inf.*).

Santìppe, 4714 (Sartipe † D). [Xanthippus.]

Satùrne, 3558 f (: disturne *inf.* : turne *inf.*); -e, 3467 (D †) (first word in verse).

Stace, 8155 f (: pace *inf.* A, space BD).

Virgile, 8155 (first word in verse).

A remarkable line is :

Virgile Ouyde (Ouide D) Omer Lukan (-can BD) and (or D) Stace, 8155 (cut out of C; no note in Austin).

---

[1] Or, *Pàndarùs it is.*
[2] Polymyte (Polymyʒt B, Polymites D) and many a (*om.* C) man to (al to C) skathe (no note in Austin).
[3] First word in the verse.   [4] Read *sauc-gard*[*e*] in A.

Note.—Besides *Iuppiter* and *Ioue*, the form *Ioues* (nom., voc., acc.) occurs. *Iuppiter*, 1318 (Iupiter C, Iubiter D), 5331 (Iubiter CD), cf. 6345. *Ioue*, 4270 f (: houe *inf.*) ; *Ioũe* (before consonants), 3564 CD, 3857 ‡ A, 4997 (Iouo B), 5778 ‡ CD, cf. 5306 ; *Ioue* (before a vowel or *h*), 3467 (Iovis D †), 3857 BCD, cf. 3564 AB, 5741, 5811, 5854, 6570. *Ioues* (before consonants), 2692 (-is CD), 2857 (-is D), 7320 (-e C ; D †), 7838 (Iouus[1] C, Ioue D), cf. 7809 ; *Ioues hath*, 6365 (-ë D).

§ 140. Synæresis (cf. ten Brink, § 266).

In proper names : *Symoỹs* (6210), *Troỹlus*[1] (568, 596, 834, 871, 1768, 2027, 2751, 3330, 3681 (?), 6035, 7404, 7483; but *Tròylùs* is the usual form). Besides *Criseỹdë* (passim), *Crisèydẹ* (1774, 4969), and *Criseydà* (169 f), there occur *Crisèijdà* (2509, 2729) and *Crysèijdë* (1734). *Dei-* in *Deiphẹbus* (*Deiphebùs, Deiphèbus, Deiphèbe*) always makes one syllable in the *Troilus* (see references in § 139, s.v.). *Phëton*, 7027, was to be expected. There is no knowing how Chaucer pronounced the name of *Pyrous*, one of the sun's team : the word occurs in 4545 : That *Piros* (Pirors B, Pirus C †, Pirous D, Pyrous G ; no note in Austin) and tho swyfte stedes thre.—*Obeyssaunce* (with synæresis of *-ey-*) is given by ten Brink as the only form of this word in Chaucer ; but *obèijsaùnce* occurs in 3320.—In *hèijnoùs* (2702) there is no synæresis.

§ 141. Diæresis (cf. ten Brink, § 267).

In Greek proper names, in *-eüs* : *Tïdeüs, Tỳdeùs*, 6451, 7166 f (Thèdeoùs C), 7295 (Thèdeùs C), 7843 f (thïdiùs C), 7856 (thèdeùs C), 7864, 8109 f ; *Tïreùx*, 1154 (Tryeux † B, Thèreùs D) ; *Cappàneùs* (7867) (Campàneùs D). *Oënonè*, 654 f (oonone B, senome † C[e], Tynome † D) is curious.

Note 1.—*She told ek how Tydeus* (Tideus BD, Cithideus † C) *er she stente*, 7848, and *Tydeus* (Tideus BD, Thedeus C) *sone that doun descended is*, 7877, suggest the pronunciation *Tidèus*. The readings are not suspicious, and Mr. Austin's collation contains no note on either line.—In the *Hous of Fame*, *Orpheüs* (1203) occurs, and in *B. Duch.* 569 *Orpheüs* (dissyl.), but the *Troilus* has only the latter (5453).—*Imenèus* (4100) is for *Hymenaeus*.

Note 2.—In 4036 A *soür* is an error : the correct reading is *sucre*.

§ 142. Synizesis (ten Brink, § 268).

The Romance dissyllabic vowel combinations *-ia-, -iau-, -ie-, -iou-, -uau-, -ue-, -uou-*, regularly retain their dissyllabic character in the *Troilus*. Thus, *-ia-* in *celestial* (972, 976 f, 6203 f); *special* (260 f, 894 f, 974 f, 1048 f); *marcial* (6331 f); *-iau-* in *alliaunce* (4588 f);

---

[1] MS. *iou* with sign of contraction (expand *ioues* or *iouis* ?).
[1] Var. *Troïlus*.

variaunce (5647 f, 7125 f, 8033 f); *-ie-* in *audience* (4732 f, 5207 f, 6598 f); *conscience* (554 f); *experience* (4125, 7620 f); *pacience* (7760); *prescience* (5649, 5660, 5683, 5726 f); *sapience* (515 f); *science* (67, 7618 f); *pacient* (1083, 2984 f, 6249); *Ariète* (6254 f, 7553 f); *quiète, quìete* (p. 72); *-iou-* in *abusion*[1] (5652 f, 5722); *affeccion, -ioun* (296 f, 4206, 4432 f, 4815); *attricioun* (557 f); *auysions* (6737 f (*-iounys* C)); *champioun* (2512); *compassioun* (50 f, 467 f, 3245); *complexions* (6732 f); *conclusion, -yon, -ioun* (466 f, 480 f, 1344 f, 2385 f, 4868 f C, 5114 f, 5946 f, 7128 f, 7366 f, 7673 f); *condicion, -ioun* (3659, 7194 f, 7330 f); *confessioun* (1613 f); *confusion, -ioun* (4785 f, 4848); *consolacioun* (708 f); *constellacioun* (5407 f); *correccioun* (4174 f); *curacioun* (791 f); *deliberacion* (3361 f); *destruccion* (141 f); *deuocioun* (187 f, 555 f); *diffusioun* (3138); *discrecioun, dyscression* (3736, 4176 f, 4868 f); *disgression* (143 f); *disposicion, -ioun* (1611 f, 6365 f, 7906 f); *dyminucioun* (4177 f); *entencion, -ioun, -ioun* (52 f, 211 f, 345 f, 683 f, 1343 f, 1380 f, 7130 f); *execucion* (3363 f, 6367 f); *illusioun* (3883 f); *illusions* (6731 f); *impressioun* (298 f); *impressions* (6735 f (*enpressiounnys* C)); *mencion* (7966); *mocion* (5953 f); *oppressioun* (2503 f); *opynion, -yon, -ioun, -youn* (347 f, 710 f, 790 f, 2382 f, 5115 f, 5650 f, 5657, 5687, 5692, 6157, 7221 f; *passion, -ioun* (3882 f, 5367); *permutacion* (7904 f); *possessioun* (2504 f); *presumpcion* (213 f); *proporcion* (7191 f); *protestacion, -ioun* (1569 f, 5951 f); *redempcion* (4770 f); *regioun* (5405 f); *reprehencion* (684 f); *repressioun* (3880 f); *reuelacions* (6729 f); *saluacioun, sauacion* (464 f, 1466 f, 1571 f, 1648 f, 6044 f (*-cyone* C)); *suspecion* (1646 f, 8010 f); *tribulacion* (7351 f); *delicious* (6806); *enuyous, enuyous* (1751, 1942, 4296, 4542); *gracious* (885 f); *melodious* (6940); *religious* (1844 f); *-uau-* in *continuaunce* (2919); *-ue-* in *casuel* (5081); *cruel, cruwel* (9, 1422, 1427, 1520, 3224, 4292, 4537, 4687, 4756, 4958, 5492, 5506, 5846, 5851, 5854, 6962, 7085, 7259, 7831, 7897, 8048, 8114, 8124); *cruelte, cruwelte* (586 f, 1076 f, 5434 f); *cruwellyche* (5966, cf. 8119); *mewet* (6557); *growel* (3553 (gruwel B, grewel D)); *-uou-* in *vertuous* (254, 891 (*-tyuous* C)); *voluptuous* (6235 (*-teuous* C)).

But there are a few cases of synizesis. Thus,—*opynyon, -youn* (5635, 5700, 5702); *entencioun* (6995 f D; cf. 681 f C); *furious*[2] (1521 D; read *furyes*); *volupteuous*[2] (6235 C); *signifiaunce* (6725 f,

---

[1] The rhymes *adown, down, toun,* show that the proper spelling of these words is in *-ioun*. Other rhymes are *lyon, preson, enchesoun, sermon, comparyson, Lameadoun*.

[2] Easily corrected by comparison of MSS. so that the synizesis disappears.

7810); *prescience* (5673, 5724); *perpetuely* (4596); *preciously*[1] (5252 C). In 1090, D reads *tempestuos* (for *tuous*?) but the true reading is *tempestous*. In *corageus* (7163 f) and *vengeaunce* (8071) the *e* after *g* is not pronounced.

Of classical proper names *Cynthia*, *-ea* (6270, 7381), *Lollius*, *Lollyus* (394 f, 8016 f), *Ixion* (6575), *Palladion* (153 f; cf. *Palladion[e]s feste*, 161) occur without, *Layus* (1186), *Palladion* (164) with synizesis; cf. *Mercurye*, below. *Monested*, *Ruphed*, *Phebused*, rhyme with each other (4713, 4715, 4716).

The superlatives of adjectives of *-y* show no synizesis : *frendlyeste*, *goodlyest[e]*, *thriftieste*, *worthiest*, *-e* (§§ 57, *a*, 59, *a*, 70, *a*). Synizesis occurs in the comparative adverb *gladlyer* (8140), but not in the comparative adjectives *frendliour* (885), *worthier* (251).

In words in which the accented syllable is followed by *-ie*, *-ien*, *-ied*, *-iynge*, the *i* may become consonantal : in the case of *-ie* this synizesis is necessary in the interior of the verse. Thus *augurye*, *contrarye* (noun) (cf. § 51), *consistorie*, *furye*, *letuarye*, *memorie*, *Mercurye*, *myserie*, *storie*, *victorie*, *comedye*, *parodye*, *tregedie* (§ 31); the plurals *aduersaries*, *contraries*, *furyes*, *ladyes* (so the genitive, § 36), *storyes*, *victories* (p. 103); *merye* (p. 113); *contrarye* adj. (§ 51), *transitorie* (3669 f). So also in the verb forms : pres. ind. 1 sg. *herye* (3793 f : *merye* pl.), *warye* (7741 f : *contrarye*); pres. ind. 3 pl. *carye* (7105 f : *letuarye*); inf. *taryen* (2104, 2707 f), *varyen* (2706 f), *waryen* (2704 f), *vnbodye* (7913 f : *parodye*); perf. part. *yburyed* (2396), *heryed* (4599, 4655), *iheried*, *yheryed* (2849, 4646),[2] *taried* (2824, 7499, 7712). *Astonyed* and *astoned* (p.p.) both occur[2] (see 1512, 1688, 3931, 8091). In one instance the p.p. *heried* has three syllables : *heried* (4098). Forms in *-ynge* occur both with and without synizesis : *burynge* (i. e. *buryinge*), *taryinge* ; *heriynge*, *taryinye* (see § 10). In 7225 we have *tarieth*. In *How thow me hast waryed on euery side*, 6947 (weryed BC, weryhed D, werreide G; no note in Mr. Austin's collation),[3] *werreyd* is no doubt the correct reading).[4]

Note 1.—In *ladyes* ten Brink (§ 257) prefers syncope *ladyes* : see the variants in § 38, VII., above. Cf. also *enemys* and *prophesies* (?) (*ibid.*).
Note 2.—Ten Brink's remark (§ 268) that *seur* (O. Fr. *seür*) is always monosyllabic in Chaucer, seems to be true; but *aseuraunce* occurs (7622 f).

---

[1] For *louelyest*, 6939 C, read *leuest*.
[2] Cf. *yhered*, 2058 A (yheried BD, iheried C).
[3] BG omit *on*, which should be supplied.
[4] Compare the context, especially *victorie* and *spille*.

Note 3.—In *As thoughte hym tho for pitous distresse*, 4286 AC (pitouse D), we must read either *pitcous* with B or *pietous* with Cp.

§ 143. Miscellaneous slurs and contractions.

This is is occasionally reduced to one syllable and written *this*. Thus,—1448 (this is D), 3778 (this seyd (is) D), 5552 (this is C, thus ‡ D), 5855 (in A read *haue ye* for *haue*), 5936 (C †), 6514 (be ‡ this C); this is, 419 ‡ D, 5965 ‡ C, 7357 ‡ C. (Cf. Child, § 96; ten Brink, § 271; Skeat, *Minor Poems*, p. 304.)

For *nas, nere, nil, nolde*, see § 124; for *noot, nyste*, see § 123.

Is it and *it is* are both found in the *Troilus*: there seems to be one trustworthy example of each:

What wonder *is it* though he of me haue ioye, 1834. In this line ABD have *is it* (i.e. *is it*), C indicates the pronunciation by by reading *ist*. (There is no note in Austin.) Cf. also *what wonder ist*, 6425 C, where ABD read *is*. In 6949, C has *ist* for *is it*, but the line is incorrect in this MS. Similarly *wast* for *was it* occurs in 3209 C, where, however, *was it* should be restored. These last two examples, though worthless as readings, have their value in determining the nature of the slur in 1834.

Ek (Eke G) som tyme *it is* a craft to seme fle (flee G), 747 ABG (Ek it is a craft for summe sumtyme to fle C, Eke it is craft some tyme to seme sle D; no note in Austin).

Note 1.—In *What nede were it this preyere for to werne*, 4773 AB (cut out of C; D†; no note in Austin), we may choose between *nedē were it* and *nedę were it*.

Note 2.—A considerable number of slurred *it's* and *is's* disappear on a comparison of MSS. Thus,—*telle it the*, 599 C; *be it*, 2060 C (cf. 7293 C); *is it* (?), 1435 A; *as it was*, 3295 A; *do it redresse*, 6403 A; *may it not*, 7926 (cf. 2242 C?); *help it*, 1405 D; *no thing it tarnith*, 1883 D; *I wil it sow* (?), 2289 C; *can it*, 5553 D; *if it so be*, 7059 C; *when that it is ago*, 1880 B (or *that it is*); *seith it is* (or *it is*) *told*, 3638 C; *soth it is* (or *it is*) *seyd*, 4054 C (cf. 6117 D); *that it is* (or *it is*) *a folye*, 6688 D; *certis it is* (or *it is*) *non*, 6771 C; *it is of*, 7038 A; *now it is wors*, 7056 A; *that is*, 1431 D; *ther is*, 3707 D, 4570 D, cf. 3872 C; *now is*, 3389 A; *weye is*, 1702 A; *what is*, 681 C; *wo is*, 694 C; *loue is*, 6307 D; *counseilt is this*, 7655 D.

Thow art is slurred once:

Thow art (Thart B Cp. John's, Thu art C, Thou art D) wys (wys(e) B, wis(e) D) ynowh forthi do nought amys, 4471. Here the reading *Thart* found in B Cp. John's is particularly noteworthy.

Not so certain is the slur of *at* in

The grete sweigh (swough B, swey C, sweyf D, swigh G) doth (makith C) it to (om. G, than D) come (falle C, fal D) *al* (om.

D) *at onys* (ones BDG),-2468 (no note in Austin). Here it is possible that either *to* (with G) or *al* (with D) should be omitted, in spite of the weight of MS. authority.

Of the running together of *I* (*he, she*) *nĕ* into *In'* (etc.), the *Troilus* affords no good example : see *y nę dar(e)*, 2946 D (I dar ABC); *I nę wolde*, 5899 C (nolde AD, nold B) (cf. 1023 f C°); *he nę kyst*, 812 C (AB om. ne); *he nę may*, 2212 C (he may ABD); *sche nę wil*, 6719 C (nyl AB, niH D). See Child, § 96; ten Brink, § 272, and *Compl. to Pite*, n. to v. 105, p. 177.

For *at the* B occasionally writes *atte*. Thus,—*atte laste*, 1230 B, 5097 B; *att[e] laste*, 916 B; *atte leste*, 7313 B; *atte meeste*, 7310 B; *atte fulle*, 209 B; see § 53. Cf. *attother*, 5096 B (at the other AC, at other D †); *the tother side*, 7050 A (that other BCD). *Atton(e)*, 3407 f B (at oon A, at on C, at on(e) D), is different. In 7732 C, for *at the writyng* read *at writyng*. In the phrase *at erste* (§ 54, n. 2) the readings are interesting,—*at erst[e]* AC, *at erste* BCp., *att erst* D †, *attę erst[e]* G : the reading of G suggests the conjecture that in *firstë vertu* (§ 54, n. 2) the demonstrative *the* has been swallowed up by the preceding *that* (conjunction),—*that the, thattë, that*.

Note 3.—A considerable number of miscellaneous slurs disappear on comparison of MSS. Thus,—*I am*, 720 A, 967 C, 1516 C, 2198 A, 4490 D; *I haue*, 6460 B, cf. 1384 A, 7549 B; *thow hast* (?), 5153 D; *he hath*, 3917 C; *ye han*, 5958 A, cf. 5469 B, 5538 C; *ye will*, 6188 D; *prey him*, 2536 C; *therfore as a*, 680 A (cf. 1321 C, 2268 D, 2341 A, 5031 C (?), 5562 D); *lete vs goo*, 6888 D; *in his armes*, 4029 D (?), 5881 D;[1] *now in a*, 1550 B (cf. 363 D, 850 C, 1290 D (?), 1320 † D, 7658 D); *the in thyn*, 5306 C (D?); *here an ensaumple*, 4863 A; *down of here*, 6876 A (cf. 474 C, 1004 D, 1945 D, 2052 A, 3263 D, 3855 D, 5346 C, 6513 C, 6733 D, 6790 C, 7275 C, 7825 A); *and yf she*, 7665 A (cf. 7629 D); *plaunte or a*, 5429 D; *sorwe or in*, 641 C; *wel for I*, 613 C (cf. 1692 D, 3151 D, 3689 B, 5320 D, 6124 D, 7128 A);[2] *natt at a bene*, 6726 D; *and at after none*, 7493 D; *can not thanke*, 3840 C; *yow with*, 3474 D. So in apparent examples of slurred *that*;[3] *whil that* (quasi *whil't*), 468 CD; *so that* (quasi *so't*), 2247 D; *thenk that al* (quasi *thenk't*) 2824 A; *wel that this* (quasi *wel't*), 2994 A; *er that he* (quasi *er't*), 4435 A; *whan that he* (quasi *whan't*), 7516 A; cf. 1437 B, 2805 C, 3073 C, 3208 A, 5138 D, 5279 C †, 5350 A, 5986 C, 6035 AB, 6170 † C, 6180 D, 6483 D, 7073 B, 7541 D, 7662 C, 8051 D. In 958 the right reading is doubtless *he that parted is* (John's ; -yd CD) rather than *he that departed* (AB) with slur of *that*. So also in apparent examples of slurred *and* : *Al day for loue* and *in swich a maner cas*, 1542 C; cf. 1239 C, 1941 C, 2184 D, 2604 C, 3651 D, 4212 C, 4232 C, 4586 C, 5770 C, 6615 D (?), 7151 D; see also the apparent slur of *than* in *leuer(e) than ben*, 7287 B. In 6139 C *I*

---

[1] In 1037 A, 4047 C, the slur *on his, in his* may be avoided, if *Troylus* be read as a dissyllable (§ 140); but in both lines *his* is an interpolated word.

[2] In 2532 no one will hesitate between What wolt thow seyn yf *I for Eleyne* sente, and *for Eleynë*.

[3] In most cases the corruption consists in the insertion of a superfluous *that*.

schal ben has the time of two syllables (cf. Scotch *I'se*), but the line is manufactured by the corrector of C.

Note 4.—It is just possible that in 4166, 4984, the scribe of B intended *thought* for a shortened *though that*.

Note 5.—*Through* (A.S. þurh) is variously spelled (*thurgh, thorugh, thour,* etc.), but is always monosyllabic, except perhaps in 7846 : *Thorugh* (Thorwgh B, Of C, Thurgh D) his (hire C, *om.* D) wol I yow (*om.* Cp.) telle. Now and then one or another MS. seems to make the word dissyllabic elsewhere, but comparison affords an easy correction (see the MSS. in 1444, 4130, 4738, 7132).

§ 144. The extra syllable before the cæsura.

In many verses of the *Troilus* the retention of an unaccented syllable (*-e, -eth,* etc.) before the cæsura would convert a masculine cæsura into a feminine, and produce the phenomenon known as the extra syllable before a cæsural pause (cf. Skeat, *Prioresses Tale,* pp. lxi ff.; ten Brink, § 307, 3). In these cases (with the rarest exception) it is possible to reduce the verse to the normal movement by apocopating *-e* or by syncopating the vowel of the syllable in question (*-eth,* etc.). In the Grammatical Chapter apocope has accordingly been assumed for such cases (in accordance with my own conviction); but, since the question cannot be regarded as settled, it is perhaps worth while to give a special section to the matter. In the following list the aim has been to enumerate all verses which the advocates of the extra syllable theory could reasonably adduce in support of their contention. Examples in which the verse may be made regular by eliding *-e* (*i. e.* in which the word after the cæsura begins with a vowel or weak *h*) have of course been left out of account.[1] The readings of D have been disregarded throughout the section, and the same is true of trivial variations, except when they concern the point under consideration.

I. Cases of -e.

I. Weak nouns (§§ 2, 3) :
This litel spot of *erthe* ‖ that with the se, 8178 (erth B).
But now of *hope* ‖ the kalendes bygynne, 1092.
For neuere sith the *tyme* ‖ that she was born, 1228 (tyde C; B *om.* the).
Right in that selue *wyse* ‖ soth for to seye, 3197 (C *om.* for).
So *bole* (§ 15, p. 47) :
Right yn the white *bole* ‖ so it bytydde, 1140 (bool B) ; similarly 4901.

---

[1] Such are 14, 44, 88, 107, 116, 118, 160, 176, 180, 189, 224, etc., etc.

Note 1.—In 889, read rather *hertę || semęth* than *hertę || semeth*; in 6823, rather *hertę || beręth* than *hertę bereth*.

Note 2.—For *wil* or *wille* (sbst.) before a pause, see 228, 861, 1564, 3465, 4362, 8000 (cf. p. 4).—*The pleyę* / occurs as the first foot of 5528, but see p. 9. Cf. also Wel-come *my knyght / || my pes / my suffisaunce*, 4151, : where there is of course no cæsura after *wel-come*.

II. Masculine nouns having *-e* or *-u* in A.S. (§ 6) :

He loketh forth by *hegge* / || by tree / by greue, 7507 (hegge B, hegis ‡ C, hegges D, hege G). Better,—*forth || by*. As to the form *hegge*, see p. 10.

From *haselwode* || there Ioly Robyn pleyde, 7537.

Tydeus *sone* / || that doun descended is, 7877. See p. 10, where ten Brink's remark (§§ 260, 261) on *sone* is corrected.

III. Feminines in A.S. *-u* (§ 8) :

And seyde || here in this closet *dore* || withoute, 3526.[1]

Here at this secre trappe *dore* || quod he, 3601.

To scornen *loue* || which that so soone kan, 234.

Blyssyd be *loue* || than kan thus folk conuerte, 308. Other instances of *loue* || with the cæsura after the second foot may be seen in 16, 46, 436, 677, 744, 1129, 1759, 1789, 1823, 1866, 1912, 3014, 3359, 3622, 4103, 4158, 4433, 4830, 5084, 5243, 5761, 6296, 6314, 6844, 7443, 8039. So perhaps, 518 : Of hem that *loue* lyst febely for to auaunce. Cf. also 3851 ‡ Aᶜ.

At which the god of *loue* || gan (to) loken rowe, 206. (BCCp. John's om. to).

Kan he wel speke of *loue* || quod she I preye, 1588 (of louē || I ȝow preie C ‡).

Ayens the god of *loue* / || but hym obeye, 6530. So perhaps, But al so cold yn *loue* || towardes the, 523 (or,—*cold || yn*); Thow koudest neuere yn *loue* || thyn seluen wysse, 622 (or,—*neuere || yn*); I that haue yn *loue* || so ofte assayed, 646 ; My name of trouthe yn *loue* || for euere mo, 7418 (ἄλλως C) (or,—*trouthe || yn*).

In *loue* || for which yn wo || to bedde he wente, 1147.

Of *loue* || that made hire herte fressh and gay, 2007 (Of loue wich that made his herte gay C).

For *loue* || that euery other day || I faste, 2251.

In *loue* || but as his suster hym to plese, 2309 (second cæsura after *suster* ?).

To feffe with || youre newe *loue* || quod he, 8052.

Note.—In *For goddes loue what seith it telle it vs*, 1181, scan *it* || rather than *loue* ||. In *Refuseth not to loue for to be bonde*, 255, scan *not* ||. In *Aquyls*

---
[1] Cf. And they that layen at the dore withoute, 3587 (lay A, leye C).

hym wel for goddes loue quod he, 2285, and *Bysechyng hym for goddes loue that he*, 3004, the cæsura is after the second foot, but there is also a pause after *loue*.—*Made loue withinne hire* (hir G) *for to myne*, 1762 ABCG, appears to be a 9-syl: verse; D reads *Made love within her hert for to myne* (there is no note in Mr. Austin's collation).—In 4586, 4587, *Loue that* (with a pause in the sense after *loue*) begins the verse.

IV. Monosyllabic feminine nouns with long stem-syllable (§§ 9, 11) :

On his *byhalue* ‖ which that vs alle sowle sende, 2819. But perhaps we should read (with GCp.) : On his half which that soule vs alle sende (see variants, p. 17, under *halue*).

But to thyn *help* ‖ yet somwhat kan I seye, 672 (helpë ‖ sumwhat C). (Or,—*help yet* ‖ ?)

Ne to thyn owen *help* ‖ do bysynesse, 795 (hele C).

To fynde vnto oure *helpe* ‖ the beste weye, 5954 (help B).

God for thi *might* ‖ so leue it wel to fare, 7322. Cf. 8151.

Withouten *nede* ‖ there I may stonde in grace, 1799.

And hast [the] lesse *nede* ‖ to countrefete, 2617 (ABC om. the, but GCp. John's have it; B om. to; C inserts to before countyrfete).

For now is *nede* ‖ sestow not my destresse, 2888.

I shal to morwe at *nyght* ‖ by est or west, 7114. Cf. 7544.

But so nyl not an *ok* ‖ whan it is cast, 2474. Cf. 2420.

In thus good *plit* / ‖ lat now non heuy thought, 3981. Similarly 4396.

And of my *sped* ‖ be thyn al that swetnesse, 1036 (speede / B).

Thow be my *sped* ‖ fro this forth and my muse, 1094 (spede / B). (Or,—*forth* ‖.)

And men cryede in the *strete* ‖ so Troylus, 1697.

Thenk (that) al swych taried *tid* ‖ but lost it nys, 2824 (BC om. that; C has on for al).

And haue my *trowthe* ‖ but thow it fynde so, 831 (treuthë ‖ but thou fynde it so C).

And be my *trouthe* ‖ the kyng hath sones tweye, 1255.

And al the *while* ‖ which(e) that I yow deuyse, 3277 (C om. yow).

A woful *wight* ‖ to han a drery feere, 13 (see p. 33).

That in this *world* ‖ ther nys so hard an herte, 5802. Cf. 6308, 7085, 8060. So also :

And by my *thryft* ‖ my wendyng out of Troye, 6292 (thrifte B). Cf. Now by my *thryft* (thrifte B) quod he that shal be sene, 3713, where the cæsura comes after *he*.

Note 1.—Several of the examples just cited have little or no significance : see § 11. The same may be said of lines in which a verbal noun in -*ynge*, -*yng* (§ 10) is followed by the cæsura or a strong pause : see 1089, 4803.

Note 2. In 4061, *And now swetnesse* ‖ *semeth the more swet[e], tho* is clearly to be omitted (with BCCp John's) : otherwise, we should probably read *swetnèsse* || *scmeth*.

V. Masculine and neuter nouns that sometimes take an irrational *-e* or a dative *-e* (§ 14).

In several instances in which a dative *-e* might perhaps be expected to occur, but in which the cæsura directly follows, no *-e* is pronounced (and sometimes none is written). That most of these instances have no significance, however, will be seen by comparing them with the idioms discussed on pp. 36-37.

Vp on his *bed* || but man so sore grone, 1642 (bedde / B).

He softe into his *bedde* || gan for to slynke, 4377. Cf. 5017, 5395, 6644, 6657, 6772. In 1152 *a-bedde* || loses its *-e* by elision or apocope before *half*.

Hath right now put to *flyght* || the Grekes route, 1698.

For ay the ner the *fyr* || the hotter is, 449.

Wel neigh doun of (on ‡ A) here *hors* || she gan to sye, 6545.

But by thi *lyf* || be war and fast eschuwe, 2103 (or,—*war* || ?).[1]

Lest yn this *town* || that folkes me dispise, 6002 (folk[es] C). Cf. 7486, 7517.

Out of the *wey* / || so priketh hym his corn, 219 (woye C). Cf. 2388, 6864, 7025.

Monosyllabic neuters with short stem-syllable stand on a somewhat different footing (see p. 38, n. 1) :—

But at the *yate* || there she sholde oute ryde, 6395 (see p. 46).

Thorugh more wode and *col* || the more fyr, 2417 (cole C, cole || more B, or col || the Cp. John's). (See p. 54.)

But al that *losse* || ne doth me no dishese, 4751 (los B; *cut out of* C; no note in Mr. Austin's collation). (See p. 58.)

The same may be said of *hewe* (p. 42) and *tere* (p. 45) :

It shewed in his *hewe* || bothe euen and morwe, 487 (hewe || on C).

For euery *teer* || which that Criseyde asterte, 3912 (tere B).

Compare also *weye, wey* (but see p. 46) :

For which that *weye* || for ought I kan espye, 6131 (wey B; *om.* † C).

Note.—It is perhaps worth mentioning that the two instances in which *borw, bourgh* occurs as a monosyllable, are before the cæsura (the other cases are in the phrase *to borwe*) ; see p. 39.

VI. *Ferde, hede* (§ 15); *smert* (p. 64) :

Whi sholde thanne of *fered* || thyn herte quake, 5269 (for ferd C). (Or,—*thanne* || ?).[2]

---

[1] In 7637, scan rather *day* || than *with lyf* ||.

[2] Cf. 6073, where the right reading is perhaps *for-ferd* (pp.) || *out* (for fered ACp., for ferde || out B, for fer C†).

Now taketh *heed* || for it is for to done, 7266 (hede / B).

The proper form of the noun *smert* seems to have no -e (see p. 64):

Ney ded for *smert* || gan bresten out to rore, 5035 (smerte B). In 6780 *smert* is perhaps a verb (= smerteth): if so, the cæsura follows *harm*.

VII. Romance nouns which have a right to -e (§§ 21, 22):

As man / bryd / *beste* / || fissh / herbe and grene tre, 2852 (best B).

A *broch* || that he Criseyde yaf || that morwe, 8024 (broche B; C †).

Was there noon other *broche* || yow lyste lete, 8051 (broch B). In 8053 scan rather: But thilke *broche* that I || with terys wete, than *broche* ||. The cæsura of 4212: But wel I wot a *broche* gold of asure, is not quite certain (*broche* || ?).

To morwe. || allas. that were a *fayre* || quod he, 3692 (fair B, fayr C).

Yf that I hadde *grace* || for to do so, 3770 (gracë had || B; C *om.* grace †).

And seyde *Nece* || who hath arayed thus, 2272 (nece || ho C).

And seyde *Nece* || se how this lord can knele, 3804 (B †; nece || how C).

But alwey good[e] *nece* || to stynte his wo, 1468 (goode nece || alwoy to C).

In 1340 read *nece* || *alwey* (with BCCp. John's) instead of *nece* || *lo* A.

That in *science* || so expert was that he, 67.

That *prescience* || put fallyng necessarie (*l.* necessaire), 5683.

God wot the *text* || ful hard is soth to fynde, 4199 (tixt ‡ is C).

    Note 1.—*Ioye* ||, 4478, suffers elision before *halt*. In 4535 : *This ioye* || *may not ywrete ben* || *with inke*, we should perhaps cut out the prefix *y-* (with BC John's), but Cp. has *i-writen*. In 6093, read *ioyë* || and *the amorouse daunce*.

    Note 2.—The reading is doubtful in 5504 : *Peyne torment* (turnement † C) *pleynt* (pleynte B, *om.* C) *wo and* (*om.* BCp. John's ; and ek C) *distresse*.

    Note 3.—In 4592 : *Bynd this* acord || *that I haue told and telle* (acorde B), *acord* may be referred to the corresponding O. Fr. form (see p. 74). *Pres* in the sense of *crowd* never has an -e in the *Troilus* (see p. 74).

    Note 4.—In *Towchyng thi* lettre || *that thow art wys ynowh*, 2108, we may omit *that* with BC (no note in Mr. Austin's collation). In *Foryaf and with here* vncle || *gan for to pleye*, 4420, we may omit *for* before *to* with BC (no note in Mr. Austin's collation).

    Note 5.—In 2917 *sire* (first word in the line and followed by the usual vocative pause) apocopates its -e (syr B).

VIII. Proper names:

Vnto *Criseyde* || that heng here hed ful lowe, 1774.

And folwe alwey *Criseyde* || thi lady dere, 4969 (or,—*alwey* ||).

This *Diomede* || that ladde here by the bridel, 6455.

And *Poliphete* || they gonnen thus to waryen, 2704.

Cf. *Pandare* || which that sente was || from Troylus, 5468 A.

Particularly noteworthy is :

Fro *Meleagree* ‖ that made the bor to blede, 7878 (Meleagre B, meliagre C ; no note in Mr. Austin's collation).

IX. *More* (sbst. and adv., §§ 64, 86), *worse* (adj., § 64) :

Nor axen *more* ‖ that may do yow disese, 1232.

By god I shal *nomore* ‖ com' here this wyke, 1515.

For euere *more* ‖ myn herte lust to reste, 1915 (mo BC). Similarly 4243, 4946.

Withoute *more* ‖ to (is † B) Troylus yn thei went, 2751.

I kan no *more* ‖ but that I the wole serue, 3232. Similarly 4035, 4115, 4156, 4654, 7731.

There was no *more* ‖ to speken (*l.* skippen *with* BECp. John's; schepe C) nor to traunce, 3532. (Or,—*skippen* ‖ ?.)

He dar *nomore* ‖ come here ayen for shame, 6130 (nomor B).

> Note 1.—In *And yf I more dorste prey yow as now*, 2521 (dorst preye B, durste preye as now C), read probably *dorste prey[e]* rather than *dorstë preye*. In *For ay thurst I (I preste* † C) *the more that I it drynke*, 406, the position of the cæsura is probably *more* ‖.

Or loue the *wers* ‖ though wrecches on it crien, 1950.

That hym is *wors* ‖ that is fro wele ythrowe, 5144.

For now (it) is *wors* ‖ than euere yet I wende, 7056 (BC *om.* it).

> Note 2.—The construction in 5144 and 7056 may be perhaps be regarded as adverbial (§ 86).

X. Monosyllabic adjectives in the "definite" use (§ 53) :

That *at the laste* ‖ the dede slep hire hente, 2009.

But *at the laste* ‖ this woful Troylus, 5034.

Til *at the last* ‖ this sorwful wyght Criseyde, 5914 (laste BC).

Al be I not *the firste* ‖ that dide amys, 7430.

> Note.—In 3407 *the laste* ‖ suffers elision before *herof*.

XI. The plural of monosyllabic adjectives and perfect participles (§§ 67-70) :

Hath lordes *olde* / ‖ thorough which withinne a throwe, 7824 (old C).

In the following instances the adjective is in the predicate and the subject refers to a single person (cf. § 69, *b*) :

Now be not *wroth* ‖ my blod my nece dere, 1679.

And ben so *loth* ‖ to suffren hym yow serue, 2996.

Now beth al *hol* ‖ no lengere ye ne pleyne, 3010.

Ye ben to *wys* ‖ to do so gret folye, 3709 (C *has* swich *for* so gret).

And beth wel *war* ‖ ye do no more amys, 4022.

And ye so *feyr* ‖ that euerich of hem alle, 6533.

> Note.—In *If ye be* swych ‖ *youre beaute may not strecche*, 1426, *ye* refers to Criseyde, and *swiche* would be surprising (swiche ‖ B).

In the two examples of *al* that follow, we cannot be quite certain that we are dealing with a plural (see § 80):

This is o word for *al* || this Troylus, 4502.
And of the furyes *al* || she gan hym telle, 7861 (furies also ? C)
Perhaps we should read *als*.

> Note 2.—In *Criseyde which that* aH *these thynges say*, 2350 (al B ; C†), and *Criseyde which that* alle *these thynges herde*, 3641 A, perhaps the only cæsura is after *Criseyde*. 3225 perhaps runs : *And this* || *yn* alle *the temples* || *of this toun*. 7857 may be scanned *She told ek* || al *the prophesies by herte* (al B, al the profecy ‡ C).

Monosyllabic perfect participles (§ 68):
Of wommen (whom ‡ men C) *lost*. || thorugh fals and foles bost, 3140.
O nece pes || or we be *lost* || quod he, 3937. (Or,—nece ||.)
Now be ye (*sing. in sense*) *kaught*. || now is there but we tweyne, 4049.
This wordes (*om*. C) *seyd* (seyde BC) || she on here armes two, 5573.
Of thinges that ben *wyst* || byfore that tyde, 5739 (wiste B; *cut out in* C).

XII. The pronoun *hire*, *here*, dat. acc. sg. (pp. 152-3).

Since *hire* is seldom or never dissyllabic in the interior of the verse, cases of apocope before cæsura present no interest. Such may be seen in 315, 370, 443, 454, 2307, 3497, 4820, 4827 (*here* || *do* A), 5089, 5100, 5149, 5192, 5299, 5305, 6480, 7599; cf. also 7948 (see p. 153).

XIII. Adverbs.

For the reason just mentioned, no interest attaches to *here*, *there* before cæsura (cf. § 89): examples may be seen in 187, 2904, 4844, 6111, 6542, and perhaps in 4658. *Whanne* in : But ryght as *whanne* || the sonne shyneth bright, 1849 (when B, whan C) (see § 88) is also of no account. More interesting are : And *namelyche* || my dere herte ye, 5996 (nameliche B, namely C); *Secundelich* || ther yet deuyneth noon, 2826 (secound[e]ly B, secundeli C) (§ 84). In the following the constructions are not certainly adverbial:
For hygh and *low* || withouten ony drede, 3260 (see § 82, n. to *lowe*).
This short and *pleyne* || theffect of my message, 5552 (pleyn C).

XIV. Present Indicative of Verbs (§ 92, V.):
But wel I *rede* || that by no maner weye, 495.
As thus I *mene* || that ye wole be my stere, 4133 (mene || ȝe wol ȝe BCp., menë || wil ȝe C).
Wherfor I *seye* || that from eterne yf he, 5640.
I *seye* || that yf the opynion || of the, 5692 (or,—*yf* || ?).
Se how I *deye* || ye nyl me not rescowe, 6594 (dye B; ἄλλως C).
Compare the plural :

For which men *say* ‖ may nought disturbed be, 1707 (seyne B, seyn C).

XV. Present Subjunctive of Verbs (§ 111):

But if that I *consente* ‖ that it so be, 413 (BC *om.* so).

And yf the *lyke* ‖ than maystow vs saluwe, 2101.

Wher so yow *lyste* ‖ by ordal or by oth, 3888 (list B, Whether ȝe wolde C).

And yf she *write* / ‖ thow shalt ful soone (soon B) see, 7662 (And ȝif that sche write thow schat sone se C).

Or yf you *lyst* ‖ no manere vpon me se, 7751 (ȝe lust no more C).

Note.—In the case of the impersonal *list* it is not always possible to distinguish the apocopated subj. 3 sg. from the syncopated ind. 3 sg. See the following verses, in which the verb in question is followed by the cæsura : 1407, 2245, 2865, 3215, 5245, 6295, 7360, 7780, and cf. § 95.

XVI. Weak Preterites (§§ 99, 102):

Or he me *tolde* ‖ who myght ben his leche, 1656 (told / who myghte B, told ho myȝte C). (Or, perhaps,—*toldë* ‖ *who myghte*).

That to hire seluen she *seyde* ‖ who (ho C) yaf me drynke, 1736.

And gan to iape and *seyde* ‖ lord so ye swete, 2028 (seydë ‖ lord ȝe smete † C).

For which she *thoughte* ‖ that loue al come it late, 3310 (tought B). (Or perhaps better,—*loue* ‖.)

What that she *thought* ‖ whan that he seyde so, 3418 (thought[e] ‖ when B, thouȝte ‖ whan C ; BC *om.* the second *that*).

For wel he *thouhte* ‖ ther was noon other grace, 5614.

Abedde *brought* ‖ whan that hem bothe leste, 4521 (C *om.* hem).

Note 1.—In 4367 : *He seyde farewel myn herte and dere swete*,[1] the cæsura is of course after *farewel*, but there is a pause in the sense after *seyde*.

Note 2.—In 5486 : *As he that felte pyte* (pitie Cp.) *on euery syde, feltë pyte* ‖ *on* (with a slur of the final -e in *pyte*) is more probable than *feltë* ‖ *pytë on*.[2]—In 7088 : *So tendrely she* wepte ‖ *bothe eue and morwe*, we cannot be sure that *wep* (strong pret.) is not what Chaucer wrote (§ 103). In 4998 : *That I the* hadde (*subj.*) ‖ where *as I wolde in Troye*, BCCp. John's omit *as*.

Note 3.—For *answerede*, etc., see II., v., n. 2, below.

Note 4.—The reading *madë* ‖, in 312, is not supported by any MS. (see variants, p. 245).

Compare also :

As she best *kowde* / ‖ she gan hym to disporte, 2758 BCp. (§ 123, IV.).

As Crassus *dide* ‖ for his affectis wronge, 4233 (§ 124, IV.).

XVII. Imperatives :

---

[1] Instead of *herte and dere swete* read *dere herte swete* with BCp. John's. C has *dere h. s.* without *my*.

[2] As he that pite hadde B ; cut out of C.

§ 144.] *of Chaucer's Troilus.* 397

Go *loue*. ‖ for old(e) ther wil no wight of the, 1481. (§ 115, III.)

And *sey* ‖ thou mayst no lengere ‖ vp endure, 2603 (seye B, sei C). (§ 115, V.)

Now spek / now *prey* / ‖ now pitously compleyne, 2584 (*sing.*) (preye B, preye ‖ and ‡ C). (§ 116, IV.)

Now *vnderstonde* ‖ for I yow nought requere, 1443 (B ‡ *om.* nought; vndyr-stond C). (§ 118, IV.)

And seyde *awake* ‖ ye slepen al to longe, 1630. (§ 118, IV.)

Now *stynte* ‖ that ye no longere ‖ on it honge, 2327 (§ 118, IV.)

XVIII. Infinitive (§ 119, X.):

A man to *loue* ‖ til that hym lyst to leue, 686 (C ‡ *om.* that).

Nomore to *speke* ‖ for trusteth wel that I, 2511 (C *has* of this *for* to speke).

Now doth hym *sitte* ‖ now gode nece dere, 3817 (hardly,—*now* ‖). But BCGCp. John's omit the second *now*; D has it.

I may here *haue* ‖ right sone douteles, 4764. (§ 124, VI.)

That it shal *come* / ‖ but they seyn that therfore, 5661. Similarly 5662.

That thing to *come* ‖ be purueyed trewely, 5717. Similarly 5726.

I moste *come* ‖ for wheder sholde I gon, 6023 (com C).

Than shal [s]he *come* ‖ that may me blisse brynge, 7021.

She wolde *come* ‖ ye but she nyst[e] whanne, 7791.

So myght I *wene* ‖ that thynges alle and some, 5730.

The folk wol *wene* ‖ that thou for cowardyse, 6775 (seyn ‡ C).

The existence of the monosyllabic infinitive form *seyn* (§ 119, XIII.) makes the following examples inconclusive:

That is to *seye* ‖ for the am I becomen, 3095 (seyne C). Similarly 3126 (seyn B, seine C).

This dar I *seye* ‖ that trouthe and diligence, 4139 (seyn C). Similarly 4779 (seyn C).

The gerundial forms *to sen, to seyn*, and *to don* are too common elsewhere in the verse to make the following examples before the cæsura of any significance (§ 119, XIII.):

He was *to sen* ‖ fulfild of heigh prowesse, 1717. Cf. 3384, 3910, 4972.

That is *to seyn* ‖ that I foryeue al this, 4020 (say C). Similarly 6037 (seyne C), 7261 (seyne C).

And soth *to seyn* ‖ she nas nat al a fo, 1769 (say C).

That what *to done* ‖ for ioye vnnethe he wyste, 4095 (don B).

Note.—In 1781, scan probably : *And what to done best were and what eschue* (C om. were).

XIX. The Perfect Participle of Strong Verbs (§ 122, X.) :
To Troye is *come* ‖ this woful Troylus, 6560 (comyn C).
  Note.—In 8161 the correct reading is : *That thow be vnderstonde* (or *-en*) *god beseche* ; B inserts *I* after *god*.

II. CASES OF UNACCENTED TERMINATIONS ENDING IN A CONSONANT.

I. *-eth* in the pres. ind. 3 sg. (cf. § 94, II.) :[1]
Fro whennes *cometh* ‖ my walyng (wele † C) and my pleynte, 408.
Whan that it *cometh* ‖ but wylfully it weylen (weyuen BC, *which is right*), 1369.
That ofte ycleped *cometh* ‖ and endeth peyne, 5166. Much more energetic than *ycleped* ‖ *cometh*.
For al that *cometh* ‖ comth by necessite, 5620 (not in C).
Nough[t] that it *comth* (comes B) ‖ for it purueyed is, 5715 (not in C).
Whan (Til C) that she *cometh* (come C) ‖ the which (and that C) shal (may C) be right[t] sone, 6754. Cf. also 7516.
Wher it *bycometh* ‖ lo no wyght on it sporneth, 1882.
Men seyn ‖ the suffraunt *ouercometh* ‖ parde, 6246 (C †). (Or perhaps,—*suffraunt* ‖.)
Ek wostow how it *fareth* ‖ on (of BC) som seruice, 956.
And yet *me of-thynketh* (mathynketh B) ‖ that this auaunt me (may B) asterte (sterte B), 1043 (cut out of C).
Whan that hym (*om.* B) *thenketh* (*om.* B) ‖ a womman bereth (berth B) here heighe, 1486.
That wher he *cometh* (comth B) ‖ he prys and thank hym geteth, 1461.
Which that myn vncle *swereth* (swerth B) ‖ he mot be ded, 1739.
Al that now *loueth* ‖ asonder sholde lepe, 4605.
Criseyde *loueth* ‖ the sone of Tydeus, 8109 (cut out of C).

  Note 1.—So perhaps in 1292 : *To suche as hym thenketh* ‖ *able for to thryue*, but the cæsura may as well come after *able*.
  Note 2.—There are no certain examples in the imv. pl. owing to the instability of the ending in that form (§ 118), but note : *But yet* (om. C) *I seye aryseth* ‖ *and lat vs daunce*, 1306 (perhaps,—*seye* ‖ *aryseth*). The same may be said of the pres. ind. 3 pl. in *-eth* (§ 97) : see *As ony men that lyueth* (-en B, leuyn C) ‖ *vnder the sonne*, 1259, and *Which that men clepeth* (-yn C) ‖ *the* (om. BC) *wode ialousye*, 7576. *Lyth* 3 sg. (§ 94, III.) and *seyth* 3 sg. (§ 94, II.) and 3 pl. (§ 97) have, for obvious reasons, not been taken into account.

[1] *Scyth* ind. sg (§ 94, II.) and *pl.* (§ 97) has been left out of account.

II. *-est* :

Thorugh Troye *rennest* || ay (*om.* C) downward to the see, 6211.

<blockquote>Note.—*Lyst, seyst* have been left out of account (see § 93).</blockquote>

III. *-en* :

Thenne wolde I *hopen* || the rathere for to spede, 865 (hope rathere C).

That men hem *wrien* (wren B) || with asshe[n] (asshen B, asschin C) pale and dede, 1624.

I kan not *trowen* || that she (*om.* B) wol write ayen, 7661 (trowë || sche C).

Ne yf she kan *here-seluen* (self BC) || distorben it, 5765.

<blockquote>For examples before a vowel or *h*, see § 136, *e*.

Note.—In the examples before a consonant, it is of course possible to read *-e* for *-en* (*here-self* for *here-seluen*; in the examples before vowels, *-e* (elided).</blockquote>

IV. *-es* :

(i.) In the plural :

Both of his *ioyes* (ioie B Cp., ioy D) || and of his cares colde, 264. The sg. *ioie* is probably right.

By alle the *othes* || that I haue to yow sworn(e), 1384 (BCD *om.* to). The omission of *to* (BCD) gives *othës* || *that*. Cp. John's appear to have *to*.

To make *amendes* (amend B, an † ende C, amendis D) || of so cruel a dede, 1427. No note in Austin : *amendes* is probably right.

It is oon of the *thynges* (-is CD) || that (*om.* BCp.) furthereth most, 2453 (D has *that*).

In gentil *hertes* || ay redy to repaire, 2847 (C cut out). D om. *ay*, but Cp. John's agree with A.

Swych *argumentz* (-tȝ B, -tis CD) || ne (*om.* CD) ben not worth a bene, 4009. (No note in Austin). Cf. 466.

That *elementes* (-tȝ B, -tis C) that ben so discordable, 4595.

The *ambassiatours* (Thembassadours B, Theem-bassatourys C) || to Troye streyght thei (*om.* B) wente, 4802.

Thembassadours (The embassadourys C) || ben answered for fynal, 4807.

Theschaunge (The chaunge C) of *prisoners* (presoneris C) || and al this nede, 4808.

O ye *loueres* (-ers B, -eris C) || that heyhe vpon the whiel, 4985.

So gan the *peynes* || here hertes for to twyste, 5791 (peyne B, peine D; ἄλλως C †). (No note in Austin.)

Of al the (that B) *londes* (lond BC, londe D) || the sonne on shyneth shene, 5901. (No note in Austin.)

His *enemys* (enemyis C) || and in here hondes falle, 6615.

400   *Observations on the Language*   [§ 144.

Note.—In some of the lines just quoted it will be observed that the reading is doubtful.—In 7397, read *sykes sore* || *adoun* rather than *sorē sykes* || *adoun*. In 8154, the question is between *steppes* || and *seēst* or *steppēs* and *sēest* : the latter scansion gives a more satisfactory line. *Knees* is of course a monosyllable in 3025 (*knees* || *and*) and 3922 (*knes* || *and*).

(ii.) *-es* gen. and adverbial :

Shal han me holly *heres* || til that I deye, 5106 (C †). See § 74.

Ther *ayenis* (aȝeyn B, aȝen C) || answere I thus anoon, 1454.

Thenk here *ayens* (aȝenis B) || whan that the sturdy ok, 2465.

Or she vs bothe *at ones* || er that ye wende (at onys || or), 2961.

So as we shulle *togederes* || euere dwelle, 5984 (shal togideres B, That we schal eueremore togedere d[w]elle C).

He hadde in herte *alweys* (alweyes B, alwoy C) || a manere drede, 6415.

Note.—The variability of form in adverbs in *-es* (§ 91) renders most of the examples given above of little significance in the question of the extra syllable.

V. *-ed* in the perfect participle ; *-ede* in the preterite :

Ful wel *beloued* /.|| and wel men of here tolde, 131.

As he was *woned* (wont BC) || and of hym self (seluyn C) to (*om*. C) iape, 3397. Cf. *woned* || *to*, 4697. See § 121, III.

Thow *mysbeleued* || and (*om*. C) enuyous folye, 3680.

For when men han wel *cried* || than wol they rowne (let hem roune C), 5249.

That ben *purueyed* || but nedely as they seyn, 5668 (not in C).

That ech(e) hym *louede* (loued B) || that loked on his face, 1071.

And ay the peple *cryede* (cryed C) || here cometh oure ioye, 1728.

I that *leuede* (hauede C) || yn lust and in plesaunce, 5155.

Ne (And B) though I *lyuede* (-ed B) || vnto the worldes ende, 6242.

Note 1.—In 6947 *werreyed* should doubtless be read (*waryed* A, *weryed* BC, *hast me weryhed* D, *haste me werreide* G) : *How thow me hast* werreyed || *on* (*om*. DG) *euery syde*. (Austin makes no note.)

Note 2.—Wherever the pret. sg. of *answeren* occurs in the form *answēred* before cæsura and the word after the cæsura begins with a vowel or weak *h*, we may read rather *answèrde* than *answēred* : there is then no question of the extra syllable (see, *e.g.*, 3767, 3974, 4019, 5351, 6777, 7491, 7533). For *answèrede* ||, cf. 4498, 5042, 5783, 7638 ; for *answèrde* ||, cf. 1964 (?), 6686.

In one line, however, the retention of a light extra syllable before the cæsura seems to be unavoidable, if the reading of the best MSS. is to be followed :

Nentendement [1] *considere* [2] || ne [3] tonge [4] telle, 6358.[5]

[1] So AECp. John's Selden B 24 ; *Nintendement* Durh.; *Ne entendement* D Phillipps 8252 ; *Ne* † *mendement* B.
[2] So ABCp. John's ; *considre* D, *consider* Durh. Seld. ; *concider* Ph.; *considered* † E.
[3] So ABDCp. Durh. Seld. Ph.; *or* E John's.   [4] *tung* Durh.; *tong* Seld.
[5] *Non* † *tendement nor tonge considere or tell* Harl. 2392. Leaf cut out of C.

Cf. And I ther (om. C) *after* / || gan rome (roman B) to and fro, 1601 (rome?).

Less certain than 6358 (for slurs are easy) are :—

What wonder *is it* (ist C) || though he of me haue ioye, 1834. For *ist* see § 143.

And yn here *bosom* || the lettre doun he thraste, 2240 (And in her bosom doun the lettre cast D; no note in Austin).

Ye bothe for the *seson* || and for the feste, 168 (BC omit the second *for*; D reads *and eke for*; no note in Austin).

O olde *vnholsom* || and mysbyleued (myslyued B, mysbeleuyd C, mysleuyd D; no note in Austin) man, 4992.

Compare :

And to *Pandarus* (-ris C, Pandare DCp. John's) || he (om. B) held vp bothe his hondes, 2059.

But to *Pandarus* (-dare BD) || alwey was (was alwey C) his recours (cours † D), 2437 (no note in Austin).

And thow *Symoys* || that as an arwe clere, 6210.

> Note.—In 2059, 2437, we are of course to read *Pandàre* (with elision) : on the forms of this name, see § 139.—Chaucer apparently pronounced *Symoys* as a dissyllable with the accent on the ultima, making *oy* a diphthong (§ 140).

§ 145. Some interest attaches to the treatment of the following unaccented final syllables before the cæsura : (1) Consonant + -*le*, -*me*, -*ne*, -*re*; (2) -*ne*, -*re*, preceded by weak -*e*-; (3) -*el*, -*en*, -*er*; (4) -*we* (-*ewe*, -*owe*, -*ow*); (5) -*y*, -*ye*. When one of these syllables stands before a cæsura which is followed by an unstressed syllable beginning with a vowel or weak *h*, it is of course easy to scan the line as a normal verse by depriving of syllabic value (by elision, syncope, or slurring) the syllable (or syllables) immediately preceding the cæsura. Thus in *He seyde he hadde a feuer* || *and ferde amys, feuer* may syncopate the vowel of the final syllable; in *He seyde o lettre* || *a blysful destine, lettre* may elide its final -*e*; in *But like a dredful louere* || *he seyde this, louere* may syncopate one *e* and elide the other, and so on. On the other hand, it may be maintained that the preferable way to scan such verses is to admit the extra syllable before the cæsura.

> Note.—I have used the terms syncope and elision above merely because they are short and convenient. In strictness, we cannot speak of *lettre* as eliding its -*e* or of *feuer* as syncopating its -*e*, unless we are ready to maintain that Chaucer's ordinary pronunciation of *lettre* was really *lettre* and not *letter* or *letr̥* and that his ordinary pronunciation of *feuer* was really *fever* and not *fevre* or *fevr̥* : and these are theses which few would

D D

undertake to demonstrate Exactly what the quality of the "extra syllable" would be in each case, if the verse is to be scanned so as to admit an extra syllable, is of course also a question that depends on the normal Chaucerian pronunciation of the words in hand. See the remark of Skeat, *Prioresses Tale*, 4th ed , p. lxii, and cf. § 136.

I. Consonant + -*le*, -*me*, -*ne*, -*re*. (For *heuene*, see II., below.) Variations in spelling are seldom recorded.

For al be that his *moeble* ‖ *is* hym by-raft, 6122.

Among the *peple* ‖ *as* who seyth alwed is, 3110. Cf. 1731, 4845.

In thiike large *temple* ‖ *on* euery syde, 185. Cf. 3382.

Out of the *temple* ‖ *al* eslyche he wente, 317. Cf. 162.

Withinne the *temple* ‖ *he* went hym forth pley[i]nge, 267. Cf. 5609 (in which insert, with Cp. John's, *al* before *allone*).

The[r]for a *title* ‖ *he* gan hym for to borwe, 488.

Vs from *visible* ‖ *and* inuysible foon, 8229.

Ne 1 nyl not *rakle* ‖ *as* for to greuen here, 4484.

Note 1.—A remarkable line is 7186: *Charitable / estatlyche / lusty and fré* (see the variants given in § 146, I).
Note 2.—In 3031 C, for *merákele* ‖ *I*, read *meruayle* ‖ *I*.

That to myn hertis *botme* (*om.* † A) ‖ *it* is i-sownded, 1620 B (boteme it is foundit † C).

And nere it that I *wilne* ‖ *as* now tabregge, 3137.

Into a *chaumbre* ‖ *and* fond how that he lay, 1641. Cf. 5394 (?).

Into the grete *chambre* ‖ *and* that yn hye, 2797. Cf. 5016.

And to the *chambre* ‖ *here* (the C) wey than (*om.* C) han thei nomen, 6877.

Right as oure first[e] *lettre* ‖ *is* now an a, 171.

And seyde *lettre* ‖ *a* blysful destene, 2176. Cf. 2232, 7761 (?).

At writynge of this *lettre* ‖ *I* was on lyue, 7732. Cf. 2146, 2178.

Note 3.—In 2091 the sense seems to make *A lettre* ‖ *in which* I *wolde here telle*[*n*] *how* imperative in preference to *A lettre in which* ‖ *I*. So in 7963: *Youre lettre* ‖ *and how that ye requeren me.* Cf. *The poudre in which myn herte ybrend shal torne*, 6672.

In feith youre *ordre* ‖ *is* ruled in good wyse, 336.

For pity of myn *aspre* ‖ *and* cruwel peyne, 5509.

Note 4.—In *That called was Cassandre ek al aboute*, 7814, *ek* is by no means a secure reading In 2314 the position of the cæsura is dubious: *Of raspre vpon a quysshon gold ybete.*

Ye may the *bettre* ‖ *at* ese of herte abyde, 6013.

And gan to *motre* ‖ *I* not what trew[e]ly (-ely BC), 1626.

And if that yow *remembre* ‖ *I* am Calkas, 4735.

I shal wel *suffre* ‖ *vnto* the tenthe day, 6260.

For *euere, neuere, leuere, delyuere*, see under II., below.

§ 145] *of Chaucer's Troilus.* 403

II. *-ene, -ere.* (Some of the words under this heading are here considered rather because they are spelled *-ere* in good MSS. than because they have any right to both *e*'s.) Variations in spelling are seldom recorded.

It was an *heuene* ‖ *vpon* hym for to se, 1722. Cf. 4093 (A †).
Thou hast in *heuene* ‖ *ybrought* (brouȝt C) my soule at reste, 4441.
It was an *heuene* ‖ *his* wordes for to here, 4584.
And seyde he hadde a *feuer* ‖ *and* ferd (ferde al C) amys, 491.
Sey that thi (*om.* C) *feuer* ‖ *is* wont the for (*om.* C) to take, 2605.
As of a *feuere* ‖ *or* othere gret(e) syknesse, 4055. For the spelling of the word (which rhymes with *keuere* inf.), see § 18.
Forwhi to euery *louere* ‖ *I* me excuse, 1097.
But as a dredful *louere* ‖ *he* seyde this, 2130 (louere ‖ seyde he C).
That hadde I *leuere* ‖ *vnwyst* for sorwe dye, 2594. (Or, *vnwyst* ‖.)
Me were *leuere* ‖ *a* thousand fold to dye, 3416. See § 64.
Amonges alle these *othere* ‖ in general, 893
Here to *delyuere* ‖ *I* holden haue my pes, 4762.
He spak and called *euere* ‖ *yn* his compleynte, 541 (euere he callyd / C). (Or,—*called* ‖ ?)
I who seygh *euere* ‖ *a* wysman faren so, 5749. (Or,—*wysman* ‖.)
Ne herd I *neuere* ‖ *and* what that was his mone, 1643. Cf. 1522, 2954 (*neuere* ‖ *how*), 4375, 4763 (?).
I may not slepe *neuere* ‖ *a* Mayes morwe, 2183. Cf. 2623, 6243, 6317 (?), 7198.
They speken ‖ but they bente *neuere* ‖ his bowe, 1946.

III. *-el, -en, -er.* (For *bettre,* see I.; for *feuer, feuere,* see II.)
But tho bygan a *lytel* ‖ *his* herte vnswelle, 6577 (his herte a lite B).
For goddes *speken* ‖ *in* amphibologies, 6068.
For thei *proceden* (-e B, -yn C) ‖ *of* thi malencolye, 6723.
And thus thei (*om.* C) *wolden* (-e BC) ‖ *han* brought hem self a lofte, 915.
For what to *speken* (-e B, spek C) ‖ *and* what to holden inne, 387.
Or nyl not *heren* ‖ *or* trowen how it ys(se), 1013 (here / B, heryn C).
And gan to *casten* (caste B) ‖ *and* rollen vp and down, 1744.
Shal I not *louen* (-e B) ‖ *in* cas yf that me lyst (*l.* leste), 1843.
Lat no wight *rysen* (rise B) ‖ *and* heren of oure speche, 3598 (Let hem not rysyn and heryn oure speche C).
As for to *loken* (looke B, loke C) ‖ *vpon* an old romaunce, 3822.
And thus shal Troye *turnen* (torne B, turne C) ‖ *in* (to B, tyl C) asshen dede, 4781.

Ne koude he sen. her *laughen* (-e B) || *or* make (-en B) ioye, 7144 (hyre se lauȝhe ne make C).

For which she may yet (ȝit may C) *holden* (-e BC) || *al* here byheste, 7554.

Who shal now *trowen* (-e BC) || *on* ony other (l. othes *with* BC) mo, 7626.

And art now *fallen* (-e BC) || yn som deuocioun, 555.

Til crowes feet ben *growen* (grow B) || *vnder* youre eye, 1488 (hem waxen *for* ben growen C).

Thanne yf I ne hadde *spoken* (speke C) || *as* grace was, 5895.

Criseyde *comen* || *and* therwith ban he synge, 6867.

To ben *vnknowen* (onknowe C) || of folk that weren wyse, 7942.

> Note 1.—The perfect participles of the verbs *sleen* and *seen* have not been taken into account (see § 122. XII., XIII.)
> Note 2.—With regard to the probability that elided -*e* should be read, wherever possible, instead of -*en*, see § 136, *a*.

My dere *brother* || *I* may the do no more, 8094. But the weight of MS. authority is for *brother deere* (*dere*): so BCp. John's. C is cut out.

I mene as loue (-yn C) an *other* || *in* this mene (*om.* C) while (wyse C), 3618.

And radde it *ouer* || *and* gan the lettre folde, 2170 (ἄλλως C).

IV. -*we*, etc.:

A *morwe* || *and* to his neces paleys sterte, 2179.

To bere the wel to *morwe* (-w C) || *and* al is wonne, 2583. Cf. 3690 (?).

He straught a *morwe* || *vnto* his nece wente, 3394. Cf. 7555.

Graunted on the *morwe* || *at* his requeste, 7312.

That neuere was yn *sorwe* || *or* (or in C) som distresse, 641. Cf. 530 B (right reading), 3932, 4527, 5171, 5541, 6540, 7405.

So lef this *sorwe* || *or* platly he wol deye, 5586. Cf. 1, 5743, 6821, 6895, 6921, 7012, 8107.

He was no *narwe* (harde C) || *ymaked* (ymasked B, imaskid C) and yknet, 4576.

Gan hym *saluwe* (salue B, seluyn † C) || *and* womanly to pleye, 2753.

Saue a *pilwe* (-wo B, pillowe D, pilowe G) || *I* (*om.* C) fynde nought (nouȝte elles G) tenbrace (to embrase C, to enbrace D, to embrace G), 6587. Read probably *pillow* || rather than *pilwe* || (which makes the verse 9-syl.):

V. -*y*, -*ye*:

Wher is my *lady* || *vnto* (to B) hire folk seyde he, 1164 (C cut out).

This knoweth *many* || *a* wys and worthi wyght, 1265.

That Ector with [ful] (ful B) *many* || *a* bold baroun, 4695 (C cut out.)
Thourgh girt with *many* || *a* (om. BC) wyd and blody wounde, 5289.
Ye god wot and fro *many* || *a* worthi knyght, 6696 (C *has* so hath *for*
  fro).
I shal therof as *fully* (ful BC) || excuse (-en Cp.) me, 3652. *Fully* is
  probably right.
> Note.—Cæsura has been assumed between *many* and *a* in 1265, 4695, 5289,
> 6696, with some hesitation.

By sort and by *augurye* || *eك* trewely (trewly B), 4778.
In *consistorie* || *among* the Grekes soone, 4727 (C cut out).
For which the grete *furye* || *of* his penaunce, 6091. Cf. 4915 BC.
In *furye* || as doth he Ixion || in helle, 6575 (ἄλλως Cᵉ).
And god *Mercurye* || *of* me now woful wrecche, 6684.
Be *necessarie* || *al* seme it not therby, 5682 (C cut out). *Necessaire* is
  also possible (see § 51).
For that I *tarye* || *is* al for wykked speche, 7973.

Here may be put the interesting verse:
In to the gardyn go *we* || *and* ye shal here, 2199.

VERSES LACKING THE UNACCENTED PART OF THE FIRST FOOT
("9-SYLLABLE VERSES").

§ 146. The occurrence in Chaucer of heroic verses lacking
the unaccented part (the *senkung*) of the first foot
can no longer be doubted.

Such verses may be conventionally called "nine-syllable verses"
even when, from ending in a feminine rhyme, they actually contain
ten syllables. The material here collected is arranged in four lists.

List I. (meant to be exhaustive) contains those verses of the *Troilus*
which are either certainly nine-syllable verses or which must at least
be seriously reckoned with before being otherwise scanned. Some of
the verses in I. may easily be emended so as to run regularly, and in
some of these a variant reading actually anticipates the emendation;
but it seemed better to include in I. a few verses that might have
been put in II. than to run the risk of excluding any which might
with an appearance of reason claim a place in the list. Under the
heading I*b* are collected a number of verses which (in MS. A) might
be scanned as of nine syllables, but may better be scanned as of ten.

List II. contains verses which in A must be read as nine-syllable
verses, but which are easily corrected by a comparison of MSS.

List III. contains a number of verses in which A is restored to order by the insertion of a single letter (or syllable) required or justifiable by grammar or usage. Some other MS. or MSS. will usually be found to furnish the required form. At the end of this list are given references for a number of similar lines from other MSS.

List IV. contains specimens of lines absolutely unmetrical in A, but curable in the same manner as the lines in III.

For the lines quoted at length in these four lists, ABCDG have been used throughout, and all the significant Cp. and John's variants recorded in Mr. Austin's collation have been registered. When no note is made of the reading of Cp. or John's, it is to be inferred that Mr. Austin records no such variants.

I.

For (ffor why D) it were (were here C) a long (-e B) disgressiou (discrecioun BG, disgrecioun C, digressioun D), 143 A. Mr. Austin notes the reading of Harl. 2392 (For whi it were of to long discuscioun), but gives no other variants. The reading of either C or D makes a normal verse : *here* may have been accidentally dropped on account of its similarity to the preceding word *were*. *Fŏr it wĕrĕ* ǁ *a lŏng*, with lyrical cæsura, hiatus, and dissyllabic *were* (§ 135, ε) is very unlikely.

Of this kynges sone of which I tolde, 261 ABCG. D reads *As of*, etc.

Shewed (Schewede C) wel that men myght (myʒtyn C) yn here gesse, 286 ABG (She † shewyd D).

First to hide (-en BCp., -yn C) his desir in (al in D) muwe, 381 (First he hid his desire in mewe G ; in the margin of G, in another hand, are the words "al for to hide," a reading which, with the change of *hide* to *hiden*, would make the verse regular)

That the (al the D) Grekes as the (*om.* G) deth hym dredde, 483 (That the grekys hym as of the deth dredde C ; Harl. 2392 seems to read *all* for *the* before *Grekes :* no other note in Austin).

That the hote fyr of loue hym brende (for brende G), 490 (stanza om. in D).

I wolę partyn with the al thyn peyne, 589 ABCDG.

Loue ayens the (*om.* C) which (wheche G) who-so defendeth, 603. *Louĕ* would cause hiatus: besides, this word is usually monosyllabic (§ 8).

I that haue yn loue so ofte assayed (asaied G, asayde B), 646.

Dorstestow (Dorestow G, Trist thow D) that I tolle (tolde BCp.

John's, told hyre C, told it D, tolde it G) in hire eere, 767. Probably read *tolde it* (or *hire*).

Twenty wynter that (or that G) his lady wyste (wist D, not † wyst C), 811.

Of (And of CDE) that word toke (took Cp. John's) hede (hed CDG) Pandarus, 820. *And of* is perhaps best.

Were it for my suster al thi sorwe, 860 ABCDG.

Next (-e B) the foule (foul D) netle rough and thikke, 941.

Alderfirst (Aldirfirst Cp. John's) his purpos for to wynne, 1062 ABDG (C cut out).

Of the sege (segee B) of thebes while (whil BD) hem leste, 1169 AG (C cut out).

How (How that G) the bisshop (bysshope G) as the bok kan (gan DG) telle (telleth *for* can telle C), 1189. G makes the measure normal.

Now (And Cp.) good (goode BG, mýn C, my good D John's Harl. 2392) em for goddes loue I prey, 1394. Read *goode em* (with hiatus) or *my goode em*.

Ther ayenis (aȝeyn B, aȝen C, ayens D, aȝens G, aȝeins Cp.) answere I thus anoon, 1454.

For his loue which (-e B, wheche G, *om.* D) that vs bothe made (mode B), 1585 (CD have *loue of god* instead of *his loue*). If ten Brink's "lyrical cæsura" be allowed, the same may be read *Fŏr his lŏue || which thăt*, etc.; but *loue* is seldom a dissyllable (§ 8).

Who sey euere (-ei D) or this so (or this euere so C) dul a man, 1633 ABG. If ten Brink's "lyrical cæsura" be allowed, the verse may be read *Whŏ sey èuer || or this*, etc. (for *euĕr* before a vowel, see § 90).

And (ȝe CD, A E) lord (-e E) he (she D, how he C, as he G, so be E) was glad and wel bygon, 1682. No doubt a word has dropped out in the best MSS. between *lord* and *he*. Cp. John's appear to agree with A.

Made loue withinne (within D) hire (her hert D) for to myne, 1762 ABCG. With lyrical cæsura and dissyllabic *loue* (see last example but one), the verse might run *Măde* (or *Măked*) *lŏue || withinne hire*, etc. The reading of D (which would make the verse normal if *herte* be substituted for *hert*) lacks authority.

I am one (oon BCp, on CG) the (of the C) fairest (fayreste BC) out of (ought of G, with-outyn D) drede, 1831. The reading of C looks like a corruption in the interest either of modesty or the more usual idiom, but may be right: at any rate, it decidedly helps the metric. *Fayrèste* does not help much.

Fro the skarmuch (scarmich B; charmys C, scarmysshe D, scarmuch G) of the whiche I tolde, 2019. *Frò the skarmùch[ë] ǁ òf the*, etc., would be highly improbable and no great improvement.

Sire (Sir B) my nece wole (wol B, wele C, wel G) do wel by the, 2042. In spite of the fact that the vocative *sire* is usually monosyllabic in Chaucer, we should doubtless read *sire* here and save the verse.

Of (Ryȝt of C, Right of D) myn owene (own B, owne D) hond (-e BD) write here (hire C, her D) right (*om.* D) now (how D), 2090 AG. Perhaps *Right* should be restored (cf. 2140).

Were hise (his BDG) nayles poynted (-ede C, -es B) neuere so sharpe, 2119.

Of (Ryȝt of C, Right of D) here (hire BC Cp., her D, lur G) hond (-e B) and yf that (*om.* D) thow nylt non, 2140. If *right* be rejected, *here* may perhaps be regarded as a dissyllable (see § 135, I.). As to *right*, cf. 2090.

He song as who seyth (seith BDG, seth C) sumwhat (se what G) I brynge, 2394. *Seyèth* will hardly do. One is tempted to combine G with the other MSS. and read: He song as who seyth se sumwhat I brynge.

If (ȝif it C, If it D) youre (ȝour D) wille (wil Ð) be (were D) as I yow preyde, 2687 ABG. *Youre* is unlikely (§ 74). The insertion of *it* (with CD) seems best.

Pleynly (-lich B, -liche GCp.) al (*om.* D) at ones they (al thei D) here (her D) hyghten (behighten E), 2708. Hardly *Pleynliche àl*, etc., with hiatus?

Dred[e]les (Dredeles BCCp., And dredles E) it clere was (cler was C, was clere D) in the wynd, 3368 AG. *And dred[e]les*, which would make the verse normal, has only the indifferent authority of E.

With a (*om.* G) certayn of here (her D, hir G, hire Cp.) owene (own B, owne D) men, 3438. *Here owene* seems highly improbable (see § 74).

Heren noyse of reynes (rayn D, reyn G, reyne Cp.) nor of thondre, 3504 ABC. *Hèren noÿse ǁ of reỹnes*, with lyric cæsura and hiatus, does not commend itself as likely.

Shul (Shal B, Schal C, Shul DG) youre wommen slepen wel and softe, 3509. *Youre* is improbable (§ 74). Perhaps we should read *shullen* (§ 123, VII.).

Reson wil (wol B, wele C, wyl D, wole G) not that I speke of (on C) shep (slep BG, slepe CD), 4250. No note in Mr. Austin's collation, though it seems incredible that Cp. John's have the absurd *shep* of A. One might conceivably scan: *Reson wil not that I* || *spėken of slėp.*

Thonkynge (Touchinge D, Thankyng G) loue he (she BCp.) so wel here (hir D) bysette, 4394. *Thŏnkyngę lŏue* || *he sŏ wel*, etc., with lyric cæsura, hiatus, and dissyllabic *loue*, is not probable. *Thonkȳngè lŏue* is perhaps possible, but *-yngė* in the interior of the verse is highly suspicious, whether in noun or participle (§§ 10, 120, III).

With the shete and wax for shame al (om. D) red, 4412 ABCG. Lyrical cæsura would give *With the shėtë* || *and wăx*, etc.

At whiche (At which B, Atte which D, Atte whiche G) day was taken Antenor, 4712 (C cut out). An unbearable verse if scanned with nine syllables. Taking a hint from DG may we perhaps read *Attę* for (*At the*) *whichė day ?*

Which that drawen (drawn B) forth the sonnes char (-e BDG), 4546.

Loue hym made (made hym G) al (alle G) prest to don hyre byde, 4824 ABCD. *Loue hym* is very doubtful.

Ector (H[ec]tor D) which (-e G, with C) that wel (-e BDG) the Grekis heide, 4838.

Of (O C) this (thilke D, ye ilke C) woful soule that thus crieth, 4979 ABG. Perhaps we should read *Of thilke; ye ilke* (C) is no doubt due to confusion between *y* and *þ*.

I that leuede (hauede C, leued D, loued G) yn lust (loue C) and in plesaunce, 5155 (stanza not in Cp.). With lyrical cæsura this would run *I that lėuede* || *yn lŭst*, etc.

Helpeth hardy man (men C) to (vnto B) his emprise, 5263 ADG.

Wende (-en BG) that she wepte and syked (syȝede C) sore, 5378.

By which (whiche D, swiche G) reson (resoun Cp.) men may wel y-se (I se John's), 5710 AB (not in C).

Of here (hire B, hir G, om. D) teris and the herte vnswelle (vnswell D, gan vnswelle G), 5808. Shall we read *here* (here possessive plural, see § 74)? Emendation (with the help of G) is easy: Of teris and the (or *here*) herte gan vnswelle.

And ther (there CG) lat (lete D) vs speken of oure wo, 5906 AB. *There* seems to be inevitable: the word is emphatic (§§ 89, 135, η).

May ye not (nouȝte G, not than C) ten (x D) dayes thanne (then G, om CD) abyde, 5990 AB. Read *mowen* for *may* (§ 123, VIII)?

410 *Observations on the Language* [§ 146.

Of vs sely Troians (Troian D, Troilus † C) but yf routhe (ȝe roughte †
G), 6152 AB.

Thries (Thrieȝ Cp.) hadde (had DG) al (alle BD, aH G) with his (hise
Cp., hir John's) bemes clere (so ABG Cp. Durham, shene D Selden,
cleene John's, clene Phillipps), 6372 (C cut out). *Thríes hádde ǁ
al with*, with lyrical cæsura and hiatus, is unlikely. It is barely
possible that *allé* (plural, referring to *snowes* in the next line) is
right, and that we may read *Thries hadde àllé.ǁ with his*, etc.

Passynge (Passing D) al (alle G) the valey (valeye B) fer (ferre G)
withoute, 6430 AC.

Thaqueyntaunce (The aqueyntau[n]se C, The acqueintauns D, The
acqueyntaunce G) of these (this BC, thes D) Troians (Troyans B,
Troylus † C, Troiaunes D) to (for to C) chaunge, 6485. Though C
alone has *for to chaunge*, yet that seems to be the correct reading.

Hath his lady gon (gone D, forȝon C, gone ȝoe G) a fourtenyght,
6697 AB.

Go (So D) we pleye (pley CD) vs in som (somme DG) lusty rowte,
6765 AB. With lyrical cæsura we might scan *Gò we pleýen ǁ vs
in*, but it will not do to separate the reflexive *us* from its verb.

Charitable (Scharite † abele C) estatlyche (statlyche C, estalich † D,
estateliche G) lusty (lyȝt lusti C) and (*om.* DCp. John's) fre,
7186 AB. With lyrical cæsura the line might run: Chàritàblë ǁ
estàtlych(e) lusty and (or *om. and*) fre: *charitablé estatlych* would
not be a real hiatus. It satisfies the ear quite as well, however, to
elide -*e* in *charitable* and make the cæsura after *estatlyche:* we have
then a pretty sonorous 9-syl. verse.

Tendre (-dry C) herted (herte C) slydynge (-yng CD) of corage,
7188 ABG.

Trewe (Trew B) as stel in ech condicion, 7194 ACDG. Hiatus ?

Sholde (-en BGCp. John's) spille a quarter of a (1 D) tere, 7243 AC.
With lyrical cæsura the verse might run *shòlden spillen ǁ a
quàrter*, etc.

Trusteth wel (-e G) and vnderstondeth me, 7250 ABCD. An easy
emendation would be to insert *me* before *wel*.

Polymyte (Polymyȝt C, Polymites D) and many a (*om.* C) man to
(al to C) skathe, 7301 ABG. Shall we read *Polýmytès ǁ and*?
Cf. *Polýmytès*, 7851 f, rhyming with *Ethýoclès* and *Thebès* (§ 139).

Graunted on the morwe (morowe G) at his requeste, 7312 ABCD.

For to speke (-en BCp., -yn John's) with hym at the leste (atte leste
BG), 7313 ACD.

§ 146.] *of Chaucer's Troilus.* 411

For to sen (se CD, sene G) yow in aduersite, 7446 AB.
Ferthere (Forther B, Further D, Ferther G) than (thanne B) this (the BCDG) story (storie B) wol (wele C) deuyse, 7457.
I comende hire wysdom (witte D) by myn hood, 7514 ABCG.
And that (that that C) Ioues (-ys C, Ioue D) of (hadde of C) his purueyaunce, 7809 ABG. Is it possible that *that that* is right? With *that Iouys* cf. the well-known *that god*. *Hadde* (C) is wrong.
Of the (a G) stronge (strong Cp.) bor with (with his C) tuskes (toschhis C) stoute, 7817 ABD.
Wrak (Venged D, Wroughte G) here in a wonder cruwel wyse, 7831 ABC.
Thorugh (Thorwgh B, Thurgh D, Thoroughe G, Of C) his (*om.* D, hire † C) moder wol I yow (*om.* GCp.) not (naught Cp.) telle, 7846.
At (Atte G) a scarmych (-e B, scharmoth C, scaimissh D, scarmusch G) eche of hem slowh other, 7871.
Peyneth here on ladyes for to lye, 7887 ABCDG. *Peyneth hère* || *on làdyes*, etc., with lyrical cæsura, hiatus, and dissyllabic *here*, is very improbable.
Of his loue I haue seyd (seide G) as (that D) I kan, 8132 AB. *Òf his lòuĕ* || *hauę*, etc., with lyrical cæsura, hiatus, and dissyllabic *loue* is very improbable.

I *b.*

Some lines in A that might perhaps be scanned as of nine syllables may better be scanned as of ten.

But the Troiàné (troyan BCG, troyanys D) gestes as they felle, 145. For *Troiàne*, see §§ 59, *b*, 70.
Al this Pandàrë || yn his herte (-t D) thoughte, 1063. *Pandare* is the reading of ABDEGCp. John's Phillipps ; Durh. has *Pandar ;* Harl. 2392 has *Al this tho Pandare in herte thoht ;* cut out in C. Hiatus may be avoided by reading *Pandàrus* (cf. §§ 126, 139). Cf. *Pàndarè* || *I*, 1044, where we may read *Pàndarùs* || *I*.
Cryseyde (Criseyda B, Cresseide C, Creseide G, Cryseyd anon D) gan al his (the D) chere aspien, 1734. Read *Crysèydè*, or rather *Crysèèjdà* (§ 140); cf. 2509, 2729, below.
Al (As D) wolde (wold BD) I that noon (no man CD) wyste (weste C, wist DG) of this thought, 1830. Unless *no man* be preferred to *noon*, read, with hiatus, Al wolde I that noon wystë of, etc. (rather than *wolde I* and *wyste of*) (cf. § 126).
Criseyda (Criseyde B, Crisseyde C, Crescide G, Of Cryseyd D) my

frend he seyde (seyd D) yis, 2509. Mr. Austin's notes the reading of E: Criseide my frende pandare he seid sir yis, but gives no other note on the line. Read *Crisèydà* and cf. 1734 above, 2729 below.

So heynous (haynous DG) that men myghte (might D, myght G) on it spete, 2702 ABC. Read, of course, *hèynoùs* (§ 140).

Criseyda (Crisseide C, Criseide D, Creseide G) my lady that is here, 2729 AB. Read *Crisèydà*, and cf. 1734, 2509 above.

Now thanne (than B, *om*. DG) thus (this D) quod she I wolde (wold D) hym preye, 2966.

So secret (secrete BD, discret G) and of (in D) swych (such DG) obeysaunce (obseruaunce D), 3320. Read *sècret* and *obèysaùnce* (§ 140).

For myne (my E) wordes here and euery part, 4173 (stanza om. in DG) Read perhaps *myne* (§ 74).

Love that with an (a E) holsom (holesome E) alliaunce, 4588 ABCG (not in D).

Loue that knetteth (cndytyth C, kennyth E) lawe (law E) of (*om*. E, and BCp.) companye, 4590.

Nought (Nouȝte G) rought (rouȝte CG) I wheder (whidere B, whider G, whedirwardes D, whedyr that C) thow woldest (wilt D) me (*om*. D) stere, 4944. The readings of C and D lack authority. A may perhaps be read: Nought rought I wheder thow ‖ woldest me stere, (cf. ten Brink's remark on the separation of subject from verb by cæsura, § 313), or, with hiatus and with syncope of -*est* in *woldest*: Nought rought[e] I ‖ wheder thow woldęst me stere.

Euery thing (thynge B, thinge G) that souned into badde (harde † G), 6338 AD (C cut out).

In a vessèl that men clepeth (clepe D, callyn C) an (*om*. C) vrne, 6674. One has little temptation to read *vèssel* and *clepęth*.

Here nedede (neded BDG, nedit C) no (none CG Cp, non John's) teris for to borwe, 7089. As a 9-syl. line, the verse would be unendurable, and *none* is surely not Chaucerian; it is probably best to read *nèdedèn* (plural influenced by *teris*, which, indeed, may even be regarded as the subject, *for to borwe* serving as a sort of complement) Cf. § 132.

Yong fresche (fresshe BG, frosch C, freisshe D) strong and (*om*. C) hardy (*om*. C) as (as a D) lyon, 7193. Read *fresshe*, by-form of *fressh* (§ 49), though this is the only case in which the form occurs in the *Troilus*.

I fynde ek (-e G) in storyes (storyies C, the stories B) ellys (ell· C)

§ 146]   *of Chaucer's Troilus.*   413

where, 7407. An impossible 9-syl. verse: read *fynde ek* (with hiatus) or *the storyes* (with B).

How myght (myȝte CG) I (*om.* B) than (thanne C, then G) do (don BC Cp. John's, done G) quod Troylus, 7652 AD. Read *thanne don* || *quod* (§ 88).

Euerych (-y CD, -ich G) ioye or (*om* D) ese (crese D) in (is in C, in to D) his contrarye, 7742 A.

Tydeus sone that doun (-e DG) descended is, 7877. Read *Tydèus* (§ 141)

Come (Com B) I wole (wolde C, wil D) but yet in swich disioynt, 7981.

Lines which in A might be read as of nine syllables as they stand, but which in that MS are so corrupt as not to make sense (*e. g.*, 400, 1928, 2720, 2925, 6326; cf. 2575, 5206) are of course not considered.

II.

In this list are included a number of verses in which A has nine syllables, but which are easily corrected by comparison of MSS.

For loue of the whan thou tornest ofte, 196 ADG. BCCp. have *ful* before *ofte*.

Or hastow remors of conscience, 554 A. BCDG have *som* before *remors*. 'Mr. Austin notes that Harl. 2392 has *som*, but registers no other variants in this line.

If thei (men D John's) ferd (-e BGCp., seide John's) yn (with D) loue as men don here, 1124 (C cut out). BDGCp. John's have *that* after *if*, which restores the metre.

Ywys vncle quod she graunt mercy, 1324 ABG. CD have *myn* before *vncle*. Mr. Austin notes that Harl. 2392 and Harl. 4912 have *myn*, but registers no other variants in this verse.

In which ye may se youre face a morwe, 1490 ABCD. GCp. John's read *which* (wheche G) *that* for *which*.

Eke I knowe of long (-e BDG) tyme agon, 1807. Read *And ek*. BCDCp. John's have the *And*.

Chese (And chese BECp., And sches C, And ches John's, And these † G) if thow wolt synge or (*om.* C) daunce (daunce synge G) or lepe, 2040. *And ches* is of course right.

Worth (-e C, Lepe E, worth thow BCp., worthe thou D, wurthe thou G) vp on a courser right a non, 2096. *Worth thow* is of course right.

But wel wot I (I wot C) yow (thow BG, thou D, that thow C) art now (*om.* D) yn (in a D) drede, 2589.

And last lasse (the lesse D, the lasse GCp. John's) nede to (*om.* BD, the to C) countrefete, 2617. Read *the lasse nede to* (or, possibly omit *to*).

He rong hem a (hem oute a ECp., hem out a G John's, hym oute a B) proces lyk a belle, 2700 AC (He rong out the processe as a belle D).

And lord so (so that BGCp. John's, how that C, so as D) his herte gan to quappe, 2899.

And to (And I to CEG, And y to D) han (have DG) right as yow lyst comfort, 2978 AB. Mr. Austin notes the reading of E, but registers no other variants in this line.

And what mischaunce (myschauns C, mischef yet D) in this world (-e B) yet (ther D, ȝet ther BCp, yet ther John's, ȝct † er G) is (this † G), 3132. Read *yet ther is*.

How this (the Cp., is this CDE John's) candele in the (this G) straw (-e E) is (*om*. CDE Jn's.) falle (yfaH D, I-falle John's, fall E), 3701. The right reading is : How is this candel in the straw yfalle.

That he cam (come C) there (ther BG) and that (that that Cp.) he was born, 3915. ABCDG all omit one of the *that*'s and Cp. seems to be the only MS. that has both of them ; yet both are needed by the construction as well as by the metre.

So thenk (thynkith C, thinketh DE, thyng G, thynk that B, thenk that Cp.) thowgh (*om*. C) that I vnworthi be, 4128. *Thenk that though that* is probably right.

Were (ȝt were C, ȝit were D) it so that I wist (wiste BG, woste C) outrely (outerly B, outerely C, vttirly D, entirely G), 4328. Either *ȝet were* or *wiste* (with hiatus).

Who-so seth yow knoweth (knowe C) yow ful lite, 4410. BDGCp. John's have *O* before *who-so* (D reads : O ho seeth ȝou knoweth ȝou but a lite).

For wistow (wistist thou C, wystestow Cp. John's, wist thou D) myn herte (hert D) wel Pandare, 4486 ABG. *Wististow* is of course right.

Of here (his D) comynge (-yng DG) and (and ek CD, and eke G) of his (here D) also, 4517 AB.

That (They Jn's.) maden (makkeden B, makeden Cp. John's, madyn CD) the (alle the C, al the D) walles (waH C) of the toun, 4783 AG. *Makkeden* is doubtless right; *al* seems to be a scribe's insertion to make metre.

In o (oone D) thyng (-e B) were and (and in BCDGCp. John's) noon (none G) other wyght, 5070.

Nay (Nay nay D Harl. 2392) god wot (woote B, wote DG; *in* CE

John's Hail. 4912 *the line begins* Nay Pandarus *instead of* Nay god wot) nought (not C, nouth D, noȝte G) worth (worthi B) is al thi (this CD Harl. 2392) red, 5160. *Nay nay god wot* seems to be right. Cp. omits the stanza.

Quod (Quod tho BG) the thridde (thrid G) I hope ywys (iwisse I hope D) that she, 5353 (C *reads* The threde answerede I, etc.).

Right a[s] (That right as BDCp. John's, That riȝte as G) when I wot ther is a thing, 5735 A (C cut out).

Com Pandare (Pandarus C, Pandar G) and (in and BGCp. John's) seyde as ye may here, 5747.

For myn honour yn swych (suche D, swiche G) auenture, 5991 AC. BGCp. John's Harl. 2392 have *an* after *swych*.

For (For when B, For whan DG, ffor whan Cp. ffor when John's) he saugh (saught John's) that she ne myghte (-t BD John's) dwelle, 6361 (C cut out).

Saue a pilwe (pilwo B, pillowe D, pilowe G) I (*om.* C) fynde nought (not C, nauȝt elles G) tenbrace (to embrase C, to enbrace D, to embrace G), 6587. Read *pillow* rather than *pilwe* (cf. § 145, IV.).

For tendresse (tendrenesse B John's, tendirnesse C, tendernesse Cp., tenderesse G, the tendirnesse D) how (-e G) shal she this (ek C, eke D) sustene, 6605.

That vnnethe (wel vnneth B, wel onethe C, welł vnnethe D, wole vnnethe G) it (vs D) don shal (schal don C, done shall DG) vs (*om.* D) duresse, 6762.

As seyden bothe the (*om.* C) meste and (and ek BC, and eke DG) the (there C) leste, 6803.

Shal (Ne shal BD, Ne schalle G, He schal C) he (*om.* C) neuere thryue (-yn C, -en Cp. John's) out of drede, 7122.

How he may best with short (shortest BDG John's Harl. 2392, schort C) taryinge, 7137. Intolerable as a 9-syl. verse.

As konnyng (-e B) as (and as BCp. John's) parfit (-e BG, tharfit C, perfite D) and as kynde, 7333.

So wel (-e G) for hym self he (he for hym self BCp. John's, he for hym seluen G) spak (-e G) and seyde, 7396 ACD. *He for hym seluen* is no doubt right.

For she sory (so sory CDGCp. John's) was for (*om.* B) here vntrouthe, 7461.

But why (*om.* D) lest (lest that Cp. John's, liste that B, leste that D) this lettre founden were, 7965. Intolerable as a 9-syl. verse.

Other lines of a similar character, when the correction is certain on comparison of MSS., are the following (in some cases the verse begins with a word or syllable that we should expect to have no accent or ictus: these instances are marked by old-style verse numbers): 652, 690, 764, 1091, 1124, 1372, 1457, 1480, 1923, 1932, 2044, 2087, 2138, 2150, 2153, 2194, 2575, 2902, 3082, 3123, 3193, 3405, 3431, 3546, 3564, 3655, 3789, 3864, 4045, 4111, 4160, 4522, 4695, 4842, 5182, 5314, 5329, 5341, 5363, 5403, 5840, 6053, 6384, 6878, 7519, 7843, 7865, 7978, 8098; cf. 7368.

III.

In some lines the insertion of a single letter (usually weak -e or -e- justified or required by grammar or usage) restores a normal line.

That *ought[e]* (auȝte C, oughte John's, owghte Cp.) wel ben (wel to ben CG, be wele D) oure opynyoun, 710.

Stond *fast[e]* (faste CCp.) for to good part (-e Cp.) hastow rowed, 962.

For *dred[e]les* (dredeles CCp. John's) me were leuere (lever to DG) dye (dethe † C), 1027. Cf. 1270, 3844, 4738, 5940, 6156, 7245, 8103, 8118.

I *rought[e]* (roughte BCp. John's, rouȝte C, roght D) nought though that (*om.* C) she stode and herde, 1032.

To *good[e]* (goode BC) mot it turne of yow I mette, 1175 (see § 14).

In whom that (*om.* G) *al[le]* (alle Cp., euery DE), vertu lyst abounde, 1244 (C †). *Alle* is surely right, see § 80, III. (cf. especially 1848, 1918, 1930, 6311).

For *trew[e]ly* (treweliche B, trewely C, truly DG, trewelich Cp.) I hold it gret deynte, 1249. Cf. 7986.

Thus *gilt[e]les* (gilteles BCG) than haue ye fysshed faire, 1413. Cf. 7447.

O (B inserts *thou* above the line) cruel god o *dispitous[e]* (dispitouse B, dispituse C, dispetous G) Marte, 1520.

Ye *dout[e]les* (douteles CG, doutelees Cp., trewly B) quod she myn vncle dere, 1579 AD.

She *thought[e]* (thouȝte C) wel (ek C, ferst D) that (this C) Troylus persone, 1786.

Be *drynk[e]lees* (drynkeles CCp., drenkynlees B) for alwey as I gesse, 1803.

Men *moste[n]* (miste C, must D, most G) axe (axen C, ask D) of (at BCGCp.) seyntes if it is, 1979.

Quod Pandarus *lok[e]* (looke B, loke DG, loke that C), alwey ye (ʒe alwey C) fynde, 2194.

And *sent[e]* (sente Cp., sent to D) you this lettre here by me, 2208.

Out of *disdayn[e]s* (desdayns B, disdaynys C, disdeynous D, disdaynes GCp., desdaignes John's) prison but a lyte, 2302.

Al *soft[e]ly* (softely BCD) and thederwardes (thiderward BCCp., thedirward G, thidirward D) gan (gan he D) bende, 2335.

Yet of (for E) hym self (my selfe E) no thyng (-e B) nold I (ne wolde I BCp.) recche (ʒit of him self ʒit wolde I no thyng rech C, ʒit of him self wolde I nothyng recche G, D = A with *wold* for *nold*), 2558.

The line is restored by reading either *hym seluen* or *ne wold*e *I*.

And shortly made (makes B, mad C, made D, maked GCp. John's) eche (*om.* G) of (*om.* G) hem his fo, 2567. Read *maked* for *made*.

Tel[le] (Telle G, Tel me CD) which (-e G) thow wylt of euerychone, 3254. Read either *telle* (which is not so common as *tel*, see § 115) or *tel me*.

So *help[e]* (helpeth BEGCp., helpyth C, helpith D) to this werk that is bygonne, 3577.

With (which † B) *pi[e]te* (piete BCp., pete C) so wel repressed is, 3875.

As she that *iust[e]* (iuste BCD) cause hadde hym to tryste, 4069.

Nought (Now C, Noo E) *swych[e]* (swiche B, such C, suche E) sorwful (soruful C, sorowful E) sykes as men make, 4203 (wanting in DG).

God *myght[e]* (myghte B, myʒte C, miʒt D, myght G) not a (oo D, o G) poynt my (of my D) ioyes eche, 4351.

Why nylt (nylte G) *thi* (thyn C, the John's, thou D) *self* (seluen BG John's, selue C, *om.* D) helpen (helpe to D, help to John's) don (doone D, to G) redresse, 5190. Read *thi seluen* (stanza om. in Cp.). Cf. 5253.

And *nam[e]ly* (namely BGD, namelich C) syn (sythe C, sithe D) ʒe two (ye bothe tuoo D) ben al oon, 5254. Cf. 6220.

Graunt (-e BG) mercy (mercie G) *good[e]* (goode BCp., god DG, iwis goode C) myn (myne DG) ywys (*om.* C) quod she, 6322.

Fro *then[nes]forth* (tennes forth B, thennes forth Cp. John's, thennes riʒte forth G) he rideth vp and down, 6924. For similar cases cf. 3009, 6970, 7016, 7034, 7248, 7258, 8080; see also § 91, s.vv. *hennes, thennes, whennes*.

Lord *whe[the]r* (whether BCG, whethir D) yet thou thenke (thow thy[n]ke ʒet B, thou thynke ʒit C, thou thinkist yet D, thou ʒitt thenke G) vpon (on CG) Criseyde, 7098. For *whether wher*, see § 138, 6.

Shal *knot[te]les* (knotteles C, knottles D) thorugh (thour C, oute D, thoroughe G) out (oute G, of D, *om.* C) here (hir DG) herte slyde (glyde C, glide D), 7132.

Hardy testyf (testis B, testy D) strong (-e DG) and (*om.* D) che‑ *ual[e]rous* (chiualrus B, chyualrous DG), 7165.

He shal no terme *fynd[en]* (fynden BG, fynde C, finde D) out of drede, 7453.

Hym self (seluen B, selue C) lyk (-e BD) a pylgrym (pilgryme D) to degyse (disgise C, disguise D, desgise Cp.), 7940 (not in G). Read *hym seluen.*

The *which[e]* (whiche CDG) cote (cote armur D) as telleth Lollius, 8016. Cf. 8187.

And *shuld[en]* (sholden BCp. John's, shulden E) al oure herte on heuene caste, 8188 (not in D).

For other examples (some harsh enough) see 1797, 2041, 3323, 4080, 4646, 5018, 5226, 5228, 5248, 6285, 6320, 6383, 6535, 6595, 6930, 7018, 7153, 7171, 7710, 7854, 8100.

Of instances in which this or that MS. (not A) has a verse that might, in its present condition, be scanned (though sometimes very harshly) as of nine syllables, but that is easily corrected by a comparison of MSS., the following will serve as examples. The necessary correction is often very slight, consisting sometimes merely in a single final -e. The list is not meant to be exhaustive. 78 C, 92 B, 93 C, 128 C, 145 BC, 147 CD, 157 B, 292 CD, 338 C, 411 BCD, 454 B, 498 B, 502 C, 623 C, 761 C, 968 BC, 1276 C, 1277 CD, 1453 B, 1473 BD, 1668 C, 1961 C, 2035 C, 2204 CD, 2206 C, 2215 C°, 2401 CD, 2417 B, 2464 C, 2535 CD, 2580 B, 2595 C, 2791 CD, 2826 B, 3239 BD, 3311 CD, 3349 BD, 3836 CD, 4624 C, 5148 C, 5288 C, 5510 C, 5763 C, 6544 C, 6694 C, 6886 C, 6935 C, 6949 C, 7135 C, 7330 C, 7339 C, 7346 C, 7423 C, 7687 B, 7842 C, 7895 C, 7917 C.—Particularly interesting is: Wherfore (-for BD, Where‑ fore C) my (A John's have *my*, BCDG omit it) lord (-e G) if my (*om.* Cp.) seruyse or I, 430, in which A and John's alone show both *my*'s.

IV.

A large number of lines absolutely unmetrical as they stand in A, and quite incapable of being read as verses of nine syllables, admit

§ 146.]   *of Chaucer's Troilus.*   419

of the simple cure just mentioned: the addition or insertion of a single letter (or two letters), usually *e* (final or interior), required or allowed by grammar or usage. Samples are:

This is the *right*[*e*] (ry3te C) lyf that I am inne, 1936.

For Pandarus (-re D) and *sought*[*en*] (soughten BGCp. John's, sou3te C, soghtyn D) hym ful faste, 2022.

And don (do on CG, do † doun D) thyn hod (-e B) thi nedes *sped*[*de*] (spedde BCE) be, 2039. Cp. apparently has *sped*. On the plural participle *spedde*, see § 68.

Wolde on (vp on CD) the *best*[*e*] (beste BCCp.) sounded (sowned BGCp., sounede C, sownyd D) ioly (*om.* G) harpe (hare † B), 2116. Read *the beste sowned* (§ 87); *the best ysowned* would also be possible.

For whi men seyth *impression*[*e*]*s* (impressyons B, impressiou[n]s C) lyghte, 2323.

Thow shalt gon ouer (to D) nyght and that (*om* G) *b*[*e*]*lyue* (belyue C, bylyve E, as blyve D Harl. 2392), 2598. On *belyue, blyue*, see § 138, 1.

Of *thing*[*es*] (thynges BCp., thingis D, thinges G John's) which that folk (-es John's) on wondren (wondre on John's) so, 2874.

Herynge here come and *short*[*e*] (schorte C, shorte Cp., for John's) for to syke, 2900.

Nyl I nought swere although he *lay*[*e*] softe, 3284. No -*e* in *laye* in ABCDG; no note in Austin.

Was euere *ylik*[*e*] (yhold B, ilik C, ylyk D, alike G) prest and dyligent, 3327.

And they that *lay*[*en*] (layen BCp., leye C, lyen D, leyn G) at the dore withoute, 3587.

But lord so she wax *sodeynlych*[*e*] (-lyche B, -li C, -ly G, sodenly D) red, 3798.

Haue ye no care hym *lyst*[*e*] (list BG, liste C, lest D) not to slepe, 3908.

Hadde of hym take here *thought*[*e*] (thou3te C) tho no fere, 3986.

Whan she his trowthe and clene *entent*[*e*] (entente B, entent clene D) wyste, 4071.

And syn (sithe C, sythe D) thow list myn *argument*[*e*]3 (-ment CG, -mentes D) blame (to blame BCDG John's), 5189. Perhaps we should read *argument3* and *to blame;* but *argumentes* is an unobjectionable form (§ 39, I).

But shortly lest this tales *soth*[*e*] (sothe BCDG) were, 5333.

She herd hem ryght as though she *then[ne]s* (tennes B, thense D, thennes GCp. John's) were, 5357 (Sche herde riȝt nouȝt thow sche there were C). (Cf. 6766, 6852.)

Cryseyde ful of sorwful (sorweful C, sorwefull D, sorowfull G, sorowful John's) pite (piete Cp.), 5393. Read either *sorueful* or *piete*.

Or elles thinges that *puruey[e]d* (-ueied BJohn's, -ueid D, -veide G, -ueyed Cp.) be, 5718 (C cut out).

And thanne (than BD, that G) at (att D, atte G) *erst[e]* (erste BDCp.) shal we ben (best D) so (*om.* D) fayn, 5983. (See §§ 54, *n.* 2, 143.)

Than (Thanne B, There C, Then G) shal (shalle G) no mete or (ne C) *drynk[e]* (drynke G) come (com B) in me, 5437.

For which Pandare (-dar DG) *myght[e]* (myȝte CG) not restreyne, 5534.

The gold *[y]tressed* Phebus heighe on lofte, 6371 (cut out in C). The correct reading must be *the gold ytressed Phebus*, but the MSS. do not have it: *goldtressed* is in ABCp. John's (separatim in B), *gold tressid* in Phillips 8252 Harl. 2392, *gold tresses* in Selden B 24; D has the diverting lection *The Auricomus tressed Phebus*, due, of course, to the intrusion of a gloss (Harl. 2392 has the gloss *auricomus* over the reading *gold tressid*, and *sol* over *phebus*); in the readings of E (*goldetressed*), Durham (*golde tressed*), and G (*golde dressed*), perhaps the lost *y-* may be discerned.

Whan Diomede on *hors[e]* (horse CD) gan hym dresse, 6400.

But syn (sithen G) of *fyn[e]* (fyne BD, *om.* G) force I (it † G) mot aryse, 6784.

Whan he was there (ther BD) as (that C) no (*om.* BG) wight (man CD, nought B, nouȝte G) *myght[e]* (myght hym BJohn's, myȝt hym C, might him D, myȝte hym G) here, 6827. Probably (with Furnivall) we should supply *hym* in A.

The lettres ek that she of *old[e]* (olde BDG) tyme, 6833. C stops the line at *sche*, but the corrector has added *oftyn tyme*.

Intendestow that we shul here (her D) *b[i]leue* (beleue CD Harl. 2392. bileue G), 6841.

With *soft[e]* (softe CG, lofte † D) voys he of his lady dere, 6999.

Conseyued hath myn hertes *pi[e]te*, 7961 (pete C, pietee Cp.). (Not in G.)

To com ayen which (-e C) yet (*om.* C) *[ne]* (ne BCp. John's) may not be, 7964. C stops the verse with *not*, and the corrector adds ȝet be.

Other examples may be seen in 1351, 1838, 2064, 2440, 2469, 2488, 2525, 2667, 2874, 3169, 3194, 3351, 3456, 4089, 4183, 4445, 4451,

4476, 4505, 4709, 4737, 5064, 5188, 5298, 5489, 5560, 5813, 6194, 6543, 6715, 6854, 7011, 7080, 7172, 7175, 7231, 7272, 7308, 7539, 7543, 7566, 7578, 7619, 7726, 7791, 7849, 7884, 8087, 8093.

On the whole matter of "nine-syllable verses," see the excellent monograph of M. Freudenberger, *Ueber das Fehlen des Auftakts in Chaucers heroischem Verse, Erlanger Beiträge*, 1889.

ADDITIONS AND CORRECTIONS.

p. 2, s.v. *hosbonde*. On the shortening of *o* in A.S. *-bónda* (*husbonda, -banda*, Chron. 1048), see Manly, p. 2.

p. 2, s.v. *stere*. The causes of the M.E. confusion of form between A.S. *stéora* 'gubernator,' and *stéor* 'gubernaculum,' are doubtless more or less complex; but one of them is perhaps the tendency (which has gone so far in Modern English) to give to the names of implements, etc., the form of *nomina agentis* (cf. *boiler, cultivator, governor, generator, pipe-cleaner, mower*, etc., etc.; in America one even hears a *dining-car* occasionally spoken of as a *diner*). Cf. also Manly, p. 3.

p. 3, s.v. *tyme*. On *somtyme, ofte tyme*, cf. § 133.

p. 3, s.v. *wele*. The Laȝamon forms are accidentally omitted (L.^{ab} wele, L.^{a} wela, weolla, wella, weole, wæl).

p. 4, s.v. *wrecche*. For *L. wreche* read *L^a. wrœcche*, etc.

p. 5, s.v. *blase*. For *bláse* read *blæse*.

p. 6, s.v. *myte*. On this word see Skeat, *Trans. Philol. Soc.* for 1888-90, p. 305. I see no evidence that the M. L. G. word ever replaced the A.S. *mite* in English. The most that can be said is that it influenced its meaning.

p. 8, *wodebynde* was put here with considerable hesitation. Both A.S. *wudubind, wudebind*, and *wudebinde* occur, apparently as nominatives, in glosses (see Wrt.-W., 137/5, 418/25, 556/39).

p. 8, *wyse*. Cf. *gyse*, § 26.

p. 9, I feel great doubt whether *feldefare* and *felofor* have anything to do with each other.

p. 10, s.v. *ache*. Insert the A.S. form *œce*.

p. 10, s.v. *sone*. See this article in *Studies and Notes in Philology and Literature, published under the Direction of the Modern Language Departments of Harvard University*, II, 1 ff. (on *sunu*, see p. 7).

p. 14, s.v. *loue*. As further instances of *loue*, cf. 16, 46, 234, 677, 1762, 3004, 3359, 3622, 3851 ‡ A^c, 4158, 4830, 5084, 5761, 6530, 7443 (old-style figures indicate that the cæsura follows *loue*).

p. 15, s.v. *shame*. Insert *L^a. scome, sceome, scame ; L^b. same, seame*.

p. 17, s.v. *chyste*. Klæber, *Das Bild bei Chaucer*, 1893, p. 392, has an ingenious but futile note in this passage.

p. 18, s.v. *help*, note But cf. "Sir, thine help now on hast!" *Arthour and Merlin*, ed. Kölbing, 1736, "O now thyn help thy socour and releef," Hoccleve, *Male Regle*, 55, *Minor Poems*, ed. Furnivall, p. 27; with which may be compared such phrases as *thin ore !*

Additions and Corrections. 423

p. 22. On *routhe, slouthe, trouthe,* etc., see Zupitza, *Anzeiger f. d. Alterthum,* II, 17, 18.

p. 31, s.v. *benche* Insert *L. dat. benche.*

p. 31, s.v. *bok.* Insert *L. boc.*

p. 31, s.v. *forward.* Insert *L. forward, forewarde,* etc.

p. 34, s.v. *game.* Insert *L*^{b}. before *game.*

p. 36, § 14, l. 6. *Scrín* is of course neuter, as is indicated below, *s.v.*

p. 38, § 14, *n.* 1. The explanation of this -*e* in neuters with short stem-syllable as derived from -*u* of the plural is Zupitza's (*Anzeiger f. d. Alterthum,* II, 11).

p. 41, s.v. *fyre.* On the form *fere* see Skeat, *On Chaucer's Use of the Kentish Dialect* (Chaucer Soc. *Essays*).

p. 47, § 15. For *myte,* see § 3, p. 6 (cf. *Additions and Corrections*).

p. 48, s v. *felawe.* Add *felawe* (before cæsura), 696 (*felow* B, *felaw* D).

p. 48, *ferde.* The comparison with M.H.G. *gevǽrde* seems to have little value. The history of the English word is very obscure, and its form doubtful (cf. p. 392).

p. 51, § 16. For *kne,* see pl. *knes, knees* (*knowes*), § 39, V., p. 105, and tho phrase *on knowe,* § 14, p. 42.

p. 52, l. 1, *first word.* For *bodig* read *body.*

p. 52, § 18. In our uncertainty as to the etymology of A.S. *cræft,* it would perhaps have been better to put this word among the *o*-stems.

p. 52, § 18. Among the neut. *o*- stems insert *soot.*

p. 60, § 18. Insert,—*soot* (A. S. *sót, n.*), 4036 f BCp. John's (sote CD, sot A) (: in hire foot, in his fote A, in his foote D). The correct reading is *sucre be or soot.* A took *soot* for the adj. (see § 46, p. 113) and wrote *sour* for *sucre.*

p. 63, § 19, s v. *cros.* On this word, see now the *New English Dictionary.*

p. 70, § 21. Insert,—thou lantèrne, 6906 (lantèrn, C, [thou] lantèrne D)

p. 71, s.v. *nece.* Add : good[é] necẹ ∥ to, 1468 (goode nece C, good[e] nece D).

p. 73, § 21. Add : sclaue, 3233 ‡ B (*read* knaue).

p. 79, s.v. *heirdesse.* I transcribe a passage from advance sheets of Professor Skeat's essay *On Chaucer's Use of the Kentish Dialect,* p. 662 : " We . . . also find the riming words *wirdes, hirdes,* in *Troil.* iii. 617, which would rime in any dialect; and I draw special attention to this passage, because the latter word is wrongly explained in *Morris,* and omitted in *Stratmann,* though it was solved by Tyrwhitt in the last century. The passage is :—

> ' But O, Fortune, executrice of wirdes,
> O influences of thise hevenes hye !
> Soth is that, under god, ye ben our hirdes,
> Though to us bestes been the causes wrye.'

The Campsall MS. writes *wyerdes, hyerdes ;* but all that we are concerned with are the A.S. forms. *Wirdes* is the pl. of *wyrd,* fate; but *hirdes* is not a plural at all. It is the feminine of *hirde,* A S. *hyrde,* a shepherd. The word *ye* is merely the polite substitute for *thou ,* and the person addressed is the goddess Fortune, who is here said to be our shepherdess. Morris's explanation of 'guardians' is clearly to be rejected. It may seem strange that Chaucer should adopt -*es* as a feminine suffix instead of the more usual -*esse*; but the context clearly demands it; and we thus have a bright light thrown upon l. 15 of the *Envoy to Scogan*, where the form *goddes* is rimed with *forbode is*. The comparison of these two passages clears up both of them." Professor Skeat's explanation of this passage from the *Troilus* (3459 ff.) seems inadmissible; certainly it is not clearly demanded by the context. *Hirdes* = *shepherds* or *herdsmen* (*bestes* in the next verse carries out the figure); the *influences of the stars* are apostrophized as well as *Fortune*, whence the plural, which may refer either (*a*) to *Fortune* and *influences*, or (*b*) to *influences* alone. The latter interpretation is perhaps better. The influences of the stars are the shepherds or herdsmen, who, under God, control us mortals, who, like the beasts of the field, cannot perceive the causes of what the shepherds force us to do.—I have never been able to accept Professor Skeat's interpretation of *goddes* as = *goddesse* (*Minor Poems*, p. 389) in *Envoy to Scogan*, 15. All the seven gods ("the brighte goddes sevene," 3) may be regarded as feeling the blasphemy against one of their number, or, if this will not do, *this goddes* may perhaps refer to Cupid and Venus. It is unnecessary to remark, in connection with the former and preferable of these two explanations, that *this* (pl.) is often used in Chaucer with little difference of meaning from that of the definite article (cf. O. Fr. *ces*).[1]

p. 86, § 31, s.v. *contrarye*. Add : cf. also 418, 637, 645 (*pl.* see p. 103), and cf. the adj. (§ 51, p. 120); cf. also § 142.

p. 87, § 31, *n.* at end. Add : Cf. 6684 (§§ 131, 139, 145, V.).

p. 89, § 33, s.v. *soueraynté*. The correct form for this line (3013) seems to be : *souereÿnëtë* (see §§ 126, 137).

p. 89, § 33, n. 1. Add : For *parde* (i.) (ii.) cf. 1040, 1451, 2493, 2608.

p. 89, § 33, n. 2. On *benedicite* cf. § 138, b.:

p. 90, l. 4. For nouns in -*ion*, -*ioun*, see § 142.

p. 92, s.v. *crois*. See now the *New English Dictionary*, s.v. *cross*.

p. 93, § 34, s.v. *pes*. For *pes* interjectionally used cf. 753 : *pes and cry no more* (pees BD, lye ‡ stylle and crye no more C).

p. 97, § 35, l. 3. For *past*, read *part*.

p. 98, § 35, I, *note*. Cf. "As thou art a man of life" (= *a lives man*), *Little Musgrave and Lady Burnard*, A, st. 10, Child, *Ballads*, II, 244.

p. 113, s.v. *merye*. On the forms of this word in Chaucer, see Skeat, *On Chaucer's Use of the Kentish Dialect*, p. 661.

p. 114. As to *lyte* in the adjectival use, cf. Manly, in the Harvard *Studies and Notes in Philology*, II, 50.

---

[1] I take this opportunity to remark that Mr. Skeat's suggestion that *olde grissel*, Scogan, 35 = *old gray horse*, is supported not only by Gower, *Conf. Am.*, viii. ed. Pauli, III, 356 ("Olde grisel is no fole"), but by *bonny grissell* = *bony gray horse* in the ballad of *Johnie Armstrong*, B, st. 20, Child, III, 369. Cf. "Mine hed is hore and al for-fare I-hewid as a grei mare," *Old Age*, st. 6, Furnivall, *Old Engl. Poems*, Philol. Soc., 1862, p. 149.

Additions and Corrections. 425

p. 120, § 51, s.v. *contraire*. Cf. §§ 31 (p. 86), 38, VII. (p. 103), and 142.

p. 122, § 52, s.v. *souereyne*. Add : But,—thilké sòueyren (*dissyl.*) purueyaunce, 5732 (sòuereyn D); cf. §§ 63, 137.

p. 122, § 52, n. 3, *l. penult*. See Metrical Chapter, § 142.

p. 123, l. 13. Add (for 1766) : seuenethe A.

p. 127, § 54, n. 2. As to *atte*, cf. § 143, where it is suggested that in *firsté vertu* the demonstrative *the* has been swallowed up by the preceding *that* (conjunction) The quotation from *Rom. Rose*, 13117-21, II, 48, should probably be replaced by " Virtutem primam esse puta compescere linguam," *Disticha Catonis*, 1, 3 ; cf. Kittredge, *Modern Language Notes*, VIII, 465.

p. 138, § 67. Add, as a note : The adj. pl. *ynowe* (with elided *e*) occurs in 3141 (inow B, ynow D), 4769 (inowe B, ynow D), 5523 (inoughe B, inow C, ynow D); see the adj. sing. *there is art ynow* || *for*, 5928 (ynough B, inow CD), cf. 7357 C. As a subst. (i.) bef. consonants, *ynough*, 912 (inough B, inow C, ynow D), *ynowh*, 6177 (inough(e) B, inow C, inough D); (ii.) before vowels, *ynough*, 881 (inow C, ynow D), *ynow*, 5904 (ynowgh B, inow CD).

p. 151. In *Wherof* artow (*ertow B, art(e) thou D*) quod *Pandare* (-*dar D*) than amayed, 5303 (*Whereto quod pandarus art thou thus amayed C*; no note in Austin), the ictus falls on -*ow* in *artow*. In

> Thenk ek how Parys hath that is thy brother
> A loue and whi shaltow not haue a nother,

5270-1 (shaltow(e) B, schuldist ‡ not han another C, shulde nat † I haue a nother D ; no note in Austin), -*ow* in *shaltow* certainly has both the ictus and the sense-accent. Perhaps we should read *thow* in both these instances.

p. 168, § 79, s.v. *oon*. In : And for a soth they tellen .xx. lyes, 6069, *a* apparently = *one*.

p. 176, § 82, s.v. *hote*. Cf. *hadde ich* (*I* CD) *it so hoote*, 5245 f B Cp. D (for hote A, so hote C), where *so hoote* is surely the correct reading (no note as to John's).

p. 189, § 85, at end, n. 5. The Northern use of *til* for *to* (of space or direction) is occasionally found : see 128 B, 506 C, 1273 C, 1999 AB, 2271 C, 2431 C (till(e) B), 2438 AB, 4423 AB, 4781 C; on-tyl, 354 C (vn-til B, vn-to AD). [Var. BC tyl.] In all these cases *til* stands before a vowel or weak *h*. In 2215 f D, *seyd hym till* (: *stonde still*) is a very bad reading. For *through*, etc., see p. 389 (and *Additions*).

p. 221, l. 1. See also § 111, III., n. 1, p. 266.

p. 242, § 100, note. On *thraste, thriste, threste*, cf. Skeat, *On Chaucer's Use of the Kentish Dialect*, pp. 668-9.

p. 246, second line of § 102. For *second*, read *third*.

p. 248, § 103. It is unlikely that, in *Til in a temple he* fonde *hym al allone*, 5609 (fond AC, fonde BD, fownde John's, ABCD om *al*, Cp. John's have it), *fonde* is to be referred to W.S. weak preterite *funde*, though John's has the spelling *fownde*.

p. 303; l. 14. For *V.* read *IV.*

p. 389, § 143, at end, n. 5. For *thourgh, thurgh, thorugh,* monosyllabic, cf. 998, 1853, 2402, 2417, 2421, 2425, 2858, 2926, 3089, 3140, 3443, 3629, 4060, 4130 4455, 4566, 4656, 4680, 4829, 7922, 7923, etc.

[Advance-sheets of Professor Skeat's paper *On Chaucer's Use of the Kentish Dialect* reached me in time to be of assistance in preparing the *Additions and Corrections.* Professor Skeat's edition of the *Troilus,* however, did not appear in time for me to use it in any part of these *Observations.* This note is added at the last moment, in the proof, to prevent possible misapprehensions.

G. L. K.]

RETURN TO ➡ CIRCULATION DEPARTMENT
202 Main Library

LOAN PERIOD 1 HOME USE	2	3
4	5	6

ALL BOOKS MAY BE RECALLED AFTER 7 DAYS

RENEWALS AND RECHARGES MAY BE MADE 4 DAYS PRIOR TO DUE DATE.
LOAN PERIODS ARE 1-MONTH, 3-MONTHS, AND 1-YEAR.
RENEWALS: CALL (415) 642-3405

DUE AS STAMPED BELOW

AUG 31

AUTO DISC AUG 0 7 1990

UNIVERSITY OF CALIFORNIA, BERKELEY
FORM NO. DD6, 60m, 1/83   BERKELEY, CA 94720

85072

682c
H83
v.3

THE UNIVERSITY OF CALIFORNIA LIBRARY

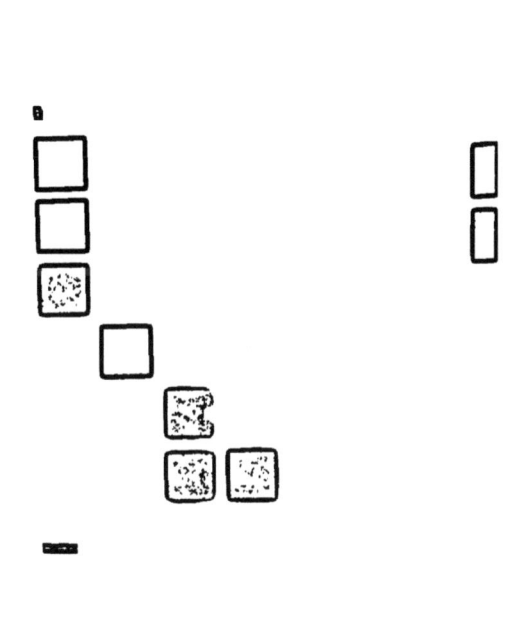

Lightning Source UK Ltd.
Milton Keynes UK
UKHW02n0759030518
322025UK00004B/15/P